MADISON CHANHANSEN

Written by
RODGER JAMES

Copyright© 2024. Rodger James. All Rights Reserved.

No part of this work covered by the copyright herein may be reproduced or used in any form or by any means—graphic, electronic, or mechanical without the prior written permission of the publisher. Any request for photocopying, recording, taping, or information storage and retrieval systems of any part of this book shall be directed in writing to the author.

This publication contains the opinions and ideas of its author(s) and is designed to provide useful advice in regard to the subject matter covered.

Dedication

For my sister Roxanne, thank you for all your effort, dedication, input and effort. It helps more than you know.

Table of Contents

Dedication iii

Introduction 1

1 CHAPTER 4

2 CHAPTER 10

3 CHAPTER 16

4 CHAPTER 24

5 CHAPTER 31

6 CHAPTER 39

7 CHAPTER 52

8 CHAPTER 60

9 CHAPTER 69

10 CHAPTER 80

11 CHAPTER 90

12 CHAPTER 105

13 CHAPTER 114

14 CHAPTER 126

15 CHAPTER 134

16 CHAPTER 144

17 CHAPTER 152

18 CHAPTER 163

19 CHAPTER 171

20 CHAPTER 177

21 CHAPTER 188

22 CHAPTER 199

23 CHAPTER 206

24 CHAPTER 213

25 CHAPTER 228

26 CHAPTER	239
27 CHAPTER	249
28 CHAPTER	259
29 CHAPTER	269
30 CHAPTER	279
31 CHAPTER	289
32 CHAPTER	301
33 CHAPTER	306
34 CHAPTER	312
5 CHAPTER	318
36 CHAPTER	328
37 CHAPTER	337
38 CHAPTER	349
39 CHAPTER	359
40 CHAPTER	364
41 CHAPTER	367
42 CHAPTER	375
43 CHAPTER	385
44 CHAPTER	393
45 CHAPTER	402
46 CHAPTER	415
47 CHAPTER	425
48 CHAPTER	431
49 CHAPTER	439
50 CHAPTER	444
51 CHAPTER	454
52 CHAPTER	460
53 CHAPTER	466

Introduction

This is my story, which cost my husband his life. The one man I ever loved. My first love, and will always be, the love of my life.

Please excuse me while I stop and wipe the tears away, as I imagine I will do so many more times through my journey of writing this… I miss him so… God, do I miss him!

I will never love another person the way I loved him. As time passes by, my mental wounds will heal. I know down inside that one day, I will fall in love again, might marry, and possibly even start a family.

I am only twenty-six years old, but with the past events, right now, that possibility isn't even a hint on the horizon. When it does happen, I shall never tell him that he takes second place—for that is my secret—and my secret only.

We met in college, and without going into great detail, over a period of almost two years, fell in love, finished school, and were married.

Four years later, single again, not by choice, but by the hands of two vile men.

I wanted to conquer everything. We are, or should I now say, both very athletic. My theory was that if someone else could do it, so could I. Craig always went along; it was not that he didn't have the physical ability, but he did, more so than I would ever have. He was more anxious to settle down than I was. I knew then he did it out of love for me. I know now he loved me far more than one could ever imagine. But he did! He gave up his life to spare mine. That is something someone, out of love, would never ask for.

We went scuba diving in the Caribbean, snow skiing in the Colorado mountains, and parachuting, which was very high in the sky, I might add. Our last journey, the final voyage, before retiring and living as normal people do, was the last. I shall never walk or hike or even jog into the woods again or anything that even resembles it.

With our jobs, we were able to squeak out a two or three-week vacation per year. This was our last (then on to thinking about starting a family of our own). The grand finale, the mother of all adventures, the one we both knew we would remember well into old age. Something we could one day tell our grandchildren. Now, there will be no one to tell!

But, then again, who would I want to tell this outlandish, nightmarish journey to anyway? Something I will live with silently until my day comes. The hot sweats at night, bolting upright in bed in sheer panic out of a sound sleep, if one would call living nightmares sound sleep.

So, you ask, "What is a living nightmare?" It is my definition of the subconscious replaying the past that is so vivid I'm living it all over again. I can reach out and touch everything again. I can smell and feel the cold, my heart racing, my lungs burning… oh God, how cold it is! I knew then I would never be warm again.

But I ran! This is what I feel the most in my dreams. Some days, the burning in my lungs hurt so bad that I just knew that this day was my last.

I had two theories on why they didn't stop. One was they couldn't let me live for fear of someone coming after them. The second was they just enjoyed killing, and the hunt to the end made it even better.

When I saw them shoot Craig point blank in the forehead, I fell to my knees, put my hand over my mouth, and screamed internally so hard my ears rang, my vision became blurred, and I nearly passed out.

I probably would have made it out of the wilderness much sooner, with a lot less effort, if it wasn't for an act of Mother Nature.

They didn't know I was there—or, at least, I don't believe they did.

We had been fishing at a small lake down a hill, about a quarter of a mile away. We had forgotten the two fish we had caught and the axe. Craig said he would start the campfire while I went back. I didn't say goodbye, nor did I even say "I love you," as I so often did before I left. It was just a short trip there and back, only to be gone minutes. Those minutes turned into history—forever. I regret so for not saying them.

Now, I have learned to assume nothing. I learned that lesson so many times before my journey was over.

The fear I was feeling at that time turned into a panic that words can't describe. I ran faster—no direction to go, just to put more distance between them and myself. The distance I did gain came slow, for they had no trouble keeping up. At the time, I was an avid runner, doing all the 10K runs in our section of the state.

Craig was always by my side, every step of every mile, always pushing me to gain seconds. It was effortless for him; he had the grace of an antelope, gliding along as if it was a walk in the park. I told him many times to go ahead. I was holding him back. But every time, I always got the same response: "What fun would that be?"

The dreaded tears are back. Even after he was gone, from saving my life the first time, he had saved it again so many countless times, even I can't remember. His memory, his voice… so I continued on.

Maybe, by now, you think I'm just babbling on. Maybe I am!

Life is so hard now; I'm back in our home. Mentally, it is as hard to go on as it was then, just not as physical. I've been told by many of our friends to go see a shrink, but what good would that do? It wouldn't change a thing—the past, my feelings, or the future.

This is why I'm writing this story. Not just to tell you my story but more so for myself. This is my therapy to help me regain some resemblance to my life back.

I will probably read and reread this over and over again—for now, I don't know what else to do.

One thing I do know is that the tears will flow forever.

Craig,

I am so sorry for what happened to you,

I will love you forever,

Madie!

CHAPTER 1

Walking back up the long sloping hill from the lake, a quarter mile from our camp, where we had just spent the last three hours fishing, I was thinking, *God, life doesn't get any better than this.* Following the man I love, my husband of several years—my life, my rock.

I was letting him blaze the trail through the underbrush. He's by far stronger and has much more endurance and ability than I possess. Not that we were walking through a jungle, but the undergrowth around the lake was denser due to the sun's ability to breach the canopy, unlike the thousands of square miles in the north country where the only thing that grows below the trees are ferns.

As we crested the hill, we could see our camp less than one hundred yards away, nestled in the ferns and trees.

Clearing the dense undergrowth and walking into the blanket of ferns, Craig slowed. I sped up so we could walk next to each other. He was carrying our two telescopic fishing rods, and I the worms we had dug up to use for bait.

"Well, how do you want your fish cooked? Over an open fire, fried? Or fried over an open fire?" he asked, smiling.

I started to laugh, and then I stopped, dead in my tracks.

Craig looked at me inquisitively as if to say, "What's wrong?"

"What's wrong? The only thing we're having for dinner is a glass of water and a toothpick."

I watched his eyes look down at my hands.

"You forgot the fish? And the axe? Madie, Madie!"

I nodded yes.

Craig started to hand me the fishing rods. "Here, I'll go back; you start the fire."

But I was already turning. I was disgusted with myself. Something so simple, a mundane task, and I forgot. Up here, close to the U.S./Canadian border, nearly three hundred fifty miles to the closest town, one simple mistake could cost us our lives.

Already three steps away, I shook my head no, raised my right arm, and gave the limp wrist wave. Not the typical beauty queen wave one sees in a parade. I was too mad at myself for that.

Not that forgetting two fish and the axe, that stupid axe, we didn't need it anyway, was going to cost us our lives.

Nonetheless, there's no room for error out here. That's one of the many things we discussed over and over planning our trip. Leave nothing behind, don't get hurt, and leave no opportunity to get sick. If we start to get hot while hiking, remove some clothes before sweating. If that were to happen, it would open a window to catch a cold.

I kept going over the rules in my head on the way back to the edge of the lake. Talking to myself as if it were changing the outcome of what I did. It couldn't! But maybe it would relieve some of my guilt for making a stupid mistake. It wasn't!

While I was sputtering to myself mentally, I was also thinking that I was getting too comfortable in my surroundings. Here, in the absolute middle of nowhere, where the only thing that wants to help you is a black bear, and that would be to eat you and put you out of harm's way from Mother Nature. But the one cold fact is that the bear doesn't realize he is the one thing in a few thousand square miles that would be of physical harm to us.

Before I realized it, I had walked the quarter mile back to the lake. I stood there for a few brief seconds, looking at the two fish hanging on the string that was tied to a small limb and the axe leaning against the tree.

One small mistake leads to a larger mistake, and that could be disastrous for one of us, I thought to myself. So, I picked up the axe, untied the fish from the limb, and started back to our camp.

Still mad at myself, walking back, I looked at the two trout we had caught. "Stupid fish," I said out loud.

As I was about to crest the hill to our camp, less than a hundred feet away, the thought occurred to me: I couldn't smell any smoke from the fire Craig was to have started.

Not thinking too much about it, the smoke could be drifting in another direction; I walked the few remaining feet to where Craig would be in eyesight. I expected him to be standing by the fire, adding a few more sticks to it.

But he wasn't!

I stopped just to head high above the ferns, so I had a clear view of our camp. I couldn't believe what I was seeing: two men standing there talking to Craig.

I was stunned! That was the last thing I thought I would see. A five-hundred-pound black bear wouldn't have surprised me as much.

Something wasn't right. As I stood there looking, Craig had his back to me. He had his right arm behind his back. The back of his wrist was against his belt. His fingers were waving back and forth, slowly, side to side, non-stop.

What did that mean?

One man was standing in front of Craig, blocking my view. The other was off to his left side.

He had long, stringy black hair with a full beard, one that hadn't been trimmed in at least two years by the length of it. As I looked him over more, his dirty, baggy blue jeans and flannel shirt, which also hadn't been washed in weeks, I imagined the second man looked the same.

All the while, Craig's fingers never stopped moving back and forth.

The thoughts started rushing through my mind. *Were these two truly mountain men fictitious characters one only reads about? Were they just two hikers like us? Were they lost?*

Craig's fingers never stopped.

As the moments passed, which seemed like minutes, my thoughts became worse. *Were they there to rob us? But how did they find us? Was it out of pure coincidence, or had they been tracking us?*

This can't be good, was my next thought. Craig was still waving behind his back, so I lowered my head, just eye level above the top of the ferns, so I could still see what was going on.

I couldn't hear their conversation. I couldn't see Craig's face to read his lips. The man on the left did very little talking. Then, Craig dropped his right arm down to his side and took two steps to his right. Was this a sign that it was okay for me to continue?

As I looked from Craig to the man he was blocking my view from, I gasped, then almost screamed. He was pointing a gun at Craig's head.

I was paralyzed. I lost all feeling and senses except for my vision. There wasn't anything I could do but stand there bent over.

Then I heard it. The loud crack in the never-ending silence, seconds before I watched Craig fall. I put my left hand over my mouth and nose to help hold the scream in. Tears instantly flooded my eyes and ran down my face. I held the long, endless scream inside that seemed to last forever. Instinctively, without even thinking about it, I knew I couldn't make a sound. My ears started ringing, and my vision became blurred as I continued screaming internally.

The only thing that happened next was that self-preservation took over automatically. I inhaled deeply, regained somewhat of my senses, and let it out slowly. The tears flowed profusely, landing on a few branches below my face as if it were raining out.

I just watched my husband brutally murdered. It was as if his hands were tied to some invisible anchor, not moving. His arms were outstretched as he fell over backward from the impact of the bullet. Then, they caught up with his body just before disappearing into the ferns.

Then, he was gone forever.

I didn't know what to do. I couldn't go forward; I had no place to go behind me, so I watched—out of horror.

The two men stood there talking to each other. They had done their damage. Why didn't they just leave? As they stood there looking around, taking in the inventory of our humble little camp, I couldn't imagine what further damage they could do to me—nothing else could be any worse.

Then, the worst happened!

I watched the man who shot Craig walk over to my backpack and pick it up. But what he did next never occurred to me, maybe because I wasn't in the right frame of mind. It is what I would have done in his situation. He found our satellite phone, removed it from the backpack, and smashed it against the tree closest to him. I stood there in disbelief at what was happening.

Then things got worse if that was even possible. He found our GPS, our lifeline, the instrument that kept us going from where we were to where we needed to go next without getting lost.

Without that, we would be nothing, lost forever. I watched him look at it, smile at his companion, and put it in his pocket. I knew now that I was lost forever. Without that, I knew I would never find my way out. I would spend my remaining days wandering around in large circles until I froze to death or died from starvation.

But even that was okay with me. My life was over; the sooner the end arrived, the more it was fine with me.

As they each went through our few articles of clothing, throwing them on the ground around them, I was hoping they would soon leave. Then, I saw them go through our food supply, putting the canned goods in a bag. I knew they were taking that along with them.

The only thought going through my mind was as soon as they left, I was going to return, bury Craig as best as I could so the animals couldn't get to him, return to civilization, get help, and return to retrieve his body. The last remaining thing in this world I could do for him.

They spent more time than was necessary as far as I was concerned. Going through our belongings several times, keeping anything that they thought would be useful to them. Our clothes didn't seem to be of much interest to them, and for that, I was grateful. I knew that before I reached civilization again, I would be in subzero temperatures, with God knows how much snow to deal with. The clothes, I knew, I would have to have if I were to survive.

Then, just as I thought it was about over, they looked as though they were about to leave. I was feeling relieved. They started walking away in the direction we had come from. But why? Had they been tracking us during the day? Or did we just happen to travel past their camp and unknowingly to us, we found them?

Luckily, there wasn't any snow on the ground yet, or they would have known, without any reasonable doubt, that there were two of us. Craig and I had talked about that several times, how unusual it was not to have snow this far north this late in the year. It is the first week of November.

They were on their third or fourth step away from our camp—that's when it happened—an act of Mother Nature.

A dead tree branch decided to fall right behind me, and it landed as close as ten or fifteen feet from my back. It wasn't a small one either. It just had to be one that made an earth-shattering, bone-cracking roar. I instantly went into sheer panic. Then, they both stopped and snapped their heads in my direction. I could read the man's lips, the one who shot Craig, there are two of them. They instantly started running in my direction.

Why I stood straight up before I started running, I don't know. I wasn't thinking proactive, just reactive. I heard one of them yell behind my back, "It's a woman. This is going to be a lot of fun."

Then, I went into sheer fear mode. I would have just as soon stayed and faced the same fate Craig had, to end my life. It had already ended when I heard the shot that ended Craig's life.

Down inside, I knew that's not what would happen to me. They would keep me alive and do unthinkable things to me for God knows how long. Probably until they got tired or bored with me or until I could find a way to escape or kill myself. The latter would be my only way out!

So, I ran as fast as I could go. I hadn't the time to give any thought to where I was going, just putting distance between myself and them. Instinctively, the only thing I knew was the path I had just traveled back to the lake. That is what I chose.

When I reached the water's edge, I thought while running in that direction, I would run around the lake. But, still in the same panic mode, my adrenaline flowing through my body at such a horrific rate, I knew I would soon burn my energy supply too quickly.

Come on, Madie, I told myself. I tried to remember the size of the lake as I ran back to it, wondering what the distance around it would be.

Trying to clear my head to think straight, I could hear them behind me, cracking the dead branches as their feet landed. It sounded as if they were gaining ground on me. So, I ran faster.

When I reached the water's edge, I turned left. I took a quick glance across the lake to determine the size of it. Then, I returned to looking at what lay ahead of me, carefully placing each step that landed. To trip and fall or, worse yet, to sprain or even break an ankle would be the end of my plan.

Running, watching the ground, I was also thinking about the run around the lake. It couldn't be more than four or five miles around it. Still carrying the two fish and the axe, very little added weight, and wearing hiking boots, I told myself, *This is just a run through the park.*

There was no way they could keep up with me. I was the avid runner here—not them. I was the one in shape. They would soon tire and give up.

My plan was to run around the lake and return to our camp. Then, I would get a warmer jacket insulated pants, and assess the situation. At that time, I would consider what to do next.

While I ran along the water, dodging the many rocks that lay in the sand, my steps automatically became in rhythm with my breathing. Two steps forward while breathing in, another two steps forward, exhaling. This is what my body knew. I mentally felt better; this is what I know. I could do this. Losing them would be easy.

Then, the thought hit me like a rock. I was leaving footprints in the sand. What good would it do to lose them visibly? They could still track me!

So, I ran up into the woods. The thick undergrowth slowed my speed. The small trees and brush pulling at my legs and arms were a definite draw on my body, but then, as I thought about it, it would also do the same for them. This would work in my favor. They would tire more quickly and give up sooner—I hoped.

I held the fish in my left hand up against my chest to reduce the drag from the brush. I managed to turn the axe around in my right hand as I ran, so I held the handle where it entered the steelhead. It was a double bit, the type that had two points on it. Craig insisted we had it for chopping firewood. That way, if one side gets dull or damaged, we can still use the other side. Craig had thought of everything but not this.

This was working to my advantage. As I ran, I used the handle to push the small trees to one side to give me a clear path to run. I could still hear them behind me, not talking, just running. I knew I didn't dare turn around and look to see where they were. I would stumble and fall, losing valuable time.

More than a mile into the run around the lake, they were still there. By the sounds of their footsteps, they hadn't gained ground on me, but they hadn't lost any either.

So, this is just going to take a little longer than I had thought—no problem!

CHAPTER 2

Relentless is all I can say about them; I'm still back there. It shouldn't be much longer before they give up.

I can see the water to my right, no more than fifty feet away. This ground had sloped up slightly from the water's edge, and, by the look of things, I hadn't reached the halfway point yet around the lake.

My body is in full rhythm with the running. Although it's working my leg muscles much more than it would if I were running at home on the road, I'm not having any problems breathing. The oxygen supply to them is keeping up.

So, my thoughts were wandering.

Why would anyone this far north in Canada want to kill us? Who are these two men chasing me? Are they outcasts from society? Or had they lived in the wilderness all their life— in which laws mean nothing to them? Can they even read or write? Why would that even matter? Come on, Madie, snap out of it, I told myself. *Concentrate on the matter at hand!*

But still, I had so many questions, ones that I will never have any answers to, at least I hope not. If I did, that would mean they had caught me.

By now, I've lost track of the distance I've run. The trees all look the same—no distinctive landmarks to judge from. As I take quick glances at the lake, maybe another half to maybe a full mile before I'm halfway around the lake.

Then, suddenly, the noise behind me decreases greatly. The cracking of the dead limbs, the scraping from the brush rubbing against their clothes lessens. It was a welcome quietness. The rumble of footsteps, one of them had just quit, given up. I wanted to smile from my small victory, but not yet. There was still one left!

I fought the temptation to turn around and look to see which one was left. But why did that matter? Partners in crime, one would do the same to me as the other.

I never heard them talk to each other. That seemed strange to me. They were still close enough, by the sound, that they were no more than a baseball's throw away. Maybe they were whispering to each other to save energy. I had no idea!

One down, how much further before the second one gives up?

All I know is that I had to get back to our camp and get some warmer clothes to survive my journey back out of here. They didn't know my plan, such as it was, which wasn't much because, at that point, I had none, one problem at a time. That's all I can deal with now.

Then, a loud crack came from behind me. *Oh my God, it can't be. He's gaining ground on me. How is that possible?*

So, I increased my pace. Was it that the one who just quit was holding this one back?

"Shit," I mumbled to myself.

Minutes passed, and I knew I was well past the halfway point around the lake. I needed seconds—no—more than that, maybe a full minute when I reached camp to find my insulated jacket and pants, but surely, by then, this one would have given up.

So, I increased my speed as much as I dared to without stumbling. Darting to the right, then left, back and forth, dodging the trees and brush, had me breathing much harder than normal. *I can do this,* I told myself. Lose him before I get back. Then, it will be much easier, as will my trip out of here.

I was guessing at my speed, by the length of my steps, that I was running a six to six-and-a-half minute mile, which by no means was a blinding time compared to what I ran when I was in a 10K race. Given the situation, I was still happy with my progress.

Thinking back, trying to remember, as I watched them scatter our clothes on the ground, where had my clothes ended up? I don't know; the only vivid memory that remains is the shot and then Craig falling backward. That one I know I will remember forever.

As I ran, I gained distance, not much, but enough by the sounds coming from behind me that he had fallen back fifty yards or more.

My thoughts went on ahead. The tears started flowing heavily. I knew what I was going to see when I arrived: Craig lying on his back in the ferns. Maybe, I hoped, I would have enough time to hug him, kiss his cheek, and say goodbye.

I stumbled and nearly fell to my knees. My nose was running profusely, and my vision was a blurry mess as if I were looking through a kaleidoscope at the different colors of the rainbow in 3D.

Adding to the fact that I was no longer paying attention to where I was going. My concentration had faded into the recent past. *Why Craig?* If I were to be captured by them, that is the one question I'm going to ask them. *Why?* Craig didn't deserve that, nor should anyone.

In the last mile around the lake, the sun was starting to set. I could no longer hear footsteps behind me. I had finally outrun him. Had he given up or just dropped off the brutalizing pace we had maintained?

As I got closer, within the last half mile, I dreaded arriving there. I didn't want to see Craig like that, but—yet—I wanted to see him again. Tell him I'm sorry for what happened to him. My emotions were ripping me apart inside, but I knew I wanted to tell him that I loved him one last time. I could see our tent up ahead. I slowed to a fast walk, knowing what was waiting there for me.

I walked up to my jacket, stopped, and picked it up. As I bent over, I saw him, out of the corner of my eye, lying there. The tears and the sobbing were instantly unstoppable. I stood up, looking at Craig, less than five feet away. The grotesque red spot on his forehead was almost more than I could bear. His eyes were open; he died instantly, never having time to close them. I was shaking uncontrollably as I walked the remaining few feet up to him.

As I started to kneel, a loud, thundering, crashing explosion erupted ahead of me. Before I even had time to think about it, I automatically looked in that direction. I couldn't believe what I was seeing. The second man, the one who had quit the chase miles back, was running straight at me. He was close enough that I could see the color of his eyes. He had been hiding, waiting for me to return.

I never straightened up. I pivoted on my heels and ran in the opposite direction, like something an animal does when being hunted. I just did it instinctively without thinking about it. As I ran, I saw my insulated pants so I stopped to pick them up. That was a big mistake!

He was coming at me with unbelievable speed. I bolted forward out of panic—just in time. Before I was at my full sprinting speed, I felt his hand slide down my back. He was unable to grab onto anything solid, and, having felt that happen, I ran even faster. My adrenaline was pumping in my body so greatly I felt dizzy. Then, things went from really bad to unbelievable—again.

The first man was flanking me from my left side. Running at full speed, if I continued on in the direction I was going, I could see that he was going to overtake me in another eighty steps. So, I veered to the right in a hard, sharp turn. What I hadn't realized was that the man behind me was no more than an arm's length away. My attention had been diverted away from him when I saw the other coming from the left. He hadn't anticipated my turn.

His presence, again, brought me to his full attention as he passed by me. He managed to get a hold of my hair. My head jerked back, snapping my neck. That brought a lot of pain that shot down my spine.

Luckily for me, his hand slipped off. My hair is shoulder-length. Any longer, he would have gotten a good handful, and the chase would have been over. I didn't have time to worry about the pain that would pass.

I tucked the clothes under my left arm. My left hand was clinched around the rope carrying the two fish. I swung my right arm, carrying the axe for momentum. They never said a word—they were like machines! I would have been a little more at ease if they were talking to each other, trying to tell each other what to do to stop me, but they weren't.

I was so scared I didn't even know if I was breathing right. I did know I was in for another long run, at least, until it got dark. Maybe then, they would give up!

By the time darkness came, we had covered several more miles. I had no idea which direction I was even going. Right now, there was only one direction to go: away from them. In the morning, when the sun came up, I would head south.

I had to slow down. The darkness wouldn't allow me to hold the speed I was going. The trees were too close. I couldn't see the next one until I was almost upon it, but I was grateful for that. If I couldn't see, neither could they. They were back there; I could hear the crunching under their footsteps, as I'm sure they could hear mine. They had fallen back, maybe forty yards, but that was just a guess.

My lungs were burning, my legs were numb, and I was sweating. The one thing Craig said over and over was: "Never sweat, Madie." Shed some clothes before that happened, but, given the situation, that wasn't possible.

Now, it had been two hours since the sunset. The temperature has dropped down to somewhere between five and ten degrees above zero. That was another guess, but it was something else that didn't matter. My survival did.

We had slowed to a fast walk. I could hear them, crunch, crunch, crunch. If they gained ground on me, I would be off in a flash and running again.

As the time and distance passed, I thought back. I now know when the second man stopped chasing me, he was going back to head me off at our camp. Also, that's why the first man slowed as we got close.

To give me a false sense of security, to drop my guard, then be captured by the other. But how did they know that? I never heard them talk. *Had they been together so long they could read each other's mind? Or were they like a pack of wolves, automatically knowing how to survive out here, helping each other in the hunt?*

That was a scary thought. *What am I up against?*

The one thing I do know that I was right about is that they had the gun and didn't shoot me. They had more than a few chances, so they wanted me alive. That scared me even more, so I walked faster.

Knowing they were good distance runners, they probably thought they would have caught me by now. That was one thing they hadn't counted on.

As I covered some ground, I continued thinking my situation over. *Tomorrow, in the daylight, would they shoot me if given the chance? Cut their losses?* They knew, and I knew, they couldn't let me live. I needed a drink of water. It was so bad it hurt to breathe through my mouth, so I breathed through my nose.

The eerie quiet out here at night was almost deafening, nothing but the ringing in my ears. I guess that's my mind's way of processing something. Adding to the fact that I was concentrating so hard—listening to the distance—ever so quiet, crunching behind me. They had fallen back more.

Then, as more time passed and several hundred yards, a startling realization occurred to me. I was barely making any sound either as I walked. A hot panic flash rushed through my body. I stopped immediately, listening. *Were they closer than I thought? Had I lulled myself into a false sense of hope? I listened—nothing. Had they stopped? Did they give up?*

I went to my hands and knees, crawling, feeling the ground cover. What I felt there was a soft, thick blanket of pine needles and some sort of moss between the ferns.

As I crawled along feeling the ground, my head ran into a tree, so I stopped. Still listening to nothing, I felt myself starting to lose control. I stood up. *Get a hold of yourself, Madie,* I told myself. To lose it now would not be a good thing.

I leaned against the nearest tree. Then, I thought I heard something barely audible. Was it a bump against a tree as someone passed—a slight step on a dead, frozen fern? I didn't know.

I did know the longer I stood there, the closer they would get. So, I started walking again. I was thinking deeply. *How could I use this newfound problem to my favor?* Then, it came to me: *What's fair for one is fair for all.* If I can't hear them, Mother Nature was returning the favor.

I made a hard turn to the right. I was guessing at least a ninety-degree turn. That felt as if I were going south, the direction I needed to be going. Any greater of a degree, and I would walk directly upon them.

My senses were at a state of high alert—my hearing was anyway. I slowed my walk, more cautious of the obstacles in front of me. Still nothing; maybe this would work. My new plan was to walk what I thought would be a mile or so, and then I would make another sharp turn. I was going to do this process throughout the night. Then, when the sun rose in the morning, I headed south.

This would work, I told myself. *There's no way they could follow me.*

Not in the darkness, and leaving no footprints, only occasionally stepping in the middle of a fern myself, but that would be easily missed. I was grateful there was no snow cover; if there was, these two men chasing me would track me down like a wounded animal.

It seemed to me that several hours passed. How many, I didn't know. Now, I wish I had brought my watch with me; it would have given me some sort of idea of how long I had survived them. As I thought on, what good would that do? It wouldn't change the outcome—flee or be caught—those were my two options, no matter what time of the day it was, so I walked on.

By now, I needed a drink so badly that my throat hurt. I almost wished there was snow on the ground to get some relief. I really wish I was given more time back at our camp, not just for the reason to say goodbye to Craig but to get a few more items: one of our canteens, a flashlight, and maybe a few items of food, whatever they had left.

Walking, step after step, I told myself: *I could do this. Walk all night and through the day tomorrow. By then, they will surely be gone.* Then, I would stop and sleep the second night of my long journey back.

Then, out of nowhere, I slipped. I threw my arms above my head, flailing like a wounded bird, and the weight of the axe in my right hand almost made me fall backward. I probably would have, but as soon as it started, it was over. Both feet hit solid ground, giving me some stability back. I spun around and bent over at the waist, releasing what uncontrollable energy was left.

Ice! I told myself. *If there's ice, maybe there's water under it.*

Now, I have a life-saving decision to make. I had the axe. Would I dare risk the chance of making any noise by chopping through it? Giving my location away wasn't an option, but neither was dying of dehydration.

What to do, I asked myself. *What if I risk the chance of chopping through the ice and not finding water? Well, at least I would have chunks of ice to suck on.*

The thought of having the cool ice melt in my mouth gave way to temptation.

I felt around the ground, found my clothes, and laid the fish on them. Then, ever so lightly, I chopped the ice. I listened—the deep sound did not penetrate through the woods—I was grateful for the thick, dense trees.

I felt around the ice and found one small indentation where the axe had hit. Then, I found one small sliver of ice and quickly put that in my mouth. OH! It tasted like heaven. It quickly melted, giving me just enough liquid to wet the inside of my mouth. I had to have more—I was like a kid in a candy store; I had to have more!

I raised the axe only inches above the ice, chopping ever so lightly. After hitting what I thought was the same spot several times, I moved over two inches and repeated the same. I felt it give way. I felt around in the darkness and found a piece of ice almost two inches long. This small amount of liquid hit my stomach—it felt so good.

After a time of chopping and eating the ice, my mouth was numb, almost to the point of aching, but I didn't care. The end result outweighed the pain. It's amazing how so little can do so good! I felt revitalized, just from the water.

I had another idea. Chop bigger pieces and put them in my coat pocket. They wouldn't melt; I now had a portable canteen without the can. After filling both pockets with ice, I stood up again. I stood there longer than I should have. No sounds coming from the dark in any direction. I felt so good, I almost smiled. I had water, which was important; I had lost my attackers, which was even more important.

I turned and started walking again; the only way to finish this journey was to get started. One step at a time—each step was one closer to home.

3
CHAPTER

The sun was soon to rise. I could tell because the temperature had fallen a few more degrees. One thing a person learns from being outside all the time is that it always gets colder before it gets warmer. Why did that happen? I don't know, but I could tell the temperature changed when I inhaled. The inside of my nostrils felt as if the tiny hairs were freezing. This meant it was at least zero or a few degrees below.

As a faint hint of red glow appeared in the sky, I became drowsy. This is the time of day when it is hard to stay awake when one has been awake all night. I was thinking back to the beginning of our trip. I started crying again.

This was to be a three-week vacation. We had driven to the last possible location in northern Canada, where we could still get a float plane to fly us as far north into Canada as possible, landing just miles short of where the tundra of the Yukon started. It took some special arranging; even as crazy as the bush pilots are, none would accept our offer. They all said it was too far north for them.

Plus, given the time of year, the first week of October, in the States, it was still fall out, with the leaves in their early stages of turning. This "far north" was different. It was in the early stages of winter. Given the differences in temperature from year to year, it could still be mild out, or it could be in the deep thralls of winter, deep snow, or even blizzards.

We finally found one pilot just before giving up. After many phone calls with him, he finally said yes. He had to take some extra precautions himself. His biggest concern would be the ice on the lake where he had chosen to land. If the ice was thin, the plane would fall through—that would be the end of all of us. He had to bring extra fuel.

By his calculations, he told us, the plane's fuel tank would be almost empty when we landed. He had to have that much more to return. But he did agree—now, I wished he hadn't.

On our flight to our destination, Craig and I both saw the eighty-pound bag on concrete lying on the floor by the side door. Neither of us asked; we had no clue what it was for.

When we reached the lake we were to land on, we were both elated. We couldn't wait to land and get started. He flew over the lake at two hundred feet. It was beautiful. The sheen from the ice looked as if someone had laid a glass plate on top of the water.

"No snow," the pilot said, "that's a good thing; it gives the cold a chance to drive the ice deeper."

Then, as he circled around, he said to Craig, "Alright, on this next pass, I want you to open the side door and, when I tell you, throw that bag of concrete out."

We were only one hundred feet above the lake this time. I had to ask, "What is that for?"

"Well, if that falls through, we don't land. Then, it's a one-way ticket back to where we started from, and you two get to pump fuel from those drums into the fuel tank."

I felt my heart sinking into the pit of my stomach. All this arranging, all the work involved, and now, so close, we could see it. It all depended on that bag of concrete. We had no idea it would come down to this.

I could also see the disappointment on Craig's face.

The vision in my memory is still so vivid! Craig went to slide the bag out the door. He gave it one shove and stopped. I could see the concern on his face.

"It's solid," Craig replied.

"Yeah, that's the whole idea. Shove it out," was all the pilot said.

Craig did! As I watched it fall toward the ice, my fingers and toes were crossed. It landed nearly flat and bounced several feet into the air, landed again, and then slid a long way across the lake. We all cheered out of happiness.

On our third pass over, we could see where the ice was severely fractured from where the bag of concrete landed, but at least it didn't fall through.

"The impact from that is far greater on the ice than what this plane would do. We'll just set this thing down as if we were landing feathers."

And he did. Not looking out, I couldn't tell when we quit flying and started rolling across the ice. Then, I realized what we were up against. I was glad we had chosen this pilot; he knew his stuff.

I remember his last words before he closed the door. "If anything happens to you, just get to a lake, call me, and give me your GPS coordinates. I will be there as soon as possible."

How easy and safe that sounded!

I bounced off a tree, bringing me back to reality. I must have been walking the last few steps with my eyes closed, dreaming of the past—just two days ago.

Now, I had no phone to call with and no GPS locator. Even when the three weeks are up, no one will know where to find me. We were to hike seven miles per day for twenty-one days, one hundred forty-seven miles. Piece of cake!

What wasn't a piece of cake were the odds of me finding that lake was greater than finding the proverbial needle in the haystack. Given the predicament I'm in now, it would be like finding the needle in two haystacks—something that just isn't going to happen. That much I knew.

Sunlight was slowly creeping in between the trees, throwing off shadows, which made it feel spooky. *You're just tired and feeling paranoid, Madie,* I told myself.

Then, it happened: a slight tinge in the middle of my back, between my shoulder blades—the feeling as if an invisible person had stuck an invisible knife there. No pain, just a weird feeling. Then, I knew they were still back there, coming for me. The tracking was slow but not impossible.

One man was trailing much further behind the first, listening for anything that would go snap, crackle, or bump in the night. He didn't want to contaminate the tracks.

They had fallen behind further than they had expected. While running, they knew now it was their turn, for they knew this part of the woods for a hundred-mile radius, like they knew the back of their hands.

They had lived there for nearly five years. They would venture away from their camp, what they now called their home, for days at a time.

During the summer months, it would even be for weeks. They knew where all the lakes, streams, and even good flowing springs were to get water. Food was never a problem, either. They knew the different paths that all sorts of animals traveled, everything from small varmints up to the large elk and moose.

They had become so efficient at hunting that they could stalk different animals and kill them while they were bedded down. They never had to use the gun, ease up and slit the animal's throat and let that animal run off; if it was a large one, then go and collect their kill.

This was different for them. This time, the hunted knew it was being hunted. They didn't panic, they didn't talk - they just followed the trail. Even in the darkness, it was easier than one would expect—for them. The semi-frozen ferns didn't bounce back after being stepped on. They remained flattened from where the footsteps had landed.

The only slow part was the bare ground between the ferns. The first man would go from plant to plant to find the next direction of travel, around the next tree. What made that process go faster was the second man was listening. When he heard a faint sound, he would step in that direction. What was confusing the second man was the sound he continued hearing. Ever so faintly, an inexperienced tracker would miss it.

Swish!

Seconds, even minutes, would pass until he would hear that again…

Swish!

What was that, he wondered.

He knew who was doing it, but what was creating that sound? Soon enough, he knew they would find out. Neither had any doubt that by sunrise, they would be close enough to their prey to find out what it was.

Amateur, the second man thought to himself. *She doesn't even realize she's doing it.*

Then, he heard one barely audible sound. If he had been exhaling instead of inhaling at the time, he would have missed it. It sounded as if it was getting closer. Then he realized that the hunted had just made a sharp turn to their right. He walked several steps in that direction, just a few feet behind the first man, then stopped.

The first man stood up, looking into the darkness in that direction. It was a feeble plot to try and lose them. The corners of his mouth turned up ever so slightly. Even in the daylight, that would have gone unnoticed. It was just for his amusement.

Never had they tracked such an opponent as this. Even with the slow pace they were moving, the blood was pumping through their veins at an increased rate. They were having fun—enjoying the moment. It was often said, between them, that the hunt was better than the kill. This time, that was without a doubt.

Tomorrow, when it was over, which he knew it would be, he was almost wishing it wouldn't be. It had been years since they had this much excitement and fun.

They didn't get cold, didn't get tired—nothing ever bothered them. They felt no remorse for anything they had done in the past. They only lived for the future.

Throughout the night, they followed the many zigzag turns, left and then right. They had long passed the water hole where the ice had been chopped up.

Clever, the second man thought. That one, he hadn't heard.

One more advantage that was in their favor was that they were heading in the direction of where they lived. If, for some unforeseen reason, this lasted more than another day, they would be no more than three to five miles away from it. That would be helpful!

The sun was starting to rise. They had closed the gap considerably. The ever so random 'swish' was getting louder. They had followed their prey long enough that by now, they knew the next move or turn she was going to make before it was made.

So easy, they thought. But what was that sound she continued to make? He wished he knew, but whatever it was, he was glad she was doing it.

They knew the direction they were traveling in. Due east—but why—where was she going? Did she even know? He didn't care; whatever it took to get the job done is what they always did.

As it continued to get lighter out, their ground speed increased. They had both learned the art of moving through the forest, making minimal noise, strategically placing each step, and never raising their feet more than a few inches from the ground. Within minutes, they hoped they would see what they had been tracking all night.

The questions I have continue to rise at an insurmountable rate. I walk, I think, mentally, keeping my brain active. The physical end of this was no problem; however, by nightfall, I would be stretching it to the limit. I would worry about that, then.

Who were these two, I asked myself over and over, never coming up with any good answers.

Were they that good that they could follow through utter darkness? If so, how did they become that good? Were they born and raised here, never knowing the difference between right and wrong, never having any laws to obey? The more I thought about it, the more I became confused by it. My best guess is that they ran from civilization, but how long ago? Another unanswered question! I would have to get smarter, like them, and learn to survive on nothing—know what was coming before it happened. I just hoped my instincts improved. If not, what's left of my life would result in hours or days, at best.

I had full sunlight, maybe twenty minutes of it. I could tell, by my already tired body, this was going to be a long day.

I came to a steep, deep ravine. As I looked down it, through the trees, the bottom seemed endless. It was a long way down. Then, as I looked across the horizon at the top of the other side, it was at least a quarter mile away, if not further. What was more disheartening was the steep climb up the other side. That would slow me down tremendously—if they were still coming, it would also be them.

I increased my speed as I descended. I could see a small stream at the bottom, still flowing. The cold weather hadn't ice-locked it yet. When I reached the bottom, I would get a long, cold, soothing drink of water. That thought gave me a little more incentive.

The trip down went fast. I stopped at the stream's edge and dropped the clothes, axe, and fish. Then I dropped to my hands and knees and started drinking. Oh, it felt so good. Though it did taste a little irony, I drank until I couldn't hold it anymore.

Upon doing that, I felt even more reinvigorated than I had been from the chunk of ice. Now, I wished I had something to carry some extra water in. But I didn't, so I didn't dwell on it. I gathered my few sparse belongings, walked down stream until I found a log to cross on, and started up the other side.

Walking up the other side, my footing slipped out from me several times, falling to my hands and knees, only to get up and go on. The incline was much steeper than it looked going down. Already halfway up, I was panting heavily, almost to the point of breaking out in a sweat, even though the temperature couldn't be more than fifteen degrees.

I was turning my feet sideways, trying to get maximum traction. I put the axe in my left hand, so I had the right one free to grab hold of trees or anything else I could get a grip on to pull myself up.

When I crested the hill, I guessed not more than fifteen to twenty minutes had passed. My legs were burning, and I was sucking in air as if I had never run a mile in my life.

Then, there it was again—that feeling—that invisible man sticking that invisible knife in my back. Something told me to turn around and look to the far side of the ravine, so I did.

At first, I saw nothing. But I didn't stop scanning the far side. What was there—nothing—just paranoia setting in? Seconds passed while I looked. My breathing quickly returned to normal. Then, I saw something move, just a quick glance between the trees. I continued to stare at that spot. Seconds later, my biggest fear returned. A cold, bone-chilling flash rushed through my body.

There they were! They walked out into a small clearing just before starting down the slope. They stood there, staring at me. It was no mistake; they could see me as well as I could see them. They didn't move—nor did I—what was next?

The confidence they were emitting I could feel clear across the ravine. That scared me; sheer panic overwhelmed me. Questions were racing through my mind again. *How did they follow me all night? They came into the same exact spot that I had.* That scared me even more.

Now, I knew that these two were better than good; they possessed the sheer cunning ability to hunt that a pack of wolves has. I turned and bolted, running as fast as possible, not looking back. I didn't need to waste the energy or time; I knew what they would be doing.

Before they reached the ravine, they knew it was there. It ran north and south, further than they had ever traveled. They didn't think she would be at the far side already; they hoped to find her at the bottom. They would catch her before reaching the top.

But that wasn't the case! They looked at each other; the man who pulled the trigger slightly raised both shoulders and then tilted his head in the direction down. They both took off at blinding speed, covering more ground than humanly possible. They didn't fall or even stumble, just dodging the trees, left to right; they descended with the grace of a speed skater, shoving off the left leg, gliding to the right and forward, then planting the right foot only to repeat the process to the left.

Reaching the bottom in less than a minute, they stopped to drink water, still carrying the food they had taken from the camp. They quickly ate a small amount of food, drank more water, and then looked up the hill. Then, they were gone as quickly and quietly as they had arrived.

The trip up wasn't as swift. They had the same problem—getting a good, solid foothold wasn't an easy thing. They ascended in the same footprints. It was easy to follow; the dirt had been separated cleanly in many places, leaving long telltale signs of sliding backward while climbing.

When they reached the top, they stopped to listen. Each man was breathing through his nose to reduce the noise so they could hear. Moments passed—nothing—then the faint 'swish.' The trigger man frowned; curiosity had him intrigued. What was she doing to make that noise? No time to ponder that thought now.

21

They were off and running, back in the same formation. The first man was quickly scanning the ground in front of him, looking at the ferns to find which ones had been flattened or to see where the pine needles had slightly been rustled.

Many times, he had ignored this marker, only to quickly turn in the correct direction. At the speed they were now traveling, he had to make quick adjustments. The daylight made it so much easier. They would close the gap on their prey, ending the chase in no time. All animals become tired after a while and give in to a walk. This one would be no different.

Now, I was scared to death, even more so than when they chased me around the lake. I asked myself, *What am I doing wrong?* I critiqued what I had done during the night; I could think of nothing. What those two men behind me did was humanly impossible.

The deep thought of what was coming behind me helped to keep me from thinking about the physical pain I was starting to feel. The drain on my body was starting to slow me down.

It took extra effort to push off of each leg as I ran. I could take nothing for granted, so I just kept running. I had made up my mind I wasn't going to stop until I fell over dead. If I was able to make night fall again, then I would walk, hoping that at some point I could step and rest, even sleep. I covered two, maybe three miles since the ravine. I could think of nothing but what was behind me.

Then, out of nowhere, a conscious thought came to me. It was as if someone was talking to me telepathically. *Madie, what are you doing? You're heading into the sun east; you need to be going south.* I stopped running and leaned against a tree.

Inhaling deeply rapidly, my body lost all of the rhythm of running. The muscles in my legs were calling for more oxygen than the rest of my body could supply. I would have to live with that, or I would not live. I looked up at the sun between the trees. I turned, putting the sun to my left, and started running again.

Now, the sun was directly at me. I had made it through the morning without seeing them. How much distance I had covered, I didn't know. I did know that the distance between each step had decreased. It was becoming a tremendous effort to keep running; I was breathing in short, quick gasps. Oh, how I so badly wanted to stop, just to rest for a short time, then to continue on.

I told myself that sunset was just a few hours away. This far north, I learned that night fall comes much earlier than at home. By three thirty, four o'clock at the latest, it would be dark, and I could rest then.

I can do that, I told myself. *It's just a thing, it'll pass.*

As time passed, the shadows from the trees were reaching across the ground to my far left. It wouldn't be long before the welcomed darkness arrived.

My running became so labored I was going no faster than a fast walk. I had consumed all the ice from the pocket of my coat. I still wanted more—however, I was too tired and too weak to be hungry. All I wanted to do was lie down and sleep.

I decided to walk, conserving what energy was left. Maybe I could walk as fast as I was running, which wasn't very fast anymore.

4
CHAPTER

They didn't stop; instinct told them to keep running. The wind continued to increase throughout the day, and they could no longer hear anything ahead of them. The stamina of their prey was astounding to them. They were breathing heavily out of their mouths, and their speed diminished. They knew they were slowly losing ground, and their hunt was pulling away—hour by hour.

They weren't worried; as long as they stayed reasonably close, they would always have the track to follow, the one thing that someone, or something, could not run away from, the telltale sign that was always left behind. It was their DNA, the sole bloodline to their prey.

Knowing now they were in this for the long haul, that fact drove them even harder. No animal they had ever tracked and killed had been so elusive. They had never failed, not even once. She was the ultimate prey!

In the early days, when they were learning the fine art of tracking, they made mistakes, but they quickly learned from them and became efficient hunters. Knowing she had no place to go, nowhere to hide, and hundreds of miles to the nearest town, she was going to lose.

The weather was changing. In their years of living in the wilderness, they had become excellent weathermen. As the afternoon passed, the wind still increased. That wasn't anything unusual, but it brought an increase in humidity. The temperature continued to rise into the low twenties.

A snowstorm was coming sometime during the night. That didn't bother them; tracking would be much easier. What they had experienced, time and time again at this time of year, was the bitter cold that followed the storm. That would last for days or even weeks until the next storm passed through.

They had no warm clothes with them. They hadn't planned on this when they left their home. They would need everything: warmer boots, gloves, hats, and heavy clothes. They knew exactly where they were, only miles from where they lived. It was now or never!

They had stopped running and looked to the north. Not only could they feel the storm coming, they could smell it, and it was going to be a good one.

After a short glance at each other, the trigger man pointed to himself and tilted his head in the direction of their home. Then, he pointed to his partner and moved the first two fingers on his right hand in a walking motion. Then, he scuffed his feet in the dirt, baring the frozen earth beneath the pine needles. The second man nodded; he knew what his partner meant and what he had to do. That meant leaving a trail so obvious that he could follow it and quickly catch back up.

They turned and started running again, each in their own direction. The man following their prey slid his feet along as he ran. He looked back at the ground behind him. It was obvious where he had been; anyone could follow him, even a blind man. Satisfied with what he was doing, he continued on.

He slowed to a walk long before dark. He was feeling fatigued; his legs had become much heavier, leaving the obvious trail. He didn't feel the need to push his prey harder. She had to be feeling tired by now also, almost to the point of collapsing. He wanted to give her the false feeling that she was alone, that they had given up. The one thing he didn't want to do was to get too close and then make some sort of noise that she would hear.

Maybe she would lie down and rest. No way could she continue on a second night without sleep; at least, that's what he was counting on!

So, he eased up, ever so quietly, carefully placing each step. He didn't know how far ahead she was, but when he did catch up, then he would know.

Moving through the darkness, literally feeling her path, he could tell that the length of her steps was short. It wouldn't be long at all now. Then, he would just sit down and wait.

The cloud cover had moved in; there was no moon or stars, just pure, utter blackness, much blacker than the previous night. He was on his hands and knees, feeling her path. His calloused hands felt indifferent to the frozen ground. This was balmy weather to them. After surviving through so many times of thirty below blasts, anything above zero was summertime up here.

The one thing that made these two men different from other people was that their mental capacity didn't register pain. Among their other abnormalities, which they never realized, they thought they were normal, but they were far from it. Their past drove them to where they are today. They had to leave civilization or pay the consequences for what they had done.

He reached their home, which was no more than a small cave on the side of a large hill. At nearly ten feet wide and sixteen feet long, it had all the amenities of a home. They had placed several inches of pine needles on the floor.

Off to one side, close to the entrance, they had built a fire pit. They also had constructed a homemade chimney that led up to a natural vent, so in the extremely cold weather, they had heat. One of their biggest finds, which was the reason they chose to remain in this area, was a coal vein that ran out of the side of the hill above them, supplying them with an abundance of fuel.

With the many lakes to catch fish and ample animals to kill for food, they needed nothing else except for some excitement in their lives. Now, they have it! This was the most exhilarating thing they had done since they had arrived. They were grateful she didn't quit easily.

He changed his boots and grabbed all the warm gear they would need. They had a flashlight, one they had never used; it was for emergencies only. Now was such a time it had to be used to get back as quickly as possible. He stuffed both pockets on both jackets, full of elk and moose jerky. Then he put a canteen around his neck.

Travel light, that's what they always did. He could think of nothing else they would need. Then, he was gone as swiftly as he had arrived.

It had been long since nightfall. I could feel my body shutting down; it was telling me I needed sleep.

But not yet, I told myself, *I need to go on just a few more miles.*

In the pure blackness I'm now traveling in, I didn't need to keep my eyes open, so I didn't. I held the axe handle out in front of me, using it as a blind person using their cane.

As it bounced off a tree in front of me, I would walk around it. I had no idea if I was traveling in the right direction anymore. It's a struggle to stay mentally focused. When I walked in one direction, I would count my steps. Then, I would try to correct my travel direction in the opposite way. Still, I had no idea if I was right or wrong.

My body was becoming so limp, and I was so exhausted I thought that every step would be my last. Falling over and passing out was a good possibility. I couldn't; I knew they were still behind me somewhere—how close remained a mystery, which drove me on.

Then, my shins bumped into something. I stopped just before tripping over it. If I had, I don't know if I could have gotten up. I bent down and felt what it was. It was a dead limb. I had a thought: *How could I use this in my favor?* Then, an idea came to me.

I laid each end in the ferns, just inches off the ground. If one of them stepped on it or walked through it, it would snap. If I had heard that, then I would have known they were too close. Pleased with my plan, I continued on.

I now have lost track of time and the distance that has passed. I didn't care. All I wanted to do was lie down and sleep, so I stopped and leaned against a tree. How easy it would be to give up now, to give in to them and let them win.

Tears started streaming down my face. *Craig, I'm sorry, I can't go on. I'm just not physically capable anymore,* I said to myself.

Then, I heard his voice, as I had so many times while running our races.

"Madie, you can do this. The finish line isn't far ahead." His voice was as crisp and clear as if he was standing next to me. That instantly woke me up. I was fully alert.

I wanted to ask out loud: "Craig, are you here?" But I knew he wasn't. I had to be hallucinating; that scared me.

I trudged on; it was an effort to pick up my feet. I never heard a snap or crack behind me. Had they fallen that far back? I had seen enough in the past twenty-four hours to know they were coming for me, in the exact same path I had used. So, maybe they found that. It was too easy for them. So, why not build a better trap, one which they could miss?

So, I thought up a new trap as I walked. It would take me some time, but I had a new plan. I searched the area for all the sticks and limbs I could find. I carefully laid them in my path, blanketing the ground. I crisscrossed the sticks as best as possible; then, I covered them with pine needles. I had the ground covered for nearly five feet. Then, on each side of that, hidden between the fern plants, I struck the ground with the axe, driving it just below the frost line.

In each slit, I stuck another limb straight up out of the ground. I did this many times on each side, something they would not be looking for after finding what I had put in the path. Or, at the very least, I hoped.

I walked on somewhere between one and two hundred yards. Then, I sat down; I needed to sleep, if only for a short while.

They had to be in the same dismal shape I was, I told myself. Maybe they had given up for the night and then continued on in the daylight. I would be long gone by then.

I sat leaning backward against a tree. I knew I wouldn't sleep long like this, but even a short cat nap would be welcomed.

At what time I fell over, lying face up on the ground, I don't know. I felt something cold lightly tickling my face, then running down both cheeks. Barely awake, I was confused. My subconscious was trying to tell me to wake up. What was happening to me? Where was I? Then, I bolted upright in a panic mode again.

Running at an amazing speed back the way he came, the flashlight made all the difference. Without it, he knew it would be mid-morning before he caught up with his friend, his partner in crime. But knowing it would be one hour max, probably less at this speed, the end result drove him on.

Moving too close to a tree while running, the clothes he was carrying made a sound: 'Swish' He smiled. Then, he knew how careless she had been, he thought. If she were hunting an animal for food, she would starve to death.

Their tracking just became faster; his new plan was the harder they pushed their prey, the more mistakes she would make without even knowing it.

Knowing the hunted, to know what it would do before doing it, always made it easier. That's what made them such efficient killers, why they survived for so long in the middle of nowhere.

Biding his time, slowing his pace to half speed, there was no sense in rushing things; his partner would return soon.

Feeling his way along, they were winning. Her pace had slowed even more since dark. He could feel the rustled pine needles, no longer lying in their normal matted position from step to step. Between the steps, a maximum of six inches of ground was covered. She was working hard to go on. It wouldn't be long.

As he crept along, he was trying to do both of their duties. Listening for what could be heard up ahead and concentrating on the ground. As he brought his hand down to feel the next step, his fingertips brushed something. He stopped moving; that didn't feel right.

Ever so slowly, he reached into the darkness, just inches in front of his face. He found it, a large stick. He followed it to the end. There, he found it was stuck in the middle of a fern. Then, he slid his hand along it and underneath. He found it to be elevated just inches above the ground. Why was this here like this? When he found the left end also placed in the middle of a fern, he grinned.

Nice try, sweetie, he said to himself, *but you'll have to do better than that.*

He slowly removed it and laid it to the side. Was this her warning sign? Is she just up ahead, resting? Now, he sat on the ground thinking. Should he risk the chance of going on further? If he did that, would he walk right up on her?

The humidity was becoming denser. It wouldn't be long before it started snowing. That could work both ways for them. On the negative side, the snow would cover the ever-so-light trail she was leaving. On the positive side, there would be footprints left in the snow.

Pondering what to do, depending on just how far ahead she actually was, also threw another variable. It would take them longer to pick up her trail again. If it were daylight, that wouldn't be an issue.

He looked up through the treetops. It was becoming lighter behind the cloud cover. There had to be a full moon behind them. With the clouds becoming thinner, it wasn't long now, the last remaining minutes of calm before the storm. How much snow would fall, they never knew.

He had nothing to do until his partner arrived, so he decided to go on. But now, he moved ever so slowly, as quietly as a ghost, feeling the space in front of him and the ground below. Every fern that came into his path, he would go around or over, if possible, feeling the ground for every small twig that would be there.

This movement caused a lot of up-and-down motion. He was tired, and his muscles were starting to feel fatigued, but he had plenty of reserves left. He inched along without a sound, pleased with himself. As slow as he was moving, at least he was moving ahead, covering enough ground.

Somewhere, not far ahead, between a quarter and a half mile, he felt another anomaly on the ground, something Mother Nature didn't do—a soft blanket of pine needles. He felt along the top of them, as far as he could reach while kneeling, but he couldn't find the other end. He sat back up, sitting on his feet.

Thinking of his next move, excitement rushed in! Never in all their years had they tracked such an admiral prey. This was becoming fun!

Delicately, he removed the pine needles in a small area. Below that, he found small sticks and twigs lying on top of each other. He slid his hand forward, below the top covering.

As far as he could reach, again, it didn't stop. He sat back up again, sitting on his feet.

Clever, he thought, *you spent a good deal of time building your little trap. But what does this mean? Are you just up ahead resting or sleeping? If so, is this your alarm clock?*

He was counting on that! If it were daylight, she could probably be seen sitting, leaning up against a tree, sleeping.

So, he did the same. He felt for the nearest tree, sat on the ground, and leaned up against it. Nothing else to do now but wait for his partner to arrive, welcoming the chance to rest but not sleep. He would need to warn his friend before coming too close and be heard. She was just up ahead; he could sense her presence.

The stress on his legs and lungs had slowed his speed, not nearly moving as fast as they had during the day. The flashlight made it almost too easy to travel, scanning it to the left and right, then straight ahead as he ran.

He was guessing at least two hours had passed since he and his partner had split up. Another guess was he was halfway back. In less than one hour, he would be back to the point where he had left them. They couldn't have gotten far, maybe two miles total.

When he did reach that point, he needed a few minutes' rest. He looked at the limb leaning against a tree, holding fern stalks—his marker.

Waiting for his heavy breathing to subside, he moved the light beam across the ground. The pine needles dragged into small piles would be easy to follow. He could walk at a normal speed now, not make any noise, and still catch up soon.

As he moved along, careful not to step on each fern, he listened—nothing. Then, suddenly, the obvious path stopped. So did he! Something had happened. Did his partner have to start running again for some reason? Or was he so close that he had to move silently? He scanned the light up ahead on the ground. What he saw there, he knew it was the latter.

Leaning against the tree, where he had been sitting for a long time in the dark. That's where he felt the most comfort, the solitude. He thought he saw something off to his left, a quick flash, then nothing. He continued to look, and moments later, there it was again.

He instantly knew what it was: his partner. He stood up, his knees lightly popped, only to be heard by him. He frowned. Thirty-eight years ago, age was something he couldn't stop. But the rest of him was solid, lean muscle, not an ounce of fat.

Eating the way he and his partner have for the past five years, no fatty foods, plus the miles of exercise every day, their bodies had no choice but to conform. They both had also learned that the body will adjust to anything. They also had no problem adjusting mentally. So, he raised his arms above his head and started waving them back and forth. He would quickly be seen. When the light shone directly in his eyes, he dropped his right arm to neck level and waved it through mid-air from left to right.

When he saw his partner ahead, waving, he felt whole again. The engine was hitting on all cylinders once more. That was the first time since he could remember that they had been apart. The duo could accomplish anything they had set out to do. So, when he saw his partner drag his hand across his throat, he stopped, only for a few seconds. Then, with added caution, he walked the remaining distance.

He handed over the clothes, boots, and canteen of water. His partner made the walking motion with the first two fingers on his right hand, then pointed ahead. Holding the flashlight, aiming the beam at the ground, his excitement grew.

"How close is she?" he silently asked.

He stretched his arms out in front of himself; his hands were feet apart. His partner shook his head no. He held his hand out, showing just inches between his finger and thumb. Then, he pointed at the ground where the trap had been made. Looking at that, he then nodded, indicating that he understood.

After putting on his additional clothing, they both drank from the canteen. They then looked at each other and nodded, silently saying, "Let's finish this."

The snow started falling through the trees; the timing couldn't have been better. With the ground illuminated from the flashlight, they walked on each side of the trap.

Crack! Crack! They both froze! The one holding the flashlight looked down at the ground. He saw the sticks protruding up out of the ground. He smiled. They just gave away their location.

He thought to himself, still smiling, *This just gets better and better!* She was an admirable prey, one with a sense of reason who could fight back. Something they never had before.

He then aimed the beam at the ground in front of his partner's feet, showing him what they had missed. Looking at the ground in front of him, he also saw the sticks. He raised both shoulders, momentarily held them there, and dropped them quickly, saying, "Oh well!"

CHAPTER 5

I was on my feet instantly, confused, lightheaded, and feeling unsteady. Too many things were happening at once, and trying to process it all at the same time, I mentally couldn't do it. Still more asleep than coherent, I concentrated on listening. I heard nothing, no more sounds, but I knew they were back, a mere hundred yards away.

So, next, I tried to figure out what was wrong with my face. I wiped it with my hands; it was wet. I looked around. *Was my mind playing tricks on me? Was it incapable, from lack of sleep, of processing all the information it was receiving at once—the end result being hallucinations?*

Now, even more confused, I could see the trees. Not great, but enough to know where they stood. I quickly looked up; it was still dark out. At that same moment, I felt the dampness hit my face.

"Oh Lord, no," I said very quietly. Then, I knew it was snowing.

Two strikes against me now. The first is their physical ability to run as well as they can. The second the snow, it would be much easier for them to follow me. Three strikes, and I would be out. I wasn't going to allow that to happen. That whole thought process didn't take more than ten seconds, but I was thinking clearly again.

Now, what do I do next? Do I turn and run? They would surely hear me. Then, it wouldn't be long before I left tracks in the snow. Or do I stay and try to hide, let them walk up on me, hoping they didn't see me? The pitcher was standing on the mound, winding up for his next pitch. I hope it wasn't going to be a strike.

I turned and bolted; running was my only option. It wasn't far up ahead before it became even brighter. I was feeling somewhat better, so I knew I wasn't hallucinating. I couldn't figure out what it was.

Then, in four steps, I ran out onto a lake. The vivid clearing was beyond all figments of imagination. I could see the glare off the ice, which made visibility good. Instantly, my next thought wasn't good; they would be able to see me.

As quickly as that happened, it disappeared. I looked to the sky as I ran and saw heavy cloud cover move in above. Then, back to nearly darkness!

I had enough time to mentally remember seeing the distant shoreline, which was a good distance away. Without the tree cover, the wind was blowing hard, which made the wind chill factor drop the temperature greatly. I didn't care; I didn't have time to be cold. Then, it started snowing heavily; I could feel it pelting the side of my face.

Things were looking up in my favor. No strike this time; I so thank God for this one. They wouldn't be able to track me now. The wind and snow would erase all signs. If I could get far enough ahead, then turn sharply and run back into the trees, the snow would hide my steps. At least, I hoped.

I ran hard on the ice, careful not to slip and fall, which was my biggest concern for the moment. Take one problem at a time, and worry about the next when it happens. I spent several minutes on the ice, happy that this was a large lake.

Then, I made the turn and headed into the trees. I was back to a fast walk when I became blinded again. I don't know how much time this has given me. I knew I couldn't waste the snow falling to cover my steps as I continued on.

I walked for hours. The fatigue had set in again; my legs were numb, feeling as though I had a ten-pound weight hanging on each foot. Sheer determination drove me on. I didn't know if I was still heading south; it just felt right.

I stopped and started stuffing my mouth full of snow. The cold, ironic taste felt good when it hit my stomach. I ate until my stomach could hold no more liquid. Then, I continued on at a much slower pace.

Moving forward slowly through the second night without sleep would be better than not moving at all. Tomorrow, in the daylight, they would somehow, somewhere, find my trail again.

Before they took their first step, they heard a faint, indiscrete sound. With the wind blowing harder, there was no way of telling if it was her or something else. They didn't care; they were whole again, a well-oiled machine that was unstoppable.

Reaching the spot where she had sat down, they stopped. Some telltale signs were there again; the heels of her boots had slid across the ground, piling up the pine needles in the direction opposite the tree. The trigger man bent down and felt the ground where it looked like she had sat; it was warmer there. He nodded his head once, stood, and quickly scanned the area with the flashlight; nothing else was there.

Before they reached the lake, the heavy cloud cover blew in overhead. They didn't notice this until they ran out onto the ice. There, they found the wind blowing much harder, and it was snowing heavily. These two combinations happening at once made the snow blow sideways—from right to left, which meant they were heading west.

He pointed the light out over the lake. With the density of the snowfall, they could see no further than ten feet. Since the beginning of the chase, this was the first obstacle they had to overcome, and it was a major one. They now knew they were going to lose a lot of time. They stood there thinking, hoping the other would come up with the holy grail plan. If they stayed out on the ice, they could easily pass by the spot where she entered the woods.

They had to return to the trees and follow the edge of the lake around, but with the heavy snowfall, time was against them. Until the snow cover on the ground became several inches deep, there would be no tracks to follow. The man holding the light shook his head. Feeling a bit disgusted, he turned and walked back toward the trees.

Where she entered back into the woods, they had no way of knowing. It could be ten feet down the edge or at the far end of the lake. They walked far enough into the trees to get out of the heavy wind. Then, they sat down; sleeping there was their only option.

When they woke, the clarity through the trees was intensified from the snow cover on the ground. The crystals gleaming on top looked as if someone had sprinkled diamonds across the snow. But they had already made their share of those, more than they would spend in two lifetimes—theirs.

They stood, stretched, and brushed the snow from their clothes. After walking around the south side of the lake, it was as they thought—no footprints left behind in the snow.

Splitting up, they walked in a zigzag pattern, one to the east, the other to the west, always meeting back in the middle. Hours passed with no results.

After nearly two dozen times meeting back up with each other, the tracker looked to the trigger man and spoke, "She walked all night." The trigger man only nodded.

As the day wore on, the temperature dropped, as they knew it would. Not knowing the exact degree, they guessed it was at least fifteen to twenty degrees below zero. They put the face masks on the hoods from their jackets and tied the string below their chin. They had the money, ample amounts of it. In the summertime, on their once-a-year trip to the closest town, they always bought the best quality clothes made for extreme weather.

They always bought the basic necessities to survive. Flour, lard, BIC lighters, coffee, salt, and an assortment of other items they thought they would need. Each year, it was always more than the two of them could pack back into their bags. Each year, they always did the same thing.

After the first year's dilemma on how to carry nearly two hundred pounds of gear several hundred miles back was solved—it was easy. They couldn't buy pack horses; they had no means of feeding them. The solution was goats, depending on the size, two large ones or three medium ones. Pack off the gear on them, tie them together, and lead them back. Once there, eat them, one at a time, until they are gone.

They learned how to tan the hides. On the days they didn't need to fish or hunt food, to pass the time, that's what they did. They had elk, moose, deer, and goat hides. Their mattresses were hides, and so were their blankets.

Several of the heavier elk hides, sewn together, made the door. It was an excellent insulator to hold the heat in the cave. They weren't trappers; they didn't believe in killing the smaller animals just for their hides. Those they only killed for the food.

They had dug a small room on the side of the hill beside their cave. It served as a meat locker, cool in the summer, and in most winters, it kept the meat from freezing.

They made their own jerky, more of it than they could usually eat. It would last much longer than the raw meat. Now, their heavy, hi-tech Thinsulate coat pockets were filled with it, knowing they wouldn't have time to hunt on this trip.

They carried fish lines and several hooks along with a few BIC lighters in the smaller pockets, as well as one hatchet, just in case. Always be prepared; Mother Nature can sometimes be ruthless.

Mid-afternoon had arrived, and they had still found no sign of a track—not the one they were looking for anyway. They had crossed the hoof prints of a small herd of elk and a few deer.

Where she had gone, they knew they would find her—it was just a matter of time.

Throughout the night, I walked. The terrain wasn't bad, with no steep hills to climb or descend. That was a good thing. I was too tired to make the effort.

I wished I had a watch with me since I had walked the past hours from the lake. *But why would that matter?* I asked myself. No matter what time it was, day or night, I had two things to accomplish: one was to lose the two monsters behind me, and the other was to return to civilization.

I thought of Craig as I walked to keep my mind occupied so I didn't think of being so tired. I cried, I laughed, I got angry—the whole gamut of emotions. The same memory, the one I always returned to, was Craig falling over backward. I knew he was dead before he hit the ground. At least I know he didn't suffer.

"Craig, I will survive them; I will give it all I have." I don't know why I said that out loud; I felt he was near. I know he heard me.

All of a sudden, I was falling, and the ground dropped from below me. It scared me to death, and I didn't know how far I was going to fall.

This is it, I thought. *Am I going to be killed when I land or crippled? Will I slam into a tree on the way down and break my neck?*

Those thoughts flashed through my mind in less than a second. Another second later, I hit the ground, bounced, hit the ground again, and slid another five feet or so downward. While sliding, I tried to get a hold of something, anything, but nothing was there but snow. My full attention now was trying to slow my descent, still not knowing how much further the bottom was. I didn't have time to panic; everything was happening too fast in the coal-black darkness.

Two seconds later, my body planed out, and I was sliding horizontally across the ice. My body spun a half-turn on my stomach before it stopped. I lay there momentarily, trying to regain my senses. *Where am I?* Then, I knew that was a stupid thought; I was in the middle of nowhere.

I slowly stood up. I felt no pain, which was a stroke of luck. I escaped this with no harm done. The only damage that had occurred was, while I slid down, the snow packed in the front of my coat and down my neck. As the adrenaline subsided, the wet, cold sensation set in. I quickly unzipped my coat and shook the snow out.

I stood there wondering, *Was I standing out on a lake again?* I didn't think so. I could hear the wind howling in the treetops around me. I only felt a slight breeze, so I was still in the woods.

I turned and cautiously walked in the direction I slid. I felt my right foot come down on something hard before my third step landed flat on the ice. It went out from underneath me, sliding backward.

As it gained momentum, my left foot went with it. I fell forward, landed face-first on a steep slope, then slid backward out onto the ice again.

"Shit," I said as I stood back up. Then, I knew where I was. I was standing in a creek, one that had washed a deep ditch in the ground over the past few hundred thousand years.

I used the axe as a climber's pick to climb up the other side. I was breathing heavily as I crested the top. I stood there to catch my breath. I was thinking it shouldn't have taken that much effort.

On another day, I would have scaled that as if it was nothing. But this wasn't a normal day! I had to stop and sleep; traveling at night had to stop. Next time, I might not be so lucky. This was as good as anywhere to do just that.

Before I sat down, I had another idea. If they were going to catch up to me before daylight, why not have another warning sign? This was the perfect spot. I traversed the slope back down to the creek on my butt. I walked the short distance to the far back, which was no more than six feet, stopped, knelt down, and swung the axe into the ice.

Not knowing how thick it was after the first blow, I tried to hit the same spot on the second swing. I did, and the axe fell through with little effort. I chopped the ice nearly three dozen times in a path no wider than three feet as I backed up to the bank behind me.

With that accomplished, I sat down, completely exhausted. I was close to sweating, and I didn't know if I had the strength to climb back up the slope again. After a few minutes of rest, I was happy with myself. If they crossed here during the night without seeing what I had done, they would fall through. That would wake me and give me just enough time to get up and run.

I walked only a few feet from the creek bank, pulled my gloves and face mask from my pocket, and put them on. That left a pair of insulated socks in reserve in one of the pockets. I set the fish and the axe down beside me, and I lay down in the snow. I was glad Craig had chosen the heavy winter gear that he had.

Everything was waterproof. The coat and pants were a smooth, soft, slippery material that the snow wouldn't stick to. They were also windproof, and I knew that sometime soon, the latter would be tested.

The snow felt so good, soft, cushiony—almost as good as if I were at home lying on my own mattress. My body welcomed the relief, and to get off my feet was a blessing. I lay there thinking before drifting off to sleep: *If they allow it, I will have to travel during the daytime only.* I was so lucky this time, plus the time and energy wasted walking in the wrong direction at night. I need every day and every mile to count.

I woke just enough to realize that I was shivering. I didn't want to open my eyes, not yet anyway, but I was too cold to lay there any longer. I opened my eyes; it was light out, so I forced myself to get up. I had to start moving to get warm and to keep to what distance I did have on them.

After standing, I stretched. I could feel my body protest; it wanted another day of rest, a luxury I couldn't give it. There's one thing I always told myself each year when we started running again: work through the pain. The body will always adjust; I just had to do it mentally, which was always the hardest part. I started walking with the sun to my left. I was wondering how many days I would have to adjust mentally before my body adjusted to this grueling pace I was giving it. Only time will tell!

I looked to the sky; the sun hadn't been up more than an hour, one hour lost to those behind me.

It wasn't long before all the aches and pains were worked out, so I picked up my pace. I was only going to run if I had to.

I unzipped my coat and untied the hood, letting it fall back. It was much colder out. The coldest day we, or I should now say I, had encountered. I knew it would come sometime soon, but only time would tell how much cold it would get.

I was hungry. I had the two fish, but I knew I had better save them for bad times. I knew if I always had the two fish, I would never starve to death. Besides, it had only been two days. I could go a few more without food. I had all the fresh snow I could use for water, plus the axe.

The next lake I came to, and all those after, I had ice to eat or chop a hole and drink water. Now, I realized the axe would be my survival tool. Without it, I somehow felt that I wouldn't make it.

The ground was no longer flat. I was now walking up and down long, slow, rolling hills. The trees were thinning out, thus allowing more sunshine through, so the ferns ceased to exist. I started to feel a little paranoid, feeling more vulnerable out in the open. I didn't like it!

But why, I asked myself. Now, with the snow on the ground, they would always be able to see me. I was letting my mind babble on; it had nothing else to do for stimulation. I was just letting my mind wander too far. I know they're back there, somewhere. That thought was always there; there's just no need to go overboard with it. The one thing I couldn't lose, besides the axe, was my sanity.

I walked for hours throughout the day. My legs started burning; they cried for a rest, but I pushed on. I thought about everything, from the past years gone by to the most current events. I even thought about my future; if I did make it out of here, what would I do? How can I go on with a normal life after living like this? No Craig by my side, no rock, no one to talk to!

I had to sit down and rest, if only for a short while. I was breathing heavily just from walking. I continually switched the axe from one hand to the other; it felt as if it weighed a hundred pounds. My arms burned nearly as badly as my legs.

I had to zip up my coat as soon as I sat. The temperature continually dropped throughout the day. Soon after dark, it would be below zero.

As I sat, I thought of the what-ifs and what-to-dos which haunted me. By four in the afternoon, it would be dark again, making it too easy to stop for the day. Would they? I doubted it. Do I risk going on and then having something worse happen to me than falling down the creek bank?

I finally decided to go on the lesser of the two evils. The odds of getting hurt in the dark didn't seem to be as great as them catching me. I ate more snow before getting up. Then, with a heavy sigh, I rolled onto my knees and stood. The wind was blowing harder from the north. Hitting me in the back wasn't too bad; at least I would know I was walking south.

I walked several hours past dark. It was much easier than the night before; the stars were shining. That gave off enough light so I could see the dark silhouettes of the trees ahead. The only danger that I encountered was stepping over a dead tree that had fallen into my path. I was more than grateful for that.

I came to a point where I just couldn't go on any further. It was time to call it a day. I survived one more, only to face the same tomorrow.

I had to get out of the wind somehow. I saw a heavy dark spot just ahead. Maybe that would be enough of a windbreak to sleep. As I walked into the clump of trees, I found it didn't. It did, however, reduce the wind greatly. I chopped several limbs off the surrounding trees, scraped the ground clear of snow, and laid a thick cushion on the ground.

Then, I had another idea. I chopped many more limbs and carried them to my makeshift mattress. I laid down and covered myself up with them. But, after piling on several inches, I found them to be heavy. They did serve their purpose, however. I could no longer feel the wind.

Was I warm and toasty? No, but I was too tired to care. I soon fell asleep. It was a fitful night of sleep. I constantly woke up shivering. I even managed to roll over under the heavy limbs, but I did sleep.

I got up the next morning feeling much better. I knew that would be short-lived. At least, in a few more days, my body will have adjusted to walking all day. It would take much longer to adjust to sleeping in the cold.

The day came and passed. I walked for miles. If I had to make some type of a logical guess, I would say I covered twelve to fourteen miles with no sign of them.

My stomach ached from the vast hollowness, but it wasn't time to eat one of the fish.

I walked down a steeper hill on the back side of the wind. There, I made another bed and slept.

CHAPTER 6

Their hunting had no success. It was getting late in the day, and in less than an hour, it would be dark, but they had no problem with that. Their walking in diagonal patterns had become much wider. It takes as many as twenty minutes to get out and then back, then wait for the other to arrive to give the news of good or bad.

Even though they were losing the daylight and wasting extra energy, they showed no emotion. As always, now that the cold front had moved through, they would have time. Maybe as many as three days before it would snow again.

Long past the point for a quick catch, they knew they were in this for the long haul, a trip toward civilization with plenty of time.

They had decided to stop and sleep for the night when it became dark. Start at daybreak, be fully refreshed, and continue. The tracker looked to his partner, then up at the sky.

"Time for one more!" He nodded, turned, and walked off.

Nearly dark, he was just about to turn and start the diagonal leg of his search back. He heard a distant tap of a tree, three rapid taps in succession. Knowing what it meant, he took off running in that direction. He ran a good distance, but during that time, it had become dark. He stopped and listened—nothing. So, he went to the nearest tree, grabbed the lowest branch, and pulled on it until it snapped.

The response came quickly: one tap up ahead and slightly to the right. When he arrived, the tracker was leaning against a tree, and he pointed to the ground. The trigger man turned on the flashlight and looked down at the tracks.

After studying them for a moment, he said, "She's dragging her feet."

Leaning against the tree, he nodded. "These are old, a day and a half ago, just after the snow."

He pointed the light at the ground again, thinking. They both knew she was a long way ahead of them, so without saying a word, they started walking in the direction she was going. Many hours later, they stopped, scraped the ground clear of snow, and laid down and slept. The cold wasn't cold enough to bother them.

Before daylight, they were up. After eating several pieces of jerky and drinking some water, they started again, but at a much faster pace. They wanted to get close before night.

Past midday, they came to the spot where she had slept. The tracker kicked the pile of pine limbs apart, then raised his eyebrows. His partner nodded.

"Somewhat resourceful." They ate more jerky, thinking in silence, and then started walking.

Her steps were lighter now, covering a longer distance between each footprint, and she wasn't dragging them through the snow. Knowing she hadn't slept there last night, they were amazed. She had walked the entire night and the next day after the storm. Her tracks were still old. With the wind blowing as it was, some of the tracks had fresh snow blown in them.

They were starting to have a little respect for her. Her determination to continue only fueled theirs. The ultimate prey was getting better. However, she wouldn't outdo them—that much they did know.

"We're still a day behind," the tracker said.

He nodded.

"It's going to be another long night."

He nodded again.

The rolling hills and thin trees had all but let the wind erase her tracks. Finding one behind a tree, sometimes several footprints in a group of trees, was all they needed. They pushed on until the early hours of the morning, when they stopped and slept.

They woke just after daybreak, doing the same thing as the morning before, eating jerky and taking a drink of water, which was almost gone now, then off following footsteps.

They were breathing heavily, walking at such a fast pace. The sun was now high in the sky. They had covered miles during the night and throughout the morning.

Her tracks were cleaner, not having as much snow in them as they got closer. That excited them. Maybe they would be able to see her on one of the rising hillsides before dark. Even if it was only a second glance, between the trees invigorated them.

When nightfall did come, the wind had slowed to a slight breeze. Still no visual contact, but the tracks were definitely fresher. They followed them until they had to stop and rest. This was a pace that they were not accustomed to. Their bodies were being pushed to the limit.

While they scraped the ground clear of snow, the tracker spoke the first words that were uttered all day, "Tomorrow."

He nodded.

Something scared me out of a sound sleep. I sat up and listened but heard nothing. Was I having a nightmare? Or did I actually hear something, and my subconscious told the conscience to wake up? I didn't know.

I started shivering, and my fingers ached. Then, there it was again. That hollow feeling in the middle of my back. Something was wrong, and I had a pretty good idea of what it was—no, who it was. This was not going to be a good day, not that the others were a walk in the park leading to the picnic. I shook my head; I had a bad feeling.

I got up and knew I had to do the most dreaded thing I had to do in the cold. I had to urinate. The thought of one's behind hanging out in this kind of weather just isn't right. With or without them behind me, it has to be done.

I walked less than a mile before I came upon a spot on the ground that had been all torn up. It looked as if two animals had fought there for some time.

As I looked at the tracks, trying to figure out what kind of animals had done this, I realized they weren't fighting; I was excited! I could see all the cracked acorn shells. They had smelled the nuts underneath the snow and had pawed the ground to find them.

I did the same thing. *Food,* I thought. I dug the snow away from the ground with the side of my foot, and sure enough, there was one acorn. I quickly bent over and picked it up. I held it in my hands, looking at it as if it were a precious piece of gold. I was happy—I was actually smiling! It's amazing how something so insignificant could make me so excited. Given the present circumstances, this meant survival, something the animals that were here before me endured every day.

I worked my way around the tree. Scratching the ground, I found more than I hoped for. The two front pockets of my coat were large, and after about twenty minutes or so, I had one full. I couldn't spend any more time; I didn't dare, even though I wanted to fill the other pocket.

Wasting time during the daylight hours would be suicide. The thought that always haunted me was how close they were. But I had to eat a few before I left. I walked up to the trunk of this lifesaving tree, held an acorn against it with my left hand, and cracked it open with the axe handle. I quickly peeled the shell away and ate it.

It tasted so good, ignoring the slightly bitter taste, just chewing on it as if I were in some fancy restaurant, eating a five-course meal. No, it was even better than that. I couldn't stop; I wanted more and more.

After eating at least a dozen nuts, I had to go. With those gone, it only put a small dent in my pocket. I wanted to refill it before walking away. Then, I heard a crack far off in the distance behind me. I almost took off running, but I didn't. Something told me it wasn't them; they wouldn't make that much noise. It was too loud and too far back. Nonetheless, I walked fast. They were somewhere back there, following me.

As midday approached again, and still no sign of them, I had been thinking while walking. I didn't know their names, nor did I want to know their names. But I had come up with my own name for them, the "death dealers," which fit them perfectly.

I also thought about the animals out here in the middle of nowhere. I could learn more from them and learn other ways to find food, but I haven't come up with any ideas yet.

With just a slight early morning glow on the eastern horizon, they were up and walking. They were getting further away from their camp than they wanted to. They had it in their minds that they were going to end it today. Even with their food drastically rationed, they only had enough for a few more days. It would take that just to get them back.

Full daylight hadn't been long when they heard a loud crack a good distance ahead of them. They estimated a quarter mile or more. They stopped for only a moment—it surprised them. Why had she been so foolish to do that? Giving herself away was just a sign of an amateur.

They continued on, thinking of what she was doing to make such a sound. Maybe another feeble attempt to make some sort of warning sign, but what during the day? It didn't matter; it wouldn't stop them, that much they were certain of.

When they thought they were about at the spot where the sound had originated, they slowed just to be sure they didn't walk into anything. Their prey was becoming better and wiser. No need for them to be overzealous and get hurt. Time was still on their side.

They walked up to the spot where she had slept. After finding nothing, they continued on, but still in a more alert mode. Her steps were at a normal stride; nothing seemed amiss. Almost at the same distance past the spot where she had slept, they heard the "crack." They stopped abruptly. A large, dead, rotten tree trunk had fallen over the path. They could see the fresh wood splinters lying on top of the snow. What did this mean? They looked at each other and then walked the remaining thirty feet up to it ever so slowly.

Standing beside the fallen tree trunk, they couldn't believe what they were looking at. It hadn't fallen over; it had been pushed. It was obvious from seeing the bear tracks on the ground around it. They could see where it had clawed the rotten wood away. The bear had smelled some grubs in the rotten wood and couldn't refuse breakfast.

They inched their way forward, one slow step at a time, checking to see which direction the bear went. With the astonishing speed a bear maintains in the first hundred yards, they couldn't risk the chance of being blindsided and attacked. They had witnessed it several times in the past few years. The bears would appear out of nowhere, attacking their prey, the victims never having a chance. Usually, it was a young deer or elk, some innocent animal not yet wise to the dangers that are always present.

The shooter had his pistol ready; they were not going to fall into that category.

Looking at the size of the tracks, they could see that it was about a half-grown bear, one that had been born late in the year and, probably recently abandoned by its mother to fend for itself. The weather wasn't cold enough yet for it to hibernate. It was just making the final rounds for extra food. They had no intention of being the main course.

They walked on, following the bear tracks. It had now turned and was following hers. They stopped again. This was as much a major problem for them as it was for her. No matter how silently they moved, the bear would know they were there. There was no escaping his uncanny ability to hear and smell.

This was something new for them—definitely a problem they had not counted on. They looked at each other again. The tracker nodded his head in the direction of going back to their home. The shooter shrugged his shoulders, answering he didn't know.

They stood there for a long time, thinking. The proximity of the bear was just too close. Now, the decision they had to make. Cut their losses and go back, let the bear finish the job they had started? If it would, there would be no guarantee of that. Let her wander on directionless, to starve or freeze to death—there was no guarantee of that either. They knew, by her heading due south, what she was attempting to do. What if she made it? There would be no place for them to hide.

Being the wanted criminals they were, it would be only a matter of time before they were the ones to be hunted down. They couldn't live with that. She couldn't be allowed to reach civilization. If the bear didn't finish it, they had to.

The tracker looked at the shooter, then in the direction of the camp. He nodded his head no. Looking in the same direction back, he nodded his head no. They were both in agreement. But now, the problem at hand is that they couldn't go forward. They had to let the bear continue on and see what would happen.

They sat down in the snow to wait patiently. Hours passed. The wind blew excessively, from west to east. That was in their favor; there would be no scent of them for the bear to detect. But it would also cover her tracks in the more open areas.

The hills were gradually becoming taller, and the tree growth was slowly becoming sparser. With all the recent turn of events, they wouldn't finish the job today. They were hoping the bear would.

The tracker felt it was safe to talk after hours of silence. Whispering, he said, "This is going to be interesting."

The shooter nodded. "We're going to have to find food."

The tracker nodded.

They had the gun, only to be used as a last resort. In their pockets, they had other means of obtaining food. That would cost them time, time that should be used to finish the job.

For the first time, they were feeling a bit uneasy.

They lost half of the day's light waiting. If the bear finished their job, it wouldn't be hard to find. No matter how much the wind blew, it wouldn't cover the mess—the blood nor the body.

It was only a short distance, and they were at the spot where the ground had been torn up badly, with bare dirt and many small piles of snow scattered about. They stopped short, confused. It looked as if a small war had taken place there. The first thought that went through their minds was the bear had caught her already. But they heard nothing—no growling, no screaming—so how was that possible? They were close enough. They would have known.

They continued on and walked to the edge of the battle. At first, they weren't sure what they were looking at. No blood, no pieces of shredded clothing. So, what had happened?

Cautiously, they walked into the middle of the spot. They looked at the ground while listening for any noise off in the trees. The bear could return, crashing through the woods with only one thought on its mind: them. The shooter had his pistol out. He was an expert marksman with it and knew he could put three or four shots in it before it did any bodily harm to them.

They saw three different types of tracks—hers, the bears, and one belonging to a whitetail deer, a large buck by the size of the tracks. Still confused, they looked on. Most of the deer tracks had been covered, some only partially by hers. The bear had wandered about covering both. They all had been through here at different times.

The tracker walked over to the tree and saw the small pile of shells. He quickly looked around and saw small pieces of acorn shells lying about. He bent down and picked up a small handful, showing them to his partner and raising his eyebrows. The shooter nodded—he understood. But the look on his face told his partner that he was amazed. She was learning—the lesson came from the buck. The next lesson would come from the bear. They were hoping it would show her how to die a grueling, painful death.

They followed the bear, following her, back into formation, which is what made them so successful at what they did. The tracker was in the lead, the shooter just two steps behind, walking step for step. He did nothing but scan the area, mainly ahead of them. He was also listening for any sound from both sides and the rear. Every ten steps, he would look in those directions. Bears have been known to circle around and stalk their prey before attacking. They had to learn that the hard way.

Once, in their first year, a huge five-hundred-pound black bear nearly got them. Right now, they weren't positive about who was tracking who. Their plan was that if the bear attacked them from the front, the tracker would drop down and give his partner a clear shot.

As they continued on, the tracker gave no sign that there was any present danger. He looked at each print that he passed by; they were at least two hours old. The blowing snow had filled in the tracks at the very bottom, just enough to know the bear was still following her. Its tracks never stopped, never varied. It just walked along, taking its time as if it were playing with her. Maybe they were waiting to attack after sunset.

They didn't like what was happening. The longer this continued, the more it could put them in jeopardy. If nightfall had come and nothing had changed, they may have gotten too close, and they could have been first.

The shooter was considering all their options, thinking and listening as he took a quick glance behind him. When he turned around, he had to stop quickly; he nearly walked into the back of his partner. His partner had stopped and straightened up. Something was wrong!

The tracker then pointed to the ground, to his left, and raised his left arm up, pointing off into the woods. The shooter followed his finger as he slowly moved it up. The bear had turned to the left. He followed its tracks off in that direction until he could no longer see them. But it was obvious that the bear had immediately increased its speed. But to catch up with whom—them or her?

The shooter tapped his partner on the back. When they made eye contact, the shooter pointed his finger at the sun and then dropped it down at the western horizon. He then pointed to the tracker, then himself, and up into the trees. Then, he shrugged both shoulders and tilted his head slightly. The tracker understood and nodded back. They might have to sleep up in the trees tonight if everything continued going the way it was.

As the day started its downward slide into night, that strange feeling never left. My senses tuned to the auditory stimulus were on high alert, and everything else was tuned out and shut down to idle mode. I didn't know what was making me feel this way.

It wasn't the hollow feeling in the middle of my back. I had heard no noise all day other than the wind. The temperature hovered somewhere between ten and fifteen degrees, so all seemed well for another day on the exterior. So, what was lurking in the back of my mind? Was it just paranoia? But that was a good thing; to become complacent would mean the end.

Tread lightly, Madie, you're walking up a slippery slope, I told myself. *Remember, they are back there.*

"Never give up; that's the easy way out," Craig told me on several occasions when we were running at one race or another.

I would be at a point during the race where I felt I could no longer maintain the pace and would slow slightly. Even if Craig was ahead of me, he could sense it; he always knew. I so wish that he was here now!

I wanted to stop and call it another day. I could tell my body was making a slow adjustment to the daily walking, but my legs felt heavy and numb. It wasn't dark yet, maybe two hours at best. I stopped and leaned against the closest tree. I didn't sit down for fear I wouldn't get back up anytime soon.

I knew my body was also adjusting to other things. Lack of a good night's sleep was one; eating was another. I had been too scared, running for my life on the previous days, to worry about food. Today was different! The near-zero calorie intake was making me feel much weaker, a very hard thing to adjust to.

Some nutritionists say we are healthiest when we are near starvation. If so, who am I to argue? I do know it makes one weaker; with no fuel to burn, a car won't run. The human body will run on empty for a long time, just not as well, not at the rate I was accustomed to.

I still had the two fish dangling on the rope around my neck and bouncing back and forth in front of me. They were frozen raw fish, which sounded pretty good right now. While standing there, leaning against the tree, I couldn't bring myself to eat one yet. The one thing I knew was an absolute certainty: things were going to get worse. I had better save them for that time.

The acorns weren't all that bad, so I ate more. This time, I ate nearly half of what was in my pocket, then stopped. I would save the last half for tomorrow. When I finished eating, I licked my chapped lips clean, not letting a single morsel of nut go to waste. I couldn't believe that I felt full. My stomach had shrunk significantly in the past few days, but it would be a feeling that was short-lived.

I looked at the pile of shells laying on the ground. I thought about saving them food I might need in a few days. I read that mice can live on dried leather for weeks. I even read that a man who was lost for days had eaten his leather boots down to the sole.

I could do that, I told myself, just like eating a piece of tasteless jerky.

There were two reasons why I couldn't: my boots were rubber up to my ankles and then insulated vortex material on the top half. If I did eat my boot, only to have a frostbitten foot, then where would I be?

Nice try, I told myself.

I walked away; I didn't care if they saw the pile of shells. I can't hide my tricks, so why bother with them? *The death dealers, always trying to deal with their trade,* I thought to myself.

I hadn't walked five minutes when some unforeseen wave went through my body. It felt funny—I felt funny. Something told me to turn around and look. My mind raced in thought. However, I had heard nothing. I felt my blood rise instantly before I pivoted my hips, back, and neck. Paranoia, nothing could be there!

I only drew in half a breath. Then, what body functions didn't shut down, the rest locked up. My adrenaline rose ten times higher than at any time in the past few days. My nerve endings were twitching so badly I couldn't even shake. Fifty feet back, behind me, stood a black bear. I would have wet myself, but that had also locked up.

If it were the "death dealers," I could have dealt with that. I was caught off guard—surprised. I was instantly in a situation I had never thought about.

Oh God, Mr. Bear, don't make this too painful, I said to myself. I knew this was it. Today is the day that it's my turn to die. My mind raced on! At any second, I would see it charge at me, then maul me to death.

When it did, I knew I had to lie down and play dead. That wouldn't be so hard to do. While it was charging at me, I would probably be out cold before I hit the ground from an overload of pure panic and lack of oxygen. I knew I wasn't breathing; I couldn't even move.

I had read that a bear is faster than a horse in the first hundred yards. I couldn't outrun it. I had the axe; I would only have time for one full swing—eat or be eaten, the rule of nature! If I miss connecting the axe in its skull, which I probably would, I would be eaten. The ever so slightly five percent chance that I had to sink the axe, I would surely eat the meat for days while I traveled.

We stood staring at each other; the seconds seemed forever to me. My panic attack only escalated, knowing I was about to die a horrible, painful death, and the time the bear was taking to do it was totally unbearable.

"I love you, Craig, I'll find you," I said softly. My life was running on fumes now.

I saw the bear tilt his head slightly, almost unnoticeable. Then, it tilted its nose into the air and sniffed several times. He was trying to figure out what kind of opponent I was or would be when he attacked. I was probably the first human it had ever encountered, an odor he had never smelled before.

He continued to sniff the air. I could see by the size of the bear that he was only half-grown. It was born late in the year and recently abandoned by its mother to fend for itself, or it was a runt of the litter. Either way, it didn't matter! It was too much muscle and raw power for me to deal with.

Any second now, this would be over with. My blood pressure had to be above the danger zone. I was seeing the little floating stars out of the corners of both eyes.

But nothing.

This long, drawn-out anticipation of a painful death was becoming far worse than the actual deal itself. *What are you waiting for, Mr. Bear?* I asked myself. If you're waiting for me to die out of fear or intimidation, you're doing a good job.

Then the bear stretched its neck toward me, still sniffing the air. I was staring so intensely and thinking so deeply; then I felt myself inhale a long, deep, whispery breath of air. Something my body did involuntarily. To me, the noise was as loud as if I was yelling. The stars faded away; now, I had an even clearer view of death.

Still, nothing!

I couldn't stand this any longer. I thought of slowly turning and walking away. What's the difference? Being attacked from behind, at least I wouldn't see it charge at me.

Then, the bear sniffed and, in the process, wrinkled its nose three times. Very quietly, I said, "What do you…"

Then, it hit me. It wasn't after me. It was smelling the fish. Or did I smell like a giant fish? There was only one way to find out. I slowly reached up around the back of my neck.

The bear slowly dropped his head several inches. *Oh God, is he going to attack now?* Reality and body functions were returning. My hands were shaking so badly, and with the heavy gloves, I couldn't get the knot untied in the rope. I grabbed the largest fish and gave it a quick jerk. The rope pulled through the gill, and the fish was free.

Now, with the left gill of the fish sticking up in the air, it looked as if it were trying to fly away, something I wish I could do. Now, I, the hunted, became the hunted yet again.

I slowly bent down, looking at the ground, but I was listening, waiting for the onslaught of the attack. I laid the fish crossways in my path. "Sorry, fish, it's either you or me. I hope it's you—no offense." I was talking to a dead fish; I couldn't believe it.

But then again, I also talked to a bear. This is what my life had come down to: talking to a bear that wanted to eat me and a fish that I had planned on eating. Eat or be eaten—talking to them was just a way to relieve stress.

I slowly stood up and looked at the bear, then I turned and walked away. *Here it comes,* I thought. I won't make five steps, then I'm lunch. I couldn't believe it! I had walked ten feet and was still walking.

When I reached twenty feet, I turned my head and looked back just in time to see the bear scoop up the fish in its right paw. It stuffed half of the fish in its mouth, headfirst, and bit it in two. I watched the tail half fall to the ground. *Oh geez,* it just made that three-pound walleye look as if it were nothing more than a small morsel of a little perch.

Five chews and the fish were gone. "How was the frozen sushi?" I said quietly.

Then, the bear put his head to the ground and opened its mouth, baring the scariest teeth I have even seen. When he raised his head up, he was looking at me, chewing. Only this time, it only took four chews before it was gone. Well, the fish bought me a few more minutes of life.

I slowly walked on. No sense in running as that would only show the fear I was feeling. Five minutes passed. I didn't know if I was still walking south; I was looking down at the ground.

As I took each step, I looked at the spot in front of me, waiting to be knocked down. I hoped that shock would instantly set in so I wouldn't feel much pain.

Time passed! *What are you waiting for, bear?* the thought continued.

I don't know why, but I had to look back. I saw the bear following, maybe twenty-five feet back, smelling the ground. He looked up at me and sniffed again. I knew, so what the heck. Chances are I won't be alive tomorrow to eat the last fish anyway.

While I was still walking, I grabbed the last fish and, with both hands, pulled it free from the rope around my neck. I dropped it on the ground behind me. Now, with no more bear food to put in his dish, I became the bear food. I walked another twenty feet or so, turned, and watched the same thing again. Now, I didn't care anymore.

Ten seconds later, the fish was gone. I said, in a normal voice, "Did you even taste it… I'm next, I suppose, just get it over with."

The bear just looked at me indifferently. Too bad I couldn't read bear expressions like one can with humans. If I could, maybe then I would know what it was thinking.

"What the hell!" I turned and walked.

As I walked, I disappeared into la-la land; I was just waiting to die. The air was crisper, I could smell the pine trees, and my vision was so clear I could see each individual snowflake. I guess this is the way it is before one dies.

When I finally turned and looked back, the bear was gone. I couldn't believe it! But why? The bear left me to live another day, just to succumb to them tomorrow. No one will believe me, what just happened, not like I'll get the chance to tell anyone. Thank you, Mr. Bear, God, and Craig! One more day of life is always a blessing, even here, in this frozen nothingness.

The moon was full. It had worked its way up in the sky for nearly two hours. I kept walking and planned to for at least another two hours if I could hold out. Adding up the time since the sun went down, the moon started to show itself on the eastern horizon, and now, I estimated, it was around nine-thirty, not that the time mattered. I wanted to put as much distance between myself and the bear as possible. I couldn't stand another encounter with it; I had no more fish. Next time, he might not have as much patience with me.

I was walking with my eyes closed almost as much as they were open. It felt as if I was dragging my feet. I looked up into the sky; the stars were dancing, and it looked as if the moon was smiling down at me. My mind's way of coping, lack of sleep and physical fatigue, it was doing the best it could.

I stopped walking. I didn't even look around. I just kicked the snow away from the ground, and with what little I had left in me, I lay down right there and fell asleep.

I was dreaming of lying in bed beside Craig at home. When he leaned forward and kissed me on the cheek, it almost felt real. Only, it was cold and wet. Something in my subconscious was telling me: "All is not right!" I didn't want to wake up; it wasn't time to leave the dream world.

Then, another sensation ran across my cheek, only this time, I knew it wasn't in a dream. It was warm and steamy. Barely mentally functioning, my eyes were still moments away from opening. I asked myself, *Two plus two?* I was no longer sleeping; one can't add to their dreams, or so I've heard.

Now, I was almost to the point of opening my eyes, and my hearing had returned. In the first few seconds of trying to figure out what was going on, before my eyes opened, I heard nothing. Then, suddenly, I heard something, but I couldn't tell how far away it was; it sounded as if it were muffled. Then, the noise grew louder very quickly. Two seconds later, I was fully alert, and the sound was on my face.

Grasping desperately, I was trying to figure out what it was. I heard several sniffs, maybe four or five, then a short exhale. I was instantly scared beyond all my imagination. The hot breath landed directly on my face. The bear had returned and was now only inches from me.

As hard as it was, I maintained a steady pace of breathing. My heart—I couldn't control—I could hear it, so I knew the bear could too. If he did, he paid no attention to it. He just made a second pass down the front of my jacket, sniffing where the fish had been. Then, I heard the sniffing move further down my legs. I don't know if he did it accidentally or on purpose, but as I lay on my left side, his nose bumped into my right knee.

I almost flinched; I wanted to scream! I wanted to jump up and run, but all I did was draw in a long, slow breath of air and hold it. Then, five seconds later, I exhaled slowly. This gave me somewhat of a calming effect, mentally, anyway. I could feel myself shaking; that was something I couldn't stop. I was about to die a horrible, painful death. That was something else I couldn't stop. I squinted my eyes tightly shut, waiting for the onslaught of pain.

Nothing happened!

There was no more noise except for the ringing in my ears, which was deafening.

I'm not sure of the time that passed. It couldn't have been more than thirty seconds, but it seemed like minutes to me. I slowly opened my eyes. The moon had dropped below the western horizon. It was still emitting enough light so that I could see a few yards away.

No bear! It had left as silently as it had entered. I was relieved and amazed how something so big could move so gracefully as not to make a sound.

It would be a while before I fell back to sleep if I slept for the rest of the night, which was a slim chance.

Was the bear following me the hours after dark? Or, had curiosity gotten the best of him, and he had to turn to check me out?

My thoughts continued: *Was the bear going to continually follow me until it decided it was time to turn me into fish food?*

Now, along with the death dealers, he would be there, invisibly, but he would be there. So, who would win? The bear or them? My odds were so low of surviving that it was probably on the negative side of zero.

I was so cold; I was shivering. I knew there would be no more sleep, so I got up and started walking.

CHAPTER 7

They stood at the spot where the bear had split away from her trail for an hour or more, each leaning against a tree, looking off in different directions. She and the bear were ahead of them, but how far? If the bear had circled around and was coming back for them, it probably would have contacted their tracks somewhere behind them. Before they reached the spot, they were waiting, so there was no need to take any chances.

Time was still on their side; they had nothing else to do. The question they didn't have an answer to was how far ahead. In the hours of waiting, had she slowed her pace, or had she continued at a fast pace?

"What do you want to do?" the tracker asked quietly.

He never looked away from the direction he was looking in. "The winds are in our favor. It doesn't know we're here… let's move on for a while."

The tracker nodded, then started walking.

It wasn't long before the daylight was gone. Her tracks were the only set they were following. They followed her for another hour, but still, no sign of the bear. Neither of them liked that much. Had the bear lost interest and moved on? Doubtful! It was still somewhere that much they had learned about bears in the past.

They hadn't survived five years out here by being careless. So, they stopped for the night. Tomorrow, they would find what had transpired during the night. Hopefully, a bloodied body is left for the wolves or to rot away. They didn't care as long as it was taken care of.

Taking no chances, the shooter said, barely audible, "I'll watch; you sleep for a while."

A small breeze was still blowing from west to east as it had all day. Neither she nor the bear would detect the smoke, so he built a small fire. If the bear was coming for them during the night, the fire wouldn't make any difference. He had his glove off his right hand, and it was in the pocket of his coat, resting against the gun, where it would stay until it was his turn to sleep.

Hours passed. The only eventful thing that happened was a full moon had risen, high enough in the sky that the reflection off the snow illuminated the ground well enough that he could see far off into the distance.

The shooter leaned over and shook his partner. The tracker instantly sat up, fully alert, as if he hadn't been sleeping at all. The shooter handed him the pistol, put two small sticks on the fire, then lay down and fell asleep.

As time passed, the tracker sat next to the fire, listening off into the darkness for any unusual noise. He understood the bears; they moved silently. The bear would be right there on them without any warning. If that were to happen, he would shoot the bear through his coat pocket. To take the time to remove the gun from his coat would more than likely mean death for one of them.

He thought about the hours ahead and what they would bring. Death? Hers? Would they have to kill the bear if it chose to hang around?

By the size of its tracks, it was a small female, borne in the previous spring. Not having a litter of cubs yet, there was a chance of her being docile, but to what point was unknown. In due time, they might know. He threw more sticks onto the fire and watched the embers float up into the trees—thinking, listening.

When the first hint of light broke the eastern horizon, the tracker stood, stretched, and kicked snow on the pile of coals that were left on the fire. The shooter was instantly on his feet. He had drawn his knife from his pocket before he was standing straight.

Then, he looked at the tracker. His partner quickly shook his head once, left and right. Realizing nothing was wrong, he returned his eight-inch hunting knife to its sheath. They began walking in the direction where they had left off the night before.

By the time the sun started to show itself, they had walked upon the pile of shells and the bear tracks. The tracks had rejoined here, coming from the east, just as they had expected. Ten feet later, they saw the pile of acorn shells.

Five minutes later, the tracker abruptly stopped and held out his right arm. His partner walked up to his right side and was prepared to shoot if necessary. He saw nothing. The tracker continued to stare at the ground. He couldn't make out the details of what he was looking at.

His first thought was this was where the attack had taken place. It only took him a brief second to realize that hadn't happened. So, what is it? He walked up further, off to the right side, and looked down at the tracks. He stopped when he reached the spot where hers had turned and was facing backward. They had met.

"The bear let her live," he spoke quietly.

Something had him puzzled. He looked at the line crossways in her path. He bent down; there he saw fish scales.

"She fed the bear fish."

The shooter frowned. "Huh?"

They increased their pace—they had a lot of ground to cover to catch back up.

Past midmorning, after several hours of hard walking, breathing heavier than normal, they walked up to a more puzzling spot. It was obvious she had laid down there and slept, but bear tracks were there at the same spot. It looked as though the bear had smelled the spot where she had laid on the ground.

The tracker stood there staring for several moments.

"How had she known the bear was coming in the dark? We're giving her way too much credit for being naïve. These tracks are old; she got up soon after she had laid down to sleep."

"Yeah, well, she can't continue at the pace she's been going, but she'll fold soon."

The shooter was becoming angry. He started walking to take the lead. Two quick steps, and he was beside the tracker. Before his third step landed, the tracker grabbed him and pulled him back.

"Shit! Look!" He pointed at the ground, just where the shooter's third step was about to land.

"Yeah, so?"

"Her track is on top of the bears, only half of it, but it covered."

The shooter dropped his shoulders and let out a long breath of air.

"She didn't know then; it walked up on her while she was sleeping," he said, looking down.

"Yes."

"The bear let her live again."

"Yes."

"Why?"

The tracker remained silent, shaking his head, then walked forward, looking at her tracks. "These are old, eight, maybe ten hours."

"Huh! We're in this for the long trip. How much food do you have left?"

"Not much."

"Nor do I! We won't catch up today, maybe tonight."

The tracker nodded and started walking.

I couldn't stop walking, though I really wanted to. Desperation drove me forward. I was tired, hungry, and physically drained, more so than at any time in the past. But I was scared by what had happened. Death could approach at any moment. The scariest thing is that I might not see it coming. I hadn't in the past, so that much I learned.

I felt weak. One good meal would keep me going for several more days. Probably, a solid eight hours of sleep would also be. I had the time to sleep from the death dealers; at least, I think I do. Hadn't they had to take the time to sleep?

By my best calculations, I was at least one day ahead of them. I would never be ahead of the bear. The bear would have to choose between eating me or losing interest and going on its own way. That much I was smart enough to know.

Clouds moved in just shortly after sunrise. The gloomy day went along with the way I was feeling. "Craig, I don't believe I can make it… my adversaries are growing, each one greater than the last. Starvation will win if the others fail."

I walked, but my mind was in a fog. I really wanted something to eat and to sleep. I stopped walking and leaned against a tree. I closed my eyes; it felt so good that I was almost sleeping and standing up.

I felt myself drifting away, mentally talking to myself, saying, *I wish this was over—live or die, let it end. Madie, reach deep down inside; you can do this. The finish line is up ahead.*

I quickly opened my eyes. I expected to see Craig's ghost present; what I had just heard sounded too real. But it wasn't; there were just more trees and more of nothing. Was it just a dream, wishing for Craig to be here?

Yes, I told myself, so I pushed on.

I hadn't walked long before I walked onto another lake. When my first step landed on the ice, I had an idea. It hit me as though someone had implanted it there and turned on the light. I could make this work, I told myself, if the ice wasn't too thick to chop through.

I started swinging the axe. With each blow that landed, pieces of ice were hitting me in the face, stinging badly. But I didn't stop—swing, chop, swing, chop—each strike resulting in removing a four-to-six-inch chunk.

After at least a dozen swings, I said, "Lord, please don't let the ice be really thick." I was rapidly running out of energy.

I had chopped an odd-shaped hole that was almost a foot and a half wide and was down into the ice roughly ten inches. While chopping, happy with the idea of spearing a fish or two, I hadn't given any thought to bait. I already knew I was going to make a spear with the axe. I stopped chopping to catch my breath and think. Worms would be too far into the ground, this time of year, to dig, so now what? I went back to chopping to finish the job, then on to worry about the next obstacle.

Panting heavily, swing after swing; I broke through. But now, the odd-shaped hole had a funnel shape at the bottom. I started chopping around the edges to open the hole. Satisfied that the opening was big enough, I now had another problem. The water was full of ice chips floating in it; I couldn't see into the water.

"Well, this is going to hurt," I said while removing the mitten from my right hand.

By the third scoop into the water, my hand was aching. I made two more scoops; then, I had to stop and let my hand warm up. Several minutes passed with my hand in my mitten. I still hadn't a clue what I was going to use for bait.

After I finished scooping out the rest of the chunks, my hand hurt so badly I couldn't stand it. Tears started to stream down my face. Carefully, I put my hand back into my mitten as though I thought it might crack off.

What are you doing, Madie? Buck up and take it, I told myself. *Sometimes, things have to get worse before they get better.*

The tingling sensation, as warm blood started to revive my hand, hurt so bad I couldn't hold the axe. I walked back to the tree line, leaning forward, holding my right hand to my chest as if that was going to ease the pain—it didn't.

I didn't have to look at many limbs before I found one that would work. It was roughly six feet long, one inch in diameter, and straight. Using my left hand, I slowly chopped it from the tree, taking my time to make sure the point of the axe landed in the same spot where the last swing ended. I was trying to get the sharpest angle possible on the tip—the sharper, the better. After trimming the small branches from the limb, I had the perfect spear but no bait.

I stood at the edge of the ice, looking out across the lake. Holding the spear was like sitting in the car with no keys, no bait, no keys, no gas. Then, just like the last time, something clicked in my mind, and I used my necklace.

Hanging around my neck was an eighteen-inch silver chain with a silver heart attached to it. Craig had given it to me on my last birthday. I took my hand out of the mitten and removed it from around my neck. I stood there, looking at it. I felt a lump growing in my throat; my eyes started to water. I remember what Craig had said to me when I opened it.

"That's my heart; no matter what, you'll always have it."

I cried. The loneliness, the loss, and however long my life was meant to be, Craig would never be here.

After several minutes of crying, I regained some composure. I wiped my eyes and started walking back toward the hole. This had to work—I needed to eat.

When I looked down into the hole, a thin sheet of ice covered the water. I could still see the bottom of the lake; the water was crystal clear. No way was I sticking my hand back in the water.

I lowered the spear into the water until it hit the bottom. Then, I raised it back up, looking at the wet line, roughly three feet deep here. Was I deep enough to draw the fish in from the deeper water? Only one way to find out! I poked a hole in the thin film of ice at the left side of the hole and lowered the chain down into the water, with the heart swinging at the very end.

I was on my left knee; my right foot was planted firmly to give me the best mobility with my right arm to drive the spear to the bottom. This had to work. I pulled the chain up and down, hoping it would give off more reflection. The heart was twisting left and right. I thought, *If I were a fish, it would look good to me.*

Five minutes had passed with no results.

"Lord, please let this work," I said.

More time passed, and my knee was beginning to ache. I continued to wiggle the chain. Then, out of nowhere, a fish suddenly appeared. It was looking at the bait. Instinctively, without giving it any thought, I drove the spear straight down into the sand. I tucked the upper end between my neck and shoulder, holding it just above the water.

For a split second, I wasn't sure if the spear had connected, but only for a split second. The fish thrashed desperately, trying to escape. I slid forward on the ice several inches; it was all I could do to hold the spear down into the sand. I was excited!

"I just caught Jaws!" I yelled.

Food—I had food.

After several more thrashes, then the fish stopped. I waited another minute to be sure it was dead. Then, I slowly started to raise it out of the water. The fish felt as if it was sliding off the spear. I stopped.

Now, what was I going to do? I asked myself.

I lowered the axe down into the water, put the head of the axe underneath the fish, and started lifting. Pulling up on the axe and guiding the spear, the head of the fish came out of the water. It was a huge northern! I was so happy I was smiling.

It was a perfect strike. The spear caught the fish just behind the gills and to the left side of the backbone.

The further the fish got out of the water, the heavier it got, and the longer it became. I put the fish onto the ice on the right side of the hole. It had to be nearly three feet long and somewhere around ten pounds. I yelled, and I danced around in a circle; I was happy!

Looking at the fish, something caught my attention off to my left, coming out of the woods. Before I had turned my head, the thought already blazed through my mind: *The death dealers.*

I looked; it wasn't. It was the bear, and it was bounding straight at me. I already knew what it was after. But still, it's an eerie feeling seeing a wild black bear running in one's direction.

I was devastated; I dropped to my knees. I went from being totally ecstatic to being totally depressed in two seconds. As I watched the bear get closer, there was nothing I could do.

When the bear got within ten feet of the fish and me, it put on the brakes. All four of its feet started sliding, then it dropped down on its butt and slid to a perfect stop right in front of my fish and three feet in front of me. To anyone else who would have witnessed this, it would have been comical, but not to me. I was sad and mad at the bear.

"Stupid bear," I said to it.

The bear had already grabbed the fish right behind the head, turned, and was walking back to the shore. It just turned and looked at me.

"At least you could say thank you." I watched it walk away. The fish was so long its tail was dragging on the ice.

"No offense, Mr. Bear, but I hope you choke." The bear never looked back.

I put my necklace back in the water, resumed my stance, and started fishing again. It worked once, and it will work again.

To my total amazement, my wait wasn't long. This time, it was a walleye, not nearly as large, though.

A fish is a fish, it's food, I told myself. The bear wasn't getting this one until I was finished with it.

I then remembered something: *Craig had put a small pocketknife in each of our arctic jackets, just in case. God bless you, Craig!*

The blade was no longer than an inch and a half, but it would work. I filleted the fish, sat down on the ice, and started eating one of the fillets. Raw fish, I would have never believed it tasted so good. It was a little bit on the chewy side, but my mouth watered with every bite. I couldn't eat fast enough.

Each fillet weighed over a pound. I managed to eat one before I was full—no, stuffed. I put the remaining one in my pocket, stood up, picked up the skeleton of the fish, and walked toward the shore.

Twenty feet into the trees, I saw the bear lying on the ground, on its stomach. It was watching me but showed no sign of getting up. I stopped and looked around. I saw no sign of even a piece of the northern left.

"You pig," I said, looking at the bear, "no wonder you can't get up."

I didn't feel that the bear had intentions of harming me. So, I walked just a few more feet toward it and stopped. No need to press my luck. I threw the skeleton of the walleye toward it. The fish landed just in front of the bear.

I walked to the south about ten feet and then sat down—time for a nap, maybe a few hours. I didn't care about the bear any longer. If it was going to attack me, so be it. I sat in the snow, leaned against a tree, pulled my knees up, and rested my head on them. I could hear the crunching of the fish as the bear ate it. I never looked in that direction. Soon, I was asleep.

I don't know how long I slept. A low, throaty noise woke me. I looked in the direction it was coming from. The bear was standing to my left, about fifteen feet away, with its back to me. Something was back there that it didn't like. Whether it heard them or smelled them, I don't know. But I did know what it was. I jumped up.

"Come on, bear, we have to go. You don't want to mess with them; they have a gun."

I was off, walking to the south.

I looked to see where the sun was in the sky, and I had slept for several hours. I looked behind me, but the bear hadn't moved. It was still looking north.

"We can't stay here. You don't have to go with me, but you have to go."

The bear turned and looked at me. It had no clue what I was saying, but I think it felt the urgency in my voice and actions. It started to follow me.

Even though I was scared of what was back there, I felt good. I had a fast pace in my step again.

CHAPTER 8

"We're getting too far away; we don't have the provisions for this," the tracker said after several hours of brisk walking.

"No, but neither does she."

"Just as long as the weather holds out long enough to finish this," he said, shrugging his shoulders, "doesn't matter how far we get."

"No, but we are going to have to shoot some food today."

They weren't too worried; the tracks were still several hours old, so they were talking in a normal tone.

"Yes, and right now, I could eat the butt of a dead skunk."

"Mmm! Soon enough, we'll walk up on an elk or a deer."

"Shit!" the tracker said in a quiet alarming tone.

They instantly stopped walking. Her tracks went from a few hours old to instantly being fresh. What they didn't like was her tracks were filled with the bears.

They remained motionless, trying to figure out what they were looking at.

Whispering, the tracker said, "They're just a few hundred yards ahead."

His partner nodded. "We gave ourselves away back there."

"Yes, we did. Who knew?"

He visually followed the tracks out onto the lake. Then, he raised his right hand and then ran out on the ice, heading for the hole. The tracker quickly looked around. He saw the two spots in the snow where fish had laid on the ice, then ran back.

He had it figured out by the time he returned. "Her and the bear have become buddies. She speared two fish and probably fed most of it to the bear."

"So, it looks like we eat bear meat tonight," the shooter responded.

The further I went, the faster I walked. I continually turned and looked behind me to see if they were coming and to check on the bear. I wasn't worried that the bear might attack me. It just followed along, about twenty feet back. I was worried that the bear might stop. It had gained a little trust in me. It might think all humans are okay. They're not, but what could I do? It had become a pain, eating all my fish. But I was starting to feel more at ease rather than enjoying its company today.

"Too bad you couldn't be a dog; we could snuggle at night." I turned to look back again. The bear was walking with the same indifferent look.

"You do look kind of scary, with that big head and those bullet-piercing eyes."

Good Lord, I'm talking to you again, I thought as I walked on.

I knew they were close behind. I wasn't as nervous as before; I guess just having some company, such as it is, was somewhat comforting. As long as I walked with the bear, maybe they wouldn't try anything.

We walked not more than a mile when the bear made a grunt. I stopped walking and looked back. Now, I was seeing more than I heard. The bear was looking back, bouncing up and down on its front feet. They were still coming, and the bear didn't like it. Then, it pawed at the ground with both feet simultaneously. That scared me! The true power of the bear was showing. It was still a wild animal, and it was agitated.

What animals lost in reasoning and analytical skills were made up for in hearing and smell. I sensed nothing. The wind was barely blowing, and the snow muffled our steps; I heard nothing.

"Come on, bear, we have to go now." I turned and started running.

I couldn't tell if the bear was following me or not. Again, I could hear nothing but my own breathing. I covered fifty feet and looked back over my shoulder. The bear was still looking back; it wasn't afraid. I had no doubt that one on two, the bear would win, though the playing field wasn't even; they had a gun.

I stopped again, this time breathing heavily. I turned sideways.

"Come on, bear, you can't stay!" I was almost yelling.

The bear looked in my direction. I waved my right arm in my direction and started running again. This time, I ran a few steps, then looked back as I ran. The bear was lopping in my direction. The thought went through my head: *I'll be darn! Did it understand me, or did it just sense my sense of urgency?*

I was running at a slower pace, constantly looking around, not to be ambushed from the side. Bear or no bear, they wanted to catch up today, right now, and end it.

As the days passed, the terrain continually grew into longer, sloping hills and valleys. The tree cover remained the same, giving an eight-foot visibility at best in a few spots along her trail. The shooter was in the lead. The temperature was the same as it had been in the past few days since the snowfall, roughly ten degrees. His glove was off his right hand, in his coat pocket, holding the gun. In a second's notice, he would have it removed and his finger on the trigger, ready to shoot whatever was necessary.

They ran up to the spot where the bear had turned. They didn't stop; their adrenaline was pumping, and they could smell victory—just ahead. In less than ten minutes, they ran through the second spot where the bear had turned to look back.

The tracker had fallen back behind his partner, about twenty feet. If, for some unforeseen reason, the bear did get one of them, the one who wasn't attacked had a split second to decide what to do and how to do it. Having to decide to run or to kill—they had never been in this situation before.

As he ran over to the spot where the bear had clawed at the ground, an uneasy feeling grew in his stomach. He knew the bear knew what was behind him and was getting close. The bear was acting like a true bear now: ferocious, fearless, and mad.

They started up a long, slow hill. He continually looked past his partner into the trees ahead. At any moment, it could happen. What it would result in, neither of them knew.

Caution was no longer the concern about being quiet. It was a matter of endurance again.

"I can smell her," was all the tracker said in a normal tone while running. This was the closest they'd been since the first day. Nightfall wasn't far away. Fatigue was setting in, taking a toll on their bodies. They had to finish this today.

The tracker rarely looked away from the view ahead. Now, halfway up the hill, the trees were thinning. He saw something move, almost at the crest of the slope. He was off and running.

I ran hard up the hill, not as fast as I wanted to go, but as fast as I could go. Breathing wasn't a problem, but my energy level was far below low, mainly in my legs. I could no longer pick them up and carry the stride I had days ago. Stopping wasn't a possibility. In the back of my mind, what they would do to me if they caught me was motivation.

I was worrying about the bear. On the final run up the hill, since the last time I stopped, I hadn't looked back. I couldn't. That tingle was back, the same eerie feeling in the middle of my back. They were getting closer. I couldn't ignore it.

Once I crested the hill, I had to look back. When I did, I saw my second worst fear. The bear was a good thirty feet back. It had stopped and was standing on its back legs. Even for a small bear standing like that, its size was massive.

I panicked. *Oh no!*

The thoughts flowed: *Was it trying to get a better view? Was it trying to intimidate them? Were they that close?*

Then, the bear dropped down on its front legs and grunted loudly.

My worst fear became reality; I saw something move further down the hill. The bear wasn't moving. This is where it decided to make a stand—one it couldn't win. I went into a daze;

I didn't know what to do. I saw more movement coming up the hill. I didn't realize that I had already walked a third of the way back to the bear. I didn't know what I was doing.

Time had stopped, and all senses were lost. The trees, the snow, and even the air I was breathing seemed to disappear. All I could see was the death dealers getting closer.

Now, I was ten feet behind the bear. *Why didn't I know? I couldn't save myself from them. How did I think I was going to save a wild bear?*

I stood dumbfounded. Then, I saw the shooter remove his hand from the pocket of his coat. He was holding the gun and started aiming it at us. I don't know if he was aiming at the bear or me. I didn't wait to see. It was as if I was in a trance.

I ran up behind the bear and pushed it on the butt, yelling, "GO!"

In a blink of an eye, with startling speed, the bear swung around in one fluid motion, knocking me down with its left front leg. It caught me just above my right hip. The bear hit me so hard that it lifted me off my feet and sent me flying in the air to my left. The pain hurt so bad I didn't know if I could breathe or not. When I landed in the snow, I slid another two feet.

Then, I heard it! I was lying on the ground, so it wasn't aimed at me. The shot rang out and echoed through the trees, the same haunting noise I heard when they shot Craig. *Oh no, they just shot the bear,* I said to myself, lying in the snow.

With the same startling speed, I watched the bear run off into the woods. I didn't think it was shot.

I didn't have time to look for blood in the snow. I forgot about the pain in my right side. I was up and running to the top of the hill again. I was swinging the axe, trying to gain all the momentum I could. Before I reached the top, I would hear another shot. This one would be aimed at me. I ran behind a clump of small trees for a shield as I reached the top.

The next shot happened. I ran for all I was worth, which wasn't much. I continued running down the opposite side of the hill. Now, temporarily out of shooting vision, I couldn't help but think, here I am again, just as the first day of this nightmare. Running, just steps ahead of death, now I had no doubt they were out to kill me. They've learned I'm a formidable opponent; the only way they would have me was dead. Their thought of taking me was long gone.

I paced my breathing, concentrating on my steps and my legs. They were not what they had once been. I had to be careful not to trip and fall.

Minutes passed, I didn't stop, and I didn't look back. I could feel myself getting hot. I had to take my coat off, never sweat. Craig had drilled that into me. I couldn't afford to stop. I slowed my pace and removed my coat as I ran. This took a tremendous amount of energy. I was careful not to drop the axe in the process. I switched it from one hand to the other while twisting one way, then the opposite, sliding out of the coat.

It was getting warmer out. *Did this mean another snowstorm was coming?*

63

They reached the top and looked in the direction her tracks were headed. There was no sign of her. They were huffing and puffing; the day had drained their energy. The shooter was still leading. He stopped, bent over, and put his hands on his knees for support. The tracker ran up beside him and stopped.

Fatigue was taking a toll on their bodies. As they exhaled, the steam looked as if they were two snorting bulls fighting the matador; mad and blowing hot air, they couldn't get past the elusive red target.

This was the first time they had started to doubt themselves.

"This isn't good; I thought we had her this time," the tracker said.

"So did I! How does she continue like this?"

"Who knows? A few more days of this, we'll have to cut our losses…"

He was in deep thought. "If so, worst case, we'll go back, break camp, and move a few hundred miles. It's a given she would send somebody back."

"No way," the tracker responded, "the only way I'll quit this is if I'm dead."

He stood and started following her tracks. Knowing his partner would be behind him, he said, "That will be the last time we see the bear."

They didn't have the energy to run. Nightfall wasn't far away. The question they both were asking themselves was: "How soon would she stop for the night?"

Two miles had passed, and dusk was settling down on them. Her tracks showed that she was still running. They were losing valuable ground.

"How does she do it?" the tracker said.

"Huh! Come hell or high water, we're walking all night if we have to. We'll catch her napping and end this."

The tone of his voice was clear, but he wasn't in a good mood.

"Another storm's coming… something tells me we won't be as lucky as last time."

In the past five years, they had seen many blizzards, snowing so hard that they couldn't see five feet in front of them. Storms where it would snow for almost two days, dumping three to four feet of snow, with winds that would exceed fifty miles per hour and wind chills well below zero.

Soon after nightfall, they reached the spot where she had stopped running and started walking. With the cloud cover, visibility was less than two feet. But not for them; they were using their flashlight.

Walking at a normal pace, it was obvious to them she couldn't. Her tracks showed that she was struggling, twisting and turning, walking right up to many trees and feeling her way around them. Soon, tonight, she would be theirs.

The wind started blowing in short gusts, like rolling waves in the ocean. The high peaks roll down into the calm lows. They could see they were getting closer as her steps were becoming closer and cleaner. She was wasting too much time feeling her way forward into the night through the complete darkness.

The tracker was following; he had nothing more to do but think. He was wondering why she didn't stop and give up for the night. Fighting it the way she was had to be frustrating at best. Downright aggravating and confused would be more like it. His legs were numb, and he knew his partner had to be as hungry and tired as he was. They couldn't stop; they were in the best situation of ending this since the beginning.

The wind was blowing from the northwest. Any sound she might make would be carried away from them. The possibility was she could be twenty yards away, and they wouldn't know it. That's what drove them on.

She had turned slightly, heading southwest. The only logical reason he could come up with is she didn't know it. To them, it didn't matter which direction she traveled. They had a compass but very rarely used it. They knew their way back when this was over. So, they pushed on. Tonight was theirs to claim—a victory after the ultimate hunt!

I didn't know why I was crying, but I was sobbing as I ran. The pitch-black obstacle course I was trying to maneuver in, the bear, the loss of Craig, and the danger of the current situation overwhelmed me. This is the lowest, most depressed I've been since that day, more than my ability to conquer. I ached all over. I was tired of bouncing off a tree only to walk into the next. I had no idea which direction I was heading.

For all I knew, I could be walking in a small circle. I tried to count my steps each time I walked in one direction around a tree and then tried to correct it before I ran into the next.

After hitting my shoulders or face on a tree trunk or a limb the first several times, I got smart. I used the axe handle, like a blind person's cane, swinging it back and forth. This cost me a lot of time. I wanted to quit for the night, but the feeling was so strong in the middle of my back that I couldn't.

I tripped on something in the snow and fell. I landed on my hands and knees. I so badly wanted to lie down and rest; I was exhausted. The wind had been blowing at a fierce, howling rate.

At times, in the more open areas, it literally pushed me. The challenges of walking blind, the wind, and the exhaustion were all becoming far more than my weary body could stand.

"Craig, I don't believe I'll survive this. It'll take a miracle if I do," I said, still on my knees.

I rolled over and sat; getting back up seemed almost impossible.

I was relaxed and at peace with the world. I felt myself drifting off. I was still conscious enough to feel the wind pushing on my back.

Madie, don't quit now; that's not you. You have never quit before.

Sluggishly, I said, "No."

I opened my eyes; I was hallucinating again. It had to be my subconscious playing games with me. That haunting voice wasn't going to leave me alone. Deep down inside, that's the only thing I had left. Memories. *For me, Madie, finish this race for me.* I stood up; that voice was so clear to me that it scared me.

My eyes were open; I wasn't hallucinating this time. I started to cry. I missed Craig more than anything.

But, if I don't, I can be with you, I said to myself.

Nothing, no response, I was going crazy—I had to be. Hearing and talking to a dead man wasn't right. I didn't realize how bad my physical and mental condition had become. Like old age, it creeps up so slowly one doesn't realize it has arrived. Only mine happened in a few days. I couldn't wipe the tears away; luckily, the face mask absorbed them.

I swung the axe handle out in front of me, checking to see what might be there before I took my first step, and then I started walking. I didn't count my steps. I didn't care which direction I went; just covering the ground would keep me ahead of them. Come morning, I will adjust my direction and head south again.

With the complete darkness and the severe wind, I hadn't realized the miracle had started. The thick arctic gear I was wearing, with the hood over my head, and the wind approaching me at an angle from behind, shielded me from Mother Nature. Even in the daytime, I wouldn't have been able to see. I didn't know that yet!

As I walked, my legs felt as if they were becoming sluggish. I couldn't pick my feet up, dragging them in the snow. That was scaring me.

Was I deteriorating so rapidly that I couldn't even maneuver any longer? Was unconsciousness just around the next invisible tree? Was the end near?

I knew something wasn't right with me. Now, my feet felt as if they were traversing through a quagmire, moving slower than the rest of my body.

I shuffled my feet along, like so many people who were lucky enough to see old age. Fear of raising one foot too high to lose their balance and fall over. That's what I've become in a few days.

I couldn't help but think the target I was aiming at was out of reach. I had become at peace with myself. I would walk myself to death, probably tonight. In my last drawing breath, the instant before I hit the ground, I would smile. The satisfaction of knowing I didn't fall prey to them.

I was numb; my body no longer ached. I was no longer hungry; I was too exhausted to care. I had been walking in knee-deep snow for some time. Then, it happened: I felt myself drifting through the air—my feet weren't moving. My body was floating forward; I was relaxed. I smiled.

The wind no longer came in gusts. It turned into an unrelenting force, unequal to anything that Mother Nature had thrown at them in the past few winters.

Her tracks were quickly becoming covered with the blowing snow. Their time was running out! They increased their speed as best they could, but it wasn't enough. They no longer had the stamina they had the previous day.

Then, the weather turned for the worse for them. It started snowing, not just the usual snowfall, but one with a vengeance. Mother Nature was releasing some pent-up energy. They were down to minutes before all signs of her tracks would vanish. They started trotting to gain the remaining distance to catch up.

Minutes later, the flashlight was useless. The tracker could feel his partner hanging on the back of his coat. Shining the beam forward, all he could see was a pure white wall of snow. He pointed the flashlight down, but the beam was unable to penetrate the snowfall to reach the ground. Their worst nightmare had arrived; it was a pure whiteout.

They could both sense her presence; she was close. Something they had acquired living in the wilderness over the years: the ability to feel something they couldn't see. Not ready to give up yet, the tracker got on his hands and knees. He held the light, and his face was just inches from the ground. He started crawling, following the ever-disappearing tracks. The progress became so slow they were barely covering ten feet a minute. With only slight indents in the snow, he had to stop many times to look to the left or right to find the next step he was looking for.

Without seeing it, he crawled headfirst into a tree. He stopped and looked back, shining the light to check on his partner. All he saw was a wall of white and then a hand reaching out from beyond and grabbing his wrist.

No sound survived the howling wind. Still holding on to his wrist, the shooter bent down and yelled so his partner could hear him, "It's no use, the tracks are gone. We'll find them again tomorrow when this is over."

He knew the shooter was right, but he didn't have to like it.

They both went to work simultaneously. They started dragging snow into a long pile with their feet, one always resting a hand on the other so as not to lose contact.

Roughly an eight-foot-long row of snow was piled. Careful not to lose their place, they walked around the opposite side and dragged the snow into the wind and onto the pile. The pile of snow would keep them out of the relentless wind. They lay down beside each other, then fell asleep, something they both badly needed.

CHAPTER 9

So, this is what it feels like to die, I thought. I felt myself floating in slow motion.

Unable to see, I couldn't tell if I was floating up or down. Then, I felt a soft, fluffy cushion underneath me; my floating had stopped, and I wasn't dead yet.

Something isn't right, I thought. *Two plus two, no, I'm not dreaming. So, what did I land in?*

The confusion I was experiencing puzzled me. I quickly tried to figure out what was going on. The wind blocked out all other sounds. Being pitch black out halted all vision, and smelling was useless. I had only one sense left to use: the sense of touch. I had landed face down, so I rolled onto my right side to keep my back to the wind. I removed the mitten from my left hand, felt the fresh snow, and wondered how deep it was. I sat up on my knees and feet. I reached out in front of me and felt the top of the snow. Then, I pushed my hand down to the ground.

To my amazement, the snow was well over a foot deep. *How long had it been snowing? How long had I been wandering around?* Now, my hand was aching from the bitter cold snow. I put my hand back in the warm mitten. Then I realized why my feet felt so sluggish; I had been dragging them through the deep snow.

"Thank you for the miracle," I said.

I swung the axe handle through the dark to see what was near me. When I brought it around behind me, it hit a tree. It was safe to give up for the night and sleep. I didn't know how much longer it was going to snow, but I did know the snow would cover me. My fear was I would suffocate while sleeping. I positioned myself so my head was beside the tree on the downwind side.

I wiggled my body so it would settle down in the snow. I laid my head down, and I felt relaxed. My legs no longer felt as if they carried the weight of the world. The wind hit only a small portion of my left side. I felt safe and secure. I was so tired I never thought I would be happy sleeping in a blizzard, but I was. That was the last thought I had before I drifted off.

When I woke, I was gasping. Something was covering my mouth, not allowing me to breathe. I opened my eyes, but they were also covered. I panicked; they had found me. Now, they were trying to suffocate me. Instinctively, my will to survive took over. My hand came up along the side of my body, trying to remove the force that was ending my life. I wasn't thinking clearly. My left arm met resistance on the way to my face.

Someone's sitting on top of me. Things were happening too fast! I was going to pass out in just a few seconds. The back of my hand slid over my face; then, I pushed it up into the air. Nothing was there, no human form anywhere. I opened my eyes, and I could see light but nothing else. I could breathe; I gasped for air, inhaling deeply several times.

Now, I was looking up through a tunnel several inches deep. I tried to move my legs, but something was on top of them. I then figured out what had happened. Several inches of snow had entombed me.

Only raising my head up, I looked around. The tree trunk had worked perfectly for a snow brake. The wind had blown the snow around it, leaving a pocket for my head to lie in. The fine powder had settled on my facemask, blocking the air. I tried to look down at the rest of my body, but I couldn't see over the top of the snow.

There were more than a few inches on top of me. I was guessing more like eight or nine. I looked up into the sky. It was still snowing so hard that I couldn't even see the lowest branch of the tree above me. Somehow, light managed to penetrate what I couldn't see through.

I felt better, but I was still tired. I didn't know how long I had slept, but there certainly wasn't any reason to get up and travel on. I would still be walking blind, as I had during the previous night. I pushed the snow away from my face and cleaned the remaining snow off my facemask. With nothing else I could do, I went back to sleep. This time, I dreamed of Craig.

When I woke the second time, the snow had stopped. The day was gone; darkness was overtaking the daylight. I couldn't believe I had slept all day. I felt even better than before because I was getting the rest I badly needed. I was stiff from lying in one position for so long. I moved my body only slightly to put the pressure points on different muscles.

I lay there, thinking, as I watched the light fade away. One more night of peaceful sleep would be a blessing. They didn't know where I was; I had been given another day of reprieve from them. I ate some snow to quench my thirst, but now, I had to urinate. I decided that could wait. I was warm under the blanket of snow, and the thought of hanging my bare feet out in the cold didn't sound like the thing to do. I didn't know where they were either. I wondered what had happened to them; they were out there somewhere, so why take a chance when it wasn't necessary?

I had nothing else to do but think of Craig. I felt my eyes water again. The question came to mind: *Would he have let me live knowing what I was going through now?*

The answer was: *Yes, the finish line is always somewhere; this one, I had to find.*

I slept through the second night. When I woke up, I felt whole again. I was starving, and I was beyond stiff. My muscles felt as though they were in the early stages of rigor mortis. It was cold but not freezing. I had to struggle to slide the lower half of my body forward, under the snow, to sit up. Then, as I slowly stood, I moaned.

I stood there for a few moments, waiting for everything to start working again. I looked around; the amount of snow that was now on the ground was bittersweet. It had saved my life and given me two nights of sleep that I needed. It was knee-deep now, and it was going to take twice the energy to walk.

I turned in a complete circle, looking. I had no idea which direction I had come from, in the dark, to get where I was. As I stood there, I wondered where the death dealers were. I had no idea of that either, but I did know what they were doing; that wouldn't change anytime soon.

Something caught my eye, maybe fifty yards away. As far as the eye could see in every direction, the snow had a pristine smooth surface, but not there, not this one spot with jagged edges that were taller than the surrounding area. I started walking toward it to investigate.

Nearly there, I stopped; I realized what it was. My heart started pounding, and my breathing increased. I felt sick—I was ready to run. I stood there like a frozen snowman. Looking around frantically for any movement, I saw none. I cautiously took a few more steps. I could see where their tracks had plowed through the snow, walking away.

The adrenaline was still pumping through my body. I walked up and stood in the spot where they had slept. I couldn't believe it. Fate had left them only fifty yards away from me, the same fate which had let me sleep longer, letting them walk away first.

I stood there looking at what they had done to survive—simple, but it worked. Now, I had a decision to make; I didn't know what to do. I looked up at the sky; it was a partly cloudy day, and the sun had not risen too far. So, I guessed which way was east; then I looked to the south.

The same exact way they went walking in. I knew they knew what my intentions were; I had no doubt about that. Still some two hundred plus miles away, at ten miles a day, meant I had approximately twenty days to go before reaching civilization.

Now, I asked myself, *do I follow them, making the walk much easier, taking the chance of walking up on them? Or do I strike out on my own, hoping they never find my tracks?*

They had found them before; the odds were in their favor, and they would find them again.

I chose to follow them for two reasons. The deeper snow would work me much harder, and the energy saved now would mean a lot in fifteen to twenty days from now. The other, I just felt better knowing where they were.

I followed in their tracks, and the two of them plowed a good trail. I continually looked up ahead, scanning for any movement. I was nervous on edge, but it was different. The hunted wasn't hunting, just following along.

I tried to rationalize what I was doing. Like NASCAR drivers, drafting to save fuel, I was learning from the best current-day trackers since the Old West. I even called it freeloading. My thoughts were clear again. I tried to analyze what-ifs: what to do if this happened, and where to go if that happens. I felt good physically.

Mentally, I was still a wreck. I would feel better dealing with the bear. I would never feel at ease with them, even if they were a hundred miles away.

I didn't walk far, less than a mile when I had to make another decision. They had split up. One angled to the left, the other off to the right. *Now, what do I do?* South was straight ahead. If I did that, it surely would be a suicide mission.

At some point, I would walk up between them. I could sit down and wait for one, maybe two days, then maybe they would walk far enough away to never find me again.

So, I stood there pondering the situation. The longer I thought about it, the more negatives I came up with. Each day, I remained out here, in the frozen nothingness, lessened my chances of survival.

Starvation, or eventually freezing to death, always lurked in the back of my mind. They might give up and backtrack; then, I would walk right into them. I knew that was always a possibility. My problems were compounding. I have to survive the present before I can move on to the next.

"I don't know what to do," I said softly. I half expected to hear a response, but I was coherent today, not walking half-dead, hallucinating, so I heard nothing. Without thinking, as if I was slightly pushed, I started following the trail that led off to the right.

I had followed it far off to the right and turned back when it did. The path led me right back to where they had met up. Their tracks never followed one another. They split up again and again. I kept following the one to the right. We did this two more times during the afternoon. I didn't know which of the two I was following; in a way, it didn't matter.

As long as they didn't know I was behind them, I was safe. If I happened to get too close, and it happened to be the shooter I was following, my odds were far less. I would be shot at with no questions asked; that was a given, just like paying taxes and death. I wasn't planning on dying today.

Now, it was almost dark. Maybe I was being overly cautious, but I chose not to go on. I was halfway back on the angled walk. I knew they would meet in the middle again, which they probably already had. I didn't know how far ahead of me they were. Possibly, they had enough time for another trip. I didn't.

Another question I couldn't answer was, "Would they continue after dark?"

Without knowing where I was, I didn't think so. They would spend the night together; I was sure of that. In the morning, I would learn more when I found the spot where they had called it a day. I would know how far ahead they were. I sat in the snow, looking up at the stars, trying to find my lucky one.

Was I an optimist or a pessimist? Seeing my husband killed and left out here with nothing, one could say that was bad. But I had the two storms just when I needed them, and I happened to sleep longer than they had. Today, I felt I was an optimist.

The wind wasn't blowing; it had turned much colder. It would be a long night, but I didn't care, sitting there in the snow. I would get to see yet another day!

I woke up much colder than the morning before. I waited until there was enough daylight to get up and start moving.

Patience, I told myself, *take no chances.*

Within two miles, I came to the spot where they had met up again. That's where they spent the night. They had built a wall of snow and had laid behind it. Then, another thought came to me: maybe they were too worn out to make another trip. Walking through the deep snow had to be tough. What if they were far ahead and had quit before dark, leaving me to walk up on them?

Too many what-ifs, I constantly thought. I had to be careful; this cat-and-mouse thing I was doing came down to a game of wits—mine. I already knew if I had to turn and run, they would catch me. I would be the one plowing through the snow, leaving them an easier path to run in. I couldn't let that happen.

We did this for two more days. On each trip, the angle out became much longer. On the second day, we only made two trips out and back, one in the morning and the second in the afternoon. I was sleeping as well as I could be at night. Each night seemed a little colder than the one before. Many times, I woke only to roll over, hoping to find a little warmth.

The third morning, I was starving. It's been over two days since the bear and I ate the fish. I was saving what I had in my pocket. I had to eat; I was feeling weak. So, I pulled the slab of fish from my pocket. It was half frozen, but it still tasted good. I only ate a third of it. Feeling a little satisfied, I put the rest of it back in my pocket, saving it for an emergency.

Today, we did something different. We continued in the same direction all day. Having never turned back to meet up with his partner, told me they were getting desperate. As the day wore on, I could tell by the length of his steps he was becoming tired. So was I! I was tired of all the zigzagging.

Losing valuable miles each day only led me further into the dead of winter when the really cold weather hit. Craig had said many times we had to be out before Christmas. This far north, the last half of December would be deadly cold.

By my best estimate, we were only covering six to eight miles south per day. We were, however, still walking ten to twelve miles a day. I was amazed at the pace he maintained. Many times, I wondered what they were doing for food.

His steps never turned to look back. They never drifted, even slightly, as if he might be looking over his shoulder. I knew he had one thought on his mind: to find my tracks. But something wasn't right! It wasn't that awkward feeling in the middle of my back like before. I couldn't explain it—this was different.

The density of the trees never changed. I always had the one hundred fifty to two hundred feet of visibility. I was now walking up a steep hill and breathing heavily; my body temperature was rising. I decided to stop and sit down, leaning against a tree, looking to the east.

It was a picture-perfect day; there was not a cloud in the sky, the snow was glistening, and there was no wind. My best guess at the temperature was around five degrees. One-half of the team of the death dealers was somewhere up ahead of me.

It was a good day to be alive, I thought, as I sat there looking through the trees. I had my axe and fish to eat. What more could a girl ask for?

I couldn't explain what I was feeling, and it wasn't going away. It wasn't a bad feeling, but I didn't like it. I looked around behind me, but nothing was there, as I knew there wouldn't be anything. It wasn't the bear; the gunshot had scared it away. I sat there, trying to figure out what it was. The only possibility I could think of was a pack of wolves stalking me, or should I say, "Us."

But that was a very slight possibility. I hadn't seen any signs of wolf tracks since the day Craig and I arrived. However, I could think of nothing else.

My thoughts drifted onto other things—food. By tomorrow, I was going to have to find more. My fishing experience had gone well, and as of now, I saw no other means. We hadn't come upon a lake in the past two days.

So, my plan was to stop and take the time to fish in the next lake I came to. I had the time. He had to be burning far more energy than I was. Patience is a virtue. Only now, patience meant my life. As anxious as I was to get out of here and find civilization, I couldn't forget that.

There it was again, that feeling, only this time it was stronger. I stood up and looked around, but nothing was there. I asked myself, *What now? What's the next obstacle going to be?*

I had no idea.

Mid-afternoon had arrived, nothing else. I walked along at a casual pace. I was trying to figure out what he was going to do. In reality, he had two choices: turn and start heading back before night, or wait until morning and then do it. It didn't really matter; I just wished I had known. So, my next plan was, if I did come to the spot where he turned, that's where I was going to sleep for the night.

I continued to walk for a good while. Although I was looking as far ahead as I could see, my mind was on something else—the unknown. Tomorrow, the next day, and even next week were all unknowns. Right now, as always, I have to deal with the present.

I wasn't paying attention as I should have been. Following his deep ruts through the snow became secondary. I didn't see anything moving. The dark shadows were growing longer, pointing to the east. I had become too complacent.

It was as if he had been dropped from the sky. I yelled! Two more steps, and I would have stepped on him. This wasn't one of the two choices. He was lying in the snow, on his side, as if he had fallen over right there. He was the one I called the tracker. I was too scared to care; I was shaking. He wasn't moving.

The thoughts began racing through my mind: *Was he dead? Had exhaustion taken its toll in the snow? Was he sick or just sleeping?*

Two seconds after I yelled, I knew. My worst fear! It was the last question that went through my mind.

He sat up. The confused look on his face only lasted a second; the surprised look lasted even less. It then turned to anger and then pure hatred.

When he made the first move to get up, I turned and ran. Again, the fear I was feeling was incomprehensible. The adrenaline rush was more than my system could tolerate. I felt sick; I thought I was going to vomit, but it didn't happen. Running off the track into a new direction would be the end of me. Then, I would be blazing the new trail, allowing him the easier path.

I heard him say, "You might as well stop and get this over with."

The calmness in his voice was cold. It raised the level of fear I was feeling to a new high.

I was pumping my arms as hard as I could. I raised my feet, bending my knees, trying to gain extra inches with each step. I didn't dare turn to look back; each step meant life. I continued down the path.

He managed to stay with me step by step. I could hear his heavy breathing. My lungs started burning. I was running with all the effort I could give. There was no rhythm in my inhaling and exhaling with my steps, as there was when I ran the races.

In races, I never ran through deep snow or with someone chasing me and wanting to kill me. I felt myself straining so hard to maintain the pace I was holding my breath. I felt at any moment, I would feel his hand grab me and pull me to the ground. I tried to look three or four steps ahead, always concentrating on what was behind me.

Several thoughts popped into my head: *How long is this going to last? Where am I going to go?*

I had only one direction to travel in: the wrong one. The one good thought was that I didn't think I would run head-on into the shooter. He was one day long gone, in the other direction.

Then, my right foot slid on something under the snow; I was going to fall. It shot out to the side, breaking the rhythm. I was unable to bring it around and plant it on the ground. My body started to fall forward after pushing off with my left foot.

This is it, I'm going down. This isn't how I planned on dying, I thought.

Now, I was nearly at the point of no recovery. Leaning out forward, I had my arms stretched out in front of me, instinctively ready to cushion the fall.

My right foot came up and landed on the ground. I had to push up and off of it if I had any chance at all to remain on two feet. When that happened, I rocketed forward. Then, I had to alter my left step, making it a much shorter step. I wasn't out of the clear yet. The momentum I gained kept me from straightening up; gravity was winning the battle with the upper half of my body. I was still going down.

I held my breath, grunted, and pushed for all I was worth with my right foot. I was heading in the direct path to collide with a tree, two more steps, and I was about to break some bones, possibly my neck. I had to overcorrect to prevent that from happening. I pushed again with my right foot and turned to the left. Now, things went from bad to really bad, and this put me off the path and out into the fresh, untouched snow.

I could feel him two feet behind me. I didn't have to look. I ran, picking up each foot, like someone would do running in knee-deep water. My lungs were burning as though they were on fire. I couldn't take air in fast enough. I was slowly losing the battle. Then, I felt his hand slide down my back; he wasn't able to grab onto anything secure. I made a hard turn to the right. The only way I was going to be able to outrun him was to get back to the trail.

"You won't make it," he said.

He already knew what I had planned. With each step, I grunted. The closeness of his voice and the sound of his raspy exhaling sent chills through my body. The adrenaline rush was long over. Pure determination to live drove me on.

Now, I could see it, the trail, only ten feet away. After four more steps, I was there, which meant I had a chance to see tomorrow! Three steps, then two, only one more to go—I was going to make it!

But I didn't. The weight of him landing on my back drove me forward. I screamed for bloody life, one that echoed for a long time through the trees for no one to hear. I landed face-first in the snow on the trail.

This isn't a good day to die, I thought.

The momentum when we landed and the fatigue caused him to be unable to hang onto me. He rolled off to the side. I hurt from the weight of him landing on me, almost knocking the wind out of me. It took me a second to inhale, getting my breathing back in rhythm.

That's all it took—he was fast, back on top of me in a flash, beating me in the back of my head. I screamed again. I tried to get up, but I couldn't. I tried to crawl, but I couldn't. I had to do something to stop the beating.

Each blow that landed drove my face further into the snow. My eyes were closed, but I could see stars. There was enough snow beneath me to allow me to twist around between his legs. I had to get on my back; then, I could at least use my arms to deflect his blows.

Fear turned into madness, the kind that was borderline insanity. I was flailing about, swinging my arms wildly. He managed to land a few good hits to my face. I tried to claw his face, but the mittens I had on made that a worthless effort. Then, he grabbed my throat with his left hand, locked his elbow, and leaned forward, forcing my head against the frozen ground. I couldn't breathe. Fear of dying sent me into pure panic. My body went limp, and the blood pressure in my head made it feel as if it was about to explode.

"If you would have given up the first day, we wouldn't have had to go through all this," he said.

Then, I saw him reach behind with his right arm, trying to find something that was out of my vision. I had to get air; my ears began ringing, and I knew shortly I would pass out.

Then, I saw it! He swung the knife around, and the blade glistened in the sunlight. He held it in front of me and stopped. I was down to seconds left in my life; I had to do something. I grabbed his left arm with both of my hands. I pulled and pushed, I arched my back and kicked my legs in the air, but I couldn't get free.

He smiled while he was taking his time. "I'm going to enjoy this. I must say, you've been the biggest challenge of any hunt I've ever had."

I felt my life slipping away. I no longer had the strength to fight. I was seeing double; everything was becoming cloudy and moving in slow motion. Seconds left, would I pass out before I felt the cold steel enter my body at whatever location he chose? I was hoping that maybe God would allow that to save me from the pain. I was no longer feeling panicked; I accepted the fact that I was going to die. I had lost, not from trying, just from fate. One step too many!

I heard a noise I couldn't explain. I couldn't tell which direction it was coming from; I was too far gone. It sounded louder; I thought maybe it was just inside me, my body's last effort to sustain life. The last thing I remember thinking was, *I'll be with you shortly, Craig.*

The next thing I saw was a big flash of black approaching off to my right. I thought I was hallucinating in the last seconds of life.

It attacked with such ferocity it was unbelievable. The noise was outrageous. He turned his head in the direction of what I thought was internal. He had heard it, too, and then I saw it in his eyes. Pure fear—he froze! It was unmistakable; it was his turn, not mine. I didn't know it yet, and it was not for another second.

I rolled my eyes to the right, just in time to see a high black flash hit him. Its mouth was wide open, and its lips were rolled back, exposing maximum capacity to sink all its teeth into him. And it did, the massive jaws clamped around his face. The speed at which the bear was moving hit him with such force it lifted him off me and into the air.

In less than a second, the bear was over me and gone. I gasped desperately, trying to get the air that my body needed so badly. I didn't have the strength to get up yet. I rolled my head to the left and watched the bear drag him off. The strength of the bear was no match for him. The bear ran, dragging him underneath it, straddling him. I heard a scream that contained more horror than one could imagine. I could see the tracker's feet flopping around as if it were a rag doll, toes up.

That's how he was going to die. There is justice—Mother Nature just held court. He had no reprieve—no parole, no gas chamber, no electric chair. I continued to watch; I was mesmerized by the horror. I couldn't believe the speed the bear had running while dragging him. It continued running another twenty feet or so.

As I sat up, my vision was returning to normal. I could hear the swishing sound of his clothes sliding through the snow. My hearing went from fading to almost nothing, then to an acute hypersensitivity. The bear stopped and pounced up and down on the tracker several times. Then, the real gruesome, horrifying death penalty was carried out.

The bear never stopped bellowing, growling, and making noises I didn't know a bear could make. The bear was pissed—no, it was beyond that! I watched it claw the top of his body with its left paw. Then, shreds of cloth flew into the air behind it. The tracker was still screaming.

Before the pieces of his clothes landed on the ground, the bear had repeated the process with its right paw. The speed of the bear clawing back and forth at his body was astonishing. All the while, it continued biting at his face and neck.

Five seconds later, the screaming stopped. The pillaging of his body hadn't. I had a front-row seat to something I didn't want to watch, but I couldn't look away. The bear continued raking its claws down his body, digging deeper with each stroke.

Now, the shreds of clothes landing on the snow were red. But it didn't stop. The longer it continued, the more vicious the strokes became. The bear was sinking its claws into his body slowly, then with a quick hard pull; it would rake away flesh and meat, throwing it into the air.

The bear continued to scream. I know my face was contorted into a twisted, scared, and ugly look of horror. Then, I saw a chunk of the tracker fly into the air. I had no doubt what it was, and I heard the bones snap. It was bloody pieces of rib bones I watched fly through the air and land in the snow.

This was the first time I was thankful for the deep snow. I heard more bones snap and then saw big pieces of red chunks catapulted into the air. The death sentence had been carried out—now, he was getting an autopsy. I was becoming sick to my stomach. This was, and always will be, the sickest thing I will ever see. I wanted to vomit, but there was nothing in my stomach to lose.

Then, it stopped. Again, I was thankful for the deep snow. His body had been pushed down into the snow, so I couldn't see it, the hollow skeleton of a man.

The bear turned to look at me. It stretched its neck out and roared; I could see its red teeth and gums. Small pieces of flesh were stuck to its nose and snout. I melted. *Was I next?* The bear had worked itself into a killing frenzy, had the taste of blood, and was highly agitated.

It took a few steps toward me and stopped. It roared at me again. I started to stand up and felt something land on my feet. I looked down; it was his knife. I remembered being seconds away from death; was I now again? I slowly got the knife and stood the rest of the way up, with the axe in one hand and the knife in the other. I was still no match for the bear; I wasn't going to try to resist if it started to charge at me.

Then, it occurred to me. That was the strange feeling I had been having. The bear was following me. It also knew he was close, so it remained out of sight.

Moments passed, and nothing happened. The bear licked its lips, sliding its long pick tongue down its snout.

"Well, am I next?"

The bear looked at me. I still couldn't read the bear's expressions, and the look on its face never changed. It continued licking away the blood, no longer growling.

"Thank you for saving my life," I said, looking at it. "I am grateful."

I was surprised the bear didn't try to eat the tracker, so I had an idea. I reached into my pocket and removed the piece of fish I had left. I held it in my hand and looked at the bear. It stood up on its back legs, and I felt my legs go weak. I could see the bear sniffing the air.

"Here, this is for you. Without you, I wouldn't be around to eat it myself. Thanks again!"

I threw the fish into the air at the bear. I guess being over-excited, I threw it with much more energy than I had intended. The piece of fish sailed right at the bear. To my amazement, the bear caught the fish in its front paws. The fish disappeared in one bite. That reminded me never to make Mother Nature mad at me.

I had to go fishing!

CHAPTER 10

"Well, if you follow me, I'll try to catch some fish, which seems to be your favorite. If not, I'll understand, so be it. I don't trust humans, either."

I turned and headed south. I wasn't sure if the bear would follow me; I wouldn't follow me either. Just some dumb blond wandering around in the middle of nowhere.

After the bloody killing, I wasn't sure if the bear would attack me, but I didn't think so. An act of kindness goes a long way, but I didn't see it that way at the time. It was just a matter of survival.

I walked a short distance and then turned to see what the bear was doing. It was slowly bounding its way toward me.

So docile, I thought, *but I will never forget what it's capable of.*

It stopped when I stopped. The bear just looked at me. I wondered what it was thinking; I tried to imagine. *What did you stop for?* Or, *Well, let's go and eat some fish.*

That's what we were going to do. I needed to find a lake. As I walked, I did the calculations in my head. I had two; maybe three days lead on my remaining assailant. We walked one day in our direction; he would do the same in his. That gave me two days! When his partner didn't show up at their rendezvous location, how long would he wait? One day?

Undoubtedly, the shooter would walk cross country to find our trail. That put me back to two. I was now in the best situation I had been in since this started. I had the time to fish and to eat. I had to feed the bear—my new bodyguard.

"I'm glad you're hanging out with me. I know you're not doing it for companionship. In your eyes, I'm just a free lunch, and that's okay. One way or another, I'm going to feed you, as long as it's not me."

I didn't look back! Talking to a bear just relieved some tension. I couldn't get that horrible ordeal out of my head. I shouldn't feel sorry for the tracker, but I did.

What a way to die, I thought. *Something no one should be a witness to.*

I plowed along for two hours or more. It was much easier walking in his tracks, but what other choice did I have? I finally came upon a stream, one with a swift current, preventing it from freezing over.

Now, I had to learn how to fish again, with a much different take. I looked into the swift water; it was, at best, two feet deep. I saw no fish. I turned to look at the bear.

"Now, what do I do?"

The bear remained thirty feet back and watched me. I walked along the edge of the stream, hoping an idea would come to me. One was how to catch fish, the other to find my way across. I couldn't get wet; it was too cold for that.

I found a small semi-deep eddy. It had a fairly thick ice shelf, maybe two feet wide, attached to the bank. Maybe there would be fish hanging out below it.

I chopped a new spear, removed my necklace, and very gingerly tested the ice. If I had a rock, I would have used the bush pilot test, but I didn't. My body's weight was the only test. I eased my right foot down on the ice and slowly shifted what I thought was half my weight. It didn't crack, so I bent down and went fishing.

I waited, with a spear in hand, nothing. I moved the necklace back and forth. Then, to my surprise, a small fish appeared out from under the ice. I thrust the spear down into the water, but I missed.

Well, no big deal, I thought.

This continued on for at least twenty minutes. I was aggravated to the point of getting mad. I stood up, stretched my back, and looked at the bear, who was waiting patiently.

"This sucks! The fish are too small."

Then, I laughed. Talking to a wild bear wasn't right, but I guess what made me laugh the most was the bear. It always had the same look—well, until it got mad.

I went back to fishing. The next fish that appeared, I got. I pulled it from the water, stood back on the ground, and danced around in a circle, whooping and hollering. A bystander would have thought I found gold.

To me, the fish was much more valuable than gold—that I couldn't eat. The fish was a small walleye, roughly a pound or more. I slid it off the spear and tossed it underhanded to the bear.

"Here you go. It's not much; I'm just trying to repay my debt."

The fish landed in the snow several feet in front of the bear. It walked forward, burying its head in the snow. It plowed through the snow and then raised its head, already chewing. By the time it looked at me, the fish was gone.

"Geez, it's going to take a lot of those, isn't it?"

I fished for another hour with just a few results. I used the tracker's knife to cut off a filet from one side of each of the few fish. I was starting to get used to raw fish. Now, I was full. I saved one small piece, just in case.

"Come on, we need to find a lake. The fish will be bigger there."

I found a log lying across the stream and walked over. When I was sure I was far enough away, I looked back. I watched the bear wade into the water and cross.

"I wish I could do that." The bear stopped at the edge and looked at me.

The sunlight was fading as I plowed on through the snow. Each step took extra effort, burning calories I didn't have and hindering my progress. My hat goes off to the dead tracker. Now, I know why he was lying in the snow two days after this, and he was worn out.

After two days of this, so will I. Hopefully, I can cover a few more miles and walk out of the heavy snow. Nonetheless, I had to do something; this couldn't go on. Five miles a day burning twice the energy wouldn't get me to where I needed to be. I will freeze to death first!

I turned around to look at the bear. It was gone. It had silently left as it had arrived. I felt a little sad, not knowing if I would see it again. It had to be close to calling it a year and hibernating for the winter.

As much as I didn't want to, I walked on past dark. The stars were out. I chose a cluster hanging in the south sky and walked toward it. I wasn't sleepy; I had two good nights of sleep in me. The only problem I had was my legs were burning.

My thoughts were long past of finding a lake when I walked upon one. It wasn't a large one by any means, but it would have fish in it. I went about the business of chopping a hole and making yet another spear. I had one more problem to overcome. The water was too dark to see the fish. I dangled the necklace on the surface. My only hope was to have a fish come up and stick its head on the surface.

Two hours or more had passed since the time I had started chopping and spearing the first fish. With almost twelve hours of darkness, I couldn't sleep all of it. I was enjoying myself. I didn't have to worry about what was behind me for tonight, and I was getting food.

This worked much better than I had expected. In no time, I had two more fish. The only reason I could come up with is the hole in the ice was letting more light in and drawing the fish to it.

I sat in a cluster of trees, using the knife to cut the meat from two of the fish. I ate until I was full, filled my pockets with the remaining cleaned meat, then laid down and went to sleep.

Something wasn't right, telling me to wake up. I heard a noise long before I consciously knew it. I slowly opened my eyes to a large dark spot standing beside me. The bear had returned and was eating the fish that was left lying on the ground two feet from me. I could hear fish bones snapping as though they were nothing more than toothpicks. I could also hear the bear's gums smacking as it ate.

That reminded me of the power it possessed, seeing what I had earlier in the day. I wasn't scared any longer. If the bear wanted me dead, it would have done so by now. I could reach out and touch it again, as before, but I knew better.

I watched the bear walk away and went back to sleep.

It was the coldest morning yet when I woke. I was shaking badly. The only way to warm up was to get up and start walking. It took me a while just to get the stiffness out of my joints as I walked. Not long after that, I started to warm up.

I've got to do something, I told myself.

To go on like this, in the deep snow, I wasn't covering the miles I needed to. Mother Nature was warning me of what was yet to come. She was just toying with me, and I knew that.

For a while, I picked each knee up high in the air to keep from dragging my feet in the snow. Only half the morning was gone, and I was already getting tired. I didn't know which was worse, walking like this or plowing through the snow.

Snowshoes would be the answer if I had a pair. I stopped to rest for a bit. I had the idea of using a thick, heavy pine branch for snowshoes, but I couldn't figure out a means of tying them to my boots. I now regret not walking up to the tracker and taking whatever I thought would be useful. He would never need or miss what I may have pillaged from him. As I thought back, I probably made the right decision.

As I stood there catching my breath, I had several ideas of what would work. Grapevines would be excellent, but I hadn't seen any since my journey began. So, I went with my next choice, bark from a cedar tree. I could peel strips from the tree; it was tough and pliable. That was my next mission. I had seen variations of what I thought were like our cedars at home.

My luck was going to run out at some point—as of now, it hadn't. I didn't walk far! The terrain was temporarily flat and heavily wooded. I found the tree I needed, so I went to work. I took the axe and chopped thin slits, eye level, horizontally on the tree.

Then, I got my newly acquired knife and cut lines, one inch wide, down the tree, making sure I penetrated through the bark. Then, I peeled the bark from the tree. I was pleased with my progress,

This will work, I told myself. I now had eight strips of bark, roughly four feet long.

I wandered south slowly, looking for just the right tree with just the right limbs I needed. I couldn't find any that I thought were bushy enough to hold my weight in the snow. So, my next idea was to use two limbs under each foot.

I chopped two branches three feet long. I laced them together, winding the bark down the main stem of both branches, then back up to where I had started. Then, I knotted the two ends together.

I repeated the process until I had two homemade snowshoes. I looked at them, thinking the small, thin branches would be too weak. I couldn't walk on these like conventional snowshoes. So, I turned them around. Now, with the stump end of the branches facing forward, they would be more user-friendly.

I went about the task of tying them to my feet. I laced the bark under the branch, over the arch of my foot, and around the back of my foot, just above the ankle. Even though I had never experienced wearing snowshoes, common sense told me not to tie my heel down. The foot had to move freely as it does when wearing cross-country skis, which I had done before.

It took a great deal of time, from start to finish, on my project. I stood there, standing on the limbs. I took one slow step forward and planted my foot in the snow, checking the lacing around my foot. It seemed secure enough, so I stepped forward with the other foot. It felt good. I wasn't sinking near as deep into the snow.

Half a mile later, I was gliding along, riding on the snow. The energy level it took to walk was reduced by more than half. My heart rate was down, along with my breathing. Maybe I could get back to walking ten to twelve miles a day as long as the lacing held together. If not, it was just a matter of retying it—no big deal!

By mid-afternoon, I felt the feeling. The bear was back there, somewhere. Bears are nocturnal, so maybe it had slept most of the day and was now catching up.

I hadn't eaten yet today and hadn't planned to. The bear would want to. Being omnivorous, the bear wouldn't care what it ate. I had only fish, so fish was the main course. I was looking forward to seeing the bear again. I couldn't possibly pet it, but at the very least, I could talk to it. I was also looking forward to finding a lake and catching more fish, not for me, but for the bear. Even if I had the Queen Mary's hull iced down with fish just to give the bear, I wouldn't be enough for what the bear had done for me.

I had to take the time to fish; I owe it that much. But the time wasted today making the snowshoes meant I would have to walk long after dark. It was a fifty/fifty chance that I wouldn't see the last of the two death dealers. If Las Vegas would be placing odds and taking bets, I had a good idea of what to bet on. That was a chance I couldn't take. My odds were less with him; he wouldn't have to get as close, and he had a gun. Deep down inside, I had no doubt he was much lower on the ethical pole of life.

I was gliding along. It felt good as I floated on the snow. Nighttime was only hours away. Something told me to turn around, so I did. To my surprise, there was the bear again.

"How do you do that? You move with the grace and quietness of a ballet dancer."

The bear was looking a little different. Maybe it was just me, but it was close to the beginning of November. Maybe following me during the day was interrupting its sleeping habits.

I sat down in the snow and removed a piece of fish from my pocket.

What the heck, I thought. *Here's some fish.*

I held it out, trying to get the bear to come closer.

Madie, are you crazy? I asked myself.

Probably so, I answered.

Now, I knew I was! I watched the bear sniff the air.

"It's not much, come and get it. I won't bite. They're the bad guys, not me."

The bear stomped the ground and made a noise. That was a little scary, so I threw the fish halfway to the bear. It bounded up to it. That was a little scary, also. It buried its head in the snow and found the fish. I removed the last piece of fish from my pocket. Now, the bear was only fifteen feet away again.

Again, I held it out but said nothing. Then, the bear walked within ten feet of me. It stretched its head forward and roared loudly. That was all I could take—way too scary.

"Okay, you win," I uttered and threw the fish at it. The bear caught it in its mouth.

"Wow, you're talented." Then, the bear walked backward a few steps.

"That's okay. I don't trust people either, especially the ones out here."

I stood and started walking.

Long past dark, I found a lake. This one was small, more in the category of a pond. I was sleepy and physically worn out for the day. The bear had hung with me the entire time.

"Time to repay more of my debt to you."

Over an hour later, the whole ordeal of fishing was over, and I had three more notches in my belt. Again, I filleted the third for me and threw the remains to the bear. It didn't hesitate a bit. Head, bones, and all, the bear chewed it up in short order.

"It's time for me to sleep. I guess you'll go and do what a bear does at night."

I had already removed my snowshoes to fish. I scraped the ground clear of snow and lay down. Soon, I was asleep.

Something woke me out of my sound sleep. I jumped up, looked around, and saw nothing. I heard nothing, either. I felt dizzy. While waiting for the blood to return to my head and the dizziness to subside, I looked for the bear—not surprised it wasn't around. I couldn't remember dreaming, so what had awakened me? I didn't know and didn't like it. I quickly went to work and tied my snowshoes on.

My goal today was no stopping, no fishing, just walking past the dark if I could physically hold out. It still bothered me on the way I woke earlier. I had to cover ground and a lot of it. Was he coming? Down inside, I had no doubt. He was only human. He had to be feeling the same as I was. If I pushed myself to the extreme limit each day, I should maintain my lead on him.

The day was over half gone. There was nothing to see but trees. I thought about the bear; something was telling me I might not see it again. Logic told me it was time for it to find someplace to hibernate for the rest of the winter. It knew as well as I that the worst was yet to come! That same logic told me I couldn't survive when the temperature dropped below zero. For now, I would be alright.

I walked on through the afternoon, thinking about several things. *The bear? Would I see it again? Craig? Who I would never see again. Mother Nature!*

One of my three races, or battles, depending on how one looks at them. I had to reach a permanent means of heat before the real winter hit. But I guess as I think about it, I could also throw Father Time in on that one. The battle is yet to come!

What was behind me was relentless, unforgiving, always coming. It was an everyday issue I had to deal with. The battle, or race, always remained at the top of the list. One mistake, be it sickness, a broken bone, or just pure stupidity, and it would be over. The other problems would never matter.

One thing running the 10K marathons taught me was to worry only about the race at hand and outrun the one behind. This was also helping me; the extra push he was giving helped the race against time.

Daylight left hours ago. I felt myself dragging each step, but I didn't stop. The bear had returned at dusk, giving me moral support and the extra drive that I needed. I talked to it more than I was silent, occasionally turning to look at it.

Many times, I asked it why it continued to follow me. It couldn't be just for the fish, and animals don't feel as lonely as humans do. It didn't understand a word I said, so why?

One more thing about this trip I will never understand, never figure out: "Why? Why had Craig and I been chosen to find these two, or them us, out here? Why didn't they just walk away? Why did they have to shoot Craig?"

I stopped and turned to look at the bear. "Why do you continue to follow me?"

My sudden stop surprised the bear. It jerked its head up and looked at me.

"I'm glad you are here; you're good company. I'm just sorry I can't hug you."

The bear continued to look at me as it usually did. I felt sad. I unzipped the pocket of my jacket. That noise the bear had already learned, it perked its ears forward.

As I removed one of the pieces of fish, to my surprise, the bear walked within five feet of me. "I'm sorry it's not much, had to ration food today."

Then, I leaned forward, stretched out my arm, and gently tossed the fish to it. Again, it caught the fish in its mouth.

I stood up and said, "God, I wish I could hug your neck. You have done much more for me than just save my life… you have no idea."

The bear sniffed the air, and it knew there were more fish in my pocket.

"You win, you can have it! I wasn't planning on eating it today anyway. I was just saving it for reserve. How can I say no to you?"

When I removed the last of the fish from my pocket, the bear took several short steps toward me, and my heart raced. It wasn't going to hurt me, but it was a bit scary. It slowly moved its head forward, sniffing.

Slowly, as though it thought I might do something, it pulled the fish, with its mouth, from my hands. "I will never bring harm to you; I hope you know that."

Then, the bear sat back on its haunches like a dog. I had to smile. I had a true friend. I slowly sat down beside it. Two feet away, in a big black furry bundle, sat more power than one could imagine. I had witnessed it firsthand.

"I'm glad you're my friend. Tomorrow, we'll fish."

It felt good to rest. Again, I worried about the one behind me.

"You know, bear, I might have just lied to you. If he catches up to me, he might bring harm to you first. You're a bigger threat to him than I am. That's the same as me doing harm to you. I'm sorry. We'll worry about that if it happens."

The bear just looked at me. I wondered if talking to it all the time gave it a sense of trust in me, along with the fish.

"You're a cheap date," I said, looking out into the darkness, "but a great buddy."

I didn't want to get up, but I had to. Two more miles, yet tonight meant a lot.

The bear quickly stood up before I had even started to move. The first thought that went through my mind was, *How did it know?* I turned and looked behind me. The bear stood up on its back legs and roared. My blood ran cold.

Oh no, I thought, *he can't be out there. How did he cover the distance between us so quickly?*

I didn't have time to be scared. The giant black bear standing next to me, swinging both paws in the air and roaring, was an unbelievable sight. I was scared to death of what I couldn't see. I was waiting to hear a gunshot. I wanted to tell the bear to get down; it was a much easier target standing erect. I remembered what had happened the last time. The speed, quickness, and power sent me sailing.

"Please get down, bear," I whispered.

Any second, I would hear a shot ring out and echo through the trees, as I had heard when Craig was killed. My emotional state of being couldn't take another. The bear ignored me. I wanted to get up and run, but if I was lucky enough to hear the shot before it killed me, I had no doubt it would be aimed at me. I didn't know what to do.

Sitting here, I would let him walk up closer and shoot both of us if necessary. My heart was pounding wildly, and my mind was racing madly. Any second, one of us was going to be shot.

"Bear, get down," I said a little louder and with more force.

Again, the bear ignored me. I was lost on what to do.

Then, I asked myself, *Had I lost? Was it over?*

This isn't how I had pictured it in my mind—if he was to get me—to die. I always thought it would be in the daylight for some reason.

The bear dropped down on all four feet, then suddenly spun a quarter turn to the right and roared again. It twisted its legs back to the left and swung its right paw in the air, roaring.

Again, it twisted back to the right, this time swinging its left paw in the air. I was confused. *He couldn't move that fast!? Why, if he was that close, didn't he shoot? Why didn't the bear attack him as it did with the one it had killed?*

The bear did this several more times. I could see that it wasn't going to give up the ground it stood on. I thanked God for the bear as I watched. My fear turned into puzzlement. What was out there? Could it be more bears? I heard nothing but the roars from the bear. Whatever it was wasn't good. The bear remained highly agitated. I felt a sense of security flow through my body.

Today wasn't the day I was going to die. I didn't move. This went on for several more minutes. The deadly silence from what was out there I didn't like. Then, the bear spun halfway around and lunged two steps forward. The light the stars were giving off, I could only see enough to see the snow fly as the bear pawed at the ground. I could see no more than that. I was amazed by the bear. The senses it had, to know or see, I wished we humans had.

Then, the bear went silent just as quickly as it had gone into attack mode, as if someone had flipped a switch. It sniffed the air, turned, and sniffed again. I was in awe of my guardian, my protector, all for just a few fish and an act of kindness.

Satisfied the present danger had passed, the bear turned and looked at me. "Thank you, again, I owe you. I don't have a clue what was out there, but tomorrow, you get all the fish you can eat if I can catch that many."

I was no longer tired. It was time to get away from the demons of the night, whatever they may be.

I didn't walk as far as I wanted to. Mentally, I wanted to walk nonstop until I found civilization, another human. Physically, I was done for another day. This one, so be it, was not uneventful. Those days I was learning to cherish.

The bear had hung tight with me, walking behind no more than ten feet back. This was new—had we crossed the line on absolute trust? Somehow, I didn't think so. I felt a sense of Mother Nature being one tick-off.

Was it safe to sleep? I didn't know. I couldn't go on; falling over in my tracks wouldn't be good. Would the new demons of the night get me while I slept? I had to take another chance. After a few hours of sleep, I would be up and gone.

I stopped and looked at the bear. "I have to sleep a while. If you would, please hang around."

I cleared the ground of snow and removed my tattered snowshoes. Tomorrow, they would need attention. I quickly fell asleep.

I dreamed. It wasn't a good sleep. I jerked several times, each time waking myself enough to shift my weight onto different points.

It was a dark dream, grey and black hues surrounding figures that had no faces, moving slowly and silently as they circled, haunting me.

Then, I woke, I didn't move, hearing nothing. I was still too tired; all I wanted to do was fall back asleep, and I did.

It was out there, my dream; my subconscious was trying to tell me. I was too tired to see the signs.

11
CHAPTER

Their plan was to wait no more than four hours past the time at the location where they were to meet up. He had done that. Seven hours later, he found the trail heading south, and then, he found what was left of his partner. He didn't get mad, didn't cry, and felt no remorse for the bloody, frozen carnage lying in the snow.

That changed everything, their plans—their future. He no longer cared what waited for them back in civilization. It no longer mattered!

Without knowing it, he went over the edge and became obsessed without feeling it. There was only one thing left in his life to accomplish now: to end hers. He no longer cared about the future or even his own life—all was gone.

The deep snow and the long hours of trailing her without eating or sleeping were taking their toll on his body. He didn't notice; he was focused on only one thing. The one thing he did know was that he was at least two days behind.

He passed the spot where she had slept, fished, and slept again. His leg muscles were stiff, turning into knots, but he ignored the pain. All he knew was to cover the distance to catch up to her. Each time he came to a spot where she had rested or fished, he still remained a day or so behind.

Then, he started following different kinds of tracks, but they were still hers. His eyesight had turned into tunnel vision. Looking only at the ground following her, everything else around him became a blur.

He stopped, looked up, and then looked around at the surroundings.

"How clever you are," he said.

He went to work making his own snowshoes. He worked quickly, smiling occasionally. The snowshoes he made were a bit different than hers. A much better quality, for he had a quarter-inch rope in his pocket. That, with many other necessary items, they had always carried with them. They had learned that through years of experience, they should always be prepared. One never knew!

Now, gliding along, he thought if he could hold out one more night with minimal sleep, he would be close tomorrow.

Two hours past dark, his plan fell apart when he fell down. His body could no longer go on. Five hours of sleep in the past two days, pushing his physical endurance to the extreme limit through the snow, he could no longer fight it. He struggled to untie his snowshoes and scrape the ground clear of snow, and then he slept.

When he woke the next day, he was beyond mad at himself; he was livid. The sun was in the middle of the sky; he had lost half a day. He put on his snowshoes and started off; nothing else mattered.

He didn't understand the bear. Why had it killed his partner and trusted her? Just because she was feeding it, fish gave no reason for a wild bear to trust a human.

There would be no stopping tonight. He had to find her and get back. Mother Nature could turn at any time. Then, out here with no protection, survival would become unbearable, nearly impossible.

I thought I heard a growl. Still more than half asleep, I tried to concentrate. *Did I hear anything or not?*

Seconds passed, and I felt myself drifting away; it was what I wanted to do. I heard nothing as I passed back into the vast darkness of sleep.

Then, I heard it again, but this time, it was much louder.

This time, I was wide awake. Instantly, I felt scared; I couldn't move. I couldn't figure out what was wrong.

I tried to look around for the bear but couldn't see it. It had been several days since I felt this way. Adrenaline was flowing through my body so quickly I felt sick.

All signs were present; the danger was near! It couldn't be the last death dealer; he would have already made his presence known.

Five seconds had passed since being awake. Then, again, I heard a low growl just past the edge of darkness ahead of me. I slowly twisted my head in that direction. The knife was luckily in my left pocket, and I was lying on my right side. I slowly moved my left hand, reaching for it. I saw nothing out there.

Then, I heard another growl off to my side, in front of me, and then another simultaneous one behind me. I didn't feel panicked. I went into the high-alert mode of listening and thinking. They had me surrounded.

Now, I knew what was out there—now and earlier—the demons of the night, a pack of wolves. It would be useless to get up and try to run. I would become their meal for the day. All I could do was try to fight them off.

The first one growled again, and soon I counted three. I wouldn't stand a chance against three of them. Again, this wasn't in my plan of how I was going to die out here. I never thought about a pack of wolves. They were the furthest thing from my mind. Maybe I could get one, possibly two, but I doubted it. The bear wasn't around; otherwise, they wouldn't have gotten so close. I was on my own to fight them, more than likely to die a horrible death. That much I knew.

I rolled over onto my stomach, then raised up onto my knees. My mind was racing with thoughts again. Should I stand, only to be jumped on by one of them instantly appearing out of the darkness? That would cause me to lose my balance and any leverage I had if I really had any at all.

I moved the knife to my right hand. I looked for a tree, wondering if I could climb one fast enough before being shredded to bits. I doubted that. With darkness prevailing, I couldn't see a tree good enough to make my escape. If, by some slim chance, I survived this, I knew from now on, I would always sleep next to a tree.

Waiting for the onslaught of pain to begin, they continued to growl. It was as if they were talking to one another, making their plan.

They were slowly moving back and forth. I asked myself, *What were they waiting for?*

Did I seem that big of a threat to them that they were uncertain? Little did they know, I was no threat at all. I would wound one; chances of killing it weren't in my favor.

This seemed to go on forever. In reality, it wasn't; maybe I was in shock. The passing of time was altered, trying to give precious moments of added time to my life. I became angry, ready to fight.

I yelled, "Come on, what are you waiting for?"

They became silent, which made me more nervous. Had that scared them? If so, only for a few seconds. Then, I saw the dark black silhouette of the one in front of me moving toward me. It stopped well within a safety zone, lowered its head, and then stretched it out forward from its neck. Although I couldn't see its eyes, coal black and vicious, I knew it was staring at me relentlessly, never blinking.

Out of the corner of my left eye, I saw the second one moving in slowly, in the same crouched position as its partner. It was leaning back, preloading the spring tension in its legs; it looked as if it was going to leap at me at any second. I didn't bother looking back to the right and behind. Logic told me it would be doing the same.

The tension I was emitting couldn't even be cut with a knife. I yelled at the top of my lungs, "Get this over with!"

The first one that attacked would be wounded; how seriously was anyone's guess? After that, it was eat-or-be-eaten!

They slowly took one step forward in unison. My mind was processing information uncontrollably. Were they just waiting to see which one of them would attack first, then the other two would move in and finish it? Or did they have some sort of ESP between them, moving in for the kill, all attacking at once?

"See you soon, Craig," I whispered.

I didn't cry. I wasn't going to give up, I was going to fight, that's all I had to give.

Another step forward, they crouched even lower. Their leg muscles were wound so tight; now, my life had seconds left.

Then, I saw the one in front of me making the leap. Perhaps I was in shock or just mentally braced, but I heard nothing. Their growls had faded away. Perhaps it was just my mind, my subconscious blocking out things I didn't need. The biggest was hearing myself scream as I was attacked.

I watched it travel through the air. I started raising my right hand. I had a death grip on the knife, ready to bury it in the wolf. I braced for the impact, stiffening my legs and leaning into the force.

Now, I could see its eyes and teeth two feet away. Its lips were curled back, showing me something I didn't want to see—long, white, razor-sharp teeth. I remember my last thought: *God, this is going to hurt!*

Out of nowhere, with unbelievable speed, a dark flash flew past me, brushing my jacket as it went past. Both front paws flew up, and the bear caught the wolf in mid-air, a foot away from my face. The bear spun the wolf over, making it land on its back. The momentum of the bear carried the wolf several feet backward.

The bear stood over the wolf, roaring while the wolf laughed. I watched the bear raise and lower its head several times, its massive jaws sinking its teeth into the wolf.

The second wolf moved in on the bear. It had forgotten about me, and now its only purpose was to try and help its partner. The bear was the bigger threat. In a flash, it had buried its teeth in the bear's behind.

My right arm never stopped moving. I was swinging it for a death blow. Instantly, I changed its direction. Suddenly, the second wolf was no more than three feet away from me, standing broadside.

I put all my weight and strength into my feet as I lifted off of my knees, placing all one hundred fifteen pounds resting on my toes. I sprang forward toward the wolf with my right arm, never stopping its swinging arch. Then, with all the effort I had, I brought the knife down to the wolf. The six-inch blade entered the wolf's rib cage on its right side.

The moment the knife entered, I fell forward onto my stomach. At the same time, I grabbed the knife in my right hand with my left. I held onto the knife with dear life. I couldn't lose it, in case the wolf tried to run, which it did.

When it moved away from the pain, I pulled down on the knife. It was unbelievably sharp. I felt the knife slice through the wolf as it pulled away, sliding down between the rib bones.

The wolf moved away from me, no more than two feet, and fell over, never making a sound. It had died with its eyes open. I was aware of a bigger commotion behind me, but that was secondary; all my concentration was focused on this one wolf.

I turned my head to the right, looking at the bear. The third wolf was up on top of the bear, attacking it. Its hind legs remained on the ground, and it was trying to bite the bear in the back of the neck.

By the time I pulled the knife from the dead wolf and stood, the growling and roaring were deafening. I had no plan of attack, and all I was going to do was help the bear. I had to. I took one step toward the fierce battle. The bear quickly spun around, trying to throw the wolf from its back.

In the process of doing that, the bear hit me. Its right shoulder slammed into my legs, sending me backward to the snow. The bear took one quick swing at me with its left paw, thinking I was one of the wolves. It missed me by inches only.

The first wolf was back on its feet, attacking the bear on the opposite side. The bear swung back around in that direction, looking for a kill. The third wolf rejoined the fight. I stood, not knowing what to do; I took two steps forward. It was biting and clawing at the bear. It stood between myself and the bear, totally unaware of my presence. I grabbed the wolf by its right ear and instantly buried the knife in its throat. That ended the attack from the third wolf.

I stood back and watched the bear finish off the first wolf. It didn't take long, and then everyone was silent. The bear quickly spun around again, still in attack mode, looking for the others for another kill. It looked at me, then at the dead wolves lying on the ground, and then back to me.

The bear walked to each wolf, sniffing them and making sure they were dead. Then, as casually as ever, it looked back at me.

My heart was still racing, and my breathing was elevated as though I was running another race. I was; only this one meant life or death.

I saw the bear wobble just slightly; I knew it was hurt. If so, how bad? I had no way of knowing. I sure wasn't going to walk up to it and look. I knew my limits. That would be exceeding the boundaries between the bear and myself.

"Are you hurt?" I asked in a light, caring voice.

Again, the bear looked at me. "I hope you're alright."

I sat down, exhausted, lost for words, and started crying. The life or death fight that just took place, and once again, the bear coming to my rescue, overwhelmed me.

Sobbing, wiping the tears just above my face mask, I said, "Why do you always come to my rescue? You are an angel."

I didn't care how cold it was; I removed my face mask. I wanted the bear to see my face. Although it was dark, I knew the bear could see me. The bear just watched. As before, I was in awe of how it could go from a ferocious fighting machine to a docile, quiet bear, as though nothing had happened.

I sure couldn't. My emotions were still flowing—scared, happy, and worried. It would take several minutes for them to subside. Before any of this happened, my worst fear returned. The bear wobbled again and almost fell, catching itself before falling into the snow.

"Oh God! You are hurt. Now, what do I do?"

The bear remained standing, and I was lost on what to do again. "I wish I could help you. Even if you would let me, I have no way… thank you."

The bear looked around, satisfied all was okay, turned, and walked into the darkness, never looking back.

Now, I sobbed uncontrollably. I cried so hard my body shook. Would I see the bear again? Would it be alright? Mostly, I cried because it had saved my life.

It took me a while to regain my composure. I sat there wondering what to do next. I wouldn't be able to sleep; too much had happened. I didn't like the idea of having three dead wolves next to me, either.

I wasn't much of an astronomer; I had no idea of what time of the night it was. I looked up at the stars; I felt so small. I think I knew which way was south. I wasn't going to sleep, so I decided not to waste the time.

I stood and reached for the snowshoes, and then I had an idea. When you have nothing, you learn to waste nothing. I had absolutely no idea how to skin an animal, but I was about to learn. The wolves' hides, as thick as they were, would make a good cover or at least a good mat to lie on to sleep. The visibility was poor, which would make the job much more difficult, but I had to try.

I didn't know which end to start on. Logic told me, always having seen deer hunters hang the deer by their hind legs, that's where I needed to start. I did, and the process was slow. I chose the first wolf I killed; it was the closest.

Now, rolling the wolf from one side to the other, I couldn't believe how heavy it was. It had to outweigh me by at least twenty pounds. Time passed, and skinning the wolf helped relieve some tension. It also took my mind off the bear. I rolled, cut, and pulled on the hide until my fingers ached. It was much harder than I had ever imagined. I almost gave up several times.

I had to do this, I told myself.

The hide was something I could definitely use. When I finally finished, I cut the hide around its neck and pulled it away from the naked carcass. As I rested, I had another idea. Two hides would be even better, one to sleep on and the second as a blanket. I rolled up the hide, picked it up, and to my amazement, it weighed at least fifteen pounds, more than I had figured. There was no way I could carry two of them with me; the energy spent carrying them wasn't worth it. It would slow me down, giving the one behind me an easier chance of catching up.

I used the rope I carried the fish with and tied the hide up. Just as I was about to put my snowshoes on, I had another idea: wolf meat. I didn't think I could eat it, but if the bear would return, it would. I wanted to be able to feed it if it did.

Now, I was thankful it was dark out. As I hacked away at the carcass, cutting off big pieces of meat, I didn't think I could have it in the daylight. I filled both pockets on my jacket, and now I was happy. I could do something for the bear if it returned. I had roughly ten pounds of meat.

I put on the snowshoes, hung the hide around my neck, and slung it onto my back. Then, I started off, heading in the direction I hoped was south.

As I walked, I thought about the bear—no, I worried about it. I hoped it would find someplace to spend a couple of days and heal if the wolves hadn't inflicted too much damage. I tried to replay the battle in my mind. The only one that I thought could have done any serious damage was the third wolf that was on top, biting it in the back of the neck.

How much muscle did it damage? I never thought about looking for blood on the snow after the bear had walked away. Now, I wish I had! I wasn't worried about the second wolf. How much harm could it do biting the bear in the butt?

In the worst-case scenario, the bear would be sore and limp for a few days. I never saw what the first wolf had done, and the bear on top of it blocked my view. So, how much damage could anything do with a black bear on top of it, chewing the hell out of it? Not much, I hoped.

The "saint" of the wilderness, that's how I classified the bear. I thought much more of it than that, but I could do nothing for it. If it lived, it would go on and live its own life. I hoped it would have a long, venturous life, never going hungry, always being safe. That's all I had to give it. Words are useless out here. Food and shelter were the only things that mattered.

By the time sunrise began, I could hardly keep my eyes open. It was time to sleep. The most recent nightmare was far enough behind me. I could relax just enough to sleep for a few hours. Then, I would have to travel hard again; I couldn't waste daylight.

The hide rolled up in the mat was frozen. Moisture, out here, didn't stand a chance. Mother Nature always turned it into a hard, frozen mass. It was her way of showing who was boss around these parks.

I removed the snowshoes, at least what was left of them, scraped the ground, and managed to unroll the hide. I couldn't believe how thick and soft the fur was. When I laid down on it, it was long enough to give me a mattress from my head to my hips. How good it felt; even though it was cold, it felt warm and soft.

I said a prayer for the bear and then thanked it again. The bear didn't know that, but it gave me some satisfaction. Then, the daylight faded into darkness. Again, I dreamed. It was always some form of grey and black surroundings, never being able to see or understand. I guess that's what my life had become.

When I woke, I slowly opened my eyes. I could tell, by instinct, I hadn't slept long, maybe two to three hours, but I felt relaxed. I didn't want to get up. The fur beneath me was almost as good as food. My hips and shoulders didn't ache from the cold ground. This was the first time I had the luxury of feeling this since I started on my journey.

I had to get moving. As I sat up, my emotions took over. The floodgates opened; I was crying within seconds—tears of happiness! Behind me lay the bear, eight feet away! It was lying on its stomach with its head on the ground between its paws. I slowly stood.

"You're back. I didn't know if I would see you again or not."

The bear looked at me, not moving. Its eyes were glassy, not the usual sharp, piercing stare.

Instantly, I knew something was wrong. I bent over, at the hips and knees, trying to show I meant no harm. I slowly walked within three feet of the bear and then rested on my knees. How much did I dare go before I crossed the line?

"You're hurt," I said softly.

I looked at the fur on the back of its neck and saw the dried, crusted blood. The fur was matted in dark red chunks.

I sat there on my knees until they started aching. I said nothing, and the bear made no effort to move. I could tell it was in pain. How much? What was the extent of the damage?

As big and thick as its neck was, I hoped the wolf hadn't gotten deep enough to do any major damage. Good or bad, depending on how one looked at it, the neck muscles were chewed badly, but in time, they would heal.

I removed some of the wolf meat from my pocket.

"Here, you want this? I brought it just for you."

Then, I laid the meat on the ground about one foot from the bear. The bear sniffed the air several times. It made no effort to raise its head; now I knew something was wrong. It refused food.

I sat down right in front of the bear. It watched my movements. I wondered what it was thinking.

"Now, what am I going to do?" I said while looking at the bear. "I owe you anything you want or need. If we were at my home, I would get you the best vet. But we're not… I'm sorry… I'm kind of useless out here."

I removed my face mask again. Tears trickled down my face; this was becoming all too frequent. The bear had no idea of how useless I really felt. If it took tens of thousands of dollars to help the bear, that's what I would spend.

"I can't even help my friend," I said as I brushed the tears away.

I sat there for two hours looking at the bear. It would doze off and then, occasionally, open its eyes to look at me.

Now, I had a conscious decision to make. Should I get up and leave, leaving behind the one who has helped me, saving my life more than once? Or should I stay and wait it out with the bear? Perhaps catch some fish to see if it would want to eat that tomorrow. That would give him a chance to catch up, putting myself and the bear in danger all over again.

I didn't know what to do. I would feel so guilty if I got up and left.

As more time passed, that's what I decided to do. It would be the best for both of us. If the bear didn't follow me, wherever our tracks split, the last death dealer wouldn't worry about following the bear. I was the one he wanted.

I stood; the tears streamed down my face.

"I'm sorry… I seem to be saying that to you a lot, but I am. If you don't follow me, I understand. I will remember you forever."

I was once again sobbing uncontrollably as I was leaving.

I didn't take the time to repair the battered snowshoes. I couldn't! I strapped them on, rolled up the wolf's hide, slung it over my back, and put my face mask back on.

Then, I turned and looked at the bear, a big mistake. The floodgates opened again. "I hope to see you again; I love you, bear. Take care of yourself."

The bear never moved; I turned and walked away.

I continued on long past dark; I was so depressed that time meant nothing. I felt nothing as if I was in a trance. I had no clue how many miles I had covered. When Craig was shot, I didn't have time to grieve. I was too busy running for my life. Time was all I had now, so it was spent thinking of the bear.

I walked and walked; eating snow for liquid became secondary, scooping up a handful as I went. Still, all I could think about was the bear and Craig. They both had saved me. My only repayment to them was to make it home. Now, as I continued, I became more determined than ever. If I failed this, in my mind, I failed them.

Halfway through the night, I was walking in auto mode. I became too tired to think or focus. I would walk around a tree just before running into it. Again, my legs were numb, and I didn't care about food.

The landscape never changed. Thick tree growth always led into another area of open ground, then short trees—always pine—looking the same, then back again. It was as if I was walking in circles. I always kept track of the moon. I watched it move across the night sky. The night had become bitter cold, without a doubt, the coldest so far.

My snowshoes had become shredded sticks. I was working much harder, but I didn't want to stop, not yet. If I did, I wouldn't get started again.

Then, something hit my left leg hard enough to knock me off balance. My left snowshoe came down on my right. I was falling forward. I tried to raise my right foot to take one step forward to regain what I was losing. But I couldn't; my feet were tangled as if they were stuck in cement blocks. I put my hands out in front of me, hoping to absorb some of the impact when I hit the ground. I closed my eyes just before landing face-first in the snow. It was an awkward landing.

My feet, still strapped to the pine limbs, were stuck up in the air behind me. I held my breath; my head was deep in the snow. My thought process was eons ahead of the fall. *What happened? What went wrong? It had to be the death dealer toying with me. I was going to suffer before I died. He just wanted to talk, to see my face before putting a bullet in it.*

This was one of the ways I had pictured how I was going to die out here. I was surprised at how fast he had caught me. He wasn't human, but I had wasted time with the bear.

Oh well, time to pay the piper, I thought. *I failed Craig and the bear.*

Two seconds later, I rolled over onto my right side and then sat up. That was the only way I could get my feet back under me.

I thought about taking a wild swing with the axe. My muscles tensed in my arms as I started lifting them, and then I let them fall to my side. It would be a useless effort. He wouldn't be that close; he didn't need to be. He had a gun!

I wiped the snow from my face and tried to clear my eyes. The cold snow stung the bare skin. It took me a moment to focus. He would be standing there, looking down at me.

Before I could see, I asked the question, the one I always asked, "Why did you do this? Why didn't you just walk away?"

There was no response. *This guy is a total psycho, playing head games with me.* That was my last thought before my vision returned.

The dark figure standing before me made me gasp for air. I had to pee badly and almost did right there.

"You're back!" I shouted.

I stood, instantly crying. I was happy and relieved. My emotions with the bear had become a roller coaster ride, up and down and back again.

Crying, wiping the tears away yet again while laughing at the same time, I said, "Stupid bear."

Still laughing and crying, glad to see the bear, relieved it wasn't the death dealer, my legs could no longer hold me up. I sat back down.

"You're a trip, you know that? I'm glad you're on this trip with me, though."

I tried to remove the wolf meat from my pocket because, after all, that's why I brought it—to give to the bear.

It took me several minutes to try to remove it from my pocket. It had turned into a frozen chunk. I didn't want to tear my pocket; I needed it. So, I took the knife and cut away small pieces until it slid out.

The bear was again sitting back on its behind, waiting patiently. It was comical; I had to laugh. "Here you go, my friend."

I tossed the meat a few feet to the bear.

What was wrong with this picture, I asked myself. *Here I am with a wild bear who continues to follow me.*

The bear had to work at eating the frozen chunks of meat. I watched it bite chunks from around the edges. The crunching and cracking noise proved to me how powerful the bear's jaw really was. I was so thankful it was my friend.

As it ate, I wondered how long it had been following me. It had been hours since I stopped. I had never looked back. Had it been with me since dark? Was it bored with just following me? It obviously wanted me to know it was there. Did it like me talking to it, or did it just want the meat it could smell in my pocket? I was too depressed at the time to sense anything was back there. More questions I will never have answers for!

I continued to watch the bear eat. I wondered about how smart bears actually were. I knew nothing about them other than that they were solid muscle—ferocious beyond all imagination and could eat you out of house and home.

I laughed again.

"I'm glad you're back, but tell me, was the big bear playing possum back there, or were you really feeling bad? Huh? Going to plead the fifth? That's okay. We'll walk until daybreak, take a nap, and then fish. How does that sound?"

I felt good! I was on another peak once again from this awful ride. It felt good to talk, even though I had only my voice to listen to. When the bear finished eating, I stood and said, "Let's go, big boy… or girl."

I didn't even know which it was, but it didn't matter!

We walked until sunrise. My best guess was three to four more miles. I was exhausted but still very happy. My snowshoes had become snow sticks, miles past their useful life. The green pine needles had long been beaten off.

"Time to sleep," I said.

The bear watched me scrape the snow from the ground and unroll the hide. I laid down and said, "Good night."

Seconds after closing my eyes, the bear nudged my feet. It startled me; I never heard it walk up. There was no wind, and with the dead silence that surrounded me, that was somewhat of an eerie feeling, a three-hundred-pound bear that moves like a ghost. I never heard of the wolves, either.

Animals' fur doesn't "swish" back and forth as I do. My snow pants advertise my whereabouts each step, saying, "Here I am, come and get me," but that was something I couldn't change.

What startled me the most was: *Is there something wrong? Did the bear know something I didn't?*

I sat up and looked at the bear.

"Is the boogeyman coming? Are you hungry again, or just not ready to sleep?"

The bear sat back, not looking around, and didn't seem agitated. I decided to lie back down, and I had to sleep.

The bear nudged me again. I woke up and sat up. The sun told me I had only slept a few hours. I felt numb, still incoherent. I was trying to make some sense of why the bear was acting like this. The wind was blowing.

"What's wrong, bear?"

I got up and instantly started making a new set of snowshoes. While doing so, I talked to the bear every so often. The second set of shoes was much better than the first. I was able to use the same lacing, so the process only took an hour.

We were off, heading south. The bear followed me like a dog, never more than three feet behind. It didn't seem alarmed by anything; it wasn't sniffing the air. Every so often, I would look back. I might not know if anything was out there, but I knew the bear well enough.

We were moving much faster, making many more steps per hour.

I should have made new snowshoes yesterday, I told myself.

It was midday, and we hadn't stopped yet. "Hey, bear… the first lake we come to, we'll fish. I promise."

The clouds had moved in, and the day had become dark and dreary. The wind was blowing much harder, and it felt as though it had warmed up. Then, it hit me: I knew what the bear was trying to tell me. Another storm was moving in; it was time to take cover.

The terrain was becoming very hilly, and I had doubts about finding a lake. I was happy with the day's progress, although it was hard to judge the miles, now going up and down the tall hills.

When I reached the top of the hill that stood before me ten minutes ago, I was panting heavily. I stopped to rest for only a moment. The trees were very sparse at the peak. Now, I knew why! The wind was blowing so hard it was a challenge for me to keep my balance. Young trees never stood a chance in this.

The wind was much colder up here. The cold gusts that hit me in the face took my breath away. That was an awful feeling. I looked at the bear looking at me. It was squinting its eyes from the fierce wind. It looked at me as if to say, "What are you waiting for?"

I didn't try to talk; the wind was deafening. I looked back to the south. I hesitated, only for a moment, to take in the view. This was the first beautiful sight I had seen since I had left Craig. I looked to the sky.

"I love you, Craig, I will try." I felt small, now seeing what I was actually facing: miles and miles of nothing.

Mother Nature, in all her glory, was asking a human to accomplish something that bordered the impossible. At least it didn't hurt to freeze to death; getting shot would. I started walking.

Just before I started down the opposite slope of the hill, a large white spot caught my attention, far off to the west of me, flat and round.

I shouted, "Come on bear, let's go fishing."

The lake looked to be a mile, maybe even two away. He would follow, so the only time I would lose was the time spent fishing.

By the time I reached the lake, it was already snowing—not a blinding blizzard, but heavy. I walked out a good distance from the shore, removed the snowshoes, and started chopping. The ice was a good foot thick, and by the time I reached the water, I had chopped through three feet of ice.

The bear sat on the ice, with its back to the wind, waiting patiently. It didn't take long before I had the first fish. I tossed it over to the bear. It was still flopping around, but even with the noise of the wind, I could hear the first crunch as the bear bit into it.

The second and third fish came quickly. They were as hungry as the bear. When I threw the fourth fish to the bear, it ate it as quickly as the first. I had to laugh; the bear's etiquette left something to be desired, eating with its mouth open and chunks of fish falling into the snow.

"You sure are a fish-eating machine! Your favorite, huh?"

The fifth and sixth fish I filleted and put the meat in my pockets. I had a feeling lakes would become more scarce in this hilly country. The bear ate the fish skeletons, wasting nothing, something that anything living in this wilderness couldn't afford to do. I was slowly learning the ways.

I kept my bearings as I walked from the lake. I knew which way was south, and I headed in that direction. We reached the tree line and continued on. I felt good; I had repaid a slight amount of what I owed the bear.

We walked several more miles. The weather had taken a turn for the worse, and it was snowing much harder. With the heavy cloud cover, nighttime would come earlier.

I wasn't paying attention to what was off to my side; I was just concentrating on maintaining a straight line to the south. The bear roared. I immediately stopped and looked back. The bear was standing on its hind legs, looking to my right. I looked in that direction.

Just barely visible through the snow was a small, steep hill; one could almost categorize it as a cliff. The bear dropped down to all four feet and walked in that direction. I followed, thinking, *Why not?*

Darkness was far away; it was as good of a spot as any to stop and wait out the storm. I even had time to build some sort of a shelter. The steep hill would block the wind, and the shelter would help block the snow.

Thank you, bear, I thought.

When we reached the edge, I looked up. The top of the slope was only fifteen feet up, but it was all I needed. The bear stood up again, sniffing into the cold wind coming out of the north. Something was up; I just couldn't figure out what.

I watched the bear as it sniffed the air, then walked twenty feet, raised back up on its hind legs, and sniffed again. This was something new. I followed; the bear wasn't alarmed, so neither was I. It repeated the same thing—now, I was puzzled. *What did the bear know that I didn't?*

We walked another twenty feet, and then the bear stopped. Then, it lowered its head, still sniffing. Then I saw it, an opening at the base of the hill. The bear walked slowly up to the opening, constantly sniffing. What did it smell? Was there another bear in there? If so, that just put me in danger.

Then, the bear walked in. It had to lower itself to clear the opening. I heard no noise, no growling or fighting.

Now, what do you do, Madie? I asked myself.

I decided to walk up and look in. My heart was racing; I was chartering new ground. The thought remained with me: there could be another bear in there, already hibernating for the winter. I looked in and waited for my eyes to adjust to the darkness. I quit breathing. I had crossed the line and was unable to run.

The cave was no more than four feet wide. I couldn't see the back of it. I still didn't know what to do. *Do I go in? Will the bear welcome me? Maybe I should just make camp out here to be safe.*

Then, the bear answered my question. It stuck its head by the opening and then backed up as if telling me it was "OKAY," all was clear.

I removed my snowshoes and leaned them against the hill. I still wasn't sure about this. I dropped down on my hands and knees.

Here goes nothing, I said to myself.

"I'm coming in," I said to the bear.

Once inside, I maintained my space by the opening. I laid the axe down beside me. I sat, leaning against the wall, and drew my knees up to my chest, trying to occupy the smallest space possible. The bear lay down against the back wall; it seemed to be okay with my presence.

It was warm inside. I lowered my hood and removed my face mask. Now, I could smell the dusky dampness, along with some other odor I couldn't make out. That's what the bear could smell outside. Now, I know why humans weren't meant to live like this; we wouldn't survive! We weren't equipped for it.

"Thank you, bear," I said softly.

I lowered my head to look outside. The snow was coming down in full force, to my dismay, another blizzard.

Doesn't it just snow a normal snowfall up here? I thought.

I removed my gloves and unzipped my jacket. The dirt beneath me wasn't frozen. On a hot summer day, it would feel cold here, but in the dead of winter, it felt warm. I was guessing it to be in the mid-thirties.

The bear was relaxed when it laid down—it took me some time. The long, slow, deep breathing told me the bear was asleep.

It was pitch black outside and much darker in the cave. I could hear the wind howl outside as the snow was piling up around and in the opening of the cave. But I was happy—this was the coolest place! I unrolled the wolf hide and sat on it. I was still just a bit uneasy about my current situation, not yet ready to fall asleep.

Then, the bear farted while sleeping. "Whoo-eee bear," I said softly.

I needed the rest, but the downtime would cost me in the end.

CHAPTER 12

He traveled like a mad, possessed man. He was shoeing hard, so hard that he had removed his jacket, tying the arms around his waist. He had to cut two poles, one for each hand, using them as a cross-country skier would. Gaining on each step meant everything.

When he came to the spot where a fight had taken place, he stopped. It took him several minutes to process what he was looking at. He counted the three dead wolves, then walked around the perimeter and counted tracks from three wolves, none of which had escaped. He found no blood out of place, just the reddened snow around each wolf.

He carefully inspected each dead animal. The first was the one she had skinned.

It was a hack job, he thought, again, how clever she was. One knife wound in the rib cage had sliced its heart in two. Was it a lucky stab, or was he dealing with more than he had given her credit for? He stood, looking and thinking.

Probably the former, he thought.

He looked at the carcass. She had stored meat, and she had an extra cover. He didn't need that; it would only slow him down. Soon, he would find her, finish this and return.

The second dead wolf lay only a few feet away, with one slice through the throat. She had killed two. The bear tracks were all over. The bear had done most of the fighting. Now, he knew the fight had taken place at night. The wolves had come for her. The length between the steps of the bear entering had caught the wolves off guard. It had become a threat; they had forgotten about her.

Smart bear, he said to himself.

He now understood the tracks he had seen earlier. The wolves were out there, following, and the bear knew it. It had split off from her. The hunted had become the hunter! He knew he had to watch for the bear. To misread any sign would mean the same fate for him.

The last wolf had been mauled by the bear, never standing a chance. It was already frozen on the outside. He removed his knife and cut it open from rib to hips. He reached into it, feeling what was inside. He smiled—she wasn't far ahead; the inner organs were not entirely frozen yet.

He was hungry himself; days had passed with no food. He peeled away the hide, sliced some meat from the carcass, and ate it raw. He then filled one pocket and started tracking her.

The day had passed. Her tracks didn't have the sharp edges he was looking for. She was traveling hard.

Like a scared and crazed person, he thought. *She couldn't hold out forever.*

He wondered how long he would be.

He knew she knew that he was still coming. He smiled. Although his body was exhausted and he wanted to return to his home, he was enjoying the hunt. He traveled most of the night. Sunrise resulted in very little progress for him. Little was the keyword, but every little bit counted. He wanted to lie down and sleep; he was struggling badly.

"How does she do it?"

He continued on.

He had passed the last spot where she had slept. The bear had split away and then returned following her.

He was close now; he could feel it. Mid-afternoon, the sky was grey and dark. He went up and down each hill she had. Two hours and he would be upon her. That drove him even harder.

Snow was coming; he could feel it. Now, he was almost running. The fierce wind was starting to erase her tracks. Then, it started to snow hard. He looked up the long, tall hill ahead of him. She was only a mile or two away.

He would find her tracks again tomorrow, after the snow. He cut long branches, making a shelter to keep himself out of the storm. He lay under it, ate more raw wolf meat, and then slept.

I couldn't see anything outside. The wind continued to blow, no doubt bringing more snow with it. Traveling was going to be slower tomorrow. My only hope was that this storm didn't dump too much snow.

For now, I was still happy. I felt so fortunate to be able to have one night at the caveman's mansion. I had the presidential suite—that's how it felt to me.

I removed my boots, which felt unbelievably good, and wiggled my toes. As I sat thinking, if I had the supplies, I would wait out winter here. *But I don't, so I can't.* The death dealer wouldn't allow that anyway, but I can always dream.

I enjoyed the luxury as long as I could. I've learned not to take small things for granted; they mean a great deal. I would never do so again. I ate a few bites of fish, thinking that the smell would wake the bear, but it didn't. I laid down on the wolf pelt. Warm, full, and relaxed, I wiggled my toes again.

When I woke, I could see light at the entrance of the cave. I felt more rested than any of the previous nights. I guess I should; I had just slept ten hours, at least. I looked back at the bear. I could make out the dark figure, nothing more. The bear was still asleep. I felt sad; I knew it would stay that way for a long time. No longer did I have a traveling partner or a bodyguard. Now, I was on my own to face the great, vast wilderness.

I knelt forward and looked outside. It was still snowing, but I would be able to travel. Navigation wouldn't be as easy; the clouds were still dark and gloomy.

I put on my boots, jacket, mask, and hood. I rolled the hide up and threw it over my back. Then, I put on my gloves. The bear never moved. It had to be in a deep sleep. I didn't want to leave this tranquility, my port in the storm. Now, it was time to say goodbye. I wanted so badly to pet the bear. I had become very attached to it but knew I couldn't. I didn't want to talk to it for fear of waking it. I was fighting away the tears.

Goodbye, bear, thanks for saving my life, thanks for being my friend, I said quietly to myself.

I continued to kneel, looking at the bear. It would go on and have many cubs. I hoped they were all as great as it was. I wondered if it would remember me when it woke in the spring.

I started through the opening of the cave. I stopped; one last thing I could do for the bear. I removed one of the slabs of fish from my pocket and laid it in the snow at the outside edge of the entrance. It would remain frozen there. The bear would smell it on the way out. It was my only way of saying "Thank you."

The wind was blowing as I stood, but not nearly as hard as during the night. I looked around, almost another foot of snow.

Great, I thought.

My snowshoes were on, and I headed south. I was glad to see all signs of our tracks had been removed by the newly fallen snow.

That didn't make me feel better, though; I was still depressed. As all roller coaster rides end, always at the bottom; that's where it ended with the bear. I wasn't going to let myself cry. I decided to put that effort into trying to get home.

Before the cave was out of sight, I stopped; I had to look back one final time, hoping to see the bear looking at me from the entrance. It wasn't.

"Goodbye! I will never forget what you did for me."

The new snow made walking somewhat harder, but not as much as I thought it would. I had to put forth a little more effort, a small piece, to pay for my life.

The day passed without anything bad happening. I hoped they would all be this way. Well, one good hope: odds still weren't in my favor. I would still bet with the Vegas odds. The death dealer was back there, somewhere.

Nighttime had come, and the cave was miles behind. Now, it was deathly quiet out, no wind. There were no clouds, just cold, too cold, but not to sleep. It was just a warning of what was coming.

I wasn't tired as I had two nights of sleep last night. Physically, I was tired, but not so much that I couldn't continue on, so I did. The one thing again I wished I had was a watch. Then, I could push myself harder. Racing the clock, running against time, was something I was accustomed to. I had to settle with the sun and the moon when it was available.

I would pick out the farthest distance I could see, going up and down the hills, then try to guess the distance to it. Then, after reaching it, I estimated the time spent getting there. It was all guesses and estimations. It gave me something to do, something to occupy my mind. So, by my best guess, I was walking somewhere around one-half to three-quarters of a mile per hour, much less than I wanted to. The problem was the extra snow.

So, being optimistic, I walked three-quarters of one mile per hour, seven and a half miles in the last ten hours. Not good, I had to do better. I needed twelve, which meant six more hours of walking to reach my goal of twelve miles per day. Sixteen hours of walking per day—not possible!

Mother Nature was playing games with me. If there was no snow, I could easily do twenty and have fourteen hours to burn each day—to fish, sleep, or whatever. That wasn't the case; I had to make do—like it or not.

I was exhausted. Again, guessing the time since the sun went down, I walked twelve hours.

Nine miles of hard work, and that was if I was walking in a straight line. Too many variables depressed me, but dying was worse. At least the miles walked kept me ahead of him!

I stopped for the day and rested, only to do it all over again tomorrow.

I found a tree to sleep beside. Never again would I make that mistake. I went through the routine, removing the snowshoes, scraping the ground, then lying on the pelt. My leg muscles thanked me, and so did my back. I ate three more bites of fish. They were big bites of raw, frozen fish, which were hard to eat. The inside of my mouth ached as I ate, and by the time I was finished, it was numb.

My daily rations, with what I had left from the bear, I had two full slabs and one day left on the one I was eating. Seven days of food—I was good to go. I would find someplace to fish on the fifth or sixth day; until then, I had no plan of stopping during daylight hours.

When I woke, the sun was just starting to brighten the eastern sky. I have learned that this was the coldest time of the day.

I was stiff and sore; it took me some time to get going. After my muscles loosened up, I was traveling along at a better pace than the day before. I credited that to being rested, but the day was young; time would take a toll on my body, and that was a given.

The rest of the day was uneventful.

By mid-morning of the next day, walking became much easier. The depth of the snow had returned to what it was before the last storm. I walked past the southern edge of the last storm. Mother Nature had given me a break, and I was thankful. The older snow was more settled, and I was able to float on top of it. Gliding along with less effort gave me added incentive. I would make the twelve miles today.

I did!

The third day was a repeat of the second. I pushed myself as hard as I could. Nothing but trees and snow and going up and down hills. In doing so, I was burning extra calories, so I ate an extra ration of fish. But the nagging feeling was back, and that scared me.

You won't catch me, I told myself.

The following morning, he was up and moving at first light. He had traveled over two miles due south. He had found no fresh tracks and was a little disgruntled. *Was he wrong? Had he misread the signs?* Everything had told him, before the storm, that he was closer than he had been in the past days.

Another two hours passed with no result. He had to go into the reconnaissance mode—search before he could destroy.

He had watched all the signs. Her strong leg was the right, always drifting to the left, ever so slightly. She was navigating, always correcting her direction. Walking past the dark is what gave that away. Without knowing it, she drifted to the east.

He turned to the left to start the zigzag pattern. He would find her; he had no doubt. As he headed southeast, searching, something told him to head in the other direction. But common sense told him to go on, so he did.

Frustrated, after several hours drifting east, he should have found her by now, but that wasn't the case. He turned, heading in his new direction of travel to the southwest.

He was breathing hard, and even in the cold, his body was hot, traveling at a slow trot. He had to find her; he was losing valuable minutes in the search. He shut out the pain he was feeling; his legs were burning, and so was his chest. He credited that to all the cold air he was inhaling, burning the small capillaries in his lungs.

She was up ahead; he could feel it. His instincts were telling him so. He pushed on harder, ignoring the dizziness. He would slow down when he rejoined her trail. He fell in the snow, wondering why that had happened. He rested for only a moment, blaming the fall for tripping on something.

Just before dark, it happened. He had found her; now, he could relax. He would still push himself, just not at the severe, punishing pace he had all day. His chest still hurt, but it was something he would turn off mentally. All he could think about was her!

The bear was not with her; he had seen no tracks. As tired as he was, he had to stay alert; being ambushed was always a possibility. That took more effort. It would be easier to walk along, makeup time, and be half asleep.

Soon, he found the spot where she had slept. Stopping for only seconds to see if he saw anything unusual, he didn't, so he continued. The pain in his chest had faded. It was now only a small tinge.

During the first half of the night, he walked at a normal pace; in the last half, he slept. When he woke, the pain was gone. But something wasn't right; he felt off. His body was one gear out of sync. He had an idea what it was, but he blew it off. He had a mission to fulfill.

Mid-afternoon, he found the spot where she had slept the second night. Come nightfall, he had to stop; his body needed rest.

He woke hours before daylight, put on his snowshoes, turned on the flashlight, and started following. Most hunters say that the hunt is better than the kill. For him, the kill would be the pinnacle of the journey. He could feel it; soon, he would have it!

I awoke at sunrise; my internal alarm clock was working well. I felt so hungry; I had to eat, so I did. Three more bites of fish. It worried me that I was consuming my food at twice the rate I had rationed for myself, but it kept my energy up. I had to be burning far more calories than I could imagine. Slowing down and conserving energy would cost me in the end.

Neither ending was a good one, I kept telling myself, a reminder to push forward every step of the way.

Four days have gone by without the company of the bear. I was beginning to feel as one would if they were out in the middle of the ocean in a rowboat with two oars, fighting surmountable odds. I had it all, as I thought. The two oars were my snowshoes. I was in an ocean of snow, and the only facsimile of a boat I could come up with was the clothes on my back.

Well, that was good, Madie. You just used up four minutes of the day thinking about that. What are you going to think about the rest of the day? I said to myself.

Step after step, I continued to lug the snowshoes. They were cumbersome and starting to get heavy. I had thought by now, my legs would have adjusted to the extra weight. But they hadn't.

Come on, legs, you have to do this! Oh no, I thought, *am I losing it already?*

I was talking out loud to my body parts.

Four days with little rest, that's why my legs feel as they do. For four days, hearing only the wind blow across the pine needles it was a reality check. Hearing the sound of my voice didn't make me feel better; it was just good to hear something different.

As the sun disappeared, I hoped I had covered the twelve miles. I had no way of really knowing for sure, but I was satisfied with what I did walk and the time spent doing it. I was exhausted worn out; I had to stop for the day. I found a good climbing tree just before visibility was lost. I had the routine down pat.

A steady breeze had blown for the past two days, but not enough to erase my existence. I looked to the sky. *How long did I have before another snowstorm came?*

They were good and bad. Walking in deep snow was a killer, mine. My third attacker, or fourth, if I counted the death dealers separately. I lay there thinking about the past and, then, of my future. Both were bleak; there was nothing waiting for me there, and there was no Craig.

Before I drifted off to sleep, I thought about his body. I started to cry; the visual I had was sickening. After the attack from the wolves, I was afraid the wild animals had eaten his body.

"I'm sorry for leaving you like that, Craig. I hope you will forgive me. I will return, pick up your pieces, and give you a grave. On the headstone, it will read: 'To the bravest man I will ever know in my life. I will love you to the end of it, Madie.'"

I tucked the hood over my face and cried myself to sleep.

He slept three hours the second night and four hours the third. He could no longer move faster than a steady walk. His body was deteriorating at a rapid pace. If he pushed himself at any faster speed, his legs and chest would hurt too badly. He was always dizzy. Then, the sharpest pain hit yet. He rubbed his chest through his jacket, hoping for relief.

"Not yet, I haven't finished this."

Throughout the fourth day, he was getting close again. It would have already been over if it wasn't for bad luck.

Before nightfall, she would be his, the ultimate prize after the award-winning hunt, he said to himself. *His body could hold out that long.*

I was out of food. During the day, as I walked, that weighed heavily on my mind. So did the question! *Do I have time?* Without food, death would come. If I stopped, death would catch up. I didn't have the senses the bear had. I couldn't smell him, and I couldn't hear him, but my instincts were telling me he was coming. How, I don't know. I never believed in ESP or hunches; it was just facts and common sense. So, why was I feeling that tingle in the middle of my back again?

I became more nervous as the day went on. I didn't like feeling uneasy. The past four days of traveling had been much better.

So, what do I do? I asked myself. *Die now or die later?*

I always remembered the Fram Oil commercial from years ago. How true it was for me now.

You can pay me now, or you can pay me later. The outlook wasn't good.

111

Another mile went, and the hills were becoming steeper. I was putting forth more effort, more arm muscle on the poles, to push myself through the snow just to maintain the pace. I had already learned it meant it was time to make new snowshoes. Another dilemma: would the time wasted be worth the time gained?

I could go for two days without eating; I had done it before. I could travel on ratty snowshoes—I had done that before, also. But that would mean burning extra fuel, and I was out of gas rationing stamps.

I stopped. I looked behind me. *So, Mr. Death Dealer, how close are you?*

I pondered the idea. I decided to take the time to make new shoes. It wouldn't take more than half an hour, maybe forty-five minutes. Each day, I was pleased with myself for covering the miles that I had. I had pushed myself, not to the extreme limit, but somewhere between extra hard and suicidal. How could he do any better?

The branches I chopped with the axe were fuller, two for each foot. I wasted no time doing that, but the cedar bark lacing was worn, almost to the point of tearing in two. I was glad I decided on new shoes, but now, I had to cut new laces. That would take time. Now, I felt rushed; I was hurrying. I had to walk about an eighth of a mile, dragging the limbs, before I found another cedar tree. I was huffing and puffing; I couldn't believe how much strength my body had lost.

I stripped the bark from the tree. I wanted to quickly lace the branches together and be on my way, but then something told me, "If you're going to do something, do it right."

"Yes," I said out loud. Then, I looked around to see if someone had spoken to me.

Another reality check, Madie, you're not losing it, I said to myself.

I did a good job lacing them up just as well; otherwise, I would be doing it again tomorrow.

I was on my way. I was relaxed, and nothing bad happened. I had just let paranoia take over momentarily.

I traveled along at least two inches higher in the snow, which meant a lot. Now, I was guessing I had about two hours of daylight left. I pushed on past dark. As always, walking became slower. I kept telling myself each step taken was one step closer to people. I badly wanted to stop for the day.

I crossed a small frozen stream, climbed the next hill, and then descended it. It was a good place to sleep, and it was several hours past dark, I gave up. I could no longer stay awake as I walked. I found a tree, did the quick routine, and then slept.

Her tracks remained fresh, even with the wind blowing, but he didn't seem to be gaining the ground he needed to catch her. He admired her stamina, making the kill even more pleasurable. His body was shutting down. He needed to rest for many days, but he ignored the signs. Everything remained shut out but the kill.

Soon, he kept telling himself, *today*.

Whatever happened afterward didn't matter! He came to realize he wouldn't make it back.

He shuffled along, just maintaining a walk hurting, his chest far worse than his legs. She would stop in the dark or soon after, and then he would catch her. That would be even more dramatic: the ultimate surprise for the ultimate kill. How could it be any better?

But she hadn't! The flashlight was growing dim. He had to use it to focus. He had two good batteries left, but he didn't think they would be needed.

He walked slightly bent forward, hoping that would ease what he was feeling. It didn't. He wasn't concentrating on it; he couldn't. Then, he crossed a small, frozen stream and stood at the base of the next hill. It wasn't as large as the others. In the dark, it looked to be two hundred yards to the top. He almost took the next step, to start climbing it, but decided this was a good place to stop and sleep.

13
CHAPTER

My internal alarm was still in perfect working order. I looked to the east as I reluctantly opened my eyes. A red and orange glow was working its way through the treetops. I was hungry, no, starving.

Get used to it, Madie; you'll have many more days feeling this way, I told myself.

The hills were gradually becoming smaller. But the wind was relentless, always coming from the north or northwest. I didn't have to face it, which was a good thing.

By mid-morning, I had found another lake. Well, the correct way of putting it, I walked upon another lake. I wasn't out looking for it. Thankfully, Canada was full of them.

Hunger won out! I had to take the time, once again, to fish. Something inside told me not to remove the snowshoes, but I had to. They were just too bulky to walk in circles while I chopped a hole through the ice. The lake was large; my guess was about three-quarters of a mile from shore to shore.

The idea came to me as I started across the ice. If he was following, and if he was close, I would see him walk out into the open as I was chopping the hole.

"Great idea, Madie," I said. I would have time to run.

Now, I miss the bear more than ever before. I half expected to see it come bounding across the ice, waiting patiently for the day's catch. I smiled.

"Stupid bear."

I chopped the ice until I was worn out. My shoulder muscles were aching, so I took a break. No water in sight. I would swing the axe two or three times, sidestep one large step, and then swing several times again. I made a complete revolution around the hole. I was always looking back at the tree line, where my trail led onto the ice. I did this several more times. Then, I dropped down on my knees to reach down far enough to remove chunks of ice.

The circumference of the hole was becoming quite large and deep. I had built a small wall of ice around the hole. I continued chopping, removing ice chunks and chopping again, but still no water. I wanted to swear, but what good would that do? I couldn't believe how much thicker the ice had become since fishing last.

The hole was now over three feet deep. It was becoming funnel-shaped, the bottom no wider than a foot. I climbed down in it, using the jagged edges for footholds. I finally punched through, striking water, after nearly four feet of ice. I stood five feet, seven inches, and felt small standing in the hole. I could barely see over the pile of ice surrounding the hole. He wasn't in sight.

I was wasting valuable time; this took far longer than I would have thought. I also knew that soon, days or a week at the most, the ice would become too thick to do this again.

Now, I was worried. *What would I do then?* Fish was my only food source in this frozen, ice-locked, butt-numbing wilderness. For the first time, I became angry. I had to shut all that out and worry about it then. I had to finish the present task. I had to put fish in my pocket and get going.

I sharpened one end of one of the ski poles with the axe. I looked to the shoreline again—nothing but trees.

Standing in the hole, spear ready, I lowered my charm necklace into the water.

The sun had crested the horizon when he woke. The pain was still there, just not as severe as it was when he had stopped. Slowly, he stood and tried to take a deep breath but couldn't. A sharp pain shot through his chest. It was going to be another rough day.

He started up the hill slowly, allowing his muscles to stretch. When he reached the peak and looked to the bottom, he knew what he was looking at. The adrenaline increased in his body; he became excited. Standing in the middle of the bare dirt, he looked at the spot where she had slept. This was going to be easy; she no longer had the protection of the bear.

The end—that's what this day would be.

He wasted no time. Now, he traveled at a pace faster than he had in the past several days. A mile at the most is how he had the distance between them.

Now, trotting along, he smiled above the pain that had already returned in full force. He had to do this: drive through the pain to conquer his greatest challenge. He had thought what they had accomplished over the past five years would never be equaled. It had been all mental ability, planning, and timing. But this physical and cunning challenge, and who could survive life longest, gave him a rush. One that had remained with him since the day this started.

He saw a large clearing coming up ahead, through the trees, fifty feet away—another lake. He followed the trail up to the edge of the ice. He stopped at the last tree and leaned against it. As he rested, he scanned across the lake but could see no dark figure traveling over the ice anywhere.

My legs were burning as I stood in the hole, straddling the small opening in the water. Each time I speared a fish, I cleaned it, put the meat in my pocket, and was always ready if I had to make a fast getaway. The first two fish were of average size. I wasn't experienced in filleting fish, so I did a hack job of it.

Being in a hurry didn't help. I had fish blood all over the front of my jacket, but I didn't care. The fourth fish was huge, and it took some time to get it out of the water.

Every couple of minutes, I glanced back at the shoreline. I was paranoid, and I knew it. I hacked the meat from the fish, and now both pockets were full. I threw the skeleton over the wall of ice. It was time to go, but I felt greedy. The fishing was fast; they were obviously hungry.

What would it hurt to catch one more, I asked myself. *It might be a long time before I have an opportunity like this again, if I have one at all.*

My back was aching as I stood in the hole, bent over, waiting to spear the next fish. I continued to wait, concentrating on nothing but looking into the water. Minutes passed, and then it happened: another fish swam up to take the bait.

He rested only a minute and then started out across the ice. Her tracks were as fresh as if she were ten yards ahead of him. He looked to the treeline ahead, following the line where her tracks were leading. She couldn't be more than a quarter mile into the woods. He increased his speed.

He was two hundred yards out onto the ice when he thought he saw something move.

I stuck the spear through the fish. It was the largest catch of the day, but still not the monster I was looking for. The spear was stuck through the fish just behind the back fin. It was thrashing wildly, and I could feel it slipping off the spear. I was concentrating deeply, moving quickly, trying to get the head of the axe under it before I lost it.

Food is a precious commodity; don't lose this one, Madie.

The fish didn't want to die. Still thrashing about after I had it out of the water, I was happy. I smiled, then sat with the spear, axe, and fish on the ice beside me, and then climbed out of the hole.

Something caught my attention: a dark spot moving in my direction. The first thought that flashed through my mind was the bear. It had returned; it could smell the fish. I was happy!

The split second of happiness turned to sheer horror. Now, I saw the monster I was looking for, except it wasn't a fish. Panic flowed through my body. My blood ran cold, and my muscles involuntarily ceased to work. He was just over a quarter mile away from me, moving at a fast pace.

He increased his speed. The dark spot was only a flash, but it gave him incentive. The burning sensation had become secondary as he moved in a slow trot.

He thought it could be the bear, but he hadn't seen those tracks for many days. So, what was it? He didn't care; nothing out here intimidated him. If it was going to attack him, he would just shoot it and go on.

Then, he knew: she climbed out of the hole and stood up. *I knew you were close, honey.* Today was the day! He watched her momentarily freeze. She was too far away to shoot at.

Just stand there a few more seconds. You'll feel no pain.

I leaned my weight toward the shore. Before I took a step, I thought about the snowshoes. I would need them, and he would catch me without them. I leaned back toward them, at the same time wondering if I would have time to put them on.

Then, I thought I could drag them into the woods; the safety of the trees would protect me from a bullet. So that's what I did. I left the poles, and as much as I hated to, I left the last fish. I carried the axe in my left hand and dragged the snowshoes to my right.

I was only a hundred yards from the trees. I couldn't believe how slowly I was moving. At least, that's how it felt, all in slow motion. I looked back, he was gaining, and I panicked. The snow on the ice was nearly as deep as in the woods. The wind hadn't done much about blowing it off.

Now, I was breathing hard. The snowshoes had become an anchor. My footsteps felt as if they were two knives slicing through the snow, piercing through the powder until they made contact on the ice, then slipping when I tried to gain traction for the next step. I looked back again; he was closer yet.

"I'm not going to make it."

Fifty yards from the trees, I started to let go of the shoes.

He saw her pick up something and start running toward the trees. The snowshoes, she didn't have them on. It was going to be easy. She would tire quickly and move even slower once in the woods. He increased his speed. Taking a shot would only waste a bullet. He would be patient. If it was the last thing he did, he wasn't going to let her escape. She was the ultimate trophy.

You can't, Madie, you need them, a voice in my head told me.

So, I hung on to them. Now, twenty yards to go, I put all my strength into each step, grunting. I was in an adrenaline rush, running as fast as I could.

Do this for me, I heard next. I was losing it, I was hearing things, and I was scared to death. This is one of the ways I thought I would die, but he was going to earn it.

I gained speed; the thought of getting shot did that for me. My mind was in high gear

How did he catch me so fast? I thought I had covered enough miles each day to stay ahead. But I hadn't! *Why hadn't I just frozen to death?* Then, I wouldn't have to endure this. The physical end was bad enough; the mental part was worse.

I ran into the trees. I had to know how close he was, so I looked. He was less than an eighth of a mile behind, so I had time to put the snowshoes on. Regardless of whether I did or not, I did. Without them, I might as well stand here and take the bullet.

He was gaining ground on her as she ran for the woods. Now, he was running as fast as he could, as fast as the snowshoes would allow, despite the pain that was growing rapidly with each step. That didn't matter.

Holding the gun in his hand, the chase was down to minutes. Just before she ran into the woods, he thought about taking a shot. One thing he had learned about hunting was to be patient. The hunted would always get close, as she would.

Just inside the trees, she would stop and put on the snowshoes; that was a given. The end! That's all he was thinking as he ran into the trees.

I threw the snowshoes on the ground, making sure the second one landed a foot away from the first. I literally jumped on top of them and, at the same time, jabbed the axe into the snow, making sure it stood with the handle up. I bent down and went to work. Wrapping the lacing around my boots with my gloves on was too slow. I needed to remove them, which would take precious seconds, seconds my life couldn't afford to waste.

I had the left shoe tied. Now, I was trying to find the side of the lacing to tie the right, and then I would be gone. I couldn't find it. I dug down through the branches, pawing at the snow underneath, trying to pull it through, but it wasn't there.

Panicked, I worked ferociously. Seconds were slipping by, and he was getting closer. I dug faster, with no luck. My thoughts were advancing to the future.

I'm coming to see you, Craig. This isn't a good day to die; the sun is shining.

I gave up. I stepped off the right shoe; I had to try and escape on one. Instantly, I thought better. I would be dead in a matter of minutes soon after. I lifted it up, and there it was, stuck in the branches toward the back.

It took another ten seconds to get it tied. That's probably all that remained of my life. I could hear him coming. The rubbing of his clothes almost sent me over the edge. I couldn't see him; the trees along the lake concealed me. I was hiding behind a small pine tree. I was hyperventilating, and the short, rapid breaths were making me dizzy. I was running before I had stood all the way up. I had no direction of travel planned; I hadn't a clue which way north or south was. All I knew was I was running in the direction of life.

I ran left and right around the small trees. They were giving me a few more minutes to live. The stress of the fast pace I was moving my body gave my mind some time to relax. I was thinking more clearly. Staying in the small undergrowth was good, but I couldn't do it forever. What would I accomplish by running circles around the lake other than staying alive and dying of exhaustion?

My outlook wasn't good. If, at some point, I turned to my left and headed deeper into the woods, the trees would thin out, and the undercover would fall away due to lack of sunlight.

I had to think about each step. I was moving faster on the snowshoes than I ever had before. I could easily trip and fall into the snow—bye-bye, Madie.

Then, the decision was made for me. I ran head-on into a deep ravine. The steep banks I couldn't navigate. It was at least twelve feet to the bottom and twice as wide. Rainwater rushing down from the surrounding hills, flowing into the lake, had created it. It was hard to tell how deep the snow was at the bottom, but that was irrelevant.

I never stopped moving. At any moment, I would feel a bullet pierce my body. The sudden change in direction put me back into panic mode.

As I expected, the undergrowth started to thin out. The fear I was feeling was beyond words, and it was growing. When it reached its peak, it would be the same moment my life ended. I was sure of that!

I couldn't hear him behind me. I wasn't thinking clearly. My ears were ringing, and my lungs equaled that with burning pain. I was moving fast.

Keep it together, Madie, I told myself.

My legs started aching. I was concentrating hard. With each step, I put all the effort I had, pushing off trying to gain ground before the next step landed.

The terrain was changing fast. I gave it no thought. All was lost except for what was coming behind me. Before I knew it, I was running across a flat, open area.

This isn't good, I told myself.

I had run into a low area. Now, a steep bank flanked my right side as I ran. I wasn't sure, but I thought I was running through a marsh void of all the trees. I looked to my left; only forty feet away were trees. Then, I looked to my right, a vertical wall fifteen feet high. No escape! Ahead was another hundred feet of nothing but a clear shot for him.

As I started a hard turn to my left, something caught my attention up ahead, just fifteen feet away. A dead tree had rotted and fallen, leaning on the bank with its top well above the top of the bank. It had been dead for some time as all the branches were gone, leaving only stubs protruding from the trunk.

I had to look back. After doing so, I wished I hadn't. There he was, just entering the clearing, less than one hundred yards back.

I had to plan and fast. Try to make the forty feet to my left or the fifteen feet ahead and climb the tree. Logic told me, in my very cloudy mind, that it would take equal amounts of time to do either. So, I chose the tree. If I could get to the top without a bullet, I could try to push the tree down, stopping his advance. Here I was again, too many "ifs."

Something wasn't right, was the thought that struck me after I had turned to run. *Why was he running doubled over?*

My mind was trying to process too much at once. The last thought didn't matter. What did was my life.

He could no longer run. His threshold of pain was high above average; it exceeded his tolerance. He was trying to trot along just to keep up. He saw what he knew he would, the spot where she stopped and tied her shoes. He followed her trail around the trees, left, then right, and back left again.

He felt himself starting to pass out. Everything became dark. He inhaled a long, deep breath to restore what his body badly needed. The searing pain that it brought with it brought him back to reality.

"Not yet," he said out loud.

Only half alert, moving forward with his head hanging down, he nearly fell into the ravine. He turned and followed her trail.

When he came into the opening, he raised his head to see. She had to be within shooting distance—she was. He tried to straighten up but couldn't. The gun was in his right hand. He thought of stopping and taking aim, but, in the condition he was in, it would be futile.

He saw her running toward a dead tree and leaning against the back. It was obvious what her plan was. He could get closer. By the time she reached the top, he would be upon her. He walked on at a slow pace, the only speed he was able to manage.

I already had my knife in my hand, five feet away from the tree. In the last step, I was going to cut the laces and free the snowshoes from my feet. The axe was going with me, my survival tool. At the slight chance I pulled this off, I would need it to go on. If I didn't, so be it.

I was so scared I was whimpering in a quiet but high-pitched tone.

As I took the first step onto the tree, I wanted to see what remained of my life. I looked back. He nearly fell. On the second and third steps up the stubbed branches, my mind was flying.

Had he used up all his strength to catch up to me? Was his body spent? Had he even taken the time to eat? Probably not! Starvation had beaten him. He was so obsessed with catching me nothing else mattered. It had to be.

I looked again, just in time to see him fall.

His left arm went numb. He became so disoriented all was lost. He momentarily blacked out. The last thing he remembered was the loud ringing in his ears. When his face landed in the snow, the cold shock brought him back to reality—the reality of the end. He was aware of what was happening and mad because he couldn't have waited a few more minutes.

He tried to stand, but his legs gave out.

Looking in her direction, he saw she was halfway up the tree, which gave him enough incentive to stand. He aimed the gun, but there wasn't enough coordination left to take decent aim. The hunt was over.

He slowly walked to the tree.

Halfway up the tree, I saw what I didn't like out of the corner of my eye. The gun was pointed at me. I was in a state of panic I had never been in before. Beyond scared, way past the adrenaline rush, and sheer determination was a small thing. Hyper-alertness, if there is such a thing, one second left. It was a good life up until this trip.

Each stub I had to grab next seemed to jump out at me in vivid color. I placed each step instinctively without looking. I had no doubt that if I looked back, I would be able to see the bullet coming at me at supersonic speed.

I was nearly running up the last half of the tree, grunting and whimpering at the same time with each step.

I always thought I would grow old, spoiling my grandchildren and drooling on myself in the end. I was drooling on myself now, exhaling madly, trying to reach the top. Everything in between was bypassed. I guess everyone wonders how they will die. Never in my wildest dreams had I pictured this.

I felt no pain; my body was functioning without feeling. Three more steps to the top, zero seconds of life left. I could see the future, arm's length away. He wouldn't let me live.

I never heard the shot; one never came. I jumped off the last step and rolled into the snow. I had one thing left to do, and that would put me back in the direct line of fire, but I had to do it.

I looked over the edge of the cliff. There he was, walking slowly in my direction. He wasn't looking at me, and he had lowered the gun.

Why? I wondered.

I grabbed the tree trunk and pulled it. It wouldn't move. The limbs had become embedded in the dirt at the top. I pulled up with all my strength. I heard a few limbs crack, which gave me more incentive. I pulled again and twisted the tree sideways. The limbs cracked again and then broke free.

I pulled on the tree as I walked in the direction away from him. Then, when I thought the tree was clear and it would fall to the ground below, I let go. I stepped back out of view. I heard the tree crash to the ground.

I sat down, and the snow gave me a soft, relaxing feeling.

I didn't know how far ahead he would have to go to find level ground to come after me. So, now, as I sat there, I wondered if I should run for it without snowshoes, and exhausted.

I sat there for several more minutes. I was getting tired of playing the waiting game. I had one question to ask, the one that has been replaying over and over in my mind.

There he was, the death dealer, fifteen feet away—unable to deal his trade, for today anyway.

"Now, what do we do?" I asked.

Silence—no response.

My breathing had returned to normal. I eased far enough to the edge to look and see if he had already started moving in one direction or the other. I saw nothing. To go any further, I would expose myself only to catch a bullet.

"Looks like today isn't your day," I said.

Again, silence.

"What, after all this time, you don't want to talk?"

The pain was so excruciating it was all he could do to make it to the edge of the cliff and sit down. As he sat there with his jaw clenched shut, his face contorted, and squeezing his eyelids closed, he heard her talking. Right now, he was unable to focus on her words. Both arms were pressed against his chest.

His grandfather, father, and brother had died before reaching his age. He had thought it had skipped him, but now he knew differently.

I sat there a while longer in silence. I heard nothing. I couldn't figure out what he was up to. After what we had gone through, I didn't see him giving up so easily. I listened intently. If he was trying to climb the rock wall, surely I would hear that, but I didn't.

I was thinking back to the beginning of this.

"So. why did you do what you did?"

Still nothing. If he was trying to make me mad, it was working.

I thought seriously of digging down into the snow, finding a large rock, and dropping it on his head. I couldn't do it, that wasn't me.

"I'd really like to know: why did you have to kill my husband? He meant no harm to you."

"Why digress here? We haven't the time," he answered.

"I think we do. So, we talk or run. Which is it?"

"You have no shoes."

"No, when you leave, I will jump down and be gone."

"You won't make it," he said in a raspy voice.

"A fifteen-foot jump for another day of life."

"That's not what I meant… give me a little professional courtesy here. We're both smarter than that."

Never having heard his voice before, I was sure he was struggling to speak.

"So, if I were to get up and come after you, why wouldn't I take them with me?"

Panic returned. I guess in all my thought process, with him being so close, that never occurred to me. I was wrong. Another day of life just became improbable. I wanted to get up and run, to get a head start on him, only to fail. I decided to stay to see how this would turn out. To die here or a mile away, dead was dead. I can't stop that.

"Professional courtesy—you're kidding, right? I owe you nothing; you're a trashy excuse of a human being. So, answer my question."

"Tsk! Tsk! Do not jump to conclusions; what I've accomplished would astound you."

"Yes, living in the middle of nowhere, with nothing, that's amazing."

"There you go again… leave no trail."

What did that mean? As vile as he was, he sounded educated.

"So, you're not going to answer it. That's fine; I'll figure out something."

"Yes… you are an excellent adversary… I did answer it… figure it out."

He was struggling, and his words were becoming more slurred. It was taking him longer to speak a sentence, and his thoughts were slowing.

"And why chase me, other than the fact that I will make it, and then, they will come for you."

"You're wasting valuable time just to give you the same answer twice. I told you that you won't make it."

He was answering me without directly answering me. So, that's what he meant.

"What am I supposed to do with this undigested ordeal?"

"Die! Then, life will digest you."

His answer was cold, somewhat shocking. But it kept the reality at the forefront of the situation I was in.

"Well… I have about two hundred miles to go. I can run the rest of my life, but I will never outrun the past. Is there something wrong with you?"

"Think your ideology will prevail? Let the chips fall where they may. What you have ahead of you, you can't beat. This was a walk in the park. In the city, there's always a reflection. In the woods, there's always a sound. In my world, there's no escape. Let's just say there's a glitch in the machine, a program error. Something I can't beat… time to close the loop."

My mind was reeling. He was giving so much, but all indirectly. Now, I knew there was something wrong with him. It took him three times as long just to speak.

"This has been no walk in the park. What's wrong with you?"

"So, we continue two for two. Okay. What Mother Nature is about to do to you…"

Then, there was a long pause, more than half a minute.

"Are you still there?"

"You can't survive. You have two weeks at best, and then it will get cold. A good day will be thirty below; some days fifty… doesn't matter."

"So, what's your name?"

"Doesn't matter."

"I've been calling you the death dealer."

"Cute… details I've planned… but not for you, time's short. Give you a little initiative. You'll find a list of numbers in my pocket. Those will make you rich beyond all figments of imagination. Maybe you'll figure it out… see not what you see, see what you don't."

Now, I was confused. I had no idea what he was talking about. Figure out what it was or his name. I didn't know.

"Thank you! You're the first one I couldn't beat. I… I admire your analytical skills. What… a way to go, huh?"

Was he dying on me or just giving me a false sense of security? I've always lived by the pretense of never assuming. The past days I had. I assumed he was just a stereotype, living in the wilderness, not being able to read or write. To my surprise, he was very intelligent, but how intelligent? Now was not the time to let my guard down.

Then, very faintly, at barely a whisper, he said, "I can help you no more."

I thought, *Help me… you've done everything but that.*

The rest felt good. Sitting in the snow, I thought of all the things he had said. He had me worrying. Many mornings, I had woken shivering. If I was moving, even with the temperature now around zero, my Arctic Gear kept me warm. Would it be later? Probably not. I never dreamed I would see fifty below. Living in Maryland, that was unheard of. Besides, Craig and I were to be long gone by now.

I felt like crying again. I wasn't going to give him the satisfaction of hearing that. I took several deep breaths, trying to overcome the sadness.

I was trying to stay one step ahead of him. If he's playing some elaborate game, waiting until dark to come after me, what will I do?

My new plan was to wait a short time and see what he says or does and then make a new set of shoes. It would take a little longer; I needed new lacing. I had just enough time before dark. It would be another long night with no sleep, staying just ahead of him.

At least ten minutes passed, probably longer. No word from below. I needed to have some sort of edge, knowing what he was going to do.

"So, what's plan B?"

Nothing.

"What? Is our conversation over?"

Still, no response.

I wanted so badly to look over the edge and see what was happening. Was I right? Was he dying? No way could I gamble.

Then, I had an idea. I got up and walked back toward the lake, about twenty yards. Then, ever so slowly, I got down on my hands and knees and crawled to the edge of the cliff. Then, I looked over, ready to retreat quickly if he was pointing the gun at me.

I couldn't see him. I had to lean out further, something I didn't want to do. My hands were within inches of the edge. I had to lean out, going over the center of gravity of my stationary points of contact. To slip now would mean doing a dive headfirst into the ground. His bullet wouldn't be needed.

I eased over and could see his boots.

Now, I was straining, and my arms were shaking, trying to hold my body up in the air. I moved three more inches forward. There he was, sitting, leaning against the rock. His hands were in his lap, and his head was slumped forward. Was he dead or sleeping? Baiting me was the first thought that came to mind.

I yelled, "Hey, I'm over here."

Nothing.

I couldn't stay leaning forward much longer. I was weakening fast.

"Take your best shot."

He didn't move. I had to lean back. Now, sitting on my knees, I was still skeptical. Neither one of us had gotten to where we were by being careless.

"Let's get this over with. How do you want to do it?"

His silence meant one thing: he was dead. But I had to be sure, so I walked back to the spot just above him.

Using my feet, sitting down, I pushed a big pile of snow down on him. That got no response. He's either dead or good. I still wasn't sure.

My next plan was to dig through the snow and find a rock about the size of a softball.

This time, I stood. I leaned over the edge until I could see most of his legs, held the rock out, and, taking perfect aim, let it go.

I watched the rock fall. It hit him on the left leg, just below the knee. The rock bounced, as did his leg. It had to hurt, but I heard no moan, no sound of registering pain at all.

He remained motionless… he had died.

14
CHAPTER

Now, I had to decide how to get down. Do I take the leap of faith and jump, hoping I wouldn't break or sprain something that seemed senseless? The day was pretty much over, so I started walking, following the cliff back toward the lake.

On the way there, I decided to go out and get the last fish I had left behind. Waste nothing; I would need all the food I could get.

It was just over a mile back to the lake. The time spent walking, I wondered what he had died from. Thinking of what he had said, which was so much, left me wondering: *A glitch in the machine, a program error.* The only thing I could think of, that onset so quickly, was a heart attack, or maybe he was a diabetic and ran out of insulin.

Like he said, it doesn't matter. I felt no remorse for him. One of my burdens had just been lifted.

I navigated through the deep ravine and out onto the lake. I found the fish and started back, following my own path to make the walking easier.

I still felt uneasy. Walking up to the man who so desperately wanted to kill me was something I didn't really want to do. When I came to the edge of the clearing, I stopped and looked in his direction. He was still sitting there, slumped over.

Cautiously, I walked up to him, ready to run at any given moment in case he moved. He didn't. My breathing had increased, and the adrenaline rush was back. I took the final two steps to him and kicked him in the legs, ready to run as if I were superhuman and could outrun a bullet.

After I kicked him, I said, "Are you dead?"

He was, but I kicked him again just for being the vile man he was. I stood there looking down at him. Then, I had another idea: waste nothing.

"You were wrong about one thing. You can help me." I started unzipping his jacket, and then I removed his hood and face mask.

It was hard to tell with his wrinkled skin, but I guessed his age was somewhere in his mid-fifties. He had a hard face; he was a hard man. I was glad he was dead.

As I removed his jacket, I thought of what he had put me through. I hoped I would be in good shape when I reached his age. But then again, it would be a miracle if I saw my next birthday.

I had to remove his snowshoes before I could get his pants off; he was sitting on them. The construction of his shoes was far better than mine, laced together with rope, a tightly wrapped bundle with no loose limbs. It took great effort to remove his pants; rolling him from side to side in the snow took a lot of energy.

I didn't like touching him; the thought almost made me sick, but I needed his clothes. Luckily, he was much bigger than me; he had to weigh nearly two hundred pounds.

His Arctic Gear was of good quality, better than what I had on it. So, when it did get much colder, I could put his on over mine, hopefully keeping me alive until I could reach civilization.

His pants and jacket lay on the ground, and I needed a rest. I started going through his pockets to see what I could find, hoping for something useful.

It was the find of the day! A flashlight that worked, twenty feet of rope, a lighter, another hunting knife, the gun, and the best find of all—a compass! I was so happy I wanted to jump up and down for joy.

"You're helping me far more than you could imagine. You lose."

The next half of my race, I was to do it alone. No bear. No death dealer. Time was now my motivator to push me beyond the limit.

I wrapped his coat and pants in a tight bundle along with the wolf's hide. Then, I cut two pieces of his rope, tying one around the clothes, and hung it over my back. The second, I put through the gills of the fish and hung them around my neck, letting it rest on my left side. Then, I tied on his snowshoes.

I started to leave. Looking back at his boots, I was trying to think of a way of what one was capable of.

I always had the same answer to the ending: to die. Whether it be from exhaustion, starvation, or freezing to death, I would still take the Vegas odds—a no-show.

I stood there looking down at his body lying in the snow. The rest of his clothes were of no use to me. I looked in his pants pockets. No surprise, there was nothing there to tell me who he was, only a single key. I had no idea and would probably never know what it was for, but I put it in my pocket. I looked at his boots; they were quality, but how could I use them?

I couldn't wear them over mine; his feet weren't that big. I had another decision to make: leave them or try to carry the extra weight. I chose to take them with me; if they became a burden, I could always leave them.

With that accomplished, I took one last look at him.

"You got everything you deserved. I hope the wolves feed well."

Then, I took his belt. I didn't need it, but it was better to have it than to not have it.

I started south. Using the compass to head in the correct direction now meant there would be no wasted steps. I couldn't afford them.

I walked well into the middle of the night with mixed emotions. The sense of being totally alone bothered me, yet I felt relieved that I no longer had to constantly look over my shoulder. I owe everything to the bear. Without it, I wouldn't be where I was. I wouldn't have survived both of them.

I stopped and ate three bites of frozen fish from my pocket. Then, I melted some snow in my mouth, cleared the ground of snow, and laid on the wolf hide. Minutes later, I was asleep.

When I woke, I felt rested, the first decent night's sleep in a while. I no longer worried about wolves; I had the gun and knew how to shoot it. The terrain had turned into slow rolling hills, each looking the same and being easily navigated.

Midday, I stopped for a short rest and took three bites of fish, then started walking again. I used the compass, looking at it when I reached the peak of every hill. The heavy cloud cover blocked any view of the sun. Something told me it was going to snow again. That no longer bothered me now since I had the compass.

I couldn't believe the difference in the snowshoes. I glided along with less effort than his. Maybe it was just psychological, knowing they were his.

It did start snowing, just before dark, not the blizzard type, just a moderate snowfall. The wind never stopped blowing anymore, each and all day, then slow or even stopped completely at night. I had grown accustomed to it.

The second day was over since I left him. I was starting to lose track of how many days it had been since they killed Craig.

"Doesn't matter," was the one thing I did learn from him. How true that saying is out here.

The third and fourth days passed as the first two did. I was walking somewhere between twelve and fourteen hours a day, to my best guess. I could tell it was starting to affect my body; I could feel the signs.

My legs were slowly weakening, and my stamina declined a little each day. I couldn't remember how many days I had run from him. I pushed on. At times, I felt myself huffing and puffing, working so hard I didn't realize it.

I remember Craig telling me, more than once, never to sweat. Damp clothes only invite sickness. With the bitter cold surrounding me, I didn't think that was possible, but he hadn't planned for this.

I was no longer worried about anything alive. The bears were the smart ones, sleeping for the winter. One shot from the gun would scare the wolves away. At least once a day, I thought about what he had told me, which was what worried me. Mother Nature was a better foe than the death dealer—even he knew that.

Only time will tell!

I woke up at daybreak. Three bites of frozen fish, and I would be off, mentally ready. My body balked at the idea. It hurt to bend over and tie the shoes on, as did the first quarter mile. My legs were stiff and aching as I pulled on the snowshoes, dragging them forward.

Come on, Madie, you can work through this, I told myself.

And I did! Soon after, my muscles stretched, and I was moving along at a normal pace.

Hours passed as I walked in a trance. The only conscious thing I knew I was doing was constantly glancing at the compass. I followed the needle due south.

The next thing I knew, after my last step, my right leg flew through the air as if it had become detached from my body. It landed in the snow much further ahead than it should have. Then, it sliced through the snow until it hit solid ground. The combination of those two things put me off balance. It happened in less than a second, and I felt myself falling into the snow.

It took me a brief moment to regain my composure. I was trying to figure out what had happened. I twisted around and sat in the snow. I looked back. There, I saw my right snowshoe sitting in the snow from my last step. I stood, brushed the snow from my clothes, and hobbled back the two steps on the left side. I picked it up and inspected it.

The frozen, brittle rope had been worn in two spots behind my heel. The past days of walking, it couldn't hold up under the stress, which was something I hadn't counted on.

Actually, I never gave it any thought. I looked behind the heel of my left boot; the frayed strands of rope told me it was just a matter of time before it would let go.

It was time to take a break, eat, and repair the shoes. All in all, the limbs I was walking on fared better; they would last a few more days. He had used many feet of rope to bind them together, which was doing the major portion of the work. The pine limbs acted only as a pad, distributing my weight across the snow.

The rest felt good as I worked diligently. I hadn't enough rope to re-tie both shoes and with the many days of traveling ahead of me, I would have done this many more times. So, I knotted the rope together, pulling enough slack from around the shoe to do so. I ate more fish and snow. Then, I was up and walking again.

The only way to get finished was to get started, I told myself.

The snow continued to fall throughout the day. Nothing heavy, but it had added up to another four to five inches on top of what was already there.

I was hoping I was walking the miles I had figured I needed each day. I had no way of knowing; if only he had our GPS with him, then I would know.

As I walked, I wondered what they had done with it. Maybe they just threw it in the snow somewhere, extra baggage they didn't need. I thought further back. The one the bear killed was the one who had picked it up. Was it with him in that bloody mess? I had never thought about it at the time, and I was too shaken up. I was just glad to be rid of him.

As I walked each day, I became more mentally numb. The only stimulation was all the thinking I was doing. Always the same thing over and over, watching Craig fall to the ground, all the good times of our four short years of marriage. How happy I was the day we were married; I had found the man of my dreams.

He never questioned me, always going along with all my little quirks, and always happy. I started to cry; I felt so bad, beyond all comprehension, the way he died. Doing it to save me, I didn't deserve it or him. Now, as I thought about it, was I lucky to be alive or not? On the slim odds that I did make it, he wouldn't be there—how lucky was that?

I walked on.

Another night arrived. I ate four more bites of fish as I continued to walk. My tongue and gums always had a tingling feeling, as if I had scalded them with hot coffee, but that wasn't the case. The frozen fish and the snow for water kept them numb, which was a small price to pay. I had many of those, and if the small prices didn't cash out to equal the big ones, I stood a chance.

By now, I've learned to tune out the sound of the wind because if I didn't, the howling through the pines would eventually drive me insane. It was the only thing to be heard, and it was relentless.

The cloud cover was a necessary evil; it did make the night turn into total blackness. But without it, it would be much colder than it was. I turned on the flashlight, illuminating the path ahead, which was a relief. But how long would the batteries last? I looked at the compass and turned it off. Every so often, I turned it on just to check my direction. Then, I would adjust it, heading due south, and turn it off again.

I learned to walk blind, but the axe handle was a perfect cane. The desolation of the wilderness was no different during the day than now. Just trees strategically placed to always be in my way. A cruel joke played by Mother Nature. I learned to walk with my head bent down. Walking into the limbs in the dark was too painful on my face. My neck would become stiff, another small price to pay.

I woke shivering harder than ever before. From now on, I would have to start wearing his clothes to stay warm to sleep. It took my muscles longer to loosen up; the pain was so bad, but I had to walk through it. I did, and after two miles or so, they felt better.

I didn't feel like eating; I was still too exhausted. It was going to be a long day.

I asked myself, *What else did I have to do?*

There was only one answer to that: stop and die. If I did die, at least I would be walking when it happened.

Hours into the day's walk, the sky cleared. The wind didn't; as usual, it blew around ten miles per hour. I didn't care, but tonight I would. Mother Nature had pulled the blanket off—it would be colder.

I didn't know why my legs were feeling so much weaker today, but they were. I had no explanation for it. I was pushing myself hard. No doubt, each day, they would slowly weaken, but at a slow rate where I shouldn't be able to notice.

The difference in one day was scary. If they declined this fast each day, I wouldn't make it. I slowed my pace, only to eat. I didn't want to. I still wasn't hungry, but my body needed fuel in the tank regardless. When I finished the last of the third bite, I was glad I had eaten. I did feel a little better, and I walked on.

It was a bad day. I was feeling depressed; snow and trees were the only things I ever saw. Up one hill, down the next, nothing ever changed. I felt as though I was walking in a frozen desert with no end. The vastness was overwhelming, hundreds, no, thousands of square miles of solitude. It was giving me too much time to think. One such thought was that it was more than I could overcome.

I stopped and took several deep breaths.

Madie, you can do this; it's just a thing. It will pass, I told myself.

What I was feeling was I knew I had to snap out of it.

To lighten my mood, I asked myself, *I wonder what day it is?*

His phrase came back to me: "Doesn't matter." I liked that. Only one thing mattered: I knew what day it wasn't—it wasn't the day I was going to die out here. The sun was going down, and I would see it tomorrow, one more day. Tomorrow never comes; that's what kept me going.

I didn't travel past dark as long as I wanted to. I had to rest and try to get a better night's sleep if that was possible. Lying in snow on the frozen ground in near sub-zero weather wasn't what I called an ideal condition for it. I had to make do with what I had. So, I removed the snowshoes, scraped the snow from the ground, and started untying his clothes. My boots! I couldn't remove them; it wouldn't be until tomorrow sometime before my feet would warm up again. Sleeping with cold feet would only add to my misery.

It was quite an ordeal pulling his pants on over mine with my boots on. I had to do it standing up; putting a layer of snow in between the clothes would be like not having them on at all. Then, I put on his jacket, which was much easier. I was glad he was much larger.

Now, I felt like a mummy, all wrapped up. The restriction from the extra set of clothes made it hard to bend at the joints, another small price to pay.

I was beginning to appreciate the small prices.

I laid the wolf pelt on the ground, and then I laid on it. Now I have an extra cushion; maybe in the morning, I wouldn't wake so stiff.

Yeah, good luck on that one, I thought.

Sleep always came quickly—the one thing I didn't have to wait for.

When I woke, it was cold; I could tell by every breath I inhaled. But I was relatively warm; only my hands and feet were cold. I debated on whether or not I should start out wearing more clothing. I decided to do so. If I got too hot, I would stop and remove them, only after taking the time to hassle with the snowshoes. I had nothing but time, even though it wasn't on my side.

I didn't eat; I wasn't hungry. My body was slowly adjusting to having no food, but it wasn't adjusting to the physical strain it was receiving.

I never thought too much about only being able to see more than one hundred feet ahead. The density of the trees never changed much, only their height. The taller ones, with their longer limbs higher off the ground, made visibility further. When the trees were shorter, their limbs resting on or just above the ground, then I could see no further than the next tree. Rarely did I ever find an open patch.

But, so what? The compass was my eyes. It could see through the trees; I was thankful for that. Without it, I believe I would slowly go insane. The trees were slowly becoming my enemy, each tree trunk looking identical as if I had walked past it moments earlier, engulfing me in a tomb of similarity. I tuned it out. My thoughts were on my body, each leg, each step, inhaling and exhaling to the next; it was all I had.

I had to remove the outer jacket just a few miles into the day and then, after a few more, the pants. I lost time doing so, but I could make it up at the end of the day, past dark.

I slept, got up, and did the same routine. I ate, but the fish supply was over half gone, and my pockets were nearly empty. So, I decided to take time and fillet the frozen fish that had been bumping me in the side the past few days. It wasn't an annoying bump; having it there meant survival.

When that was finished, I stepped onto the shoes and started off. My pockets were full again. Luckily, the last fish was a large one, so I was good for a few more days.

The wind blew much harder, always at my back. The gusts were as hard, if not harder, than any I had experienced before. And the cold, slowly heading in the direction I didn't need. Mother Nature was warning me, as the death dealer had. "You won't make it," I remember him telling me. Well, it wouldn't be from lack of trying.

Then, it started snowing again. Only this wasn't going to be a normal snowfall like the last. It came too fast and hard. Within minutes, it was snowing so hard I couldn't see past five feet, and with the severe wind, it snowed sideways.

I turned and looked to the west. All I could see was snowflakes flying past my face. I didn't stop. I held my compass in the palm of my right hand and tied the compass on a string around my neck. To lose that would mean to lose my way, then my life.

Then, it got worse! No one could have ever told me it could snow this hard. If they did, I wouldn't have believed them. Growing up in Maryland, we didn't see much snow.

I clenched my hood tight around my head. It was designed to wrap around the face, and the drawing had a slip spring-loaded clasp, instantly locking it in place. No need to worry about tying knots. Whoever designed it obviously spent time out in the cold.

I ran into a tree, only looking at it for a split second before I ran into it. I held the axe handle out in front of me, but I couldn't see it. It was as if my hand had been cut off at the wrist. Everything passed that disappeared into the snow.

Craig and I studied, read, and learned what to do in various situations in case of an emergency. During a blizzard, one wasn't supposed to walk for fear of being lost. It was recommended to sit tight and wait it out. How much more lost was I going to get? I almost laughed; Mother Nature's cruel little joke backfired on her. I was already there and had been for more days than I can remember. From the beginning, it was all I knew.

Now, it was no different than walking past dark. I had done that so much that it was second nature. Without the compass, I would have had to do what was recommended, so I continued.

Just like in the dark, walking was slower, but I was still walking. Hours passed. The snow became deeper under my feet, but it gave me a sense of peace. I was in my own little world. The only thing I concentrated on was the axe handle, bumping into the next tree so I could walk around.

Every few minutes, I would find the compass hanging from my neck. I would hold it within inches from my face to see it and adjust my direction.

Now, I wished I had left the extra set of Arctic Gear on. While I walked, I was getting cold, which was a first. I had the severe wind to thank for that, one for Mother Nature.

You're not going to beat me, not yet, not today anyway, I said to myself.

Daylight turned dark. The snow didn't stop. I was exhausted; it took much more energy to walk blind. I had no way of knowing, but I hoped I had walked ten miles. It felt like I had walked twenty—I only wished.

I fumbled around in my pocket and removed the flashlight. In the heavy snowfall, it wasn't much good, and I didn't want to waste the batteries. As slow as my travels were, I decided to stop now that it was dark. The distance gained wasn't worth the battery power lost, constantly looking at the compass.

I removed the shoes, and then I dug a wall of snow to block the wind. I put on the extra clothes and sat behind the wall. I couldn't lay down for fear I would be covered with snow during the night and suffocate to death.

CHAPTER 15

I backed into the snowbank as far as I could. Then, I tied his hood up over mine. It came with a chin strap complete with snaps. I wrapped it around my face and snapped it onto the right side of the hood. It also had real fur sewn in around the outer edge. Thick, long hair, probably from some domesticated, raised fox.

So, now, I had only two inches around my eyes exposed to the bitter weather. I looked out ahead of me; I could see nothing. I waved my right hand inches from my face, and I couldn't see that. I sat there in my own little world, surrounded by darkness. My knees were drawn up near my chest, and I laid my head in the valley between them.

I tuned out the sound of the wind. I could feel a stream running down my face. I knew this couldn't be fixed—there would be no lights to guide me home.

Craig, I want to talk to you. You will always be the missing piece of the puzzle. Without you, there is no future. This makes no sense. I can't do this anymore; I'm sorry. I'm floating on a tidal wave, and I will drown soon.

This is how I foresaw one of the ways I would die out here. The snow will swallow me, then so be it. She's too powerful a foe, another one for Mother Nature.

It was too early. My system wasn't used to going to sleep so soon after dark. My body was thankful for the rest, but now I had nothing to do but think. It was worse than the physical abuse. As I started to drift off to sleep, my thoughts came randomly. They had a mind of their own. The last one was, *Craig, I love you! Please come home.*

Maybe that was my way of saying: "It would be alright to die tonight."

As I dreamed, everything seemed so real. I never woke, but some of them were hard, borderline nightmares, rousing me just enough to end it.

Sometime during the night, I stretched my legs out and leaned back. That's the way I woke up. My headache is what woke me. I opened my eyes to solid darkness. *Why did I wake up early?* Then, it hit me. I was slowly, silently, and painlessly suffocating. I was breathing used air, mine. The lack of oxygen caused the headache.

The snow had drifted over my head. I tried to raise my arms to clear the snow away from my face. They moved sluggishly. *Was I just minutes away from the point of no return?* That scared me. Now, I was wide awake. Then, I realized I was buried.

Near panic, I jerked my arms up through the snow and cleared my face. It wasn't as easy to stand up, as if the snow was trying to hold me down, saying stay here, give in, and let Mother Nature have her way.

When I stood, my feet burned, and there were a thousand needles in each foot kind. I bent over and then forward, hoping that would lessen the weight on them. It didn't. I waited for the pain to pass.

While doing so, I looked around. I had tunnel vision, looking through the small opening both hoods made. I couldn't believe what I saw. The snow had drifted over me. The depth equaled that of the top of the pile I had made. The surface of the snow was smooth, wiping away all signs that I was even here. I couldn't distinguish my pile from the surrounding snow. My tracks from the night before were gone. She made a gallant effort to erase me.

I thought of what the death dealer had said to me, "Leave no trail."

"Not this time. You're going to have to do better."

She had tried to finish me, never to be found.

My feet were freezing. The pain had eased some. As soon as I started walking, the blood flow would warm them.

The early morning stiffness and aching in my muscles became a ritual. I moved slowly, digging through the snow, looking for the snowshoes. I couldn't remember exactly where I had left them. I used the axe, my multi-purpose tool, to scrape the ground under the snow.

When I found them, I picked them up and hit them with the axe to knock the snow off. Then, I gave them a good inspection. I wasn't happy with what I found; all the small branches were broken, and many of them were missing.

I slept past my usual wake-up time, so visibility was good. I looked out past the spot where I had slept. I guessed that about two more feet of new snow had fallen. I had to have good shoes.

As much as I didn't want to, I had to make new ones. The time lost making them I would gain back plowing through the snow. I tried to re-tie the new limbs as he had; construction meant everything.

The snow had stopped, but, of course, the wind hadn't.

"Is that all it does up here, snow and blowing wind?" I asked.

"Yes," was my answer. That's why no one chooses to live up here.

After a long time spent making the new shoes, I was ready. Now, I realized several more days had been added to my walk. It took longer to accomplish anything. The snow was light and fluffy, making it a drag to walk through—literally.

I was slowly sinking in the tidal wave. Mother Nature was starting to win the little things, and today she was relentless. The clouds were starting to move out. That was a good thing. The sunshine peeking through the cloud cover was making me feel better mentally. But the wind had increased, blowing harder than it ever had before. No less than thirty miles per hour, and that was a conservative guess.

With each step I took, I watched the loose snow being whisked away. The way it does when it's blown across the bare ice on a lake, turning into fine dust and then disappearing.

I was happy with my new shoes. They were almost as good as his. Only by sheer determination and long hours would I make ten miles today and each day after. I needed to lose some weight. Then, I laughed at that thought. I was doing that each and every day.

His boots, hanging around my neck, were the only cargo I could discard. I hated the thought of doing so, but they weighed at least five pounds. By the end of the day, they would feel double that. I stopped and lifted the string, tying them together over my head.

My feet had never warmed up. If only I could put them on top of mine. They were high-quality boots, and they were probably the best. They didn't have removable liners; the thick inner soles were sewn together. I thought if I could cut all that out, I could slip the outer shell over mine. I bent over, placed his boot next to mine, and found it wasn't possible. My boots would never fit inside. Though he was taller than the average man, he had small feet. My bad luck: the little things sure had taken a turn.

I stood there and removed the laces, the only thing that could be of use to me. While doing so, the wind nearly blew me over several times. Her fury was growing. Why was she so angry with me? I had done nothing to her but invade her privacy. I was trying desperately to correct that. I dropped the boots into the snow, and they instantly vanished under the surface.

Gone forever, never to be seen again, I thought, as I would be if Mother Nature won.

I continued on. When I reached a spot where I could see ahead, no matter how far, I looked at the compass. Then, I would pick out a spot or a tree and head for that. It was the only thing I had to do.

I walked through the day. I had to take several breaks, not to eat, but to just rest. It was exhausting work. Even with his clothes on, I wasn't hot by any means. I just wished my feet would warm up. I thought they would have by now.

I continually switched the axe from one hand to the other. The empty hand I tucked up inside the sleeve of his jacket, keeping it from the wind.

Just before dark, I stopped for another rest. I decided to eat, having not done so all day. It would be easier now than trying to do it in the dark.

As I ate, I watched the daylight fade into twilight. I had a new plan. I thought it was a great idea, giving me something to do in the dark. I would count my steps, and each time I reached one hundred, I would turn on the flashlight, check my compass heading, and start over.

I soon became bored with that. My thoughts wandered, forgetting where I was in the count. The reason they wandered was because I was getting tired and exhausted; I couldn't concentrate. I couldn't stop, not yet. The pain in my legs grew, and the rest of my body was limp. Mentally, I was going into neutral, the body's way of adjusting.

Finally, I could go no more. I felt like crying, but I was too tired to do so. The wind continued to blow. I turned on the flashlight to find a spot out of the wind.

I walked on; my steps were only shuffles. I wasn't at the point of dying from exhaustion, not yet.

How many more days can this continue? I asked myself.

I found a clump of small pine trees. I walked to the downwind side of them, which was much better but not totally out of the wind. Again, I piled the snow, this time against the trees, and sat down. I laid the pelt on the side of the pile and leaned against it.

I sat there thinking, *How many days do I have left?*

I used his answer again, "Doesn't matter," and I knew it really didn't.

At least I didn't know the day I was going to die. If I were to wake up one morning and someone said that today was the day, I wouldn't bother trying. Tomorrow morning, if I do wake up, I will do it all over again.

I looked at the sky. Tonight, I could see the stars, and they looked so small, as I would if they were looking at me. A small dot in a sea of trees, wondering how far the shore was, riding the tidal wave that was killing me.

I was miserable sitting there. I hurt so bad; it even hurt to move. It was also miserably cold, with the temperature hitting a new low. She was adding to her count, which was growing each day. How many more would it take until the big one arrived? The Vegas odds had to have doubled or tripled by now. I wished I had a phone, but I would bet the ranch, the bank account, and whatever I owned that I would be a rich, dead person.

I wrapped the outer hood over my face; even my eyelids were aching. I lay there hoping to fall asleep soon, maybe fall into a light coma; then I wouldn't hurt, and my pains would drift away. They did, and I slept, but not well. I woke frequently, shivering, and my body's way of telling me not to sleep too deeply caused my heart rate to drop. It wanted to stay warm, and the only way of doing so was to pump blood into all parts for heat. It wasn't doing too well.

I woke at dawn. I felt like I hadn't slept at all, and I was still tired. Knowing what the next few minutes were going to be like, I hated getting up. But I had to get started as God had given me another day.

I stood and moaned loudly, almost yelling. The pain in my feet was unbelievable, and my legs, hips, and back weren't going to let me forget they were still there. I became nauseous, and I would have vomited if there was anything available in my stomach. I felt dizzy and lightheaded. I started to fall, but I caught myself.

Getting up a second time would be worse than what I was going through now. I took deep breaths, and the bitter cold air hitting my lungs shocked me back to normal.

Now, I had to take the first step. I couldn't stand here all day. I started toward the shoes. I cried; I didn't know how long I could stand the pain.

After the ordeal of tying on the shoes, I looked at the compass and started out. In the first hour, I didn't cover much ground, but my muscles were slowly giving in, facing the fact that they had another ten or twelve hours of work ahead.

By midday, I was back to normal, at least normal for here. Not normal if I was at home. I had to do something for my feet; I was slowly losing them. They ached all the time. Moving along at a steady pace, I didn't want to break the momentum, so I didn't.

The next few days passed the status quo. Nothing ever changes in the wilderness. Maybe an occasional snowstorm and, of course, the temperatures do and were. Something I couldn't change, though, was my food supply; it was running low. I would have to do something in a few more days. I had crossed lakes but didn't fish. I didn't need or want to.

I wasn't thinking as much as I used to. I had worn out the past and didn't worry about the future. The compass and my steps were all I concentrated on. I wasn't delusional; I had enough wits about me yet to know I was becoming delirious.

My feet no longer ached as bad. I tried to forget about them, but what I had left in me was directed toward walking south.

Then, something happened. Something reconnected in my head as though someone had just placed it there out of nowhere. The idea was to cut pieces of the wolf hide and wrap it around my boots, hopefully giving my feet a little more time. I did it using the knife for the first time in two or three weeks. I found out how much dexterity my hands had lost. The lack of use, other than squeezing the axe handle, or the lack of food, or the cold, I didn't know which.

It doesn't matter, I told myself. Nothing did anymore.

I used some of the rope I had taken from—I couldn't remember what I called him anymore—tied them up and put the shoes back on. They were becoming very ragged again. As soft as the snow was, I would have thought they would have lasted longer. I didn't know if I could make another set; I wasn't sure I had it in me.

Automatically, I stood up and started walking. I don't know how much time passed before I realized I didn't know which direction I was walking in. I looked at the compass, and my shoulders dropped. I was walking due west.

Come on, Madie, keep it together, I told myself.

What time of the day it was didn't matter. In the back of my mind, I knew I was slowly losing it. I walked; that's all I knew.

I wasn't paying attention to the trees or the terrain, just the compass. I treated it as though it was the most valuable thing in the world. In mine, it was. I would look at it through the small opening in front of my face. I watched the ground, never more than three or four steps ahead.

I watched the right snowshoe travel forward across the surface of the snow. Watching each step mesmerized me, placing me in a trance, shutting out the aches and pains, and helping me forget how bad things were. How close was I to cashing out? Then, I watched it land, disappearing in the snow. It went past the point of breaking the rhythm of connecting with the ground.

In a flash, I felt myself falling forward.

What happened? I thought, only inches into the fall. My body automatically reacted.

Trying to protect myself, I put my arms out in front of me in hopes of cushioning the landing. I took a deep breath and tried to take a quick half-step with my left foot, hoping to regain my balance. It was a miserable attempt. I watched my arms sink into the snow through my small window of vision. I squeezed my eyes shut and grimaced just before I landed face-first in the snow. I landed with a very quiet 'poof.' That's the only way I could explain it.

Nothing hurt. I fell below the surface of the snow, and everything instantly became dark. I tried to grab hold of a solid surface below me and then around me, but nothing was there. I panicked; my arms were flailing around.

I started swimming, trying to reach the surface, but the harder I worked, the further I sank into the snow. I became more panicked; I had thirty seconds to hold my breath. I continued to struggle. I tried to stand by pulling my knees up to my chest, but nothing was working. The blood pressure was rising fast in my head, and I knew I couldn't hold my breath much longer.

Then, I knew the tidal wave had just swallowed me, pushing me to the bottom in hopes of holding me there. Now, my head felt like it was going to split open. It could no longer take the lack of oxygen. I quit struggling, let my body go limp, and gave up.

"Please take me! I can't do this anymore," I said silently.

Seconds passed. It was a good day to die—Mother Nature had won. I heard his voice, right beside me, as clear as day, "Madie, when have you ever quit anything? That's not you. Not the Madie I know."

I turned my head sideways as if I was going to see him. My body inhaled, doing it on its own. The will to survive took over. There was just enough air inside my hood and around my neck to give me the air I needed. I just put the last chip on the table, giving me a little more playing time. I decided to live.

I reached down and grabbed hold of my legs behind my knees and pulled. That brought my chest up close to my feet, and I got a hold of each main stem of the snowshoes and pulled again. This brought me up over the center of my feet.

With all the strength I could find, I directed it to my legs and stood up. When my head broke through the surface of the snow, I inhaled loudly, drawing in all the air my lungs could handle. I exhaled and quickly did it again. The pain in my head faded away. I was alive but not free. How ironic that was; I would never be free from this, even in death.

I looked around, trying to figure out what I was in—as far as I could tell, nothing. The ground had swallowed me for no apparent reason. I reached forward, stretching as far as I could, trying to find something solid to hold onto in the snow. There was nothing. There I stood, rib deep in white quicksand. I had my shoes beneath me so I would sink no further in the fluffiest snow I had ever seen.

"Well, Ms. Nature, you set a trap. It didn't work, not this time."

Wow, my voice! The first time I heard it, well, I'm not sure. It was possibly two weeks. It was raspy, bordering between bad and gone.

Doesn't matter, I thought. I had bigger problems and more than one.

I worked my arms up out of the snow with the axe in my left hand. My next plan was to swing it in the air while reaching forward as far as it would go. Maybe I could sink it in the frozen dirt far enough to get a good hold and pull myself free. It did!

Freedom was two arm lengths away. Slowly and gently, I pulled on the axe handle. I felt myself move an inch, then two; it was working. But I never moved the third inch; the axe broke loose. No big deal, I just swung it again. As I pulled again, the axe let go.

After several more failed attempts, I was breathing heavily. I rested for a moment and thought. The only thought I had was, *Why couldn't I sink my axe deep enough to slide free of the snow?*

Then, it dawned on me: my snowshoes. I had two anchors on my feet. No, it was more like two buckets of concrete trying to pull me to the bottom. I had to lose the shoes. If I did cut them free, it meant never getting them back. I could have made more, but I needed the rope; I didn't have enough for another set.

Always the same dilemma out here, walking along the edge of death. I wouldn't have made it without them, but I couldn't have been free with them. There had to be another way! I stood there thinking for the first time since the first day of this mess. I was thankful no one could see me; I looked like an idiot.

I thought, *Well, sometimes we perceive what we are. Everyone creates their own problems.*

I had definitely created mine.

I could think of only one thing. I had to get the shoes to the surface; I had to save them. Right now, they were saving me. I took a deep breath and then held it. I knelt down into the snow, back into the darkness, grabbed hold of each of the main stems, and jumped up.

When my weight was suspended off, I pulled up on the front end. I had enough air left in my legs to do that two more times, and then I stood up to breathe. It was working. I didn't gain much, but I did gain.

Finally, something was going right. I did it again and stood. Now, my shoes were resting at a forty-five-degree angle in the snow. I repeated the process a third time. It was hard work, and I was back to huffing and puffing, but I felt better. I was standing with my waist above the snow.

The fourth attempt brought the tips of the shoes out of the snow. I stood leaning forward to offset the angle of the shoes, and then I swung the axe. I had a much better range of motion with my arms. After the axe was buried in the frozen dirt, I hung onto the handle.

Instead of pulling my body forward, I lifted my legs, trying to pull the shoes free. It worked! I took small, short steps, and when I reached level ground, I fell over. I lay there, resting, thinking how close that was.

Breathing heavily, I said, "You'll have to do better than that."

She would; that was inevitable.

I was up and moving. Why bother to sweat the little things? I had bigger fish to fry.

The alertness and energy level soon faded. Back to the same routine, looking at the compass and walking around trees. Soon, another day will have passed. I made the best of it. I ate as I walked.

By my best estimate, I had three more meals left, so there would be only one meal a day until I found more food. I had the gun; I knew how to shoot it, but I never saw anything to shoot at.

Every two or three days, I would see tracks from a deer or a rabbit, but that was the only thing I saw. They knew I was there and were long gone before I saw them. Besides, I had never shot anything in my life before, and I didn't know if I could do it now.

I was beginning to hate the night; they were becoming brutally cold. It was as if they were having a contest to see which one could be the coldest. The sunshine meant a lot; even on cloudy days, the sun managed to raise the temperature.

I wasn't traveling as long past dark as I used to; I didn't have the energy. Each day was slowly eating away at my body. It felt like Father Time was joining in, taking sides with Ms. Nature to do me in. As much as I hated to admit it, they were winning. His words echoed through my memory several times each day: "You won't make it."

That drove me on. I was always a little hardheaded. I was going to show them all if it was the last thing I ever did. If I didn't make it, it wouldn't be the last thing I ever did—I tried.

The nights always humbled me, as it was doing tonight. Of course, the wind was blowing; that was a given. I had to invent a new way to try to sleep, but the lack of sleep hurt me as much as all the miles I was walking. I had to slow the little things down as much as I could. I still scraped the ground clean of snow.

My new addition was a pile of small pine limbs underneath me; then, the wolf pelt covered the upper part of my body, and on top of that, many more pine limbs. I didn't know if it would help, but I had to try something.

The weight on top of me was more than I expected. As I lay there, I didn't think I would be able to turn over or even shift my weight while sleeping.

Oh well, I thought, *maybe I can get a few hours of sleep before the stiffness set in.*

I did, but it did, also! I woke up during the night. How long I slept, I didn't know. My muscles were screaming, and I had to shift my weight. I stretched my legs out, but I couldn't roll over on my side. But I tried and managed to move a few inches, which was enough; the pain subsided. I wasn't ready to give in to it; I fell back asleep, shivering.

Getting up each day was a necessary evil. I was lying under my blanket of pine limbs, shivering my butt off. I hated the thought of getting up, as I did each morning. Nothing new; what the next few minutes would bring was a given. I slept a little better; I almost felt rested.

After enduring the pain and the stretching, I inspected the shoes. I could get one more day out of them, so I was off. As the day wore on and I became mentally numb, I thought of the miles I had already walked.

How many? I had no way of knowing how many more I would have to walk. With any luck, within a few days, I would walk upon a logging trail.

Those few days came and passed. Now, I was out of food and found no logging trail.

I told myself, *Maybe in a few more.*

It had to be just a matter of time. My feet were slowly easing up on the pain each day. That wasn't a good sign, but there was nothing else I could do for them. I could no longer feel my smaller toes on each foot. I knew what that meant.

Jack Frost had teamed up with Ms. Nature and Father Time. I was beginning to dislike them. How many more foes would I encounter before this was over? So, I continued to run from the Grim Reaper—he was the worst of them all.

Right now, my biggest quest is to conquer food. The severe cold drove the ice much deeper. I didn't have the strength to chop a small crater on some lake, so that was out.

Another day passed, and I found no food. I was starving, and my energy level in the tank was nonexistent. I stopped and sat down in the snow. I looked at the sky; the sun was shining. It was much too pretty of a day to die, and I had a few left in me. After that, it was anyone's guess. I would probably fall asleep one night, never to wake up. I had to have food to provide heat.

Why did the ideas keep popping into my head out of nowhere? I didn't know, but they did. Somewhere out there, something was on my side, maybe my guardian angel, trying to balance out the scale.

His belt, I had his belt. I could eat that—not much nutritional value there, but better than nothing at all. I pulled it from my pocket and started cutting it into small pieces. I wasn't sure if the dye would make me sick. I was back walking on the edge of death. To starve to death in the days ahead or die tomorrow from poisoning, dead was still dead. I thought about that more and more as time passed.

I chewed on a piece of the belt, and it was bitter. The more I chewed, the more it swelled in my mouth. Then, I swallowed, knowing only time would tell. I put another in my mouth, got up, and headed south.

CHAPTER 16

Before dark, I took the time to chop my limbs and make a small hut under which to lie. I was down to walking in only daylight; my body could handle no more. Time was running out; I was wearing out, and the cold was becoming unbearable. My hands ached, mainly my fingers, and it felt like they were on fire.

Each blow from the axe hurt so bad it was hard to hang on to it. I looked at it as a small price to pay for life, such as it was. I was lonely all the time, constantly shivering, and I was weak and aching, making each step a burden. My mental status was failing.

I lay under the hut, knowing I had to try something else. The weight of the limbs lying on me made my body ache even worse. I thought I had done a good job giving myself just enough room inside to roll over.

Outside, I had put a thin layer of snow on top to help keep the wind out. The only thing wrong with it was that it took far too much time to build and that I didn't have energy. I was fighting a losing battle. I had nothing but time—but time, I didn't have. My only purpose in life was to walk, and I had the rest of my life to do that. If I didn't find civilization soon before my body was totally wasted, this hut, or the next one, or even the one after that, would become my coffin, and I no longer care.

I would sleep a short time, and then the shivering would wake me. All I could do was roll over and pray that sleep would return quickly. It always did; my body was begging for sleep. The internal will to survive was still there. I would soon wake again with my body telling me it needed heat. I knew shivering caused friction, which was the muscle's way of providing heat. I hated shivering, shaking uncontrollably, burned energy I didn't have. I was on a downhill slide, and I was in the express lane.

The cramping in my intestines woke me in the middle of the night. It was bad, bad enough that I forgot about being cold, one pain canceling out the other. My only fear was I would get diarrhea, and a little of that would cause me to dehydrate. My system was too delicate to stand much, but I would probably freeze to death first. Bare skin exposed that long wouldn't be good.

I lay there hoping it would pass. Eating pieces of the belt wasn't such a good idea. It had to be the dye, whatever chemicals it took to make it, but my system didn't like it. Luckily, it passed because I had nothing in me to lose.

I was up but hated every moment of it. I slowly walked back and forth, trying to loosen the knots in my muscles.

Another day, another mile, I told myself.

The thought always remained close: *How many more? How many did I have left in me?*

I walked, pushing myself. When I walked, I had heat. But I always felt weak and tired, one creating the other. Each time I rested, which was several times a day now, I shivered. Another quid pro quo, one canceling out the other—a losing proposition.

I had to have food, which was my biggest thought. I looked at different trees, wondering if I could eat the bark from any of them, but decided against it. I was eating snow like it was going to vanish on me, trying to offset the hunger pain, which only made my tongue raw. Another give and take; the little things were adding up fast.

I had to rest again, guessing it was somewhere around mid-afternoon. It was another cloudy day with only a small breeze. If there was such a thing as a native around here, they would say it was a calm day, but not me. A calm day would be sitting in a heated house next to a warm fire, drinking something hot.

Yeah, right, dream on, that's wishful thinking! I thought. That was a thing of the past.

It seemed as if I had been out here, walking nowhere, for years and years. I was slowly forgetting about how real people live. In the back of my mind, I would never see that again.

I didn't want to get up; resting a few more minutes wouldn't change a thing. I sat there, thinking of all the people at home. My friends and my family, what were they thinking? What did the pilot think when we didn't show up at our rendezvous point? Had they sent a search party out for us?

I never saw a plane and never heard one off in the distance. But I wouldn't have; we were to walk west, and I ran south. Without GPS, I would never have found the exact spot to meet them, and he wouldn't have given me the time.

I sat there deep in thought. *There had to be a way out of this. If I could outrun and survive him, I could find something to eat.*

I thought about the bear, and I heard that bear meat is good. If the bear was still tagging along, though, there was no way I would eat my friend. But now, I was glad I didn't have that option.

So, I was back to the belt, but the dye was making me sick after only two bites. I removed it from my pocket, and it was tempting. I looked at it, rolled it over in my burning fingers, and to my surprise, there was no dye on the back of it. Now, I had another idea. I had two knives in my pocket; one of them had to be sharp enough to slice through the leather, trimming away the surface that was penetrated with dye.

I went to work, but my fingers weren't working, which made the process slow. I sliced the leather in half, the way I always remembered the way my father ate a piece of cake. He would cut the bottom half off and eat it first, saving the top half with frosting for the last. He said that was the best part. *A piece of cake—how good would that be!*

The dye had penetrated nearly, but not quite, half the thickness of the belt. I got to eat the bottom half of the cake, which was okay, better than no cake. I put a piece in my mouth. It wasn't bitter, just dry and tasteless. It took a long time to soften it up before I could start chewing.

While doing that, I cut up another six pieces and put five of them in my pocket. When I finally got to swallow it, I started on the second, and then, I was up and moving. Chewing on the leather gave me something to think about other than walking, which was a relief.

By the time I stopped before dark, the five pieces were gone. I made a shabby hut, crawled in, and cut more leather. This time, I used the wolf pelt to cover the opening. Then, I slept, shivered, and slept again. I lost count of how many times I repeated that process through the night. Each time I woke, at least I knew I was still alive.

I woke up before sunrise. It was beyond being bitter cold. They had a new winner. I'm not sure how cold it is, but like he said, "A good day would be thirty below." It had to be that.

I crawled out of the hut. I moved so slowly that one would have thought I was ninety years old if one was watching. Once outside, it was even colder, if that was possible, but it was; it wasn't my imagination. Even a few degrees, my ragged body could detect.

I turned on the flashlight and inspected the shoes. They were in shambles. I had walked on them days past their usefulness. I was going to make a new set before I started off. I guessed the leather helped because I didn't get sick. I felt as though I had two ounces of energy, so I cut more while shivering and using the flashlight.

I was beginning to miss the feeling of being watched. I couldn't see how prisoners in solitary confinement could take or even hermits. The lack of interaction with other people quickly takes a toll. Unlike the prisoners, I had my freedom. I also had my own solitary confinement—another paradox—so many out here.

Everything became a chore, taking twice if not three times as long to do. I thought of my last paradox. *I have all the time I need.* Time is what I didn't have! It hurt to hold the knife and apply pressure on my hand. I had to continually switch from left to right.

Finally, I had cut a dozen pieces, roughly one inch long, and that was the easy job. I couldn't even guess how long it was going to take to cut four limbs and tie them together. A twenty-minute job for a normal person, but I was no longer normal.

Well, heck, what else did I have to do? I said to myself.

There was only one answer, always the same: *Die soon enough.*

Tears ran, freezing to my face mask, even under the hoods, trying to chop the limbs I needed. I couldn't believe the pain. Today was far worse than yesterday. With the speed of my deteriorating body, I was no longer in the fast lane. I felt I was on the autobahn with failing brakes. This would be the last set of snowshoes I would ever make; that was a given. Either I would find life other than mine, or I would find life with Craig.

I tried so hard to tie the rope around the limbs. I just couldn't get them to move; my fingers were unable to apply enough pressure to do a good job. Mentally, I was working hard. The movement slowly loosened my muscles. By the time I finished, sunlight was peeking through the trees. I stood, looked at the compass, and headed south.

I couldn't feel my feet, and I wasn't even sure I had anymore. Occasionally, I would land hard on one of the shoes, and then I would feel a burning sensation, letting me know they were still there.

I walked for hours, constantly eating pieces of the belt. I had doubts that it was doing me any good as my energy was long gone. I was dragging the shoes through the snow. I stopped and rested. If Ms. Nature dumped another heavy snowfall on me, it would be the end of me. I didn't have the strength to travel through it.

I was frequently switching the axe from hand to hand, and my fingers ached. Then, I dropped it. I was back to walking in a vegetated state. I was two steps past the axe before I realized it. My mind told me both arms were light; then something registered that something wasn't right. That's when I figured it out.

Like my body, my mental process was slowing. I stopped and looked back. I saw the axe handle sticking vertically out of the snow. A small wave of panic flowed; I couldn't be without the axe. I wouldn't survive! It was more important than the gun and equal to food. The little things were telling me how delicate my life was, walking on a high wire, sliding along the sharp edge of a razor.

One mistake would mean failure. I had to make a small circle to get back to the axe, but the snowshoes had no reverse. The little warning of dropping the axe made me realize I must take better precautions. My hands would only get worse, as would my mind. How long would I walk next time before I realized I had dropped it? I stood there looking at the axe, sticking the handle up in the snow. It was hard to think clearly, but I tried hard. My mind was in slow motion, and I knew it. I was trying to think of a way to not lose the axe, which was my lifeline.

As slow as the thoughts were coming, at least they still were. The idea finally came to me: I had his shoelaces. I tied them together. Luckily, they were long enough, which was one thing that was in my favor. I tied both ends to the handle and put the loop around my neck. Slowly, my life spiraled out of control. I had saved the axe—I wondered if I could save my life—as I walked on.

I ate more pieces of the belt and melted snow in my mouth. I couldn't get enough water. The leather, the extremely dry temperatures, and starvation were all dehydrating my body.

Days passed. I no longer tried to keep track because I no longer cared; I was exhausted. Nothing ached anymore; something inside me learned how to turn it off. I didn't know if I was in shock. It was as if my body just shut down the parts that had become a problem. I didn't care; I had no energy. I would walk for an hour, and then I would have to rest, only to struggle to stand and do it all over. The miles slowly faded behind me, each day becoming fewer; each day, my life faded in front of me.

The terrain became flatter, which lifted my spirits. I knew I wouldn't be able to traverse the steep hills I once traveled. I didn't have the strength to carry my weight up them. The little things meant so much. I was walking, bent over, leaning forward. I didn't know why I couldn't stand straight; maybe, just deep down inside, I didn't want to.

The belt was down to being about ten inches long. I couldn't eat any more of it. It just tasted too horrible. I spent more time shivering than not, but walking was producing just enough heat. I hated walking; it had become such a great effort to do so. I hated the thought of stopping and sleeping each night, which was also miserable due to the extreme cold.

Paradoxes, paradoxes, I thought, *why do they have to be so many?*

The wind was gusting severely, and black clouds were moving in. The humidity gained a point or two, which meant only one thing. I collapsed in the snow, landing on my knees and then rolling onto my right side. I lay in the snow.

Why don't you just take me? I thought. Then, his words returned from the far corners of my memory.

"You won't make it," he had said twice to me. It was all I needed. Words like that stated directly at me I had never liked; in fact, it had always infuriated me throughout my life. Slowly, I stood and started south.

I walked with my hands inside the sleeves of his coat. I thought about tying them shut, but I could only tie one, so I didn't bother.

I could feel my feet swelling; there was no pain, but it was uncomfortable. It was obvious what that meant; the blood was pooling in them. The frozen tissue was unable to return the blood back to my legs. Now, I was down for a few days.

Soon, blood poisoning would ruin the rest of my body—well, what's left of it anyway! The patience my foes have; they are relentless. They're in no hurry, slowly pecking away at me each day. They tried to end this quickly by burying me in the snow but failed. Now, they're winning. I just hope God gives me the grace to smile the moment before death. I will have won the war, and I'll be with Craig.

As the darkness settled around me, I started to look for a place to sleep. I needed a group of small trees to help block the wind. In my feeble state of mind, I was still amazed. Nothing ever changes out here: tall trees, short trees, and always another tree. It would be easy to go insane looking at all of them. Without the compass, I probably would.

I was almost glad that I could stop walking for the day. Rest felt good until the aching cold settled, which had become worse than walking, which I hated even worse. Now, I had developed a wheeze in my chest. Each breath I inhaled rattled my lungs, and it was setting in fast. I was weak and needed food.

Soon, real soon, or I would become too weak to walk. The race was on, the crowd was cheering, and the finish line was close. Starvation was in the lead. Freezing and blood poisoning were a close second. Now, I had pneumonia settling in, and I was a mess—irreparable. Like old cars sent to the crusher to be recycled, I wouldn't be sent anywhere; I just recycled where I died.

It hadn't started snowing yet, but I was pretty sure I would see new snow by morning. I started making a place to sleep if sleep was possible. I stuck the snowshoes in the snow, pointing up, making it easier to find them in the morning. It took so long to get things accomplished. I had the ground cleared of snow and then the limbs.

I slowly removed the axe hanging from my neck. I dreaded what was coming next, but I had to do it. I half-heartedly swung the axe, and when it connected with the limb, a shock wave of pain rushed through my body. I yelled. I swung again and yelled again.

By the time I finished chopping the first limb free, I was crying. My hands were rebelling, telling me they were no longer capable of doing physical work. But neither was the rest of my body. I chopped—I cried. I chopped again, and I cried again. By the time I finished, there was a river of water running. I cut three limbs, which wasn't enough for good coverage, but I would make it. I packed snow on top of them and then over my exposed legs. I might survive the night if I could keep the wind off of me. Then, I thought, *"Might,"* that's the key word here.

I was too cold to sleep. The shivering and aching wouldn't allow it. So, I turned on the flashlight, aimed the beam, and slowly moved it across the ground in front of me. It was a waste of time and battery power, but I had nothing else to do. I moved it from left to right and back again.

Then, out of nowhere, something moved into the light. I flinched. A natural reflex! I thought I was going to be attacked again. If it had been another wolf, by the time I flinched, it would have already been over. But it wasn't!

It was a rabbit, the first real live animal. I couldn't believe it was true! *Two plus two equals four,* I thought. I wasn't dreaming. My next question: *Am I delirious? Seeing something that wasn't actually there?* The rabbit hopped once, totally unconcerned that I was there.

Food, I thought next. I slowly removed the gun from my pocket. I did this slowly, not because I was afraid I would scare it away; I couldn't get my fingers to move right. Now, I was holding the gun out in front of me in my right hand. The gloves were too fat to fit inside the trigger guard. It seemed as if it took me forever to pull my right glove off with my left hand.

Any second, I thought I would see the rabbit hop away, but it didn't. The cold, burning steel of the gun hurt my hand. Now, I was aiming it at the rabbit. *Could I do this?* I've never killed anything before. I was having second guesses. A wave of sadness hit me: *The poor rabbit.* I had to have food.

As I pulled the trigger, the amount of pain that shot up my arm was unimaginable. More pain than I had ever felt before in my life. The powder flash momentarily blinded me.

A split second before I lost eyesight, I saw the rabbit roll in the snow. I no longer cared about food. The recoil from the shot sent my hand flying backward up over my head, and I could no longer hang on, causing the gun to fly through the air, landing in the snow somewhere behind me. I no longer cared about it, either.

I screamed for all I was worth. I pulled my right hand up to my chest, holding it with my left. I fell over onto my right side, crying harder than I ever had in my life. My hand felt as though it had been smashed in a large vise.

From my wrist to my fingertips, everything throbbed; I could count each heartbeat. I thought the skin in my palm and my fingers were going to split open. With each heartbeat, I could feel my hand swell. While I cried, I took short breaths, and the pain grew. I could feel myself passing out. As the shock in my hand lessened, the pain continued to grow. I screamed; I couldn't take much more.

When I came to, I had no idea how long I had been out. I was glad I had. The pain was bad but not unbearable. I lay on the ground, waiting for it to leave. It was a great battle putting the glove back on, but what little heat my body could give it would help.

As the pain eased, I thought, *That was a really good idea, Madie. What's your next great stunt?* There would be none.

I pulled the three limbs off using my left hand. Then, I stood, retrieved the flashlight, and looked for the rabbit. I found it only six feet away from where I was sitting under my blanket of pine. The poor thing died with its eyes open. The sadness I felt for the rabbit was greater than my pain. I stood there, looking at the rabbit and the snow-covered with blood. The tears ran. This was the first warm-blooded thing I had ever killed.

I'm sorry, bunny, you didn't deserve this, you poor thing. I dropped to my knees. I had a bittersweet feeling. I was excited to have food. God sacrificed the rabbit to give me one more day.

Until now, I had serious doubts that I would have enough strength to last until tomorrow. I tried to hold the knife in my right hand, but I couldn't. It would be some time before I was able to use it again—if at all, my time was short.

I managed to use the knife with my left hand. It was the most disgusting thing I have ever done. This rabbit had brought two firsts for me. I put a piece of the meat in my mouth, gagging, but began chewing and gagging again. It was warm and mushy, but it didn't taste bad; it was just the thought of raw meat. I managed to eat both back legs and then put the front legs in my pockets for food for tomorrow.

The small amount of food made me feel much better. It's amazing how the little things mean so much. Finally, one for me. *Thank you,* I thought to whoever up there had helped me.

17
CHAPTER

The night was unbearable. I slept—if that's what it was called—maybe more like short cat naps. I woke up the last time for the night. I was in the seventh level of hell, only there was no heat. I was far below that; the cold, burning, searing pain reeked through my body. Ms. Nature had to have the upper hand; she couldn't stand the fact that I had food.

I was so stiff I couldn't stand.

Another new winner, I thought to myself, *a night colder than the one before.*

I was glad I didn't know the actual temperature. How long did I have before hypothermia set in, taking control of what was left of my body? At least it didn't snow; I was thankful for that. The little things were keeping me alive.

It took all the effort I could find just to stand. I was pretty sure I would set a Guinness record, the first person still alive with rigor mortis in their joints. I couldn't move, I wasn't in pain, I just couldn't move. That wasn't a good sign. I didn't know what that meant, but I knew what that was telling me. The congestion in my chest had increased dramatically overnight.

Soon, even though Craig and I wouldn't lay beside each other for all of eternity, we would be with each other. That's all that mattered.

It was unbelievable how much time it took me to tie the snowshoes with my left hand, but I didn't care. I had to focus on each little movement. It was as though I was drunk; the eye-to-hand coordination was gone. My brain was the last thing to go, and now it had started. I had a feeling I would be walking around in a vegetative state before the end. At least I would feel no pain.

I fumbled for the compass. There was no sun, but I knew south wasn't in the direction I thought it was. I pushed myself, taking the first step and then the second. I could feel both feet rolling from side to side in pools of blood under the skin. It felt like I had balloons filled with water from the ankles down. My feet were gone, but there was no pain. I would walk until I took the last step. I would be dead before I hit the ground, and that became my new mission. There would be no sleeping tonight; I feared if I laid down, I would never get up.

I would walk a short distance and then stop to rest. I did so, leaning against a tree, standing up. My energy was gone, so I did this many times in the morning. I thought about the rabbit. It gave up its life for nothing; I was too far gone and too far from home. Each time I rested, I heard his words, *"You won't make it."* He was probably right. But that made me move on, more than he would ever know.

By mid-afternoon, I was barely moving. It hurt to breathe; my lungs were functioning at far less than half capacity as the bitter cold was slowly freezing them. As I walked, I tried to occupy myself, so I came up with my own poem.

There was a ragged woman who walked a ragged mile to survive a ragged end. Craig, I'm nothing on my own; please let me come home.

I said that over and over. I had to keep my thoughts on something so when I did fall over, I wouldn't know it.

Something wasn't right; I stopped to look around. Something other than what I had been looking at, which was the ground just three feet ahead of each step. The pine trees were gone, and the ground was flat like a tabletop, as far as I could see. Birch trees were abundant, and a few hardwood trees were mixed in. I rested as I looked around.

I wanted to sit down so badly, maybe even sleep, but I wouldn't let myself do it. *You won't make it,* echoed through my head. He was still there, pushing me. I walked on, far more bent over than the past days. Maybe it was helping me keep the momentum moving; I couldn't tell.

I walked a good while, and then it happened. I fell over. I felt myself bounce in the snow. I lay there, not trying to get up, hoping to fall asleep, freezing to death while doing so.

For the first time, the snow felt good, like lying on a bed—my death bed. I had accepted that, the ragged end with no more little things. They've tallied up and drew the equal sign, which was the big one. I looked around; I wanted to know what my cemetery looked like. Then, I looked at the area close to me, which would be my burial plot. Not only would I have no headstone, but neither would Craig.

I'm sorry, Craig, I failed you, I thought. Everything was shutting off and closing up. The sign had been hung: going out of business. I closed my eyes, waiting.

I was delirious. I was back running a 10K race with Craig. As always, he was three steps ahead of me. He never slowed, even toward the end of the race.

Then, he yelled at me, "Madie, what are you doing? Now is not the time to slow down; the end is just up ahead."

I jumped. I heard that plain as day. I opened my eyes, but he wasn't there, and I wasn't running the race with him. Was I hallucinating? But my eyes were closed.

"What do you want from me? I gave it my best shot; there's nothing left." My voice was nothing more than a crackling whisper, and my throat was raw.

"I want you to finish this."

That did it. I never believed in ghosts. I do believe in angels, but they don't intervene. I know I heard what I heard. It was a battle standing back up, but I managed. I wanted to get two sticks to use as crutches, but I wouldn't be able to hang on to them. So, I was back to walking until I fell over dead in my tracks.

I didn't know what time of the day it was, but it didn't matter. My steps were nothing more than shuffles, covering only inches per step. My feet were failing fast; it now felt like I had bags of water under them. I tried to move my fingers but couldn't. But I continued to walk, taking quick, short breaths. It felt as if I was going to suffocate any minute. *There was a ragged woman who walked a ragged mile to survive a ragged end.* What was the rest? I couldn't remember the end.

I wouldn't see tomorrow because I wouldn't survive the night. I walked because that's all I knew what to do. I was waiting for death—the grim reaper.

Then, I walked out onto a lake. I was yards from the shore before I realized it. I stopped and realized I hadn't covered more than a mile since I heard his voice. It had taken a very long time, though.

I looked to my left at the shoreline, which was nothing new. Just another lake like I've seen before. When I reached the halfway point, I realized it was much bigger, more than a mile to the south shore. I started out on my death march.

There was a ragged woman who walked a ragged mile to survive a ragged end. I don't know why, but I liked saying that; it kept my mind occupied. I covered only four steps and then looked to my right. Why, I don't know. I guess because I had nothing else to do.

Now, I knew I was hallucinating. I had to be! I saw a dark object out on the ice only yards from the shore. I stopped, but it didn't move. It had to be a deer or a lone wolf. I continued to look. My thoughts were moving in slow motion. It still didn't move. I looked away.

Two plus two. It took much longer for the answer of four. I wasn't dreaming. I looked back and saw that it was still there, only a quarter mile away.

What was it? I asked myself.

I had the usual answer: *Doesn't matter.*

Then, I thought I saw it move only slightly. I watched and thought. I couldn't see wasting the energy to walk over there only to have it run away. I needed to go south. I tried to raise my arms to scare it away, but I couldn't. They wouldn't rise any higher than my waist. They were in the beginning stages of what my feet and hands had gone through.

Well, it doesn't matter anymore, I thought. *What's a quarter mile out of the way? Dead was dead, and tonight is the night.*

I started walking in the direction of the dark figure.

Halfway there, I expected it to run into the woods at any time. I continued on at a snail's pace. I wanted to yell at it to satisfy my curiosity and watch it run. I couldn't; I tried to speak, but only a crackly whisper escaped me.

Why won't you just let me die and get this over with? I thought.

At least, in the woods, the next tree was only several feet away. Out here on the lake, it was a monumental task. *It's too far. I'll never make it to the other side.* I was drained and exhausted. I could barely find enough strength for the next six-inch step and the one after that. I wanted to sit down. But I didn't want to stop on the lake. I wanted to die in the woods. I guess I had privacy there, my graveyard sanctuary.

As I got closer, it looked like a human. I shook my head, trying to clear it. *Was I seeing clearly?* I sure wasn't thinking clearly. I had to be hallucinating. Maybe it was my nightmares haunting me during the day, the death dealer trying to get me.

Then, it stood up, and I was less than two hundred yards away.

Human, I said to myself. I didn't feel happy or sad; I was too far gone and moving in my vegetative state.

He was looking in my direction as I walked toward him. I was less than fifty feet away. He had a box sitting on the ice and a fishing pole—he was ice fishing!

"Hi there!"

I said "Hi," but only in a whisper. I knew he didn't hear me. I walked closer.

"I don't see many people out here. Where you headed?"

I didn't try to talk. I walked up to him.

"Hi, I'm Jim."

I stood there looking at him. His voice sounded so good. "Can you help me?" It hurt to talk even though I was barely whispering.

"Sure, are you lost?"

"No."

"What do you need then?"

"Can you tell me where the nearest hospital is?"

His look went from happy and friendly to a quizzical frown.

"Yeah, sure. The nearest town is twenty miles away, but it's another thirty to the closest hospital."

It took me several moments to do the addition in my head. I felt my shoulders drop several inches. My whole body slumped. It was too far, five days if I were healthy, but now, at the speed I was moving, it would take more than ten.

"Thank you." I took one step and stopped.

"Which direction?"

"Due south."

Huh, how ironic, I thought.

I wouldn't see tomorrow, I was sure of it. But I wasn't thinking clearly, if at all. I had to get to the finish line; that's all I knew. I looked at the compass and started walking.

I took several more steps and then stopped. "Would you do me a favor?"

"Yes," was all he said.

"Tell our friends we didn't make it… I'm sorry." Then, I turned and slowly started walking.

"Wait, I can help."

I stopped again, turned halfway around, and looked at him. It took too much effort with the snowshoes to turn all the way. I saw a worried look on his face. He had only a stocking cap on his head. He was clean-cut; I guessed him to be in his late fifties. He had on heavy winter gear but wasn't dressed like I was.

"Aren't you cold?"

"No, I came out to fish for a couple of hours. When I get cold, I'll go back. I get a little stir-crazy being inside all the time. But, enough about me. Are you cold?"

"I'm frozen."

"You said, 'We.' Is there someone with you?"

"Not anymore."

"Does he need help? I have a snowmobile and…"

"No, there's nothing you can do for him. Besides, what's left of him is too far away."

My throat was killing me from speaking. He stood there for several seconds, looking me over. My mind was numb, joining in the parade with the rest of my body. Now, he had a worried frown on his face.

"How far away can we send somebody?"

I had to think for a minute. I had long past lost track of the days. I barely remembered how many miles I estimated I had walked.

"Maybe two hundred and fifty miles."

"Oh my God! You've walked that far?"

"Yes."

He walked toward me. "You've got blood on your jacket. Are you bleeding?"

"No."

"You're not hurt?" he asked, looking at my jacket.

"No."

One-word answers didn't hurt as much. "Yes, I'm frozen."

He grabbed my arm. "Come on, I'll take you to my house. It's not far away, less than a quarter mile in the woods."

I was thinking a little more clearly, maybe because I was with someone. "I need to go to the hospital. Can you give me a ride?"

He looked at my snowshoes but didn't question them. "Yes, you're in luck. I'm a retired doctor. I have a few supplies with me; I would feel lost without them."

"Yes, you can't help me here." I started walking in the direction of his tracks leading toward the woods. He still had his arm wrapped around mine.

I shuffled along. I would see tomorrow, but I still couldn't move any faster.

He didn't ask and never said a word. I felt myself being lifted off of the ground; he was carrying me. I had taken my last step ever on my own two feet.

He was strong for his age. It was obvious he kept himself in shape. He never slowed, walking in the deep snow and carrying me with my snowshoes still on. He barely broke out of his normal breathing pattern.

My eyes were closed. I laid my head on his shoulder with my face at the base of his neck. I had truly been saved by a stranger. I didn't cry; there were no emotions left in me. I was as close to being an empty shell as possible without being dead.

I counted the cadence of his steps with his breathing. Two steps inhaling, two steps exhaling, and I could feel his heartbeat. How I wished I was in Craig's arms! My trip from hell was over. Now, I would have to face my new life from hell. Nothing would ever be the same, emotionally or physically. But I was alive. I had made it; I had survived the impossible.

"You're a good man," I whispered.

I don't know if he heard me. He never acknowledged me, and I never opened my eyes.

"We're almost there. I'll get you inside and see what shape you're in."

"Not… good."

It felt as if he had increased his speed. I had to be getting heavy by now, but, as I thought on, maybe not. At five foot six inches tall, I weighed one hundred twenty-seven pounds when this started. *Not now! How much weight did I lose? What had my body deteriorated to?*

His house was a small log cabin with two stories and a wrap-around porch on the front and two sides. A large front window faced toward the lake. He carefully sat me in a chair close to the front door.

"We'll get these… I guess snowshoes off your feet first."

"They saved my life."

I watched him try and untie them. The knots were too tight and frozen. "I wouldn't have gotten this far."

I dug and slid one of the knives from my pocket. He was looking down, and he didn't see me handing it to him.

"This was one of the death dealers." I had it lying crossways in my hand and couldn't close my fingers.

He looked at the knife, then at me, and back to the knife. I could tell he had many questions to ask but said nothing. He took the knife and cut the rope around each foot.

"Wow, it is sharp, a lethal weapon."

"Only the owners were lethal."

He frowned, stood, and opened the front door. Then, he turned and picked me up.

"I can walk."

Down inside, I really didn't want to.

"No need to, that's what I'm for."

He carried me inside and sat me down at a massive and beautiful kitchen table. With all the clothes I had on, I couldn't feel the heat I had been longing for. He went to close the front door. I fumbled at the zipper on the outer jacket. With the heavy gloves on and the frozen sticks that were once my fingers, I was failing badly.

On his walk back from the door, he noticed.

"Here, let me get that for you."

He unclasped the chin strap and removed the first hood, sliding it behind me. I noticed a slight frown on his face. Then, he unzipped the outer jacket, and the frown grew, but neither of us spoke. He removed the left sleeve and then the right. He leaned me forward and removed the jacket from behind me, dropping it on the floor beside us. He undid the pants, wrapped his right arm behind my back, and lifted me off the chair. The nylon material offered no resistance; the pants slid to my knees, exposing the second pair.

"My, two sets of clothing, you were prepared."

"They kept me alive. They belonged to the second death dealer."

"Who?"

"One of the men who killed my husband."

He started the process over with the second jacket. When he went to pull the sleeves over my hands, it hurt, and I moaned loudly. The inner seal was too tight. He walked to a drawer next to the sink, removed a pair of scissors, and returned.

"Don't cut my clothes; I want to save them." I tolerated the pain, to speak.

He looked at me. "They're of no use to you anymore."

"I want to save them. It's all I have left."

"Alright, well, let's remove the gloves first."

I had no idea of what was coming next. He started pulling on the tip of the glove on my index finger on my right hand. I muffled the yell, and he stopped. As he pulled on the second, third, and fourth fingers, I moaned loudly. The glove had slid only a quarter of an inch.

"Do the thumb first."

He pulled, and I yelled. He returned to the fingers. I tried very hard not to be loud. I gritted my teeth, but I couldn't help it. The moaning and yelling helped relieve the tingling and pain in my hand. It felt as if I had thousands of needles trying to poke through my skin.

"We really need to cut them off."

"No," I was breathing heavily, "I can do this!"

I didn't want to tell him; he would think I was an idiot. *Maybe I am?* Craig had bought them for me, along with the heavy winter gear. I couldn't destroy them.

"Just get a hold of the fingers and thumb, and don't stop pulling until it's off."

He did, and I yelled at a level I didn't think I was capable of. I laid my right hand on my right leg. I leaned over and pushed down on my wrist with my left arm. The pain was so intense I had my eyes squeezed shut, and I held my breath. I became sick and started to dry vomit. It took well over two minutes for the pain to ease.

Slowly, I lifted my head up and looked at him. He never moved and never said a word. He had a look of sadness and fear mixed together. He was looking at my hand. I looked down at it, and what I saw, I was not prepared for.

A mixture of colors combining one, something the Crayola crayon company had not yet named, a dark blue, black, purple, and maroon hue combination, reaching nearly to my wrist. The fingers and hand were swollen to twice the size, explaining why the glove had such a problem getting off. My skin didn't look like skin, just a charcoal chunk of frozen meat.

"Please, let me cut the left one off."

"No!" I looked down.

"I can't stand the pain for you."

"No."

When it was removed, I had to scream again. I sat in the chair, leaning forward, holding both hands suspended in the air. I was close to fainting, and if they were to be bumped or touched, that would have put me over the edge.

"That's it. I'm cutting the inner seals to pull the coat off."

I didn't argue. He carefully cut them so as not to touch my hands.

The coat was off and lying with the pants on the floor. The face mask was next. Things continued to decline. I felt him reach for the bottom of the mask at the base of my neck. He lifted it up over my chin, but something was wrong. It was pulling on the skin on my face and around my nose.

"Wait! Something's not right."

He stopped and leaned his face closer to mine. He lifted the mask away from my upper lip, trying to look underneath. He shook his head, and I knew it wasn't good.

"Pull the back up and over first."

He did. I closed my eyes as I felt the material, and something brushed down my face a second before it jerked my head backward. I yelled, "Ouch!"

Then I felt something run down my face on the right side of my nose, then past the corner of my mouth and down my chin. He quickly turned, took one step to the sink, and got the towel lying there. He held it against my face. Then I looked down at the face mask lying on my lap. My fear vanished; it turned to horror. The face mask was inside out, and I saw more than half of my hair stuck to it.

I took a deep breath.

"My hair? Why did it fall out?" I calmly asked.

Doesn't matter, I had bigger problems. What did I feel running down the side of my face? I could see Jim dabbing my face, but I couldn't feel it. Why? Questions were piling up faster than I could ask them.

It must be blood. I had to ask, "Is that blood?"

"Yes."

"Not good, huh?"

"No."

I was the one with a sore throat and could hardly speak. Now, he was the one giving the one-word answers.

"Why?"

"Why, not good, or why blood?"

"Well... both."

I could feel my hands start tingling, and a low level of pain was creeping in. They were trying to come back to life. But I knew by their looks that they were *The Day Of The Living Dead*—zombies imitating life.

"Severe tissue breakdown answers both of your questions."

I could tell he wasn't telling me everything; he answered me without telling me anything.

"Come on, Doc, tell me what you're avoiding. I can take it, especially after what I've just been through... you have no idea."

He was shaking his head.

"Your nose, cartilage, and tissue around it... have died. Not to go into great medical detail, but the blood had nowhere to go."

"As black as my hands?"

"Yes."

"I fear my feet are much worse," was all I said. The pain in my hands was increasing.

He unlaced both boots. As he started pulling the right one off, he never looked up.

"Does that hurt?"

"No."

Both boots were off, and I could tell, even with the socks still on, my feet were swollen badly, but I already knew that.

The right sock came off first, and he started moving faster, removing the second one.

He mumbled, "Oh my God!"

I could barely see my toes, and my feet were swollen much more than I had expected. The skin was stretched tight, and they were twice the size they should have been. They weren't as black as my hands, more of a reddish purple.

He lightly poked my right foot with his finger, but I didn't feel it, and my skin didn't give.

The years of professionalism were coming through. He worked methodically, asking no questions and just diagnosing. He cut my blue jeans up to each knee.

"Are my feet frozen solid?"

161

"Yes. When you said, out on the lake, that you were frozen, I had no idea."

"How could you? You saved my life; that's all that matters."

"Not yet."

He stood quickly, looked across the countertop, and then around the rest of the kitchen. I watched him as he took one step and then stopped. He looked to the front door and then back to my feet.

"You're not going to like me very much, but you have to go back into the cold."

He went to the front door, opened it, and started back to me.

"Why?"

It was the last thing I wanted to do, but I said nothing else.

"I imagine by now your hands are tingling."

"Yes."

"As your body warms up, it will immediately try to start healing itself, something that's not possible. Blood poisoning will wreak havoc on your internal organs. Your liver will become damaged, and your kidneys will start to shut down. If they haven't already… when was the last time you urinated?"

I had to think that was something I never kept track of. "I don't know; that's something I avoided as long as possible. It was just too cold."

"When?"

"I don't know. For the past few days, I haven't eaten much snow. My throat is too raw, and it hurts too much."

He asked nothing else. I was lifted off the floor, chair, and all. He sat me down in the middle of the doorway, facing the cold.

Now, with no heavy clothes on, I was instantly cold. I started shivering. I turned and looked at him; he was in the living room looking for something.

"How long do I have to stay here?"

My body was already aching, and I bent forward, trying to protect myself.

"Until the helicopter gets here and takes you to the hospital."

"I said there was nothing you could do for me here."

I was looking out at the lake.

"Yes, you were right. I had no idea. I'm sorry."

"It's not your fault, it's theirs."

18

CHAPTER

He had already dialed the number and had walked to the far end of the kitchen, talking into the phone, with his back to me. Whatever he was saying, I didn't care. Dying here in this chair, or in a hospital bed, or living life as a cripple, my life was over.

His phone conversation was short. He was walking toward me.

"The helicopter will be here in one hour; it's coming from Montreal. That's the closest hospital that has the capability of handling something like this… I'm sorry, the proper way of saying it is the closest one that can help you."

"It's okay, Doc. Why the big hurry? Why don't you just drive me there? I want you to tell me the truth. Remember what I asked you out on the lake?"

He nodded. "It still stands; tell them I'm sorry."

We were silent for a moment, both thinking our separate thoughts. "Where am I?"

"Fifteen miles north of a small town called St. David-de-Falardeau, roughly four hundred people live there. It's the last town before nowhere begins."

Craig and I chose Quebec. It was straight north of Massachusetts, desolate and untouched by humans.

"Yes, I know. We set down on a little lake at the north end of the Mistassini provincial reserve. We were to be there for only two weeks. We had a GPS and were going to hike due west fifty miles and be picked up again."

I was shaking violently. Parts of me might have been frozen, but at least the rest was warm in the heavy gear. The only protection I had on now, from the bitter cold, was a pair of blue jeans and a flannel shirt. My head was hanging down with my forearms pressed against my chest. Both hands were hanging forward in mid-air, offering no heat. I was afraid to bump them against anything.

"Can I have a blanket at least?"

My whole body was aching.

"Not yet."

"Your home is going to get cold. Just put me out on the porch and close the door."

"It's fine."

He had put one of the kitchen chairs beside me, as close as possible, and was sitting on it.

"What day is it?"

"Thursday."

"No, the day of the month."

"The eighteenth of December."

My thoughts were slowing down again. How fast the body reacts in self-preservation. Doing the math was a problem.

"Thirty-one. We arrived there on November eleventh. It took me thirty-one days to walk two hundred fifty miles… what does that average to?"

He was silent for only a moment. "Eight miles a day."

"Not good."

"No, I would say that's not good. It's amazing—astronomical, the last step before humanly possible starts in winter time."

"Each day I always thought was my last step." I was shaking, and my body was going numb. My hands had quit tingling; they were now aching.

"You said it was their fault. Who are they?"

"I named them the death dealers; there were two of them. I never knew their real names… all of this because of the stupid fish I forgot. We caught fish for dinner that night, and I left them hanging on a tree. I had to go back and get them."

I went on and told him the story, going into great detail. I had to pause several times to wipe the cold tears away. I lost track of time; reliving the past was still so vivid in my mind. I went on and on about the bear, the only truly good thing that happened to me, saving my life and being a good companion. I didn't look back at him; I just talked, and he just listened, never saying a word.

"It's time to get you ready. The helicopter should be here anytime."

Then, his phone rang. He answered it and listened, then said, "Thank you."

Then, he stood. "Ten minutes."

"What? Do you have ESP?"

"No, a watch."

"I'm numb; I can't move."

"You don't have to… that's an incredible journey, one few could survive from. I'm honored to have met you; you're an amazing woman."

Somewhere in the middle of my story, he had wrapped a heavy blanket around me. I was too involved in reliving the past to notice. He lifted me out of the chair and slid it back into the kitchen with his foot. Then, ever so carefully, he closed the front door while still holding me. While carrying me back to the lake to meet the helicopter, he talked to me, and I listened.

"It's going to be warm in the helicopter. We're going to give you a sedative to slow your system down. It won't put you under; you'll just feel very relaxed."

"Doesn't matter; I've learned to accept what comes and goes."

He was silent for only a moment. "You never told me your name."

"Madison. Madison Chanhansen. Call me Madie; my friends call me Madie. Thank you for saving my life."

Again, I had my face buried in his coat at the base of the neck. I heard the thump, thump of the helicopter coming over the treetops. I started to cry; I had made it.

"You saved yourself. I'm just here to put you back together."

What's left of me, I thought.

My future flashed through my mind. I would miss running the 10K marathons, and I would miss Craig. Mother Nature had won, in a way. Without a doubt, after seeing my feet, I would lose them.

"You don't have to go with me. What about your home?"

"It will be fine. I could never walk away from the bravest woman I will ever meet."

I cried. I never considered myself brave; I was just unlucky and scared.

The helicopter landed on the lake, just yards from the shore. He turned his back from the rotor wash that covered us with snow, trying to protect me.

"Kind of like the blizzards you experienced out there," he said loudly over the noise.

I barely heard him.

"No, not too bad."

I had my arms around his neck, crying.

The people from the helicopter ran, carrying a gurney. I was whisked up and put inside in no time. The door was closed, and I felt us lifting off the lake. I closed my eyes; I was on my way to face a new life.

"We're going to start the IV. You'll begin to feel very sluggish," Jim said. I never felt them stick the needle in my arm.

Jim was right. For the first time since having the bad fortune of meeting the death dealers, I felt relaxed. My muscles didn't ache, and my hands and feet didn't hurt. My body felt as if it was floating in a pool of warm water. I don't know why, but I started crying again.

One of the nurses, a female, put her hand on my shoulder. With a concerned, sad look, she asked, "Madie, is everything alright? Are you in pain?"

"No." I couldn't wipe the tears away.

My arms were too heavy to lift. "I'm happy to be alive, but I feel guilty. Craig should be here with me."

She looked over at Jim with the look of: *What is she talking about?* Jim shook his head. We both knew what it meant. I wanted to say that I wasn't fragile—you can talk about my past. I didn't, it didn't matter.

"What's your name?" I asked. I could feel my words becoming slurred.

"Sarah, and this is Mike."

She looked at the man sitting to her right.

"Hi, Mike. Thank you for coming out here to help me."

"Our pleasure," Mike said, "so we have a little frostbite, hey? Not a problem, we'll get you fixed up in no time."

"Yes, I couldn't beat Mother Nature."

My eyes were heavy. It was a struggle to keep them open. I saw a slight frown on Mike's face as he turned and looked at Jim.

"Mind if we take a look?" Sarah asked. "Are you warm?"

I shook my head no, then yes. It was easier than talking.

I looked at the ceiling. I didn't feel the blanket being lifted from my feet.

"Oh my God," Sarah said.

Then, she whispered, "It's the worst I've ever seen."

She looked back at me. "Don't you worry, honey, we'll take care of you."

Jim nodded. I didn't know if it meant yes, they'll take care of me, or it's the worst they've ever seen. Probably the latter.

The rest of the flight to the hospital was quiet. I wouldn't let myself fall asleep. I fought it all the way. I wanted to hear the final prognosis as if I didn't already know.

We landed, and I was whisked inside; they knew I was coming. It wasn't utter chaos as I would expect. Every move was calculated and precise. They'd gone through this countless times.

Jim disappeared. I was placed on a large examination table, my clothes were quickly cut away, and a sheet was placed over me.

I was talking, not to anyone in particular. I was more out of it than with it. I was rehashing my story, not for them but for me. The only way I could cope with it. I felt guilty; I had made it, but Craig hadn't.

I heard the door open but didn't look in that direction. During the whole time, several nurses were working on me at once. I didn't stop talking. I wasn't nervous, just sad.

Then, I heard Jim's voice: *"I want a complete analysis ASAP. Tell the lab her blood work takes priority."*

"Doctor, she's delirious. She's been telling us quite a story, sleeping in subzero weather, eating raw fish that she speared herself, and two men chasing her day and night. And how she befriended a wild bear who happened to kill one of them," the nurse said.

"It's all true," the doctor said, looking at me.

"Oh my God!" she replied.

"I want to take a bath," I said.

"Madie, we need to get you into the operating room as soon as possible."

"Please, let them give me a bath. It's been thirty-some days, and I smell like a goat."

Our eyes met. "What's a few more minutes going to matter?"

Jim smiled.

"Okay, how can I say no to you? When they're finished examining you, take a quick one," he turned to the head nurse, "you know what to do."

"Thank you for saving me. I will never forget you."

Jim looked at me and frowned. "You're not going to die."

"It doesn't matter."

I relaxed and let them do their thing. I must have nodded off because the next thing I felt was being lowered into a portable tub of water. I opened my eyes, and there was a whole room full of nurses surrounding me, each one holding an arm and a leg to keep them out of the water, another one tending to the IV line hooked to my arm, and the last one holding a sponge.

The water was only lukewarm, but it still felt good. The bath only lasted a minute, two at the most. I saw a mirror along the wall.

"Before you put me back on the table, I want to take a look at myself." Then, they lifted me out of the portable tub, wrapping a large white towel around my body.

The nurse nodded. She seemed to be in charge of all of the others working on me. They held me in front of the mirror. "Take the towel off."

They did—I gasped. What I saw was that I wasn't prepared for it. I knew I had lost a lot of weight, but it had gone beyond that. There was no muscle mass left on my body, and I could count each rib.

I could literally see each bone in my body, and my skin was so transparent that it was wrapped loosely around each bone. My hip and pelvic bones were grossly protruding, showing hollow spots where there weren't supposed to be any. My knees, shoulders, and elbows stuck out as if they had been reformed. My face looked old; my cheekbones looked twice their size. Dark, sunken eye sockets and my eyebrows were gone. But what looked the worst were my legs from the knees down.

They were as black as both hands and were puffy and swollen. I was sure if a needle was stuck in them, they would squirt blood due to the pressure under the dead skin. Now, it was clear to me why I had no energy left to walk and why it had become such a challenge.

I was a mess—a walking skeleton—I shouldn't be alive.

I nodded. Even though I was out of it, I could still mentally process what I was seeing.

Thank you, Craig, for pushing me on. I wouldn't have made it, I thought.

The nurses placed me back on the table and put a sheet over me. Before I knew it, I was left alone, the solitude which I had grown accustomed to, and I had years of it ahead of me.

My eyes were closed. The bath, the drugs, the soft mattress, and the warmth had me relaxed. I wasn't asleep; I could hear things going on and people talking off in the distance. Time no longer mattered. I didn't have to contend with Mother Nature or battle with Father Time. The miles walked were now a thing of the past. Everyone creates their own problems, and I have created mine. It was my idea, the trip of all trips, one I would pay for for the rest of my life.

No Craig! A feeling of guilt I would never overcome, no matter how many shrinks I would see, would ever cure me of that.

Jim walked in, holding several sheets of paper, no doubt test results. He looked somewhat down.

Neither of us said anything for a moment.

"I'm not a wimp."

He tried to smile but only accomplished a small grin. "No, you've already proven that. I need to tell you before we operate on you."

"Give it to me, the real version with no sugar coating."

"No, I wouldn't do that to you. I hardly know you, but yet, I already consider you a dear friend."

"Come on, Doc, give me the news."

"My friends call me Jim."

Then, he raised his eyebrows and inhaled deeply.

"Your kidneys have suffered damage from blood poisoning. We'll filter your blood during the operation and then see what happens in the days to come. Your liver and pancreas have minor damage, but nothing you can't overcome. You have a severe case of bronchitis and strep throat. You're severely dehydrated and borderline diabetic, again from your pancreas, and a mild case of hypothermia. That's just on the inside. You're going to lose both feet…"

He paused. "I believe you already knew that. We'll know more once we put you under and start operating, but I believe you'll also lose your right hand and all of the fingers on your left. We can maybe save your left thumb. You're going to have to undergo several operations of plastic surgery on your nose. I believe your upper lip will survive, but there will never be much feeling in it."

He paused again. "I'm sorry."

I nodded my head. "It's just a thing, it'll pass. When are you going to start operating?"

"For someone who is about to lose both feet and basically both hands, you're taking it very well. You have a good attitude—all the people who come here should take after you."

Then, he thought a moment. I didn't ask.

"They're setting up the operating room as we speak."

"Are you doing it?" I asked.

"Yes, I'm going to help you, but yet, I feel guilty."

"No need to. Now, you've saved my life twice. I owe you," I said.

"Is there anyone you would like us to call parents, brothers, or sisters?"

"No. My parents have been gone for several years, and I was the only one."

"What about your husband's parents?"

"He never had any," was all I said.

No need to go into detail there. "So much for retirement, eh Doc?"

"Jim, remember my friends?"

I liked Jim. He was so modest and down to earth.

"What about your wife?"

"There isn't one. I've been divorced for eight years."

Then, Jim slid the chair that was sitting in the corner of the room up beside my bed and sat in it.

"There's plenty of good prosthetics available in the states. I will find one for you when the time comes."

Then, he was silent again, deep in thought. I could tell he was somewhat sad. "As weak as your system is, the operation is going to be hard on you. You're looking at a fairly long recovery time."

"I have nothing else to do; it doesn't matter."

Then, I went on to tell him how I came about coining that phrase. The death dealer—how right he was.

Then, I asked, "How long will the operation take?"

"Six to eight hours," Jim replied.

I nodded.

"I need the rest. I haven't had six good hours of sleep in a very long time. When I wake, I will feel like running a marathon."

Then, I smiled, trying to lighten the mood.

Jim smiled, although it was weak.

"Cheer up, Jim. I'll plow through this, one way or another. What's going to be hard on me is no Craig. That I don't know if I will ever overcome."

Jim looked into my eyes. "You're an amazing woman."

"I think I've heard that before."

I smiled. "Maybe from you."

"Yes."

The nurse came into the room. "We're ready, Doctor."

19
CHAPTER

I woke up and slowly opened my eyes. I looked through the narrow slits in my eyelids. The white light blinded me, so I closed them again. My next thought was, *Was I approaching the pearly gates?*

Nothing on my body hurt, and I wasn't warm or cold. I tried to move my arms and then my legs but couldn't. I could feel nothing. I listened but heard nothing.

This is it, I thought.

I didn't survive. I was confused, and my thoughts were scrambled.

Where was I? Was I dreaming? Did I die in the wilderness?

Nothing was clear to me. Then, I tried to swallow, which hurt. The pain was severe. I was still alive. I realized I was in the hospital, but what part of it I didn't know. I tried to talk, but nothing happened.

As I lay there, I could think and hear but nothing else. My face itched, but I couldn't scratch it. I moved my cheek muscles, trying to relieve the itching sensation. My eyes were still closed, but I sensed someone standing beside me.

"Madie, you're in the recovery room. It will take a few minutes for you to fully come around. I will stay here with you," a soft female voice said.

"Please, scratch my face."

I could feel myself saying that, but I didn't hear it. Nothing happened. It was obvious to me the nurse didn't hear it either.

"You came through the operation very well. I was with you the whole time."

As I lay there, I thought, but I didn't fight it.

I could feel my thoughts coming through more clearly.

How well could I be? I'm limbless, well, half limbless anyway. Digit less, for sure, I thought.

I mumbled. I knew what I was saying, but it just wasn't audible.

She patted my shoulder. "I'm still here. It will be confusing for you for a few more minutes."

It was! I had never been put to sleep before. This wasn't like waking up after a night's sleep.

She patted my shoulder again. "Take deep breaths, that will help you."

I opened my eyes, ignoring the pain. I squinted.

I can do this, I said to myself.

More minutes passed, and I looked around the room. Finally, I tried to speak again. I looked into the nurse's eyes.

"Can you scratch my face?"

She smiled; she had heard me. "You have a bandage over your nose. That's what you feel. Can you tell me what part itches?"

I nodded no. I wiggled my cheek muscles, and this time, they moved.

"Is the tape bothering you?"

I could feel her pulling on the corners of the tape.

Relief!

I nodded yes.

"I can fix that for you. I'll use a different kind of tape."

She smiled again.

She was trying too hard to be nice. I didn't need babying, but I didn't tell her that. I didn't want to hurt her feelings or to sound rude.

Hours passed. I fell in and out of sleep; each time I woke, I felt better, telling myself incremental amounts, one step at a time. Now, I had another two hundred fifty miles to go. This time, it wouldn't be on my feet. I had another battle to overcome: what the first two hundred fifty miles had done to me.

I was asleep when Jim walked in. The nurse was gone. "Madie, are you awake? I need to tell you a few things."

I nodded.

"How are you feeling?"

"Crazy. My feet itch. Could you bring them in here so I could scratch them?"

Jim smiled.

"That's a first. It's not an uncommon thing for someone to say that their feet itch when they no longer have them. You're not crazy, but no one has ever asked me to bring them back."

I shrugged my shoulders. "Why is there a bandage on my face?"

172

"We had to remove most of your nose. Remember?"

"Most of it?"

"Yes, it will be fixed in due time."

"How am I going to blow it? It's gone."

Jim smiled. "It still works. We just removed the skin and cartilage, the outer shell. It has no functionary purpose other than cosmetic."

"Oh well," I said.

Jim frowned, becoming serious. "We had to remove both feet five inches above the ankles, where we could find good, live tissue."

"Well, that's good. At least I won't walk with a limp."

Jim laughed. "We did save your left thumb and forty percent of your left palm."

I raised my left arm.

"We're going to keep a close watch on it; you could still lose it."

"How long do I have to pee in a bag?"

That got a slight reaction from Jim.

"Well, until you're able to get around on your own. My guess: two months."

"Those nights, lying in a snow pile I had dug for protection, trying to sleep, I was so cold, I ached. Most of the time, I shivered so hard that it kept me awake. Down inside, I didn't think I would see this day. All I could think about was that I had lived to see another day. That was always the challenge.

"To walk as many miles the next day as I could, plus walking, kept me warm, but it wore me out. I looked forward to resting at night, but yet I hated it. So, this isn't so bad. Peeing in a bag because I have no feet to get up and go to the bathroom with will always be better than that. Come what may, I learned out there to live with what was given. An axe, and on the days I had two pockets full of fish, I felt fortunate. When they were empty, I still felt fortunate. I was still walking south."

Jim stood there listening.

"The morning I left the cave and the bear, I left a big slab of fish in the snow for the bear. When it wakes in the spring, it will find the fish. I hope it remembers me; I will always remember what it did for me. I will always remember you."

Now, the tears were flowing again, and I couldn't wipe them away.

"Thank you." I raised my right arm and wrapped the bandage around it to catch the tears.

"Here, let me get that for you."

I tried to smile in appreciation. "Just like the times ahead, when I'm alone, I'll adapt."

"Yes, I have no doubt about that. You have already proven that. You wouldn't be here if you couldn't."

"The one thing I've learned is that the body will adapt. You just have to do it mentally; that's the hard part."

Jim nodded. "I've never heard it put that way, but you're right."

"I'm not tough," I said as I wiped more tears away. "I cried more times than I can remember out there."

"You're only human, but you are the toughest person I will ever meet. I wouldn't want to try to keep up with you. You would have left me in your dust out there."

Jim smiled. "It's only temporary. You'll be walking by summer."

Days passed. I was eating three meals a day. I didn't like the idea that a nurse always had to feed me, but I had no choice. I was feeling better, and I had energy; I just had no way to use it.

The nurse brought a tray in. It was dinner, mashed potatoes and gravy, Salisbury steak, and corn. As she was feeding me, she talked, saying, "I'm sorry. I know hospital food isn't that good."

"Don't ever let anyone tell you it's not. This is the best food I've had for a long time. Sure beats raw frozen fish."

She became serious. By now, I was certain that it had gotten around the hospital of my ordeal. "Yes, I'm sure it is."

"I really do like it," I said. "You have nothing to be sorry about."

She didn't know what to say. I felt like it was a rule among the hospital staff to ask no questions. Maybe they felt uneasy about it, with me lying here with only stumps. Maybe they felt sorry for me and didn't know how to handle it. Several different nurses tended to me, never asking a question. The last thing I wanted was for them to feel sorry for me. The river will continue to flow—life will go on.

So, I decided to break the ice, but this time around, it wasn't with the axe. "I've had several different nurses helping me, and I do appreciate it more than you know. Why don't any of you ever ask me any questions about how I ended up like this? It's like you're afraid to talk about it."

She looked away from me, and then I knew I was right.

"Well, we are. We've had frostbite patients here before, but never someone like you in such bad shape. I don't want to make things worse. We're here to help you."

Then, she looked at me sadly.

"Did Jim, I mean the doctor, tell you not to talk about it?"

Down inside, I didn't believe he would.

"No."

"Did he tell you about the things that happened to me out there?"

"Yes… well, some of it. He didn't go into great detail."

I was right again.

"Jim is a good man. He saved my life. If he wasn't out ice fishing that day, I would have walked right past, never seeing his house."

"Oh yes, everyone here, including the other doctors like him."

Then, she loosened up a little and leaned toward me.

"We can't say that about some of the doctors if you know what I mean."

I nodded. "There are always one or two bad apples in the bushel."

She laughed. "Yes, there is. I'm still on the afternoon shift tomorrow. What do you say? Can I sneak in some real food? What have you missed most?"

"That would be great."

I had to think about that for a minute. "How about a large pizza of your choosing, and you can help me eat it."

Her eyes lit up. "Sure, that would be great, extra cheese for starters."

I looked at her name tag, "Connie." Before, I didn't bother. I had to get more involved, so they wouldn't feel uneasy. I was going to be here for a while.

"I wasn't lying. The hospital food isn't that bad. But pizza is better." I smiled. She wasn't so bad.

"If you don't mind, what was it like out there?"

"I don't mind at all."

Then, I paused for a moment, thinking.

"Lonely, the last half of the way, the first half was scary. Running for my life, and it was always cold. I guess that's obvious."

Then, I went on and told her the story, in reverse from the end to the beginning—the cliff notes version. Several times, I saw her eyes become wet. Then, when I told her how Craig died, she cried. Tears flowed down both of our faces.

"I'm sorry; I didn't mean for you to cry," I said, wiping away mine with my bandaged stumps.

"I couldn't have done what you did. I wouldn't have made it."

"I would have said that before it started. You would be surprised what you can do when you're forced to."

She nodded no, wiping her tears and trying to regain composure. "You're an amazing woman, Madie."

I had heard that before, but I still didn't think so. "So are you, Connie, helping people each and every day, some who are dying? That's amazing."

Then, she cried again. "Thank you, but I will never equal you."

"I disagree. But there is one thing I don't like, and that is to be babied. I can take it."

"Oh no! It's nothing like that. We just didn't know what to say. We do now."

I smiled. "You guys are the heroes. I ran because I didn't want to die. How brave is that?"

"Who wouldn't? Few would have survived. I don't see how you did."

"Not very well," then, I held up both stumped arms, "the price I had to pay."

"A small one for life," she said.

She was right. The river will continue to flow. I just had to learn a new way to row.

CHAPTER 20

Three more days passed. Jim continued to check on me three to four times a day. The bandages were removed daily, and my stumps were cleaned with medicine and re-bandaged. Each time, Jim spent extra time inspecting my left hand.

"Both legs and your right arm are doing great. I was never worried about those. Your left hand is still questionable. We'll still need a few more days to be sure. We're pumping you with as many antibiotics as we can," Jim said.

"I do know it's starting to ache more."

"That's good, it's trying. Do you want me to have the pain reliever increased?"

"No, not yet; pain is good. I know I'm still alive."

Jim smiled. "If it gets too bad, let me know."

"I want you to know how grateful I am to have you. You have your own life to live, and yet you choose to stay here and help me. Don't you want to go home?"

"No, miss out on helping you get better? Not a chance, you're stuck with me."

I cried yet again. I didn't know what to say.

"Then, you deserve a medal. What, I don't know, but a big one."

Jim pushed up his lower lip. "No, you do. I know if you were at war, they would decorate you with so many medals you couldn't carry them."

I was at war—a personal one—one that I would never win.

"You never complain. Not once! You have a positive attitude."

"Only on the outside," I said, "on the inside, it's a train wreck. Something only I can deal with."

Jim nodded again. He was a good listener. He would make a good shrink. Then, he removed a small notepad from the front pocket of his hospital coat. Then, he wrote something as I watched and then handed it to me.

"This is my cell number. It's always with me, and it's always on twenty-four-seven. I'm here for you. If you ever need something, personal or medical, call. I will be here as fast as possible."

That did it! The floodgates didn't just open; the dam broke. The tears gushed like they never had before. All the grief I was holding in rose to the surface. I couldn't catch my breath. I shook violently. I wanted to get up and hug Jim, but I couldn't do that. I could do the next best thing.

Crying my eyes out, I started to sit up and slide to the edge of the bed, but I couldn't. I had forgotten that I didn't have any hands to push with. Jim moved quickly to the edge; my movement caught him off guard. The tubes running in and out of me tangled, but I didn't care.

Jim reached for them, freeing them from the sheet and blanket covering me, and he was leaning over me. I wrapped my arms around his neck and pulled myself up to him, using my forearms. I buried my face at the base of his neck. I continued to cry so hard I was shaking him. Jim said nothing and hugged me back. It felt good, human contact, something I hadn't had for a long time.

Gasping for air in between the outbursts, I tried to speak.

"I… I can't e-even give him a-a decent b-burial. The-there won't be-be anything l-left of him," I continued to gasp for air, and the shaking became worse, "he s-saved m-my life. I-I couldn't help him then. I-I can't help h-him now. I'm so sor-sorry."

Jim didn't move, nor did he speak. I must have been making quite a commotion. The door had been left open, and the next thing I knew, there were two nurses standing in my room, just inside the door. How long, I don't know. They both had tears running down their faces and said nothing.

I didn't stop—I couldn't. Once it started, it flowed.

"I'm lost, and this can't be fixed. He's not by my side. We were supposed to travel into the future together to the last page. The death dealers took that away from us."

My crying slowed, and I could breathe. Jim's coat was soaked with tears. I felt like a babbling idiot.

I looked at the wall behind Jim. "I'm not brave. I'm an emotional train wreck."

"Who wouldn't be?" one of the nurses said.

I looked at her; she had a Kleenex and was wiping away her tears.

The crying wore me out. I slept until Connie woke me, standing beside my bed, holding a large, flat box. Before my eyesight had processed what I was seeing, I smelled it.

"Mmm, that smells good," I said.

She smiled. Then, she laid it on the rolling table, opened it, and inhaled deeply.

"How many slices?" she asked.

"Two—for starters."

While she was removing the pizza from the box, she said, "I heard you had a bad day."

"God, am I everyone's topic of conversation around here?"

"Honey, you are the hottest thing that's ever been here since I've worked here anyway."

She smiled.

"You're not the typical, grumpy old fart that's never satisfied. We have a lot of those. So, yes, that's a good thing," she said, smiling.

I could see she was sincere. Connie's a good person, and I like her. "Well, thank you for being truthful. I owe you for half the pizza."

"Nonsense, I'm happy to do it."

I ate the two slices of pizza; they were huge, and I was stuffed.

Connie also ate two. When she finished, she said, "The rest is yours. Eat it when you like."

"Tell you what, why don't we share it with the other nurses on duty?"

She agreed. Soon, my room had four more nurses in it, and I learned their names. They were all nice. They all thanked me as they started to leave.

"Don't thank me. It's Connie we owe this to," I said.

Time passed. I looked forward to Jim's visits each day. But, as each day passed, the feeling I had for mealtime increased. I hated it. I didn't like having to be fed. In between meals, I thought about it. I might be a cripple, but I'm not an invalid. Just because I no longer had any fingers to hold a fork didn't mean I couldn't feed myself. I had to figure out something.

Just then, Jim walked in as Connie was feeding me.

"This really sucks," I said.

Jim frowned. "Are you referring to the food, being in the hospital, or not being able to get out of bed?"

"None of the above."

Then, I laughed. "I guess I did leave that kind of open to speculation. Not being able to feed myself."

"Oh, that!" Jim smiled.

"What, you don't like Connie?"

I knew Jim was kidding. "Connie's a sweetie. I don't know what I would do without her. I just want to be able to do the simple things again."

"Not for some time."

I nodded. Down inside, I thought there had to be a way.

Jim sat, and we talked while I finished eating. When Connie left, Jim removed his doctor's coat. I knew he was planning on staying for a while, and I liked that.

After a while, our conversation turned to my health.

"Looks like you might save your thumb, but it will be very sensitive for a long time. It will be very useful. You'll learn to do everything with it, much better than having no fingers at all."

I nodded.

The next morning, sitting up in bed, I was staring at the wall in front of me, something I did a lot. My head itched. I rubbed it with my right stump, but it was one of those deep itches that required one finger to apply a good deal of pressure. The soft bandage wasn't getting the job done. I saw the ink pen lying on the table next to my bed, the one the nurses used to fill out the day's menu. I had another use for it. I dragged the table over the bed and, with the tray in front of me, I leaned over and picked up the pen with my lips.

After several attempts, I managed to slide one end of it under the ace bandage wrapped around my right arm. Then I scratched. The hard end of the pen felt so good I couldn't stop. It was as if the itch had legs and was moving around on my head.

Then, I had an idea. This worked. *Why wouldn't it work to hold a spoon or a fork?* Then, I could feed myself. It would take something a little more elaborate, but it was doable.

I waited patiently for Jim's next visit. I was excited! How something so small meant so much!

I had time to plan on what to ask for and who to get to help me. Jim could get the job done. He was the one with the connections.

When Jim finally arrived, I didn't ask him right away. We chatted as we usually did.

"You seem a bit more cheery today," Jim said.

"You noticed—that obvious, huh?"

"Yes."

"Well, I have a favor to ask."

"Anything, remember what I told you."

"Could you call the company that makes the prosthetics and have them send someone here?"

Jim stood there looking at me.

Then, he said, "You're not ready for that yet; you haven't healed enough."

"I know." Then, I told him my idea.

Jim smiled.

"What you're asking for, what you need, sounds more like something a local machine shop would make. I don't see a problem with it. I'll call one, as long as you don't ask them for something to attach a set of rollerblades to."

Then, Jim laughed.

"Hey! I hadn't thought of that. Thanks for the idea!"

Then, I laughed. It felt good even though I knew I wasn't healed enough to try and move on my own.

"You'll fall and break your neck."

"Well, at least I won't break an ankle or any fingers when I land."

Jim smiled again and then shook his head.

Later that day, there was a knock on my door. I couldn't see the entrance to know who was there; my door was always open.

"Come in." The nurses never knocked, and I was anxious to see my visitor.

A man walked to the foot of my bed. "Hi, I'm Pete. I was called by your doctor."

The man looked sheepishly at me, almost as if he was afraid to talk.

"I have my own business, and, well, I've never been asked to do anything like this before."

I held both arms out, showing him the stumps. "So, you know my problem."

Pete looked down at the floor. "Yes, I'm sorry."

"All I want to do is be able to feed myself."

Then, I laid my right stump over the table and rolled it over the bed in front of me. I bent over and picked up the ink pen with my lips. Again, it took me several tries to slide one end of it under the ace bandage.

Pete stood there watching me like he was frozen in place.

When I succeeded in placing the ink pen, I said, "This is where I got the idea. My head itches a lot. Can you make something that will hold a spoon or a fork?"

Pete looked at my arm for several seconds, then at me, and then back to my arm. He said nothing, but I could see the wheels turning behind his eyes.

"Yes, I think so. Can you give me a few days?"

I smiled, trying to ease his tension. "Don't worry, I won't run away."

Pete looked down at my legs; I knew I had failed at what I was trying to accomplish.

181

"Don't look so sad; you're here to help me."

"Yes, but I've never made something to work on a person before."

"Relax, Pete," I said smiling, "if it doesn't work, it's no big deal."

Pete didn't move. "How sore is your arm?"

"It's not, just the end is tender."

"I'm," Pete said slowly, "I'm not trying to invade your personal life; I just needed to know so I know what my guidelines are on what to make."

"I understand. You're helping me, so ask away."

"Well, I, uh, see that your left-hand bandage looks different."

"Yes, I still have my thumb on that hand and about a third of my palm, at least so far."

"Is it sore?"

"Yes, very much so."

"Would you like me to make something for that hand also?"

"Sure! I was only thinking my right, but that would be an added bonus." The little things, how they mean so much, now I was even happier!

"I will be back in three days."

"Thank you. Thank you so very much. You have no idea what this means to me."

I waited patiently for three days like a child, counting down the days until Christmas. Now, it was the morning of the third day. I've been in the hospital for a month, and hopefully, soon, I can feed myself. The first step of a long journey; now, like then, out in the frozen wilderness, one step before the next. Come what may, I will accept it!!!

Jim walked in. "How are you today?"

"Ask me again this evening, and then, I can give you the correct answer."

"Well, I've been thinking. Since we've removed your stitches, you've been doing remarkably well."

Jim started removing the bandage on my left hand.

"I have a proposition for you."

Then, Jim looked at my left hand, rolled it over, and looked at the palm. "It's going to be some time yet before this heals completely. I think we can leave the bandages off your legs and right arm from now on unless it makes you feel uncomfortable. If so, we'll leave the ace bandage on; your call."

"Everyone around here knows what I look like without them, so that's fine. If I should ever go out in public one day, then I will."

"You will, one day, go out in public again."

I was waiting patiently to hear Jim's proposition.

"We need to keep your left hand bandaged."

"Okay."

"Not because of the surgery, but because it healed fine; we just don't want you bumping it. A bruise, at best, would set back the healing process a couple of weeks. In the worst-case scenario, it would damage the tissue, which is already very vulnerable, to the point where it would go the other way. With a bad bruise, what would happen is the muscle might retain too much blood and…"

"Alright, Doc, I get it already. I want to hear what you had to say when you walked in here."

I smiled.

"Well, you're in no shape to live on your own. With supervision and someone looking after your hand each day, sort of an assisted living environment, you can get out of here. Do you want to come and live with me for the next few months?"

That did it—the dam broke. I cried tears of joy this time. I couldn't talk. Even if I was capable of doing so, I wouldn't have known what to say.

Jim smiled. "I don't know if that means yes or no, and you don't know how to tell me."

Crying, wiping the tears, I nodded yes.

"Good, then, it's all taken care of."

"But why? I'll be such a burden on you. I can't dress myself or even take a bath, not to mention all the other things."

"It's all taken care of. I've hired a local woman to come in once a day and do all the things you need. I'll cook. I'm pretty good at fried eggs and peanut butter and jelly sandwiches."

I laughed.

"Peanut butter and jelly sounds good—beats a glass of water and a toothpick. Some days, that's all I had. I'm in! I don't know what to say other than thank you."

"No thanks needed. I look forward to it. We leave tomorrow."

"But Pete hasn't come back with the gadget I asked for yet."

Jim looked at his watch. "He'll be here in less than a minute."

Before I could say another word, Pete walked in.

Astonished, I looked back at Jim. "Do you always run everything on such a precise schedule?"

"Yes, it could mean the difference," Jim paused, carefully choosing his words, "of a good outcome or a bad one."

"Yes, I'm thankful you do. If you didn't, I would have walked past your house that day."

Pete walked up beside my bed carrying a box. My thoughts were racing, wondering what he had in it and if it would work.

Pete was all business but still uneasy about being around me. Jim stepped back, standing in the corner, and watched.

"I came up with a simple plan. Several of us actually tried it. After a little practice, we got fairly good with it."

Good Lord, I thought, *what is it with men giving such long, drawn-out explanations today? Get it out of the box.*

I smiled. Pete reached into the box.

"I started with a three-inch wide leather belt and cut it down just long enough to wrap around your arm. It's adjustable; the reason for this is to grip your arm well enough to stay in place without causing any pain."

Pete held it in front of me. The black leather strap had two short spikes sticking up on one end. There were several sets of holes on the other end, and a square tube was attached. On that was a funny-looking little spring.

Pete carefully wrapped it around my right arm. Then, he slid two holes over the pins sticking up and then twisted it slightly on my arm.

"Is that too tight? If it is, I can loosen it."

"No, I think that's fine."

Then, Pete reached back into the box. "This is all 304 stainless steel, easy to keep clean."

Then, he removed a fork and spoon. Each had a square tube attached to the end. He then put his index finger next to a small indentation on the tube.

"This little pocket here locks into this spring-loaded ball," pointing to the square tube on the strap, "you can't see the steel ball. It's inside."

Then, he slid the square end of the spoon into the tube attached to my arm, and I heard a "click."

"There, now, it's locked in place."

He lightly tugged on the spoon, but it didn't move.

I wiggled my arm in the air, and the spoon was secure. I grinned from ear to ear—this was going to work.

"This is wonderful!" I said.

He held the fork. "This works the same."

I looked at Jim. "I can't wait! I'm going to get a huge bowl of chocolate pudding."

We laughed, except for Pete.

"Watching you the other day with the ink pen, I decided it would be too hard for you to attach this with your lips, so I made another strap for your left arm."

Pete then removed another leather strap from the box. This one had a funny-looking scissor attachment to it. He strapped it to my left arm, being much more careful. My left arm was still bandaged.

"Let me know if this hurts."

After it was strapped to my arm, the three of us looked at it.

Then, Pete removed the spoon from my right arm and laid it on the table in front of me.

"Now, all you have to do is push the gripper over the tube of the spoon and pick it up. Then, you can lock it in place."

I did, and it worked, to my amazement. I held it in the air, looking at it.

After two tries, I had the spoon inside the tube on my right arm. "You might have to wiggle your right arm just a bit to snap it in place."

"Click."

"Now, just pull your left arm straight back."

I did, and the holder broke free. Tears streamed down my face.

"If I could stand, I'd hug your neck." Something so small meant so much.

With the tears still flowing, I said, "Whatever I owe you won't be enough."

Then, Pete smiled. "You owe me nothing. It's the least I could do."

I looked at Jim and then cried my eyes out.

It took some time to get myself together. After I did, Pete and I said our goodbyes.

When Jim and I were alone, I looked at him.

"Thank you for getting this done for me. I'm sorry you never got to meet Craig. You two would have gotten along well with each other. You are both a lot alike—quiet, strong, and easy to like."

Jim nodded. "I'm sure we would have. How about I order that bowl of chocolate pudding for you?"

The dark but happy gloom that was hanging over me was lifted.

"That would be nice. You better tell them to bring a roll of Visqueen with it; this could be messy."

Jim laughed. "I'm on it, be back soon."

When Jim returned, I was nervous. He sat the bowl down on the table in front of me. "Would you like me to leave? No audience?"

"Are you serious? No, I want you to stay. I can do this."

I did. I moved my right arm very slowly, concentrating deeply on every little move. Pete was right. After a short time and several spoonfuls, I got the hang of it.

"Look at you, you're already a pro at this," Jim said.

"I don't know about that. But it feels good to be able to feed myself."

"Like I said, soon enough, one step at a time, and soon you'll be walking again."

Jim walked in as I was eating a bowl of oatmeal. It was 6:30 AM. "So, what brings you here so early?"

"Well, we have a lot to do in a short amount of time. After you eat, we've got to get you dressed. But first, they wanted to do this for you."

All of a sudden, nurses started walking into my room. It was like they were appearing out of nowhere. Five-six, then I stopped counting. Then, Connie walked in, pushing a cart. On it was a huge cake with more lit candles than I could count. Then, more nurses followed in behind her.

I looked around the room. I had only seen some of them once or twice, but I remembered all of their names.

I looked down at the cake and read what was written on it: "Good luck, Madie, we will always be behind you."

I laughed, and I cried. While crying, a card appeared in front of me. "If this is a mushy card, I'm going to bawl my eyes out."

Everyone laughed, but I was serious. Jim opened it and read it. It was more than I could take. I did exactly what I said I would do.

"To the bravest, most courageous, and determined person we will ever know. We're proud to call you our friend."

I could barely see, looking through the wall of water that covered my eyes. I could see that Jim's eyes were glassy.

"If it wasn't for this man, I wouldn't be alive. He chose the right time to endure the cold and ice fish. He carried me up to his house. I knew at the time I had only hours to live, and I accepted it. Now, look, I'm here with you. I will never forget any of you and what you have done for me. I'm the one who is proud to call you my friend. Thank you, and for the cake."

Most of the nurses were smiling, and more than half were wiping their own tears.

Magically, a knife, plastic forks, and paper plates appeared, and Connie cut the cake.

Slowly, I removed the spoon and attached the fork. Everyone applauded, and again, I cried.

After everyone ate a slice of cake, my room thinned out. As each nurse left, they hugged me. Some even kissed me on the forehead as they said goodbye. My eyes never dried out, but I tried to maintain them.

Connie and Jim were the only ones left. I looked at Jim. "You said we have a lot to do, and now all this."

"Yes, we're leaving today, this morning. It's all set up. The helicopter is waiting."

Then, a woman walked in, one I had never seen before, and she was carrying clothes.

"We got you a set of warm clothes to wear."

I shook my head in disbelief! Everything was happening so fast, I was speechless. I knew I was leaving; I just didn't know it was going to be so soon.

21
CHAPTER

The winter air was just as I remembered it. But, then again, how would I ever forget it? It was cold and crisp, but after seven weeks in the hospital, it was refreshing.

I looked at the sky; not a cloud to be seen, and not a breeze even stirred. How ironic! When I had wished, day after day, for it not to blow, it did. Now that I didn't care, it won't. Mother Nature—she plays a cruel joke.

I sat in the wheelchair, looking out at the helicopter. It was running and waiting. The snow was deep. Much more had fallen during my stay.

I was wrapped in a blanket.

"What are you waiting for?" I asked Jim, who was standing beside me. An attendant was standing behind the wheelchair.

"The van was supposed to be here to give you a ride out," Jim answered.

"Nonsense, it's not that far. I can take it if you guys can."

"I'm game," said the man behind me.

"Madie, it's below zero. It will get cold once we get in the rotor wash."

I looked at Jim with the look that said: "I can't believe you said that."

"Like I'm going to get frostbite on my fingers."

"Okay, let's do it," Jim replied.

It took only minutes to get to the helicopter and then inside. I couldn't believe how quickly my stumps started aching, but I said nothing.

The ride back to Jim's house was pleasant. The serenity below was much more beautiful now than when I had walked through it. I'm learning fast to enjoy what I had taken for granted— the little things.

As we covered the miles, my thoughts drifted back to my long journey. I always had the same question, one that I would never be given an answer to.

Why was I allowed to live? Three people died foolishly, two I didn't care about. One I will never get over.

We circled Jim's house before landing. Sitting, waiting on the lake next to the shore, were three snowmobiles. Each had a small trailer behind it, and smoke was coming out of the chimney of the house.

"Is there anything you haven't thought of?" I asked Jim.

He smiled. "If there is, I haven't thought of it."

I smiled, trying to hide the sadness. Something else I will never understand: why was Jim being so kind to me? One day, I will ask.

We landed. The ground crew went to work as if they had done this many times. I was placed in one of the trailers, and what little luggage we had was placed in another trailer along with the wheelchair. I looked over to the general area where Jim had been ice fishing; the hole was long gone. Snow had covered any signs that we had once been there. Now, I was glad I was wrapped in a blanket from head to toe; no one could see the tears flow.

The spot where I had been given another chance at life, I will never forget.

The sled I was in pulled right up to the front steps, and he shut it off. Before I had a chance to thank him, I was being lifted out of my seat and carried up the four steps onto the front porch. The front door opened, and a woman, smiling, stood there.

"Hello Madie, everything is ready for you," she said.

"Geez, you guys are treating me like royalty."

She smiled again.

"I'm glad you didn't roll out the red carpet; I would have run away."

"Madie, this is Mary, the lady I told you about."

"Hello, Mary."

"I hadn't thought about the red carpet, sorry," Jim said.

"I didn't know you were close enough to hear that; I was kidding."

"I know," Jim grinned, "I think we've thought of everything else."

They sat me on the sofa. The man who carried me said nothing. I thanked him.

"These two men are Jonathan and Jerry. The man at the door is George."

I thanked them also.

"Well, I have coffee and hot chocolate made. Of course, there's a little brandy or Canadian Club to mix with it."

"Yes, please, we would like you guys to stay and have a warm drink with us," Jim said.

The three men agreed.

Jim and Mary had produced a short-legged tray and placed it over my lap. Then, an extra-long straw was laid on the tray. The tray had a non-slip mat on it. I wondered how many more things Jim had thought of. With time, I will see.

I had the hot chocolate with brandy and then another. By the time I had finished the second one, I was glad I had a small glass. I was feeling a little buzzed; I blamed it on the straw. Drinking alcohol through a straw always got one drunk quicker, or so I've heard.

The men had unzipped their bib overalls, and their coats and boots were piled at the door. They were talking and laughing, telling stories, some of which included Jim. And I sat back on the sofa and listened.

Mary sat at the kitchen table, always making sure the men had their glasses filled when needed. She was a small, thin woman, somewhere around fifty years of age. I guessed she weighed about one hundred twenty-five pounds, but she was attractive for her years. Black hair, dark eyes, and a pretty smile—one that made her face light up when she did.

Time passed quickly. The men talked louder and laughed more. I was thankful to be in good company. One day, I knew I would have to go home and be alone. For now, I cherished what I had.

Mary came over to the sofa and sat next to me.

"The men have lived here all of their lives. They can go on forever telling stories of the past."

"How does Jim fit in?"

"Well, through the years, when he was around, he's had them help him build this place. They were always willing because they always had plenty to drink. That was all they ever wanted for payment. Of course, there was always a steak to eat or a hamburger. Jim always made sure of that."

"I haven't known Jim for too long, but he does seem like a very generous man."

"Honey, you don't know the half of it," Mary replied.

The men never stopped talking. They were unaware of our conversation going on.

"One time, a young boy wandered off and got lost. The four of them searched for two days before they found him nearly five miles from here. Another time, an ice fisherman had a heart attack out on the ice, and the lake is quite a ways from here. They all went racing there on the snowmobiles and kept him alive until the helicopter got there and took him away. There are other stories, but I don't want to bore you."

I liked hearing them. Then, it occurred to me why they were so efficient about getting me from the helicopter into the house; they had done things like this before.

Then, a thought hit me as I was staring at the floor.

"I would like to hire you guys."

They became silent, looking at me.

"When winter breaks, I will pay for your trip, and you, and whatever else you need. I would like you to find the remains of my husband and bring him back so I can bury him."

They remained silent, still looking at me.

Jim spoke to break the silence, "I'm sure they would be glad to Madie."

"Hoo-wee, that's a lot of square miles to cover," Jonathan said.

"I have the exact GPS coordinates memorized and the name of the lake to land on. It's the one thing they couldn't take away from me. They got everything else."

Once I started, I couldn't quit.

"The days I ran from them, I never understood why they did what they did. They could have walked out of our camp, and we would have never seen them again. They were professionals, very good at what they did. They could track me even after the heavy blizzards would hit. There were times I was a day, probably two ahead of them. I slept very little. They always found me."

By now, many teardrops had landed on the tray, but they said nothing.

"That stupid bear was my friend and companion. It always let me know they were close long before I could see them. It saved my life more than once. The one thing Mother Nature couldn't control. She tried to get me every day. She was more relentless than the death dealers. I never knew their names, so I named them that because that's what they were. There were days I was so cold and hungry and scared I wanted to die.

"Fear of what they would do to me made me run. The bear killed the first, and I believe a heart attack got the second one. Then, I was just cold and hungry. Then, I went on for Craig; he would have wanted me to. There were times I heard him, in my head, always telling me the end was just ahead. Sometimes, I thought I was going crazy. I owe him that; I can't leave him up there, all alone, for eternity."

I kept wiping away the tears with my right stump.

"If you guys don't want to, I'll understand. Maybe you know someone who would."

Jonathan spoke again, "I'm in, come hell or high water, he will be found."

I looked at Jerry and George. They nodded yes and looked sad.

"We will do it for no charge, that I guarantee," Jerry said.

"We can be up there and back on the same day. So, don't worry, we will take care of everything. Winter won't break until late April; we'll go then."

It was now the end of January.

Sadness overwhelmed me. I cried hard, and in between sobs, I said, "I'm sorry I ruined your story telling."

"Madie, we're here because of you. This is your day; you do whatever you want," said Jerry.

Then, I cried even harder. So many people went out of their way to help me; it was more than I could take.

The men soon left. Again, I apologized to Jim and Mary for ruining the day.

Jim's reply was, "No apology needed! Don't worry, they'll be back so many times, you'll get tired of them."

"I doubt that they seem like nice men."

"The best! I would trust my life with them," Jim said.

Days passed, and we each fell into a routine. Mary was a blessing, arriving each morning at 7 AM. She doted over me constantly. I continually tried to tell her to quit doing so that I would be fine.

I always received the same answer, "That's what I'm here for."

First thing, she would dress me for the day and then brush my hair. Jim always cooked breakfast for us. Then, as Mary would put it, she would doll me up. Along with the new clothes that were in my closet from the very first day were other things I needed. More makeup than I will ever use, toothpaste, and on and on.

Each day, I thanked Jim and Mary; I knew she had a hand in getting everything.

Each afternoon, I would sit in a wheelchair and stare out the large picture window, which faced out over the lake. Sometimes, I would watch Jim ice fishing, but mostly, I thought of the recent past; it still consumed me and probably would for a very long time.

Sometimes, I cry, sometimes not. I always felt guilty for more than one reason. I was the one who was alive, which was bad enough.

Even worse, it was me who had come up with the idea for the vacation. I also chose the area. The worst part was watching Craig die and saving my life. How he knew they were what they were, I will never know. I think about that each day; maybe it was from the conversation they were having. Craig was a very good judge of character; maybe he just knew. He was a brave man—the saddest part is—no one will ever know.

I became fairly good at moving myself around in the wheelchair, using my forearms as hands to spin the wheels.

The bathroom I used had been remodeled to be handicap friendly. That had also been taken care of before we arrived. It was clear to me that Jim had put a lot of thought and effort into preparing things. I didn't know how I would repay him for everything. Money would be an insult, and thank you would never be enough. One day, I would think of something, but for now, it was secondary.

The days Jim caught fish, that's what we would eat for dinner. Cooked fish was much better than frozen, raw fish. But we always ate well. Between Jim and Mary's cooking, they ran the gamut of variety.

I was nearly back to my original weight, but the muscle tone wasn't there. I hated having to huff and puff from helping to get from the wheelchair into bed, onto the sofa, or into the bathtub. Lack of exercise, nothing I could do—for now.

One afternoon, Jim was in the recliner reading the newspaper, and I was on the sofa looking at a magazine. Mary kept us supplied on her daily visits. Jim didn't ice fish today. It was snowing so hard the lake couldn't be seen from the house.

No one seemed concerned but me. I chose to remain silent. The wind was howling, and from my past experience, this was going to be a substantial blizzard. The first since I arrived at Jim's.

Mary was in the kitchen putzing around. Whatever she was doing, it smelled wonderful. I worried about her getting home.

As I continuously kept looking out the window at nothing but white, my nightmares of me being out there in it grew. How, or why, I had lived through them, I will never know.

Why my emotions were taking over, I didn't know. Insecurity, I suppose.

Finally, out of nowhere, I said, "You kept all my warm gear, didn't you?"

I hadn't seen it since I arrived.

Jim lowered the newspaper. Looking at me, he saw instantly something wasn't right. "Madie, are you alright? You're very pale. What's wrong?"

I shook my head and then looked out the window for the hundredth time.

"It's really bad outside. I think this one will last for a long time. It's what I feared and hated the most. I always thought it would be the end. How will Mary get home? She will get lost."

I didn't look away from the window.

"Mary can wear my warm clothes if she wants."

"Madie, please don't worry, we are safe."

"But it will get so cold, and it will be so hard to take."

Why was I saying what I was saying? I had no clue.

"I'm worried."

"There's nothing for you to worry about," Jim said in a calming voice.

Instantly, Mary quit doing what she was doing in the kitchen and walked over and sat by my side, saying nothing.

My eyes became damp. "It's really bad outside."

Mary picked up my right arm and held it in both her hands.

"Don't worry, Madie. We have made plans for this. I have enough things here to last me a week or more. Up here, it's inevitable. Storms like this happen a lot. I'm not going anywhere."

My past was still present. I could remember all the pain, each little detail of what I felt and went through. "Well, I don't need much to eat. I will be okay eating every couple of days."

Jim smiled at me. "I would like to show you something if you want to get back in your chair."

I was shaking for no real reason. I was inside a warm home. I nodded.

Jim pushed my wheelchair through the kitchen. On the far wall was a door that I had never been through. Jim opened it and then pushed me through.

Once inside, I was speechless. The room was roughly ten feet by ten feet, and shelves went from the floor to the ceiling on each wall. Each shelf was at least two feet deep, and each was loaded with food to its capacity. More cans, boxes, and bags of food than a small grocery store stocked. In the center of the room, sitting on the floor, were several fifty-pound bags of flour, sugar, potatoes, and rice.

"See, there's nothing to worry about. There's enough food here to feed an entire family for the winter without leaving."

I cleared my eyes. "I'm sorry. I guess I was acting kind of foolish."

"No, I understand. Besides this, there's a small room out in the back of the shed that contains some frozen things. Plus, there's a one thousand-gallon tank, buried in the ground, of fuel oil. If, for some reason, that fails, there's enough firewood to heat this house for two months. That is also in the shed."

"That's a lot of firewood."

"Yes, the guys and I refill it each summer, plus there's back up for that. It doesn't matter how much snow is on the ground; all we have to do is call the helicopter in. We could be out of here in no time."

I shook my head in disbelief. "There's nothing you haven't thought about."

"If there is, I don't know what it would be."

Mary, who was standing behind us in the kitchen, spoke, "This is what we do up here; always be prepared. Mother Nature is unpredictable."

"Yes," I said, "and relentless. When she's one-on-one with you, she will always win."

"She didn't win with you," Jim said.

I held up both arms. "It was a tie, but in the big picture, she did."

Dinner was over. We had eaten mashed potatoes and creamed peas, and what had smelled so good earlier in the day, while I was temporarily losing it, was homemade bread. In our conversation, while eating, I learned Jim had all the kitchen machines possible. Jim said the bread machine "makes life easier."

For dessert, Mary had made a homemade apple pie, my favorite, and there was ice cream with it.

"We do eat well," I said.

"Yes, as you may have noticed, I try to eat only red meat once a week. I never get tired of fish, and there are dozens of ways to prepare it," he said.

"That's fine by me. Fish is one of my favorites, not to mention I'm the moocher here—it sure beats the glass of water and a toothpick. I had so many days out there."

It was still snowing hard outside. I could see the snow bouncing off the windows, and three feet past, complete darkness had consumed everything. I closed my eyes, remembering the times it was so dark at night during the blizzards I couldn't see my hand in front of my face. The aching cold my body felt; it was as if I could now feel my feet and hands ache, and I wanted to rub them. I opened my eyes and thought I would see them.

Jim was watching me but asked no questions.

"Mary, you don't know how much I would like to help you clean up and do the dishes; I feel guilty."

Mary smiled her charming smile. "That's what the dishwasher is for."

Jim's cabin wasn't large, not what one would expect a doctor to own, but it had all the luxuries. What Jim had told me was that it had the basic things to conduct life.

"If it's okay with you, I would like to see my clothes."

"Sure, I have them packed in a box upstairs."

There was only one bedroom upstairs, complete with a bathroom. It was Jim's. I used the one in the back. An office slash spare bedroom was in front, off the living room. That's where Mary would be staying until the storm broke.

"I knew one day you would ask for them. I'll be right back."

The stairs that led up were open, and I watched Jim go up and disappear. I was nervous. I hadn't seen them in over two months. It was inevitable; sooner or later, I would. No time like the present to get it over with. I guess the blizzard triggered it, reminding me of the nightmare I went through.

Jim sat the box down in front of his recliner. I was almost sweating. Mary sat in a French chair facing us, and I could see by the expression on her face she didn't know what to say.

Jim opened the box, and I started shaking. Then, I told myself, *This is crazy. It's what kept me alive. No harm is going to jump out of the box.*

My arctic suit came out first, the jacket, and then the bib overalls. It was dirtier and scratched up more than I remembered. There was a lot of blood on it from the earlier fish I had caught, which is now worse for the wear. I stared at them as Jim held them, and then I reached out with my stumps, and Jim handed them to me.

I sat there holding them in my lap, almost hugging them.

"The day we bought these, Craig had insisted on them. They were the warmest and the most expensive. I remember telling Craig that they were overkill; I didn't need that much because we wouldn't see that kind of cold these were made for. You know what he told me?"

Tears flowed. They said nothing, letting me talk.

"I can remember it like it was yesterday. Craig said, better safe than sorry. You don't have to wear it if you don't need it. One more way he saved my life."

I looked back at the box; I knew what was next.

"Go on," I said to Jim.

Jim removed the jacket next to the death dealers. Even though I had worn it on the last half of my journey, I started trembling.

Mary gasped.

It was appalling; the front of it was covered in dried brown, crusty blood, much more than I remembered. It was also very dirty. Whether it was from me or him, I couldn't remember. It was full of scratches and tears. It looked as if it had been worn through a long war—a battle that had been fought hand to hand.

Then, Jim removed the pants. Unlike mine, these were only waist-high and looked nearly as bad as the jacket.

Jim saw me shaking.

"Madie, when I packed these in the box, it occurred to me. I don't believe you would be here today without them. That was a smart thing you did when you took them from him. They kept you alive. Without the extra set of clothes, the rest of your body would have ended up like your hands and feet."

I nodded.

"You wouldn't have survived the nights by what you have told me."

"No, I tried his boots, but they wouldn't fit over mine. I don't know why I didn't get his gloves. Maybe I would still have fingers today. Huge mistake on my part; I just didn't think about it."

"Again, by what you have said, you did pretty well; given the situation you were in, you had the presence of mind to get what you did. It saved your life."

"The day I ran from our camp, I had no idea what I was in for. I ran for my life; that's all I knew about what to do. I really thought after a day they would give up."

"Who would? There isn't a person alive who has been put in that situation. Truth be told, there aren't many people who would have done as well as you did."

Next were my hat, gloves, and boots. I could still remember what the boots felt like on my feet.

I looked down at the empty space below my stumps.

"They got me home, they served their purpose."

"Yes, they did," Jim replied.

"Day after day, I walked in those boots, which were hard for me to believe, even now. The axe, where is it? It kept me alive."

"It's upstairs, too long to fit in the box. Do you want it?"

"No, the first three weeks, it was my security blanket. As long as it was with me, and I had fish in my pocket, I knew I might make it. Then, the ice got too thick, and I couldn't chop deep enough to reach the water. The day that man died, I would have eaten his boots if they were leather, but they were rubber. He had rope in his pocket, and his snowshoes were better constructed than mine. I took his shoes, and with each pair I made after that, I made them like his.

"Each set only lasted five or six days. My hands hurt so badly when I made the last pair; I had no doubt they would be my last. I couldn't hold on to the axe, and out of lack of food and energy, I lost the will to survive. The last few days, I was just walking, just waiting for death to come. The natural instinct to survive took over, and I kept hearing Craig's voice telling me that the end was near. He was right. I had nothing to do with it; it was his voice and you who saved me."

"You saved yourself, Madie. I only had a small part in it," Jim said.

"I never saw your house, but something told me to look to my right. When I did, I saw a black object. At first, I thought it was an animal. Thank God it was you. If I haven't thanked you for all you've done for me, I am now. Someday, I will even the pendulum with you."

"No need to. I've told you many times it's an honor to know you."

I shook my head.

"I'm just a lost soul. What seems normal is not what it seems. My truth is, at best, an untold story, one that can never be told."

"Only if you want it that way; that's up to you," Jim said.

I started crying, wiping away the tears on my shirt sleeve.

"One day, I am going to set up a room in my house, a shrine for Craig. I'm even going to put some sort of bear in it. We took several pictures of us together up there. Hopefully, they'll still be good in the camera after the snow melts. I took one of Craig, who was wearing jeans and a flannel shirt. That one I will have made into a life-size picture and put it on the wall in that room."

22
CHAPTER

Mary bathed me every day. It was a major hassle getting me in and out of the tub, but as the days continued to pass, I got stronger. My stumps had also become less tender, and I was able to help Mary back and forth.

"Tomorrow, I think I'll take a shower," I said, trying to maintain a straight face.

Mary looked at me with the look of saying, "Are you serious?" But she didn't respond.

I laughed.

"I'm kidding, although it would feel good. I've been here. How long has it been? Three weeks? You're always so serious around me. You never ask me any questions about what I went through."

"I don't know what to say or ask. I'm here to help you, so that's what I do."

"Well, you're definitely a much better cook than I am, and you have the patience of Job. But please feel free to ask me anything. A little one-on-one conversation with another female would be good; I'd like that."

Mary grinned.

"You're much too quiet."

"Thank you," Mary replied.

"For what? I'm the one who should thank you every day."

"For the compliment about my cooking, Jonathon does most of the cooking at our house."

"Jonathon, is your husband?" I blurted.

"Yes."

"I didn't know that. See, after three weeks, I learned something."

"We always have moose, goose, rabbit, or venison for dinner. We have a freezer full of it. I could bring some if you would like."

"Eat Bambi or Thumper? I don't know, I've never tried it."

Mary laughed as hard as I've ever seen. "You forgot Mother Goose."

Maybe she was finally going to loosen up around me, but then she became very serious.

So, maybe not.

"I don't know what I'd do if I lost him. I love that man more than anything. To see Jonathon brutally murdered like that, I would fall to pieces. I wouldn't be able to run. So, that's why I've never asked any questions."

"I did fall to pieces, doing so while I ran. I couldn't stop; even if I wanted to, my body wouldn't let me."

"The day you arrived, I wanted to cry. I spent the first few hours one breath away from tears."

"So, that's why you were so quiet."

"Yes, and it wasn't just from seeing you like that or what you went through. It was me—what would I do if I lost Jonathon? I couldn't bear it. I'm sorry for telling you that."

"No need to be; you didn't do this to me."

Then, we both were silent, each thinking our private thoughts.

"Does Jonathon know this? I mean, how deeply do you love him?"

"No, he knows I love him, and he treats me like a queen."

"Mary, I want you to do something for me. Tell him! Sit him down, look him in the eyes, and tell him. One day, he could be gone. That was my mistake; something else on the list that I can't do now and will take to my grave. Please, do it tonight."

Mary cried. I reached up from the bathtub and wrapped my arms around her neck.

I whispered, "Life's too short, enjoy what you have."

Then, both of us bawled our eyes out.

The next day, during bath time, Mary talked more than usual. She seemed a little more chipper. I didn't ask if she told Jonathon; it wasn't my business.

I wheeled the wheelchair into the bathroom. After Mary got me undressed, she slid the curtain open on the bathtub and smiled.

Inside the bathtub, a tall stool sat in the center. I was speechless.

"You said you wanted to take a shower. Now, you can."

I didn't know if I should laugh or cry.

"It should be the right height. I think you can put your legs down on the tub if you need to for balance."

That was it; my eyes glazed over. "Thank you."

The shower felt good. The pulsing water hitting my body relaxed me. My left hand had healed enough so that I could start using it. I carefully squeezed the bar of soap between my thumb and what was left of my palm. Mary had carved a groove in the center of the bar, a thumb hold, to lock the bar of soap in my hand.

When I first saw my left hand, I thought it was extremely grotesque. It still is, but I have gotten used to it, and I'm glad to have it. It is the only thing that has kept me from being totally helpless.

So, now, this is another first. My first shower and the first time to wash myself—piece of cake.

My legs were stretched out straight, the stumps resting on the bottom of the tub. The hot water hitting me in the face blended with the tears, washing them away. Vanishing—as had the gallons of previous ones. One day, maybe I will stop crying as much. Time will tell!

I was almost finished and was proud of myself for accomplishing such a simple task. Then, I dropped the soap; it was no big deal. I started to call Mary but decided I had to fend for myself. Soon, I would be home alone with no Mary to call for. So, I started to retrieve the bar of soap myself.

Big mistake.

I adjusted my legs directly beneath me and slowly transferred my weight onto them. I could feel the end of my leg bones, the stumps, as I tried to stand on them. They felt awkward.

Instinctively, I flexed my leg muscles, trying to maintain balance, but nothing happened. The pressure from the weight of my body on the tender skin stitched up over the ends began to hurt. Nothing. I couldn't stand the short time it took to pick up the bar of soap. My right arm was on the shower wall, and my left was on the stool, trying to maintain stability. The pain was increasing, so it was now or never.

The bar of soap ended up covering the drain in front of me. I bent down and reached out with my left hand to pick it up. I felt my left leg slide backward, and I tried to correct the problem by shifting more weight onto my right leg. It happened so fast I didn't have time to flinch.

Both legs started sliding in opposite directions. I reached back with my left arm, trying to get a hold of the top of the stool to slow my fall. All I succeeded in doing was pulling it over with me. My knees buckled, and my body hit the tub at the same time as the stool. The momentum of my body, when my butt landed, slid me forward. I started to gain speed as my right knee was traveling forward.

At the same time, I was falling backward. Then, I felt a "thump." The back of my head hit the edge of the seat of the stool, now lying on its side.

I saw stars.

Without thinking, instinctively, I thought I still had two good hands. I tried to pull myself back up, but they slid down the walls of the shower. I was in a fog, not quite sure of what was going on.

Within seconds, the shower curtain flew open. Mary was bending down to help me up. My arms and legs were flailing about, trying to get a hold.

Mary grabbed me. "I'll get you up."

I relaxed.

Mary pulled me up into the sitting position first. The back of my head hurt, and a headache was growing fast, so I squinted my eyes.

"Oh my, you've cut the back of your head," Mary said quickly. She was holding the back of my head with her right hand.

I was sitting upright in the tub. She turned the shower off with her left hand. "Don't move a muscle."

I watched Mary turn and grab the towel from the rack. Her right hand was covered with blood. I started to reach back with my right arm but then stopped, remembering I had no hand.

Two seconds later, Mary had the towel against my head, applying pressure.

"Let's get you up on the side of the tub," she said.

She reached around me, below my arms, and pulled. I was surprised at how strong little Mary was. I pushed with my legs.

Sitting there, Mary wrapped my bathrobe around me using her left hand. She never let go of the towel with her right.

It took some effort for both of us to coordinate our movement, but I finally got both arms into the sleeves.

My back was facing the room. I heard the wheelchair hit the edge of the tub. "I'm going to pull you backward into the chair."

Mary was still in the panic mode. She handled the situation gracefully, as a nurse of ten years would.

Mary stood behind the chair as she pulled me into it.

I was still in a daze and looked down at my legs. They were hanging over the edge of the tub.

"Lift your legs, Madie; I'm wheeling you out of here."

I did, and the strain of doing so made my headache worse.

"Ooh, instant headache," I said.

I closed my eyes.

"Not good," Mary said. I felt myself being briskly wheeled into the kitchen.

We stopped beside the kitchen table, and I opened my eyes.

"Madie, can you hold the towel for a few seconds?"

I nodded.

I watched Mary run three steps and open one of the kitchen drawers. I couldn't tell what she removed, so I watched her run for the front door.

Mary took one step outside, and I heard a loud horn blow for two seconds. Then, Mary ran back inside and up to me. She set the can on the table, "air horn." She then took over holding the towel.

"Jim will be here shortly."

He was! I watched Jim through the window, run up the front steps, and across the porch. He never stopped running, and even with his heavy boots and clothes, he covered the distance through the house in no time. He looked at me, then to Mary, and back to me. He had already figured out what was wrong.

Jim was huffing and puffing. Breathing heavily, he said, "Let's take a look at it."

"It's not good," Mary said.

I felt the pressure from the towel go away.

"No, that's a pretty good gash," Jim said.

I heard a cupboard door bang open, and then I saw a small white plastic basket on the table. It was full of brown glass bottles, and then a larger one was set beside it. It held rolls of tape, gauze, and an assortment of pads and bandages.

Then, Jim popped the hasps of a white enclosed metal box with his thumbs and opened it.

"You guys sure are making a big deal out of nothing," I said.

Jim never took the time to close the front door behind him. The rush of cold air felt good; it relieved me and brought me back to my normal senses.

"Madie, you have a deep cut in the back of your head. It's about an inch long or longer, and bone is exposed."

I didn't say anything; I felt embarrassed. I let Jim do his thing.

"This is going to burn a little, Madie." I watched Jim remove a small can from the basket.

"The first thing we have to do is stop the bleeding; you're bleeding profusely." So much for the shower and being clean.

I felt something being sprayed into the cut.

Not too bad, I thought.

"This will stop the bleeding. Then, I will numb it before I clean it."

We waited a minute, and while doing so, Jim removed his jacket with Mary's help.

Jim sprayed it again and then reached for another bottle from the basket. "This is going to sting a little more; it's a topical deadener. It will numb your skin before I give you the shots to completely numb it."

It did; I took a deep breath to counteract the pain.

Mary had several rags that she had soaked with hot water. I couldn't see her, but I sensed she was handing Jim what he needed without him asking. The bloody rags piled up on the table beside me.

The steel box contained all the sharp instruments.

"It looks like you have enough stuff to perform surgery," I said.

"If need be, I could," replied Jim.

"Okay," Jim said after he removed a string and needle from the box and a small brown bottle from the basket, "this is going to burn a bit."

"Time to pay the price of my own stupidity."

Once again, it did. I tensed every muscle in my body, the only defense I had against the pain. We went through this four more times, and by the last time, the pain had decreased.

"There, the rest you won't feel. How are you doing?" Jim asked.

Mary had reverted back to what she had been the first day I arrived. Having spent so much time with her, I had come to know her well, but this wasn't like her.

"What's wrong, Mary? You're not talking."

Her voice crackled.

"This is my fault. I'm here to help you keep things like this from happening. I did a horseshit job of it."

Hearing Mary say that shocked and surprised me.

"Mary!"

Then, I regained my composure. "It's not your fault."

"Yes, I hadn't thought of the bottom of the tub being slippery. I should have had a rubber mat down for you."

Then, it occurred to me, seeing the air horn on the table, that there were more contingencies and precautions around in the house than I ever imagined.

Jim scrubbed, shaved my hair around the cut, sutured, and wrapped my head with gauze. They worked meticulously.

Before it was all over, my emotions got the best of me, always balancing on the fine line of total collapse. I reached up with my left arm and wiped the tears away.

"Madie, what's wrong? Am I hurting you?" Jim asked.

"No! Why do you two do so much for a freak show like me? I don't deserve it, or you two. You're way too nice to me."

"Madie, you're not a freak show. We do this because we like you, and we want to."

That did it! My emotions fell off the fine line and crashed. I bawled my eyes out yet again. Will the day ever come when there are no more tears?

Mary hugged me, and Jim pulled one of the kitchen chairs beside me and sat in it. He held my right arm in his hands.

I looked at them; they were covered in blood.

"You're a mess," I said.

"It's only blood. Physically, you are one of the strongest people I will ever meet. I have told you that before. It will take some time, but you will get stronger. Anyone who has gone through what you have would be a wreck. We're here for you, whatever you need."

I gushed tears, which seemed like gallons.

"All for a stupid bar of soap," I said. I leaned forward and hugged Jim, and then I hugged Mary.

"Thank you. This wasn't your fault. Besides that, it's only a small cut."

Then, I had to lighten the mood. I was the one who had put it in the tank. "Looks like I'll have to cook dinner. I disrupted Jim's fishing. I wonder how much they charge for pizza delivery up here."

They laughed.

"Oh, about two thousand dollars," Jim replied.

"Ekes, it better be really good pizza, and extra cheese should be included for no extra charge."

They went to work cleaning up the kitchen. More medical supplies had been used than I would have ever thought. I sat in the wheelchair, feeling useless.

When Jim had the medical supplies packed up, Mary said, "Go, I'll finish. The fish are waiting for you."

Jim smiled. "Jonathon's a lucky man."

"Yes, he is," I said. Then, too, I wondered if he knew that.

23
CHAPTER

I had wheeled myself into the living room. The sun was shining as I sat in the far corner facing out, reading a book.

Mary had finished cleaning up, and I began hearing the bangs and clangs from various pots and pans. It was three thirty in the afternoon.

My body didn't feel right, and it wasn't from the fall in the bathtub. I felt a sharp stab of pain in my left hand, moments later, at the end of my right leg.

"Mary, maybe we should eat early today."

"Okay, is there something wrong?"

She walked around the corner so she could see me at the far end of the living room. "Are you okay?"

"I'm fine. There's a storm coming, another bad one. You should be at home with Jonathon, not stuck here like the last time."

Mary looked out the window. "Are you sure?"

"Pretty sure."

Jim returned shortly after four, carrying two walleye fish.

"Wow! Those are nice ones," I said.

I wheeled my chair into the kitchen.

"We'll eat in twenty minutes," Mary said.

Jim looked at her, wondering why it was so early.

"Madie says another storm is coming."

Jim looked at me with the same look he had just given Mary.

"Are your bones aching?"

I nodded. "I felt the pressure drop, causing my sinuses to pop a couple of times."

"What? That's how we predict the weather around here?" Mary said, smiling.

"Whatever works, works for me," Jim said. "What's for dinner?"

"Pizza," Mary answered.

I smiled. Down inside, I wanted to cry again.

"These won't cost thousands, only one veggie, the other half pepperoni, half sausage and mushrooms. I didn't know what Madie likes."

"Mary, you are a saint."

"The least I could do for letting you bang your head in the shower."

"Maarrry," I said.

"What?" she answered.

"We already had that conversation."

"I know, but it didn't work."

"I'll call Jonathon; tell him to come and get you. He can eat pizza with us," Jim said.

Jonathon arrived, and we ate. Jim and Jonathon talked and laughed. It was a pleasure being in such good company.

By now, I was using my left hand to hold the fork. I was still using the gadget on my right, sometimes to hold the knife and other times just for backup.

Their stories never ended. Always about fishing or hunting, an encounter with a wild animal, or someone lost or hurt. I liked them all, except for my own. Mine is a living nightmare, and I didn't want to talk about it. I sat silently and listened.

It was almost dark out. Mary and Jim had cleared the table and put the dirty dishes in the dishwasher.

"Well, Mary, should we go?" asked Jonathon.

"Yes, I suppose so."

Mary put on her heavy clothes and boots. Every day, she had driven herself, on her snowmobile, six miles. The one lone path, which was called a road, never plowed in the wintertime.

"You riding with me or driving yours?" Jonathon asked her.

"I'll drive; it's not snowing yet."

"I'm glad it will be by morning," I said.

"Maybe so, but I hate not being here."

"I'll be fine. See you in a few days," I said.

We said our goodbyes.

Later that evening, Jim and I were sitting in the living room.

I had to ask, "So, why aren't you married? The single women are surely missing out."

"We all create our own problems, and I created mine. I don't blame her; it was my fault."

Instantly, I felt guilty. I went too far and crossed a line that wasn't mine to cross. I wanted to crawl into the crack between the boards on the floor.

"Stop, I shouldn't have asked. Your personal life isn't my business. I'm sorry."

Jim did it again. It had been so long that I forgot about him doing it. He pushed his bottom lip up, making the top protrude. Something he did only in deep thought, contemplating. The first time, with me, was the outcome; now was the answer. It was out of my control, and I was floating in the middle of the ocean, waiting.

"I let my job consume my life, and she fell into the background. I went home two days before Christmas to spend the holidays and found the 'Dear John' letter."

"Do you still love her?"

I couldn't stop. I knew the first rule when digging a hole. When you're in one step, stop. So, why didn't I?

"That was a long time ago."

"Well, do you?"

Jeez, Madie, stop, I thought. I needed to get the roll of duct tape and cover not just my mouth but my whole face to hide my embarrassment.

"Sometimes, we burn bridges when we don't even know we're doing it. She's remarried; that's enough for me. You will always be a true friend."

Jim smiled.

The wind was increasing; I could hear it howling outside, an all too familiar sound. Mother Nature was venting, letting off just a little pressure before she released her fury.

"This is going to be a bad one. She's still upset with me because she didn't get to finish me off."

I was glad that the conversation had taken another path.

"Well, she won't win, not to worry. Wintertime is definitely hers to claim. I just look at it as though she just huffs and puffs; she eventually goes away."

"Not with me, she won't," I paused, "never! The battle was staged and ended in a draw."

Maybe it was just me being paranoid again, but I felt there was something different with this storm. I had the eerie feeling she was coming back for me.

"Well, I'm going to bed; good night," I said.

"Do you need some help?" Jim asked.

"No, I can manage. Thank you anyway."

"Good night then," he said.

It felt like I had been asleep for only minutes. I was walking down the freeway, not a car, house, or another person in sight. Miles ahead of me was the forest. I heard a train blow its whistle from inside the trees, and I had to go there.

I was inside the forest, walking further into the dense trees. It was dark and gloomy but relaxing. As I walked, I was getting older and older, something was sucking the life from me, and I knew it. I stumbled. Too tired to go on, so I laid down on the soft floor of the forest; it was time to sleep.

I was dreaming in my dream.

So, when are you coming home? a voice asked.

I am home, I responded, *I will always be here.*

Why am I so alone? I asked myself. I didn't understand, and I was confused.

I woke in my dream, and it was snowing. I wasn't cold, and I was walking again.

Now, I felt my thoughts racing in an uncontrollable turmoil, and I woke. I bolted upright in bed into the sitting position. Still confused, I looked around my dark room. I was warm and safe. My attention was drawn to the outside. I heard the wind beating on the house, knocking on the door, calling for me.

Slowly and quietly, I got into the wheelchair. I then rolled myself into the living room and looked out the large front window. I saw the snow rubbing against the glass. I had to go there.

I carefully rolled through the house, making sure not to bump into something and wake Jim. I stopped in front of the door. Something was calling me, beckoning me to come out. Slowly, I opened the door.

I rolled out onto the porch like a ghost into the fog of night. Pure blackness lay ahead of me. I couldn't see the contrast of white snow in the black night. The cold wind took my breath, and the bitter cold stung my skin. Why was I here? I wanted to get up and walk further into the darkness. Then, I realized what was different about this storm. She had returned to claim me.

"Madie, are you alright?"

I flinched. The sound of Jim's voice startled me.

"She won't get me, not this time or ever."

I wheeled back into the house, and Jim closed the door behind me. I felt sad but mostly embarrassed. In the dark room, I was glad Jim couldn't see my tears streaming down my cheeks.

"Am I going crazy, losing it? I would change my name, but she would still find me. I felt myself being drawn outside."

"What you went through, your emotions are still lost. No, you're going to be fine."

I watched Jim walk through the dark to the kitchen table. When he returned, he handed me a Kleenex.

How did he know? I thought.

"Thank you," I said.

"Do you want to talk? We have all night," he asked.

"No, I'm sorry for waking you. I'm not going to do a death dive off the porch. I just had to look her in the eye and let her know she got as much as she's going to get from me."

I had to be going crazy. I was talking about Mother Nature as if she was a living creature. In my head, I guess she was.

"She has claimed many lives through countless years. More than anyone will ever know. Once, when I was vacationing in Florida, I had a chance to talk to a fisherman, the captain of his own boat. He was half-tanked, but regardless, when he started talking about the sea, he shared his thoughts. He just talked as if I wasn't there. The gaze in his eyes looked far away. I believe he was standing on the side of his boat, looking across the vast miles of the ocean.

"To condense his story, he told me that one has to respect the ocean. When you're out there, you never let your guard down. Always be prepared, even on a calm day. When the storm gets bad, never give up, never do anything stupid, and always look out for the crew.

"When he finished, he just stood up and left. I felt as though he had left something out there or someone. So, I sat there alone, thinking the frozen north was no different. Instead of drowning, you freeze.

"Death comes in different forms—that is the only difference. So, what I'm trying to tell you is that you looked her in the eye each and every day you were out there. You didn't let your guard down, and you didn't give up. What more could you have done? Nothing," Jim said.

"I didn't take care of my crew," I said, thinking of Craig.

"The forces of nature weren't behind that."

"No."

"You did an exceptional thing, almost superhuman. You survived and found your way out from the middle of nowhere."

I sat there listening to Jim and all the things he had said. He was making me feel better, but I would never be normal again, physically or mentally. I would never be the old Madie again.

"Running for my life from the death dealers, I never had time to worry about much else. I knew I had to eat. Usually, at night, I cried myself to sleep. Craig was always in my thoughts, as he is now and will be for the rest of my life."

Then, I was silent, reliving the past and the memories that will haunt me forever.

Jim remained quiet also, waiting patiently to see if I wanted to go on.

I did.

"The last half was even worse. I know that doesn't seem possible, but it was. I was lonely, tired, and cold."

I went on and on throughout the night, saying the same thing—most of what Jim had heard before. Talking about it was my only salvation from falling over the edge. My only security blanket, each time I thought about Craig, I felt warm inside. He was still with me!

It was early morning, and soon, daylight would show what Mother Nature was giving us. We went to bed.

Sitting at the kitchen table, we were drinking coffee. It was mid-morning. "Thank you for listening to me babble on all night. I'm sorry for keeping you up."

Jim shook his head, "That's what friends are for."

I felt my throat gurgle, and my eyes started to water. I wasn't going to cry this time. "A true friend you are, plus a whole lot more. You're in the saint status."

Jim smiled. "No, not hardly."

It snowed throughout the day. Jim made two trips outside, shoveling off the front porch each time. On the second trip out, I watched him fade away into the blowing snow, heading for the shed.

Twenty minutes later, I heard the snowmobile pull up beside the house and behind the fireplace. Then, I heard a door open and heard Jim stacking firewood in the box beside the fireplace.

How convenient, I thought.

Throughout the day, I watched him open the door from the inside and refill the stove with wood. I saw that it was getting low but thought nothing of it. Now, I knew!

The stove was a plus. The inside of the house was toasty warm. This was the first time he had used it since I arrived, and I wondered why.

Once Jim was back in the house, I didn't feel so on edge. I was worrying over nothing, and I knew that. He was an old pro, experienced in this extremely harsh weather.

"The fireplace is a nice added luxury, kind of cozy. You should burn it more often."

Jim smiled his kind, warm smile. "Well then, we will. There's more wood out there than we will burn all winter."

"The next sunny day, will you take me out there? I would like to see what things look like from the outside."

"Sure, I would be glad to. I will do more than that. You can go and sit on the lake and ice fish with me. If you feel up to it, we can take the snowmobile and ride into town; it's only nine miles away."

"I'd like that."

Inside, I wasn't quite sure if I was ready.

The rest of the afternoon we spent playing cards. It was a slow process. I used a stack of books to lean my cards against. I would slide each individual card over the edge of the table so I was able to grasp it with my thumb.

My left hand ached all the time, and much more so if I bumped it. Using it made it burn, but I was glad I still had it. It was a small price to pay, so I said nothing.

We were finished playing cards, and Jim had kicked my butt. We were sitting at the kitchen table, and I asked, "When will I be able to be fitted with artificial limbs?"

Jim frowned.

"Each person is different. It depends on how the healing process goes. It takes time; even though the skin looks healed up, it's still tender. It takes weeks, even months, for it to toughen up. The body weight pressure on the skin inside the prosthetic could easily tear it open. If that were to happen, it could set you back another few months."

"I'd really like to start walking again. Realistically, how much longer would it be?"

"One more month, by the end of March."

I became excited! Four more weeks! Much sooner than I had thought. "I can't wait! The wheelchair needs to go."

"I would expect that from you. Professionally speaking, that's what every doctor wants to hear. You wouldn't believe the number of people that won't try. They just give up and live the rest of their lives the way they are. There's been so much tremendous progress in prostheses; it's unbelievable. Some people still think of it as a peg thumping down the street. Nowadays, you can walk past someone with an artificial leg, but you don't even know it."

"What about two?"

"Well, that's where the real test comes in. It takes a lot of therapy and training, but mostly willpower. I have no doubt in you."

I do, but I didn't let Jim know that.

24
CHAPTER

It took Jim half of the day to dig out from the storm. I watched him do a great deal of shoveling. Ninety percent of the work was done with the tractor and the snow blower. His snow blower was not a small one; it was equipped with a heated cab, and he blew a path from the shed around the front of the house and down to the lake, which was nearly twenty feet wide. Then, he started on the lake. When he finished there, he had cleared two acres of ice.

A high pressure had moved in. It always did after a storm. That's what chased the blizzard away, and now the sun was shining. The wind was calm, but the outdoor thermometer registered as twenty below zero.

Burr, I thought as I watched through the front window, cozy and warm from the heat from the fireplace. Why anyone would choose to call this home and spend their entire lives here was beyond me.

And I used to think where I lived was cold. Now, I realize it's just a walk in the park.

Mary arrived on the third day; I was happy to see her. She parked her snowmobile in front of the house. She came walking in the front door carrying a box.

We hugged.

"I'm glad to see you," I said. "More food, like there isn't enough in this house?"

"Did you guys survive the storm, okay?" Mary asked as she set the box on the counter.

I hesitated. "Yes, I guess so. For my life, I don't see how you do it."

Mary laughed. "It's just the way it is."

She opened the box.

"No, no food; I picked up something I overlooked," then Mary removed a long rubber mat full of holes from the box, "a mat for the shower, no more slipping and falling down."

Then, Mary removed a much smaller box. "Soap on a rope, just for precaution. I don't know of anyone who doesn't drop the soap in the shower."

I felt bad, making Mary get extra troubled because of my stupidity.

I watched her go to the kitchen drawer and remove a pair of scissors. Then, she cut one end of the rope away from the bar of soap and smiled.

"There, we'll tie the loose end to your wrist, no more bending over."

"Mary," I said slowly, "you're in the saint status with Jim. You two do way too much for me."

"Nonsense, we want to."

I felt the gurgle in my throat again, but I fought it off.

"Thank you."

We talked girl-talk for over half an hour.

"How long has Jim been out on the lake blowing snow?" Mary asked, looking out in that direction. "He likes his ice fishing, well, fishing in general. As soon as the ice melts off, he's out there in his boat, black flies and all. I guess you could say he's a fanatic. He says he decided to stay here years ago because of our company. I believe it was because of the fishing."

Mary smiled. "We would be lost without him. He's the greatest Yankee ever who came to visit and stayed."

"Well, he definitely is the toughest," I said, thinking about just going through the last storm and never seeing the thermometer rise above zero for weeks at a time.

Mary shook her head. "No, there's some tougher than him."

I knew what Mary meant.

"Thank you for the compliment, but it's not true. I only ran because of what I thought they might do to me. Reaching civilization and living wasn't considered. I ran because I had a pretty good idea they would rape me and do other unmentionable things to me for as long as they could. Maybe weeks, even months, until I could find a way to escape or kill myself—probably the latter. Look what it cost me. Now, I'm a freak show. Each time I look in the mirror, I look like a major wart hog."

"Madie, you don't look like a warthog. You're a beautiful woman. Don't ever think anything different."

"I have half a nose, and my nostrils are twice as big as they should be. I'm the queen freak."

"No, Madie, you're not," Mary said quietly.

"Sorry! I'm not feeling sorry for myself; just facing reality. Some days, it's rather tough."

"Oh, I almost forgot," Mary reached back into the box and removed two packages, "I brought venison and rabbit. Which would you like to try for dinner? I can cook both."

Oh no, I thought, *Bambi or Thumper.*

"Why not? I ate raw fish, which was rather chewy. At least this will be cooked. Which does Jim prefer?"

"He likes both, it doesn't matter."

"Let's cook both. I'd like to help if I can."

"Sure, you can fry it."

I felt good; I was doing something productive. With great effort and a big mess on the stove, I managed to turn them in the frying pan, sitting on the stool while doing so.

We ate, it was actually good. I liked them both and complimented Mary's cooking.

"Jonathon's a much better cook than I am. He's the one who showed me how to cook this kind of stuff when we married. Besides, you were the one who cooked."

"Yes, with a lot of help from you."

Then, I was silent, thinking. I would have eaten them raw along with the fish; I just wasn't given the chance.

The dishes were done, and then I took a bath with Mary's help, and then she went home. Jim and I sat in the living room talking.

"Mary said you're an avid fisherman. Is that why you moved so much snow on the lake?"

"No."

I read his expression; something was up. "So, why then?"

"We've got company coming, possibly in a day or two. We never set an exact date before you and I left the hospital, just sometime this week, whenever he could get away for the day."

Now, my curiosity was up. "Well, who?"

"Another doctor. I had to make room for the helicopter to land."

"Wow, a friend of yours?"

"No."

"Are you sick?" I asked worriedly.

"No." Jim smiled.

Now, I was confused. It was too early for me to be fitted with prosthetics, so what could another doctor do that Jim couldn't?

Jim read my thoughts.

"He's a plastic surgeon. He's going to look at your nose and see what it will need to be repaired."

Jim smiled.

A jolt of excitement rushed through my body. Jim never ceases to amaze me. "Why didn't you tell me before now?"

215

Jim shrugged and grinned, like the kid who got caught with his hand in the cookie jar. "If I gave you all the good stuff at once, you would have nothing to look forward to."

I was beaming, happy! I couldn't believe I was going to get a new nose so soon. "That's something to look forward to no matter when it's given. Wow, I can't believe it!"

Another thing Jim had thought of, something he had prepared for long before it happened. "Thank you."

"You're welcome."

I waited patiently the first day, trying to conceal my excitement but failing miserably. The helicopter was a no-show.

The second day ended up as the first. My disappointment had to show, but Jim showed no concern.

The third morning, we were sitting at the kitchen table, drinking coffee. "It's torturing you, isn't it?"

"Yes. It shows that bad, huh?"

"Yes, he'll show up today, so don't worry."

I nodded. "I won't have to look like a warthog, not that that I'm going anywhere. Even if I lived in town, I wouldn't."

"Self-esteem means a lot, one of the stepping stones on the way to healing."

I knew what that meant; it was another thing Jim had planned. It was going to take more than physical healing for me to survive this, to go on with life.

"You understand everything, don't you?"

"The world's got you down right now. You're resilient; you will get better. I've come to understand one thing about you: you're an angel, and they don't die. They go on, regardless."

I lowered my head. The sadness I felt from the kindness of that man.

"I'm no angel. I don't understand you. You have me on a pedestal where I don't belong. I'm just an average person. Your kindness overwhelms me."

Just then, we heard a snowmobile race up in front of the house and stop.

"That sounded a little too fast for Mary," I said.

"Yes, and a little too early, something's wrong," Jim said.

By the time Jim stood, Jonathon had raced through the front door.

As Jonathon closed the door, Jim asked, "Who?"

"Ed, he didn't get home last night."

"Oh, dear God," Jim said.

"Jerry and George are packing the gear we need, hoping you will help. We thought we'd break up in teams of two."

"Who's Ed?" I asked.

"He's what we call, up here, a long-line trapper. He travels fifty miles a day. The problem is he has two lines, covering each one every other day."

"So, you don't know which one he's on," I said, understanding the big problem.

"He's run the same two lines for over twenty years, and he knows every square foot. The real problem is we don't. He's shown us on the maps, but it's not the same," Jim said.

Silently, I said to myself, *Poor Ed, it's not looking good.*

"His snowmobile probably may have quit on him, and he's hiking it back. Best case scenario, it got dark, and he holed up for the night," Jim said.

"Have you heard the weather? There's another storm coming, and it's moving fast. It's going to start later this afternoon. The bad news is this one's worse than the last. Are you in?" Jonathon asked.

"Just when I thought it couldn't get any worse," Jim said worriedly.

Jim looked at me, out to the lake, and then back to me. I could see his mind reeling.

"Go, I'll be fine. I know what it's like out there. Find him."

Jim frowned.

"Hey, I'm warm, and I have food. You'll be back tonight."

Jim nodded.

I watched Jim get dressed in his Arctic Gear; it didn't take long. I tried not to show the concern I was feeling for them.

They knew what they were doing, I told myself. *This isn't a first for them.*

Jim stood at the door for a moment, looking at me.

"I'll be back as soon as possible."

I smiled, trying to relieve his concern. "Mary will be here soon; I'm fine."

Jonathon nodded. "She was getting ready when I left."

I heard the snowmobiles drive away. Now, I was alone for the first time since I found Jim. I was deeply worried, not for me, but for them. With another storm coming, things can always get worse.

I read the book Mary had given me and listened to the helicopter. Mostly, I worried for the four men. I knew what they were facing: surmountable odds with Mother Nature bearing down on them.

Relax, I said to myself, *they have snowmobiles, and they're traveling in pairs. They'll take care of each other.*

Mary arrived, and hours passed. The day became darker and more menacing as noon arrived. As usual, the wind grew in intensity as the storm approached.

"Mary, you should go home before it starts snowing. I would hate to see you try and get home in it."

I could see that Mary was torn on what to do.

"Well, I should stay here with you," she answered.

"No, no way! You need to be home when Jonathon arrives. He will need you. Remember what I told you? You need to be there for him."

"Yes, but you shouldn't be alone either."

"Let's face reality here. I have years ahead of me being alone. I will be fine."

Mary left right after lunch. The arrival of the helicopter was secondary. If it ended up as being a no-show, I didn't care. My thoughts were with the five men battling the elements.

Ten minutes before two o'clock, I heard the distinctive sound of the helicopter approaching. I had given up on it, showing the storm was closing in on us, and they didn't have long.

From the window, I watched the blades come to a stop, and then two men got out. I wheeled over to the front door; the handle looked new. It wasn't the commonly used doorknob—it was a handle with a thumb push lever. Then, it occurred to me another of Jim's long list of things he had thought of. I'm sure at the time it was installed, it was just for "in case." Today was the case.

I opened the door just as the two men stepped off the ice and onto land. As they got closer, I said, "Come in, it's awfully cold out there."

It was obvious to me who was who. They walked side by side up the front steps. They were dressed basically the same. The man on the left had more of a military look to him, the pilot.

I backed the wheelchair into the living room as they walked in. I spoke to the man on the right first.

"Hi, I'm Madie." I held out my right arm to shake hands.

The doctor hesitated for a second, looking at me.

"Go ahead and shake, it won't break."

I smiled, trying to ease their uncertainty.

"Hello, I'm Dr. David Bryant, and this is Mark Feldon."

I shook both their hands.

David looked around and asked, "Is Jim here?"

"No, he's not. A long-line trapper didn't make it home last night. There's a team of four men out searching one hundred miles of trap line."

"I've heard stories about Jim doing that. Now, I know they're true. Takes a courageous person to do that and survive."

"Yes, but the problem is a bad storm is about to hit us, which makes finding him alive pretty slim after the storm is over. You shouldn't stay long, or you won't make it out of here. Worse yet would be to have it close in on you while you're trying to get back just before it starts snowing. The wind will increase tremendously, and then it will go downhill from there. I don't want you to be another statistic just because of me."

"I've heard your story, and yet you made it."

"Yes, only by the grace of God and help from unbelievable things."

I was quiet for a moment. "Really, you shouldn't stay; we don't have long."

"I believe you; if anyone would know, it would be you. I'll take a look and take a few pictures with me if you don't mind."

"You're here to help me, do what you need to."

I looked at Mark. "There's hot coffee in the kitchen; help yourself."

"I will, thank you," Mark said.

David studied my face. He prodded and poked and then took a series of measurements, writing down notes as he did so. Then, he removed a camera from the case he was carrying with him.

The camera was so close to my face that I could feel the cold radiating from it.

"I'm going to shield your eyes. It's a little bright being this close."

Then, he wrapped an ace bandage around my head. I was in complete darkness, sitting in a wheelchair.

"I'm going to take one picture at each angle, each side, up and down, and one exactly in front."

I heard the shutter click five times, and then he removed the ace bandage. "There, I hope that wasn't too painful."

"No, not at all."

"Good, then we'll be on our way. Tell Jim I will call him."

"I will. Thank you; this means more to me than you know. But please hurry, Mother Nature is kind to no one. She shows no mercy."

David nodded, and we said our goodbyes.

I watched the helicopter lift off and fly away. I said a short prayer for them.

Minutes later, it started snowing.

Within half an hour, it was snowing heavily; all was not well.

Four thirty in the afternoon, and the men had roughly eight hours of search time. I sat in the wheelchair, looking out the front window, hoping that was enough.

"Please make it home," I said.

Please be safe, I said to myself.

Within the hour, it was a raging blizzard. Two in one week, my heart grew heavy. I could feel it sinking in my chest. Visibility was gone, and I could no longer see the huge oak trees in the yard, which were only ten feet away.

Anxiety set in, and I ran the gamut of emotions, tears included. If I had feet, I would have been out there with them. If I had feet, I would go look for them!

I was too nervous to eat. I tried to read, but I was unable to comprehend the words, so I gave that up. With all the nervous energy I had, I had to do something, so I wheeled out into the kitchen and decided to make hot chocolate.

The dishes in the dishwasher were clean, and the microwave was at eye level, all within reach. Very clumsily, I sat the glass in the sink. Using my right arm, I pulled myself up so I could reach the faucet with my left hand, and I filled the glass.

So far, so good, but now, there was a problem. I had watched Mary memorizing in each cupboard, on each shelf, where things were kept. The third cupboard door left of the sink, and the second shelf up sat the box of hot chocolate, far out of my reach. I started to give up on the idea, but then I thought twice.

What else have I got to do? I asked myself.

Now, I had two choices: to pull myself up on the counter, hoping I could sit there, or try standing on my stumps, hoping I could still reach. I chose to stand.

I gripped the edge of the counter with what little was left of my left hand and slowly pulled myself up. I felt myself teetering, rolling on bone, and the pain from standing on my stumps hurt unbelievably but not unbearable. I only had to stand on them for a few seconds, long enough to open the cupboard door and grab the box of hot chocolate.

I couldn't reach the handle, so I pulled on the bottom of the door, and it swung open. The pain intensified rapidly. I couldn't believe how tender the skin that had been sewn together to cover the end of the bone was. I reached for the box on the second shelf.

Once, I stood five and a half feet tall. I had no idea, until now, how much shorter I was. Four foot ten, at the most. I couldn't reach it. I flopped back into the wheelchair, disgusted. My first attempt at doing something on my own was a failure. The first of an endless supply, and I was mad.

Get over it, I thought.

I sat in the wheelchair, thinking.

Then, I had a third choice. I wheeled the chair up parallel to the counter. Now, all I had to do was momentarily stand on the seat and retrieve the box.

Slowly, I pulled myself up and tucked my legs underneath me. Then, I stood, using my left hand as a crutch as I stood. The pad on the seat didn't hurt nearly as much as the bare floor. Now, I had the box in my hand and slid my thumb under the lid.

Two things went wrong: the lid popped open, and the box started to fall. I leaned forward, trying to stop its descent, an involuntary reaction and a bad mistake.

From there, things went downhill, and they went into the express lane. The wheelchair rolled backward, forcing me to fall forward. I reached out with my right arm, trying to grasp the counter.

Mentally, I could feel myself flexing my fingers, reaching for the countertop, but it missed. My arm caught nothing but air. Now, I was at the point of no return. The left side of my body was facing the cupboard.

Before I had time to react and save myself with my left arm, my head slammed onto the edge of the counter. My forehead and cheekbone, on the left side of my head, took the brunt of the impact. I felt the hit but hadn't had time to register the pain yet.

I was concentrating too hard on what was coming next. A split second later, my left shoulder collided with the counter, and my momentum increased its downward spiral toward the floor.

The impact on my shoulder spun me around in midair. I was flailing about as I continued my descent as if I could get a handhold on something, a natural reaction in a state of panic.

The right side of my body took the next big hit as I slammed onto the kitchen floor. I bounced once and slid forward a few inches.

I was dazed.

Two plus two, four, I said to myself.

I wasn't knocked out; I was still with it. Then, my mind did the involuntary body scan. The pain was instantly there, and my face hurt the worst.

"Oh crap, that hurt," I said.

Instantly, I brought my left land up to my face, trying to rub it to relieve the pain. The pain in my left shoulder couldn't stand the quick movement, pain outweighing what it had set out to do. It went limp in midair, losing control and stability; my hand slammed into the bruise I had just received on my face. I yelled, and then I rolled over onto my back.

With both shoulders throbbing, I let my arms lay on the kitchen floor, and I closed my eyes. I could feel the swelling start around my eye.

Minutes passed while I waited for the pain to subside.

I put my elbows beneath me and pushed myself up into the sitting position. I could already see the puffy sacks above and below my eye.

Oh great, I thought.

Then, I rubbed my face and then looked at my left hand. No blood, which was a good thing. I looked at the wheelchair, which had rolled backward and stopped when it hit the stove.

I sat there, thinking, *What is the best way to get back in it?*

As I thought about it, the pain in my shoulders eased, but the pain in my face increased.

I slid on my butt the six or so feet across the kitchen to the wheelchair. The safest way back into the seat was to stand. I put my knees underneath me and straightened my hips. Both forearms rested on the seat of the wheelchair.

It was against the stove, unable to roll any further. I leaned forward, applying much of my upper body weight on my elbows. I drew my left leg up, and the stump made contact with the floor.

The solid jolt of the bone making contact ran through my body. That was something I wasn't used to. No cushion, no spring-loaded tension that ankles give—clunk. My right leg hit the floor, and I put my left and then right elbows on the arms of the chair. I stood, my socks pivoted nicely on the floor, but not without pain.

I sat on the chair. *A graceful ending to a disastrous beginning.*

I rested, breathing heavily. The time spent lying in bed and now sitting in the wheelchair was taking a toll on my body. My muscles were wasting away. I would soon have to do something about that.

I rolled alongside the counter. Most of the bags of hot chocolate had spilled from the box and scattered about on the counter. It felt awkward always using my left hand. I wasn't left-handed before, but now I had to learn to be.

I replaced the bags in the box; the last one I used my teeth to tear open.

Sitting in the living room, my face pounding, I drank hot chocolate. I waited patiently to hear the roar of the engine when Jim returned on the snowmobile.

Hours passed, and nothing. Deep inside, I wasn't planning on it. With the blinding snow, it would be impossible for anyone to navigate. I hoped they were safe. Surely, they had packed gear to stay warm for the night. They weren't rookies like I was.

I was still worried.

Midnight came, and the wind was howling. I was too nervous to go to bed. I slowly paced back and forth in the wheelchair. I stopped and turned the front porch light on.

Looking out the window beside the door, I could see the porch post. Past that was a wall of white. The snow blocked all possibility of any light penetrating it. This was a much worse storm than the last. Jonathon was right, and yet they set out anyway.

I don't know how hard the wind was blowing, but guessing at the speed of the snow flying past the light, it was severe. A conservative guess was fifty to sixty miles per hour.

I started to leave the porch light on, but then I turned it off. They weren't coming back tonight.

It was 1 AM, and I decided to try to sleep. Clothes were on, and there was no shower. I lay down on the couch and used the blanket hanging on the back.

A small, dim light on the stove cast just enough light to give a few shadows in the living room. I stared at them, listening to the wind and worrying about the men.

I woke and looked at the clock hanging on the wall: 7:53 AM. I looked out the front window and saw it was still snowing. My heart sank.

"Unbelievable! Does it ever quit up here?" I spoke.

Why did I think about the bear? I had no clue. I pictured it inside the cave, sleeping, warm, and out of harm's way—smart bear.

I hoped the men were doing the same. I wondered if they found Ed; if not, Mother Nature surely would have been able to put another notch in her belt.

I lay on the couch alone in the house. I already didn't like it.

"Get over it," I said silently, "I have years and years of it to come."

The morning passed, and I spent it in the wheelchair, pacing from one window to the next. Then, I would make a lap around the kitchen table and start all over again.

Lunchtime came and went, but I was too nervous to eat.

My left eye was nearly swollen shut. I ignored the pain, but for something to do, I wheeled into the bathroom to take a look at it. It was a deep red, and within a day or two, it would be black.

"Oh great! How am I going to explain this one?" I was looking at myself in the mirror.

My nervous energy was building. I rolled up to the refrigerator, opened the door, and saw the leftovers from Mary's last dinner. I ate it cold, something I had acquired a taste for. I wasn't all that hungry, but it was something different to do other than pace.

Now, four o'clock in the afternoon and less than an hour before dark. I thought back to all the days I spent walking here, always cold, always tired, and most of the time hungry. I hoped the men had made a decent shelter and had food for the second night.

I made another trip to the front window. It was hard to tell how much snow had fallen from the storm. With the wind blowing so hard, the snow was piling in drifts around the house, leaving a wind-whipped tunnel between the house and snow, some of them nearly level with the bottom of the window. The bottom of the window was five feet above the ground, and the drift on the side of the house, which was downwind, was growing more. It had to be at least seven or eight feet tall.

Another guess, but I would say two feet or more of fresh snow on top of the three that were already there.

I had no way of contacting Mary to see if she was as worried as I was. How many times had she been through this? Probably more than I could imagine.

I read, and I paced, and then I read, and I paced. By 8 PM, I was tired of doing both, so I lay down on the couch and slept.

I heard it in my dream: *The death dealers were chasing me on snowmobiles*. And I was on foot. I was running frantically. I couldn't see them behind me, but they were getting closer and closer. I ran harder, ignoring the searing pain in my lungs. I tried to look behind me but couldn't.

At any moment, I felt that I was going to be run down. I was about to lose the race. I looked ahead, and there was no place to go but straight through the trees and deep snow. If only I was in my running shoes, on bare pavement, then I would stand a chance.

Now, I was yelling and running as hard as I could. The snow had become so dense I felt as if I was running in quicksand. I couldn't look back; the snowmobile was too close, and the noise from the engine grew.

I felt myself quiver and then jerk. I was wide awake and sat up. It took me a brief moment to realize I was inside the house, warm and safe.

Then, I heard it! This time, it was real, the sound of a snowmobile.

Jim was back! It was dark outside, and my emotions went from a panicked horror to excited happiness.

I glanced at the clock: eleven thirty-seven.

I was still confused, not fully awake yet, and things were happening so fast.

Why now? Why at this time of night? I thought.

I looked out the window. The light shining from the snowmobile gave me enough to see that it had quit snowing, and this all happened in less than three seconds.

The snowmobile stopped in front of the steps, and then the engine went dead.

I thought of how the mind plays cruel jokes, part real, part fiction, but now I was wide awake.

I hobbled, hopped into the wheelchair, and started toward the door. I was so happy I couldn't stand it! The house was dark, and there was no way I could see myself smiling from ear to ear.

I got to the door as it opened. I moved in reverse as Jim walked in so I wouldn't be run over.

"You're up?" Jim asked.

I was still smiling. I leaned forward, held out both arms, and leaned farther forward. Jim understood; he had already hugged me when the door slammed shut.

"Yes, since you left. I'm glad you're back and safe. I worried about you guys, risking your lives when you didn't have to."

Jim stood. I could see his grin in the dim light from the stove.

"Madie, we weren't risking our lives; it wasn't that bad out there."

"Are you serious? The worst blizzard of the season, and it wasn't that bad? Right!!! What if one of you froze to death out there? You endured some pretty rough weather. I was really worried."

Jim's face became serious.

"Madie, what we endured was nothing compared to what you did. We had a tent and heat, food, and fuel for three days. On top of that, we each have our own top-of-the-line GPS, four snowmobiles, and one two-way radio per team. So, if it came down to where we were destitute, we could still drive out in the middle of a storm. Madie, you did the impossible. A superhuman feat doesn't come close to saying what you did. I know of no one who survived what you did."

I quickly scanned my memory of my trip, but this wasn't about me. "Nonetheless, you were out there. I was here, and I was worried."

Then, I thought of what Jim said, and I asked, "So why didn't you?"

"Didn't I what?"

"Drive out in the storm."

"Well, the obvious. The GPS tells us where we are and what direction we need to go, but it doesn't tell us where the trees are. Can't see, you know."

How well did I know that?

"So, what did you do at night?"

"Played cards and told more stories. Now, we have another one to add to our list."

"Played cards!" I blurted.

Then, I laughed. "Here I was doing the wheelchair pacing thing, and you were playing cards!"

"Yes, we travel well prepared."

"I know that now. I guess I should have known."

Jim was already removing his boots and heavy clothes.

"So, what about Ed? Did you find him?"

"Yes, but poor old Ed didn't fare so well. He didn't make it. He was gone when we found him. The autopsy will tell, but I'm guessing it was a heart attack. He was gone long before we found him, frozen solid."

My heart sank. I didn't know Ed, I'd never met him, but I felt bad for him. "I'm sorry—another one for Mother Nature."

"He died doing what he loved. We talked about that. Ed wouldn't have wanted it any other way."

"Well, I'm glad you're back."

Jim turned the light on, and then he saw my face. A concerned, worried look registered on his face. "Oh my God! Are you alright? What happened?"

"The neighborhood grizzly bear and I didn't get along."

"Yeah, sure."

"Honest, you should have seen the bear; he didn't fare either."

"Shower again? There are no grizzly bears here."

"No." I didn't want to tell Jim, but it was coming.

Jim walked over to me, turned the light on beside the sofa, and inspected my face.

"No, did you fall getting in or out of bed?"

"Hot chocolate." I didn't want to give the details.

"No thanks, don't try to elude the answer."

"That is the answer," I said.

I watched Jim look to the counter, up to the cabinet, and then back to me. "That was on the second shelf. Why didn't you have something that was within reach?"

"I thought that was within reach. It wasn't graceful, believe me."

"Well, nothing is broken. Live and learn."

CHAPTER 25

Several more weeks of winter passed behind us. Each storm that came diminished in intensity. The snow continued to pileup outside. After each storm, Jim ritually removed the snow from the barn to and around the house, then down to the lake and out to his favorite fishing spot. He fished relentlessly, each day for roughly two hours. Rarely did he return empty-handed. I didn't get tired of eating fish. It's cooked by Mary and Jim in more ways than I knew it could be. I like all of them, but I now, and always will, have a new outlook on food. Taste is just purely for pleasure. The body doesn't care as long as it doesn't make it sick.

I was starting to get restless, being inside since I arrived, and I needed to get out. It wasn't mentioned again about getting out and going to Mary's for dinner. I wanted to ask but felt that I would be too forward by doing so.

Jim returned from his daily fishing trip. He had a good day, three walleye and one northern. As usual, I sat by the kitchen table and watched him clean them. His method was much more efficient and neater than mine. Jim used an electric filet knife. He would start behind the gill, cut down to the backbone, and follow that to the tail. With the skin still attached at the base of the tail, using the knife, he would flip that over. In one nonstop, smooth motion, he would continue down, removing the meat from the skin. Then, a small, sharp handheld knife was used to cut around the ribs, removing them. The fish was quickly flipped over, and the process was repeated. Each fish took less than one minute to clean.

I had never cleaned a fish before; therefore, mine was a hack job, but the raw, bloody meat kept me alive.

"Can I go fishing with you tomorrow?" I asked as Jim was cleaning up.

Jim paused for a brief moment, "I don't see why not."

I had a good idea of what he was thinking. "I'll just sit there and watch you. I don't want to fish."

Jim said nothing.

"I can slide out there on my behind." I was silent for a moment. I couldn't read Jim's expression on what he was thinking. "Well, I can."

"Madie, you can go fishing anytime you want; all you have to do is ask. I've been waiting, letting you do things on your time, and no, you're not sliding out there on your butt. You can ride."

I smiled; I was happy—the little things.

The next morning, I couldn't wait. I tried to show no emotion about going fishing, but I think it showed. Jim and Mary went about their business as usual.

"What day is it?" I asked. "I've lost track of the day of the week." I had a long time ago, but I didn't tell them that. I had no need to keep track, and I wasn't going anywhere.

"Saturday," Jim replied.

Lunchtime arrived. We were sitting at the kitchen table eating. I heard the sound of snowmobiles approaching. The noise grew louder as they drove around to the front of the house. I counted them as the drivers turned off the motors. One, two, three. I wondered who was there. I looked across the table at Jim and then Mary. They showed no concern for our guests out front.

Now, I wondered what was going on. I heard the footsteps coming up the steps. Next, I would hear the knock on the door. *Why wasn't Jim getting up to go to the door and see who was there?* I thought to myself.

I was the only one looking at the front door, but the knock never happened. The door opened, and then Jonathon, Jerry, and George walked in.

"Can't catch fish sitting there eating," Jerry said.

"You're early," Mary replied.

Now I knew why Jim and Mary were acting the way they were. Something was going on, but I hadn't figured it out yet, and obviously, I was the only one who didn't know.

"Yeah, we got tired of working on our tans," Jonathon said.

I laughed. It was five degrees above zero, a real heat wave.

Mary got up, walked over to Jonathon, and kissed him on the check. "You've never had a tan in your life. Would you guys like something to drink?"

George, who I considered the quiet one, spoke.

"We brought our own," patting his chest pocket. "For medicinal purposes. And to keep the nip away."

Then, George looked at me, "The only medicine that combats the cold."

Everyone laughed. It was Saturday, and it was going to be a good day.

I looked at the two culprits sitting at the table with me. "So why the big secret? Carrying on all morning like nothing out of the ordinary…."

Jim cut me off, smiling. "It's just a little surprise. Thought we would have our own little fishing derby this afternoon, Mary included."

Mary smiled.

"And you! I thought we were friends; us girls are supposed to stick together."

They got a big chuckle out of that.

"Fishing derby, huh?" I asked, looking at Jim.

"Yes, winner takes all; looser has to clean and cook fish," Jim said.

"What does the winner get?"

"All the fish they can eat."

I looked at my stumps. Now was the time to add in on their little charade. "What does the loser get?"

"All the fish they can eat," Jim laughed.

"I see. I hope everyone here likes peanut butter and jelly." They all laughed again. "I can toast the bread to make it special." The laughing didn't stop.

"Not to worry, we've got you fixed up," said Jonathon.

What did they think of this time? I had to ask, "What? A sign that says, 'Hey fish, jump in Madie's bucket," I said smiling.

"Better than that, you'll see."

The three men left before Jim, Mary, and I. They went out to the lake to auger holes through the ice.

Jim and Mary stayed behind to help me get dressed.

"The gear I wore here will be fine," I said.

Jim shook his head, "No, you've got new ones to wear."

I watched Jim get up from the table and walk up to his bedroom.

When he returned he was carrying new insulated coveralls, black with silver striping around the thighs and biceps, very nice looking.

I sat staring at them, dumbfounded. I didn't know what to say.

"Sooner or later, I knew you would need these," Jim said, holding them up for my approval. "The silver stripes glow in the dark."

I wondered how long they had been here, another of the many things that had been thought of. "Jeez, guys, you never cease to amaze me. I don't know what to say. A thank you right now would be like leaving a dollar tip on a hundred-dollar bill, but thank you." I looked at the new

Arctic gear Jim had bought for me. "Wow, it's really nice," it really was. It was a far better quality than the death dealers, which was even better than mine. But, then again, we had no plans to be out in subzero weather.

Jim handed them to me. I could tell by the weight and texture they were of good quality, the best. "I know this is kind of a cliché, but you shouldn't have; mine would have been fine."

"You deserve it. You've been dealt a bad deal, and I'm happy to do it," Jim said.

Tears formed. "But why? I'm nobody. I still have a hard time grasping why you do so much for me, why I was allowed to live, and why everyone treats me like a queen when, in reality, I'm a freak show." I wiped my nose, what was left of it, and then my eyes.

"Madie, one thing you do not ever forget: you're more than somebody. You are a queen, if nothing else, the endurance queen. You were allowed to live by your own perseverance. You outlasted them; by sheer willpower, you survived."

I shook my head 'no.' "I outlasted them only because I was scared to death."

"Nonetheless, it still took superhuman stamina to travel that far." Then Jim was silent for a while. "You know the night we were out looking for Ed? You were talked about quite a bit. It was mentioned several times that if we were looking for you, we had no doubt we would find you alive, that is, if we could have kept up with you."

I laughed, "Yeah, right, you have the snowmobiles."

Mary chimed in. "People around town still talk about you, and they keep asking when they get to meet you; you're a celebrity."

"Yeah, right," I said again. *But what else did they have to talk about in a small town?* I thought.

"Come on, let's get you dressed and go have some fun," Jim said.

By the time we were dressed, the snowmobiles returned to the house. I wondered how they timed it so perfectly.

Like before, Jonathon, Jerry, and George went to work, picking me up and carrying me outside. Then, they placed me in one of the sleds behind a snowmobile.

"You guys need to start your own shuttle business. Call it Deep Woods Taxi Service," I said after they sat me down.

"I think we'd starve to death," George said.

"What kind of medicine are you taking?" I asked.

"Doctor Jim Beam. Jerry has Nurse Brandy. Do you need a shot?" George asked.

Everyone was laughing. I was between a laugh and a cry, a happy cry. "You guys are the best," I said.

We drove out onto the ice, and they went to work again. Six wooden benches were placed beside the six holes. I was surprised they had six holes bored through four feet of ice so fast. I looked around. Over to the side lay a large two-man motorized ice auger. "If I had had that with me, I wouldn't have been so hungry. The last time I chopped a hole through the ice, it took me at least two hours."

They looked at each other, not knowing what to say.

I did it again; I ruined the mood. I had to stop doing that. "I'm sorry, I was just thinking out loud."

"You can think out loud anytime you want to," Jim said.

It was at least five degrees below zero, but none of the men had hats on. The sun was shining, and the wind wasn't blowing, so I guess for these people who have lived here all their lives, it was a warm day.

I was placed on a bench next to a hole. They all stood around me, and I wondered why. How was I going to hold a fishing rod? Let alone reel in a fish if I caught one. Why weren't the others going to one of the other spots to start fishing? I had so many questions, and then they were answered. Jonathon walked up to me, holding a fishing rod and something else. I didn't take the time to see what it was. I looked at each of their faces, and each one held a smile.

"Here, we got you fixed up." He held out a short pole with a huge reel on it. "This is motorized. All you have to do is push the button down to wind the line in. Push up on the button to let the line out."

Well, that's fine, I thought. But how was I going to hold onto the pole? Before I could ask, Jonathon was placing a leather belt around my waist.

"This is what the deep-sea fishermen use to haul in the big ones."

"Man, I hope there isn't any fish in this lake that big. If there is, it will pull me down through that hole," I said.

They laughed.

"No, but there are some pretty big northerns in here," Jim replied.

"How big?" I asked.

"Fifteen to twenty pounds," Jim answered.

Jim stayed beside me for a while. He baited my hook and helped me get the line through the hole. The reel worked perfectly, just a slight 'hum' when I pushed the button. We watched the bait disappear down the hole.

The end of the pole sat nicely in the pocket on the front of the leather belt. I held the pole up with my right forearm, my left ready to pounce on the button if I caught a fish. "Thank you," I said quietly to Jim.

Jonathon, Mary, Jerry, and George were fishing. I watched Jim, he was looking around slowly, and then he would look at each one of them. Each time, he would look at the shore. I was curious as to what he was thinking and he was unaware that I was watching him.

I wanted to say, 'You better start fishing if you don't want to have to clean them,' but I didn't. I watched the show; I had a front-row seat. I waited patiently, waiting to see what Jim was up to.

He walked about fifty yards to the right of us and then looked to the shore again. "Would one of you guys help me auger a hole here?" He asked.

"What? The last hole's not good enough?" Jerry asked.

"Uh, oh, I smell a skunk in the wood pile," George said.

"I can see this isn't going to be fair. The skunk has a home-turf advantage. We're the ones who are going to get skunked," Jonathon said.

I looked at Mary, and she was smiling from ear to ear.

Jim shrugged his shoulders innocently. "Well, it's not that I don't want to clean fish. I want to eat them."

"Oh, I see. So that's how it's going to be. We cast the first stone before the first fish is even caught," Jerry said.

I decided it was my turn. I started whistling, "Here, fishy, fishy, fishy."

They laughed hard. Everyone was having a good time.

"Mmm… peanut butter and jelly is sounding good. I think I'll have mine filleted."

They roared.

Down inside, I was sad. Craig would be at the height of his glory if he was here. Only if I thought; I hid my feelings because I wasn't going to ruin their day.

"The way I see it, Mary, Jerry, and Jonathon will catch three, maybe four if they're lucky. George, one if he's really lucky," Jim said, laughing.

"Hey, wait a minute, I'm a good fisherman," George said.

Now, Jim was laughing hard again. "Well, you asked."

"No, I didn't," George replied.

"Oh, I'm sorry," Jim said.

An hour passed; the home turf advantage seemed to be working out. Jim had caught double the fish over anyone else. He was right about George, he hadn't caught a fish yet, but neither had I.

I was a little nervous when we started fishing. I was worried about getting cold before we were through. It's amazing how the body doesn't forget, but I settled into the cold air as though it wasn't there.

Another half hour or so passed. I wanted to catch at least one fish. No doubt I was going to catch the least amount. I knew that before leaving the house. They weren't going to leave me to clean the fish.

"This really sucks. Does the fishing derby give handicaps as they do in golfing?" I asked.

Everyone was silent. "I mean, one of my fish ought to equal four of yours."

"Sounds good to me," Mary said.

"Why not," Jim said, "poor George is the one who's going to be cleaning fish."

"Looks that way," George said.

"I'd be kicking some butt if I could fish the way I did out there," I said.

"How did you catch fish without a fishing pole?" Jerry asked. "I always wondered."

"Has anyone got anything shiny?" I asked.

"You bet," Jerry answered.

Jerry stood up and opened his fishing box. He removed something and then started walking toward me. "Pull up your line, and I'll hook this on it."

I did, and the hook was bare. "Darn, I didn't know I had lost my bait."

"No, you won't. You're at a big disadvantage here. Walleye only nibble at the bait. With the pole and, well, you can't feel them bite." Jerry said.

Jerry didn't say what he was thinking, but I knew what he avoided. I had no hands or fingers to feel.

I watched Jerry remove the single hook from the line and then attach a large, shiny, artificial lure with a treble hook on the end to my line.

"There, that should get you one."

I lowered the line back into the water.

Jerry went and sat back down.

"After I finally got a hole chopped through the ice…" then I was quiet, thinking. Sadness was always with me and, on occasions like now, it took precedence. I wasn't going to cry, not this time. "Craig bought me the necklace I'm wearing. I used it for bait. It would lure the fish up to the hole."

"But you didn't have a pole or a hook," Jerry said.

"I used a spear; I would put a super sharp point on it with all the strength I had. I would make sure the spear went through the fish at least a foot, sometimes more. Most of them would try to swim away, but the edge of the hole prevented that. I would hold on to the spear until they tired out."

I didn't need to look around; I could feel the others looking at me, waiting for me to finish my story.

"I couldn't drag them up through the hole without the axe. I put the head of the axe underneath them; that way, they didn't slide off the spear."

"Smart thinking," Jerry said.

"It was the second or third day the bear was following me, and I don't remember which. I had just tossed my first catch in the snow beside me. While it was still flopping around, the next thing I saw was the bear running straight at me. I was scared to death.

The thought went through my mind: this wasn't one of the ways I foresaw dying out here, and that it's going to be painful. I would have jumped into the water, and I looked, but I wouldn't fit through the hole. So, I just froze, not because I wanted to; it was involuntary. The bear slid to a stop beside me as it grabbed the fish. It ate several more that day. That was the day it started trusting me."

I was so deep in thought telling my story that my vision was secondary, just a blur.

"I filleted the last two. The bear even ate the skeletons. The next few days after that, I always made sure I fed it fish. Either give it food or be food, I thought. But you know the funny thing is, the day I watched the bear kill one of the death dealers, it never ate any part of him."

I failed. My eyes and nose were streaming, gushing torrents of water. "The bear attacked him with unbelievable fury. It kept biting at his face and neck while it tore the rest of his body apart with its claws. His chest was an empty cavity when the bear finished with him. The bear turned and looked at me and then growled. I thought I was next. It was as if someone flipped the switch off, it casually walked away as if nothing happened. I was shaking so badly I didn't know if I could stand. It was the second worst thing I've ever seen."

I looked at Mary, and she was in tears. No one said anything. "I'm sorry. You guys don't want to hear my stories."

"But we do, they're fascinating," Jerry said.

"They are far better than anything we have to tell," George said.

"All of ours together will never equal yours," Jonathon said.

I looked at Jim, he remained silent, but he'd heard most of them in the hospital.

"The bear saved my life more than once. It was Craig's love that kept me vertical long after I should have been face down in the snow frozen solid."

I had forgotten about fishing, even though I was still holding the pole. All of a sudden, I felt a tremendous pull on the fishing pole. Instantly, I tensed the muscles in both my arms, and I didn't have time to think about the rest of my body. I was pulled off the stool I was sitting on. I landed on my knees and then my elbows. My face stopped inches from the ice. I could hear the reel unwinding as the fish pulled the line out.

Everyone came running in my direction. I didn't know if they were checking on me to see if I was hurt or if they didn't want me to lose the fish. I didn't have time to ask.

The fish was obviously a big one; it kept taking line, and the reel continued to sing. Jerry reached down and did something to the reel. "There, that will slow it down a bit."

Whatever Jerry did made the pull on my arms greater, and I lay there on the ice. I looked up at him with a frown.

"I set the brake tighter. Don't want him pulling all the line out of the reel," Jerry said, answering the question I didn't ask.

They helped me up and sat me back on the bench while I continued to hang onto the pole. It was quite a feat for all of us.

"This one's going to be huge," Jim said.

"What is it? I didn't know there were sharks this far north," I said.

They laughed.

"No, it's going to be a Northern," Jim said.

"Don't lose him!" Jerry said excitedly.

"What do I do?" I asked. I had no idea.

They talked me through it. Several times, I asked one of them to take the pole, but they would have no part of it. They told me it was my fish to pull in.

After fifteen minutes, the fish gave up, and I was exhausted. "How are we going to get jaws up through the hole?" I asked.

Everyone was grinning but me; I was too tired.

Just as Jim said, it was a Northern, and huge was an inadequate description for it. The fish weighed nineteen pounds, fourteen ounces. It was a whopper!

"I can't believe it," I said.

Jim removed a camera from the pocket of his jacket. They tied a rope around my wrist so I could hold the fish up. "Everyone, get around, Madie," Jim said.

After the picture was taken, Jonathon said, "Take several extras. Mary and I want one, and one will have to be put on the wall at the grocery store."

I wanted one with Jim and myself, so I asked.

When the pictures were over, so was the fishing. Jim had caught the most with six. Jonathon and Jerry each had four, and Mary came next with two. Poor George – zero – just as Jim had said.

"How did you know?" I asked.

"Know what? Oh, the fish count," Jim replied, "Well…"

George cut him off, answering it for him. "He knows every square inch of this lake, where the fish hang out and where they don't."

"Maybe so, but I've never seen a Northern that big caught on this side of the lake."

"Well, Madie, by pounds of fish caught, you win," Jonathon said.

"Yes, but Jim caught the most."

"We knew that would happen before we started," Jerry said.

We rode the snowmobiles into town to Jonathon and Mary's house. There, we had the fish fry, complete with French fries, coleslaw, and hush puppies, something I had never had before. Everything was delicious, and we all ate our fill. More than we normally would eat.

The word got around town fast. Soon many visitors started flowing through Mary's house. Not to eat fish, to meet me. I was cordial, but down inside, I didn't care much for it. I would have rather done without it, but I owed this group that much as much as they had done for me.

Visitors flowed through the house about as much as the drinks flowed. Some stayed quite a while, while others only passed through.

I sat back and watched. The more people that stayed and talked, the happier our group seemed. It was clear to me that Jonathon, Mary, Jerry, and George were the locals.

They knew everyone personally. I was also amazed at how much alcohol Canadians can drink without getting drunk. Jim kept it in moderation. He fit right in. He asked about their children or grandchildren as he talked to different people.

The people who visited didn't know how to take me. I didn't know if it was what I went through, or the condition I was now in, or maybe because I was an outsider. More than likely, it was all of the above.

Every so often, I would catch one of the women standing off in a corner staring at me. I always wondered what they were thinking. What I wanted to say is, 'Yeah, I know I'm a freak show,' but I didn't. It wasn't their fault. No matter where I go, even when I'm at home, people will stare.

Maybe the woman who stared at me felt sorry for me. To me, that was worse. I didn't want that from anyone. I would prefer they thought of me as I did—a freak show.

I was looking at a group talking across the room. The next thing I knew, there was a woman standing beside me.

"Madie," a timid, quiet voice said. "I'd like to shake your hand."

I looked up. It was the woman who had been staring at me earlier. Here comes the pity party.

"I'm sorry for bothering you. I would like to shake your hand, the bravest woman I will ever meet. If you ever decide to write a book, I would like you to sign my copy."

I looked into her eyes. This woman was sincere. I held out my left hand.

As grotesque as it was, she took my hand in both of hers. She didn't shake it; she just held it and smiled.

"I'm sorry. I don't know your name."

"Linda. It's an honor to meet you."

I smiled. "I don't know about that, but thank you."

"No one will ever equal what you did." Then she was quiet.

I could tell she was deep in thought.

"Ed was my brother. He would stop by my house every day. He talked about you often. He would have enjoyed meeting you."

I could see her eyes watering. Everyone has to endure tragedy in their life. "I'm sorry, Linda. Jim told me about it."

We talked for a long time. I had another new friend.

CHAPTER 26

We were starting to have a few days of about thirty-two degrees. The snow had settled down to a foot and a half deep. Winter would soon be over. I would have to face the reality of the rest of my life soon.

I was scheduled to have my nose fixed next week on Monday. As the winter passed, I wasn't as worried about my appearance as I had been in the beginning.

But I was still excited! It was now the second week of April. At home in the States, the grass would be turning green, and the early spring flowers would be making their appearance.

Jim had made all the arrangements. The helicopter would pick us up on Sunday. We had two rooms set aside for us at the hospital Sunday night. I was to go under the knife at seven a.m.

My time here was coming to an end. I was going to miss this group. The plan was I was to return here and heal for three to four weeks. Jonathon, Jerry, and George had made the preliminary plans to return and find Craig depending on Mother Nature, on how she gave up her final hold on winter. I dreaded that day, but again, I wanted him out of there. I couldn't wait—the last, absolute final thing I would ever do for him.

I continued to cry myself to sleep at night, more so now than before. His remains would be in a black rubber bag inside a plastic container. I would never see them, but knowing they were in there would be devastating. I already knew that the day I saw it, I would go to pieces, and that is a given.

I had talked to a few friends at home and to a few colleagues at work. I told them I was doing fine. I was physically, but psychologically, they would never know.

That was for me to deal with, me alone and no one else.

My job was waiting for me, they said, whenever I returned. They knew my condition, but the reality was out of their reach until they saw me. How would I ever function normally again? Sure, I would have artificial limbs to walk on, but how could I ever be able to sit at a computer or even write a letter? The daily routine would be impossible without hands or fingers.

Mother Nature gave up or was she just resting, waiting for the next time to pass through? Would she ever give up? My answer was 'no,' as I sat in the wheelchair outside, in front of the house.

Sunday morning, eleven a.m., it was already thawing out. I was sitting, waiting for the helicopter to land. I was in deep thought. I was anxious about getting a new nose, but my thoughts were in the past. The cold days and the colder nights, the aching and burning she had put my body through. Why now, today, was she being so generous?

The sun warmed my face. The men had already gone to work when we heard the helicopter approaching, out of sight below the tree line. I watched it land on the ice.

As always, it went like clockwork. They didn't speak. When it came to this kind of stuff, I saw a different side to my friends. They were very efficient. Someday, somehow, I would repay them. I was proud that they considered me a friend.

As soon as the skids touched down on the ice, the three snowmobiles instantly started their engines. I was in the sled behind the first snowmobile, and our luggage was in the second sled. Jonathon, Jerry, and George were the drivers. Mary rode with Jonathon and Jim with George.

The rotor only slowed to half throttle. Jim climbed in first, stowed our luggage, and moments later I was lifted into the air and placed inside.

I started to cry; the kindness from my friends was overwhelming. Mary smiled and held my hand. "You'll be back in a few days," she said, shouting over the noise.

I nodded my head. I looked at the three men standing there, and then I waved goodbye. The door was closed, and we lifted off. I watched them grow smaller and smaller as we flew away.

Jim held my arm. "You're on your way to starting your new life. You'll do well."

I was quiet on our flight to the hospital, thinking about what Jim had said to me. 'My new life.' I'm a true believer that we all have a purpose in life. Some people are destined to be alone; was I one of them? Why was I chosen to live? That question is always on my mind. Why was Craig chosen to die? Was Craig's purpose in life to save mine? If so, he had fulfilled his mission gracefully. So many questions that I will never have answers for.

I looked at Jim. "Thank you from the bottom of my heart and beyond. I have no way of telling you what all this means to me. I still don't understand why you have done so much for me."

Jim smiled. "I'm proud to have the opportunity."

Again, I cried. The measurement on the scale far exceeds its limit when weighing the kindness and generosity of this man.

"You saved my life. I wouldn't be here without you."

"Madie, you and you alone walked out of the wilderness. Don't ever forget that. I'm only here to help you heal."

I could no longer talk; I was crying too hard. I was thinking that that was debatable; I wouldn't have lived another night. The hospital was out of my reach. In a way, you did save my life.

I was gasping too hard, so I didn't tell him that.

The operation went well. I had a nose, some of which was from a cadaver. I didn't ask. There was a time in my life when I would have refused such a thing; it seemed far too gross. The thought of wearing a part from a dead person would have been unimaginable. That time wasn't that long ago, but then, eating raw fish and sleeping with a wild bear was incomprehensible. Now it's just a thing, no big deal. I will always be a freak show, but at least now I won't look like a wart-hog freak show.

I was in a great deal of pain, and it hurt to move my head; far more pain now than after my last operation of losing two feet and one and a half hands.

I didn't complain. The end result was the next finish line. When I talked, I didn't move my lips. As I lay in bed, I moved my eyes but nothing else.

Jim and Dr. Bryant, who performed the operation, both said it would be short-lived. In two days, three at the most, the pain would subside, and in two weeks, the swelling would be gone. Shortly after that, the bruising would fade.

I didn't care. What else did I have to do?

I got to know some of the nurses as before, and, as before, even the nurses who didn't attend to me would come in and visit. After the first day I was a celebrity here also. Word travels fast.

The third night, Jim was sitting in the chair next to my bed. He never left my side until it was time to sleep. He sat back and watched the parade come and go and never said a word. I believe most of the nurses were unaware that he was a doctor, but that didn't bother him.

"You get to remain anonymous through all of this. I wish I could," I said.

Jim shrugged his shoulders. "You should go and give speeches about your journey. You'd make a great deal of money."

"That's the last thing I want," I said.

Jim smiled at me. "Your call, I only suggested it. You're already famous."

"Look what it cost me to get here," I said.

"You'll have the rest of your parts soon, just not the originals."

"I wasn't talking about that. If Craig was still here, maybe I would consider it."

"I'm sorry, I didn't look at it that way," Jim said.

"I know. It's just that he gave up his life so I could go on. I have a hard time dealing with that."

"As would any normal human being," Jim replied.

"I would give my blood and all of my tears if I could tell him thank you and kiss him goodbye."

Jim nodded.

After five days, I got to leave the hospital. Dr. Bryant told me that wasn't a normal hospital procedure; enough time hadn't elapsed to be sure the operation was a success. But, given the fact that I was in the hands of a great doctor, I could go. Jim would take good care of me—those were his exact words. I wanted to add to that. Beyond Jim being a great doctor, he was a far greater man, one who gave all to help others. But I didn't; if he didn't know that already, it was his loss.

We landed on the lake. The men and Mary were already there, waiting. I wondered how Jim did it. He was always with me. I never saw him on the phone talking to anyone. While we were waiting for the guys outside to open the door, thoughts kept rushing through my mind. How were these helicopter rides being paid for? I was never asked to sign any papers at the hospital, never asked whom I had insurance with and consent forms I never saw. Down inside, I knew. I didn't know what to do about it—hopefully, one day, I would.

At least, this time, the group said hello. They all hugged me and told me that they were glad to see me back, but that didn't lessen their efficiency. I was still whisked away with blinding speed and carried inside the house before I even had a chance to get cold.

Mary already had coffee and hot chocolate ready. Mostly, the drinks flowed, stories were being told, and laughter was abundant. This was the happiest I felt since Craig and I spent our last hours fishing on the lake. I remember it well and will until the day I die.

My nose was wrapped with gauze and tape, over an inch thick. It was easiest for me to drink through a straw. I couldn't drink alcohol; I was taking too much medication to fight any infection that might set in and ruin my nose.

The hot chocolate was good. The companionship and infectious happiness that radiated from the group was all I needed. At this point, my life would never be better. The reality always loomed in the back of my mind, it was inevitable. The rest of my life was already predetermined, thanks to the death dealers.

Days passed. I was going to keep my nose. The swelling was almost gone, and Jim changed the dressing every day, inspecting it closely each time. The feeling was returning, but Jim told me I would never have as much as I once did. I didn't care; things like that didn't concern me.

The weather was getting warmer. The men were coming by late in the afternoon every day. They would grill outside on the deck, some sort of wild game, but it was always good. I was turning into a true wilderness woman. Something else I thought I would never do, being a true city girl as I was or once was. We would play cards most nights. I was turning into a decent poker player. I had no choice. It was either that or losing my money to them. When it came to poker and winning money, they showed no mercy toward me. I was thankful for that, and I wouldn't have wanted it any other way.

George was usually the big winner. He just sat back and grinned. They always harassed him, and he would just grin more. The fishing derby was even brought up once, on how badly he did. George didn't mind. His reply was, "Yeah, well, that's like going to the casino thinking you're going to beat the house—not going to happen."

"What are you saying, George?" Jim asked.

"That lake is your casino. The odds are always in your favor."

Everyone laughed, but they all agreed. Then Jim was the one who grinned.

The snow had melted down to less than a foot. In some places, the ground could be seen. My days were becoming short here.

I wheeled around, parading my new nose. A slight hint of purple lingered in places, but that would soon be gone.

It was discussed during our last poker game whether they should make the trip north now before the ice melted too thin for the helicopter to land. I told them about the bush pilot we had hired and how he determined the ice was strong enough for his plane to land. They all liked that idea.

Another problem was the snow, how much more was still on the ground over two hundred miles further north, covering what they needed to find.

It was determined to wait two more weeks and then fly up on a reconnaissance trip. I asked them to please let me pay them, now having to make two trips would be too costly to do. They would have no part of it. Then I asked to at least let me pay the pilot, but I got a firm 'no.' My final plea was to pay for the fuel—I lost that one also.

The two weeks passed in slow motion. I waited with much anticipation and I had mixed feelings. I would be glad to have Craig back. I dreaded having to bury him in a black rubber bag. I was happy about finally going home, but being there alone was a harsh reality. Leaving my new friends was one-sided. It was going to be a sad day.

It was still dark outside and the group was sitting around the kitchen table eating a large breakfast Mary had prepared. It consisted of ham and eggs, pancakes and sausage, toast and hash browns. She had brought homemade donuts and two gallons of strong hot coffee. It was five-thirty a.m., we wouldn't see daylight for another hour, and another thirty minutes after that the plane was to arrive. Today was the day, the one I couldn't wait for, but the one I didn't want to see.

The talk wasn't the usual banter of storytelling and laughter. It was semi-serious out of respect for me.

I had no doubt why Mary fed the men so well. Up and back in one day, she wanted them full in case anything happened.

I listened. They were prepared, even for the unexpected. Each man had two days rations of freeze-dried, instant food.

I asked, "Have you ever had to eat that stuff?"

"Only once, after the last dozen times," Jerry said, smiling, trying to ease my tension. It wasn't working.

I don't know how Mary does it. I looked at her. She held no look of worry on her face, only concern. But, then again, that might have been for me. She had complete faith in these men, as I did.

The past few days were unseasonably warm. With the exception of the piles of snow Jim had made, the snow had melted away.

Much talk of speculation passed back and forth across the table. There was a good possibility the ground would be bare at our camp when they landed. If so, it would be a one-trip job.

I wanted it over with. Inside, I said a prayer, asking for the snow to be gone.

My breakfast was two cups of black coffee. My stomach was in too much turmoil to handle food.

Jim chose to remain here with Mary and myself. I was grateful, although I hadn't asked him to. Having him around would help calm my nerves throughout the day. He knew that also, but he used the excuse of carrying a fourth man on the plane was excessive weight.

Jonathon, Jerry, and George didn't try to persuade him to go; they knew as well.

As the first sign of sunlight broke on the eastern horizon, the men were getting their final things packed. It wasn't much; in fact, it made me a bit nervous to see how small the supply was. Everything fit in one small cardboard box. No extra clothes and no overnight gear. It wasn't mentioned, and I didn't ask, but I was sure they each had some sort of defense with them, just in case.

It had frozen overnight. I was wheeled out into the yard, and I watched the steam float away as they spoke. I was in no condition to feel the cold. The men stood around the four-wheelers, the summertime mode of transportation, waiting for the plane.

I hadn't asked who they had talked into making such a terrible trip. I had left that up to them.

I looked into the only trailer they used to haul the small amount of supplies out to the plane. There, I saw the plastic container, and I gasped. The reality of seeing it for the first time broke my heart. Odds were, the next time I saw it, Craig would be in it.

I could no longer hold back my emotions; they broke through like a volcano. I cried until my stomach hurt.

No one spoke.

Mary stood on one side of me and Jim on the other. Seconds later, the faint growl of the plane was heard, and it was approaching fast.

Through my sobs, I said, "Please, don't leave him up there."

The sadness was apparent on the three men's faces. "We won't, Madie. We won't," said Jonathon.

I wanted to jump up and hug them for what they were doing for me.

The plane made a tight circle overhead as we all watched it fly back over the lake. I recognized the plane.

The next thing we watched was something falling from the plane, hitting the ice, and bouncing. It repeated that many times before it came to a stop.

It was a rock. Through the tears, I had to laugh; I knew who the pilot was.

Looking away, watching, Jerry said, "There are old pilots, and there are bold pilots, but there are no old bold pilots."

I laughed again and so did everyone else. I knew these men were in good hands and they would have a safe trip.

The engine was turned off before the plane came to a complete stop.

"If it's not too much trouble, I'd like to go down and talk with Randy."

Jim looked at me, then down to the plane and back to me. "How about I go down and bring Randy up here?"

"Ok, I just want to thank him. It won't take long." They were on a time schedule, and the pilot had to be back at his base before dark.

Before Jim had driven all the way out to the plane, Randy was running toward the house. I wondered why.

Jim returned with Randy on the four-wheeler.

Randy quickly got off and walked up to me. "Madie, I'm so sorry, I'm so sorry. I couldn't find you. The day we were to meet, I waited all afternoon. You didn't show. I kept going over and over in my head and recalculated the coordinates I had to make sure I had the right location. I was sure I did. I returned the next day and flew around for awhile, but still nothing. Several days later, I returned to see if you were there, but you weren't. I spent many sleepless nights thinking you might have died out there. I'm so sorry for what happened to you. There isn't an outpost anywhere that hasn't heard about you. They all blamed me, and so did I. I'm truly sorry."

I was surprised by this and didn't know what to say. I hadn't given it a thought of what it would do to someone who was responsible for picking us up. "It wasn't your fault. You should know that, and tell them also. Thank you for making the extra trips in trying to find me."

He shook his head no. "I owe you some money," he said.

"For what?" That surprised me even more.

"I didn't finish my job. I want to give you half of your money back."

I could see by the expression on his face that my ordeal had eaten away at him. "No way, you're finishing it now. I'm the one who should be paying you. Thank you for doing this for me."

Again, he shook his head no. "Word traveled through the bush camps that you needed a plane; no way was I going to let anyone else do it."

I cried again. More generosity from people I didn't know.

"Whenever you decide to go home, I will fly you back to our base camp. There, we have a land plane, and I will fly you to the airport."

Water gushed, and I was back to being a mental wreck.

I spent the morning silent, and my nerves were in turmoil. One would have thought that I'd expect Craig to come walking through the front door when they returned. But it was far worse, a plastic box and only bones. The wolves would have picked him clean by now, and I guess that's what bothered me the worse. Mother Nature has no respect for the dead in the wilderness.

Silently, I condemned the death dealers and myself. If only I could have done more for him, somehow returned and buried Craig, kept his body from the wrath of nature.

Jim and Mary left me alone. I had to deal with my demons myself, and they knew that.

By lunch, I was wheelchair-pacing. The end result was already a fact in time, unchangeable. But still, I had to spend the sad, nervous energy that was inside me. I looked at the clock on the wall at least a dozen times an hour. The day was passing far too slowly.

I was sitting, looking out the front window.

Mary walked up behind me, "Would you like some lunch, Madie?"

I wasn't hungry.

Jim quit reading his book and looked at me.

"No, thank you," I said.

"Come on, let's go for a ride on the four-wheeler," Jim said.

So we did. I hung on to Jim as we rode through the woods. We rode for miles, and it was relaxing. The place that I had to fight for my life, the place that claimed parts of my body and consumed Craig's—the place I said I would never return to now relaxed me. I squeezed Jim tight. No words will ever describe what I felt for this man.

We returned after two o'clock, they would be back soon.

"Can we sit outside and wait?" I asked.

"Sure, anything you'd like," Jim answered.

Mary brought out two cups of hot coffee and some of her donuts. "You haven't eaten all day," she said.

The three of us sat there enjoying the sunshine.

Anticipation grew. "I hope nothing went wrong," I said.

"They'll be fine. There's more experience in that plane than one will ever find anywhere," Jim said.

I had no doubt Jim was right. But I still worried.

Twenty minutes later, the sound of the plane was heard. My heart skipped several beats, and I started shaking. Was Craig with them? I hoped so. I couldn't go through this again.

No rock this time. Randy banked the plane around the west side of the lake, leveled it off, and brought it in for a landing, heading straight for us.

My shaking became worse. The plane came to a stop twenty feet from shore. I watched the side cargo door open on the plane, and Jonathon and George got out. Then, they both turned to face the door—what did that mean?

Now, I was trembling. Was Craig in there? Did he finally make the trip out?

Jim got on the four-wheeler and drove out to the lake. He arrived just as Jonathon and George turned to face the plane.

Mary remained with me. "My stomach is in such a knot I think I'm going to be sick," I said.

Then, I knew. I gasped, and I grabbed Mary's arm. She said nothing. I couldn't take my eyes off the plane. I watched the six-foot plastic box slide out of the plane. George lifted the lead end, and the box continued sliding out. Then Jonathon lifted the trailing end. Craig was in it by the way they were handling it, there was no question.

I watched them load the temporary casket into the trailer.

I couldn't help myself; I cried and shook uncontrollably.

The five men manually pushed the plane around, facing back out onto the lake.

The plane throttled and then was gone, but I hardly noticed.

The men stood out on the ice, talking long after the plane was gone. I watched the hand gestures and the arm movements through blurred vision. I had no way of deciphering what the conversation was.

I had a good idea, but right now, I didn't want to know the gruesome details.

Jim listened, taking it all in. Occasionally he would nod with the story of their trip, the details.

The four-wheeler started with Jerry driving, George sitting behind him, and Jim and Jonathon rode in the trailer next to Craig.

'The true pain begins,' I said to myself. They pulled up beside me, and Jerry turned the four-wheeler off.

I quickly glanced at their faces. Each one was somber. I looked at Jim last, and he nodded his head 'yes.' A closer to what I already knew.

I stood on my stumps, leaned forward, and fell toward the trailer. By the time I caught the side, five people rushed to my side.

I laid my left hand on the top of the box. To my touch, it felt warm. Craig's love, his love of life, his soul, was still reaching out to me. "I will love you until the end of time. Thank you for saving me. Thank you for pushing me forward when I had nothing left. You guided me here. God will take care of you now. Go in peace. You no longer have to worry about me. Now it's my turn to take care of you."

I looked at Jonathon, Jerry, and George. "I can't thank you enough for doing this for me."

My pillowcase remained wet throughout the night. I slept very little; all I could think about was Craig lying in the box, locked up inside the cold shed behind the house. He was safe now, safe from Mother Nature and what she controlled.

The next morning, plans were made and messages sent. Tomorrow, Randy would return, fly Craig and me to his base camp and then on to the airport. From there, back to the States and home.

Jim wanted to go with me, but I told him no. I had to do this alone. Craig and I started this together, and that's how we were going to finish it.

27
CHAPTER

Perception isn't the reality. What they saw on the outside this morning wasn't what I was feeling inside. I felt sick, and my mind was in a fog. I tried to hide the shaking, and I didn't cry. I remained strong, although I wasn't walking through the wilderness, cold and stiff; I wish finishing our trip—the final leg home for Craig and I.

The entire group had arrived at Jim's bright and early. My bags were packed. Jim wanted me to take everything that he had bought for me, but I said no. I would be back, and I would. I would need them then. Maybe in the fall or early winter, I'd have the pleasure of their company again. I told them that I was already looking forward to it. I would miss them dearly.

Randy was due in at nine in the morning, and from there, we had three hours to get to the airport to catch the plane home.

The local funeral home had been contacted to pick Craig up. Two days later, I would bury him. A small, quiet funeral was what I planned, just a few close friends we had and nothing more.

I thanked everyone at least six times while we waited outside for the plane. Despite nervous energy and trying to remain steady, I acted like I had things under control.

Like I thought earlier in the morning, *perception isn't the reality.*

Randy didn't circle the lake, and he didn't drop a test rock. He flew in from the south, dropped in just over the treetops, and landed on the ice fast, with unbelievable grace.

We were already waiting at the edge of the lake.

Now, I had to say goodbye one last time without going to pieces. It would be a miracle if I didn't.

The engine stopped, and my anxiety grew. The men went to work. Craig was loaded first as I watched, barely breathing, and then my luggage, which was two cases.

My head was spinning, and my ears were ringing. I was next. I took a deep breath and said to myself, "Please, God, help me get through this." Then, I heard it again. I was losing it—one step from entering the nut house. It was clear as day, 'Madie, you can do this, it's just a thing.' My subconscious brought up old memories. I had heard Craig tell me that so many times.

It helped. I hugged Jonathon, Jerry, and George, kissing them each on the cheek and saying thank you more than once to each.

And then Mary… I embraced her, more than a hug, I squeezed her tightly. I could feel my throat tightening up and my eyes watering. "You've done more for me than anyone will ever know. There's no way I can tell you what you mean to me. I have no words that can thank you enough."

Mary stepped back. It was the first time I had seen tears stream down her face. "I would do it all over again. It was an honor to help you. You've become a dear friend. I will miss you," then she cried.

I had to look away. I had one more to go; now wasn't the time to lose it.

I looked at Jim. Too late, before I even started to hug him, I was crying. We hugged, and minutes passed, but I couldn't let go and speak. I cried uncontrollably.

Finally, I regained just a slight bit of composure. "Without you, none of this would have been possible. You have done more than save my life. That alone was enough, but you chose to do more. There hasn't been a day gone by that I think of the day you saved me. I felt that was my last day on this earth, I knew that and I had accepted that. Then, there you were."

I cried hard again. I wasn't finished, but I couldn't breathe.

Gasping and talking at the same time, I said, "Somehow, you will be repaid for your kindness. That is my promise to you."

Jim was smiling when we finally let go of each other. He was also wiping tears away; he didn't speak, and I understood why.

"Enough of this sob fest," I said, trying to lighten everyone's mood.

On the outside, it worked, for me included. They all grinned.

"Time for Craig and I to go home."

They put me in the front seat beside Randy. I could have sat in one of the back seats, which would have been much easier. They didn't face forward. There were two small benches, one on each side, facing toward the center of the plane. Then, I would have had to stare at the plastic box all the way there. I was thankful they went to the extra effort.

I was strapped in, and the door was still open. Smiling and crying at the same time, I said, "The dearest friends I will ever have, thank you."

Then, the door was closed.

The engine roared to life.

I waved goodbye, and then the plane moved forward. Instantly, they were behind me and then out of sight.

Then, I bawled my eyes out. I let the sadness flow from my body.

I hardly noticed the plane lifting above the treetops. The roar of the engine and the shaking of the plane made me feel like I was in a dream. Soon, I would wake up and be at home with Craig lying in bed beside me.

"If I would have found you, this wouldn't have happened," Randy said.

The sound of his voice brought me back to reality. Craig would never lie next to me again. I looked at Randy.

"I'm truly sorry. I want you to know that," he said.

"It was already over, two weeks before you were due back. This wasn't any fault of yours," I said.

"Well, I don't feel that way."

I quit crying. "They smashed our satellite phone and took the GPS. I would have never found that lake. So I walked south, the only thing I knew to do."

Randy nodded.

I went on and told him everything. Why, I don't know, it didn't make me feel better. It wasn't going to change anything, just drag up miserable memories, but still, I went on and on.

The next thing I knew, I felt the plane descend, and the engine slowed. We were coming in for a landing. I didn't notice the terrain below during the entire trip.

This time, we landed on a concrete runway. When the plane came to a complete stop, I looked and saw a twin-engine plane not far away. I looked around more and saw that up ahead was a very nice, large building. Behind it was another lake. There were about a half dozen planes, or so, sitting at various places, waiting to go to work.

"Wow, this is really nice," I said.

"Thank you. I wish we had time to show you around inside. Even though this is only a base camp, there are rooms to stay all night in and a nice restaurant. Many people travel through here during the warm months," Randy said.

Where all the men came from, I had no idea. All the doors opened at once. Each one said 'Hi' or 'Nice to meet you,' and then they went to work. In less than two minutes, Craig and the luggage had been placed into the next plane. I was sitting in the wheelchair being pushed toward that plane.

Then, they started asking me for my autograph, something I hadn't expected. *Why*, I wondered, *I'm not famous. I'm just another person.* I looked at them, and I counted five. Randy stood back; he wasn't one of the group.

The man standing closest to me was holding a pad of paper and a pencil. I couldn't believe it. Still confused, I asked, "Why?"

"Because it's you, everyone has heard your story," he said.

How, I wondered. "What do you men do?" I asked.

One of the men said, "We're all pilots, ma'am. It's a pleasure to meet you."

"Dear Lord," I said to myself, still not understanding. But I figured I owed them at least that. They were helping me out of the kindness of their hearts. I held up my arms, "I have nothing left."

I saw the disappointment on several of their faces.

Who was I to not return the kindness? "Ok, I'll try, but it won't be much." I squeezed the pencil between my thumb and the palm of my left hand. I asked each of their names. As I signed paper after paper, on each one I wrote their name and thanked them for helping, and then I signed my name at the bottom. I wasn't left-handed; it would have been neater writing if I was.

"I'm sorry it's not too legible," I said.

Then, they asked for a picture, and I agreed… if I could have one.

Now, they were all smiling. Randy held back as the group gathered around me. I looked at him.

Knowing what I was thinking, Randy said, "Someone has to take the picture."

I was placed in the seat behind the pilots. It was a ten-seat plane, and I was told that I would have two pilots this time.

Randy got in as they sat me inside. I had to ask, "Why didn't you want in the picture?"

"I don't deserve it; I failed you," he said quietly, not to be heard by the other men.

I don't think he said that for my benefit; he truly believed it. I felt my throat gurgle, and I swallowed, fighting back the temptation to cry. "I already told you," I said.

He didn't acknowledge me. The co-pilot got in and closed his door.

On this plane ride heading to the major airport, I couldn't see the plastic box. It was in the rear cargo storage area. That hadn't eased a thing for me. I continued the cycle, crying and then stopping for a while. Then, I would start all over.

So much pain and sorrow. Like I told the death dealer, "I can run the rest of my life, but I will never outrun the past."

It was bothering me that Randy was carrying so much guilt. He was just caught in the middle, a no-win situation for him. Finding me then would be like me going back now to try to find the bodies of the death dealers.

This plane ride was smoother, quieter, and had much more comfortable seats. I had to do something for Randy before saying goodbye. "Do you have a camera on the plane?" I asked.

"Yes, ma'am," the co-pilot answered. "I brought it with me." Now, he was smiling as he looked back at me. "Everyone wanted this seat, so we drew straws. So here I am. Thank you for letting me help you."

Thank you, I thought, but now, who was confused here? I was the one being helped. I didn't respond.

I thought for a few minutes. "I'm sorry, I forgot your name."

"Doug, ma'am."

"Doug, would you take a picture of Randy and me when we land?"

"Yes, ma'am," he said.

We had parked in the private plane area of the airport. In the background we could hear the big jets landing and taking off. As I was being pushed toward the terminal, Randy was lagging behind. I asked Doug to stop. "Time for a picture," I looked back to Randy. I saw the hesitation in his face. "Please, stand here beside me."

Randy did, and the picture was taken.

"I'm going to return this fall. I'll pay for the picture. I think an eight by ten would be nice."

Randy nodded and then hugged me. He whispered in my ear, "I'm sorry."

Again, I couldn't prevent the tears. "Thank you for your help," I said. "Goodbye."

It was quite the ordeal getting through the airport, now with the added extra security. I didn't go through the front door. So, entering the way I did, one would have thought that I was a criminal. I left those behind in the pine trees and snow, but I didn't tell them that. The sharp edge these security guards seemed to be working on would have been suicide, and I would have been detained. I was going to finish our trip, and that was now my mission. I remained silent. I did everything they requested and answered all the questions they asked.

I had a first-class seat. Not because I wanted one, I didn't, but the aisle was too narrow for the wheelchair in coach. I was pushed down the tunnel and into the plane first before general boarding started. The flight attendants, two females and one male, took a quick glance at me. I read their thoughts—how were they going to lift me from the chair to the seat? They quickly recovered, and their professional training kicked in. They were the only humans who prevailed over everything.

My wheelchair came to a stop at the third row of seats, that's what I had requested, and a window seat at that. I wanted to remain anonymous. I didn't want the other passengers staring at me, the freak show.

My eyes were swollen and, I assume, very bloodshot. They'd had time to become that way since I left Jim's. Two plane rides, crying most of the time. I imagined I looked like a wreck. I could hear the flight attendants talking behind me, but I wasn't focusing on what they were saying. I was thinking about what I had to do next. It would be much easier for me to do it on my own. There wasn't room for two people, and myself, to fit in the small space in front of the two seats. I stood on my stumps, carrying half of my body weight on my arms and using the seats as a crutch.

"Oh, my God," one of the female flight attendants said.

The human factor, again, had caught her off guard.

I took the three steps to my seat, pivoted, and sat. I moaned loudly. Pivoting on my stumps sent a bolt of pain up my body. I hadn't done that before, but I wasn't expecting what I just felt.

The three attendants looked to be in panic mode. Two of them started talking at once.

I raised my left hand, waving them off. "I'm fine," I said, trying to lower their stress level. The sight of my grotesque left hand did just the opposite; they momentarily froze. "I'm fine, really." I wasn't thirsty, but I knew if I asked for something to drink, they would feel as though they were helping me. "I could use something to drink if that's not too much trouble."

It worked. They hurried away as if they were attending to the president.

The plane was full, and I felt us being pushed backward away from the gate.

Each plane ride, each leg of our journey, became mentally worse for me. Almost home, the hardest part of all. Tears constantly dripped into my lap. I continually looked out the window so no one would notice. I had to face the biggest demon. Far greater than the two death dealers, Mother Nature, with her bitter cold and deep snow, was nothing; going into our home, seeing the pictures of us together on the wall above the fireplace and Craig's clothes hanging in the closet. His personal things would drive reality home, the inevitable I had to face and something I couldn't run from.

I fought the constant urge to bawl my eyes out. I would do that enough when I was home; now wasn't the time. I had already drawn enough attention just by my physical appearance.

Drinks were being served. In no time, the flight attendant had worked her way back to the row I was in. After asking the gentleman sitting next to me what he would like, it was my turn. I turned to look at her. She momentarily stared at me. The tears and puffy, bloodshot eyes were worse, I had no doubt. Seconds later, she regained her composure again.

"Could I have apple juice, please? And I'll need a straw if it's not too much trouble."

She complied. I didn't look at her when she sat the glass on my tray.

I could see the man looking at me out of the corner of his eye. He watched me intently, trying to be courteous. Something I would have to get used to, the staring.

"It isn't easy, believe me," I said, trying to break the ice between us. *Confront the problem head-on,* I thought.

"No, I imagine not," he said. I was thankful he was polite. He didn't ask any questions. "If there's anything I can do to help, I will."

He was dressed in a nice suit, a businessman, a professional, very cordial and reserved. Somewhere around fifty, I guessed.

We had our choice of dinner. A turkey sandwich or a full meal, Salisbury steak, mashed potatoes with gravy, and broccoli. I had to pack my eating utensils in my luggage for security reasons, so I had no way to eat. I wasn't all that hungry; my stomach remained in a knot, so not eating didn't matter.

She was back, and it was my turn. When she looked at me, I read her expression. She asked, "Ma'am, are you alright?"

I thought, *How do I answer that—yes and no?* Yes, physically, I was fine. No, inside, I wasn't. Both arms were lying in front of me on the tray. I twisted both of them in a slight turn, indicating I didn't know.

She took that gesture with a different meaning. "You can't eat, I didn't know." She was caught off guard again. She probably hadn't dealt with many people in my condition, if any at all.

"I'll be fine," I said. But she continued to stare at me.

"How about I cut a turkey sandwich up for you?"

I nodded. I knew she was just trying to help.

She returned. Again, she asked, as she set the plate down on my tray, "Ma'am, are you alright?" in a soft, caring voice.

I looked away from her and down to the plate with the turkey sandwich cut into small pieces. "I'm taking my husband home to bury him."

She looked at me, not knowing what to say.

"Oh, no, you're her. You're Madison! I didn't put it together until you said that. I should have known. I'm so sorry."

Why was she being so apologetic? She had done nothing wrong. How did she know? I turned my head and looked at her, frowning as if to ask, 'How did you know?'

"When you were in the hospital, fighting for your life, all the newspapers ran a huge article about you. That was quite awhile ago, I nearly forgot," she said.

I wished she had, but now I knew. Although I was never asked to do any interviews with all the staff at the hospital, it wasn't hard for someone to get my story.

She walked away.

"To everything, there is a purpose. Now, I know why I was asked to take this flight. All expenses paid by a colleague who knows a colleague who knows another," the man sitting next to me said.

I looked at him, confused, not understanding.

"I'm a doctor. Not one that heals cancer or diseases."

"You're a shrink?" I asked.

"Yes. I prefer the term psychiatrist; it doesn't sound so harsh."

A quick, small chuckle escaped. "He thinks of everything, and it must be something he does constantly." Jim was behind this. I didn't know whether to be mad at him or applaud his kindness. I thought about it, and it was left up to me, my option, to do what I felt most comfortable with. I had the right to walk away or go forward.

Before I decided which path to choose, the man said, "Who would he be that you referred to?"

"Jim. The man who saved my life—the man who put me back together," I said. I went on and told him my story. No details, just how I became what I am today.

Then, I asked him his name. He told me it was Gary, Dr. Gary Barns.

He didn't treat me like a patient, lying on the sofa in his office. We talked, having a normal conversation. He asked many questions, but none were of what I felt about my situation or anything else of that nature.

As the plane started to land, he removed a business card from the breast pocket of his jacket. "If you ever feel you want someone to talk to, I'm available."

I held his card in my thumb, thinking. Now was the time I had to decide which way to jump from the fence. "The hurting time is just beginning; the healing time comes later." That's all I could say.

Gary nodded.

I was last to exit the plane. My wheelchair was rolled up next to my row of seats. I butt-hopped into Gary's seat and then into the wheelchair. The three attendants were standing around me. Both pilots had left their seats and were standing by the door, waiting for me to exit.

As I was rolled up to them, the closest pilot said, "It's a pleasure to meet you."

There it is again. The freak show that I am, everyone's always staring, yet they always wanted to meet me. Go figure. I smiled. "Thank you for getting us home." I shook both their hands. They didn't seem to mind my grotesque left hand.

When I was rolled through the gate, I saw a butler-dressed man standing off to the side. I thought that was odd. Then he started walking in my direction.

"I'm here to take you home, Madie. I have a limo waiting outside," he said.

Now, it was my turn to stare; I wasn't expecting a limo driver waiting for me. My mouth fell open, but no words came out. 'Jim! Jim planned this,' I said to myself.

"Can I ride in the front with you?" I asked.

"Sure," he said with no hesitation.

On the way home, the sadness returned. Quietly, I said, "When we get to my house, I'll have to pay you with a check. I have no cash."

He shook his head 'no.' "It's already taken care of."

The tears flowed. "I'm sorry," I said. I wondered if the crying would ever stop. Not for a long time was my answer.

We pulled into my driveway, and the part I was dreading the most was next. I had my house keys in my left hand, and I had to do it—face my biggest challenge.

The driver unlocked the front door and pushed me inside. "Thank you for your help and kindness. Please, let me get my checkbook. This will be for you."

"No, ma'am. That has also been taken care of."

I should have known. "Thank you again."

Now alone, I rolled the wheelchair slowly into the living room. Everything was just as we had left it eight months ago. The house smelled musty, and then it occurred to me the electricity was still on. I rolled into the kitchen and turned on the faucet in the sink, and the water flowed. I hadn't given a thought about paying the utility bills while I was gone, yet they weren't disconnected due to lack of payments. Then it occurred to me I broke down and bawled my eyes out. I was still finding things Jim had thought about. What else had he done for me? I had no idea.

It took ten hours, since I left Jim's, to get home, and I was beat. I unpacked my bags and took a long bath, sobbing the whole time.

Two more hours passed. Everything I did took much more time than it once had. I didn't care. What else did I have to do?

Then, I crawled into bed... literally. I could remember the last time I slept in this bed. Craig was next to me. How excited we were to be starting our trip the next day, the mother of all adventures, the grand finale—now, to me, the trip from hell. Craig's grand finale—saving my life. Never again would I feel him lean over and kiss my lips goodnight. Never again would I tell him I love him. I do tell him that every day. I just don't get to look into his eyes when I do.

I cried myself to sleep.

I woke later than I had planned; it was nine a.m. I called the funeral home before I got out of bed. I had only one thing to accomplish that day; if it took all day, then so be it.

They knew my physical condition and were coming to pick me up in one hour. I got dressed and brushed my hair. I didn't bother with makeup, and there wasn't time. The time at Jim's house, I didn't bother with it unless Mary had wanted to fuss. Now was not the time for me to start; I was afraid. If I tried now, it would only add to the freak show appearance. That was something that was going to take much practice.

While waiting, I promised I wasn't going to break down. The next two days were for Craig.

They arrived right on time. Two men helped me into the car. It was a white Cadillac Deville with a white leather interior. Both men sat in front wearing a suit and tie, the standard funeral stereotype.

In the office of the funeral home, the first order of business was to sign all the forms. Then, I picked out a casket from pictures in a book. I was told it wasn't necessary to have a formal casket because there would be no showing at the funeral home. By my choice, there would be no open casket—by choice from the death dealers. They tried to talk me into something just a bit more elaborate than a pine box. I would have nothing to do with it. This was Craig's resting place for all of eternity, and he deserved more.

I chose an oak casket with elaborate scrollwork. It was Craig, and it fit him to a 'T.' A preacher was to give a sermon at the grave site, the final thing that would be done for him on this earth.

Then, I was given some news I hadn't expected nor had I given any thought to. I had to speak to the federal authorities before the funeral could actually take place. The FBI – it was still a murder case. The funeral home director told me that, given my situation, it was just a formality. It was set up to take place at one o'clock.

I was nervous and scared as I waited for whoever was going to show up from the FBI. I had no idea what they were going to ask me or how they were going to act. I had never dealt with anyone of that caliber.

I was sitting in a restaurant not far away from the funeral home. That's what was decided on where we would meet. I didn't care for it much, doing such a private thing in public.

CHAPTER 28

I chose the table in the furthest corner there was. The driver from the funeral home would return when I called.

The short time I sat at the table alone, my nerves escalated, doubling with each passing minute.

Finally, I saw two men enter the front door. There was no question as to who they were. Clean-shaven, well-cut hair, suit and tie. No smiles, no talking, and they didn't look around. Their only mission in life was to make me nervous. They walked directly up to my table.

"Madison Chanhansen?" the FBI man asked.

"Yes, that's me."

"Hello, I'm Agent Netz, and this is Agent Healy."

No first names, no cordial greeting, just stiff and coarse. I was too nervous to smile. "Pardon me for not standing, but I can't." I held my left hand out to shake theirs.

"Yes, we know." They didn't ask if they could sit and join me; they just did so.

"We have a few questions we'd like to ask you," Agent Netz said.

Right to the point, no informal talk, I thought to myself.

"We understand your husband was murdered."

A knife was just plunged into my heart. The cold, sharp, piercing edge took my breath away. 'Keep it together,' I told myself. "Yes, that's correct."

"Your husband was killed somewhere at the north end of the Mistassini Provincial Reserve?" Agent Netz asked.

"Yes."

He just twisted the knife.

"Yes, the autopsy shows he was killed by a 38-caliber shot to the head. Do you own such a gun?"

He just removed the knife and plunged it in deeper. "No!" I almost yelled. *Do they think I killed Craig?* I thought. I told myself to keep it together.

"Then you walked roughly two hundred fifty miles, which is just outside the small town of St. David de-Falardeau?"

"Yes."

"Seems a little far-fetched, doesn't it?" Agent Netz said.

That did it – no more togetherness on my part. Without even thinking I went to stand up. My stumps didn't make contact with the floor. "Look, if you think I killed my husband, you're wrong. I didn't. Besides, look what it cost me." I held both arms up. "Do you want to see my feet? Sorry, they're not there."

"Believe me, we've seen people do extreme things for insurance money," Netz said.

Now I was furious! I took a deep breath. "So, that's what this is about—me. Not trying to figure out who the two men were. Well, let me ask you this, Agent Netz. Why didn't I just walk to our rendezvous point, wait the two weeks, and then fly out?"

"Well, I don't know, ma'am," Netz said.

I went on and told them everything in great detail. It took over an hour. The waitress came by several times to check on us. Both agents refused each time. They remained silent, listening, no longer asking questions.

By the time I was finished I was crying. It hurt to drag up the harsh memories. "I'm sorry you don't believe me. Yes, it is a little far-fetched, as you put it, but it's something I can't change."

Their expression had changed; now, they looked human.

"I wish their bodies could be found, or what's left of them anyway. But I have no idea where to tell you to look."

"That would be nice, but that's a matter for the Canadian Mounties. That's out of our jurisdiction." Then they stood. "We already knew. We just had to hear it from you. We would have known if you were lying or not." Then he held his right hand out. "I would like to shake your hand—probably the toughest woman I will ever meet."

I shook both their hands. "I wish people would stop calling me that. I was too scared and lonely. What choice did I have but to walk until I died?"

They nodded their heads and left.

I sat there for a while longer thinking, how did they know? The FBI doesn't leave the boundaries of the United States.

I called the funeral home.

Now, it was time to go to the cemetery and pick out a plot to lay Craig in. On our way there, the endless flow of tears amazed me—nonstop. The body never seems to run out.

I didn't buy just one, I bought two. I wanted to be next to him when my time would come. Then, and only then, we would be together again.

The few friends from where Craig and I worked were coming to the graveside funeral. The day was warm, and the sun was shining. The grass was green and freshly mowed. Midday in Massachusetts was always nice. Flowers were everywhere throughout the cemetery. Memorial Day was coming, and family members would be remembering their lost ones.

I had arrived early. I sat in my wheelchair next to Craig, lying in his beautiful carved oak casket. The casket was sitting on the aluminum stand, waiting to be lowered into the cement vault and sealed for all eternity.

It was an hour before everyone was to arrive. I wanted the extra time to be with him. I had my left hand lying on the casket, and I was talking quietly to him. I heard a car pull up behind me, but I barely heard the doors close. I wasn't through, and I needed more time with him. Days, or even weeks, would have been fine with me. While I talked, I wiped my eyes and nose with one of the many Kleenexes I had brought with me.

Then, I felt a hand on my shoulder. "Madie," I heard a voice say.

I turned to see who was speaking to me. I yelled, and I couldn't believe the group I was looking at. "Jim!" I instantly stood, turned, and took two steps before falling into his arms. I cried harder than I ever had before. Through my water-filled eyes, I saw Mary, Jonathon, Jerry, and George. "I… I can't…. believe you guys are here!" I was shaking, gasping for air. I was so happy they were here that I ignored the pain. I went from Jim to Mary and hugged her for a long time, then on to Jonathon, Jerry, and George. I held each one for minutes and never stopped crying. I tried to speak to each one as I hugged them, but only slurred words came out. I continued with deep sobbing gasps. Then, George sat me back in the wheelchair. I continued to cry—happy to see them and sad, the last time I would be with Craig.

I held Jim's hand in my left. Mary was holding my right arm. "I can't believe you guys made the trip. This is the nicest thing anyone could ever do for me. Thank you. You're the best friends anyone could ever have. I'm the happiest person alive to have you as friends. It would be lonely and miserable without you."

I couldn't stop crying and, by now, even the men had tears in their eyes.

"This is the hardest part for me. I would go back into the frozen wilderness and lose the rest of what I have to have Craig back and not go through this." I continued on crying uncontrollably. The gate was open and there was no stopping what was escaping until it had all run out. "Craig would have really liked all of you. He'd be right there running around the woods with you, saving people. I couldn't save him. He'd be fishing every minute with you; he would have liked that." I went on crying; the gate wasn't empty yet.

When I finally looked around our friends were there standing beside and behind me, and they all had tears. How long had they been there? How much of my carrying on had they heard? Doesn't matter; it was all true.

The preacher came around and spoke to me. Then he walked to the far side of the casket and gave the eulogy. It was beautiful; it, too, was Craig to a 'T'.

I had gone through a dozen Kleenexes by the time he was finished.

I hadn't planned on talking, but I did my final goodbye. "Craig," I paused, "The future was ours to explore. It went to the last page. I'm lost and lonely, and I hurt. The wrong done to you I can never put right. I will never outrun the past. Thank you for helping me outrun them. Without your love, I wouldn't be here. You lost your life-saving mine. You saved my life twice. From this day forward, my promise to you is that I will start a new book. In it, every day will be you. My love for you I will carry to my grave – that is another promise to you. If you're not too busy, check in on me from time to time – I will know it, as I did out there." I laid my left hand on the casket and was crying softly. "My memories of you will take me forward. Goodbye, my love."

I looked up at Jim, and he was crying. I nodded, and he understood. I was pushed back to the cars behind us. I never looked back; my memories will always take me there.

We stopped at the cars, and I thanked our few friends as they came by. Then, to my surprise, last in line were the two FBI agents.

"I'm surprised you're here, thank you."

Agent Netz spoke. "After hearing your story yesterday, how could we not be?"

Craig's life, even in death, touched everyone.

"If you ever think of anything that might help us find the names of those two men, please call. We'll do whatever we can." Then, he handed me his card.

Agent Healy shook my hand. "I'm sorry," and he also handed me his card.

I rode with Jim and the group from the cemetery. Luckily, he had rented a Suburban, so we had plenty of room. We went back to my house. "My feelings for all of you almost equals how I feel about Craig. This means more to me than you know. I'm sorry, I have no food in the house. I haven't had time to go shopping."

"If you're up to it, we'll stop at a grocery store and buy something," Jim replied.

"For you guys, I will do anything, whatever you want." Now I was crying again.

The four men went into the grocery store, and Mary stayed in the car with me. Quietly, she said, "This will be interesting. They can't buy venison or rabbit in there."

I smiled through the tears. "Yes, they are the greatest group of guys I will ever know."

Mary held my hand.

The men grilled steaks and drank beer. Mary handled the baked potatoes. I wasn't hungry, but I picked at my food to show appreciation for what they had done. The conversation wasn't their normal during dinner—no laughing or storytelling. I wished they had; it was what I always expected from them. They were doing it out of respect for me.

Our house, I should now say mine, was large—four bedrooms and three baths. I looked around at the group – there was no way I was going to let them stay in a motel.

"There's four bedrooms, and I'm not about to let you go to a motel. I'll take the couch."

They were silent, and the men took quick glances at each other.

"What? You think I'm letting you leave after all you've done for me?"

George spoke, "It's not that. You think we're letting you sleep on the couch? Oh, no."

"Sleeping on the couch is better than all the nights having a snow mattress put together," Jerry said. "I'd be honored to sleep on your couch."

I thought about the nights I had a snow mattress. "You're right, I'm sorry."

"Madie, it's a unanimous vote. If it's alright with you, we'd like to stay for a few days and help you out. Get groceries and make things around here a little more user-friendly. Maybe even mow the lawn if you'd like," Jim said.

I resisted the feeling growing in my throat. "I'd like that."

Dinner was finished and the dishes were in the dishwasher. They all got up and headed out to the car to get their luggage. I asked Jim to stay behind.

When we were alone, I started. "I want to thank you again for all the things you did for me that I never thought of. You paid all the bills while I was gone. I never gave the utility bills a thought, and someone has been mowing the lawn."

"You're welcome. As I have said before, it's been my pleasure."

"And for buying the plane ticket here and the limo ride home."

"That wasn't me. Give credit where credit is due, and that was Randy."

I nodded; another to add to the list. When things returned to normal, I would start to repay them – it was the least I could do.

Five large suitcases were carried into the house. Jerry returned last, carrying a large box, and sat it on the floor in the kitchen.

Jim spoke for him. "That's your things, the ones you wanted me to save. The day you arrived at my house frozen, you wouldn't let me cut them off you, despite the pain you were in. I didn't understand why, but now I do."

The tears ran down my cheeks. "Thank you."

Three days passed, and the men worked diligently. The door to the bathroom was made wider, as was the door that led out to the garage. From that door to the left, a ramp sloped down to the garage floor along the wall. I was told it was temporary and that they would remove it when I got my new feet. The two steps straight ahead were left in place. The glass door on the bathtub was removed so I would have easier access, and a shower curtain replaced it.

Mary cooked, feeding the men well. She made many trips to the grocery store. With my supervision she rearranged the kitchen cupboards, placing what I would need within my reach. The rest went to the top shelves. Down inside, I knew I wouldn't be doing much cooking.

The fourth day was a surprise. My vehicle and the suburban made the trip to the car dealer. It was to be sent out to have temporary hand controls installed for gas and braking. It took extra planning to do both with my left hand, but it was do-able.

While doing so, I was stared at a lot. I didn't know if it was because of my looks or because they doubted that I could handle it. I was nervous about driving. Sitting there, watching and listening, I had told myself that I would make at least a hundred trips around the neighborhood before entering into the mainstream of traffic and society. By then, I hoped to be accustomed to the staring.

The fourth night was the last we were going to be together. Their flight out, going back home, left early—seven forty a.m.

I made sure Mary had bought plenty of alcohol. Dr. Jim, Nurse Brandy, beer, and whatever she had a craving for.

Mary cooked. I wanted to send them back with a special meal. For all the work they had done, I bought a prime rib – twelve pounds. Six lobster tails, portabella mushrooms, lettuce, and all the fixings that go with it, wild rice, and steamed cauliflower. I helped with the cooking. At times, I felt the wheelchair was more in the way than my help. But I enjoyed being in the middle of things.

Some of the men helped from time to time. But mostly, they sat around the bar, drinking, watching, and talking. I made sure their glasses stayed full.

Dinner was elegant. Everyone, including myself, ate a lot. The laughter roared as more stories were told. I fought back happy tears this time. I loved this group. I was going to miss them.

Jonathon leaned back in his chair. "Boy, I was so hungry I would have eaten the butt out of a dead skunk."

"Jonathon!" Mary yelled.

Everyone roared. They oohed and yucked, but they all laughed.

"But I must say this was much better… much, much better."

"I'm with you, Jonathon. I would have finished up with a toothpick," I said as the laughter continued.

Everyone helped clean up, and it was finished in no time.

"This is quarter poker night, isn't it?" I asked.

The men started talking at once, but they all agreed.

"I have to win some of my grocery money back," I said, laughing.

George spoke, "Oh, no, missy, dinner was for our cat carpenter work. You're on your own now."

The laughter started.

"Yes, when the quarters hit the table, it turns to one owner, and that would be me," Jerry said.

The commotion grew as the banter increased. But I was curious, so I asked, "Cat carpenter? I haven't heard that before."

"Yeah! We do shitty work, then cover it up," George said.

I laughed the hardest. Tomorrow, reality would hit, but for now, I was going to enjoy the time I had with them. I had been taught that lesson the hard way.

"You guys did excellent work. Thank you," I said.

"Everyone but George," Jerry said.

"Hey, wait a minute here. First my fishing, and now this? The abuse I take."

The laughter continued. I had watched the men the past few days. Although I wasn't sure about George's fishing, he was the best carpenter in the group, and the men knew that. They were always asking him questions on how to do things.

I was the big loser of the night, a whopping eleven dollars and twenty-five cents. It took three hours of enjoyment to accomplish that.

As the cards were being put away, I was getting the ribbing.

"It will take us another two hundred years of this for me to feel even with you guys. I would give it all to you this instant. All you have to do is ask." The reality was approaching.

Mary put her arm around me. "We have loved you from the beginning, and that's all we need."

Tears flowed.

Jim spoke, "If you did that, it would take all the fun out of this. Friendship is far greater than money. In the end, money doesn't matter, but friendship does."

"There are so many things I'd like to say. I don't know how or where to begin. What's worse is, words can't express what you've done for me, there and now here. Thank you for everything."

Before we went to bed, it was agreed upon that I would visit them the last week of September and stay through October.

The next morning, everyone was up at five, showered, packed, and ready to leave by five thirty. This early in the morning, they would beat the thirty-minute drive to the airport.

It was time to say goodbye again. Again, I promised myself I wasn't going to cry. I kept telling myself it was the end of May, and in another four months, I would see them again. Everyone was standing in the living room by the front door. Each one took their turn. They lined up and filed past, giving hugs and kisses. I told each one thank you for the help. In some fashion or another, they all heard that I was going to miss them. I had to grit my teeth several times. Several more times, I squeezed the wheelchair with what was left of my left hand. I remained strong, and my eyes dampened, but I didn't cry.

Then, they were gone.

Then, I cried uncontrollably for a very long time.

When I finally finished, my stomach muscles hurt, but I didn't care. Although they weren't here, I had friends who cared for me.

The house was immaculate, thanks to Mary. Coffee was made, waiting to be drunk, and again, thanks to Mary.

Two cups were gone, and I didn't think I could handle a third. I wheeled over to the coffee maker and turned it off. It was going to be a long day and turn into a longer week.

For the next few days, I had my own little pity party every hour or so. By the end of the third day, I decided I was going to go visit Craig tomorrow at the cemetery. It was only four miles away; I would call a cab.

It was a perfect day, seventy-five degrees, with a slight wind blowing from the northwest and not a cloud in the sky.

The cab driver was very friendly. When we arrived at the gravesite to drop me off, he removed the wheelchair from the trunk, unfolded it, and placed it beside me.

"I can handle it from here. You're very nice." I tipped him and asked, "If you're not too busy, would you return in two hours and take me back home?"

"Yes, I will make sure of it," he said.

I wheeled through the grass and up to his grave. The ground was bare, and the flowers that had been left were gone. The headstone wasn't to be delivered for two more days. The cement pad was there, in the dirt, waiting.

What a lonely site, I thought as I looked around. The quiet stories of the headstones... never to be heard... only read. The name, the date they arrived, and the date they left. Good people that meant so much to their family. If words were given in one sentence, I wondered what they would say. For Craig, that wouldn't be possible for me. How would I begin? 'The most giving man one could ever ask for.'

I was alive, and he wasn't. Maybe it should read, 'This life ended so his wife's could go on.' I started to cry. It would take the entire back of the headstone to explain.

As I was crying I said, "Craig, my dreams fell fast. There's no turning back and going forward is going to be awful without you."

My head slumped forward, and my arms lay in my lap. I cried and cried and cried.

"I'm sorry. I'm so sorry for what happened to you; you didn't deserve it."

He was lying in there, and I was sure he could hear me.

I sat there, in a trance, numb. My mind was in neutral, lost to the world, lost in my new life.

The two hours were gone. It felt as though I was there only minutes. I heard a car drive up behind me. I turned and looked; the cab was back. Silently, I said, "Goodbye, I'll be back soon."

The driver walked up behind me. "Ma'am, are you ready to go?"

I wanted to say 'no.' "Yes," I answered.

He pushed me back to the cab and helped me get in, saying nothing. The puffy red eyes, sitting alone for two hours in the cemetery, he didn't need to ask. The trip back home was silent.

Pulling into my driveway, I asked, "What's your name?"

"It's Tore, ma'am," he answered.

"That's an interesting name. I'm Madie."

He tried to smile, but only a weak grin resulted. "Nice to meet you. It's Greek. My mother was full-blooded. My father was American. He always said he couldn't resist her charm and still does, along with her firecracker personality and her gift to talk."

Sounds like they still love each other, I thought. I saw a ring on his left hand when he helped me at the cemetery. "I see that you're married. Do you still love your wife?"

"Oh, yes, very much. She's very understanding. I work odd hours, sometimes working double shifts. We can always use the extra money. I do it for them. But I don't feel the need to tell her that. We have two girls, three and five, and they look just like her."

"Never ever lose that Tore. It can be taken away instantly."

"I understand. Seeing you at the cemetery crying broke my heart. One doesn't need to ask questions about why. I don't need to know how. Just that it happened is sad."

I sat in the backseat, staring into the past. "He was shot – right in front of my eyes. I couldn't stop it, and now, I have to live with both memories."

Tore lowered his head, either in thought or not sure what to say.

"The hurting time has begun, and I don't know what to do. Each day brings a little more misery. I'm still searching for something I will never find." I wanted to babble on, but I didn't. I would become tired of talking about Craig. Strangers, the ones who never knew him, would tire of hearing me talk about him.

"Thank you, Tore. I will call again."

"I will be waiting," Tore said.

29
CHAPTER

Three weeks passed by. The hours in each day seemed to move in slow motion, but the days were escaping fast. I couldn't decide if that was good or bad. My life was on hold, heading in no one direction.

I was spending a great deal of time moving around the house on my knees. It was faster, plus I needed the exercise to rebuild my muscles; they were shot. If I was going to walk again, I had to be able to hold myself up. I would clean the house, dust, vacuum, and do laundry, whatever was needed this way. The handicap I had to overcome on my knees was much easier than the one I had with my hand. At times, I caught myself reaching out with my right arm, which was useless. It took time trying to do things with my thumb and palm, but I was getting better at holding the furniture polish can and pushing the spray nozzle.

At first, I would tire quickly. As the days passed, my endurance grew. I could now go over an hour before I had to stop and rest.

I found a few things my right arm could do, such as carry the dirty clothes or the sheets from the bed to the washing machine. I could use the stump to swish the dust cloth over the furniture, but other than that, not much else.

Twice a week, I would go to the cemetery to visit Craig. Tore always drove me. Each time, I would leave in tears. That never got easier – a handicap I would never overcome.

I was lying in bed, ready to get up, waiting to face another day. Then, an idea came to me. I could see no reason it wouldn't work. Basically, it would be the same as walking on the prosthetics.

I got out of bed and walked on my knees to the linen closet. Even though walking around on my knees was vertically challenging, the wheelchair was slowly becoming a thing of the past.

I removed two towels from the closet. I had to get dressed next. Shorts and a T-shirt were the attire for the day. Zippers and buttons were a nightmare. At times I would become so frustrated at trying to accomplish something that physically wasn't accomplishable. At least I didn't have to worry about shoes.

Rug burns on my knees were something else, another reason to try my idea. They wouldn't go away until I could walk. If not, I would have to invest in knee pads.

I headed out for the other end of the house, carrying the two towels in my right arm. The duct tape was out in the garage, in the junk drawer under the workbench.

I opened the door to the garage. The two steps down from the utility room were tough. Something I couldn't do gracefully. Going back up the steps was much easier.

I stopped at the kitchen table. Sitting on the edge of the chair, with my stumps resting on the floor, I folded each towel into thirds. I placed the first towel on the floor under my left leg. Now came the hard part. I put my right arm through the roll of duct tape to hold it. I thank the lord Mother Nature didn't get my thumbnail on my left hand. My thumb had become a more valuable tool than the axe was out in the wild. I peeled the edge of the tape back and then used my teeth to hold the tape. Using my left hand, I unrolled about six inches of tape. Each step of the process became harder. I lifted one corner of the towel with my left hand and then used my right arm to hold it in place against my leg.

It took what seemed forever to get the towel duct-taped around my leg. By the time I finished the second one, I was huffing and puffing.

Now, I had pads on the bottom of my legs, and I stood. I remember once when I was a child, I tried to walk on stilts. It wasn't easy, downright awkward. That's how it was now as I stood. The pads under my legs felt good, but my balance was off. I needed my toes back for stability.

I leaned forward and placed my right arm on the bar top to help steady myself. I took one step forward. I remembered what happened to me at Jim's, and I didn't need to repeat that now.

Then, I took another step slowly. I was shaky, but I was going to do this. I followed the bar around to the sink and then onto the stove. I felt no pain at the end of my stumps. The only problem I had to overcome was the towels were a bit slippery on the floor.

I teetered back and forth with each step. Now that I no longer have my feet, I realize how much balance they give to the body.

I headed for the living room, using the kitchen wall for support. I wanted to walk on the carpet to see if the added traction made it easier.

It did. As I slowly walked around the room, I used each piece of furniture to steady myself—from the recliner to the rocking chair, past the sofa, and onto the television.

I made three more laps and was feeling more confident. Down the hall, I went. I could use both arms there, bracing them against each wall. Turning around was another problem I had to conquer. Mentally, I wanted to pivot on one leg. I could see that wasn't going to work, and I started to spin out of my pads. So, I took baby steps. My right leg moved forward while the left inched backward, so much effort to do something that once was simple.

Back to the kitchen, I went. I was beginning to feel at ease. My newfound mobility was a good thing. I was going to walk until my legs became tired. I wondered how long before the stumps started to hurt. But from what I saw on the internet looked to be about the same. The weight from the body was nestled inside a pocket of the prosthesis. Time will tell. I was going to be ready, physically, by then.

Three more laps around the house. My legs were somewhat tired, and I could have made more, but I had to stop; the towels had become too loose to go on.

I sat back down on the kitchen chair and removed the towels. There had to be a better way.

I had no plans for the day, pretty much the same thing as each of the past days. I could do laundry and clean the house only so much. They were never dirty when I did. If I could think of a better way to pad my stumps, I was going to make a trip to the grocery store, and then on to the cemetery. Today, I would take flowers.

I sat in the chair for a while, but I could think of nothing. There wasn't anything around the house that would work. One idea I had was a pair of waders. Stuff the padding into the boots and tie the top around my waist. How stupid would that look? I was glad there weren't any.

The only thing I could come up with was taping the towels to my legs with massive amounts of duct tape, but that would hurt. I put the pads back on my legs and headed to the closet for a pair of jeans.

I was finished, and I stood. Then I smiled. The first thing I had to get at the store was a massive amount of duct tape.

I looked as if I had snow boots on, without the toes. I couldn't tell where the towel ended above my ankles, but it worked. I made three more laps around the house.

Then, for the first time, I walked outside. Three steps into the garage and I stopped since I suddenly felt insecure. I had nothing to hang on to. I looked around the garage for a temporary crutch. The thought came to me, *If I was out in the wilderness, I could use the axe to chop a stick, or the axe.* Neither was an option now. No dead sticks. If I used the axe in public, I would be arrested for being a crazy, axe-wielding woman—freak show added for no extra charge.

I took inventory of what was in the garage. The usual stuff: a rake, a snow shovel, broom, hedge trimmers—too short—and a dirt shovel. Without feet, I would never use that again.

I shuffled to it and then carried it to the workbench. I determined how much of the handle I would need for a cane and then sawed it in two.

Now, I had my crutch, a stick cane. Whatever worked, something I learned out in the middle of nowhere.

I headed down the driveway. When I got to the street, I turned and walked back. My new mobility was much more than I had planned.

The sun shining on my face and the fresh air gave me a better outlook. Two more trips to the street. I felt good, but my legs were becoming tired. I went back into the kitchen and sat in the chair.

While I rested, I made a grocery list and a list of a few other things. That list was short, but so was the grocery list.

I thought about where to go. My first trip out, being much sooner than planned, would be simple. I decided to go to the Super Target. It would have everything I need. And regardless of where I went I would get the stares, the quiet conversations behind my back, whispering, talking about me. I would be the topic at many dinner tables tonight. So, what, I didn't care, and then I grinned. I could give them something to really talk about, like, 'Hey, I ate raw fish and a lot of it, and one rabbit included. I even slept with a wild bear.' Who would believe me? No one. The only thing they would believe was that I was some kind of a crazy woman.

I called the cab company and asked for Tore to pick me up. I was told he had the day off. They said they would send someone else. I thanked them and hung up. This was going to be interesting.

I had twenty minutes before the cab arrived. I walked to the bathroom, brushed my hair and my teeth, and put a light coat of makeup on. I wanted to spruce up the freak show appearance a little. I still cared, not as much as I used to. If they had seen me the day I walked out on Jim's lake, they would have called 911.

Now, they wouldn't be looking at my face, something I couldn't change, no matter how much makeup I put on.

I was excited going to the store, something I didn't do in the wheelchair. Now, I wondered which would draw more attention—a crippled lady in a wheelchair or one walking around with no feet. Either way, it didn't matter to me. I wasn't crippled, just missing a few parts. What I had worked on, why not use it?

I stood in the driveway, waiting for the cab. I used the remote to close the garage door and put it in my pocket. I couldn't carry a purse and use the cane. Then, I thought of something else I had to get—a shoulder purse, one with a long strap that I could hang over my neck.

The cab pulled into the driveway, and I headed for the back door.

The driver jumped out. "Oh, my! Let me help you," the driver said.

"I'm fine, I can do this." Then I paused. "Well, maybe you could open the door for me."

We pulled into the parking lot. As we drove toward the entrance, I took a deep breath as anxiety was building. Maybe this was a mistake. I wasn't worried about falling down. That was something I had done dozens of times in the snow. I didn't care if people watched me do it, and I wasn't worried about what they thought.

It was just that this was my first time out, in public, alone.

The cab slowed and then stopped. Now, I was as nervous as I was the day I went to take my driving test. I couldn't fail then. As all sixteen-year-olds, a driver's license was a big deal. I couldn't fail now. If that were to happen, I would be a hermit for the rest of my life.

I sat in the back of the cab and looked around. The people coming and going were numerous. Rushing through the business of everyday life, and I was about to give them a show.

I watched the people push their carts, full of merchandise, leaving the store. It hit me – a cart could be my crutch. It would also shield me somewhat. I would look like a short old lady trudging along.

"If you'd like, I can take you back home," the driver said.

I looked into his rearview mirror and saw he was looking at me. I could read the expression on his face, and I knew what he was thinking.

"No, I can do this. I just need to get one of the carts," I said.

In a flash, the driver was out of the cab. He walked to the nearest cart abandoned by its former user in the aisle we were parked in.

I opened my door as he pushed it up to the cab. I got out, thanked him, and paid the driver with a large tip.

I took another deep breath and began pushing the cart, heading for the door.

I walked through the automated front door. Now that I was inside, I didn't feel so vulnerable. Why I felt that way, I didn't know, but I had to get over that. If I could once walk through the wilderness alone, I could walk across the street.

Eight months had passed since I had last been inside this store. I still remember it well. I headed down the aisle in front of me, then turned and down the next one, eventually ending up on the one the duct tape was on. That was a bigger priority than food.

I put two rolls in the cart. With that done, I headed for the section that the purses were in. As I walked there, I relaxed. I was starting to enjoy my shopping trip. I stopped at various places and looked at things on the shelf that caught my eye.

By now, I felt like a normal, average woman out shopping.

On one side of a long aisle was nothing but purses of all shapes, sizes, and colors. What I needed made the selection limited. I didn't want anything fancy, and I wasn't too worried about the color.

I was deep in thought as I was looking at which one I wanted to buy. I felt a tug on my pant leg and looked down. To my surprise, there stood the cutest little girl, maybe three to four years old. She had long blonde hair, with such a head full that it made me think that that was something one would see on a girl much older. I looked into her bright blue eyes. She had a look of serious concern in them.

"Lady, are you alright?" she asked in a quiet, timid voice.

I smiled at her—so innocent. "Yes, I'm OK."

I saw her mother turn at the end of the aisle and head in our direction, moving much faster than normal.

"But you have no feet," the little girl said.

"Mia! You shouldn't bother that lady," the mom said.

Now I could see her face turn a little shade of red, obviously embarrassed.

The mother wouldn't look at me. She reached for the girl's hand. As she started pulling the little girl away and walking back in the direction she came from, the girl's body pivoted in that direction, but her head remained fixed on me. "What happened?" she asked.

"Mia, I told you not to bother that lady."

By now, they were several steps away. "It's OK. If you don't ask, you don't know. She means no harm," I said.

That surprised the mother and she stopped, not expecting that I was willing to talk.

"I'm sorry, she doesn't mean to be rude," the mother said.

"She's not. Something to be said of the age of innocence; it's not a bad thing." The little girl was still looking at me, still curious. "They were frostbitten, and the doctor couldn't save them," I said.

"Oh, my, I'm sorry," the mom said.

"Don't be. It's not your fault," I said. I raised my right arm. "See, my hand, too," I said, looking at the little girl.

She looked at me. I saw no look of grief in her eyes, just concern.

"Does it hurt?" she asked.

"No honey, not at all. I'm Madie," I said to both of them.

"Mommy, what's frostbitten mean?" the girl asked.

"It's when your feet get so cold they freeze," the mom answered.

"Didn't you have boots and gloves on? My mom always makes me wear them when it's cold out." She was still taking all of me in, the four-year-old mind trying to grasp reality. "Your other hand, too?" she asked.

It didn't matter what the mother thought. She would soon turn and run, and I would never see them again. I stuck my left hand out, "Yes, see, it's kind of messed up."

Mom gasped. She put her fingers over her mouth, trying to recapture what had already escaped. Her power of observation lacked her daughters.

"I know it's kind of ugly; I'm sorry," I said, now feeling guilty about what I just did. Mia would talk non-stop at the dinner table tonight, and I would be the topic.

Mia let go of her mother's hand and walked directly toward me. I quickly glanced at her mother, expecting to hear her call Mia back, but she didn't. She stood there mesmerized. Mia took hold of my left hand in her right. "It's not ugly, it's just different," she said. Then, she rubbed the top of mine with her left. She looked directly into my eyes. "Really, it's not, and it's still your hand. You're a nice lady."

Was this little girl clairvoyant? Did she hold some mystical power not seen by others? The soft touch of her hands on mine, the small fingers, and tender skin. Her sincerity was unconditional, and I felt my legs buckle. My eyes watered. Flashes raced through my mind of what would have been—Craig and the children. Who wouldn't want a little girl as kind and caring as Mia? That part of my life was gone. Now, my nose was running as the tears increased.

Unaware of the effect she was having on me, she looked at me. "Mom said if I was good, we could go to McDonald's after shopping. Do you want to come with us?"

That did me in, a combination of a laugh and cry escaped. The laugh part was only to hide the cry. It took all I had not to break down; so much kindness from a little girl who didn't know me. Trying to help Mom out of the uneasy situation she was just put in, I answered, "Oh, I don't know, Mia. I'm sure your mom has a lot to do." I let go of Mia's hand, but I couldn't say goodbye. I quickly turned and faced the cart. I had to get away before losing it.

I didn't get far. By the second step, I was bawling my eyes out. My legs grew weaker, and my shoulders slumped. I shuffled my stumps, trying to stifle the sound of my crying. I was a freak show, yet everyone was so nice to me.

I got to the end of the aisle; the purse no longer mattered. I wasn't thinking about which way to turn, and I was thinking about what Mia had said last. 'Mom said if I was good,' I couldn't imagine her any other way. Her kindness came from her heart.

I started to turn to the right when I felt a hand on my shoulder. I stopped and turned. Still crying I looked at the mother, then down at Mia. Mia was looking at me. I saw no sadness or pity on her face, just her big blue eyes as if they were looking at a normal person. I was wrong about Mom turning and running.

"You're welcome to join us, really," the mom said.

"I'm sorry, I didn't mean for this to happen. I just thought when people would see me, they would go the other way."

She nodded.

"You have a wonderful daughter. But, no, thank you, I'm not fit to eat out."

"It doesn't bother Mia. I've just learned a valuable lesson from her. It won't bother me," she smiled. "We would be honored, huh, Mia?"

Mia nodded. "I'm going to have a happy meal. You can have one with me."

I laughed. Mia's charm was a gift. I wanted to cry again, only this time, it was because of happiness. I didn't.

"We have more shopping to do. How about we meet there in an hour," the mom said.

"That would be fine. But please, tell me your name," I asked.

"Sharon. I'm Sharon. I should have told you sooner. It's just…"

I cut her off; no need to explain the obvious. "I know. Thank you, Sharon."

I watched them walk away. I felt better, so I returned to the purses.

Everything that was on the shopping list was in the cart. Now, I needed one more thing. I had no idea what to get; I've never bought something for a four-year-old before.

I narrowed it down between a toy and a book. I ruled out a toy, and I was totally lost there. So, I walked to the book section. My entire time spent shopping; I was either thinking about what I needed or the innocent, unshakable look on Mia's face. She was truly one of a kind. So, I didn't notice the people that were staring at me, I'm sure there were plenty. Hopefully, I had new friends, and I didn't want to mess it up. I started to get a book for little girls, and then I saw a book on dogs and cats. I went with that, all the kids like animals.

I headed for the checkout. On the way there, I noticed, for the first time, that I was walking like a stick person, barely bending at the knees. As I thought about it, that's what I was—digitless. The floor was freshly waxed, making it just a little slippery. Subconsciously, I was correcting for that.

I stopped just before entering the aisle to the cash register. It took me several minutes to call another cab.

When I started to walk up to the cashier, she came around the turntable and met me. She had obviously been watching me. "Here, let me help you," she said.

At first, I didn't know what to say. "Thank you. I didn't mean to make a show," I said. Just by being in public I was doing just that.

"You're not. Just glad I can help out," she answered.

I had two of the plastic bags full hanging on my right arm. I stood at the front door of the building, waiting for the cab to arrive. I ignored the people entering and leaving the store. They would take one quick glance at me and quickly look away as if they were embarrassed—human nature.

When we pulled into the parking lot of McDonald's I saw Mia and Sharon through the window. Mia quickly waved to me, and I waved back.

I didn't see the curb next to the cab. I was trying to manipulate myself, the two shopping bags, and my cane as I closed the door. I had to move back one step to close the door. Then I tripped over the curb and fell down. I landed on my butt and then rolled over on my left side. One of the grocery bags split open, and the contents spilled out onto the sidewalk. *Oh, great,* I thought, not thinking much of it.

By the time I started to get up Sharon, with Mia in tow, came out the door. "Here, let me help," Sharon said.

I was disgusted with myself for not seeing the curb. "Here I am again, making a show, just what I wanted to avoid."

"Nonsense, everybody falls down."

Mia picked up the book I had bought for her. Of course, that had to be the bag that broke open. "You like dogs and cats, too," she said.

'Well, I did something right,' I said to myself. "I bought that for you, Mia. I was going to give it to you inside. A surprise, but I guess I kind of messed that up, huh?" I said as I stood up. Sharon was picking up the remaining groceries.

"No, you didn't. It's just as nice outside," Mia said, looking directly into my eyes again.

Wow, so much insight from a four-year-old, I thought. "Do you like it?" I asked.

"Oh, yes," Mia answered.

"What do you say to Madie, Mia," Sharon said.

Mia walked three little steps up to me. Then she held her arms up, wanting me to pick her up. I didn't know if I could do it and maintain my balance, but I had to try. She was such an adorable, loving little girl; who was I to deprive her of that, myself included?

I wrapped my right around Mia, squeezed, and lifted her. My left hand was on my homemade cane and I used it to maintain my balance as I held Mia. I constantly felt the feeling of falling forward, and I missed my feet.

I wanted to hug Mia for a very long time, but I set her right back down. "I felt like I was going to fall over, I'm sorry. I wouldn't want to do that holding you." I smiled.

"That's ok. I can sit by you inside."

I looked at Sharon, and she smiled. I was taken aback. When she smiled, her looks changed; she went from beautiful to an especially gorgeous woman. She had a smile that would halt hundreds of men in their tracks. She was holding the groceries loosely in her arms.

Neither of us had paid any attention to the cab driver. He was standing behind us and held out a bag. "Here, use this one. I already ate my lunch," he said. I thanked him, and we went inside.

They ate while I drank a Diet Coke from a straw. Sharon had gone to the counter and brought it back for me. I was starving, but I didn't want to make another show. Truth be told, I didn't want to gross them out; my eating utensils were home.

Sharon and I talked mostly about Mia. Mia showed no concern over that. She did sit by me. Occasionally, she would point out a dog or cat in the book, saying, "That's a pretty one." She held my left hand in her right. I wasn't sure if Sharon was aware of this. "Is she always this affectionate?" I asked.

"No, normally she's very shy. She's taken a liking to you," Sharon said.

"She's an amazing little girl. I can see she takes after her mother."

Sharon smiled. "Thank you, but something tells me the two of us don't equal you."

'Then or now, there's nothing left of me. I can't even eat in public,' the thought continued. I said nothing, and I was relieved when she didn't ask.

We were finished, and Sharon gathered up the remains and headed for the trash. I reached into my pocket for my cell phone. It took me several attempts to flip the phone open.

"What are you doing?" Sharon asked.

I looked up and she was looking down at me. "Calling another cab," I said.

She shook her head no. "Mia, let's give Madie a ride home."

"OK, I'd like that," Mia said.

CHAPTER 30

I was home alone. Sharon and Mia had come in but didn't stay long. We exchanged phone numbers and I was looking forward to seeing them again.

During the time spent at McDonald's and the drive home, Sharon had become more comfortable around me, not the panicked mother she was at Target.

We sat at the kitchen table before they left. Sharon never asked what had happened to me; I thought she would, but I was glad she didn't. I didn't know how I was going to answer her. But if we continued our friendship, I would have to do just that. I sat at the kitchen table, resting my stumps, thinking. I would just tell her the truth; no sense in lying to her, what would that prove? In my case, the truth would not set me free. The truth hurts, but it's still the truth. I continued thinking. I remembered what I had told the last death dealer: *I can never outrun the past. The past is my truth.* And I made a promise that I would go on.

The longer I sat at the table, the more depressed I became. If I didn't get up and do something within minutes, I would be crying.

So, I stood, and sharp pains shot up both legs. I had exceeded the limit of what my legs could take for the day. I hobbled to the wheelchair and sat in it. I was too tired to crawl on my hands and knees the rest of the day. Then, I removed the pads from my stumps.

I put the few groceries away; while doing so, I thought about the day. It hadn't turned out nearly as bad as I had thought it would.

I ate and then went into the living room and crawled onto the sofa. I spent the rest of the night watching movies.

When I woke, it was only one forty seven. I removed the blanket from the back of the sofa, covered myself up, and turned the television off.

When I woke the next time, it was just beginning to get light out. Even now, as it did out there, my internal clock was still working. I looked at the clock on the wall: six twenty-two. I dropped my head back down on the pillow, wishing my internal clock would break. I had nothing to do today; why couldn't I sleep just a little longer?

I was wide awake, and falling back to sleep wasn't an option. I got up, got in the wheelchair, and headed for the bathroom.

I took a long hot bath, soaking in the hot water. I remembered back to all the mornings when I woke as the sun was coming up. I was cold, stiff, tired, and hungry, yet I faced another day and moved on.

Now, I was none of those, yet I had to face another day and move on, part of my promise—one that I would never break.

I got dressed and put a light dusting of makeup on. I'm not sure why, but I would have no visitors. I guess I did it because it felt good. I would have to get much more coordinated with my left hand before attempting the lipstick. If I were to try that now, my lips would be twice their normal size with jagged edges. That, without question, would put me over the top in the freak show appearance—a twisted clown in a horror flick. That I didn't need. I was already halfway there.

I took two ibuprofen before leaving the bathroom. I was going to walk again today. Hopefully, that would ease the pain before I started.

I rolled out into the kitchen and made a pot of coffee, then sat back in the wheelchair. "Well, that took all of an hour," I said. Now, I had no idea what I was going to do the rest of the day.

While the coffee was brewing, I started on the pads for my stumps. I folded the towels and got one of the rolls of duct tape. Then, I got a pair of scissors and proceeded to cut the end of my jeans off. The extra length only got in my way.

By the time that was finished, the coffee was made. I poured a cup and then went to work. Like yesterday, it was quite an ordeal. I got disgusted several times; the tape was sticking everywhere but where I wanted it to. I almost cursed Mother Nature several times. Why hadn't she left me with a thumb or finger and a right hand? Then, things would be four times faster than they are now. But she hadn't. Somewhere, in some unseen place, she was laughing at me.

Three cups of coffee and thirty minutes later, I was finished. I slowly stood. The pain was there in my stumps, just not as much as it would have been without the ibuprofen.

I took slow, short steps, waiting for my body to adjust. Now, as it did then, it did. The body always adjusts to what it's given. Like the dozens of times in the wilderness, I had to do it mentally.

Each day, I passed by the box Jim had brought for me. It was still sitting on the floor beside the television. It was long, nearly five feet, but only two feet wide. My past – what kept me alive. Sooner or later, I would have to open it. Removing the items would be painful. Today was the day.

I made several laps around the house, trying to build my courage.

I slid the box across the floor and sat in the recliner. I removed the tape, breaking the seal. I looked at the box. It was larger than necessary to hold what I knew was in there.

Before I lifted the first flap, I removed the charm necklace from under my shirt. I squeezed it, 'This is for you, Craig,' I said to myself.

I took a deep breath and then opened the box. My jacket was on top. I removed it, laid it in my lap, and looked at it. It was even a little dirtier than I remembered. What I hadn't noticed before was all the small rips and 'L' shaped tears in it. Running in the dark, slamming into the trees, and snagging the tree branches had taken its toll. There were over a dozen little holes in each of the sleeves and many more across the front. I shook my head as I thought back. If there was a hole for every time I ran into something, there would be no jacket left at all.

Then, I removed the pants; they weren't as torn. The limbs at that level had died and fallen off the trees. I looked back into the box to see what was next. I cringed – memories flashed in my mind – before and after I started wearing his jacket. It kept me alive, but it was a total wreck. Brown, dried blood, and huge tears that I don't remember doing. The right pocket was half torn off. The left sleeve had a small dried chunk of something on it. It took a severe beating on the rest of my trip. I didn't feel any of them happen. It was far worse than I remembered seeing the day Jim took it off of me.

I was proud of myself. I had kept it together. The worst part was over, or so I had thought. I looked back in the box. The axe – I would have starved to death without it – was lying on top of the now brown snowshoes. I removed it. I had to squeeze my thumb hard to maintain a grip to get it out of the box. I looked at the blade. Even with all the ice it chopped, it looked the same as the day I had gone back to the lake to get it.

Now, my eyes watered. Remembering the frostbite and the starving would never be as painful as memories of how quickly one remembers. I didn't want to let go of it, my lifesaver. I laid it in my lap, the security blanket of my past.

I went back to the box. In the front left corner was a plastic bag I didn't recognize. It was a white kitchen garbage bag from Jim's house. There were several things in it. I sat it in my lap, on top of the axe handle, and opened it. Instantly, I was crying hard or harder than I ever had; I couldn't breathe. It was as though Craig was as close to coming back to life as possible. On top were two of his flannel shirts and then one pair of his jeans. I remembered exactly where they were, and they were in his backpack the day I started running. Something the wild animals had no use for. I held the shirts up to my face, hoping I could still smell him on them. He was long gone; something else Mother Nature had taken care of. The snow, the cold, and the fresh air had removed him.

I gasped between sobs. The pain and the love were unbearable. Why the men chose to bring them all the way here I didn't know, but I was glad they had.

I finally got myself together enough to look back in the bag. My vision was blurred looking through the tears. The camera—they had found it. I held it on top of the shirts. What was inside it held more value than any amount of money could replace—Craig. I had taken many pictures of him and there were several of us together. Now, I was glad we had spent the extra money for the model with the timer. Those I would take to my grave with me.

The remaining items in the bag were my clothes of mine and the compass. I sat the bag on the floor. Sadness grew as I continued to cry. So much love – so much lost.

I finally quit crying. The pieces of rope were all that remained on top of the last set of snowshoes I had used. I could tell that they were dried and brittle. I left them in the box.

I thought of the knives, the ones I had used to clean the fish. I set the things in my lap on the floor. I went back to the death dealer's jacket and felt the outside of the pockets. I found them in the right pocket and removed them.

I looked around at everything by myself. Every single thing that was here kept me alive. Without any single item I wouldn't have made it, including Craig's clothes. The memories and the promise I made to him pushed me on.

I sat there a long time, looking at everything. The memories flowed, and details of certain events remained clear. The most painful one was watching Craig fall backward. Everything that happened after that day, combined together, didn't equal that.

I blew my nose, wiped my eyes, and then cried some more. I was in deep thought. Then, out of the clear blue, I thought of the list—the piece of paper the last death dealer had told me about in his pocket. Why, now, I remembered that I don't know.

I bent down to get his jacket, thinking that if the list survived the trip, it would be a miracle. I sat his jacket on my lap. I reached inside the ripped right pocket, but it wasn't there. If it wasn't in the left pocket, it wouldn't bother me, just something that disappeared along with him. It wasn't in the left pocket. To my surprise, I found the piece of paper in a pocket inside the jacket. I removed it and looked at it. I had no idea what it was.

It held what he had said it did. A list of numbers, but what the numbers meant, I had no idea. There were ten lines with a series of numbers in each. I stared at them. Were they combination numbers to some sort of a lock box – I didn't think so. Maybe phone numbers, but they weren't in the right numerical order, so that ruled that out. Another thought came to mind; maybe they were overseas phone numbers. I ruled out numbers for addresses.

Then, I thought of what he had said just before he died, 'See not what you see. See what you don't.' Were these numbers a code? Something I had to break before I could understand what they meant? I was confused. It was going to take much more time and thought than I wanted to spend right now.

I stood. Another memory flowed from nowhere. The nowhere being some hidden, forgotten place in a very dark spot in my mind. That's where a lot of the bad events went. But they would never go far enough, or deep enough, to where they weren't able to resurface. His words were clear, 'Those will make you rich beyond all figment of imagination. Maybe you'll figure it out.' I sat back down and looked at the list of numbers. Was he just playing some sick, perverted joke on me? Was this his only way to get even with me, in death, what he couldn't accomplish in life?

I looked at the numbers, but I was at a total loss. I had no answer.

If it were true that these numbers meant something, why tell me? My curiosity grew as I remembered his words. I would have thrown the list away, but his tone of voice when he said, 'Maybe you'll figure it out,' held no sarcasm. I believe what he said was true.

I sat there a while longer. What else do I have to do? Not much, I decided, so I decided I would try and figure out the numbers. If I couldn't, or if I ran into a dead end, who would know?

I carried all the items into the spare bedroom. The problem was the spare bedrooms were upstairs. I had to walk across the great room to get to the staircase. It was a large room in which Craig and I had turned into a library/office combination. Its next function was going to be my wilderness sanctuary. A place I could go when I was feeling down – the only place where I would feel close to Craig.

I had a good idea of how I was going to set it up, but first, I had to retrieve the pictures from the camera. I would pick out the best one of Craig and then one of the two of us together. I would have to find someplace that could make them into life-size portraits.

On the far wall, opposite the door, a life-size picture of Craig would be the first thing I would see when I entered the room. The left and right walls would have a picture of us together.

Somewhere in between, I was going to display the arctic gear on mannequins. The axe, compass, knives, and snowshoes would also be displayed.

Somehow, somewhere, I would buy a stuffed bear or at least a bear rug to remember my friend. Our friendship was brief but long enough to save my life.

If someone else saw this room when I was finished, would they think I was crazy? Obsessed to the point where I've lost it? Probably so, but it would be my therapy. It was that or visits to the shrink. It was out of the normal path in the house; no one would see it.

It took three trips, the last one being the hardest. I left the snowshoes in the box and dragged them up the stairs. They were too brittle to remove. Like the Christmas trees, I remembered being young, the pine needles falling off by the hundreds. I didn't want that to happen to the snowshoes. I had to find a way to preserve them.

I was back in the kitchen looking at the list while coffee was made. As I thought about it, the only thing I questioned about what he said was it would make me rich beyond imagination. I doubted that. If that were true, why were they living in the middle of nowhere, the place where it got so cold you couldn't function? Why not someplace warm in the tropics, some little island that no one visited?

They meant something, or he wouldn't have told me about it in his last moments of life; I have thought about it dozens of times and replayed our conversation over and over in my mind.

What he was saying, he knew he was dying long before I did. Maybe it was something he had accomplished in his life. He either wanted to share it with others or just make them aware of it. An invention of some sort – a cure for some disease – a trust fund. The list of things went on and on. It could be anything, or it could be nothing. The only way to find out is to figure out what the numbers meant.

I drank a cup of coffee as I thought about it—where to begin. The only way to get finished was to get started, as I did each new day walking out in the wilderness. This was a little different – no walking, just thinking.

But first thing today, I was going to the cemetery again. I hadn't been there for several days, and I wanted to talk to Craig.

I called the cab company, and Tore would be here in forty-five minutes. I couldn't wait to see him; he was a good man.

While I was out, I thought I'd spend some time with Sharon and Mia, so I called. We agreed to meet at noon at the pizza parlor.

I packed my eating tools in my new purse and wrapped my stumps. I worked hard and never rose up to rest. This job was a real struggle; too many things to hold with one thumb. I was huffing and puffing and barely made it before Tore pulled in. I had to come up with a new design of stump pads, some sort of slip-ons with an easier way of fastening them to my legs.

I heard Tore pull in as I was reaching for the door. By the time I closed the door, he was entering the garage, and I assumed he was coming to my rescue. I smiled at him.

"Wow! Would you look at you? I'm looking at you, and I don't believe it." He was quiet for a moment, watching me as I walked toward him. "Does that hurt?"

I laughed. "No, it just adds to the freak show appearance. It's so much easier to get around this way than with the wheelchair."

Tore frowned, "You're not a freak show. You should be awarded for doing it."

Why I was being so lucky to be surrounded by good people, I wasn't sure. Tore didn't baby me, nor did he feel sorry for me the way I wanted it. He wanted to help, what all good people would do.

"Let me open the door for malady. It's an honor to have you ride in my chariot," he said with a bit of a hacked accent.

We both laughed. "Yeah, right," I said.

"Well, it is. It may not be a chariot, but I am honored—seriously."

Now, I didn't know how to laugh or cry. I got in the back seat and remained silent.

On the way to the cemetery my mood sank, knowing the fact I was going to see Craig. Jim and the crew in Canada, Sharon and Mia and now Tore. The few people I've met since the death dealers have become instant friends. Almost to the point of being too nice to me, and I was feeling guilty.

I wasn't watching the scenery go by, and I was too deep in thought. "Mother Nature was never this kind," I mumbled.

"What did you say? I'm sorry I didn't hear you," Tore said.

Tores' voice brought me out of my trance. "I was thinking out loud, talking to myself. I do that now, but I never did that before."

Tore nodded. I watched him frown in the rearview mirror. "What did you mean, Mother Nature wasn't this nice?"

"I thought you didn't hear."

"I heard it, but it didn't make sense to me."

"It doesn't to me either. What hurts the worst is it never will." Now, Tore looked confused. Do I spill my guts and tell him the story, or leave him confused? He was too nice, so I decided to give him the reason I'm the way I am. "Mother Nature did this to me—frostbite."

No expression changed on Tore's face. I watched him from behind as he looked forward, driving through the traffic.

"Your husband also?"

"No, he was murdered."

"Oh, man, I'm sorry. I barely know you, but you are a tough lady. That I knew from day one. You've been through a lot."

Tore left me at the cemetery and would return in an hour and a half.

I walked to Craig's grave as I heard the car pull away. I was thinking of what he had said, but I thought of something different. If he only knew I wasn't tough. I ran, and I couldn't save the man I was going to talk to.

"Craig, I'm back. I wanted to tell you how much I love you. Every day arrives with a new list of reasons why I believe you still exist. The people I meet are so kind, and I wish you could meet them, you'd like them. I can see a part of you in each of them." Now, I was crying again. I went on, "Each list has the same thing at the beginning—You. God, if you are listening to me, make sure Craig knows how much I love him. He was a wonderful husband. I wish I could have him back." I was crying harder, but I had to tell him. "I would give what's left of my arms and legs to hug his neck one more time. I would give my life just to kiss him on the cheek and say goodbye." Now, I couldn't breathe, and my chest was heaving. Tears were running down my face. "Craig, I miss you each minute of every day."

I sat in the grass, looking at the dirt where Craig lay. Six feet and an eternity away—so close but so far. I spent the rest of the time thinking of the past. Sometimes I cried, sometimes I smiled. Even when I smiled, though, I was sad.

Tore returned. I stood and looked at the grave, "I'm sorry I cried so much. I'll be back, and I'll try to do better next time." Wishful thinking on my part.

Tore knew I had cried a great deal while he was gone. That was clear to me by the look on his face. Humans can hide emotions, but sadness is the toughest.

He opened the door, and I thanked him. "Will you take me to the pizza parlor on Meadowvale?"

"I will take you wherever you need to go. I was thinking while I was gone, would it be alright if I brought a camera and had a picture taken of us?"

Tore got in the cab and started driving out of the cemetery. I was wondering why, so I asked, "What in the world would you want that for?"

"What I know about you is probably just a drop in the bucket that is overflowing with water. The two things I do know are massive. I don't see how you do it, but you do. What's back there in the cemetery is insurmountable, and seeing you now is incomprehensible. If it's ok with you, I'd like to put the picture on the visor." Then Tore lowered the visor, "Right here beside this picture of my wife and daughter."

I was still confused. He answered me without any real reason why. "Why would you want to do that?" I asked again.

"I have this picture for two reasons. I love them to death; they are my life. The reason I go to work every day. On the bad days, when I have jerks for customers, and I'm working a double shift, thinking, this just isn't worth it."

I was listening intently. How well did I know that? How many times did I ask to die? Going on wasn't worth it, but I said nothing.

"You're a rock, an inspiration. I mean, when I think I'm having a bad day, now I'll have two pictures to look at. I'll look at yours first, and then I'll know what I have to endure is nothing compared to what you do. I have no excuse to feel depressed, and then I'll look at theirs and smile."

My eyes watered. "Not now," I told myself. I'm going to see Sharon and Mia. They didn't need to see me crying. "So, what's the second reason?" I asked.

"Well, you might think I'm stupid or something. If I'm in a bad crash, I want that to be the last thing I see before I die."

That did it, the straw that broke the camel's back. I bawled my eyes out. "That's the most honorable thing I have ever heard. It's not stupid; don't ever think that." I took several deep breaths and wiped my eyes. "I'd be honored to have my picture on your visor."

But why did people continue to think I was invincible? I was no rock, maybe a basket of pebbles, none of which connected to anything. "Stop at the next store that sells cameras, and I'll pay for it. I know someone who will be glad to take the picture."

He did.

We pulled up in front of the pizza parlor. "Wait here, I'll be right back." I went in the front door and waved to them, then motioned for them to come to the door. I asked Sharon and she agreed to take the picture.

We walked out the front door. I introduced them, and Tore and I leaned against the cab. I asked Sharon to take a few extras, telling Tore that I wanted one. Then I had an idea: Why not get a picture of Sharon, Mia, and myself? We stood in front of the pizza parlor, and Tore was at the helm. He took many pictures, one was of me holding Mia, she had asked for that.

We were finished and Tore and I said our goodbyes. He took one step and stopped. "This has been the best day I've had at work. Thank you," he said.

I waved, and then he turned and left. My eyes were wetter than normal.

"He seems like a nice man," Sharon said. "Will you tell me what that was all about?"

We walked into the pizza parlor and Mia was looking at me. She sensed something wasn't right, but she didn't ask. She held my hand as we walked past the tables and customers.

People stared at us, but she wasn't embarrassed as most people would have been. I was her friend, and I was proud of that.

Mia colored on the back of the paper placemat. I told Sharon the reason for the picture. I noticed a small hint of sadness on her face. "Wow! That's amazing. What one does for a living doesn't show their true character. I'm learning a lot, thanks to you."

I wondered what she meant. Maybe I would have a chance to ask later.

The pizza arrived – half cheese, half vegetable. "I'm sorry if I make a mess. I'm not the greatest at eating." I fumbled with the strap as I wrapped it around my right arm.

"Sometimes I make a mess, too. That's why we're sitting by each other, so we won't get any on mom."

Sharon and I burst out laughing, but Mia didn't see the humor. How did she do it? I determined it was a gift she was born with.

As we ate, I talked about Tore. I told Sharon the things he had said about his family and how much love he held for them. I could see the more I talked, the sadder Sharon became.

Not knowing why, I stopped. She never asked about me and why I was the way I am. A thought occurred to me—maybe she didn't want me asking questions about her.

I offered to pay for lunch in return for a ride home, but Sharon wouldn't hear of it.

In the driveway, Sharon wouldn't come in. I didn't ask; maybe I offended her. I hugged Mia and said goodbye to Sharon. No future plans were made.

As I walked into the house, a sad feeling flowed; would I ever see them again?

31
CHAPTER

The first thing I saw when I walked into the kitchen was the list of numbers lying on the bar. I carried it with me as I walked into the bedroom. I sat at the computer and turned it on. While I waited, I thought about the endless possibilities of what the numbers meant still overwhelmed me. I looked at the first line and shook my head. Finding a needle in a haystack wasn't nearly as hard as this; one already knew what the object was. The area to look in was already determined—the barn. If need be, one could remove a single stalk of straw at a time; it would take a great deal of time, but by process of elimination, the needle would be found. I had nothing, just an imaginary piece of bait. The needle, if it existed, the barn pretty much covered the planet Earth. Maybe this was just a wild goose chase. His words were clear as day, 'Maybe you'll figure it out.' I believed him. The way he said it, the tone of his voice, I didn't believe he was lying. The first line read, "41 27 18/88 11 49." They sure looked like padlock numbers or combination numbers to a lock to me. If that were true the goose chase was already over. I never knew their names, so I didn't have any way to find where they were from. Not being able to do that, I couldn't eliminate it down to a state or city. Even then, the impossible held true. What intrigued me was the slash and second set of numbers.

I stared at the blank screen, where to start, one strand of straw at a time. Physically, I wasn't computer friendly. I rolled the mouse, clicked on the Internet icon, and the screen came to life. The easy part was over. Some people say they fat-fingered the keyboard when they made a mistake. I thumbed it to do death. I typed in mathematical equations. Now I felt small, pages full of various mathematical equations. It was asking me if I wanted chemistry, physics, algebra – the list went on and on.

I sat back in the chair, "I don't know," I said. What I was looking at didn't look right. Samples on each screen didn't fit the simple numbers on the list. I ruled out that possibility.

Next, I went to codes—not much there. I was never too good at math. That much I did know. Still, I had a nagging feeling the ten lines of numbers had nothing to do with math. That brought me back to my original thought. The search engine brought up padlocks. Again, pages of manufacturers and brand names. As I scrolled down each line, I read everything there was about that individual padlock. I learned a lot about them: shank length, shank diameter, and the hardness of the steel—some of which could stop a bullet. Some were re-keyed, meaning the lock had to be relocked before the key could be removed. But nowhere could I find one combination lock that used a set of six digits to unlock it.

I sat there staring at the screen, but I wasn't looking at it. I was too busy processing thoughts to focus on vision. The lock idea was ruled out, and I was kind of glad because if it had been that, I would have finished. The hunt was over.

Somehow, I had to pick up the pieces that were left to find. Nothing in life is easy. I learned that when it came to dealing with the death dealers, the 'not easy' part intensified ten-fold.

I was getting nowhere, and I was going in the express lane.

I typed in astronomy and spent another hour there. Looking at numbers, dimensions, and anything I could find. Nothing rang a bell, and I felt like I was nearing the end of the express lane. I could see the cement wall, but I wasn't ready to crash and burn yet.

I turned off the computer, walked into the living room, and turned the television on. I was watching it without really watching it. I was thinking about what my next step would be. It had to be a code to break. That, along with the math, was not my area of expertise. If it was a code, numbers to be broken down into letters might tell me something or maybe lead me to the next step.

An entire two-hour movie passed by on television, and I had spent it in deep thought, but I hadn't come up with a plan. Many times, I thought back to that day. One thing I truly believe is if the death dealer had ten more minutes to live, he still wouldn't have told me what it meant. He was too much of a cynic. I knew that, now, by something else, he had said, 'You wouldn't believe the things I've accomplished.' He was self-absorbed, alright, bragging about something, but I can add to that. A self-absorbed piece of trash who deserved the fate he received. I was getting angry at him for his egotistical attitude and myself for not being able to figure it out.

I went to bed and tried to read, but my mind wouldn't turn off. Thoughts and ideas were coming fast. I made a list. Tomorrow, I would call Jim, I needed to, just to say 'hi' and 'how have you been?' Now, I had another reason. With his connections there, he would know of someone who would sell me a bear rug or a complete stuffed bear. That would go in the wilderness room, a reminder of a brief friend.

The next call would be to the university to try and find a name for one of the math professors. Then call him or her and try to set up an appointment.

Then, I would call the prosthetic company and set up my first visit. Jim had given me the phone number before I left his house. I was ready – I wanted to be tall again. Plus, the freak show bit was getting old. Physically, I was getting much stronger, and by the time I went, I would be back to normal. Well, normal as far as muscle tone goes, anyway.

I had to call Sharon first as I thought about it. I felt bad about our visit. If I had done something to offend her, I wanted to apologize. That is, if she would tell me. Maybe it was my appearance – more than she could handle.

I was pumped! I had something to do tomorrow, several things actually. I gave up on going to sleep.

I had brought the list of numbers with me and they were on the nightstand. I slid the list over to the edge with my thumb and got a hold of it. I studied the list for a very long time. I read and reread each over and over again.

27 18/88 11   49
39   3 10 104 17 23
40 53 31   75 12 25
40 38   2   73 59 17
27 42 51   82 19 19
37 22 54   93 33 21
32 37   8   96   5 39
34   7 18 118 48 57
29 59 13   95 20 34
42 16 14   71 29 40

I read them so many times I almost had them memorized, but that's all I had. Then I started reading each column vertically and that's when it hit me. The fourth column – none of those numbers were below sixty. These numbers didn't belong to a combination lock. From what I had seen earlier on the Internet, none of the numbers went above sixty. I was excited! Now, I knew what I didn't have, which gave me more incentive. The fifty remaining numbers didn't go over sixty.

The death dealer was playing a game with me. I knew now it was a game that could be solved. I heard once, and I don't remember where or when 'The impossible only takes a little longer and costs a little more.' I thought that was strange at the time. The bottom line, nothing is impossible and I wasn't giving up on this one.

I turned the light off.

My internal alarm clock was right on time. I looked at the clock on the nightstand: five fifty-five. I felt that the sun and I raced each morning to see who rose first. I think I was excited before I even woke. I didn't have to lie in bed the ten minutes to become coherent.

I headed for the shower. My stumps hurt, but I didn't have the pads on. Along with my daily multivitamin, two ibuprofen had to be taken. I might not get to leave the house today, but I wanted to be prepared just in case. If Sharon didn't want to meet for coffee which was what I had planned, and meeting with one of the professors, the chance was next to nil. I would stay home. Talking with Jim would happen unless they were out saving someone. This time of year, that wasn't as likely.

I was bathed, dressed and had the freak show makeup applied. Seven-fifteen, maybe a little too early to call Sharon. I would give her fifteen more minutes.

I hobbled to the kitchen. There was coffee left over from yesterday, so I poured a cup and put it in the microwave.

The cup of coffee was gone. The first call of the day was the only one I dreaded. Maybe it would be like the bear's friendship, brief. I really hoped not.

The phone rang on the other end; I was nervous.

"Hello," the tender voice said.

"Mia! How are you today?" I was surprised and didn't expect her to answer.

"I'm fine. Are you? You don't sound the same. Are you hurting?"

Wow, unbelievable, I thought, a truly special child. "Do you have a busy day?" I wanted to talk with her for as long as possible, but I had to cut to the chase and get it over with.

"No, I don't think so."

"Can I talk to your mom?"

"Yes."

Now, yelling, "Mom, it's for you," and then silence.

"Hello," Sharon said.

"Sharon, it's Madie."

Silence. *Not good* raced through my mind. I didn't wait. "If I offended you yesterday, I'm sorry. I'm really sorry."

Again, silence. *I'm going to miss you and Mia,* I thought.

"It's not that you didn't. I was just sad listening to the cab driver and how much he thought of his family. Do you want to meet this morning?" Sharon asked.

"Yes, I would like that. Would you like to come here? Mia can watch television."

Sharon agreed, and they would be here in an hour. I still didn't have a clue what the outcome would be.

I dumped what was left in the coffee pot and made a fresh one.

When Sharon and Mia walked in, I could see immediately Sharon was uneasy, as she was on the first day we met at Target.

We did smiles and hellos. We then took Mia into the living room to watch television, and Sharon and I returned to the kitchen. I didn't ask and poured two cups of coffee.

I sat at the kitchen table beside her and could see a slight tremble in her hands. This wasn't about me or Tore.

Sharon started into her coffee. I decided to let her determine the next move. Then her eyes watered. "You're probably wondering why I never asked what happened to you. I wanted to, so many times, I just couldn't. Then, questions would be asked about me. Questions I wasn't ready to answer. I knew sooner or later you would know."

I watched one single teardrop fall into her lap.

"My husband and I have split up. He's been living in a motel room for over a month. It's killing me. I don't know what to do."

I was just blindsided. I didn't see that one coming. 'What do I say?' I asked myself.

This time, Sharon didn't let the silence linger. "The past two years, we have grown apart. We didn't argue or fight much, just the usual disagreements. To make the story short, his name is Kevin, and Kevin decided he wanted to try living apart for a while. I didn't try to stop him."

I watched several more teardrops fall. She still loved him, but I asked anyway. "Do you still love him?"

She nodded yes. "Very much. I can't imagine divorcing him."

"Do you two still talk to each other?" I asked.

"Yes, every night. He calls and talks to Mia, and then we talk."

"Good talk or bad talk."

"Sometimes it's good, other times it's just talk. We never fight." Sharon said.

Kevin still loves her, and that was obvious to me.

Sharon was much better at holding the tears back than I was. How many countless times had I bawled my eyes out in the past? I sat there watching her continually taking quick glances into the living room. I didn't know if she didn't want Mia to see her crying or if she did it because in there sat her strength. The reason to go on—I had mine, and he was in the cemetery.

"Do you want a divorce?" I asked.

"No."

"Does he?"

"No, at least I don't think so. That's never been discussed."

Then, Mia walked into the kitchen. She sat on my lap, and our discussion was over.

When we said our goodbyes to each other, Sharon looked no better than when she arrived. I was sorry I couldn't help her. How could I? I was no shrink.

293

My next call went to the university. After many explanations and being put on hold the same amount of times, I was put through to the department I needed – math. I was told that I would probably have to leave a message. No surprise about that. I heard the phone ring as I was thinking about what to say without sounding crazy.

"Hello, Professor Lehn," a voice said.

I was caught off guard again, surprised, a live person answered. I stuttered for a second, but then I got it together. "Hello, my name is Madison Chanhansen." Without great detail, I explained what I had. "Would it be possible for you or someone else there to take a look at it?"

"That's an unusual request, but I don't see why not. I'm free for another hour, and then I have a class. If you can get here before then, I'll start on it for you."

Things were happening much faster than I had thought they would. Surprised, I said, "Yes, thank you!" Then, the professor gave me directions to the building his office was in.

I quickly called the cab company and, in doing so, decided I needed to put their number on speed dial. I told them it was urgent and was told that Tore was on his way.

Now I was in the panic mode and hurrying around. I was dressed but had no stump pads. Tore would be here long before I could finish them. The trip across town to the university would take forty minutes and it was going to be cutting it close.

I gathered my purse, towels, tape, and a leather jacket. I quickly wrote a copy of the list of numbers. The original, with his handwriting on it, was staying with me.

The purse hung around my neck. With the stick cane in hand, I hobbled out to the driveway. Moments later, Tore was racing into the driveway.

He jumped out of his cab. "I was scared. I was told it was an emergency. Are you alright?"

I smiled. "Yes, we need to get to the university by eleven. Is that possible?"

Tore grinned, "You've got the right man."

On the way there, I taped the towels to my feet. Flopping around in the backseat made it much harder than sitting in a chair at home. While doing so, I explained briefly why I was going there.

We made it with twenty minutes to spare. Tore pulled the cab as close to the front as he could. "You did a wonderful job." I paid him, saying, "Thank you."

"At your service, malady." Tore smiled at me.

I walked down the long hall following the directions Professor Lehn gave me. His office was three-quarters of the way down, and I was wasting time walking so slowly getting there. I saw his name on the placard on the door. It was open, but I still knocked.

"Come in," he said.

I walked in and saw the look on his face—shock—totally caught off guard.

"I'm sorry. I should have told you when we spoke on the phone. I'm Madison."

The professor quickly stood and walked around his desk. I thought maybe he was trying to make up for his blunder. I wanted to tell him there was no need to.

I had put the light leather jacket on in the cab, not because it was cold out, to look a little more respectable. He reached out with his right hand to shake mine.

"That too," I said. I held my right arm up. The leather sleeve went limp at the end of the stumps. "The left one's kind of messed up, but it works. Is it alright if I shake your hand with that?"

He looked at my hand and then back to me. Total disbelief was all over his face. He had never seen anyone like me, but who has?

"Yes, that would be fine," he said.

"Again, I'm sorry for not telling you. I know I'm a bit of a freak show." I smiled. "We're short on time; here's the list." I handed the list to him.

"Please, sit." He studied the list as he returned to his chair.

"Thank you." I sat. "That took a load off my feet." Wrong thing to say.

The professor looked at me with a blank look. "I'm kidding, just trying to let you know that I'm fine."

"How long have you been like that?" he asked.

"Eight months. It started when I acquired that list. Not from a friend, let's just say an acquaintance."

He looked at the list for a very long time. "I don't believe this is some sort of a mathematical equation, but I'm not positive yet. Like you said, it could be some sort of written code. That is out of my area."

My shoulders slumped. Before I could speak, he said, "I know who would. If you can leave this, give me some time. Give me a number where I can call you. I will… no, I have another idea."

I perked up as I watched the professor pick up his phone and dial.

"Yoon He, this is Morgan. Something's come up at the last minute. Can I collect that chip you owe me? Would you teach my eleven o'clock class for me? I have the material I was going over here on my desk. Ok, thanks. See you in a minute."

I was really excited now, but I tried to remain calm on the outside.

Professor Lehn hung up. "We help each other out. The students like him; he's much younger than me, and they can relate to him more."

I looked at him. He was your typical looking professor—mid-fifties, salt and pepper hair, and reading glasses perched on the end of his nose. What made him look his age was the tweed jacket. "Thank you. This is much more than I expected."

Yoon He walked in. His appearance fit his name—black hair, a small build, and a slight tan to the tone of his skin. I was guessing Japanese. Yoon He was smiling.

"Yoon He, this is Madison," Professor Lehn said.

I stood. Yoon He's smile quickly stopped. "Don't worry, I get that look all the time. It's nice to meet you, Yoon He." I stuck my left hand forward, and Yoon He shook it.

"Nice to meet you," Yoon He said, and his smile instantly returned.

Yoon He took the material from Professor Lehn and left; he had five minutes.

I sat back down.

"Let me make another call to Professor Schaut. If he doesn't know, possibly he will know someone who does."

"I want to thank you for taking the time to do this and for disrupting your busy schedule. I wasn't expecting this kind of service. I will repay you."

The professor waved me off. "No need to. One class won't be missed. Besides, to tell you the truth, we never get asked for outside help. This is kind of interesting. I'm glad to do it."

The professor made the call and hung up. "This is your lucky day. He will be here in fifteen to twenty minutes."

We talked about what, I'm not sure. I was too excited. The time vanished—where to, I had no idea. Professor Schaut came storming in, and I wasn't sure if he even noticed me. He was tall, several inches past six feet. He had no jacket or tie but was dressed impeccably with heavy starch in his shirt. His pants had to be micro-stitched, not a wrinkle to be found.

Professor Lehn handed him the list of numbers, "Edward, this is Madison."

Edward raised his head. His deep, dark, penetrating eyes looked at me. "Hi, how are you?"

His deep voice matched everything else. I couldn't read his personality. My first impression was he was tough, no games—tell it like it was. Now, I wondered if I was a nuisance to him, something he'd rather not be doing.

"I appreciate your help. At first, I thought this was something in math. Then, I leaned toward something written in code. I searched and researched everything I could think of. I had no luck, and that's why I came here for help."

Edward never looked up from the list. I wasn't sure if he was even listening, so I stopped. I looked at Professor Lehn and gave him the look 'Now what?'

Edward didn't move, and I could see the wheels turning behind his dark eyes. I grew uneasy. It seemed to me, as the moments passed that he forgot to breathe. The silence was sharp. What would happen if someone broke his concentration?

Edward broke it himself. He reached into his pocket, and I watched as he removed a cell phone and flipped it open. Then he pushed two numbers. "It's me, how long before you're free? Alright, I'll call you back." He hung up. "Come on, let's go eat lunch."

I could see a slight twinkle in his eyes – did he already know?

"You two are hungry, aren't you?" Edward said.

I didn't know what to do. I looked at Professor Lehn for help.

"We always eat lunch around here. Believe it or not, the food is really good in the cafeteria."

"We have an hour to kill," Edward said.

"I'm in, but I insist on buying. You're taking the time to help me. It's the least I could do," and I stood.

"Oh, my God," Edward said. "Here, let me help."

Well, he didn't want to run, I thought. "I get that all the time, but thanks, I got it." I smiled; maybe I had misjudged him.

"The cafeteria's a good quarter mile away. Are you going to be alright?" Edward asked.

"I'll be fine as long as you don't run. I didn't bring my jogging shoes."

Edward laughed. "Ha! Good one."

I looked at Professor Lehn, he had a look of unsure what to think. Of the two, I found Edward had a better sense of humor.

Curiosity was killing me. "You know, don't you?" I asked.

Edward grinned. "No, I don't know. I could get a group of people on it and let them start crunching those numbers. In the meantime, I could send it to some people I know. They could send it through the computer and see what it spits out."

He kept saying 'could.' I was hobbling fast to keep up with them. "But you keep saying could, I think you know," I laughed. "I would have bought lunch anyway, without the drama."

"I like how you think," Edward smiled. "But, what I know and what I think I know aren't always the same. I enjoy your company."

"Fair enough," I said.

I insisted on going last in line so I could pay. As I slid my tray along the buffet, I was careful what I ordered. I had to use a fork.

The men carried my food and drink to the table as I paid. The truth was, I was too anxious to be hungry.

As we sat at the table I wanted to ask Edward who he had called, but didn't. 'Patience, soon enough,' I said to myself. I was already farther ahead than I ever thought I would be.

"So, Madie, do you mind me asking what happened to you? At first, I thought a car wreck, but I ruled that out," Edward asked.

I was really glad to see he didn't feel awkward around me, unlike Professor Lehn. "No, I don't mind. Why did you rule out a car wreck, just curious?"

"Your left hand… it doesn't fit the scenario."

"No. You're right, frostbite, and my nose isn't the original one either."

"Oh, my God!" Edward replied.

"I don't know how much to tell you; I don't want to gross you out."

"You're a beautiful woman, Madie. How could you do that?" Edward asked.

"For what I'm about to tell you. You two are helping me, going way out of your way to help someone you don't know. Have I told you how much I really appreciate it? I do. If either of you want me to stop, tell me. If I get to talking too long, let me know." I started at the beginning of our trip. I told it like it was, and every so often, I would come out of the deep trance I was in. I would look at them. Professor Lehn sat in his chair with his hands in his lap, looking at me. Edward was the only one of us who finished eating, and now he was staring at me. Without my missing body parts, who would believe me? I went on, and the napkin was a good Kleenex.

I was to the part where the death dealer was dying. Edward's phone rang. "Crap! For all the inopportune times for my phone to ring."

I watched his large hand engulf the phone, and with one flip of his thumb, it was opened.

"Hello, yes, we're in the cafeteria. You need to be here and hear this." Edward didn't say goodbye; he just flipped the phone shut. He looked at me and said, "Please, go on."

I looked to Professor Lehn for approval. "Yes, do. I wouldn't miss this for the world."

In less than a minute, I was back in my deep trance. Far into the story, I stopped. Remembering something that I knew then, I was just too far gone for it to really sink in. "My feet were gone, two frozen, solid chunks of flesh. I could no longer feel them as I walked. The only way I knew my weight had transferred to the next step was the muscles in my thighs. I asked to die. Then I could smell smoke. Soon after, I found out it was coming from Jim's house, the man who saved my life. At the time, I thought it was my body, the last gasping breaths of death." I went on, telling them what I had said to Jim when I found him and what he had done to save my life. I wasn't like Sharon; I couldn't remain strong, and I cried.

I finished. To my surprise, there was another man sitting behind me. I looked at him.

He half raised his right arm, attempting to wave. "I'm just sorry I missed the first part."

"What an amazing story. Your will to survive exceeds the realm of humanly possible," Edward said. "Madie, this is a good friend, Sam. Sam, this is Madie."

I waved back. Blowing my nose and wiping tears, I didn't see the need to speak.

"Sam, this is the list of numbers Madie has." Edward handed it to him.

Sam studied the list as the rest of us watched him do it.

"The only thing I know, which isn't much, is the fourth vertical row of numbers doesn't go below sixty. The other five don't go above it," Edward said.

Sam nodded in agreement.

"The ten horizontal rows mean nothing to me."

"Well, they wouldn't if," he stopped.

"What? What do you mean?"

"These are GPS coordinates."

I grew ten inches as I straightened up. "Are you serious? Are you sure?" I asked.

"Yes. See GPS coordinates. The first read the latitude set of numbers and then the longitude set of numbers. If the large space between the two sets of numbers wasn't provided, I wouldn't have figured it out so fast."

"That's what I thought they were." Edward looked at me, "I wasn't sure, that's why I called Sam. He's a geologist and teaches geology here."

I couldn't believe it! I was so happy I wanted to jump up and down. Even if I had feet, I wouldn't have done that. I was sitting with three professionals – I had to act like one.

"The first set is 41 degrees latitude; the second number is in minutes, and the third number is in seconds. So, it reads 41 degrees, 27 minutes, and 18 seconds—same for longitude, 88 degrees, 11 minutes, and 49 seconds. Relatively easy."

I was beaming. I remembered the death dealer's words, 'Maybe you'll figure it out.' I had, in a roundabout way. I removed his handwritten list from my purse. Looking at it, I said, "No, it doesn't look too hard. The numbers in degrees don't range too far apart from one another."

Sam raised his eyebrows. "Latitude lines north or south of the equator always run parallel with it; longitude lines run north and south. They move east or west around the earth connecting with prime meridian, which is the north or the south pole."

That much I knew.

"If you divide the circumference of the earth, which is approximately 25,000 miles, by 360 degrees, the distance on the earth's surface for each one degree of latitude or longitude is 69 miles.

As you move north or south of the equator, the distance between the lines of longitude gets shorter. At 45 degrees north or south of the equator, one degree of longitude becomes 49 miles in distance. But that's not the case here. None of the latitude numbers go above 45. North of the equator, the 45-degree mark is just at the United States/Canadian border. South of the equator is halfway down South America. Without a chart, I can't be exact. But those numbers….." Sam thought for a minute. "So, what I'm saying is," Sam looked at the numbers, "the lowest number is 27, the highest is 42, latitude." Sam removed a calculator from his pocket and punched in some numbers. "15-degree variance, times 69 miles per degree, is 1035 miles north and south. Longitude variance is much greater, 47 degrees. So, there the distance is 3243 miles. You're looking at a distance of covering an area almost the size of the continental United States."

That much I didn't know.

I just lost the ten inches I grew and then some. My shoulders slumped. "Wow, this just became harder," I said. I had figured it out alright. The plot, whatever it was, thickened. What I had just figured out became much harder. "Maybe it's time I bag this."

"Why? I said it's not that hard. After dividing each degree into minutes and seconds, you can go even further. Each second can be divided into tenths or hundredths. That would allow you to find something the size of a penny. Or even thousandths, which would get you down to a piece of thread. Unfortunately, those aren't given."

"So, why tell me that? I'm already depressed enough," I said to myself.

"For whatever reason, those weren't needed, or they would have been on the list. Another thing you need to know is six satellites are used to obtain these coordinates. The seconds will get you down to about a ten-by-ten-foot area, give or take a few feet, barring no mountains blocking one of the satellites. If so, the area increases in size," Sam said.

I was silent, sad, and depressed, thinking of what to do next.

"You can go on the Internet, type in latitude and longitude, and then each set of lat and long set of numbers. That will give you the general location. To find what's there just buy a good quality GPS and go drive around until you find the spot."

The needle in the haystack—it can always be found, but was it worth it?

I said my thank yous and goodbyes.

32

CHAPTER

I was sitting on the sofa, thinking and resting my legs. The extra walking and the faster pace than usual had the skin on my stumps raw. But that was secondary. Did I really want to go all over the country on a wild goose chase, unsure of the outcome? Something I had to seriously think about. The list lay on the coffee table in front of me, taunting me. So far the worst human being that lived hadn't lied to me. I felt no remorse for him dying or what happened to them after.

I called Jim. Hearing his voice would cheer me up, and getting an update on what the rest of the crew was doing would be good. I missed them all terribly.

"Hello."

I could hear the wind blowing, making it sound as though we had a bad connection. I also heard water splashing. Within one second after Jim said hello, I knew where he was – on the lake fishing. "Jim, it's Madie. How are you?"

"Great. Fishing is good, but to be honest, I miss you. We all do. Each day, we talk about you. Everyone wants you to come back already. How about you? How are you doing?"

I had never told them about the list. I hadn't thought about it at the time. I wouldn't now. If I didn't pursue it, why waste the time?

We talked. During our conversation Jim caught a fish, a nice three-pound walleye, he said. Now, I wished I was there. Freshly cooked fish, nothing better no matter who cooked it, Jim or Mary. I asked about her. Jim told me that she really missed me, that she even had tears on their way back home.

I told Jim I would be there in two months. I said goodbye and hung up. Now, I wasn't sure if I felt better, happy that I talked to him, or sad because I missed them.

I sat on the sofa, remembering the past. I always feel so good when I think of Craig and the crew, yet I still cry, as I am now, for no other reason than missing them. Craig would never come back, and I was the reason he was dead. A pang of guilt that would never leave and that I would be buried with.

I turned the television on. I channel-surfed all the way up and back down and then turned the television back off. Nothing looked good, mainly because I didn't want to watch.

'What to do, what to do,' I said silently. I didn't have to decide which way to jump from the fence anytime soon. Today, I made a big step; now, do I choose to jump in the direction of doing something, making the next move? As the saying goes, the grass isn't always greener on the other side. I could add to that; it's just as hard to mow. In this case, it would probably be harder. Curiosity was killing me, as it did the cat. How many of the nine lives did I use out in the wilderness? I didn't keep track. However many, it didn't matter. I was still here. Why worry about one more?

I got up and moaned. The pain in my stumps hadn't eased a bit. Slowly, I made my way to the computer.

It was on and waiting for me. I did what Edward told me to do. I typed in latitude and longitude. Up came the screen full of questions. I scrolled down the list and then clicked on 'Finding Locations by Coordinates.' The next screen appeared. In the first empty box I typed in the first latitude number on the list – 41 27 18. For the next empty box, I typed in the longitude number – 88 11 49. I scrolled down to 'Find Location.' Then I clicked the mouse again and within two seconds, up popped the next screen giving me the location. Not knowing what I would find, I wasn't surprised when it showed me a map telling me West Chicago, Illinois. Now, I knew where the where was. But what had I gained – what was there? What was I looking for? A building, a business, a home – the possibilities were endless.

I entered the next GPS coordinates. 39 3 10, 104 17 23, clicked the mouse, and up came Denver, Colorado. "Huh," I said, thinking. Remembering what Edward told me, 69 miles for each degree. On the longitude scale, I just moved 1104 miles west… for what?

The third set of numbers took me to Philadelphia, Pennsylvania, the fourth to New York, and the fifth to Tampa, Florida. Edward was right.

The last five sets of numbers took me to Springfield, Missouri – Dallas, Texas – Los Angeles, California – Houston, Texas, and Boston, Massachusetts. That pretty much covered the United States.

Next I typed in United States land area – 3,539,341 square miles. Now, I kind of liked the idea of just finding the needle in the haystack. The odds were much better there, and I knew what I would be looking for.

I leaned back in my chair, staring at the computer. Why would such a list exist? What could they have possibly done or known? Each step I progressed was nothing more than a lateral move. I learned nothing other than the fact that I now had ten haystacks to sort through.

Something wasn't right. If I went all over the country on this wild goose chase, I'd be like the chicken – running around with my head cut off – blindly – running into dead ends.

The phone rang. I jerked; it scared me. This was a first. Since I had returned home my phone didn't ring. I made my way to the phone. "Hello," I said.

"Hello, Madie. This is Professor Lehn."

I was surprised. Why was he calling me? We had just talked hours ago.

"Hi, Professor. What a surprise hearing from you already."

"Yes, well, I couldn't get you off my mind. What an incredible story, you accomplished the impossible."

"It's funny you say that, I was just thinking earlier about 'the impossible,' this list I have. The impossible just takes a little longer and costs a little more. Look what it cost me."

"Yes, I'm sorry. Your journey, what a thing to overcome. Edward and I talked about it in great length after you left."

I didn't even make it to the dinner table, I thought.

"So, the reason I'm calling is that I would like to have you come to the University and speak."

My mind was reeling. I didn't see that coming twice in one day. "I…"

"About your journey, that is, if you're up to it. If not, I understand," he said.

"Wow! I don't know." I could think of so many reasons not to. "I've never stood in front of a group and talked before. Who would want to hear? I would bore them to death."

"Oh, no, Madie, it's incredible. I wasn't in the least bit bored. At times, I'm not sure that I was even breathing."

"Can I think about it?"

"Yes."

"How many people are we talking about?"

"You would draw a big crowd, around one hundred fifty to two hundred people."

"Are you serious? I was thinking dozens and not many of those." I didn't know if I could stand in front of that many people and talk. I would turn into a different kind of basket case. If Craig were here, he would be behind me one hundred percent. Now, that's the reason I would be up there. I would do it for him, his memory. "Yes, I will do it. Just understand I might not do as well in front of a large group."

"Just be yourself, Madie, you'll do well."

"OK. I ask one thing, not too soon. Please, give me a few weeks."

"Consider it done. I'll keep in touch. You tell me when you're ready."

After I hung up, I wondered what I had gotten myself into. Could I do it? I could always say no.

One more call to make, the last on the list—the prosthetic company in New York, downtown Manhattan.

303

I got up and went to the desk. The phone number Jim had given me had laid there since they had left. I carried the piece of paper out into the kitchen.

I dialed and waited. As soon as I told the receptionist my name, she cut me off.

"Ms. Chanhansen, we've been waiting for your call. Everyone has been wondering if something had happened to you?"

She talked to me as though I was a long-lost friend. The 'Ms.' Part was incorrect, but I decided not to correct her. "No, I just wasn't ready physically. I guess I am now."

"Everyone has been excited to help you. There are so many options for amputees now, you wouldn't believe it. The technology here is growing so fast. The most recent is water resistant. We even have custom silicone services. Every product we create is as unique as the person using it. Our attention to detail in our handcrafted products makes it look as if it were your actual fingers. We make sure that comfort goes hand in hand with functionality."

Wow, for a receptionist, she makes a good salesman, I thought.

"We even have choices of feet if you are a runner. We have many clients who run 10K races."

That got my full attention – running. Would I be able to do that again? "But I've lost both of my feet, several inches about each ankle," I said in doubt.

"That doesn't matter. We've been in business long enough to have those problems worked out. We even have foot shells to cover the prosthetic feet. That allows you to wear shoes. So at work or out to dinner, anywhere in public, no one will know the difference."

Sold, this might be better than I thought. "No more freak show," I said.

"Ms. Chanhansen, don't look at it that way."

"Well," I decided not to go into details. The stares I get, "I have lost both feet and my right hand."

"Yes, we know, that's why we're excited to help. Most clients have lost one limb, but very few two. When they leave here, after therapy, they look normal. They are all very happy to have a real working hand again or to be able to walk. The ones who have lost both feet say it's so good to get out of the wheelchair."

I was even more excited! I'll have a new pair of running shoes complete with feet to put inside of them.

"So, when can we set up an appointment for you?" she asked.

"I'm sorry, I didn't ask your name," I said.

"I apologize, that's my mistake. I was just so happy you called. It's Andrea."

I liked these people already. Jim had set me up with a good company. "Well, anytime is fine with me, Andrea. Just give me some time to make arrangements to get there." Now, my mind was thinking of details—bus, train, too far to get a taxi. My new car fitted for handicapped users was not due for delivery for several weeks yet.

"That's already taken care of, plus your motel room during your stay. We will send a car to pick you up and return you home," Andrea said.

From Massachusetts to downtown Manhattan is roughly one hundred fifty miles. That was asking a lot, but I assumed transportation would be added to the final bill, so I didn't ask. "That's wonderful," I said.

"We tell our clients it's one to three days for fitting. In your case, it will be a full three days, possibly four. Today is Wednesday. Can we set you up for Monday? That way, you can spend Sunday traveling and get settled in the motel room."

"That sounds great to me. I don't want you to go out of your way to fit me in so soon, though." Everything was happening so fast.

"We're not, like I said, we've been waiting for your call. That way, you can be home by Friday night at the latest," Andrea said.

It wasn't like I had anything else to do. "OK, I'll call and make arrangements at the motel."

"No need to. I will do that for you. We want to make this as pleasurable as possible."

I hung up and sat back in the kitchen chair – then it occurred to me. She said it's already been taken care of. Jim. Was there ever anything that he didn't think of? I wanted to cry. How would I ever repay him for all his kindness?

CHAPTER 33

The next morning, I awoke but kept lying in bed. So much to think about… the list that covered ten locations all over the country, going to be fitted for feet and a hand, and worrying about Sharon. She still loved her husband. What Jim had done for me, I would, in return, do it for Sharon. The kindness, the caring, whatever it took, I would help.

I got up, dressed, and drank what was left of yesterday's coffee. Then, I went back to the list. On the computer, I re-entered the first GPS coordinate; again, it brought up West Chicago, Illinois. I magnified the screen, drawing closer to the exact location. It even gave me the name of the street. The map also showed me how to get there. I printed it out. Then, I shrank the screen, showing me the bigger picture. That allowed me access to directions from the closest main interstate.

Then, I sat back. I stared at the computer, thinking for a long time. One of the many things I wasn't was clairvoyant or psychic. Nothing jumped out at me. I also wasn't smart enough to figure it out. Then, I smiled. "I hope you cook for all eternity," I said. If I never figured this out, I've lost nothing. I beat him, albeit there was only half of me left, but I still beat him. The satisfaction in that outweighed this. I hoped the wolves ate well.

I went down the remaining nine locations on the list, always giving me names of streets, or highways being the only variance—big deal. Now with ten maps to the ten locations, step two was completed.

Would I bother going on to step three? What would that be? I thought about calling Agent Netz and Healy at the FBI. Would they even bother with it? What if there wasn't anything there? I had no credibility with them, and I had no proof. I decided against that idea because of too many ifs.

Time passed; mentally, it stood still. I was so deep in thought that everything else was lost. I came up with several wild ideas, none of which held water. Down inside, I still had that nagging feeling as I did earlier. These numbers meant something, something big. Why would he have them? In his dying words, why would he tell me about them?

I also had many negatives to this. If it was important, why hadn't they already reaped whatever this list contained? Why were they hundreds of miles north—hiding—if that was what they were doing? Were they wanted men and escaped to Canada to avoid being captured by United Stated authorities?

Nothing made sense, and I was getting a headache. I regretted not ever knowing their names. Then, it didn't matter, but now it does. But even at the time, I had no way to know or mark the locations where they had died, even if I wanted to. Something else I now regret.

What did the death dealers know? What were they hiding? What kind of mess would I get myself into if I pursued this? My headache was getting worse, and I needed more coffee.

Before I made my first move to get up, my phone rang. I flinched, mentally I was far away. The ringing brought me back. "Hello."

"Hello, Madison, it's Sharon."

"Hello, Sharon! What a nice surprise having you call."

"I just wanted to call. It's been bothering me since I left yesterday. I shouldn't have troubled you with my problems. I'm sorry."

"Sharon, you have no reason to be sorry. Everyone needs someone to talk to every now and then." Lord knows I did. How many times did I bend Jim's ear? I'm sure I said the same thing over and over.

"Well, I don't know your past. It hasn't been kind to you, that much I do know. So you didn't deserve to hear about mine. You've lost more than me losing my husband. Again, I'm sorry."

Then, it hit me, I know what to do for Sharon. "Losing a husband is far more important than my physical condition, Sharon. Don't ever forget that. I have to be gone all next week, but I'll return on Friday. I'd like to do something for you if you'd let me."

I could hear the quivering in Sharon's voice. "Alright, but don't feel that you have to."

"I don't, I want to. A lot depends on your husband. If you both agree, I'd like to invite you two over to dinner the following Saturday night."

"I'd like that. I'll ask my husband and get back to you. What day are you leaving?"

"Sunday."

"If you don't hear from me tomorrow, you will by Saturday. If he says no, can I come alone? I'll get a babysitter for Mia; she likes that."

It won't accomplish what I had in mind, but she didn't know that. How could I say no? Sharon still needed a friend. "Sharon, try to talk him into it. If you can't, then it will be just you and I."

I could hear the relief in Sharon's voice, as if she wasn't sure if he would accompany her. "Good. I'm already looking forward to it. Do you want me to help with dinner?"

"No, I can handle it. Although it won't be much, just so you're forewarned." I already knew what dinner would be. After having talked with Jim, I missed their kind of food. Fish, I would prepare it in Mary's favorite way—baked. With wild rice and sautéed mushrooms, fresh broccoli, and a salad for starters. And a nice bottle of wine – I could handle that. It would be my first big meal since arriving home.

After hanging up with Sharon, I went back to the list. There had to be something I was overlooking in the ten locations, some similarity or a clue, a hidden message that would give me something else to go on.

I retyped each GPS coordinate into the computer again. Slowly, I studied each location and each spot. I compared the names of the streets with one another. I even compared the sea level elevation with each of them. Also, what I couldn't figure out was why the GPS numbers always brought me down to a street and that it seemed to be in the middle of it. Why not in a field or woods up in the mountains or out in the desert? Was the name of each street a clue to the answer and the actual physical location meant nothing?

I spent a good hour studying the names of the streets, trying every possible solution to break the letters down into different words. The words I did come up with I couldn't even make into a sensible sentence. Then I looked at the words I did have. Maybe combined, they meant or led me to one answer. I failed there, as I was failing with every idea I had.

Then, I compared the names of the streets to the cities. I even cross-referenced them with one another one – another dead end.

I decided to go back to the beginning and start over. I went to the search engine and brought up longitude and latitude. This time, I went into greater detail. I studied and read everything that was there. As Edward had said, so did the Internet. To get an accurate reading, one needed all six satellites. Tenths, hundredths, even thousandths would pinpoint that even further. After the third number – seconds, I wasn't given the luxury of further information. It was leading me back to the physical location, to the same spot of nothing. I was getting nowhere.

I wasn't giving up—never. Whatever was there, at the physical location or something else in all the numbers, I didn't care whatever it was. But whatever it was, I felt I had to find it. Hopefully, that would lead me closer to the names of the men who killed Craig. They had received their justice. Mother Nature had been the judge, jury, and executioner, and I was the witness. But I still wanted to know who they were.

My thoughts drifted back. Mentally, I watched each of them die again. She had gotten it backward—the one who pulled the trigger should have received the gruesome, painful death by the bear. The other, the lesser of two evils, should have died of a heart attack.

But she had come after me for no other reason than that's what she does. At certain times of the year, it's not nice to fool with Mother Nature. She turns into a real nag. But I did. I wasn't given the choice.

I went back to the list. The only way to solve the next problem of either—something actually being at the GPS location or a clue in the numbers was to go to one of the spots on the list and take a look. The closest one to my home in Massachusetts was Philadelphia, Pennsylvania, just under one hundred miles away.

That was my next plan. The following week, after returning from New York City, I was going there. How, I didn't know yet. Then it dawned on me. I wouldn't be able to find the exact location without a GPS.

Now, or should I say, again, I wish Craig was here. He was the electronics wizard. I was clueless. He was the one who always figured out how to hook up and operate the DVD players, surround sound system, and the new computer… whatever. I didn't have the patience for it. Craig already knew how to operate a GPS. He had researched and studied all the options available before our trip.

Now, it was my turn. The search engine brought up the first page. There, I had several selections: Lowrance Automotive, Garmin Street Plot, and the Magellan Roadmate. I was blind, sitting in my house, and feeling lost. I started reading. The first on the screen was the Lowrance Automotive iWay. It told me all I had to do was choose a city, state, and address. The iWay does the rest with visual and audible clues for every turn along the route. The unit automatically has a re-routing to correct for missed turns or detours. The built-in GPS receiver antenna continually updates the display screen to show progress within ten feet of your actual position. The color monitors are sunlight-viewable with 320k 240-pixel clarity; whatever that meant, I had no idea. More studying, the other two models were basically the same.

I sat in front of the computer, thinking about what I had just read. I wasn't sure if that was what I needed. Sure, it would get me anywhere in the country by address only. I studied it some more. Nowhere did it say finding a location by GPS coordinates.

There had to be more. I clicked the mouse on the 'Find More' icon. The screen exploded, and now I had more options available than imaginable, twenty-seven to be exact. These were made for fishing. But as the options grew, so did the price. As I read all that was available, I was amazed. When it came to fishing, these did everything but the dishes. Built-in water temperature reading, advanced fish symbol ID, adjustable ping speed, and sonar graph mode. The list went on and on. I continued reading it.

Then, I found what I was looking for. Well, what I thought I needed. Navionics and Lowrance map compatible. I looked at the model number—Lowrance LEX-111chd. I could buy it for $2,249.00. Geez! But I was interested. It also had the features of twelve parallel channel GPS and precise GPS receivers. For another eighty dollars, I could buy a software package called Mapcreate. I skipped over the features it had for fishing. Why I wanted it because it said it had excellent land detail with major highways, city streets, rural roads, and railways included in the software. A searchable database of up to two million points of interest.

This is what I needed if I was to go to the first location. To see if anything was to be made of the list, of how big of a wild goose chase I was on.

I had to know. I bought it. The order was confirmed, and I was told it would be delivered in seven to ten days.

The further I was getting into this the more interested I was getting. I remembered what the dying death dealer had said to me, 'Maybe you'll figure it out.' I had to know who they were. Then, it would go down in the records, the ones who had killed Craig. So, if it was at all possible, I wanted to tarnish their names for all eternity. I owed that to Craig. The only payback I could do to them.

Friday morning, I rose with the sun. I had nothing to do as I thought about drinking my morning dose of coffee. Tomorrow, I would pack.

I needed to go talk to Craig. I had two reasons to go, it would be over a week before I got another chance, and the headstone was to be delivered yesterday. I wanted to see if it was engraved correctly.

Tore dropped me off at the cemetery. The day was warm and sunny, and a strong wind blew from the southwest. I decided to stay for two hours. Tore would be back between eleven and eleven-thirty.

As I walked toward Craig's grave, I saw his headstone. That sight hit me like a ton of bricks, applying so much pressure to my chest I couldn't breathe. My life temporarily stood still.

I walked the final steps up to it. Then I started shaking, it was beautiful. I couldn't overcome the reality that it was final. I began a torrent flow of tears.

The headstone marked the spot where Craig would spend all eternity. I couldn't stand it. Now I was standing in a vacuum that was sucking all the air. I couldn't breathe. My lungs weren't strong enough to inhale air. Seeing the headstone was the same thing as seeing Craig lying in the casket. I wasn't able to do that. I never dreamed it would be so hard.

His name was engraved in white letters. I knew that somewhere, he was talking to his neighbors, laughing and listening. That's what he did, and it was his gift. His charm would enthrall them, as it did me. I had memories, something that passersby didn't have. All they would see is his beautiful dark granite marker with the date he was born and the date he died. They missed the fortunate opportunity to be charmed by his presence.

The ones who saw the engraving on the back of his headstone would understand. It was there to let them know what kind of a man he was in life.

The man who lies here understood more about life

than one could imagine. He asked of nothing. He lies

here because that's the kind of man he was, so I could

go on. I know he's smiling and content with what he did.

I will love you forever.

Now I was crying so hard I was seeing stars, and my knees started to buckle. Time was lost, and my body could no longer go without oxygen. I didn't care. I dropped to my knees and put my left hand on his gravestone before falling on my face. I instantly inhaled and felt the cool calmness that Craig always emitted. Somehow, he saved my life again.

I was still crying. "Craig, it's so hard to move on, but I will do it for you. You moved on for me. There are days I wish we could have gone on together, but that wasn't the case. My heart remembers and the tears I live with."

Now, I was sitting on the grass at the side of the headstone, facing it. "Physically, I can no longer feel, but in my mind, I will always feel your touch."

I sat there, silent. The minutes passed by.

"Craig, I'm trying to find out who they were. The one who killed you left me a clue. There's not much to go on, but I have to try. What little I've learned gives me more questions with no answers. What they did to you makes no sense. What he gave me makes no sense. I'm not as I once was, but that no longer matters. If at all possible, I will figure this out. Then I hope you will rest easy. That is my promise. You let me live, and I owe it to you."

I moved so I could see the face of the headstone. "I need you. This is the saddest thing I've ever done. I have so many things to tell you. What I regret is that I never said anything to you when I walked away—I love you. Those three words haunt me. Why didn't I say them then? All I can say now is that I'm sorry for not doing so."

The crying never fully quit, and now it was gaining intensity.

"This is my fault. The guilt I have I will never outlive." I was back to gasping for air, and my stomach ached from all the crying.

I saw Tore pull into the cemetery from the road. Where had the two hours gone? I must have fallen asleep, or more like fallen into a trance, remembering all the memories.

I stood. "Goodbye, I will be back."

CHAPTER 34

I sat in the back seat of the Cadillac Deville, a white one. My luggage was in the trunk. The driver introduced himself as Todd when he arrived at my house to pick me up.

Now, we were on our way to New York. The trip was roughly two and a half hours. I wasn't nervous. Being fitted for artificial limbs was no big deal. Even if it was, things that used to bother me didn't anymore.

We had been traveling for almost an hour. Todd hadn't talked much, just answered the few questions that I had asked. I couldn't tell if he was nervous being around me or just being professional. The silence was a little too stoic. "Todd, do you work for Advanced Arm Dynamics?" I asked.

"Who?" Todd asked.

"The place where you are taking me to in Manhattan—Advanced Arm Dynamics."

"No, ma'am, I was just hired to pick you up and take you to your motel. I heard rumors that someone would have to drive you back home. I wondered why at the time; now, I know."

Well, now I knew he was nervous being around me, the freak show. "What do you do for a living, Todd?"

"I work for a limousine company. I drive a limo all night and sleep during the day."

I was right on both thoughts. In his profession, he probably didn't have conversations with the clientele. "You're out of your routine today."

"Yes, ma'am. It's a nice change, though, first time to drive into New York."

We were silent for a short time. "I suppose you see all types of people driving a limo."

"Yes, well, I thought I had. Business people, obnoxious drunks, the snooty rich people—until now—I'm sorry for what happened to you."

I watched the rearview mirror. Todd never looked into it to look at me. I knew what he was thinking, like all the others who saw me, 'I wonder what happened to her.'

I waited, but Todd never asked. I watched in the mirror; Todd's eyes never wandered away from the road ahead. I thought, *He's good, a professional.*'

"Frostbite," I said, answering the question he was never going to ask. Todd never flinched. The only thing that moved was his arms, continually making minor adjustments to the steering wheel to keep the car on the road. *Wow, he's really good, a true professional.* "It doesn't bother me to talk about it."

"I don't know what to say. I thought I've heard it all until now. Another first—two on the same day from the same person. Like I said, I don't know what to say."

"But you didn't even acknowledge I said anything."

Todd shrugged. "I've learned not to. I've had women get naked in the back of my limo many times. I've even had some do the horizontal bop in the back seat. I learned in the early days not to look. When I did, they reported me, saying I was invading their privacy. I always got in trouble, almost got fired once."

"How ridiculous! People can't act civilized, and you get in trouble," I said.

"You don't know the half of it; that's why I just drive."

"So, that's why you talk to everyone in the third person."

"Yes, five minutes of interaction, and I never see them again."

"I know I'm a freak show, but not by choice. I try not to act like one."

"No, ma'am, you don't."

"And please, stop calling me ma'am. It makes me feel old. I'm only in my twenties. My name is Madie."

"I know. I'm sorry."

"Well, we have more than five minutes together. If it's fine with you, we can have a normal conversation."

"It is. You're a beautiful woman, life wasn't good to you."

I flinched. I didn't see that one coming. I guess I wasn't professional. The next thought I had was—is Todd hitting on me?

Todd still hadn't looked in the mirror. "I'm not working you, just stating a fact. People, well, men, can't even compliment women anymore. Women think it's either sexual harassment or the man is coming on to them."

I wasn't giving Todd enough credit. He was more intelligent than I thought. "Thank you for the compliment. I don't feel that way anymore. Some people stare, and others walk in the other direction."

"People have become so rude; it's all about them. Society is slowly going downhill."

"Yes, that may be true, but there's still a lot of good people out there," I said. Thinking about Jim, Mary, and the rest of the guys, they don't come any better than that. "A very good man saved my life."

Todd remained quiet. I couldn't read his expression in the oblong little mirror. "Are you married, Todd?" I asked.

"No."

"Ever been?"

"No."

He was back to answering the question with no further input. I decided to stop asking, wondering if I had said something to offend him.

On the drive into the city, even for a Sunday, the traffic was heavy. I had been home for almost six weeks, and it felt good to get out. Seeing something different made me feel better, even if Todd wasn't talking.

I watched the overhead billboard. We took Ninety-Five through New Jersey, turned east on Nineteen, and went through the Holland tunnel. From there, we went north on the Avenue of the Americas to our final destination, the Rockefeller Center, the place where I would be staying.

As we pulled up in front, it only took me a second to know this was above normal as hotels go. Jim spared nothing. I would have to call him when I settled in and thank him.

Just as Todd shut the engine off, my door was opened. I was greeted by a middle-aged gentleman with all smiles, a dark gray suit and tie, and shoes that sparkled. "Good afternoon, Ms. Chanhansen. It's nice of you to join us this week. My name is Svenson."

Wow, not only were they waiting at the door, but he also knew my name. "Good afternoon. It's my pleasure being here."

Before I started to get out of the car, a second man arrived next to the car, pushing a wheelchair. I had all intentions of walking, but I decided against it. I didn't want to make a bigger show than they were already giving me.

By the time I sat in the wheelchair, Todd had my luggage removed from the trunk and had placed it next to the car. Then he closed the trunk.

I had folded a hundred-dollar bill in fourths. I wanted to tip Todd, and it was the least I could do for him. It was in my left hand, tucked between my thumb and the stump of my hand. I reached out with my hand to shake Todd's. "Thank you," I said as we shook. Now, discreetly, I slid the bill into Todd's hand. I watched him casually put his hand into his pocket. He never looked to see what it was and, again, I thought, a true professional. "I'm sorry if I offended you. That wasn't my intention."

Todd started to say something but then stopped. For the first time, I saw an expression on his face. "You didn't, don't think that," he said.

"Have a safe trip back. I'm grateful to you for doing this for me."

Todd nodded, "You're welcome."

Then, I was turned and wheeled toward the door.

Once inside, we went straight to the elevator, bypassing all the formalities of checking in. I wondered why, so I asked.

"That's not needed, Ms. Chanhansen. It's all been taken care of," Svenson said.

I should have known—silly me.

Before we entered the elevator, Svenson gave orders to several people. Somehow, I believed he was more than just a doorman, but I didn't ask. I didn't want to show my ignorance or offend him.

Svenson opened my door, and a second man rolled my luggage in. I almost gasped—what I was expecting was a single room with a king-size bed. What I saw in front of me was a room fit for someone important or rich. I was neither. To the left side of the room, a huge leather sofa with matching chairs at the end, a massive wood coffee table, and end tables surrounding it. As I continued looking around the room, at the far end, hanging on the wall, was the biggest flat screen TV I've ever seen. To my right sat another sofa, only this had such thick cushions on it; it looked as though you would sink out of sight if you sat in it. Between the oak bar to my right and that sofa, a recliner sat with a perfect view of the flat screen.

Svenson pushed me further into the room. Then, I saw the bedroom to the left. It was as large as the living room, only it had a great deal of open space. Both rooms had sixteen-foot ceilings.

Now, I was totally amazed as I was wheeled in. Another flat screen hung on the wall facing the bed. Another half-sized bar sat in the corner.

"Both bars are fully stocked, so help yourself. The maid will come twice a day, and your laundry will be cleaned, pressed, and returned by the end of the day. I do say we have an excellent chef, and the food is superb. The menu is complete, order anything you want any time of the day," Svenson said.

He slowly pushed me toward a door into the bathroom. We stopped just in front of it and then Svenson opened the door. My heart skipped a beat. A black marble floor that had white inlaid lines through it with so much polished gloss, it looked as if there was an inch of glass on top – and that was just the floor. A full-length counter that contained two sinks covered with marble to match the floor. A full-sized whirlpool tub also wrapped with marble and two full length mirrors on two sides. Beside that a shower the size of my bathroom at home with three sides of frosted glass.

"I hope this is satisfactory. If anything needs to be changed to accommodate you, just let me know."

I couldn't speak. I didn't know if Svenson thought it didn't meet my approval because of that.

I had seen elegant things in my day, but nothing like this. The room was overwhelming. I tried to remain calm when I spoke, "This far exceeds my needs. Everything will be fine," I said.

"Oh, and there's one more thing, well, actually two. Another half bath is off the main room and a laptop computer with DSL hookup for you to use."

Svenson pushed me back into the main room. The second man, who had carried my luggage in, had already left. He pointed to the door that led into the half bath.

"The bath is in there. The maid will be up momentarily to take care of your things. Just tell her where you would like them. Also, we have a female therapist on call for you, if you need help bathing or for anything else."

I thought, *No one helps me at home.* However, I didn't want to insult him. "My! You've gone out of your way. I don't deserve all this, but thank you."

"Well, someone sure thinks so. This has all been pre-arranged for you, and you're welcome. I'm the general manager here. Call me if you need something, even if it's in the middle of the night." Then Svenson handed me his business card.

"You treat me like I'm someone special, I'm not," I said. "Thank you again."

Svenson looked at me. "You are. We will take care of you." Then he walked to the door. He stopped and looked at me. "All your meals are on the hotel, so please, eat all you want."

I couldn't help it. I cried after Svenson left. The 'someone' who thought I was special was a given. The hotel paying for my meals was an added plus for the tears.

I opened my cell phone and called Jim.

The second ring hadn't finished. "Hello."

I heard Jim's voice, which added to the flow. "Why did you do all this for me?" I was so upset I didn't even say hello. I heard Jim laugh. "I didn't need this much," I said.

"It wasn't just me. It's from all of us, everyone pitched in. In fact, they're all here now and, of course, we're having fresh fish, celebrating for you."

Jim must have held the phone out, and I heard the crew. They all started talking at once. Now, I was bawling my eyes out. "Here, they all want to talk to you."

Sobbing into the phone, I spoke to George first. "You need to get back up here; they're killing me at fishing."

I laughed while crying. "Thank you, George, you're the greatest."

Then, Jerry and Jonathon. I thanked each of them twice.

Next, I heard Mary's voice. Instead of feeling worse, hearing her, I felt better. We talked for a long time. I got the details of what was going on, something the men didn't feel was important, just part of their everyday life.

Now, I felt part of the gang again. Although I wasn't there, I wasn't left out. I promised Mary I would be back as soon as I could. I missed them.

Jim was back on the phone. "Well, then, you got the low down on all of us. What about you?"

I don't know what it was about Jim. The tears were streaming down my face again. It wasn't just the fact that he had saved my life and gotten me the most dedicated professionals to repair me. He really cared. "Jim, I don't know if I've told you this before. You're a good man. No one else would ever do the things for me that you have. Everyone should have a friend like you. You don't know how proud I am that I do."

"There's no one else who deserves it any more than you do. We all feel that way—you're a special lady. We all want you back here."

I couldn't talk. The endless flow of tears was relentless.

Jim waited patiently while I got myself back together.

"I feel pretty humble. I'll never be able to return the kindness you have given me."

"Just come back, and that's all we ask."

Sitting in my room, alone and crying, I felt good. I was glad I called.

I spent the rest of the night thinking about the list of locations. I wanted to tell Jim about them but decided against it. The same thought always came to me. What did I have? Nothing. Where would it lead? Probably nowhere.

Would Jim think I was crazy for even considering it? That was questionable. Jim was an intelligent man, so his answer could go either way.

At eleven o'clock, I turned the light off. I wasn't worried about what I would go through tomorrow. Whatever it was, so be it.

5
CHAPTER

I woke at the usual time, between six and six fifteen. They were to pick me up at eight o'clock at my room. By choice, I would have rather met them in the lobby at the front desk. I didn't like the idea of them thinking I was a helpless invalid. But for now, I would go along with it.

I showered, dressed, and drank two cups of coffee.

Now it was seven. I had an hour to burn, so I wrapped my stumps and headed for the lobby. As beautiful as my room was, I wanted to get out and get a little exercise.

The elevator door opened, and I walked out. It was off to the side of the reception desk where two people stood behind doing their daily duties.

I slowly strode out into the lobby. They were either too busy or just accustomed to having guests coming and going to notice me. It felt good to stretch my muscles. I continued on.

I walked up to a large cherry coffee table that sat in front of a much larger sofa and matching chairs. For some unseen reason, I stumbled as I turned to walk around it. I fell forward, catching myself with both arms landing on the coffee table.

I straightened up, looking in their direction while doing so.

I could see the expression on both of their faces. The woman gasped; the man standing next to her didn't know what to say.

"Are you alright, Ms. Chanhansen?" she asked.

Wow! She knew my name. "I'm fine; I just tripped."

"Here, let me help you." She started around the end of the very long counter. "Why didn't you call and ask for assistance," she said.

"Because I didn't want any," I said. "Really, I'm fine. I wanted to get out and stretch my muscles."

That didn't satisfy her, and she continued. I didn't know what to do. I wanted to be cordial, so I stood there and waited for her to walk up to me.

"Please, let us call some help for you," she said, standing next to me. "We're to be at your beck and call any time of the day or night."

Jim, I thought. I looked at the name tag on her jacket. "Sandra, no one helps me at home. I don't feel that I have to bother you."

"But that's what we're here for; you're not at home now," Sandra said.

I could see she didn't want to take my pleas' for no help. "I have to learn to do this on my own. How else can I go on with my life?"

That seemed to pacify her. I wanted to tell her about the dozens of times I fell out in the wilderness, landing face-first in snow that was thirty degrees below zero, but I chose not to.

"Well, ok. You know where we are if you need help." Then, she turned and walked away.

I turned and headed back toward the elevator. I saw that was the fastest way to diffuse the situation.

I spent the remaining time waiting in my room. From now on, I would walk up and down the hall if I wanted to get out of my room and walk.

One minute after eight o'clock, there was a knock on my door. I didn't let my door completely close when I returned. I was sitting at the desk surfing the Internet. "Come in, the door's open."

In walked a woman followed by a man pushing a wheelchair. Both looked to be in their late twenties, possibly early thirties, and both were dressed impeccably. I expected the standard-issue white uniforms; boy, was I wrong. Now I felt underdressed in my black jeans and white dress shirt.

"Hello, I'm Jennifer, and this is Dan."

I held out my left stump and shook their hands. I watched them closely, and neither flinched. People like me were an everyday part of their life, I thought.

"Are you ready? You have a long day ahead of you, but it will be a good one," Jennifer said. "We'll be with you the whole day. Fitting and training are what we'll cover today. There's so much available you won't believe it."

Again, I thought of the past. A long day consisted of getting up with the sun and being so tired, sore, and stiff, then walking through deep snow into the wee hours of the morning or until I could no longer go. That was a long day. This was going to be a breeze. "I'm ready. I think I should be able to handle it," I said.

Dan pushed the wheelchair up next to me. I really didn't want to use it, but after the little episode down in the lobby, I gave in. Besides, I didn't want to freak them out. "I really appreciate you coming here, but I feel this is somewhat out of your way. I could have gotten there by myself."

"Probably so, but we're here to help you from start to finish. That's what we do; if we did anything less, we would feel that we weren't doing our job," Dan said.

I smiled. They seemed nice enough and sincere.

As we passed through the lobby, I looked at Sandra. She smiled. I wondered if she knew where we were going. Probably so; she seemed to know everything else.

Dan helped me get into the backseat of the limo. The driver was already sitting behind the wheel, and Jennifer sat next to me. We waited for Dan to put the wheelchair in the trunk. "This isn't the usual vehicle we use for transportation. This was all pre-arranged."

I lowered my head. *Jim,* I thought. Yet another thing added to the list.

"Ms. Chanhansen, is anything wrong?" Jennifer asked.

Slowly, I shook my head. "No. How can I possibly show him the gratitude he deserves?"

"Show who, Madison?" Jennifer asked.

"The man who set this all up. The one that saved my life and who is the kindest in the world." My eyes watered. I fought it back; now wasn't the time. I wasn't going to let them see how weak I was.

Jennifer looked lost, confused. "He sounds like a special person. I'm sorry I didn't get to meet him."

"You have no idea." I would have babbled on, but I was saved when Dan opened the door to get in. I was thankful.

"All set," Dan said and sat next to Jennifer.

I was looking at my stumps lying in my lap. I didn't look up, but I could feel the uneasiness quickly filling the inside of the car.

"I like the way you wrapped your legs. Keep them warm, good idea," Jennifer said.

I was sure Jennifer was just making conversation, trying to lighten the mood. "That's not why I did it," I said, wiping my eyes.

We pulled in front of a large four-story building. As the inner city goes, it had a spacious front entrance.

Enough with the pampering, I thought. When Dan got out of the car to retrieve the wheelchair from the trunk, I followed him. I didn't know what they were going to say, so I didn't give them a chance.

When my stumps made contact with the concrete, I stood and started walking toward the front door.

They both started talking at once. Dan ran in my direction to help. "Ms. Chanhansen, don't you want to use the wheelchair?" he asked.

"What if you fall? Wouldn't that hurt?" Jennifer asked. I could tell by the tone of her voice she was shocked.

I smiled. This was obviously something they hadn't seen. "If I fall, I'll get back up. No, that's what the pads are for." I continued on.

"What the heck. Who needs a wheelchair?" Dan said.

"I can see this is going to be an easy week," Jennifer smiled at me. "You wouldn't believe the patients that come here and struggle. All is not lost."

That made me feel better.

The past kept returning, along with the memories. My definition of struggling was trying to stay alive. Everything else is just a thing. "It all depends on what one did in the past to show how they will deal with the present," I said no more.

I watched them look at each other. They didn't understand what that meant.

We walked up to the receptionist's desk. Clare Cummings was the name on the placard sitting in front of her. I signed the guest book; my handwriting was almost legible, and I apologized for it. Clare was friendly, pretty in her mid-thirties, and also dressed to a 'T.' She asked if I would like coffee, if my room at the hotel fit my needs, and if I needed anything else that wasn't provided. I answered all the questions as fast as she asked them.

Then, I was ushered to an office.

Jennifer sat next to me, "The first thing we need to do is fill out these forms."

"Is everyone always so friendly around here?" I asked.

"Oh, yes. We try to make this as painless as possible. Some people arrive here very nervous, and some are even scared. It doesn't take them long to realize this is very relaxing."

"The painful part is already over with. As for being scared, I don't think that will bother me again," I said.

"I don't know what happened to you, but whatever it was, it wasn't good. Hopefully, time will heal that," Jennifer said.

I wanted to tell her that in two lifetimes, time would never heal this. I didn't; I felt I was being too coarse, and they were being very nice. I smiled.

The forms were all signed, and I wondered what was next.

"Well, the choice is yours. What would you like to work on first? Getting new feet or a new right hand? I will tell you that it will take more time and therapy with the hand."

I didn't need time to think about it. I wanted to walk normal again. "New feet, if it's alright with you, I want to walk as normal as possible again."

Jennifer smiled. "By the time you leave here, no one will ever know the difference. You will look and walk just like anyone else."

I didn't know about that, but it had to be better than now. "I'm more than ready to lose the freak show bit," I said.

"You're not. People just don't know how to take someone who is out of the norm."

How well I knew that.

We walked down a long hall, passing many doors on each side. "I'll give you a quick tour before we get started."

I read the lettering on each door as we passed them—Research, Development, Engineering, Lower Extremities, Arm/Hands, and Physical Therapy. Jennifer opened the door to Engineering, "This is where it all begins."

I was surprised. The room was small, with four computers and three people sitting behind them. In the middle of the left side of the room was another door that was open. Beyond that, I heard a noise coming from inside the room.

"Engineering and Development work together. Actually, they're one department," Jennifer replied.

I could hear the discussion grow louder in the other room.

"After it's designed, the product is sent out to be manufactured and then returned here to be tried and tested."

Now, the conversation was becoming heated. Whoever they were, they were just short of yelling at one another. I walked in the direction of the door.

"Sometimes it takes a lot of discussion to work the problems out," Jennifer said.

"No need to make excuses on my part. Whatever it takes to get the job done," and I walked into the room. They instantly fell silent. Now they had a look of embarrassment on their faces, the two men standing there, looking at me from head to toe.

Jennifer quickly followed behind me. "I'm sorry, Ms. Chanhansen. You didn't need to hear that."

"Please, call me Madie, no sense in being formal all week." My appearance had the effect I thought it would. Their expressions went from embarrassment to shock.

"Wow! Look at you. This is a first. No one comes here in your physical condition walking."

"Well, the way I see it, I'm not a cripple, just missing a few parts. Why not use what you've got?" I didn't ask them what they were arguing about, probably something technical in which I didn't have a clue.

"I'm sorry," the second man said.

"For what? You're only trying to make it better for people like me."

"What a positive attitude. Madie, it will be a pleasure working with you," the first man said.

"I'm sorry," the first man said and then walked into the Engineering room.

We left through the door of the Development room. In the hall, I said, "I'm ready. I want new feet. Taping these pads on every morning is a pain."

"Ok. You're in charge. Think of us as only here to aid you."

We walked into the room of Lower Extremities. To my surprise, the man who had said it was going to be a pleasure working with me was already there. He read my thoughts, "All the rooms are connected. Again, let me apologize. My name is Glen."

I shook Glen's hand. "It's nice to meet you. I'm ready to do this. I have places to go, and I don't want to look like this when I do."

"Alright. The first thing we do is show you an actual prosthetic limb of each option available. There are several."

I smiled, trying to ease the tension that carried over from the other room. "I know, I got on the Internet at home. I would like to run 10K races again one day."

"Well, then you know we fabricate each prosthetic limb for the individual user. That takes a little time, but when you leave here, we'll both understand what fits you best."

I frowned. I was hoping to leave here with new feet.

Glen saw that. "Maybe we can get it done this week. We'll certainly try."

On a table at the back of the room sat at least a dozen variations of feet. Glen led me to it. "All of these are made of an advanced composite material, very tough and durable." Then Glen picked up something I didn't understand. "This is a delta twist shock absorber, and it comes in two models—the 4R120 and the 4R121-30. The difference in them is the way they connect to the foot. Each model is made for moderate to high-level activity. What it does is counteract the strain of torsional loads on the residual limb caused by everyday activities, such as getting in a car, walking on uneven surfaces, or even in crowds. Think of it like the shock on your car; it makes the ride smoother. How it works is it has interchangeable elastomer plates. Red is soft, this one has yellow plates installed for medium duty and green plates are hard. They allow you to adjust internal and external rotation independently, creating a softer, more elastic internal rotation at heel strike and a firmer, more bio-mechanically correct rotation during toe-off." Glen looked at me. "Are you with me so far?"

"Barely."

"After we get you fitted with feet, we'll install each set of plates and let you walk around. Then you'll see the difference. At that time, you can make the choice."

I was trying to keep up. I watched and listened intently to Glen.

Then, Glen picked up something that looked like a hockey stick, only it had a very short handle. "You said you're a runner; there's a foot for that." Then, he handed it to me. "This is called the sprinter. As you can see, there's no connection at the ankle like some of the flat feet here. The curve at the ankle location absorbs the shock or load. It flexes, I should say, then as you lift off into your next step, it unloads, pushing as your ankle and calf muscles would."

I already liked this one. It would work perfectly when I started running again.

Then, Glen picked up another from the table. "This is called the 'Advantage DP2.'"

I looked at it. It had a flat foot with a round tube roughly ten inches long with a round connection at the top. Then, it became clear to me what that was for—to connect to the shock absorber. I said nothing.

Glen sat that one back on the table and removed two more. "This one is the 'Luxon Max DP,' and this is called the 'iE61 Custom Pylon Foot.'"

"They look the same as the first."

Glen smiled. "Yes, but there's a difference. The iE61 Pylon Foot has a narrower foot with a greater arched heal." Glen stood it on the table. "See, this connects with the ground as the human foot does."

I could see the gap under the arch.

"The heel flexes just enough to absorb shock as the heel does. How tall were you before your accident?" Glen asked.

Accident! It was more of a tragedy. "Five eight," I said. They weren't here to listen to my story; senseless murder was the term I had for it.

Glen went on showing me a number of flat feet, each having a certain function. I was so involved I never noticed that Jennifer had left the room. She had remained like she said she would; she had sat back, watching and listening until now.

When she returned, she said, "Lunch has been delivered. Are you ready to take a break?"

Lunch! It's that late already? Where did the morning go? I thought. I looked at Glen.

Glen said, "I'm ready. Are you, Madie?"

"Sure." All I could do was go along. My mind was in a fog with all the information I was given.

We walked into a very large and quite elaborate kitchen. The table was mahogany with a dozen chairs around it. At nine chairs sat covered plates with real napkins, silver, and glasses. "What are we having?" I asked.

"Rib eye steaks, baked potatoes, salad, and dessert," Jennifer said.

"Geez, do you always eat this good at lunch?" I asked.

No one responded right away, and that gave me my answer.

"Well, no. Usually, it is subs or pizza or burgers," Jennifer replied.

Jim was the reason for this, I had no doubt. "Excuse me, I need to go to the restroom." I took m purse with me, strapping the leather holder on.

I returned and sat down. Everyone was sitting waiting for me. "Please, go ahead, don't wait for me." I slid my thumb under the cover and removed the lid. There sat the thickest, juiciest steak I had seen in a long time.

"Madie, would you like me to help you cut your steak?" Jennifer asked.

"No, thank you, I'm fine," I said.

Everyone else removed their covers. I could sense they were watching me out of the corner of their eye. I picked up my purse from the floor, sat it on my lap, and removed the knife. I snapped it in place and returned my purse to the floor.

The room was deafly quiet.

I had to say something to start the conversation. "Is everyone always so quiet when they eat around here?" I smiled. Then I started cutting my steak, holding the fork in my left hand it went rather smoothly.

"What an interesting piece of equipment," Glen said.

"Yes, well, when I was in Canada, I spent a long time in the hospital. I got tired of having the nurses feed me all the time."

"Did you design that?" One of the engineers asked.

"No, I came up with the idea, and someone else designed it. That's out of my area."

"Wow! That's really cool," he said.

"That's definitely another first—two in the same day from the same person," Glen said.

"I could go on and give a long list of firsts. I did what I had to do. I'm not here to tell you my problems, and you don't want to hear them," I said.

"Is that where you had your accident, Madie?" Jennifer asked.

"It wasn't an accident per se. Mother Nature did this to me, something I couldn't escape. She was relentless."

"We try and ask what happened to every patient that comes here. Most people tell us, but some, very few, don't want to talk about it. If you don't that's fine by us," Glen said.

"I'm afraid if I start talking, I won't quit. I'll get to babbling for a long time."

"How long can it be? We'll listen," Chad said.

I started in. Every time I tell the story, the memories become more vivid. I can feel the pain and see events, even the minute ones that mean nothing. I can feel the cold and fatigue sucking the life from my body.

I had to stop several times to wipe away the tears. As always, I lost track of time. It felt like I traveled in time, back there living it all over again, always so engulfed that the present stood still. Once, I was crying so hard again that I had to stop for a moment. I looked around the table, everyone had finished eating, but that didn't really register to me. All I noticed was that they were sitting there in a trance, staring at me. Jennifer and Sam, the receptionist, were wiping their own tears.

I finished. "I'm sorry. You didn't need to hear that." No one spoke. "What time is it?" I asked.

That seemed to bring them back from their trances. One of the engineers looked at his watch. "One thirty," he said.

"Now, I'm terribly sorry. I wasted an hour and a half of your day." I couldn't believe I talked for that long. I felt embarrassed. "You asked, now you know."

"Madie, we've heard stories from people about car crashes, industrial accidents, losing limbs from disease, but nothing ever like that. That's incredible. I would sit through it again just to hear it all over," Glen said.

That did it. I bawled my eyes out. I couldn't understand why everyone thought my story was amazing. *It's just me; I gained nothing by surviving,* I thought.

We were back in the room, and Glen finished showing me the remaining variations from the table. He was more reserved, but I could tell his heart was more into it.

"I know what you need, if you allow me. I will fit you with two different sets, one for running and the other for everyday use. They will interchange fairly quickly."

"That's fine with me. Whatever I leave here with will be wonderful. People will no longer stare at me. I will be starting a new life."

Jennifer came walking into the room carrying a pizza box. "Here, this is for you. I felt bad you only got to eat one bite of your steak at lunch. We all feel bad. We asked you to tell us your story, and you didn't get to eat."

I smiled. "You didn't have to go out of your way for this. Missing one meal doesn't bother me. It was nothing to go three or four days without eating out there."

"Believe me, we're going to take care of you. Now I know."

I knew what she meant; I didn't have to ask.

I ate several slices of the pizza, sitting in a barber's style chair while Glen took all sorts of measurements of both legs.

We both finished at the same time. "It takes several days to custom fit a prosthetic limb to a person, and you have two. I think we can speed that time up for you," Glen said.

CHAPTER 36

I sat in my room thinking about the day and about the list. I made up my mind that I was going there as soon as I got home. The GPS would be waiting in the mail for me. My curiosity was getting worse, and I had to know. I had nothing else to do, so I had no excuse.

Jennifer and Glen insisted I take the rest of the pizza with me back to my room. I ate the rest of it. Luckily, it was only a medium size. I had to get my new feet soon so I could start running before I started turning into a large size. That wouldn't be good. I didn't eat the crusts; somehow, that made me feel like I was cutting back—yeah, right.

I made mental plans. Saturday night, I would cook for Sharon and her husband. Their business wasn't my business, and they had too much to lose—a family.

My next problem was how I was going to get there. I wanted to do this alone, and if it was a flop, I didn't want anyone along. They would think I was crazy. I already looked the part walking around the way I was. *Maybe I am,* I thought. Then, again, nothing ventured – nothing gained. I have nothing to lose.

I wanted to call Jim and the gang again to thank them again. I decided to wait another day or two. I didn't want to be too redundant, even though I didn't think they would get tired of hearing from me.

I got on the Internet; something kept calling me back to the list of locations. I had them stored on the icon on the desktop; one double click, and there they were—all ten of them. I sat back and looked at them. The nagging feeling returned as I looked at them; something wasn't right. More ideas kept coming to mind. Now, I was going down the path of illegal doings. Could they be meth houses? Actually, manufacturing the stuff while I sat here thinking about it? Or some sort of storage facility or warehouses holding drugs waiting for delivery?

My thoughts continued on. Eight of the ten on the list were major cities. Five of those had over one million in population. Did that mean something?

Could they be running some sort of an illegal car ring, a chop shop, or a high-end car racket? I remembered what the death dealer said, 'It will make you rich beyond imagination.' I ruled out the car scenario. I kept going back to the drug thing. I couldn't think of anything else that would produce that sort of wealth. If it was, I wanted no part of it. That led me to another thought. If it was, could I get shot when I got there? Walking into the middle of a drug business was the last thing I wanted. I couldn't run away.

So now I wondered if I needed help. I could think of more reasons not to take someone along than to do so. I've already gotten one person killed in my life; I wasn't going to get two, not out of my stupidity. The original reason I had from the beginning—there might be nothing there.

Now, more than ever, I wanted to call Jim. I had no doubt if I told him about it he would insist on going along. Jonathon, Jerry, and George would also go along. Strength in numbers, but that strength wouldn't equal the bad guys – if they were there.

I decided to remain silent. This was my venture to do alone. I was going, and I wasn't putting anyone else in harm's way.

Then, the phone rang in my room. I jumped; it scared the crap out of me. I was in deep thought of thinking bad things. That was the last thing I expected.

I put the phone to my ear. "Hello."

"Madie, it's Jim."

My heart went from racing fast to racing even faster. My emotions went from fear to excitement in just three words. "Jim! What a surprise!" just short of yelling.

"I had to call and see how you were. Did you have a good day?"

I told Jim about my day. I skipped the part of my storytelling at lunchtime. "I don't know what we are doing tomorrow. Maybe they are working on getting a new hand, and they didn't tell me. They also didn't tell me about lunch, maybe they didn't know how, but I did. Thank you, everyone enjoyed it. Why do you do so much?" Jim didn't answer me. "Well, there's another reason I called. We've got a surprise for you tomorrow. I'm not going to tell you; that would ruin it, but you'll see."

My stomach knotted, and my throat tightened. "You've got to stop doing this; it's too much."

"For you, it's never too much. We all talk about you all the time. We're proud to know someone like you and even prouder that you call us friends."

That broke the door down, the one I was trying so hard to keep closed. I cried. I managed to say, "I'm the one who is proud that you're my friends. All of you mean the world to me. This would be unbearable without you, especially you, Jim."

"Well, the only way I see it for you to repay us is to come here and live with us. We've all talked about it. Everyone wants you here. Professionally speaking, I could help you during your rehabilitation. You'll need extra care during physical therapy, so what better place could you do it?"

He had me there, and there was no better place. "I have two things I need to do when I leave here. They will take several days, maybe a week. When I'm finished, I will let you know, and then I will come. I want to… being alone every day isn't fun. I'll call."

"Good. I'll send Randy down."

We said goodbye to each other. Alone in my room, I cried.

The next morning, I walked the hall, several trips up and down. Getting to the first location and what I would find was all that was on my mind. If it went bad, I wouldn't have to worry about calling Jim. The plot next to Craig's grave was already paid now, waiting for me. If something did happen to me, so be it. But could I do it to the friends I had in the north? It would devastate them. Was I being selfish? I had to know and I would be careful, for them and for Craig.

When I walked into the lab, I knew something was up. Jennifer, Glen, and the four engineers were there mulling around. Each one looked as though they were the cat who ate the canary.

Glen spoke, "We stayed last night after you left and finished both sets of feet for you. The Sprinter for when you run, and we chose the 'iE61 Custom Pylon Foot.' We decided that would fit you best. We will install the '2C5' foot shells to those and then you can wear real shoes. Within weeks, no one will ever know, by watching you walk, that you have artificial feet."

"But you must have stayed all night. Why did you do that?" I asked.

"How could we not? Your story gave us the incentive. If you could do what you did, we could do this. If it makes you feel any better, we were home and in bed by midnight."

It didn't.

"Well, are you ready to walk on feet again?" Glen asked.

I wiped my eyes. "More than you know."

Sam walked into the room. I couldn't read the look on her face, but she was looking at me as if I were the Queen of Egypt or the most expensive call girl she had ever seen. She stood there a moment, looking at me. Then she looked at all the others in disbelief.

"I just got a call from the restaurant; they're catering lunch. No, that's not the correct word. They're cooking lunch. They just received twenty pounds of fresh walleye flown in from Canada. They will deliver at noon," Sam said.

I bawled my eyes out. That was the surprise Jim had told me about. "I… I don't know why he keeps doing this. He called last night and said there would be a surprise today, but I had no idea it would be this," I said.

"Wow! Walleye, my favorite," one of the engineers said.

"You must be pretty important to whoever is behind this," another engineer said.

"No, he is. It's Jim and the rest of them. I'm not important, just lucky to know them." I went on and told them what I hadn't yesterday in the story, how they would go out in the severest weather and rescue people.

"Not to put a monetary value to this, but it must have cost a small fortune," Glen said.

I told them about Randy and his plane service. "Randy told me he feels what happened to me is his fault. It isn't. I wasn't able to get to the lake we were to meet at. I was too busy running for my life, plus the fact that they had taken our GPS, I would have never found it." This I had also left out.

No one spoke.

"There I go again, rambling on, things I'm sure you don't want to hear."

"No way, like I said yesterday, we would listen to it all over again. Yet we're still hearing new things." Glen shook his head. "It's beyond amazing. I don't believe there are many people alive who would survive what you did."

I had regained composure. "You'd be surprised what you can do when you're forced to." I looked at Sam. "I'm nothing special, believe me. I just have great friends. I wish you could meet Jim, than you would understand. He's the one that's special." My eyes watered, thinking of the past. "I can never get right what I got wrong. That man makes it bearable."

"Let's get started. I want to be tall again," I said.

Glen showed me the two sets of feet they had ready. "We have something relatively new. It's called the 'Reduced Friction Donning System.' Before this came along, a cotton sock was used. This is much more superior. The cotton stockinet was placed over the limb when wearing the prosthesis. The problem was it would create intense friction against the skin, making it difficult for patients to pull the residual limb into the prosthetic socket without tissue irritation or misplacement. The Reduced Friction Donning System is constructed of a state-of-the-art material which enables the residual limb to slide smoothly into the prosthetic socket with significantly less effort or irritation."

I was impressed that Glen knew his stuff. I wondered how many calls Jim had made to find these people. "So, what you're saying is, I can wear the artificial limbs longer?"

"Yes. How the Donning System works is that it's placed over the residual limb and drawn through an opening in the socket by the attached weighted lanyard. The reduction of resistance that Donning allows is for proper positioning of the limb in the prosthetic socket so that the overall comfort is greatly enhanced. It comes in six standard sizes, and the same is used for upper limbs."

I tried three different sizes. When the proper size was determined, I had to install it several times to make sure I did it correctly. This was done with much help from Glen.

"When you've learned to use your new hand, you will need no help," Glen said.

We went into the next room, which was used for training. The floor had a thick padded carpet. In the middle of the room sat a low set of parallel bars, much like the gymnasts used.

I sat in the chair at one end, and Glen and Jennifer took their time placing my new feet on me.

"Now, this is going to feel very awkward for you. You'll feel as if you're going to lose your balance and fall. That is normal. Jennifer and I will be on each side of you. You'll also have the bars to hang on to for stability."

I stood. Standing there, I felt myself swaying back and forth, like I was standing on a bridge in a strong wind. I could feel the muscles in my legs constantly adjusting to correct the motion.

Holding tightly onto the bars, I took one step. "I feel like the jolly green giant." Then, another step. This was totally different from walking on the stumps that I had grown accustomed to. The third step, and it felt really funny now. As my weight shifted from leg to leg I wasn't sure of the feeling. I couldn't feel the contact with the floor. Jennifer and Glen held on to me tightly. With each step, I felt as if my legs were going to buckle beneath me, sending me to the floor.

By the time I reached the end, I was breathing hard, so much for the exercise I did and all the walking beforehand.

"Do you want to stop and rest a moment?" Glen asked.

"No."

It took me a long time to turn and face the other direction. I was putting most of my body weight on my arms. Then I headed to the end where I had started from.

When I reached that I was nearly sweating.

"Let's sit in the chair and rest a minute," Glen said.

"No, I can do this," I said. Another complete trip down and back, and now my arms were burning badly. It was either time to rest or start trusting my legs. I chose to trust my legs.

"Let's take a breather before you fall."

The sweat was running. "No, not yet." Slowly, I transferred my weight from my arms to my legs. I stood there, allowing my body to adjust. "Let go of me; if I fall, so what? I will get up again." They did. I took one step and wobbled a bit, then another and another. Jennifer and Glen held their arms out, waiting to catch me if I fell.

"Believe it or not, the hardest thing to deal with is I feel so tall."

"That's normal; it will take a little time to mentally adjust to that," Glen said.

I started walking again. Halfway down, my right arm slid off the bar, and I fell into the bar on my right side. I was surprised that my legs helped me up.

I was feeling good that I was walking. Several more trips back and forth, with no major mishaps. I was regulating my breathing, taking long, slow, deep breaths and then exhaling. I was soaked, sweating like I had when I ran the 10K races.

"Madie, you really need to stop and rest for a while," Glen said.

"No, I'm walking out of here today on my own."

They could see the determination I had and they didn't try to stop me. They never left my side.

I continued, down and back. My turning was becoming much faster. I looked at the chair each time I returned to the beginning. That drove me down and back.

Time passed, and I felt my leg muscles getting weaker. "Could I get a drink of water?"

I stood, resting, while Jennifer left. When she returned, I drank the glass empty. "Thank you. This is much harder than I imagined."

Jennifer never tried to stop me. It was always Glen, and I wondered why.

I pressed on. With the exception of not being cold, I felt like I was in the wilderness again. Each step forced me to take another. If I stopped, I would fail. The only way to finish was to keep going.

"Madie, you've got to stop. You've been at this for two hours," Glen said.

"If I had stopped out there, I wouldn't be here," I said.

"But Madie, you're not. You don't have to do this in one day," Jennifer said.

She spoke, I thought. "I didn't fail then, and I'm not going to now. You have no idea how hard that was. This is nothing compared to that."

After several more trips, I was reaching my limit. I remember sitting in the snow to rest on the last few days of my journey, only to get up and go on. I would do it now.

Then, Sam walked in. "Lunch has been delivered."

Breathing deeply, I was exhausted. "I will stop for that. Fresh walleye is the best."

"Good, let me run into the other room and get the wheelchair," Glen said.

"No. Never again. I will walk." I held a poker face. Inside, I was nervous, leaving the security of the bars and going on my own, something I had to do sometimes. Falling didn't bother me; it was the failure. I didn't want them pampering over me.

Glen moved the chair out of my way. He was on my left side, and Jennifer was on my right.

I took the first step and then the second. I wobbled, but I concentrated on the feeling in my stumps. That feeling told me what was going on. "My legs aren't wobbly; it's the rest of my body," I said.

"That's right. It takes days for the body to adjust to the new information it is receiving. You have very strong legs, I've been watching. I'd be safe to say probably the strongest I've seen from any patient," Glen said.

I smiled. All the walking had paid off. Slowly, I took another step. When each foot made contact with the floor, I paused, waiting for the mental process to do its thing. I felt like a robot in slow motion. I moved very rigidly like, with no fluid movement in my knees or hips.

Now, the hall leading to their kitchen seemed much longer. The fresh walleye from Canada was the finish line. I was going to eat it while it was still hot. I increased my pace, but while doing so, I almost fell several times.

I walked into the kitchen, and the engineers and Sam started applauding. Some were clapping, and others were cheering me on—all this because of two vile men. My life was nothing to applaud. This is the end result. I smiled at them and kept my thoughts to myself.

"This walleye is fabulous," Jennifer said.

"It's like no other. I learned to love it during my time there. We ate it at least four times a week. Now, I would eat it every day." I went on and told them about Jim's lake and the fishing derby we had.

Everyone ate and ate, 'oohing' and 'aahing' while doing so. The conversation was slow while everyone ate, which was a sign of good food. Jennifer was the exception – she barely spoke all morning, and now she was a chatterbox. I wondered why and I wanted to ask her.

The fish was baked with Jim's favorite recipe. I'm sure the cook was given strict orders on how to prepare it.

When everyone finished, I couldn't believe nine people ate almost twenty pounds of fish. The rice pilaf and steamed vegetables were hardly dented.

"That was totally amazing. By far the best fish I have ever eaten. We need to do something for Jim," Glen said. Everyone agreed.

"You? I owe that man more than anyone could imagine. Saving my life is really a small thing compared to what he has done for me since. My friendship is all I have."

"That is all that matters, Madie. You could pay him back monetarily, but what would that mean to him? You wouldn't be in his or their lives. Nothing is greater than friendship or love," Jennifer said.

She was right. My thoughts went from Jim to Sharon. I sat thinking it over. I was going to call Sharon tonight to see how she and Mia were doing. I was looking at my hand resting in my lap. The ugliness of it and what had happened led me to all of this. Somehow, I knew Craig was behind it, smiling.

"Madie, what's wrong?" Jennifer asked.

Very perceptive, I thought. She noticed things no one else did. "Nothing. If you guys would give me several minutes I will walk down and get my phone. Then we can call Jim and you can see for yourself, when you talk to him, what kind of a man he is."

The engineer who was in the argument the day I arrived said, "Here, please use mine."

"I'm sorry. I don't remember your name."

"It's Doug, and no, we're sorry. Normally, we don't intertwine with the people who come here. Some were never formally introduced. This is different, and I might add, a real treat."

I learned their names yesterday at lunch, and I had ruined that. "Thank you," and I dialed. "If he's not out saving someone, he's fishing or with his friends," Jim answered, and we talked. I thanked him over and over while wiping away the tears.

The phone made its way around the table. Everyone talked to Jim for quite a while, much longer than a first conversation with someone they had never met. Everyone explained to Jim what they did and thanked him as many times as I had. He had to be getting tired of hearing it, but Jim would never say so. I could see him sitting in his fishing boat, holding the fishing pole and smiling. I cried.

I stood up and started clearing the table. It was one-twenty. "I'm sorry. Please, accept my apologies. This is the second day I have wasted your time. I'm sure you have more important things to do."

Everyone stood. Instantly, they started helping clear and talking. "Are you serious? This is the greatest," Doug said.

Each had a positive comment. Sam said, "You need to write a novel. It would be an instant number-one bestseller."

Everyone agreed.

I smiled, turned, and slowly walked out of the room. I didn't want them to see me cry this time. Writing a novel was the last thing I wanted to do right now; telling strangers that I watched my husband murdered and that I ate raw food was my business.

Jennifer caught up to me in the hall. "Madie, what happened?" She saw the tears.

I wasn't going to tell her. I asked the question. "You don't talk when we're working with Glen, but then, when we're out of that atmosphere, you do. Why?"

Jennifer smiled. "We offer people who come here more than new limbs and physical therapy. My job is to help with psychological counseling. Each person is different. Some people are an emotional basket case when they arrive. The trauma they suffered, added to the fact they had lost a hand or leg, they have trouble. I determine what would work best for them by their state of mind. That allows us to present training techniques in ways that best suit the person. I also help the person determine whether they might need further psychological or medical support in coping with the emotional issues when they leave here."

A shrink, I thought, but I didn't say that. "I could care less that I've lost my feet and right hand. I will walk again, and it's just a thing. No one can bring Craig back; that's my loss."

335

"No, they can't. I'm sorry." We kept walking. "To tell you the truth, when I heard you were coming and had the severe loss you had, I was worried. Then, after hearing your story, I felt small, and I didn't believe I could help you. Then, after seeing you this morning," Jennifer was quiet for a moment, "I'm without words. You're the best I've ever seen, and not just physically either."

"I'm battling this emotionally, more than I let show. It's Jim that's helping me."

"Yes, I see that," Jennifer said.

The rest of the afternoon I walked, taking short breaks in between.

Glen was worried about skin irritation on my stumps from my weight. As the day wore on, the pain grew. I didn't tell them.

The last hour I walked circles around the room while Glen actually sat in the chair.

"It's amazing, one day, and you have it mastered," Glen said, watching me.

"Oh, I thought you were still full from lunch," I said.

"Well, that too. Tomorrow, we work on a hand. It's a little harder to master."

I raised my eyebrows.

"Well, maybe not," Glen said.

CHAPTER 37

I was back in my room by four-thirty. I sat on the sofa and lifted my feet up, resting them. I leaned back against the armrest, and it felt good to give my legs a rest. I looked at my new feet. Glen had fitted the prosthetic limbs with foot shells in my size so I didn't have to buy new shoes. Then, magically, a new pair of shoes arrived in my size. I wasn't walking as slowly and mechanically as I had been earlier. By Friday I hoped to be walking as I did before Mother Nature claimed what she could.

I sat there, twisting my legs back and forth, watching and listening to my shoes click together. I smiled. I couldn't wait for Jim and the gang to see me. Mary would be excited; another bawling fest would follow. Oh, well, so be it.

There was a knock at the door just as I was beginning to relax. I had no idea who it was. I hadn't ordered food yet. I got up, and now, in that short amount of time, my stumps let me know they needed a break. I opened the door. The porter was standing there holding a large bouquet of flowers. I watched him look at me from my feet up, then down the hall.

"I'm sorry, I've got the wrong room," he said.

I smiled, thinking, *I got up for that.* "Not a problem."

"Oh, my, look at you! I don't have the wrong room, just a new you. You really look good. I'm sorry I didn't recognize you at first."

"That's ok."

"Here, these were delivered for you."

"Thank you."

I sat them on the bar and read the tag. 'Congratulations! Walk on. Can't wait to see you. The Gang!' I couldn't believe it. Now, the surprises were coming twice a day. I looked at the flowers through watery eyes. They were making me feel very humble.

I had to call.

Jim answer.

"Hi, Jim, it's Madie."

"Hi! I wasn't expecting to hear from you."

"This has got to stop, the wonderful lunch and now the flowers. I'm starting to feel guilty."

Jim laughed. "The flowers were Mary's idea, and, of course, we went along with it. Don't ever feel guilty. You deserve every bit of it."

I cried, and Jim waited.

"I didn't deserve what happened to Craig, and I don't deserve all of this now."

"Why?" Jim asked.

"I'm here, and Craig isn't, that's why."

"Who wouldn't feel that way? Remember one thing: You didn't pull the trigger. I know that sounds harsh, but it is a reality check. The guys and I have talked several times. We have an idea, but it's up to you. It's your call. We know your starting point and that you are headed roughly due south. If you like, with help from you, we will go up there and try to find one or both of them. As I said, that's strictly up to you. Maybe from dental records, they could be identified, giving you some satisfaction and closure in this. If you say yes, we will need all the information you can remember. The number of days that elapsed to the day the first one met his end to topographical landmarks such as lakes and how close together they were. The size and shapes, hills, valleys, the density of the forest – anything at all you can remember. Rocky slopes and the size of the boulders, we have access to all the maps, nothing is impossible. You have proven that to us. What do you say – can we try?"

I was quiet, thinking deeply. So many thoughts were coming to me at once. They'd put a great deal of thought into this. If anyone could do it, it would be them. I would be putting them at risk if I did. One life was lost there, and I wouldn't want to be the reason to lose another. Let the past be the past; it wouldn't change the future, even if one was found and identified. But it would make me feel better, and I did owe that to Craig.

The thoughts were still coming when Jim said, "Madie, you still there?"

"Yes. I don't know, that's asking too much. Something could happen to one of you and no dead man is worth that. You guys mean more to me than I can tell you."

"Yes, there's always that chance every time we go out. One thing you need to remember is that there are four of us. We will have full gear and enough electronic equipment so that we will always know where we are. We will have maps along with heavy-duty communications so that we can call in help if needed. Also, we will go in warm weather. You had none of that."

Jim had me there, but I still didn't know. "I don't know. The odds aren't in our favor of finding a needle that's nearly impossible to find. That's a lot of ground to cover."

"Not really. We could narrow it down to a fifty-mile stretch, maybe five miles wide. That isn't so much."

With that definition, it didn't sound so bad. "Can I think about it for a day or two?"

"You can think about it for as long as you want. It is possible – remember that. Plus, we can fish in some lakes we've never seen before. That's always good. So see, we can even catch fresh, good fish while we're there."

"Believe me, there's some whoppers in some of those lakes. I remember fishing on one lake, which was nearly three miles long, east to west, and a mile wide. That's a rough guess, mind you, but that's where I caught the biggest fish—a huge northern!"

"See, that's something. A good landmark to go from," Jim said.

"If I do decide to let you do this, there's one thing that isn't negotiable."

"And what's that?" Jim asked.

"I go to."

"Oh, Madie, I don't—"

I cut Jim off. "I did it then, and I can now."

"Ok, it's your call. I'll tell Jonathan, Jerry, and George."

I sat in my room. Now, I had two things to think about. The list and the trip back into the wilderness. The odds favored Vegas on both items; finding anything at all in either venture was slim to none. The difference, though, was my trip was mine to risk alone, and I accepted that. Asking them to traipse around in the middle of nowhere was totally different.

I asked myself a question, "What would be gained if they did find one of them?" I had to think about that one.

I walked into the lobby just before seven. Wednesday morning, and my week was nearly half over. Jennifer stood at Sam's desk. "Good morning, Madie. You look good with your new shoes," Jennifer said.

"Good morning. Sam, how are you?" I said.

"I'm wonderful. I told my husband last night that this is the best week that I've ever worked here."

I was the topic at their dinner table, I thought. "Well, I really need to get another hand. It took me forever to get my feet on. Good thing I woke early."

"All you have to do is call. You have the number for assistance, and Dan will be here in no time," Jennifer said.

"No, I have to do it alone. I have many years to come that way."

I could see Jennifer didn't know how to respond to that.

I walked into the room across the hall from where I had spent the last two days. Glen was waiting, standing by a table that held robotic-looking hands.

"Good morning, Madie. Would you like a cup of coffee before we start?" Glen asked.

"Yes, please. I missed mine this morning. Well, really, I ran out of time; I didn't want to be late."

I sat on the tall stool next to the table while the three of us drank our coffee. They talked, and I listened. While listening, I thought about the conversation with Jim. I still hadn't decided.

"Madie, you seem distracted this morning," Jennifer said.

'Not much gets past you, does it?' I smiled. "I'm ready to go to work."

"Alright, Madie, here we go. There's so much more available now; everything I'm about to tell you will overwhelm you. First, the fitting process we do is in three phases: the interface phase, the control phase, and then the alignment phase. The fitting takes one to three days. Why the big variance is the patient's capacity, and the prosthesis they choose determines the interface phase we create for a prosthetic socket. That is the foundation of any successful prosthesis. This is broken down further with multiple diagnostic interfaces and special techniques, including friction-free donning socks for optimal fit and comfort. Similar to what is used on your legs. On completion of that phase, the control phase is initiated. For a myoelectric prosthesis, electrode sites are identified on the patient's residual limb and transferred to the diagnostic interface. Then electrodes are mounted in the diagnostic interface to maximize the patient's EMG signal output for a body-powered prosthesis, harness, cable and housing are attached to the frame of the prosthesis. Then, the control phase is complete when optimal control and comfort have been achieved. Are you with me so far?"

"Geez, I don't know," I said. "What is a myoelectric prosthesis?"

"An electric hand, you will have moving fingers capable of grasping things. Let me back up for one moment. The alignment phase involves the fabrication of a rigid frame and attachment of all components to maximize function and cosmetic restoration. So now, here are the options available in hands."

I watched Glen remove a claw-like-looking item from the table.

"What you have is known as wrist disarticulation, which means at your level of amputation, you have no wrist movement. That problem has been solved for you. This model, called the Electric Greifer, comes in four models. Only one works for disarticulation, Model 8E34=6, so the choice is easy."

It looked like a flat hand with one upper and one lower finger.

Then, Glen removed another hand from the table. This one looked much more like something belonging to a robot. Two upper fingers and one lower and attached to the side of it was a small round cylinder.

"This is called 'DMC Plus Hand.' I believe this model will suit you better," Glen said.

"Do the fingers actually open and close?" I asked.

"Yes, they do. How that happens is this." Glen handed me a small cylinder with a flat wire leading to a flat round disk on the other end.

"See all the short pins extruding on the end of the controller; those plug into the hand. The disk on the other end sends the signal telling the hand what to do. What tells the disk what to send to the controller are muscle contractions. Sound complicated?"

"Yes."

"Well, it's not. You flex the muscle in your limb, and the fingers open and close. Flex another muscle, and the wrist rotates. I'm here to take care of the complicated stuff. You have the hardest part: learning how to control it. It will come automatically, and after time and much practice, you will be using it like you did your real hand. Now, you need to hear the details of what makes it work. Two independent measurements and regulating systems proportionally control speed and grip force at all opening widths. Speed and grip force are determined by the level of the muscle signal. Should the muscle signal vary, speed and grip force are proportional to the changed muscle signal. This relationship between muscle signal and speed and grip force more closely mimics the natural hand. For all amputation levels above wrist disarticulation, passive wrist rotation uses a friction ring, similar to what I explained to you yesterday in the ankle, but not exactly. More involved, after gripping once with maximum force in the 'DMC Plus' control mode, the EMC signal required to open the hand will be slightly higher. So why, do you ask? This reduces the risk of the hand opening due to unintentional muscle contraction. I could go further into detail about how we make that work, but I won't. I will have everything adjusted correctly by the time you leave."

"Geez-oh-pete! I had no idea!"

"I know that's a lot to ingest. You have to know how it works to make it work," Glen said.

"It's not just that. I had no idea of the level of sophistication."

"I've only touched the surface, and there's one more thing."

Oh, great, more info to retain. "I'm afraid I won't remember all this."

"The wrist rotator has six different operation modes. Eventually, you will tell me which one you are comfortable with."

"This is much more involved than feet," I said.

"Yes, it is. But it's well worth it. We have a lot of hours of work ahead of us."

Glen worked diligently. Time became non-existent. Sam walked in and said, "Lunch is here."

"We were just finishing up with the donning socket—a long way from the finish line."

"No surprises today?" I asked Sam.

"No, subs. As wonderful as it was, we can't keep eating like that. Well, at least I can't."

We ate, and surprisingly, I was hungry. I had a turkey on wheat with tomatoes, lettuce, and spicy mustard. I watched the clock. No long stories. I didn't want a long lunch. Fifteen minutes later, I looked at Glen. "I'm ready to get back to work if you are."

"What, no story today? I was looking forward to it," Paul said.

"Not much left to tell," I said.

"Well, we've got another forty-five minutes. Lunch is an hour long, and I'd hate to waste it," Paul said.

"Well, I didn't tell you everything about the bear." I had only told them the beginning and how it had killed the first death dealer. "But I want to leave here Friday with a hand, and by the things Glen told me this morning, it's going to take more hours than what's left."

Glen spoke up, "I'm willing to work late into the night if you are. That's up to you and what you can endure."

"Please, if you don't know me well enough by now, you will. I don't believe you can hang with me." I was tempting him; Glen had opened the box. I wanted a new hand. "I believe I could work straight through midnight until tomorrow night."

Glen lowered his head. "I don't think I could. I know you well enough to know that, and I have no doubt."

"Two of us will assist, however long it takes," Paul said.

I looked at him and then back to Glen.

"So, what do you say? You've got our curiosity up about the bear," Paul said.

I had all intentions of keeping it short, but that didn't happen.

This time, I didn't cry. They heard all about the bear. Even though it saved my life, had become a companion and friend, and was the only good memory of my trip out, I wasn't sad about talking about it. It was another thing I had lost during that time, but let the wild be wild.

"Come on guys, it is one ten, time to go back to work," I said.

Paul shook his head. "That's just utterly incomprehensible."

Sam walked over to me and laid her hand on my shoulder. "You ever need anything, no matter what or where, I hope I'm the one you call."

I need Craig back. I need my old life back. It would be nice if I had my feet and hands back also. But that can't happen. I smiled. I didn't want to hurt her feelings. "Thank you, that's kind of you. I hope to spend a lot of time back in Canada with Jim and the rest of the crew. Sounds kind of funny, huh? Going back to where I lost everything. When I'm here in the States, I will keep you in mind."

The rest of the day, Glen, Paul, and Rod worked on my hand. They would fit, adjust, re-fit, and re-adjust, only to try a different part or a different sensor, which led to re-doing the process all over. Then, as I felt we were getting somewhere, yet again, one of the three would throw a wrench into the gears. A new wrist rotator would appear, or a longer controller would be placed slightly on a different muscle location inside the donning sock. Then, as I thought, *Maybe this time,* a different colored friction ring was placed inside the wrist rotator, changing the control movement, of which I had very little.

Sam returned. "Before I leave, would you like me to order food for you, or are you going to call it a day?"

I looked at Sam, then Glen. "I had no idea there was this much involved."

"We're just getting started, like I said, normally one to three days. Usually, it's three."

"I want to stay, but I don't want to interfere with all of your personal lives. You guys make the call."

"I thought it was already a done deal. You told us more at lunchtime, we're staying."

"Even if you hadn't, I would have," Glen responded.

"Rod?" I asked.

"Let's eat. If we work all night, can we hear another venture tomorrow?" Rod said.

I felt bad, so much devotion because of me. "Pizza, and I'm buying."

"Are you crazy? No way, that's part of the package," Glen said.

"What package, yours or Jim's?" I asked.

"A package is a package. It's already… well, let's say, it's taken care of," Glen said.

We ate. I paced the floor, and it felt so good to get out of the chair. Three large pizzas were devoured by the time we finished.

Hours passed, and I felt like we weren't getting anywhere. The men were constantly talking, discussing options, placement, and muscle contractions. I listened; I was learning a lot. "Something else I haven't told you."

They stopped what they were doing and looked at me, waiting to hear. "The end of my nose isn't real. Well, it's not a factory issue. It had severe frostbite; I went a long time looking like a warthog," I said.

"Wow. The doctor did an excellent job. I didn't notice," Glen said.

"Something else Jim took care of. Dr. Bryant did the work, and Jim assisted. I owe that man everything for my life." I went on and told them about my first conversation with Jim and how I had told Jim to tell my friends back home that I didn't make it. And when he said 'I can help you' and my reply was 'you can't help me, I'm frozen.'

I did this because I felt that they needed a break, and I was thinking about Jim -that always made me feel better.

No one said anything. I looked at each of them, and Rod was shaking his head.

"I can't thank you guys enough for all that you're doing for me," I said.

"That's what we're here for. The extra benefit we're getting from this is you. That's our satisfaction," Paul said. Rod and Glen agreed.

The tears formed, and I quickly wiped them away.

It was eleven p.m.

"You guys want to call it a night?" I asked.

They looked at one another, each waiting for the other to reply.

I gave them an out, "I am."

"I'd like to make a few more placements and adjustments if everyone's game," Glen said.

We worked until one a.m.

I walked into my room at one twenty-two, and I was beat. In five short hours, I would be up facing another day.

I couldn't believe how tired I was, and I had done nothing but sit. I thought back to the countless, endless days that I moved along, dragging the heavy snowshoes, too tired to keep going but too cold to stop.

I brushed my teeth and lay down on the bed to rest a moment before taking my feet off and putting on my pajamas.

The next thing I knew, the phone was ringing, and all the lights were still on in my room. At first, I thought I had only slept for a few minutes. Groggy, I couldn't figure out why the phone was ringing. By the time I reached the phone, the thought had come to me that something was wrong; something drastic had happened to one of the men up north. "Hello," I heard a click. "Good morning. This is your six a.m. wake-up call." It was Sandra; I couldn't believe I slept through the night. "Thank you," I said.

Instantly, I sat up, and I had to hurry. Getting undressed, showered, and redressed was going to take more than an hour.

Dan was waiting in the lobby when I arrived. I was ten minutes late.

"I'm sorry I'm late."

I walked down to the lab. The door was opened, and I walked in. Glen, Paul, and Rod were there working. They looked much more refreshed than I felt. "My, you guys look all bright-eyed and bushy-tailed this morning."

"You bet," Paul said.

"I'm into this. Ready for another seventeen-hour day—I am," Rod replied.

"Geez."

"You had your morning coffee?" Glen asked.

"No, I slept late. Could you strain the water out and main vein the caffeine for me?"

They laughed.

"I don't believe I feel quite as lively as you. Coffee would be great."

"I know I'm speaking for all of us, this is great, having the opportunity to help you. You, without a doubt, will always be the biggest celebrity we will ever have here," Paul said.

I felt small. Somewhere deep inside me, was telling me Paul was speaking from his heart. "I'm nobody, but thank you for feeling that way."

"You may never be a big movie star or some famous person otherwise, but to us, there will never be a more important person to grace our presence," Glen said.

My eyes watered. "You're the heroes here. Without you helping me, I wouldn't, or couldn't, function normally again. I thank you."

By lunchtime, the major things were completed—the donning socket, the DMC hand, and the controller were agreed upon, and the location where the controller was to be placed. The location of the controller against the muscle in my arm took forever. One sixteenth-of-an-inch movement, in one direction or another, amazed me at how much it changed how the electric hand worked. As I flexed my muscles, I watched the hand open or close. At first, I felt like a spastic—uncoordinated. But now I had operated the hand countless dozens of times, and I still couldn't coordinate it correctly, but I was getting better. The men worked meticulously.

"This is still amazing to me, so much involved. I had no idea," I said.

"The problem is there's more. Hopefully, by the end of the day, you will be learning how to use your new hand, and then we'll install a myobock electrode. Then you'll see drastic improvement in sensitivity as well as superior noise filtration which the latter won't seem much to you, but it does. Bottom line, it improves smoothness. To get to that point, we call the electrode frequency filter—the voltage frequency that operates the hand and the filter frequency have to be synchronized. No big thing—just more time. We want you to go home tomorrow fully functional," Glen said.

"Will I be able to drive?" I was already thinking about my trip to the first location.

"Well, yes, after time working with your new parts. Tomorrow, I wouldn't. Maybe in a week, possibly two, you can," Glen answered.

That wasn't what I wanted to hear.

Jennifer hadn't spent anytime with me since I had made the comment to her yesterday. Now, I felt I had offended her, and I felt bad. I would apologize to her the next time I saw her. What I had said was still true and always would be. I just should have been more subtle about it.

We ate. I had asked for a giant-sized chicken salad with honey mustard dressing and water. I had to stop eating the way I was. If I didn't, I would have to order heavy-duty feet to support the extra tonnage. Unless it was fish, that wasn't fattening and, as they say, 'bland food.'

"You're doing quite well. By dinner time, we should be finished, and then tonight, we'll spend as long as you want learning how to control it. In the morning, we'll fit a silicone hand to it. It will fit perfectly. It will match the size of your real hand, giving you all the functions you need, not to mention they are very stylish—four fingers and a thumb, which draws much less attention than having an exposed bare claw."

"I will have it mastered in no time."

Glen laughed as he took a bite of food. "I have no doubt about that. Just remember, it's not as easy as walking on your feet. We have some unusual tests to run you through. You conquer those, and you can handle anything."

I had to – for countless reasons.

"By the way, we have a surprise for you tomorrow. You'll see."

I didn't ask what; I knew I wouldn't get an answer. As I thought about it, it was probably some huge send-off party, with many flowing tears on my part.

The afternoon went as Glen said. We had finished before five p.m.

Glen walked me up to a small table that had been set up in the corner during the afternoon. He removed a large towel covering it.

On the table sat a dozen eggs, a small stack of paper cups, and a pencil. *How strange,* I thought.

"Ok, Madie, are you ready? First test, remove one of the eggs from the carton," Glen said.

Paul and Rod watched on. *Piece of cake,* I thought. I reached for the first egg. I held on to it and started removing it from the carton. Three inches later, the egg exploded, sending egg goo all over. "What is it? Trick eggs?" I asked.

"No, you unknowingly used too much pressure holding the egg. Don't feel bad; that happens to everyone. Next time, when you contract the muscle in your arm, use less force. Remember, the prosthetic hand can do everything a human hand can," Glen said.

I held a towel in my left hand and wiped the slimy mess from the claws. Then, I contracted another muscle, and I watched the hand rotate at the wrist. "What an eerie feeling," I said to myself.

The second egg shattered, and so did the third.

"You're trying too hard, Madie. Slow down, think about the muscle in your arm," Glen said.

I did and went slow.

Now, I held the fourth egg in my hand. I did it! I smiled. Ten seconds passed, and the egg remained intact.

"Ok, good, now rotate the wrist," Glen said.

I contracted another muscle. My wrist started turning, and the egg split open. Now, I was frustrated. "Geez, why can't I do this?"

"That's not uncommon either. When you started rotating the wrist, more energy was sent to the grip. Not to worry, within a week you'll be doing everything with your hand normally. The thought process will become second nature."

The fifth egg I held on to. I rotated my wrist until the palm was up, then I started rotating it back. Splat – more egg mess. "I hope everyone likes scrambled eggs, looks like we'll have enough of them."

They laughed, but inside, I was more determined.

Within an hour I was doing much better, but I still didn't have it mastered.

"Now, test two. We'll let that arm rest for a while. See these thin paper cups? I'm going to fill them with water, and all you have to do is pick them up," Glen said.

Now I knew better – this was no piece of cake. "This is going to be a mess."

I grasped the cup, and before I had it lifted from the table, the cup collapsed. Luckily, they had a large pan beneath it to catch the water. "Oh, crap!" The second and third ones ended as the first.

After eating dinner, we worked all night on my motor skills. Glen did most of the coaching, but Paul and Rod occasionally gave suggestions.

"We should do this more often," Paul said. "Normally, we don't interact with the patient. I'm learning a lot, and there's things here I see that I can work with. We're always looking for things we can do to make it easier for the user."

I worked with the eggs and glasses of water, and slowly, I was getting better.

"See the pencil there on the table – pick it up and write your name," Glen said.

After a time, I finally managed to pick it up. I tried to write my name but only scribbled.

"Remember, you can rotate your wrist. That will give you the angle of a normal hand," Glen said.

That helped. Now, at least, I could read the scribble.

I worked on that for an hour.

"Now for a more difficult one. The condition of your left hand will make this much harder. So, if you can't do it, don't worry about it. See if you can tie your shoe. Not that you'll ever have to do it. Your shoe will stay on your feet and give you the dexterity you need. But there's always buttons, zippers, things in every day life that we take for granted."

How well I knew. The things I used to do automatically I now had to think about.

I tried, but I couldn't. Now, I was mad at myself for not being able to. Before in my life, there was nothing I couldn't do. Now, I had trouble with the simple things.

"If she would have left me with just one finger on my hand," I said angrily. I tried again and again to pull the lace through to make the bow and finish the knot. I kept dropping it. Now I was mad. It wasn't my right hand that was failing – it was the left. There wasn't enough left of my palm to push the lace where it needed to go. "This is aggravating, burned by Mother Nature," I said loudly while sitting up.

The three men looked at me, not knowing how to respond.

"Well, figuratively speaking, I don't know what it feels like to be burned, but I do know what it feels like to be frozen. She's a real mother." I laughed, and they just looked at me. "That was supposed to be funny. Guess not, huh?"

CHAPTER 38

I walked into my room just before eleven p.m., complete with my new hand. I wasn't ready to sleep since I had too much to learn. Practice and more practice was the only way to get the end result I wanted. I turned the television on for noise and then called room service.

"Could I get six eggs fresh out of the carton? And several more paper cups? The four I have in the bathroom won't be enough."

The voice on the other end asked, "You don't want these eggs cooked?"

"No, fresh and runny," I said.

"Yuk," the voice said.

I laughed. "I'm not going to eat them. I will show you to satisfy your curiosity."

A few minutes later there was a knock at the door. I opened it, and there stood a man in his early thirties wearing a white shirt and a white apron. It was clear what he was. "Are you the one I just talked to on the phone?" I asked.

"Yes. I don't normally answer the phone, but I wasn't busy," he said.

"You cook," I said.

"Yes. Excuse me. I should have removed the apron. I was going through a long list of reasons why someone would want raw eggs at this time of night, and I didn't think about it. So, are you going to show me?" he asked.

The door opened from left to right. I stood in the opened door holding the inside handle with my new hand, out of view from him. "I'm Madie, and you are?" I asked.

"Troy. It's nice to meet you, I think."

I laughed. I could see the big question mark on his face. "It's nice to meet you, Troy. Come in."

I walked slightly behind Troy. "We need to go to the sink at the bar. I said I will show you, and it could get messy. You're my first audience."

Troy frowned. I walked past him, turned, and walked behind the bar. Then Troy sat the six eggs, still in the carton, on the bar. I held my right hand up so he could see it. I saw the slightly shocked look on his face. "A little weird?" I was trying to ease the surprise.

349

"Yes, well, I've never seen anything like that before," Troy said.

"Don't worry, neither have I until today. If I can use it with a fair amount of proficiency I'm going home tomorrow. So, that's what the eggs are for. I need lots of practice; I'm not too good with it right now." I set the carton of eggs beside the sink and opened the lid with my left hand. Then, I reached for an egg with my right hand. After clamping the three jaw-like fingers around the egg, I slowly lifted it out of the carton.

Now, I held the egg above the sink, "Pretty cool, huh?"

"Wow!" Troy said slowly, staring at my hand. "I had no idea something like that was made."

"Watch this. It's the coolest part and also the hardest." I rotated the wrist.

"Holy shit! That's really cool… and amazing!" Troy said.

Then, I crushed the egg. I dropped my head and tried to think of what movement I had done wrong.

"How does that work? You're a real bionic woman."

"Hardly, there's a small pad called the controller inside the socket." I raised my shirt sleeve to show him. "I flex different muscles to move the hand. As you can see, I haven't gotten it figured out yet. For some reason, when I contract the muscle to rotate the wrist, I'm applying too much pressure on the controller to close the grip. The result is scrambled eggs."

"Wow! Incredible."

"It will be incredible when I can use it correctly."

"Well, maybe you're; I have an idea. So, you don't drink alone; I will clock out now. The end of my shift is midnight, but we're not busy. No loss in leaving thirty minutes early."

I watched Troy call down to the kitchen. When he hung up the phone, he walked to the bar.

"Let's see what you have in here." Troy whistled, "Just about everything. You do drink, don't you?"

"Oh, yes."

"Two drinks always help to relax a person; any more than that, one starts going the other way. Maybe that will help you. Sweet drinks or blended with soda?" Troy asked.

A drink would be a good idea. It's been a long week, so why not? "I don't care, just not too strong. Then, it won't taste good."

Two drinks later, and after learning about Troy and his wife and little boy, I decided to try again. I did much better. I held the egg while rotating the wrist for over a minute before crushing the egg. "I believe your theory works."

350

"You'll get it. I wish I could stay, but I have to get home. My wife worries if I get home late; she worries too much. I love her to death, and it's better than having one that doesn't care," Troy said.

"Don't ever stop and take nothing for granted. I know I had to learn the hard way."

I tried to tip Troy when he left.

"Are you crazy? I should pay you for seeing something that cool."

After Troy left, I worked on the eggs for a long time. Slowly, I could see an improvement. Then, I switched to the paper glasses filled with water. That was much harder, and several times, I got disgusted with myself. Many times, I told myself it was time to go to bed, but I didn't. I couldn't; I had a task in front of me. I would sleep when I felt I was doing better.

Hour after hour passed. I was into this too much to feel sleepy. I went from the egg to the glass of water, then to writing my name. That became the easiest. My penmanship would never be the same, but at least now I could read what I wrote.

I never stopped. I continued to cycle through the exercises. I was now getting to where I could open and close the fingers while rotating the wrist. I was proud of myself and happy. I thought it looked pretty cool.

Now, I was walking around my room, picking everything up and setting it back down. As I strolled around the room, I realized I hadn't been this happy in a very long time.

I was too excited to sleep, and now it was four-thirty a.m. I made a pot of coffee with the help of my new hand. Things were much faster now. Holding the tin foil bag of coffee in my left hand, I removed a knife from the drawer beside the bar. I slid the knife through the bag and sliced it open. Before, at home, this process would have taken ten times as long. I just couldn't believe the difference in having two working hands again.

I gripped the bottom of the tin foil bag with my right hand, rotated the wrist, and poured the coffee into the coffee maker. I wanted to jump up and down like a high school cheerleader over something so small! I smiled.

While I waited for the coffee to brew, I worked on tying a shoe, which was still difficult. I worked at it until I started to get mad—mainly at myself—something so simple. Silently, I talked bad about Mother Nature.

I showered, and then the first thing I did was put my right hand back on. Slowly, with much concentration, I used it to help get dressed. The flexibility it gave me was wonderful. My socks and pants slid onto my body gracefully. No more going back and forth, from side to side, with my left hand to complete the task.

Then, my shirt—I wanted to look extra good today—my last day. The buttons were a major problem. I still had to use my thumb to push the buttons through the hole. I knew in due time, I would be using my new hand to accomplish this.

The coffee was gone, and I was ready for my last day. Between the caffeine buzz, the emotional high of using my hand, and my last day, I went out and paced up and down the hall. I had to burn off some energy.

It wasn't even six o'clock yet. As much as I wanted to go home today, I wanted to get to the lab early and show Glen and the rest what I could do.

I turned the television and lights off in my room and walked down to the lobby. There I asked Sandra to call me a cab.

Sandra became concerned, "Is there something wrong? You usually leave at seven."

"No, everything's fine," I said.

"You look different today," she said.

"Maybe because I'm taller," I replied.

Sandra looked into my eyes, started to say something, and then smiled.

I think I knew what she was referring to but chose not to say.

As I rode in the cab the thought occurred to me the door might be locked. Glen might not be as early of a riser as I was. So be it; I could wait.

I paid the cab driver and walked toward the door. I looked to the sky. A hint of white glow was starting to appear. So many mornings, I had seen this, wondering if I would see another, wondering what the day would bring. More snow, more pain? Always more loneliness. Today was going to be a good day, and I could feel it.

I half expected the door to be locked, but it wasn't. I walked in, and the lobby was dark, and no Sam. The hall lights were on, so I headed down toward the lab.

When I walked in, I surprised Glen. "Holy Moses! I wasn't expecting that," Glen said. Then, he looked at the clock on the wall. "What are you doing here so early?"

As excited as I was to show Glen what I could do with my hand, I chose to play it cool. "Oh, not much, the last day, you know. I didn't know if you'd be here or not."

"Usually, no, but there were a few things I wanted to do and get ready before you arrived—so much for that."

"So, what are you working on?" I asked.

"Mainly, your hand as long as you're here, mind if I take a few measurements?"

"That's why I'm here; I couldn't sleep." I was beaming. I couldn't wait to show Glen.

"I think I know what size silicone hand you need. But to be exact, I can take a measurement on your left arm, from your elbow to your wrist. We want to keep everything proportional, you know."

Glen didn't smile or gloat. "I was right," he said matter-of-factly. He knew his stuff.

Glen handed me what I would call a rubber hand, complete with wrinkles on the side of the palm between the thumb and index finger. The fingers actually curved as a normal hand would do. It was an empty shell – a glove for my robotic hand. It looked good. "You know, if this hand had fingernails, it would look almost real," I said.

Glen looked at me as if I were crazy. "Not a bad idea. Tell that to Paul and Rod when they get here. That's their area."

"My area for what?" Paul asked as he walked in.

I told him my idea. "That could happen." He thought for a moment. "I would have to differentiate between a man's and a woman's hand, but it could happen."

Glen took the hand back. "The steel ring at the base locks onto the hand." After some effort, the silicone hand was locked onto my steel hand. Now, I felt even better. It didn't look like a real hand, but it would draw much less attention to me.

"I haven't even made coffee yet this morning. Why don't you move the fingers back and forth and get used to it? It's a little different; nothing you will notice until you pick something up. That will be easier for you, you'll see. The silicone gives you a better grip. It's not as slippery as the bare metal fingers. I'll be right back."

Glen left, and I felt a little apprehensive. All the work I had accomplished during the night just changed. Paul had also left the room. I went to the table and reached for one of the tools lying there. I picked it up; Glen was right. The tension left; the small screwdriver I held in my hand felt more secure. I laid it back down and worked the fingers back and forth. The thumb, index, and middle fingers were the only three that moved. The fourth and little finger stayed extended, something a normal hand wouldn't do. *A small price to pay,* I thought.

I continued moving the fingers, watching the silicone hand as it contracted and expanded. Something didn't feel right. The more I moved the fingers, the more sluggish they became. I concentrated on the muscle controlling it. The harder I tried I didn't get any better results. I tried to rotate the wrist and it barely moved. Something was going wrong, but I didn't know what.

Glen returned. I was looking at my hand, and then I looked at Glen. By the expression on my face, he could see that something wasn't right.

"Something the matter?" he asked.

I nodded. "Something happened. It's barely moving no matter how hard I try."

Glen held my arm just above the wrist. He used his left hand and held the two fingers. "Squeeze my hand."

I did. I felt no resistance. "What did I do?"

Glen looked at me with a puzzled look. "That's strange." He moved his left hand away. "Close your hand." I did, and it hardly moved. "Wow, that's a first. The battery must be going dead; it must be a bad battery. They usually last ten to twelve hours under constant use."

"Battery? This thing has a battery?" I asked.

"Yes. Where do you think the current comes from to move it?"

Then, I knew. I had drained the battery using the hand all night.

Glen removed the silicone hand. "This is one of the many things we have to go over today. It just moved to the top of the list." Then Glen removed my hand from the wrist socket. "This small cylinder on the outside of the hand holds the battery." Glen unscrewed the cap.

"I thought that was where I could store my lip gloss," I said, then laughed.

"Yeah, right."

"Seriously, I thought that was just a part that helped to move the fingers."

"It is. You could say that's your motor."

Now I knew. Glen replaced the battery. "I still don't understand. That shouldn't have happened."

I remained silent. I wanted to tell him so bad it was killing me.

Paul returned, and Rod was following him. "I see everyone's an early riser around here," I said.

Glen put my hand back together. I worked the fingers. Using extra force, they opened and closed really fast. "That's a big difference," I said.

Glen looked at me. Now was the time. "Can I hold an egg?"

"Sure, I'll go get some," Glen said.

I had an idea. With the extra grip the silicone hand gave me, I knew I could do more.

Glen returned and sat the carton of eggs on the table.

"Toss me one," I said.

Glen looked at me. His eyes said it all, *Are you crazy?* Out of the corner of my eye, I saw Paul and Rod turn and look at me.

"It will get all over you," Glen said.

"Maybe so, but it will wash. Throw me one."

Glen shook his head and removed an egg from the carton. I was about five feet away. I watched the egg float through the air. I held my right hand out, palm up. I watched the egg land in it and instantly closed the grip as I let my hand drop to absorb some of the momentum. I held my hand back up, rotated the wrist until the palm was down, and then rotated it back up. I opened and closed the fingers twice and then tossed the egg back to him. I smiled from ear to ear.

They all started talking at once. Rod clapped. Paul said, "That's the fastest I've ever seen anyone do that. You're a quick study."

'Not too quick,' I said to myself.

Glen smiled. "Now I understand. There wasn't anything wrong with the battery." Then he frowned, "Did you sleep at all last night? Let me answer that—knowing you, no."

I smiled again. "I couldn't wait to show you guys."

"That's totally amazing—off the charts. It takes most people days and days to do that," Rod said. "Now I know how you survived; you don't quit." Rod shook his head, "Up all night."

"I couldn't. Craig wouldn't let me. I kept hearing his voice in my head – 'don't give up, Madie, the finish line is just ahead.' In the beginning, I promised him two things. One was that I would make it, but, toward the end, I wished I hadn't. All I wanted to do was give up and die. The second, I don't know if I can fulfill."

No one spoke. They didn't ask, and I was glad. I wouldn't have told them.

"Last night was enjoyable. What a big difference. I had to do it. You three have gone beyond your call of duty this week. It's my way of showing you how much I appreciate it."

We worked, drank coffee, and talked. I was shown ways to improve my control of moving my hand. Glen made minor adjustments during the process.

Many times, I caught Glen looking at his watch. I thought nothing of it.

It was almost nine o'clock. Glen gave me another exercise to work on, and then he went over to Paul and Rod, who were sitting at a table working. He spoke quietly to them and then left. Still, I thought nothing.

Glen returned. He nodded at Paul and Rod and then walked toward me. "Ok, now a hard test." He picked up a ball with a handle that was on the floor. "Sit in the chair. This is a twenty-pound exercise ball. I want you to lift it from the floor. It will show you two things. The first is that the hand will not fall off. The second thing is how strong the hand really is. You will learn that it will become a real hand to you. Lift it as many times as you can." My back was toward the door.

I sat in the chair. Slowly, I lifted the ball from the floor, not knowing what to expect. I felt the pull on my forearm, but nothing happened. The grip didn't break free, and the donning socket didn't slide from my arm.

"See, just like the hand you used to have," Glen said.

I sat the ball back down. I lifted it several more times just to be sure.

Glen was behind me. "Madie, you have visitors."

I turned and yelled. Then I jumped up! I was talking loudly, and I was sure the words I was saying made no sense. Instantly, I was crying and laughing. The tears clouded my eyes. I ran the short distance and slammed into Jim. I hugged him for all I was worth. Through the tears, I saw George standing beside him. Paul, Rod, Sam, and Jennifer were standing behind them. I cried so hard I couldn't talk. Then, I hugged George and then back to Jim.

I was so happy, and through the crying, I said, "What are you doing here?" I was still in shock, and my heart was pounding. There was so much I wanted to say and so many things to thank Jim for. "This is the greatest thing I could ever ask for." I continued to cry as I went back and forth, hugging them both.

"Ok, this has to stop, or you're going to have me crying," Jim said.

I laughed. "Glen said there was going to be a surprise today. I had no idea it was going to be this. But why?" I asked.

"That is for me to answer. I asked them. The reason I asked them is your condition. I've learned enough about you to know you'll do ok on your own, but it goes further than that. I probably wouldn't have if you had only one prosthetic limb, as most people do. You have three. Legs are the easiest to become injured. Sores, blisters, and muscle bruising, all have to be tended to if they should appear. That's not uncommon until the tissue toughens up. I also know you well enough that you'll push yourself through it, which isn't good. Hands are more likely to need minor tweaking here and there. They are temperamental at first. After a few adjustments, they seem to settle in and work fine for years under normal use. I couldn't let you leave here without returning at least twice a week, and that would be after several days of therapy. So, the call to Jim. If he hadn't been a doctor, this wouldn't have happened. He can look after you and tend to all your medical needs," Glen said.

I listened intently and was thinking about my plans—Sharon and her husband tomorrow night and the trip to the first location. I was in no position to negotiate. "Ok." I hugged Jim again. "Why didn't the rest of the gang come with you?"

Jim answered that one. "George is the technical one of the bunch. He's going to take a crash course today to learn how to do the adjustments you might need down the road."

"Yes, it isn't that easy. I will give you our phone number. George, you call if you ever need or have a question about anything," Glen said.

George smiled the smile I remembered – always kind. I walked to George and hugged him again. While doing so I said, "George, what would I ever do without you guys?"

"What would we ever do without you? You're a major part of our lives. You're not leaving," George said.

I broke down, crying even harder this time, holding George the entire time.

When I got myself together, I said, "Thank you, everyone in this room. My life was destroyed. Without you, I would have failed, but now I have hope."

"Madie, at first, I was really worried about you. You had all the bad tucked away where no one could see, where no one could get to. The trauma you endured was much greater than your physical condition. I didn't know how you were going to get through it, but now I do. Going back with your friends, I will never worry about you. The love you have for them is obvious to all, and I can also see that it is returned ten-fold. You don't need someone like me. You have them—the greatest thing of all. They will take care of you," Jennifer said.

How perceptive she was! She knew more than I thought.

I cried more. "Another sob fest. I do that a lot. Jennifer, you're the greatest shrink anyone could have."

Sam was wiping tears away, but Jennifer was more refrained. Her eyes were wet. "Except for you – you have them."

"Not to be the killjoy here, but we have quite a bit to cover yet today," Glen said.

George, Paul, and Rod were over in the corner, sitting in chairs. George was being shown the prosthetics I had. Glen, Jim, and I were back in the center of the room where I had spent the last two days. Everything was back to normal.

My right leg was removed. Glen told Jim what to look for, what could happen, and all the different things to remedy the problem. Then, Glen removed the left leg and donning socket. I looked at both stumps. I felt naked, and I wanted my feet back.

Glen showed Jim how to install the donning socket on my right leg and then the foot.

Now, Jim had to replace both things on my left. After two tries, Jim had it.

"What is it with you guys? People usually struggle with this. You two breeze through it," Glen said.

"Jim's an intelligent man. He struggles with nothing," I said.

They both looked at me. Glen said, "I don't believe you do either."

"Believe me, I struggled every day."

"You're alive. Compared to everyone else, you breezed through it. They wouldn't be, me included," Glen said.

I wished they'd been there, watching me fight for every step and sleeping in the snow.

"Never judge the condemned. Mother Nature had my number, but God said no. That's the only reason I'm here."

I paraded around for Jim. I caught another egg, and I was happy to show him what I could do.

Then, it was lunchtime.

Sam, Jennifer, and the entire group went out to a three-star restaurant. It was impressive, and the meal was fabulous. Several bottles of wine were consumed. Everyone talked and laughed. In a way, I was sorry that the week had come to an end. But I had other things to do – fulfill my promise to Craig. I only hoped I could accomplish the task.

I sat back and listened to the stories that were told. Jim and George with their rescuing events and Glen and the engineers told events that had happened with patients.

"Madie, you're dealing with all of this marvelously. I don't see how," Jennifer said.

"The way I see it, we struggle with two things – living and dying. Everything in between, the small things, we just deal with. My physical condition I can deal with." I wanted to say that I wished Craig was here to coach me, but I didn't want to ruin lunch.

Everyone stared at me.

"You are the most amazing person we will ever work with," Jennifer said.

I laughed, trying to downplay her comment. "I doubt that. You just haven't met the people out there who are far more amazing than me."

On our ride back, Jim asked, "George, how are you doing? Will you be able to learn enough to help Madie?"

"Whew, I don't know. It's incredible stuff. Honest answer? No," George said.

"I'm not worried, George. I have faith in you."

Glen rode with us. "I have an idea. We'll pack an extra hand and foot and give you all the technical information involved, and you can work with those. When you feel that you have it, then you can send them back. That's another first—we don't normally do that."

"Thanks, I'll need it," George replied.

39
CHAPTER

Jim, George, and I were in the back of the limo, and Dan was driving. I could see he wanted to say something to me when we got in, but he didn't. I credited that to having people around he didn't know.

The goodbyes went better than I thought. I thanked and hugged everyone there. I told them many times how grateful I was. I kept it short. I had done enough crying around them. I was really grateful I didn't have to go back.

We used the ride to relax. Jim and George were drinking a beer, and I had a glass of wine. George had two one-inch-thick stacks of paper lying in his lap—his manuals. One for my hand, the other for my foot, and he was reading away.

"George, you don't have to cram that all in right away," I said.

"What! Are you crazy? I had no idea this technology was available," George replied.

I laughed. "That's what I said."

"Pretty cool stuff. Gets involved."

"Like I said…."

George cut me off, "What if something goes wrong? I'll feel bad if I can't help you."

"Then, I'll limp, and I can manage without a hand."

"Not while I'm around."

George continued to read while Jim and I talked. The conversation hadn't come up yet about me returning with them. I hadn't decided how I was going to tell Jim, so I just started in. "Jim, I need a week before I can come and stay with you."

Jim frowned.

"I have a few things I need to do," I told him about inviting Sharon and her husband for dinner tomorrow night. "The other is a promise I made to Craig. I can't break that; I couldn't live with myself.

Jim was quiet, and I could see he was thinking.

"Seven days, and then I will be there. That is my promise to you."

"Why don't George and I stay with you? You can do what you have to, and then we can return together."

Now, it was sink or swim—the big decision. My mind raced. It would be good for me if they went along, my personal bodyguards. But if things went wrong, they could be injured or killed. What if the numbers mean nothing or something I couldn't figure out? Two to one in favor of them not knowing. "No. But thank you. I started this alone, and I want to finish it alone. The worst is behind me."

Jim nodded. George was now paying attention to us.

"It has something to do with the two men who killed Craig," Jim said.

I gulped. Jim was highly intelligent, and now I realized he had other skilled traits. "Yes. For the first few days, that's all I could think about when they weren't several steps behind me. I've played that scene over and over in my mind, hearing the gun crack and watching Craig's body drift backward. I now believe time can be altered. I watched him fall in slow motion. The horror of what I had just seen—his body floating backward toward the ground. He just kept falling and falling." The tears and my nose were flowing. "I wanted to run up there and catch him, and I knew I had time. Before he hit the ground, I wanted to say to him that I loved him. I saw his body land in the soft ferns, and he bounced once. Then I knew he was dead. I screamed so hard inside my ears rang, and I felt dizzy. If I had a gun, they would have been dead. I wouldn't be here today; my life would have been over. I would have lied down beside Craig and killed myself. There, in the middle of nowhere, we would have spent eternity together… the way we were meant to spend our lives. So, please, give me seven days."

"Whatever you need. I don't like it, but you are our friend. You know what you're doing," Jim said.

Do I? What would he say if he really knew? I had a good idea.

"I don't like it either. You need to be with us, plus the fact that something might happen to your new hardware," George said.

"I'll be fine," I said, trying to ease their worries.

George went back to reading. Jim and I were quiet, each thinking our own thoughts. Mine involved my promise and now I had to move faster on my plans. Seven days wasn't much time. If, for some reason I found nothing at the first location, I had planned to go to the second and third over a several-week period, thinking the thought if I had survived the first. If not then I would see Craig sooner. That wasn't really losing, but in another way, it was. The death dealer's real names wouldn't go down in the books for what they had done. Their sentence had been carried out, but I still had to hold court and find them guilty. I had to find their names.

Jim and George insisted we stop and eat dinner before we got to my house. Without saying, it was no fast-food place. They had Dan Map Quest restaurants in the area on the On-Star in the car.

We pulled into the parking lot of the restaurant. "I don't know if we're dressed properly for this place," I said.

"I believe we are. We're not wearing jeans, and they'll accept our business," Jim said.

"Is there anything you do normally?" I asked.

"Yes, every day, but we don't get out much, do we, George?" Jim responded.

George nodded 'no' while looking at the building. "We'd have to travel a couple hundred miles to find something this nice at home."

We ordered our main entrée, and then we were brought a barrage of appetizers. First, a bowl of clam chowder soup, and when the last person finished, that was me, a large basket of specialty crackers and several types of cheese spread. After that, four large baskets of homemade bread and rolls followed by huge plates of house salad. Following that was a plate of oysters, from which I refrained—shrimp cocktail and herring. I was stuffed, and the main course had yet to arrive.

"Guys, I can't keep eating like this. I can feel my body growing as we sit here," I said.

Jim smiled. "Our personal celebration for you."

"Yes, but…." Jim stopped me.

"As long as you have us for friends, you'll never be hungry again."

I said no more, thinking I'm going to get fat.

Jim and Dan had steak, George had prime rib, and I went with the fish special—Mahi-Mahi. It was delicious.

When we finished, George sat back in his chair and moaned. "We're going to have to call a tow truck to get me out of here."

Everyone laughed.

I started digging in my purse, looking for my credit card as I wanted to pay. My wallet was at the bottom. I started with my right hand; grasping the smaller things on top was a bit of a problem. I switched to my left hand, and I was still pawing around with not much better success. I had to use my right hand, and that's what it was for. I couldn't get below the small stack of papers lying on top. I managed to close the fingers on them and removed them. I laid them in my lap, in front of the purse, close to my knees. I returned to the mining job in the purse. Finally, I saw the fingers clamp around it. I could sense Jim was watching me.

"What are you looking for?" he asked.

"This," and I held the wallet out, "now the real hard part."

"Are you doing what I think you're doing?"

"Well, if you think I'm after my card—yes."

"I suggested we stop and eat. I should pay," Jim replied.

"Please, let me get it. After all you've done, I want to do this."

"Alright, but it makes me feel guilty," Jim said.

I shifted in my chair. Before I could respond to what Jim said, I felt the papers slip from my lap and land on the floor. Another test. Could I pick them up? I didn't want to take an extra amount of time trying. At home, it wouldn't have mattered, but in this nice restaurant full of people, it would.

George saw the hesitation on my face. "Here, I'll get it."

I watched George reach down, and in one smooth motion, he got all of them, something I once could do. "Thank you, George," I said.

George slightly frowned when he looked at them. I looked to see what he was looking at—the list of the GPS locations. To my misfortune, that had to be on top. Maybe George wouldn't know what it was, but his frown deepened.

"GPS coordinates," George responded.

It took him all of three seconds to figure out what it was after all I went through trying to do so. I should have known. *Geez*, I thought. George continued to look at the list.

"These numbers are all south of the border and range over quite a distance. I'd say most of the United States."

Holy cow! My next thought was *busted. How am I going to explain this?* I was impressed with George's intelligence, another person I had underestimated. He was always the quiet one of the group. Never assume.

I said nothing. I didn't know where to go from here. I sheepishly looked over to Jim.

"That also has something to do with it. I hope you know what you're doing," Jim said.

"Crap," I said silently. As for the part of knowing what I'm doing, the jury has come in – no way. I'm as lost now as I was out there, and to tell Jim and George that would end it – that couldn't happen.

"How can George and I let you traipse around the country alone?" Jim asked.

"I'm not. I'm trying to figure out who they were. I want the names of the men who killed Craig." I was in the dark grey area there, but it wasn't a real lie. "I made the promise."

That seemed to pacify Jim because he was quiet.

"Have I told you how much I really do appreciate all you've done for me?"

"Yes, more than enough. It's us that appreciate you… I still don't like it," Jim said.

Shoot. He still hadn't let go of it even with my trying to change his thoughts.

362

"I'll be fine." That wasn't a lie. I had two possibilities—figuring it out or having the worst thing happen to me. If so, I would be with Craig, another good place.

CHAPTER 40

I was nervous. The table was set, and the salad, bread, and baked potatoes were ready. The walleye was laid out on the cookie sheet, seasoned, and ready to go into the oven. The wine was poured – I was sipping on my glass, trying to deaden my anxiety a bit. It took much persuasion to talk Jim and George into leaving for home earlier in the day. I told them about Sharon's situation and that I wanted to try and help them. Another thing I had to do alone. That was what they finally conceded to, only after a lot of disagreement.

I had never met Sharon's husband. I didn't know if he was a jerk of some sort or worse. I wasn't worried about my cooking or what he thought of my appearance. What I was nervous about was I didn't want to turn into a blubbering idiot. This wasn't about me. But they both had to know what they'd be losing.

The doorbell rang. I took a deep breath and opened it. There stood Sharon, her husband, and Mia. Mia I wasn't expecting. I had hoped she would be with the babysitter. What I had to say shouldn't be heard by a child.

"Hi! Come in," I said, looking at the three of them.

They made no effort to move. Sharon slowly looked at me from my feet to my head.

"Madie! Look at Madie, Mia. She's tall," Sharon replied.

Mia nodded.

I smiled. "Yes, I had new parts put on this week."

"You look really good, Madie," Sharon said.

I could tell by the tone in her voice she meant it. "Thank you."

"I'm sorry, this is my husband, Kyle," Sharon said.

"Hi, Kyle, it's nice to meet you." I held my right hand out to shake his.

Kyle paused, looking at the artificial hand, and then shook it. "I've heard so much about you. Even for never having met you before, this is also a surprise for me," Kyle said.

I tried to apply just enough pressure against Kyle's hand when we shook. He didn't flinch or grunt, so I guess I did alright. "I know it's a little odd looking—the hand—I hope you're not offended."

"Oh, no, not at all," Kyle said.

Mia stepped up and took my right hand. "It's alright." She held it in her left hand and slid the tiny fingers of her right hand over the top of it. "It really is—it's you. It won't offend people."

My mouth fell open. The wisdom far exceeded the age. I wanted to pick Mia up and hug her forever. She was a special child. I smiled. "Thank you, Mia. I hope everyone sees me as you do."

"They will. You're special." Mia then walked past me into the house.

A sad happiness overcame me. *Not even in your league,* I thought.

The television was turned on for Mia. The three of us sat in the kitchen, drinking wine and talking. With what little I saw of Kyle, he seemed alright, not the jerk I had expected.

We ate, and Mia was back in the family room watching the Disney Channel. So, I started. I had no real plan to follow. "The reason I asked you over for dinner tonight, although this isn't about me, I wanted to tell you my story. Why I'm now the way I am and alone." I started on how Craig and I met and everything we did in our few years of marriage. Then, I started at the beginning of our trip.

"I never said I'll be right back, goodbye, or I love you. I regret that more than anything I've ever done in my life – each and every day. There's never a day that goes by that I don't think about that. I hope Craig forgives me." Now I was crying. They didn't know yet, but they didn't ask. "Each and every single day, I think about him. Each and every single day, I want him by my side. Nothing will ever put right what I did wrong. It's my fault he's dead. I should have yelled and started running; maybe that would have distracted them. But I just stood there. I watched them shoot Craig in the head." I was, again, crying so hard I could barely talk. "My… my life was over from that day on."

I went on and told them the rest and they never spoke. At several different times during my story, Sharon wiped her eyes. I told them all about the death dealers.

"I wanted to die every day I was out there. I wasn't going to let that happen in the hands of them. My promise to Craig was that I would make it out. Now, look at me. Maybe this is Craig's way of getting even with me—or Mother Nature's—or both. I know I deserve it. The guilt I carry consumes me."

Mia walked out into the kitchen and stood by me. I was still crying, and she started to crawl up into my lap, so I helped her. Her tender innocence and act of caring overwhelmed me. I cried harder and hugged Mia to my chest. I didn't want to let her go—my security blanket. "This is why this isn't about me. You have something that is very precious. You have a daughter whose wisdom amazes me. You two obviously still love each other, so don't throw away what you have. Life is too short. What you have could be taken away from you at any time. Every day, all day long, I feel so bad for Craig. I regret so much when it comes to him. I had to learn the hard way. That's the reason you had to listen to my story. What you do from this point on is up to you two. That's all."

I watched Kyle take hold of Sharon's hand. "I don't know what to say. There's nothing to be said that would make you feel any different. One thing I can say is that's unreal." Kyle looked at Sharon.

Sharon was staring at me. "Madie, it's not your fault. The blame lies on those two men. You would have done the same for Craig," Sharon said.

She was right on both counts. The reason I had to try and find their two names. But I said, "Tell that to my conscience – that will never change."

I watched Sharon look at Kyle and smile. Kyle said, "I'd like to start again if that's alright with you. You and Mia do mean the world to me."

Sharon smiled, and I watched the tears form in her eyes. "We want you home tonight," she said.

I had finally done something right.

CHAPTER 41

Sunday morning, I was excited, nervous, and worried. Four thirty a.m., and I was wide awake. Lying in bed, I was thinking of what the day would bring. Good or bad, I was going. The only real plan I had was the route I was going to take to get there. Go east on Interstate 70 and then get on Interstate 85. That would take me up along the coast to Philadelphia. Once I got close, I would let the GPS take over and guide me the rest of the way.

I wasn't worried about driving; my new limbs would get me there. It was the fact that I was starting a new journey. Unlike the long walk through the wilderness where, toward the end, I didn't care what happened to me – this was for Craig. The anxiety was killing me. It was far worse than the pain I felt in the freezing sub-zero weather trying to sleep.

The same question I always kept asking myself during the past weeks—what would I find?

I packed a small bag just in case: an extra pair of blue jeans, one shirt, a toothbrush and toothpaste. That was it. If all went well, I would be back before bedtime.

Six a.m. I was backing out of the garage. My stomach was full of butterflies as I eased the car out onto the street. Then, I put the car into drive. "You can do this, Madie," I told myself.

Two hours max, and I should be there, I thought as I drove away. The worst two hours I will spend since the day I watched Craig die.

I looked back at our home—the best part of my life spent with Craig there. Sadness weighed heavy in my chest. This could be the last time I would see it. If so, I tried. Never returning didn't bother me. Now, it was just a house, a shelter. It ceased being a home without Craig.

Silently, I said goodbye. If fate had it so, this was my last day, and I failed Craig. All wasn't lost; I would be with him.

I turned right at the end of the street. Several more turns and several more miles, and I would be on the interstate.

It was a warm August day with only a few spotted clouds. I kept telling myself it was a good day, but a good day for what? That was to be decided before lunch.

Before I got on the interstate, I stopped at the gas station, went in, and got a cup of coffee—the high-octane—black and the dark roast blend. It wouldn't calm my nerves, and I knew that. I wanted all the caffeine I could get. For some reason, I felt I needed to be on high alert. What good that would do was more than likely a waste. I couldn't outrun a bullet if it came to that. I wasn't in shape to physically outrun another person, nor, in my condition, could I fight. But I still needed all the senses I could obtain. Like before, out in the middle of the wilderness, I wanted to see my attacker. Look them in the eyes; only now ask why. Something I got no answer for out there.

I drove out of the gas station and headed for the entrance ramp to the freeway.

The traffic was heavy but I paid no attention to it. I was in a trance, a self-preservation mode. I had to get to the finish line to see what was there.

The hot coffee went down smoothly. I nearly crushed the Styrofoam cup, popping the plastic lid loose with my new hand. Nervous energy. I left the lid off so I could see if I was distorting the cup each time I lifted it out of the cup holder.

I set the cruise at the seventy-mile-an-hour speed limit. I was on my way.

I rolled the passenger window halfway down. The warm wind blowing in felt good. Mother Nature was being kind, something she wasn't nine months ago.

By the time the coffee was half gone it no longer tasted good. My nerves were a mess. I was scared now, much more than I had been when the death dealers were chasing me. The unknown was far worse. What I could see I could deal with – at the time I ran away – now I was running into it.

An hour passed, and I was trembling inside. If I had a real right hand, it would be shaking. The left one couldn't, and I had my thumb wrapped around the steering wheel in a death grip. The stump of my left palm was aching, as was my left forearm. I tried to ease my grip. I told myself – the sun was shining, it was warm, no bad guys were chasing me – mentally, that didn't help.

An empty train moving through the night, I was the ghost rider. That's what my life felt like right at that moment. The occupants in the cars passing me were totally unaware of what I was going through or what I was trying to accomplish. I didn't care. My life's mission was to try and right the wrong for Craig.

Down inside, I knew Craig wouldn't want me to do this. He was far easier going than me. That's what I loved so much about him. If he was alive, he wouldn't let me do this, but then again, if he was alive, I wouldn't have to.

My mind was packed full of all the things that could happen; they were endless. God might have given me style and grace, but right now, I was sure he didn't give me enough common sense. I was scared to death. I was getting closer.

'What you'll find there will make you richer beyond your wildest imagination.' I remember the death dealer's dying last words. The money meant nothing to me. Craig does, and will, for the rest of my life.

Each time I thought about it, I always thought the worst. Meth labs, money laundering businesses, and even by some far chance, teenage slavery for prostitution. It had to be something very bad, very illegal, to be that lucrative. The second reason I thought was the death dealers weren't honorable men. They had murdered Craig.

So, I had a pretty good idea: I was walking into something I might not be able to walk away from.

So be it – we all create our own problems. I definitely created mine. The unseen wound I have is too deep, far beyond bone depth – this is for Craig.

I got to the city limits on the interstate. I turned on the GPS and watched the numbers slowly click away. Both longitude and latitude were moving in the direction I needed. I had preset the numbers I needed to be at in the GPS at home. I hit the 'Find Location.' Now, a computer voice would tell me when to take the next turn.

I was in the right lane, going slower than the speed limit. A voice in my head said, 'It's not too late to turn around and go back home to the peaceful tranquility of security.' I missed the best part of my life. It was over before it happened, and I had nothing to go back to.

I wasn't sure how many miles I had left to go. It wasn't many but guessing, maybe ten to twenty max. Now I was feeling nauseous, as though I was going to be sick. I started to pull over because I could feel it. I took several deep breaths and made myself relax. That helped some.

I watched the traffic as I drove. I listened intently to the GPS, and for almost two miles, it said nothing, which made it worse.

"Next intersection, turn left," the computer voice said.

I flinched and then made the turn. This was another four-lane road in a business district with stoplights every few blocks. I watched the fast-food joints, gas stations, an occasional strip mall, and other small stores go by.

"Where was this leading me?" I asked myself. To some answers, I hoped.

At the next intersection was another stop light which was red. At the corner was another gas station, and my nerves were working overtime. I felt like I needed to stop, so I pulled in to use the restroom.

I parked the car on the side of the building. The place was relatively busy for mid-morning; half of the twelve pumps were busy. I walked into the store and it was also busy. I went straight to the restroom.

When I walked back out, I wandered through the store. I didn't want anything as I looked at the items on the shelves as I passed by them. The customers, as well as the clerks, were unaware of what I was going through.

I bought a roll of breath mints – for two reasons. One was a token for letting me use their restroom and the other, I guess, was I didn't want the coroner to think I had bad breath. Like I was going to breathe on him after I was dead.

I got in the car. I sat behind the wheel thinking before I started it. Death was always on my mind. Expect the worst, and then when it happens, it won't be so bad.

I dialed Jim's number. If I was down to the last hour of my life I wanted to hear his voice once more. I wanted to say thank you for being there, as he was once again.

"Hello."

"Hi, Jim, it's Madie. Are you out fishing?" I wasn't going to tell him the real reason why I called.

"Yes, caught a few already—Northerns."

"Northerns! I thought your choice of fish was walleyes."

"Well, it still is. An old timer passed through town two weeks ago when I was there. He got to talking about how his mother used to boil it in pickling spice, and then they would dip it in a bowl of melted butter and call it the poor man's lobster. Sounded pretty good, so I thought I'd give it a try. I'll let you know the outcome when you get here."

"Sounds wonderful!" and it really did. I wanted our conversation to go on forever. "Another fish recipe to add to your repertoire."

"Yes, I wonder why I didn't think about it."

"I called to let you know how much I appreciate all that you have done."

Jim cut me off.

"Are you doing what I think you're doing?" he asked.

"Yes," I answered.

Jim was silent. "You don't have to do that. Like I told you, it could be dangerous. It won't change the past or your future."

He was right. But the one thing it could change is how I felt. Right the wrong, for Craig. "I know, but I have to, you know that."

I could see Jim nodding his head yes in the silence. "You're a survivor. Otherwise, I wouldn't have let you go alone. Nonetheless, I still worry about you."

I wiped the tears from my cheeks. "I look forward to spending days with you fishing. It will be relaxing."

In somewhat of a stern voice, Jim said, "If I had my way, you would be now."

"This isn't about me, it's about Craig." I was quiet, thinking, "I think I'll take up hiking when I get there." Then to lighten the conversation, I said, "But only in fair weather, I'm a sissy, you know."

It worked. I heard Jim chuckle, "Yeah, like I'm a city slicker."

That he wasn't. We said goodbye to each other.

I started the car and looked at the GPS. "Time to get this over with," I said.

I drove down the street following numbers that I had no idea what they meant. I was more relaxed after hearing Jim's voice.

Little did I know, lurking in the distance behind me, that a car was following my every move. It knew how to blend in with its surroundings.

This road took me several miles. The traffic lights faded away as did the businesses. Then, I was told to take a right turn, so I did. Within a mile or two, the scenery changed and I didn't like what I was seeing. The residential area faded away. As best as I could, I guessed I was northwest of the downtown. I drove on for several more miles. No voice to tell me what to do.

Now, I was driving through more open areas in a much older part of town. A variety of small businesses stood here and there on each side of the two-lane street. Some sat behind fences with locked gates, and others sat in the open. They ranged from a tire store to electrical repair, auto mechanic, body shop, and even a junkyard.

The traffic remained moderately heavy, and I was thankful it was daytime. No way would I have chosen to do something like this at night. I would be the only car here then, on some deserted, forgotten street until the next day.

Another mile passed before I heard, 'Turn left.'

This street led me into an industrial area. Not the more modern structures with the steel siding, manicured lawns, and the concrete or stone billboard in the front lawn letting one know who they were.

These buildings were from the World War Two era. Several stories tall with brickwork and many individual windows made up the outer walls. A sign hung above the front entrance showing their name.

Many were empty, long abandoned by the previous owner. Now, I really didn't like what I was seeing. What would I do if I ended up at one that looked empty? What if it was locked? Too many 'what ifs,' but I knew that going into this.

I was too busy paying attention to what I was passing by to look at the numbers on the GPS. The next thing I heard was 'destination ahead.' Involuntarily, I almost slammed on the brakes. I was so scared I couldn't breathe. I let off the gas pedal and slowed down. I looked in the rearview mirror to see if there were cars coming up behind me. There was one lone car more than a quarter mile back—if it was of no concern to me.

I looked from building to building as I drove. Now, I was only traveling twenty-five miles an hour. I still expected the worst at any moment. It wouldn't have surprised me to see men run from one of the buildings, yielding guns ready to shoot at me.

That didn't happen, but I was still foreseeing it. Would it happen when I entered one of the buildings? Would I get my answer just before I died? The thoughts continued until I heard the GPS 'destination two blocks ahead.'

I was breathing heavily and had long forgotten about my artificial limbs. My right hand was squeezing the steering wheel with a death grip.

I was moving forward at ten miles per hour. At any moment, I was ready to floor the accelerator and speed away.

It would be no crack house, but a meth lab and a few other options still were a good possibility.

Then, the GPS said, 'Destination obtained.' I stopped in the middle of the street. Of all the things I thought I would see, I wasn't expecting what I saw, not in my wildest dreams. I looked to the right side of the car and then to the left. There were no driveways or buildings, no fences. What I saw was absolutely nothing—an open area all around me. I was still breathing heavily as if I had just finished a 10K race. The closest building was several hundred yards away. There had to be a mistake. How could this be? Did I enter the numbers wrong? I checked them – 40 53 31 latitude, 75 12 25 longitude. They were correct. Even though the GPS read the same numbers maybe it made a mistake, a malfunction somewhere connecting with the satellites.

I needed to get out and stretch; my nerves had my muscles in knots. I could foresee nothing bad happening, so I got out. I walked in front of the car and looked around.

I watched the car come up behind me and then pull around to the side and stop. The man behind the wheel rolled the passenger window down.

"Are you alright?" he asked.

"Yes, I'm fine."

"Are you lost?" he asked.

"No." Just confused, but I didn't tell him that.

"Do you need me to do anything?"

Again, I said, "No."

"Well, have a good day."

I said nothing and watched him drive away.

I looked to both sides of the road again—huge grassy, open areas were all that were there. I decided to get back in the car, drive down the road a few miles, and re-enter the coordinates again.

I did. I turned the car around, pushed the 'find location' button, and drove slowly forward. Within a mile, the voice said, 'Destination ahead.' When I reached the same spot I heard the same thing as before. I stopped. Could there have been some former building here? Now demolished since they had done whatever it was they had done? I rolled the car slowly forward and watched the third digit and then the second on the GPS slowly move over the location. So how could that be? By all indications, what I needed to see was right in the middle of the road. Common sense told me it could be anything to either side of the road, but the coordinates wouldn't be correct.

I stopped the car and backed up. The numbers again matched for the third time. I got out again. Frustrated and mad, I looked around. I looked in the grass on both sides of the road – nothing.

I was deep in thought as I glanced at the asphalt. Nothing but cracks in the well-worn road, which I didn't give much thought to.

I heard a car door shut behind me. I quickly turned to see who it was. It was the same man who stopped before. I hadn't watched where he went when he previously left. Now, mysteriously, here he was again.

"You can't find what you're looking for?" he asked.

"No. I guess it's been removed long ago," I said.

"Are you sure I can't help?"

"No."

"So, you're going back home then?" he asked.

What a strange question to ask, I thought. "I don't see that's any of your business," I said.

"Yes, you're right. Well, I hope you find whatever it is you're looking for. Have a good day."

I watched him drive away. At first, I thought he was strange, maybe even odd. I thought no more of it. I looked around once more. I would pick up the pieces and go home, but the problem was there weren't any pieces to pick up. Then, it hit me—I had failed. The death dealers led me on another chase, and this time, the outcome wasn't good. I leaned up against the car. "I'm sorry, Craig, I failed you."

As I leaned against the car, I looked down at the blacktop, defeated. Something I didn't like. My eyes absently followed a crack across the road as I thought about the death dealer. The more I thought about it, the madder I got. I wanted to call them every name in the book. But that wasn't me; I wasn't made that way. I always lived by the rule—don't get mad, get even. They had gotten away with another one or a continuation of the first one. There would be no restitution for Craig here.

I was in no hurry to drive home. I got back in the car and sat there. I didn't want to leave. Maybe I was just grasping for straws; call it an intuition, but I felt something wasn't right.

I felt sad. "Craig, I need you. I'm slowly dying without you," I said. I wiped a single tear away. I know what he would say if he were here, "Why are you giving up so soon? You're just getting started." I laughed at that thought. He was always pushing me to do better or go faster. I needed him now.

Reluctantly, I put the car in drive and watched the preset numbers on the GPS fade away.

CHAPTER 42

I started driving back to the expressway. All the GPS destinations kept running through my mind. I had memorized all ten cities and their coordinates. I now had a new plan. There was no reason to go home—nothing there but the physical things. I had my check card and visa with me, and the toothbrush and toothpaste, what else did I need; nothing that I could think of. So, I was going to the next closest location—Boston, Massachusetts. 42, 16, 14 latitude, 71, 29, 40 longitude, so I entered those coordinates in the GPS. It even gave me the distance, two hundred and seventy miles. I might be far behind in this race, but it wasn't over. Craig was always right; too early to give up. Maybe whatever was there had been torn down or even burnt to the ground? Or, if the death dealers were doing something illegal and the police or feds had found out about it, they had removed the problem in the past without the death dealers knowing about it. They had been in Canada a long time and things change as time passes.

I felt better as I headed north on Interstate 95. Traffic would be heavy, especially around New York City, which was less than an hour away. I didn't mind, and I was in no hurry. My plan was to find a motel for the night, possibly in Boston, if I decided to drive that far. I had no intention of driving after dark. Then tomorrow, in broad daylight, find the second location.

So, I drove along enjoying the sunny afternoon with the windows rolled down on the car. I had new hopes even though now I had more unanswered questions. With the first location a bust, that answer went to the grave with each death dealer.

I relaxed and let my mind wander. I always thought of the past, and I guess that's because I was trying to figure out the present that had to do with the past. Then I thought about the bear and smiled. I wondered if it had found the fish I left when it woke. If so, I wondered if it remembered me. I will always remember it. I also always wondered if it was a male or female, something else I would never have an answer to. If it was a female, I hope she raised a few cubs this summer that were just like her. If it was a male, well, I hoped it enjoyed doing whatever it is male bears do in the wild.

The last death dealer's words kept haunting me. I remembered all that he had said. It was as fresh as if he had told me an hour ago. What haunted me the worst now was, 'if you're smart enough to figure it out.' Maybe that was the itch I couldn't scratch back there, what I had a funny feeling about and didn't know. The problem is, I still didn't know. How could I be smart enough to figure it out when nothing is there?

I wrote that location off as a lost cause. I had a scared but excited feeling flowing through me about the next one. I could still die, or I could find something. The latter is what drove me on, and I had to know. Curiosity killed the cat; maybe it will be Madie too. I can't fix the past, nor can I fix the future, but I can try to fix the wrong.

As I drove through Connecticut, I decided to call Jim and give him an update on what was going on, no need for him to worry when there wasn't anything to worry about.

The phone rang only once. Jim answered, "Hello."

"Hi, Jim, I called to let you know I'm ok. I found absolutely nothing there."

Jim was quiet. To break the silence, I asked, "So, what are you doing?"

"Well, I just made three gallons of fish soup. I invited everyone over for supper, and you should be here also," Jim answered.

"Fish soup!" I didn't know if that sounded good or not. "Another new recipe?"

"Yes, it's actually quite good. Potatoes, onions, all the fish you want, and half and half for the cream."

Now, it sounded good. "Wow! That does sound good. Your repertoire grows. You should start your own cookbook—Fish only." I heard Jim laugh. He didn't sound as worried about me being alone out here as he had been before. So, I asked, "You don't seem as concerned now as you were when you left?"

Jim was quiet again, and now I knew that meant something. "I'm not going to lie to you. I already knew on the way to the airport that I was hiring a private investigator to follow you. I told him under no circumstances to let anything bad happen to you. He's already called in twice."

That explained a lot, the man coming back and asking the strange question. I should have known that Jim thinks of everything. But never would I have guessed that. "Why do you waste your money on something so useless?"

"You're not useless, Madie. You're my friend, and you mean a lot to me."

How could I be mad at him? I couldn't. "So, is he following me now?"

"Ask me no questions, and I'll tell you no lies."

That meant yes. I didn't have to pursue the conversation any further. "Jim, I'm a big girl. I can take care of myself." In the situation I was in, I wasn't sure, but I didn't want him to know that. "Please, call him off and save your money."

Jim responded, "Just keep driving north. You can be here in a day and a half."

"You know I can't do that; this is for Craig."

"I know, but I still worry."

"You're a good man. I'll call you tomorrow."

I kept looking in the rearview mirror. He was good, always out of sight. The traffic had gotten heavy, and all three lanes were full. I kept trying to remember what kind of car he was driving. At the time, that didn't concern me. All I remember is that it was tan and a four-door. I would remember when I saw it, but I never did.

It was late afternoon but hours before sunset. As I drove north through Connecticut, I started thinking of ways to lose my tail. As I passed each exit ramp, I thought of pulling off and racing through the side streets or even trying to hide behind a restaurant or a gas station. Somehow, I didn't think that would work. He was obviously experienced at what he did then he would be on to me. Once that happened, there would be no escape. "Alright, buddy. I've run from foes much greater than you." I didn't know how yet, but I had plenty of time to think of something. "Just play it cool," I told myself. The difference was they were trying to take my life, and he was trying to prolong it. I didn't need him then, and I don't need him now. I started this journey alone—nine months ago and over a thousand miles away—and I was going to finish it alone. I did appreciate what Jim was doing for me, but, in the end, I would save him money.

Downtown Boston wasn't far away. I was in the middle of Providence, Rhode Island, on 95. The green overhead billboard said Boston 50 miles. I would have time to sightsee or even shop. I didn't know my way around the city, so I would take a cab and do it the easy way. Then, it hit—the idea I was looking for—out of the clear blue, and it was so simple. Sometime in the middle of the night, I would call a cab, walk out of the motel, and disappear. How simple it would have been there, in the wilderness, if I could have done that. I would still have my hands and feet.

I have to have a rental car to continue on. Once I got to my room, I would call and reserve one.

I was in the motel room and all had gone well. I stayed on the south side of the city. Not knowing which direction the GPS would take me the next day, there was no need to double back. I was tired of driving, hungry and I needed a drink, possibly two. I chose a large twelve-story, top-of-the-line motel. The greater amount of people made it easier to blend in.

When I parked my car, I got my small bag and removed the GPS from the dash. It would be a while before I returned to my car. I decided not to leave the motel, and shopping was out. To call a cab now would give him ideas he didn't need to have.

I brushed my teeth, fluffed my hair, and headed for the bar.

I sat at the end of the bar where I could see the entrance. Watching the people walk by I would remember what he looked like if he chose to be bold.

Halfway through my second drink, he was. I watched him walk in and directly up to me. He smiled and sat down next to me. From my past experience, I wanted to get up and run; common sense told me he meant no harm.

"Hi, I'm Wes," he said. He held his hand out to shake mine.

I was a bit offended. "Do you want the artificial hand or the one that's grossly disfigured?" I said as I held out both hands.

That startled him. He didn't know; maybe he would leave.

"You already know, Jim told me. No need to play hide and seek anymore. To answer your question, it doesn't matter. Whatever you feel more comfortable with."

He recovered quickly, and I dropped both hands. "No sense in getting friendly. We won't be around each other too long."

"So you're not going to let me help you?" Wes asked.

"No."

"Jim said you would say that, but I had to ask, you know."

Deep down, Wes didn't seem that bad of a guy. "So, how did you know I was in here?"

"I watched you walk in here," he answered.

He was good, I never saw him. I eased up on my attitude, and I had a new plan. As long as he didn't know, I wanted him to think I was a poor, helpless woman. "So, if that's not enough to freak you out, wait until you see this." I swiveled in my bar stool, facing him. I held up both legs just enough so when I pulled up my jeans, he could see the poles that were my legs. "You've got me; I can't even run away from you."

"Bad accident?"

Wes slowly looked at me, from my feet up to my face. I don't think he believed that. I shrugged my shoulders, "So now what?" I asked.

"That's up to you. I was paid to follow you and make sure no harm comes to you. Whatever it is you're doing, I'll help."

"Yes, I found that out. But I don't need your help. Jim is just wasting his money."

"That's for him to decide."

"Maybe so, but I have some say so in this."

"So what you're saying is you don't want me around."

"I prefer the hide-and-seek method. If you can't seek, Jim will no longer pay you."

I got up out of my bar stool, I decided I would order food from room service. "Have a good life."

"What makes you think I'll never see you again," Wes replied.

I smiled as I walked away with my back to him so he couldn't see. He was smart.

"Just so you know, I have my ways."

So do I. Compared to the death dealers, you're nothing. I didn't respond to him. I didn't wave; I just walked away.

In my room, I ordered food since I was starving. I was hard on Wes; he was just doing his job, and Jim was just worried about me. I wasn't upset with either of them.

While waiting for the food to be delivered, I called the car rental company and rented a mid-sized car. The only place that was going to be open in the middle of the night was out at the airport. I told them I would be there around three a.m.

The alarm clock on the nightstand next to the bed went off at two a.m. I got up and took a shower. The motel's shampoo and soap would do for one day, better than nothing. While in the shower, I thought a motel as nice as this would have a shuttle service to the airport. No need to call a cab and draw any extra attention. Without a doubt the shuttle bus had come and gone throughout the night. Hopefully, Wes would be in the back, where I parked the car, watching it.

While I dressed I made a pot of coffee and dried my hair, both provided by the motel.

I couldn't help but think about Wes. Was he sleeping in his car with one eye open, watching for me? Good chance he was. After four hours of sleep, I felt pretty good. I had time to kill, so I got in the elevator and rode it down to the fourth floor. From there, I found a stairway at the end of the building facing the parked cars in the back. To my surprise, there was a window looking out on each floor. Now, I didn't have to wander around the parking lot looking for his car. I had to mess with him and let him know that I had dealt with better adversaries than him. If he was sleeping in his car, I was going to wake him, laugh and tell him I was just checking on him, making sure he was ok.

Slowly, I looked at each car, and there were dozens. I started at the row of cars closest to the building. When I got to the end of the row, I started on the next one. After several minutes, I found it—a tan Ford. I was positive it was his, parked three rows away from mine and off to the side. I studied it for a while, but he wasn't in it.

For some reason, I didn't think he was far away, so I went back to my room. I found a piece of paper and wrote on it. Then I went out to the parking lot. Quietly, I walked to my car. I had parked it in the last row, along the grass and bushes. I put the note on the windshield under the wiper blade with the writing facing out. He would see it and read it, and I would be long gone.

I started to leave, but something glistening behind my car caught my eye. Quietly, I took several steps to the back of my car. A shiny strand of something suspended in the air reflected the light. I looked closer. I couldn't believe what I was seeing. If I hadn't spent the time with Jim out on the lake, it would have taken me longer to figure out what it was. Instantly, I knew—fishing line. It ran from the back of my car out into the darkness of the bushes. I looked closer still. The line was tied around a magnet, and the magnet was stuck to my license plate, his way of knowing when I left, or so he thought. I wasn't sure if he was sleeping somewhere out there in the dark or if he had some sort of warning system to wherever he was. It didn't matter. I smiled. 'Not this time. I've outrun worse,' I said to myself. Without making a sound, I walked away.

I went to the lobby, checked out of my room and asked for a ride to the airport car rental. I was told the driver would be in front in a few minutes.

I stood at the front door, holding my one small travel bag. As I waited, I kept looking behind me. Not a single person showed up.

The shuttle pulled up in front. I walked out and got in before the driver had time to get out. If he didn't see this, I was gone. Besides, how could one man watch both ends of the building? As we drove away I couldn't help but look behind. This time of the night, there was no other traffic. That was helpful. We drove over a half mile, and we were alone.

I sat back and relaxed. Now, on to the finish line – alone – just as it had started.

Twenty minutes later, we pulled into the Hertz Car Rental. I removed a twenty from my wallet. "Thank you. I'm sorry I got you out so early," and I handed him the money.

He smiled. "Thank you," he said, emphasizing each word.

I got in the car, plugged the cord of the GPS into the cigarette lighter and stuck the suction cup on the dash. Now, the GPS was looking at me. I turned it on, hit 'enter,' and waited for it to calculate the coordinates. It was far too early and way too dark to go looking. I used another function on it. I typed in restaurants, and within seconds, it told me of all the eating establishments in the surrounding area. I found a waffle house less than five miles away.

On my way in, I bought a newspaper, I was going to be here awhile. I drank several cups of coffee before ordering food. During that time, I read the first section of the paper. I tried to waste all the time possible before the waitress became upset with me.

Two eggs over easy with ham, hash browns, and whole wheat toast. I wasn't sure I could eat all that food, but it would run the bill up, giving me an excuse to tip her generously.

Another hour passed, and it was nearly five-thirty. The place was starting to fill up with customers. Now was the time to leave before I wore out my welcome. I left another twenty lying on the table when I left.

Within the hour, it would be light out. I sat in the car thinking. I hoped Jim wouldn't be too mad at me for what I did. I wasn't mad at him; he was just trying to protect me. I put the car in drive and headed for the exit. A voice automatically said, 'Turn left.'

Before I got on the interstate, I pulled into a gas station. I didn't need any more coffee, but I needed to use the restroom. Then I returned to the rental car and sat. I needed to waste more time; I needed daylight.

I thought back to all the times, lying there in the snow, shivering and aching so bad from the cold I couldn't stand it, waiting for the sun to rise. Only to get up and struggle through the day, being so cold and aching so badly I didn't think I would see nightfall. I looked down at my right hand. Nothing ached now except for my heart, and that wasn't from the cold.

I watched the sunrise, and it was peaceful. How long would it be before Wes figured out I wasn't coming back for my car? It didn't matter.

My phone rang, and I looked at the caller ID. It wasn't Jim. "Hello?"

"I read your note."

It was Wes. He must have read my mind, but I knew it wouldn't take him long.

"That wasn't nice," he said.

I smiled. "The part about leaving the note or the fact that I'm long gone?"

"Go back to Mayberry! Where's that?" Wes said, somewhat disgusted.

"Where you're from. Remember what I told you? We wouldn't be seeing that much of each other. I don't need you."

"Other people think so."

"Yeah, well, not me. I escaped two men that would make you look like a novice, no offense to you." I listened to the silence on the other end. "Were you fishing last night? Obviously, you didn't catch anything. You should have tied it to my car and the other end around your neck, and then I could have gone trolling."

"I underestimated you. That has always worked in the past."

"Wes, you seem like a nice guy. Go back to Mayberry or wherever you're from."

Wes was silent again, probably trying to figure out why he failed.

"Another thing I said last night. If you can't seek, Jim won't have to pay you. I'm sorry if I've been hard on you. I don't hold anything against you, but I have to do this on my own. Jim didn't tell you the story, and I'm not going to. Have a good life." I hung up the phone, started the car, and drove away.

After twenty-five minutes of following the directions from the GPS, I was almost there. Only this time, I was on a four-lane highway. The traffic was heavy due to the morning rush hour. I was west of town on Hwy 2. Every mile or so, there was a traffic light. Huge buildings sat far apart on each side of the highway on their well-groomed, expansive acres. I didn't bother to see what kind of businesses they were or their names since that wasn't my concern. The numbers were.

'Destination ahead.' I slowed down and got dirty looks and grimaces from the drivers as they went around me. This time, I had a feeling it was going to be one of the businesses. I would walk in the front door and ask what kind of service they performed or provided and go from there.

'Destination reached,' the GPS said. I wasn't expecting it so soon. I turned on the right blinker, pulled over to the shoulder, and stopped. I looked left and right. "You've got to be kidding me!" I yelled as I hit the steering wheel with both hands. No buildings, no driveways, just open road. I looked at the GPS, and the third number was off a few digits. I looked in the side mirror but the traffic was too heavy to back up – but I did anyway. I put the passenger's side of the car over on the grass. This gave me a good four feet of clearance from my car to the traffic.

I only had to back up fifty yards, and then the numbers matched. I stopped, and this time, I said quietly, "You've got to be kidding me." This didn't make sense, any of it. Something had to be wrong with the GPS coordinates. I sat on the side of the road, oblivious to the cars speeding by me. I looked around and saw nothing. It was almost identical to the first spot. I turned on the emergency flashers and got out. Even though I was blaming the GPS for being wrong, it wasn't. Today's sophisticated electronics don't lie. I was now beginning to think the death dealer did. What could be so important in these two spots when there was nothing there? I stood in front of my car, trying to think of something, anything that connected the two locations. The only thing they had in common was nothing. I looked for a storm drain, a manhole cover – anything out of the ordinary. The only thing I saw was an empty pop can and a piece of paper. I picked that up. It had been there so long the ink was faded. I walked to the back of the car, but nothing. I leaned against the car, and my phone rang. "Who in the world is calling me," I said frustrated. It had to be Jim checking on me. The caller ID showed otherwise. "Hello," I said in a disgusted tone.

"You must have known; it's me. You sure sound like it."

It was Wes. "Now, what do you want?" I asked.

"I know you don't think much of me, and that's ok. I called to tell you I'm sorry for treating you the way I did and for what happened to you. I called Jim since we talked and he told me your story. I'm truly sorry."

I was quiet, wondering how much Jim had told him.

"Sounds like you're on the side of the road somewhere."

"Yes."

"Any success this time?"

"No!"

"You sure you don't want my help?"

"No, I can take care of myself."

"Yes, I have no doubt about that."

"Wes, I'm sorry for calling you a novice. You didn't deserve that; you're not."

"Compared to you, I am."

"And I'm sorry for treating you so badly last night."

"So we're even?" he asked.

"Yes."

"OK then, I'll buy lunch."

I laughed. "I don't think so. It would be harder for me to lose you next time." While I was talking with Wes, my eyes followed a perfectly straight crack in the road, from the gravel to the painted white line in the center of the road. There, it stopped, and so did my thoughts.

I hung up with Wes. I drove down to the next light, less than a half mile away, and turned around. I reset the GPS and headed back in the direction I had come from and watched the numbers. As I drove past the same spot, the numbers didn't match. Whatever had been there was definitely on the other side.

I had to use the restroom again, so I started looking for a restaurant. Within a few miles, I found one. I went in, used the facilities, and then sat at a table and drank more coffee. The reality was hitting home hard. I was on a wild goose chase, and I was losing so bad that I couldn't even see the goose; it was so far ahead. I could see the dead death dealer sitting on the ground, leaning against the cliff and laughing at me. I was getting closer to calling him all the names I could think of. I still had that nagging feeling that something wasn't right, so I didn't. I was beginning to think I wasn't smart enough.

I sat in the booth alone, staring at the wall for a long time, thinking of all the possibilities I could have found. I wasn't planning on what I had found. Now, I had to make a decision. I had two choices: give up and go home, giving the death dealers' names a free ride through eternity, or take one more chance. I wasn't ready for the previous to happen. I was down, but I wasn't out. I still had one more strike to go. If I found the same thing at the next location, they won. The next closest location on the list was Chicago, Illinois. It would be a day-and-a-half drive. On the scale of time in my life, that was nothing. For Craig, it was everything. I paid my bill and went to the car. Rental or not, it's what I was driving there. By some chance, Wes didn't return to Mayberry; I didn't need him hassling me. I got in, and then I called Jim.

"Hello, Madie. Will we see you in another day?"

Sometimes, caller ID is a bad thing. "No. The reason I called is the second location didn't tell me anymore than the first. I have to check one more for my peace of mind. It's a good day's drive or more."

"So, are you going to tell me where? I'll still worry but at least I'll know where to come looking for you if something happens."

"Are you going to sick Wes on me?"

"No, I sent him home."

"Well, then, yes. West Chicago. I hope to find something there for Craig's sake."

"So do I. Can I fly down and be with you? I don't like the idea of you being alone."

383

"Thanks, Jim, I'll be ok."

"The rest of the crew is getting anxious for you to get here. They have several things planned."

Now, I was curious. "What?"

"A three-day hiking trip with a fishing tournament while doing so. George wants some redemption from the last one."

"George, how's he doing? Has he got the technical stuff figured out yet?"

"Oh, yes. He's ready for you."

We said goodbye, and I headed for Chicago.

43
CHAPTER

The trip to Chicago was uneventful, just the way I wanted it. I drove straight through, which was nearly seventeen hours, with only necessary stops gas and bathroom breaks. Junk food and drinks were my diet. I ate because I was bored, nervous, and frustrated. Now, it was past midnight, and I was tired.

I drove north on Interstate 294, and that's what the GPS told me to do. I saw several signs for motels at the O'Hare Airport exit. It looked as good as any to stop and stay for the night.

I pulled into the Sheridan, parked the car and carried my one little bag with me to the reservation desk. Now, I wished I had packed better. I went all those weeks trying to escape death in the same set of clothes. It didn't bother me now that I had to go a few days but being in public, around people, did. They would think I wasn't right, some sort of a crazy lady. In a way, they would be right on both assumptions. Surely, I had to be crazy for what I was doing, running around the country looking for ghosts, sent on a wild goose chase by a dead man – three, actually. Two of which I wanted to crucify, the third for redemption – myself – I was trying to redeem myself.

I got the room key, headed for the elevator, and pushed the up button. The first thing I was going to do was take a long hot bath. Soaking in the water, I hoped, would take the stiffness away.

While I soaked neck-deep in three-fourths of a tub of hot water, my thoughts were consumed in the ten locations. I was missing something. Maybe these spots were just clues to something else. What if I was too involved in looking for some kind of a physical structure? I thought back to the first locations. I had looked around fairly thoroughly, I thought. The dying death dealer did say, "If you're smart enough to figure it out." That's what haunted me: the way he said it and the tone he used. Was it because he knew he was about to die, and this was his only way to get even? I didn't think so. Why, then, didn't he just tell me? I had the answer for that because he was a vile man, cruel to the center of his bones and then some, far beyond his physical being. My body was feeling better, but mentally, I was no better off.

Lying in bed, I was warm, safe and secure. I felt myself dozing off. Maybe tomorrow the next spot would produce something. How could three spots in a row be nothing? Just before I fell asleep, I thought, *If I were standing next to his dead body, I would kick the crap out of him until I resurrected him from the dead and got some answers.'*

I woke. No alarm clock and no wake-up call. When I fell asleep, I had told myself I had to get up early, and I did, five forty a.m. No daylight, but my internal clock was still functioning.

I made a pot of coffee which had become my only staple most mornings. I didn't feel like eating, but then again, I didn't feel like much. Less than five hours of sleep, and I felt a little sluggish. How many times had I felt this way then? To add to that feeling, I ached physically; I was gone. I was frozen, yet I managed to go on. I had no reason to complain now, and I was too close. The end—good or bad—was today; I had to finish this.

I put on the same wrinkled clothes. They weren't dirty, and they didn't smell, so for now, they would do. Another day without a little make-up wouldn't. I called down to the front desk and asked where I could find a store – a Target or a mall – anything that would sell what I needed. To my surprise, I was told that the motel kept a supply of just about everything needed. This close to the airport they catered to their guests. Someone was always left without their luggage, a common everyday thing.

I re-attached my legs and hand, got dressed, and waited for the knock on my door. They wouldn't be long in delivering what I needed.

Now I felt whole again. Make-up applied and limbs attached, I was ready to find my answers.

I checked out. As I walked out to the rental car, the sun was just starting its early morning climb up in the sky. The temperature was just right, cool but not cold. The air had a clean, crisp aroma to it. It was a good day, and I was ready.

I started the car and pushed the on button on the GPS. I took a deep breath to relax, which worked, but only momentarily. By the time I turned the car onto the road, anxiety was back.

I knew the routine by now; the GPS and I got along fine. I no longer stared at it. The early Wednesday morning rush hour traffic was already flowing, something I remembered combating in a former life. Maybe one day I would return to work – maybe. For now, I had more than enough. Everything Craig and I bought with loans, the house and both cars, were set up with an insurance policy. If one of us were to die, everything was automatically paid off. I had the life insurance money also, a great deal at that, which was another thing Craig insisted on. At the time, I told him he was crazy; nothing was going to happen to either of us, but old age, I had said. It turned out I was the one who was crazy. I've recalled Craig's words many times, 'You never know. Better to have it and not need it than to need it and not have it.' Never in my wildest dreams had I thought it would have resulted in this.

I watched the traffic and the landscape as I drove along, turning when told to do so. I kept my mental bearings. Now northwest of the city, more north than west and my trek never took me off major highways.

The GPS told me to turn right at the next intersection, and I did. I looked at the new surroundings. This road was a two-lane major road. I was now heading east on 176. In less than a mile, I drove through a small town called Wauconda. Then I saw a sign that said Lakewood Forest Preserve, two miles away. Traffic had become moderate. The residential area supported houses, just not as many as the inner city. Another mile passed. 'Destination ahead.' I panicked, I froze, and I couldn't believe what I just heard. The GPS said that I had one more mile to go, which would put me in the Forest Preserve. That couldn't be good, no buildings, no houses, nothing but trees. I had a bad feeling, "This can't be happening," I said. My good day was going bad fast, and I wasn't even there yet. I slowed down to prolong what I had a good idea of what was coming.

I started into the Preserve, as I knew nothing but huge trees. What I didn't know was how far to the other side, but it didn't matter. What I was looking for was going to be somewhere in here. Going no more than ten miles an hour, I turned on the emergency flashers and waited. Then I heard, 'Arrived at Destination.' I stopped in the middle of the road and shook my head. I looked around, "Are you serious?" Trees… nothing but trees. A few cars went by while I sat there. I didn't know what to do. My mood was quickly going into the tank. His words came back to me, again, for the umpteenth time, 'See not what you see, see what you don't.' My feelings instantly turned to anger. "What in the hell is that supposed to mean?" I yelled loudly. I slammed my right fist onto the dash three times, much harder than I thought. What I saw on the dash surprised me, an indentation the size of my fist and it didn't even hurt. My artificial hand turned into a bionic. "What am I supposed to see?" I said, still yelling. I looked to the right side of the car and then to the left side. Nothing that Mother Nature didn't put there. No way could the death dealers have been here. I wish they were here now; I'd hang them from the trees, only I'd do it the slow, painful way. I wouldn't put the knot at the side of the neck where it snaps the bone, causing instant death. I'd put it in the back of the neck, behind the head, where they kick and squirm in the air while they suffocate to death. I felt some life go out of my body, and my shoulders sank. Ten pounds was just added to my body. I sat there, trying to make some sense of this, but there was none to make. I got out of the car. This was my last chance, and I failed, but I wasn't ready to leave yet. I walked behind the car and looked around. Failure wasn't an option; it was reality. As I paced up and down the road in short distances, I was feeling worse. I wanted to cry, but I wasn't giving in to them. In the end, they had beaten me, as Mother Nature did, slowly and painfully. The knot was placed behind my head, and I was suffocating, doing it while I was breathing. Then I walked to the front of the car, and everything looked identical to what was behind the car – nothing. I could no longer hold back what I was feeling—grief and failure for Craig. My eyes started to water. The man I loved so much, who I'd have given my life, I couldn't repay him. So much love, so much loss. I started crying so hard I couldn't hold myself up. I dropped to my knees in front of the car. As I continued to cry, I sat down on the gravel on the side of the road. I leaned back against the bumper, drew my knees up to my chest, and laid my head on my knees. Gasping, I said, "Craig, I made a promise I couldn't keep. This one I can't finish without you. I feel you watching and I know you're upset. I want one last hug, to look you in the eyes and say I love you and goodbye. I don't know if you'd want that. If not, who would blame you? I'm certainly not the one to be judgmental after letting them kill you." I couldn't breathe. The lever on the trap door was about to be pulled. I felt that I was the most worthless person alive. "There's nothing left for me to do. If you were here, you'd figure something out, but you're not." I was staring at the ground, thinking of the past. Over and over, my mind continued to play the scene when the death dealer shot him. I continued to look at a piece of electrical wire sticking out of the gravel while doing so. The strands of copper had been stripped of their plastic protective coating. I kicked at it with the heel of my left foot as I cried. The only thing that ever truly meant anything to me and I couldn't bring justice to him.

As time passed, I quit crying, and several cars passed. My mind had shifted into neutral, and my body was numb. Time was lost. I didn't want to leave the last connection of hope for Craig, but there was no hope.

I continued to drag the heel of my shoe back and forth over the wire, a piece of scrap that somehow managed to bury itself in the side of the road. I thought of nothing as I kicked the gravel loose and pushed it away. The bare end of the wire was probably from the snowplows in the winter, scraping the end each time it passed over it. I wasn't thinking about the wire, probably just a short length, as I continued to work at it. Idle time it was just a vent for what I was feeling. Some people smoke when they're worried or nervous. Right now, my relaxant was the wire. I had several inches of gravel removed, thinking it would become free at any moment. When it did, I would get up and leave and return home for the rest of my life.

A car stopped in the opposite lane. The man driving rolled down the window, "Ma'am, are you alright?" he asked.

My eyes had to be puffy from all the crying, and my cheeks red. "Yes, I'm fine."

"Are you sure? Has your car broken down? Do you need some help?"

"No, the car is fine. I'm fine, really." I could see that he didn't believe me.

"Well, why are you sitting on the side of the road in front of your car?"

"Just looking for something that isn't here."

"What was supposed to be here?" he asked.

He was asking a lot of questions. I would never see him again, so I told him, "An answer for my husband."

"Why didn't he come and look?"

"Because he's dead." That did it, and he asked no more questions.

"I'm sorry, be careful."

He drove away. I continued to sit in the dirt, thinking of all the feelings I was feeling—anger, frustration, sadness, loneliness, guilt; the list went on. I could see that I was ruining my shoe. I continued to put a great deal of pressure on it as I dug the gravel away. It was just a stupid shoe; it could be replaced. I wanted that piece of wire. By now, I had dug a ten-inch-long trench. The closer to the road it got, the deeper the wire went. I had to have that wire. I started crying again, and I couldn't even do this right. I kept thinking it would become loose any minute. I got up and walked into the woods. I looked around for a big enough dead stick to use as a pick. I couldn't stop crying and wiped my nose on my sleeve – I didn't care.

When I returned, I dropped onto my knees and wiped my eyes on the other sleeve. With both hands, I drove the stick into the ground, breaking as much dirt loose as possible. Each blow only resulted in a small handful of dirt. With each drag of the stick out of the trench, I was so involved in what I was doing that I didn't notice I was piling the dirt up on my lap. I continued to jab and drag, and I continued to cry. People say they believe me—the two FBI men, the crew up north, Sharon and Kyle—but I would never have real proof.

Ten minutes had passed, and my arms were aching. The trench had only become a foot and a half long, but it was now over a foot deep, and it was angling down at a steep rate. I stopped to rest. The trench was still a good three feet from the road. While I rested I studied the end of the wire, four large strands inside a thick black casing. The end that was exposed to the elements was brittle. I peeled the outer casing away. Inside was one red, one black, one white, and one green. I thought that was odd. The first thought that came to mind was the DOT had placed this here for the automatic counter that counted cars as they passed by on the road. But why would they do that on a small secondary road? I ruled that out, plus it was too deep. By the looks of it, it was running under the road.

I had quit crying. I dug as though I was possessed. The dirt had spilled off my lap and was now piled up on both sides of my legs. Still I was getting nowhere, just a deeper hole. Then it hit like a ton of bricks. "See not what you see; see what you don't." Those were his words; maybe there was something under the road. I had no idea what, but there had to be something there, something that couldn't be seen. I stood and walked out onto the road. Then I saw it again, a straight crack – more like a manmade seam. I had seen it at the previous spots, it just didn't register. It ran from the side of the road to the center. I followed it, and at the center, it made a ninety-degree turn and ran down the center of the road. Roughly thirty feet down, it made another ninety-degree turn and ran back to the same side of the road. Now, standing twenty feet behind my car, I realized there must be something down there. Hidden in plain sight, under asphalt, where no one would find it. I had to know. What if I was wrong? So what? I needed a better tool, and I wasn't leaving until I knew. I went back to the hole I had started digging, replaced the dirt, and packed it back in place by walking on it. I was going to find someplace to buy a shovel. While I was gone, I didn't want anyone to notice what I had done.

I looked at the clock on the radio when I had left. I looked at it now when I returned and found one hour and twenty-seven minutes had passed. It took me longer to find a place to buy a shovel than I thought. It seemed to me it took approximately thirty minutes. Time flies when something good comes one's way. That was a presumption on my part, but I was hoping. I left the car running and turned the emergency flashers on. I got out of the car and retrieved the new shovel from the back seat. As I walked to the spot where I had started, I wondered how this would work – operating the shovel. My left hand with only the thumb to grip the handle, and my right hand, well, I wasn't sure. If I could close the fingers around the handle and keep them locked in place would be the next test.

At times, I was so involved in removing the dirt that my right hand would slip down on the handle. I was forgetting, mentally, to maintain muscle contractions on the pressure pad. I dug, but the excavation was slow. My left hand offered little to no use at all. Many times, I would use my left forearm to lift the heavy end of the shovel out of the hole. Still, it was slow going. Several times, I had only half of a shovel full of dirt, but I didn't care. I was excited and anxious to see if anything was there. I was working my way down the wire, and I lost track of the time. The trench was still two feet from the road and three feet was opened up behind me. Now, I was over thirty inches down into the ground.

Midday traffic was light, and I was glad for that. The few cars that had passed by continued on. I had an answer ready if one would stop and ask what I was doing. I would tell them that I worked for the state doing a routine maintenance check. The car had out of state plates on it, and if they would notice, I had an answer for that also.

The gravel had turned into clay, and it was hard. The trench was one shovel width wide. Now I was on my knees, leaning over, trying to dig. I tried to jam the shovel deep into the ground, with each strike, as hard as I could. The clay didn't give much, a handful of dirt at a time. I'd pick and scrape the dirt back several times before I had a pile big enough to remove from the trench. The sun was high in the sky, and the temperature was in the mid-eighties. I was sweating and panting, breathing at a rate that was one step away from inhaling rapidly.

One foot away from the road, the trench leveled out just over three feet deep as I followed the wire. Digging was exceeding my physical capability.

I stopped to take a breather and assess the situation. My next plan of action was to take the easy route, start back at the top of the ground for the last foot, and dig toward the asphalt. When I reached the edge, I would continue down. It seemed like a good plan. The finish line was still the same, but the dirt had to go away.

How quickly I had forgotten how easy it was to sink the shovel into the gravel compared to the clay. I reached the edge of the asphalt in what seemed to me in record time. The trench was only eight inches deep, and I started going straight down. On another foot, I hit the clay again. No sign of anything other than more dirt. So now, at somewhere around two and a half feet deep, I stopped for another break. My body was starting to ache. I saw nothing. I had two choices, well, three, actually. One was to start digging under the road, the second to continue going straight down and the third choice wasn't an option, not yet anyway – quit and go home. I chose number two. No more than a foot, and I would reach the wire.

The clay was miserable, dense, and moist. It would stick to the shovel. Many times, I had to lift the shovel out of the trench and hit it on the ground to break the dirt loose. Finally, I reached the wire. To my dismay, it made a sharp ninety-degree turn, running straight down into the ground. I was starting to get tired.

I stood up and stretched, letting the blood flow back into my legs. The what-ifs were racing through my mind. There were too many. One, it was much deeper than I could dig; two, it was further under the road; and three, there was nothing here. I wasn't ready for number three.

I started back at the edge of the asphalt. Now, as I dug down, I was angling in under the road. By the time I was a foot down, I was almost a foot in under the edge of the road. I dug on.

A car stopped. This time, a woman was driving. I hid my left hand.

"Do you mind if I ask what in the world you're doing?"

I smiled. "No, not at all. I work for the DOT. We randomly pick roads to see how they hold up under conditions. Then, we study the sub-structure to see what works and what doesn't." I smiled again, trying to play the part. It sounded good, anyway.

That pacified her. "Ok, good luck."

I watched her drive away. I went back to studying the substructure with the shovel. By now, I was getting so thirsty I couldn't swallow. I didn't think of water when buying the shovel. I ignored it. I told myself it was just a thing. From lack of a good grip, my left hand slid on the wooden handle each time I jammed it in the dirt. I was getting a large blister on what was left of my palm and a small one on the inside of my thumb, but the pain didn't stop me; I dug as if my life depended on it. My sanity sure did. If I did find something, whatever it was, I would never remove the guilt.

Now, I was down to the level of the trench where I had left off, a good two feet under the road, and still nothing. I was growing despondent. I looked at my left hand. No longer were the blisters there; they had been torn open. Ripped pieces of flesh split open, and blood was oozing. One of the tears went deep. The skin was weak from the extreme surgery it had gone through. It would probably never be the same. Now, from this, it had a long way to heal again, but I hadn't called it quits yet. I took a few minutes to rest, but I had to go on.

I started digging again. I was practically lying on my chest on the ground to reach the bottom. I dug another six inches down and was just about at the limit I could go. With two more weak jabs of the shovel, the pain in my hand was becoming unbearable. I felt like crying; I was losing. Anger won out. I gripped the shovel with my right hand, and with all the strength I had, I thrust it back into the dirt. 'Clank.' To my surprise, it struck something I didn't expect. Could it be a rock or some sort of foreign object? I was hoping not. Now, with newfound energy, I went back to digging. After nine or ten partial shovels full of dirt, I could see something. I wasn't sure what it was, but it wasn't a rock. I dug more. Now, I had several exposed inches of metal. I was going down the side of it, right beside the wire. Then, after four more inches deeper, I stopped. I went back to the spot where I had found it. I dug the dirt away, moving up. It didn't take long to find where it had stopped, and then I dug in under the road. Soon, I found a horizontal surface. I had the corner of a large metal box. I had no idea how deep the vertical wall went down, but I did have a good idea of how far it went underneath the road—the reason for the straight seam running perpendicular down the middle of the road. I wanted to stand up and dance around, whooping and hollering, but I was too tired. I ached, and my hand burned unbearably. I stood there thinking about what I had found. I still had no clue, but I had found something. "See not what you see; see what you don't." His words echoed in my head. I smiled.

I walked to the far end, thirty feet away. I wanted to dig down there to see. I couldn't use my left hand; it wouldn't let me. It was shot, already used far beyond its limits. *Now, what do I do,* I thought. *Where do I go from here?* Now, I wished I had let the doctors remove my left hand. An artificial hand in place of it and I could go on, but that wasn't the case. Who could I call for help? If I told them I wanted to dig up the road, they would think I was crazy. I had proof, just not enough. It would take someone who I didn't know, who was high up in authority, to give permission to do what needed to be done. Even then, I wasn't sure if one would need a permit or some sort of legal document from a judge to dig up government property. The DOT wouldn't like, that I did know. I was still as lost as when I started. Someone, somewhere, would listen; I just had to find that person. Still standing at what I thought was the opposite end, I had to have more proof. Now, I wished Jim and the gang were here; at least, they would help dig.

Then, I had an idea. A metal detector, surely it, would detect that much metal down there, which was roughly four feet from the surface.

It took a lot of work and twenty minutes to replace the dirt. Holding the shovel handle with my right hand, I used my legs to help push the dirt back. My left hand was done, now it was burning so bad I couldn't stand it.

I started the car and used the GPS to locate the nearest motel—seven point eight miles. I started driving. I was worn out; every muscle I had left was either aching or stiff. I could hardly hold up both arms to steer; my lower back ached severely, and so did both legs. I hadn't worked that hard in a very long time for that length of time. I was dirt and grime from head to toe, and I believed I could plant potatoes in my hair. Each time I moved my head I could feel dirt fall out of it. My left hand was the biggest casualty. The blood had dried into a thick cake on it and the dirt added in made it look much worse than it really was. But the open raw flesh still burned. I followed the directions. Mentally I made a list – shower, new clothes, food, along with a gallon of water, find a store to buy a metal detector, bandages, and the most difficult thing of all – find someone who would help me. I had a huge order to fill before the day was out. It was already past three thirty. I wanted someone there tomorrow to start the process, whatever it took to dig up the road, with perhaps a large machine of some sort. The permission from whoever would be the slow process.

CHAPTER 44

I drove to the motel. It was nothing small; it was quite an elaborate building set next to a golf course. The place was bustling with people. I was so preoccupied thinking of all the things that had to be done that I had forgotten about my appearance. I walked up to the registration counter. Immediately, the two girls behind the counter freaked out. They both started talking at once. I was sure their voices were three octaves higher than normal. The girl closest to me looked at my face, down to my hand, and then back to my face. "Oh, my gosh! Have you been in a car accident?" Before she finished her sentence, the second was already speaking. "Have you been beaten up or raped? Do you need us to call the police?" They both stood there wide-eyed, staring at me.

"Abducted? The police will be here within minutes." The first added to their list.

I couldn't believe all the wild ideas they were coming up with. Before they had come up with a half dozen more and called out the National Guard, I raised both hands and smiled. "No, I just had a flat tire. I fell down a steep hill, changing it." I was impressed with myself for coming up with such an answer spontaneously.

They still weren't totally convinced. "But your hand—Oh, my God—it's bleeding. It's gone!" The first girl was still freaking.

A thought occurred to me. What would they do if I detached my right hand and both legs and laid them up on the registration desk? They'd fall over—graveyard dead. Then, I would be the one who would have to make the call. I didn't. "That's from a previous accident. I'm fine, really. I just want a room if that's ok."

"Yes, whatever you need. We're here to help." The first girl went to work on the computer.

Now, while I had them in a weak state, I thought I would take advantage of their offer. "If it's not too much of a bother, my luggage was lost. Could you help me find someplace to buy new clothes? I'll pay with a credit card. And I'll pay the motel if you have some bandages and antibiotic ointment I can have. It's really starting to burn." That wasn't a lie.

"Oh, no," the second girl said, "that's on the house." Instantly, she picked up the phone.

Both girls went above and beyond their job duties. They had my size and list of clothes I wanted. I was told the clothes would be delivered to my room in an hour or a little more. By the time I had finished checking in enough bandages and gauze had been delivered to supply an army of ten. Then, as I started for the elevator, a man walked up to me. He was dressed in the standard golfing attire—a polo shirt, yellow pants, and white golfing shoes to match. "I heard you need my assistance. I was in the bar having a few cocktails. I'm a doctor."

Now my mouth fell open. How did he know? I looked at both girls.

The second girl looked at me. "We know our clients."

"Thank you." I really didn't want his help, but they had done so much, so fast, I couldn't say no. "I really need to take a shower first," I said.

"By the way, my name is Dr. Malley. My friends call me Lee."

"Hi, I'm Madie." We shook hands. While doing so, I saw a slight frown on Lee's face. He noticed my right hand, not because the glove on it was dirty, but because of what it was. His professionalism took over, and he said nothing. We agreed that when I was finished taking a shower, I was to call down to the bar, and he would come up and dress my hand.

I showered and called Lee. He answered. I told him not to be shocked that I was missing more than just my right hand. I had a robe on, one that the motel supplied for me. I was just amazed at how fast they moved and got things done. Room service arrived at my room minutes after I had. The robe and a pitcher of iced tea were delivered. It was nearly gone when Lee arrived.

When I heard the knock on the door, I got up. The robe, on a normal person, would have been far above the floor, but my artificial legs were lying on the bed. The robe on me drug across the carpet. I looked like 'Thing' from the Addams Family, gliding along the floor with no feet visible; only I waddled. "Come in, Lee. Thank you for taking the time to help me."

Even though Lee was forewarned, he still looked at me surprised. "Boy, you weren't kidding."

I walked on my stumps back to the chair and sat down at the round table in the corner. Lee went to work. He examined my hand.

"This is torn worse than I thought. The skin is still tender. By the looks of it, it hasn't been too long since surgery, maybe six months."

"Yes, you're close," I said.

"Mind if I ask what happened?"

He was kind enough to help. How could I say no? "Frostbite, all the way around," I said.

"Wow. That extensive, you're lucky to be alive."

I didn't respond.

Another knock on the door, "It's open," I said.

Room service—one of the cleaning ladies walked in carrying a large bag. On it said JC Penny—my new clothes. I couldn't tip her; my right stump was tucked inside the robe and Lee was in the middle of wrapping the left. "I'm sorry, I can't tip you this minute."

Lee quickly looked at me, "Here, I'll get it."

I watched Lee hand her a twenty, and she left. "When you're finished, I'll repay you."

"How about when I'm finished, you come down to the bar and buy a couple of rounds of cocktails? My golfing buddies are there, but they won't mind."

"You have a deal," I said.

Lee left and my list of things to do was dwindling fast. I sat on the edge of the bed, resting. I was almost too tired to get up, and my body was feeling weak. I used the time to think of who I should call. That list was so short—it contained no one. Even if I got the DOT involved, there would have to be some sort of law enforcement there. The death dealers were behind this. The only link to them, right now, is what I found under the road. That was, as of yet, still to be determined. Then it came to me – the FBI guys – Agents Netz and Healy. I had told them if I ever remembered anything else, I would call. I had their cards in my purse.

I called and got an answering machine. I left my name and asked if they could call me back right away. I headed for the bar, a drink or two would relax me, maybe even take some of the pain away.

I walked into the bar. I spotted a group of men sitting at a table in the back along a long glass window that overlooked what I assumed was the eighteenth hole. I saw Lee sitting with them. I walked up to the table. I saw Lee raise his eyebrows on my walk there. I credited that to being clean and having new clothes. Lee stood, and then the others followed. Introductions went around the table.

The waitress walked up and asked what I would like. "A round for everyone, and I'll have a Long Island iced tea." I wanted the extra alcohol.

"I like her already," one of the men said.

My hand was bandaged. They wouldn't know of my deformities unless Lee had already told them. "It's the least I could do. Lee helped me." I held up my hand, "Changing a flat tire."

The men talked and laughed. By the way, they were acting, the round of drinks I bought definitely wasn't their second. They talked about their golf scores and who did what on different holes. I drifted in and out of the conversation, mainly out. I was thinking of the next thing on my list—a metal detector. I really wanted to know if I was right. Was the thing under the road as big as I thought?

By the second round, I was feeling better. I joined in on their conversation, mostly answering the few questions asked of me.

Then, I asked, "Would one of you gentlemen know where I could buy a metal detector?"

Several of them started talking at once. Lee looked at me. "You're in luck. Terry here is sort of a treasure hunter. He owns one."

"Yeah," said another man. "It's not like he doesn't have enough money; he can't spend what he has."

Terry smiled. "Don't pay them any attention; they're just drunk."

Terry caught some flak over saying that, but it was all in good fun. They sort of reminded me of my friends up north.

Another man spoke up, "I'd buy you one, but I'd bet a hundred Terry's is in his trunk."

"Pay me the hundred; it's in the back seat," Terry said.

What luck! "Could I borrow it? I only need it for an hour. First, you'd have to show me how to use it," I said.

That did it – all the men got up – everyone was going. *This is going to be interesting,* I thought.

At the car, Terry removed it. The men had carried their drinks with them; they were regulars. Neither the bartender nor the waitress questioned them.

Terry turned it on. "That's all there is to it. Sweep the wand across the ground. If there's metal there, it will find it."

Another one of the men removed a coin from his pocket and tossed it out in the grass. "He'll find it." Terry started walking that way. Carrying their drinks, the others followed. Lee and I were last.

"You would never know," he said.

I looked at him. He saw I didn't understand what that meant.

"Your physical condition—you don't even limp," he said quietly.

"Thank you… for not telling the others."

Terry found the dime in less than a minute. I was thinking, "How deep can it pick up something? Will it go down three or four feet?" I asked.

"Sure, depending on the size. A dime, maybe not, but something bigger, probably," Terry answered.

I didn't want them to go, but I didn't want to go alone. I was drained, and my body needed to rest. "Would you guys like to go on a short road trip? Only eight miles, there's something I need to check on. But first, let's go in, and I'll buy one more." They were more than happy.

There were six of us. Lee drove, he seemed to be the only sober one of the bunch. We all got in his Cadillac – a white Deville – something I would expect a doctor to drive. Omitting Jim – he was a truck kind of guy, given the location he lived in.

We pulled up to the GPS location, and I looked at the freshly dug dirt. The men never stopped talking. I had an explanation ready as everyone got out.

"There's a pumping station under the road. I work for a private consulting firm, and we really need to know how big it is. It doesn't show up on any of the blueprints."

There was enough traffic passing by. I was worried about one of them getting hit as they walked around on the road like they knew what they were doing.

I showed Terry the corner where I had dug. "It starts here. I believe it goes to the center of the road but how far down is anyone's guess. Will it be able to detect it?"

Terry whistled, "With that much metal, this thing will beep like a crazy woman in a traffic jam. No offense."

"None taken," everyone was laughing. I was on pins and needles, and I was about to know.

Terry started across the road, making wide sweeps as he walked slowly. When he swung it to the left, we heard one loud, constant tone. When he moved it to the right, it stopped. The edge was obvious. When he went past the center of the road, it stopped. Then he turned and started down the center of the road. I stopped breathing. He continued sweeping from left to right. With each right swing, the noise stopped. The rest of the men stood in the road watching. A car had to slow down to a near stop to drive by. It honked its horn at us.

"Hey, we're working here. Can't you see that?" The driver flipped him off. "Boy, you'd think some people think they own the road," he said.

We were the ones at fault, but I said nothing. My skin was tingling.

Ten feet down and the metal detector continued beeping. I wasn't breathing, and the anxiety weighed so heavily on my chest that I couldn't. Fifteen feet down, the detector still beeped.

Lee walked up beside me. I could feel his presence, but I couldn't look away from Terry. "The freshly dug dirt is a funny-looking flat tire. You dug a long time, but your hand couldn't take it."

I said nothing. I wasn't letting him in the loop.

"Is there something else down there besides what you said?" he asked.

"If you don't ask questions, I won't have to lie to you. But, to be honest, I don't know."

Lee nodded.

"I'm grateful for what you and your friends are doing for me. I really am. I'm sorry I can't tell you anymore right now. If anything becomes of this, you'll know."

Lee nodded again.

Twenty feet down, and nothing changed. I was right – I had to be. All signs were saying so. Twenty-five feet and still going. I was feeling relieved, and the pressure was lifting. I took a deep breath. Lee and I followed along on the side of the road as Terry slowly continued to the thirty-foot mark. "It should stop, make a ninety-degree turn, and come back to the edge of the road," I said quietly, watching and listening.

At the spot where I had visually marked, it did. Terry went one step further, and the metal detector ceased to make noise. Terry stopped and backed up one step, then swung to his left. The music started again, and I almost smiled. Terry started toward the edge of the road. The swings to the right—no noise—the return swings to the left, and it was clear where the edge was.

"How in the world did you know that?" Lee asked.

I held both hands in the air, palms up—one of the prices I had to pay. Lee didn't understand, and I wasn't going to tell him.

"Whoo wee! That's awfully big whatever it is," one of the other men said.

This was the happiest I had been in a long time. I wanted to jump up and down, maybe even do the Saint Vidus's dance. Internally, the adrenaline was flowing, but I remained cool on the outside. "Thanks, guys, especially you, Terry. You saved me a lot of time. The drinks are on me, as many as you want," I said.

They all smiled, and one man said, "Sounds good to me."

At the bar, I gave the waitress my room number. I told her to keep them coming until the last man leaves. I was planning on having my share and then a few extra. I was celebrating what was still to be determined. I was getting somewhere, and that's all that mattered.

I was into my third drink and feeling no pain when my phone rang. I didn't recognize the number on the caller ID. "Hello."

"Ms. Chanhansen, this is Agent Netz returning your call."

I looked at several of the men and pointed at the phone. Then I stood and started walking toward the door. I dropped the phone. As I quickly bent down to retrieve it, I couldn't believe I did that to an FBI agent. I was feeling good, but I didn't think I was drunk. "I'm sorry, Agent Netz. I dropped the phone." I was embarrassed. "Please, forgive me." My hand didn't feel right, not that I could actually feel it. The fingers weren't gripping the phone right. *The alcohol,* I thought.

"No harm done. I was curious as to why, after all this time, you called."

Here it was, my chance to sell what I had learned and make it sound believable. "I found something that links the killers to my husband, but I need your help. I don't know how to go about it. I don't have a clue as to who to go to and start the process. I also don't know what to do after it's found," I said.

"What did you find?" Agent Netz asked.

The question I was dreading. "That's the problem; I don't know."

"I'm confused. You found something that might give a name but yet, you don't know what it is?"

"I know where it is." By now, I had reached the elevator. "It's going to take someone with a good deal of say-so to do what it takes. It's under a county road, a two-lane highway, to be exact." I hoped by now he was interested.

"Where are you?" he asked.

"Chicago, Illinois. It's massive—twelve feet wide and thirty feet long. All of it is under the eastbound lane."

Several moments of silence.

"Sounds a little bit out there. How do you know it's not something belonging to one of the municipalities?"

"If you saw where it was, you'd think differently, but it isn't. You have to believe me on this. There's something inside there and it belongs to them. I don't know how else to convince you. It's going to take more than what I'm capable of. Please help me." Now I was begging.

"Well, I can get in touch with the department in that area, and they can send an agent out there to check it out."

"But, I'd prefer you were here."

"It's out of my area. My boss wouldn't agree to that."

"But, you're the FBI. You can go anywhere, can't you? You started the case, and I'd really like to see you follow it through. All I can tell you is that it's going to be substantial. Please believe me."

"I just don't think I'd get the approval to fly there."

"Tell your boss I'll pay for you and Agent Healy to fly out here tomorrow, I'm that sure."

"Let me make some calls. No promises. This is stretching it."

"The one thing I do know is that you won't be sorry. Please, come."

"I'll call you back." Then he hung up, no goodbyes.

My nerves were back on the fence, teetering back and forth. In this situation, there was no good side to fall. I couldn't fail. I started to go up to my room. I had to go back to the bar and say good night to the men and thank them once more.

When I walked back in, Lee and Terry were the only ones left. I walked to the table.

Lee spoke, "The others had to go. They wanted me to say thank you for the drinks and the trip."

I sat down, half of my third drink still sitting there, and I gulped it down. I needed more sedative. "I'm sorry I had to rudely get up and leave; that was the FBI."

Lee raised his eyebrows. "Wow! Has to do with that flat tire?"

I smiled.

"So, how did you know that flat tire was there?" Lee asked.

Lee seemed nice enough and honest. I had only known him for two hours. I wasn't going to tell him everything. "It cost me more than you could possibly know. You've seen my physical condition. My husband lost his life. He was murdered, and I had to watch."

I needed another drink--more bottled sedative.

"I'm sorry. Where did this happen?" Lee asked.

"Canada, very far north. That's the reason for my physical disability."

"What is your physical condition? You look fine to me," Terry asked.

My hands were in my lap. After a lot of struggling, I removed the glove from my right hand and held it up in the air, closing and opening the mechanical fingers. Then, I tried to rotate the wrist, but the alcohol was impairing my efforts. I couldn't get it to move correctly. I lifted my right leg up and lifted my pant leg far enough to expose the pole. I repeated that on the left. "Most of the nose is from a cadaver. The only visual freak show thing is my left hand."

"I never noticed. You carry yourself well. I did the glove but paid no attention to it," Terry said.

"Thank you. A lot of practice. I walked a long way to get this way. Mother Nature wasn't kind."

"How far?" Lee asked.

"Two hundred and forty miles."

Lee whistled. "How long did that take you?"

"Thirty one days."

Lee shook his head, "That's amazing."

"Without a doubt," Terry added.

The waitress brought another round of drinks. "Thank you, you're great," I said. I was glad she had interrupted the conversation.

The conversation had drifted away. By the time the drinks were gone, I was ready to go to my room.

"So, what's down there, if you want to tell us? Curiosity has the best of me," Lee asked.

400

"Not near as much as me. I don't know. If it turns out to be nothing, then I have failed. Put me in the trash. Another thing I couldn't do." I felt tears forming in my eyes.

My original plan was to drink until I couldn't lift the glass. I stopped after the fourth. I was barely drunk, two before the trip and two after. I had to be clear for the second call. I was ready to call the airlines and book two tickets.

"I need to go back to my room. You two have been kind, thank you."

"We'd like to be there, or at least know if you find anything, if you get to dig it up."

"Deal, it's the least I could do."

I got into my new pajamas, removed my feet, and sat on the bed. I didn't have to wait more than an hour before the phone rang, which was sitting in my lap. "Hello."

"Ms. Chanhansen, Agent Netz. I talked to my boss. He had to go to his. He then had to call the man in charge in that area…"

I thought, *Come on already. All I need to know is if you're coming or not.*

"After the politics, a few favors, and a string or two pulled, I'm flying out there on the first flight out. I'll land at O'Hare at 8:40 a.m."

"Oh, thank you. You don't know how relieved I am."

"Why me, if you don't mind my asking?"

"I know you, and I trust you. You can get this job done; it's just not going to be easy."

I went to sleep happy. This had turned out to be the perfect day.

CHAPTER 45

I was up at six and glad not to be hungover. I was showered, dressed, and ready to go by seven. Agent Netz was coming to the motel to pick me up, but he wouldn't be here until nine-thirty at the earliest. I paced the floor, then I went down to the lobby and paced; I even went outside – the weather was beautiful. No one could ask for a better day, no clouds – no wind, somewhere in the mid-seventies.

I went back in, walked into the restaurant, and ordered coffee. I took cup after cup, but I wasn't thirsty; I was wide awake without it—it was just nerves.

At nine a.m., I went back outside and sat on the bench by the entrance. By nine-thirty, my bladder was severely strained, so I went in and took care of business and was back on the bench by nine thirty-five.

At nine fifty, I watched a car drive into the parking lot; it had government written all over it. There were two people inside. The license plate was a standard Illinois issue. Agent Netz got out on the passenger side—the driver I didn't know. I walked toward them. FBI agent or not, I hugged Agent Netz's neck. "What can I say? You have no idea what this means." He was slightly embarrassed.

"This is Agent Wheeling, out of the local office."

"Hello, I'm Madie."

Agent Wheeling smiled. "Yes, I've heard all about you. Quite an ordeal you went through."

"Still going through. I've lived this non-stop since I returned home. Maybe, finally, I can come up with a name for the two who killed Craig."

"So, tell us again what you found?" Agent Netz asked.

"I'll show you; it is eight miles from here. Do you need to check in first or have coffee?"

"No, we're ready," Netz said.

"I need the shovel, just in case."

On the drive there, I sat in the backseat. "It's going to be a long day—maybe a lost one."

"So, what's there?" Agent Wheeling asked.

"I wish I knew. It's big, whatever it is. I'm not crazy, that much I do know."

Agent Wheeling laughed. I liked his personality; he wasn't as stuffy as Agent Netz.

We pulled up to the spot where I had dug. I took a deep breath, and I was shaking as we got out. They walked out on the road, looking a little puzzled. I walked to the loose dirt on the side of the road. I pointed down at the small crack in the road with one agent standing on each side of me. "It starts here and goes to the center of the road." I walked in that direction as they followed. "It turns here and goes down the center." As we made the thirty-foot walk, they stayed at my side, looking. "Then it stops here and goes back to the side of the road."

At the edge of the road, they looked around, saying nothing. I had more proof, and they needed it. "Last night, I had a man run a metal detector over it. It detected what you see in the seams. We can do it again." I started for the car. "If you open the trunk, I'll get the shovel and show you."

I started digging in the loose dirt. I couldn't use my bandaged left hand, and I was struggling, but I had to show them.

"Here, let me do that. What kind of a man would I be if I stood here and watched a woman do that with a bandaged hand?"

I smiled. "I did it yesterday, and that's why my hand is bandaged today."

Agent Wheeling worked the shovel like a pro. He's had plenty of experience, and it was also clear to me that he was in shape and strong.

Within five minutes he was almost to the bottom. "I can truthfully say that I loosened it up for you."

"Yes, you did," Agent Wheeling smiled.

"Geez, it took me hours yesterday."

"Well, Ms. Chanhansen, I know of your situation. I'm surprised you did it at all," Agent Netz said.

He said that in a complimentary way. "Madie, please call me Madie," I said.

Then, we heard the shovel hit the steel, and the agents looked at one another. Agent Wheeling dug for another ten minutes, making the exposed metal much larger than I had had it. He stood and looked at Agent Netz. "Now, what do you want to do? It's your call, and I'm only here to assist."

Agent Netz stared at the ground. "It still could be something belonging to the street department."

I shook my head no; the GPS coordinates didn't come from there. "Not this."

Agent Netz stared at me. Somewhere inside, part of him believed me. "Before we go digging, we need the county road commission and the street department out here. Tell them to bring all the drawings they have for this area."

Agent Wheeling made the calls. When each department heard the FBI was requesting them, they said they would be there right away.

They were – within twenty minutes. The road commission pulled up first. He got out of his truck, walked toward us, and looked around.

"Where are your drawings?" Agent Netz asked.

"There aren't any. What are you looking for?"

We showed him, and then introductions were made. FBI – ask questions later. His name was Mike.

"That's not ours. We didn't put it there – I mean, why would we? It's got to be the streets," he said.

Within minutes, another truck pulled up. 'Street and Sanitation' was painted on the side of the door. That man got out carrying a thick, rolled-up tube of papers. This time, introductions were made; his name was Adolf, and then we showed him.

"What in the world is that?" he asked.

"That's why you're here, you tell us," Agent Netz said, still stuffy but blunt.

Adolf laid his tube of papers on the hood of his truck and unrolled them. There were literally dozens of drawings stacked up. He started paging through them, stopped at one certain page, and then looked around. He held that page with his left hand and continued through the stack with his right. He stopped the second time and shook his head. "I'll show you." He flipped back to the first drawing he had with his left hand. "This is the sub-division on the east side of the forest preserve. You can see here the sewage system runs parallel with the forest. Nothing enters it from that side." Then he turned back to the second drawing. "This is a mile away. It runs west. The first one ran south. They don't connect. That doesn't belong to us, which I pretty much already knew. Forest preserves are off-limits to just about everything except electrical. But that has to be above ground in them."

Agent Netz followed the wires running along the side of the road. I thought I saw a slight bit of relief on his face.

"So what is that?" he asked. Then he stared at me, thinking.

'The death dealers,' I knew that much. I remained silent, watching.

Agent Netz looked back at Mike. "You're sure that's not some steel re-enforcement for the road, maybe bad ground or something?"

"No, no way. If the contractors hit a soft spot, they're required to dig down until they find solid subsoil. I promise you we didn't put it there."

"Ms. Chanhansen here says it goes to the center of the road and then thirty feet down. Would either of you have a detector to verify that?"

"Yeah, sure, I do," said Adolf. He opened one of the toolboxes on the side of his truck and removed something that looked nothing like Terry's.

We all watched. He started at the hole and then walked toward the center of the road. The tone on his detector had a much higher pitch than Terry's. "Wow! A strong signal. Four feet down. It's thick, that's for sure."

His was much more sophisticated than Terry's. When he was finished, he had confirmed what I had already told them. Still, I remained silent, waiting patiently to see what was next.

The agents looked at each other. "I say start digging," Agent Wheeling said.

"You're going to dig up the road? At whose expense?" Mike asked.

Agent Netz looked around. "How about we start at the side of the road? We'll dig away the dirt along the side and see what we have."

Sounded like a good plan to me, one step closer.

"I can't make that decision. You'll have to get that," Mike said.

Netz looked at Wheeling. "We'll have it in an hour," Wheeling said and returned to his car.

Adolf left; it didn't concern him. The rest of us stood around, waiting for the call.

It took almost ninety minutes for Agent Wheeling's phone to ring. The conversation was short. "It's a go. We'll have the search warrant and a permit in less than an hour."

Netz turned to Mike. "How soon can you have a track hoe out here to start digging?"

"Hour… two at the most," Mike responded.

"I like one better, if you can do it."

Agent Netz was softening up. It was lunchtime; my nerves had settled, and I was getting hungry. Mike left to go and line up the equipment.

"I'm ready to eat lunch, anyone else hungry?" Wheeling asked.

"I am," I said, and Agent Netz nodded in agreement

"We all can't leave, not with that exposed."

He was right. "I'll stay," I said.

"I'll stay with you, just in case the equipment shows up," Netz said.

Agent Wheeling left. Burgers were decided on. Agent Netz and I went to the tree line and sat down. "You're not as hard as you were when you got here."

"I know. I'm sorry for that. You have to understand that it took me quite a bit of talking to get here. I had a lot on the line. Not my job, but definitely my credibility. Each person's boss up the chain of command asked the same thing – what do you have for proof? The only thing I could tell them was your word. I believed you, but I must say I was skeptical on the inside."

"Thank you for believing me. It would be much easier if we knew what was down there."

Soon enough.

An hour passed, and our food was gone. Most of the conversation was about what could be down there.

"Madie," Wheeling said. "So, how did you know that was down there? Finding that one spot has far worse odds than winning the lottery."

"The man who killed my husband told me moments before he died. I don't know why; maybe he was bragging. Maybe he didn't want it to go to waste. It's something illegal, I'm pretty sure of that, that's the reason I wanted Agent Netz here. I'm sure he didn't believe my story back then. But why in the middle of the road, in the middle of practically nothing? I'm doing it so I can figure out who they were, closure on a senseless murder I can't even prove."

"What did he die from?" Wheeling asked.

"He ran himself to death. A heart attack, I think, something else I'll never know for sure. I ran for almost two weeks, and he was never far behind. Some days I could see him."

The semi arrived. The piece of equipment was much larger than I expected. Behind that, Mike followed in his truck, and behind Mike another truck with the same logo on the door.

By two o'clock, the digging had started. Now, I wished I hadn't eaten; my stomach was doing things that weren't normal. I had to sit down; even my sticks for legs had turned to rubber, but I couldn't leave. Like everyone else, we stood close enough to watch every dig from the huge machine. The east lane of the highway had been closed off, and orange pyramid cones were placed up and down the road. A man stood at each end directing traffic.

The machine started about ten feet past the spot where I had dug. As it dug its way toward the spot, it went deeper. I was in awe; with one swift scoop in less than five seconds, it had removed ten times the amount of dirt that took me hours to dig.

Now, it had dug its way several feet past the edge where it started, and I guessed to be about ten feet down. The operator was good. He dug along the steel wall just inches away. He was told to stop. Everyone walked up to the hole and gazed in. I looked around at the faces, and each one held the same expression – bewildered – as I had been since I started on the journey.

Agent Netz told the man driving the machine to dig the trench wider and then dig down until he found the bottom.

Within minutes, the hole was twice as wide, and he was back to the spot where he had previously stopped. Anticipation was killing me, and I could hardly stand it. With each scoop removed, I expected something—what—I had no idea. A boogeyman couldn't jump out of the dirt and get us, but with the death dealers, one never knew – mainly me. The rest didn't know how vile they were. I walked up to Agent Netz and put my right hand on his arm. It was the first time I was sorry I couldn't feel with that hand. I needed the security. Quietly, I said, "If anything jumps out of there, promise me you'll shoot it."

Agent Netz smiled. "Nothing is going to get you, I promise."

"You have no idea what I dealt with." I could feel my face getting hot, and I was feeling sick.

Agent Netz looked at me; his look became concerned, but he said nothing.

One scoop down, then the second moved to the right, equaling the first in depth. That continued as we all watched. Deeper and deeper, the bottom wasn't in sight. The hole was so deep the driver had to remove dirt in front and back of that spot. He needed more room to move the bucket as it went further down.

My senses were on high alert, yet I was quickly dying. Thoughts were running through my mind like a wild stampede. What could be in there that was so tall? We already knew the length.

The metal wall was exposed fifteen feet down, one of the men had said so. To me, it looked huge, deep enough that if I fell in, I would never be found.

Agent Netz yelled up to the driver, "Keep going until you find the bottom."

He did. After several minutes and many scoops, it was finally clear where the bottom stopped. A wall of dirt started under it. The driver lifted the boom up and swung it away from the hole. The pile of freshly dug dirt was growing fast. At the bottom, on the far side, it had spilled over to the tree line.

Everyone walked up to the edge of the hole. Standing on the blacktop, we looked down. The man, who I didn't know that had followed Mike there, whistled, "Would you look at that."

I did, I couldn't look away. I couldn't believe how deep it was. Then, the man removed a tape measure from his belt, leaned over the hole, and started reeling out the tape. We all watched it go down. When it hit bottom, he whistled again, "Seventeen feet to the bottom with four feet of dirt on top." He looked at both FBI agents, "What do you have here?"

"I don't know, but we're about to find out," Netz said.

I looked to the left and right. The trench was as long as it was deep and five feet wide. This was only the beginning. I leaned over further to look at the steel wall. It was rust brown, and, by the looks of it, it had been there for a while. "How long has this been here?" I asked.

Everyone looked at Mike and the other man. Mike held the bill of the hat he was wearing and scratched his head with his hat. "I can't be sure, but by the looks of it, years. The metal has started to pit with rust. That's all I can tell you."

The decision was made to dig to the far end, expose the entire wall, and then go from there.

Agent Netz said, "What in the world are we standing on," to no one in particular.

I was pulling out all of my previous thoughts. It was too big for a stash of money or drugs. The wild speculations had been kicked aside after the first location when there was nothing there. "Could it be a nuclear bomb or something of that nature?"

Agent Netz looked at me with a shocked expression. "Right now, we rule out nothing, but thanks for the good feeling you just gave me."

I shrugged my shoulders, "That's why I wanted you here. They were ruthless beyond definition."

"God, I hope not," Agent Wheeling said.

The machine dug its way down to the center. It was just past three thirty.

Netz, Wheeling, and I had walked around to the far side of the trench where the digging had begun. We stood there looking down into the hole at the massive steel wall.

"How are we going to get in there? Cutting torches would do it, but would we be causing a major catastrophe, killing everyone in the area?" Netz asked.

No one spoke. The machine continued to dig as we watched.

My phone rang, "Hello."

"Madie, it's Lee. The receptionist said you haven't checked out yet. Buy you a cocktail?"

"I can't."

Lee could hear the noise in the background. "Where are you?"

"At the spot, you need to see this."

"Terry and I are on the way."

I walked over and stood between Agent Netz and Wheeling, and we watched the digging progress.

"We could get a crane out here, lift that out of the ground, and truck it to a controlled environment. There, with enough equipment, we could x-ray it and see what's inside," Wheeling said.

"Yes, I have thought of that. What do you think of the idea of drilling a pinhole toward the top and sticking a mini camera in there?" Netz asked.

"That's an idea. Worst case scenario, if Madie's right, that wouldn't hurt anything," Wheeling said.

Dear Lord, if I was right. "What's the shelf life on one of these?" I asked.

"I don't know for sure. Indefinitely, I suppose, given it's in the right environment," Netz said.

"This doesn't have the right environment." I was thinking of the wire that started all of this.

Agent Netz was to my left. He saw Lee and Terry first. "You don't belong here."

I put my bandaged hand on his arm. "They're with me. They helped me last night; that's how I knew it was as big as it is. Terry has a metal detector."

More introductions. The agents were nice but cool to them.

"This is it, guys. To be determined yet as to what's inside," I said.

"Good Lord, it's massive," Lee said.

"A lot more than what we found last night, that's for sure," Terry said.

The machine worked its way down. Only three feet left to dig before it reached the end. Lee and Terry had left. I looked to the top of the giant pile of dirt; it was unbelievable to me—all of that dirt. "How did they get that thing in the ground?" I asked myself. I was nauseous—beat mentally and physically. I walked over to the pile of dirt and sat on it. Three feet and then what—the bomb squad, the geek squad with their side crew, the peep squad to look in a window that isn't there? I looked at the cloudless sky. "I wish you were here Craig; I need you. Forgive me, will you? If not, I don't blame you."

The agents stood on the road talking, discussing strategies. It was past five. I saw a pizza delivery car stop down the road. The driver got out carrying a stack of pizza boxes. I wasn't hungry; I drank a sixteen-ounce bottle of Diet Coke.

By the time that was finished, the trench was just past the steel wall. The operator had dug a ramp leading up out of the hole—one bucket wide. Then, he backed the machine up about ten feet and shut it off. After hearing it all afternoon, the quietness was deafening. I didn't get up; we still had a long day ahead of us, so why waste the energy?

I was overrun with emotions—so close. I didn't realize I was taking short, rapid breaths. I kept thinking of Craig – and the death dealers – the thing that had led me to this spot.

The FBI agents stood on the road looking down. Mike and the other man walked down the road and into the hole. I had a front-row seat as I watched.

The other man walked to the center of the steel wall. "Regardless of what's in there, this has to come out. It can't stay under the road forever. It would eventually rot and fall in."

"Who are you?" I asked.

He looked at me funny. "The county road commissioner," he said.

"Oh. I didn't know."

"Look at this!" Mike shouted. Everyone snapped their heads at him. "There's a seam here."

I didn't know what that meant. But like the others, the two Feds, one state cop and a few others that had arrived throughout the afternoon, I headed that way. Agents Netz and Wheeling started walking down the trench, and I followed. The rest stayed up on the road, looking down. I stood behind Agent Netz, looking over his shoulder. Mike was on his knees in the dirt, and he had gloves on. Slowly, he brushed the dirt away from the side, following a crack in the metal. It was barely visible. It started at the bottom. Mike followed it up the side, and six feet up, it stopped. He followed the now horizontal seam to the right for two feet, then it made another turn and ran back down to the ground.

"I wonder if there's more along the side," Mike said.

The county commissioner slowly walked down the side looking. Mike remained where he was and was still brushing the seam with his hand.

At the other end, the county commissioner said, "Nope, that's the only one."

"Look at this," Mike said again.

Agents Netz and Wheeling leaned in to get a closer look.

"There's two one-inch welds on each side. See this one?" Mike asked.

I looked about a foot above the ground.

"There's another one about a foot below the seam running across the top," Mike said.

We leaned in to get a closer look. Now, the Feds were breathing on Mike's neck.

"And there's two more on the opposite side. I guess that's our door in," Mike said.

"Don't semis travel this road?" I asked.

They looked at me like, what does that have to do with it?

"I'm not an engineer, but however this thing is built, it's built well. Think of the weight it's been holding up," I said.

No one said anything.

"Clever. Men, just dig a small entrance and remove what's inside. Then replace the dirt and be gone," Agent Wheeling said.

"Looks that way, odds are whatever was there is gone," Netz said.

"No, it's still in there." I thought of what he told me: *It'll make you richer beyond your wildest dreams.* "It's not nuclear either. Everything we see here doesn't add up," I said.

"Can you guarantee that?" Agent Netz asked.

I had nine more locations stored away. As ruthless as they were, they didn't have the means to steal the bombs. "Pretty much," I said.

The geek squad and the peep squad weren't going to be called. Now a maintenance man with the road commission was. He was told to bring a generator and a grinder. It would be thirty minutes before he arrived, more downtime. Whatever was in there was still in there. The waiting all day was taking its toll on me. I felt like Mrs. Humpty Dumpty – soon to fall apart, never to be the same.

Another county truck arrived and pulled up along the edge, just above the door. Even though with the lucky find of the entrance, saving who knows how many hours waiting into the night, I was getting cranky. I wanted to know what was in there, their names, and what kind of evil things they had done. I was back sitting on the dirt pile, looking at the door. I heard the generator start up. Then I watched an electric cord drop over the edge, and within minutes, the man was grinding away.

I couldn't believe it. In five minutes, he was done. I stood without thinking about it. Mike handed the man a hammer and chisel, and the man drove the chisel into the seam. With each blow of the hammer, a loud, deafening, hollow echo rang out. It sounded like the noise went for miles and then returned as the next one was sent away.

It didn't take the man long. The side he was chiseling on moved away from the wall, less than an inch, but it was moving.

I walked to the trench and then down. I stood behind the FBI men. Another inch—I couldn't breathe. I watched Mike and the man stick their fingers behind the plate of steel and begin pulling on it. As it opened further, they moved it back and forth. Now, it was a foot out.

They pulled harder. I could see the strain on their faces. "Watch yourself. This thing's about to fall," Mike said.

Two more pulls, and then it broke free. It fell at an angle and then landed against the far wall of the trench. Each agent had a flashlight ready. Agent Netz stopped at the opening and looked inside. He said nothing, then walked in with Agent Wheeling following. Mike and the other man moved away. I wanted to go in – I needed to go in. But I waited to let the experienced men give the all-clear. Again, I didn't breathe. I wanted to hear if they spoke. It seemed like it was taking forever. I could hear the soles of their shoes as they walked on the steel. 'What!' I wanted to shout. Then I heard the creaking of an old spring, but still nothing.

Moments later, Agent Netz appeared at the opening. "Madie, you'd better come in here."

Oh, dear God, I thought. What? Is it good or bad? Bad was my answer; the death dealers were involved. I walked to the opening and put one foot in. I was lightheaded, and I was about to know. I walked into the darkness, and it took just a moment for my eyes to adjust.

"Look at this," Agent Netz said.

I looked in the direction he was pointing at with the flashlight. I saw it, but it took my mind several moments to process it. I leaned forward and stared harder – two doors with handles in the center. That meant one opened to the left and the other to the right. At the top of each door was a small window. With that processed, I said, "Looks like the back end of a truck."

"Not just any truck. This one's special; it's an armored truck," Netz said.

"And it belongs to Brinks," Wheeling said.

I heard his voice from far up ahead. His voice echoed off the bare metal walls. "Oh, man! It just got worse. It went from grand theft to murder. The driver is still sitting behind the wheel."

I couldn't speak. I thought, 'An armored truck? An armored truck!' Now, I knew. It all became clear to me: *You'll be rich beyond your wildest dreams.* "It's full of money, not just a regular shipment, that's for sure."

"Yes, look inside." Netz stood on the back bumper. I heard the creak again, dry, rusty springs from under the truck, longing to be used again. "There are bags upon bags in there."

I stepped up on the back bumper. The only handle to hold onto was the door, and my right hand was acting funny. I ignored it. The light penetrating the window was poor. I did see a large pile of canvas bags tied shut. We stepped down. "Do the doors open?"

"No, they're locked, just as they were while traveling," Netz said.

"So, where's the man who rides shotgun? Isn't there always two men per truck?" I asked.

"Good question," Netz said. "Maybe he was one of them, and maybe he was paid off to disappear."

We could hear Agent Wheeling banging and clanking around from up ahead. "Boy, there's practically no room around this thing. Whoever designed this thing put a lot of thought into it; just the perfect size to fit an armored truck. The front bumper—well, in fact, the whole front end of the truck is smashed in. Looks like it crashed into the front wall – hard."

I needed to see. At the doorway, I asked Mike if I could use his flashlight.

Back inside, I looked around on my own. The passenger side of the truck was only three inches from the wall. I walked to the driver's side and looked down, at best ten inches of clearance. I could see Agent Wheeling by the driver's door, struggling just to move.

The 'much planning and thought' statement from Wheeling was an understatement. I slowly scanned the side of the wall with the flashlight. There was a big i-beam standing vertically every foot, from one end of this prison box to the other. I looked up to the top. Sitting on top of each vertical i-beam, another beam ran horizontally across the ceiling to the opposite wall. "That's how it held the weight of the traffic," I said. My unanswered questions only grew at a rate that was overwhelming me.

I now knew what was at the other locations and in them. There was nothing here that could give me the names of the death dealers. No evidence that they had any part of this or were even here. The GPS locations from the second one were the only link. "How are we ever going to find out how long this has been in here?" I asked that, just thinking out loud.

"That's easy," Netz said. "The tag on the license plate expired five years ago."

"Plus, one phone call to the Brinks Company and they can give the exact day and time it disappeared. We're getting somewhere, and it just takes a little time. We'll know."

Another question I didn't have an answer for. Why were they waiting so long to come back and claim the stolen money? Why were they living in the middle of nowhere—the most unforgiving place imaginable?

Agent Wheeling came stumbling out between the truck and the wall. "Amazing. Totally amazing!"

"The first thing we need to do is call Brinks and tell them we have one of their trucks. We need them to open it. They'll need another truck here to transport the money to FBI headquarters."

"I want the DEA here also with two cars, with two agents in each, to escort the money back. Agent Wheeling, can you get a crew out here to completely go through this truck for prints or find any other evidence? That has to be done before anything is touched inside."

"My boss has been waiting for my call. He won't believe this. If I wasn't standing in here, I wouldn't. This is totally unbelievable," Wheeling said.

Mentally, I agreed. I could feel I was about to start crying. There wasn't going to be any restitution for Craig from what I was looking at. My throat started to swell and I was swallowing at the rate of once every two seconds. I wasn't going to lose it in front of the FBI men. I walked outside and then up the trench. I didn't stop walking until I was behind the dirt pile and out into the woods. There, I sat down and leaned against a tree. I tucked my knees into my chest, and I cried hard for a long time.

Agent Netz broke the solitude surrounding me. My world had now become a three-foot radius around me. Now, it was time to leave me with the trash. I wanted to go back to that spot, lie down where Craig had died, and go with him. I looked up at him through my flooded eyes. He had his gun out, and I couldn't understand why.

"Madie!" Netz said.

I wiped my nose, as lady-like as I could, without any Kleenex. "What's wrong? Why are you holding your gun?"

Agent Netz looked relieved and holstered his gun. "We called and called, and you gave us no answer. I thought something happened to you. You were never out of sight all day, and then you disappeared."

"Something did happen. I failed. But, not to worry. The two men behind this are long past dead. I watched both of them die days after they shot Craig in the head. Have you ever watched someone you love die, Agent Netz? It's not a good thing. As time passes, mentally and physically,

413

you deteriorate to nothing. I watched them murder my husband, Agent Netz, and I did nothing to stop it. I promised Craig if I would survive them, I would find out who they were. It's what drove me to walk out of there. I have nothing to prove it, only my word." Now, I had myself crying hard again.

"I believe you. I did then, too, when I first talked to you. All is not lost. We have something to go on now."

"I don't see what," I said while crying. "They were vile men. Now I have to add to that, they were highly intelligent." Now, I was bawling my eyes out again. "How did they manage to do this, Agent Netz?"

"I don't know, but you can count on us using all the resources we have. We'll figure it out." Then Agent Netz bent down and helped me up. "Come on, you're a part of this. I'd like you here throughout all of it."

CHAPTER 46

It was past dark. I had walked in and out of the steel tomb at least a dozen times as the men worked. While outside, I paced back and forth. It took the crew – whoever they were and whatever department they were from – nearly two hours, dusting for prints and going through everything with a fine toothed comb. As I had known, nothing unusual was found, just money and two lost souls.

Eleven bags had been removed and hauled away. They were never opened. The body of the second man was found lying on the floor against the back doors. I didn't want to see them. I had seen enough death. I saw the two black body bags carried up the trench, put in an ambulance, and taken away. Their wives and children, if they had them, would suffer all over again, thanks to me. They would have to endure the grief all over again. Like me, it would be a closed casket.

It was decided that the road was to be closed. The road crew would work into the night and remove the dirt around it. At sunrise, a huge crane would be delivered. It would lift the steel tomb, with the truck still inside, out. It would then be taken away to where I didn't ask.

Agent Netz wanted me to go back to the motel for the night. I asked him if he was, but he wasn't. He was staying until it was hauled away. I made my decision; he was staying, and so was I.

A portable lighting unit was set up. Now, the area was brighter than it had been during the day. The machine operator worked much faster. By four a.m., all the dirt had been removed, and the top, both ends, and the opposite side were exposed.

Before sunrise, a crane drove up the road. To say that it was huge wouldn't do it justice. I counted ten sets of wheels on one side. It literally dwarfed the machine that had completed the digging. Behind the crane were two semis—the first one carried a huge hunk of steel and a forklift. The second had more wheels than I bothered counting. It was empty. That one, I assumed, would haul the steel tomb away. It bothered me that there were nine more. I didn't know how Agent Netz would take it, but sooner or later, I would tell him.

Three men, definitely professionals, moved smoothly and efficiently. By the time daybreak could be seen on the eastern horizon, they were set up and ready. To everyone else's surprise there were lifting hooks on each end – I wasn't surprised. I had seen what they were capable of long before this.

Two men walked across a plank onto the steel box. Each man was carrying large black nylon straps. The diameter of them was the size of my arm. They walked to the opposite ends and placed a large metal hook in the lifting eye. The crane lowered its cable, and the lifting straps were connected to it.

I watched the others huddle around one of the men with the crane. I walked over to see why. He had a radio clipped on his belt, and the microphone was attached to his shirt collar. He was talking with the man operating the crane.

We heard the engine rev up, and from the microphone, we heard, "Here we go."

I watched – nothing happened. Seconds later, I had thought I would see it starting to rise in the air. I didn't. "Why isn't he lifting it?" I asked. I had eased my way through the men so I could stand beside him.

"He is," the man said. "There is a scale in the cab. As the cable slowly tightened, he watched the scale. It told him how much weight was being lifted—a safety precaution—can't exceed the lifting capacity of the crane."

"Thirty thousand," we heard.

I couldn't see anything move – the box, the cable, or the hook, which was half the size of me.

"Forty thousand." Moments later.

"Fifty thousand." No one seemed concerned.

"Sixty thousand." Geez, sixty thousand pounds, and the tomb still rested in place.

"Seventy thousand."

If the others were nervous, they didn't show it, but I was. I asked, "How much can that crane lift?"

"One hundred tons," the man with the microphone said. He was watching the box intently.

"Seventy five thousand."

"How much can those straps hold?" I was expecting them to snap at any moment.

"Ninety thousand each," he replied.

"Wow," I said. They knew what they were doing, so I relaxed—some.

Then, we saw it move… ever so little.

"Finally, just short of seventy eight thousand," we heard through the microphone.

It wasn't long and the steel tomb was hanging high in the air, then swung around and lowered onto the waiting truck.

I watched it disappear down the road.

"Well, you're done here. It looks like I've got a big hole to fill," Mike said. He was looking a little frazzled around the edges. "Never in my wildest dreams. I have driven over this road hundreds of times in the last five years."

"Huh! That's exactly what he said," I said.

"Who?" Mike asked.

"The man who put it there, only his statement was directed to the money, nothing else."

Agent Netz and Wheeling were as dirty as I was. Their ties had been removed hours ago, and they needed a shave. They wanted to drop me off at the motel. I asked them what they were going to do. I was told that an empty warehouse was located, the box was to be unloaded there and then the truck was to be removed. Everything was to be dissected again.

I had to go. Deep inside me, there was one more mile of hope; it wasn't over—not yet. "Can I go with you? I want to be there if anything at all is found to tell us who they were."

"Sure. You've been a real trooper through this. I really thought you would have given up long ago," Netz said. "We've got time to stop for breakfast or just coffee if you want."

"If we did thirty days and nights non-stop like this, it would be nothing. If I hadn't done it then, much more would have been frostbitten. I wouldn't be here showing you two more dead men. That I couldn't stop. I didn't stop them from killing Craig. I had to make it out of there and find out who they were. Please, guys, find something from this; it's all I have. My life is looking out the window – nothing to be seen, just white haze and dark static. I made a promise." One I was beginning to think I couldn't keep. "Breakfast – I'll buy."

We ordered. "Just for my personal curiosity, how many days did you run from them?" Wheeling asked.

"I lost count, fourteen, maybe fifteen, but I'm not sure. There was never a day I didn't travel less than twelve hours. The days I knew they were close, I would go eighteen. Two days, I remember going non-stop through the night and on through the next day. They always found me; they had the advantage. The deeper the snow got, the harder it was for me to keep my ground on them. I was plowing the trail, and they followed in my footsteps. One of the many things that saved my life out there was I made my own snowshoes. With each blizzard, traveling became so much harder. When I started using those, I was back to eight to ten miles a day."

I hadn't gotten tired of telling the story and I went on. The food was brought to our table as I went on talking. I stared at my plate. I moved the food all around, thinking back, reliving it all again. I was no longer hungry.

Agent Wheeling asked how the first death dealer died.

"I befriended a half-grown black bear, only out of luck. The fish I speared for food I would feed to the bear, only out of fear at the time. I wanted it to eat the fish – not me. The day he died, he had caught me. I was screaming from sheer panic; he was on top of me, pounding on me. I hadn't seen the bear since the day before. Then I saw a black flash, then that one, and the bear tumbled into the snow. That bear literally shredded him, the most awful and gruesome thing I had ever seen."

I told them just about everything but the end. I realized they had finished eating, and their plates had been removed. I stopped as the waitress returned to our table.

"You didn't eat anything," she said.

"Please, would you bring us a to-go box," Netz asked her.

I shook my head, "I'm not hungry."

"But you haven't eaten since when – two days ago?" Netz asked me.

I shrugged, "It's only food. Many times, I went four or five days."

"Not now, you don't have to," Netz said.

I shrugged again.

"That's just amazing," Wheeling said.

"Every time I tell the story, that's the response I get. It's not amazing. The whole deal was just luck. In the first half, I ran from fear. I knew what they would do to me. The second half I did for Craig. I've babbled on long enough; let's go see what you can find."

"I believe there's more. What aren't you telling us?" Wheeling asked.

"Not now," I said to myself.

When we drove into the warehouse, my mouth fell open. Now, the steel tomb looked even bigger. There was a group of men all around working – at least a half dozen.

"Who are all these men?" I asked.

"They're like us, only specialists in different areas," Wheeling said.

We got out of the car, and I was astonished. I tilted my head back as I looked up in the air. The top of the steel tomb was raised into the air, almost straight up, and was hinged on one end. The other end was way up, I didn't know for sure, but guessing fifty feet or higher.

One of the men hurried over to us. "This thing is unbelievable," he said excitedly.

My eyes followed the lid back down to the box. There, on each side of the box, were two long hydraulic cylinders holding the lid suspended in the air.

"It's self-contained. There's a high-volume pump and tank inside. All we had to do was hook it up to electricity and turn it on. You won't believe how fast the lid moves." He was still hyper.

We heard the pump turn on, and within three seconds, the lid slammed shut. The noise echoed off the walls inside the warehouse forever. I wondered if those two men heard the same thing when their fate was sealed.

Then, it was raised back into the air in the same amount of time.

"Holy Be-Jesus!" Agent Wheeling said.

"Yes. It's clear the truck was driven into it; the smashed front end tells that story. I know what you're thinking—why drive an armored truck into a hole in the ground—why not just stop? They didn't. The smashed rear end tells another story. Once it's removed, we'll learn more. By preliminary examination, it hit the wall somewhere between thirty-five and forty-five miles per hour. Everyone has their theory, well, just speculations. One is it was pushed from behind by a larger vehicle. We'll check for flat spots on the tires. The next one is some fast-acting agent was released, and they fell asleep or died just seconds before driving in. We'll find out more when the autopsy is finished. After this much time has passed, it's going to be almost impossible to determine if they died before or after going into the hole. Another one is the speed the lid opens; it only took two to four seconds to open it upon arrival of the truck. A vehicle could have been staged there facing them with the bright lights on, momentarily blinding them, provided this occurred at night. Another is that the two men in there weren't driving, that their bodies were staged, or someone seized the vehicle long before and killed them instantly. There are so many questions. By many, I mean the more we learn, the more there are," the man said.

"That's what I've been telling myself for the past eight months. Now, I have twice as many. This is a massive undertaking. How did they pull it off without anyone knowing?" I said.

The man looked at me, and I could see the expression on his face. "Who are you?" he asked.

Agent Netz picked up on it also. "This is Ms. Chanhansen. She's the one who told us that it was there."

"I only told you something was there; I had no idea what it was," I said.

"Now there are more questions," the man said. He looked back at the steel box. "This is a good one. Without a doubt the strangest one I've ever worked on. I only hope we can come up with all the answers."

So did I, for Craig. "You don't know the half of it," I said.

"You seem to be quite knowledgeable about this. Stick around. We'll have questions for you," he said.

"Don't worry, I'm not going anywhere. I need answers as much as you do," I said.

"Why?" he asked.

"Your first answer – the men behind this killed my husband, and now they're dead."

"What were their names?" he asked.

I looked at Agent Netz, "That's what I need – that's why I called Agent Netz."

"Oh, geez! This is getting better," he said.

"So, you know mine, what do they call you?" I asked.

"Oh, I'm sorry. Al, they call me Al." Al rubbed his cheek. He might have been FBI; I wasn't positive, but he was definitely a lab guy, and I liked him.

"I have a list of questions that added up during the day yesterday. How did you know that was there? Did he tell you?" Netz asked me.

"No… well, yes, but not exactly. He gave me a set of numbers and nothing else. It took several weeks to realize they were GPS coordinates. Then, I had to figure out where they were. I drove to Chicago and then to the site. When I arrived there, there was nothing there. The two things he did tell me were, 'See not what you see; see what you don't.' That statement went through my mind dozens of times while I was there. I couldn't figure it out and I gave up and sat down on the ground in front of the car. I cried my eyes out, and while doing so, I started kicking at a wire sticking out of the ground. Then, I became obsessed with it and started digging. So I went and bought a shovel. The further I dug the deeper it got and the more determined I got. Then I realized, 'See what you don't.' The cracks in the asphalt confirmed that there was something down there."

"I'm impressed," Netz said.

Throughout the morning, I sat back and watched. Whatever questions they asked, I answered. The back of the steel box was cut away, and the truck was removed. My body was getting numb, and my eyes burned from lack of sleep. I had to be with them if anything was discovered.

Agent Netz sat down beside me, "Nothing yet."

"I have many more questions that there are no answers for yet. How did they know that truck would travel down that road at that exact time? How did they shut the road down without anyone getting suspicious? When it happened, why didn't those poor men call in? I would assume those trucks are watched by GPS at all times. Why didn't whoever was on the other end know where the truck disappeared? I found it."

"Those are all good questions. One's that I have asked myself, and I don't know. We'll find out, believe me," Netz said.

I did; I was counting on them.

"Look at the logistics that had to be worked out with months of planning and tens of thousands to complete it. The bill alone on the crane yesterday was eight grand. They had to pay to get the hole dug and then the road replaced. God only knows what that box cost them," Netz said.

"Whatever the total cost was to them was only pennies on the dollar. Look what they had gained. The other thing he did tell, that I didn't tell you a while ago was 'it will make you rich beyond your wildest dreams.' I'm guessing millions."

"You're probably right, Madie. I'm glad you trusted me for this. This is big." For the first time, I saw Agent Netz smile. "I might even get a raise out of this."

All I wanted was two names.

By the time we are finished they should let you retire. When we were finished here is when I decided to tell him there were nine more to go. In a way, that depressed me.

Late in the afternoon the guys in their blue lab coats had the armored truck completely dissected – nothing.

Agent Netz walked over to me, and was looking very haggard. "It is four ten and I have a room I haven't used yet – but in bad need of. Let's go get a shower and a two-hour nap. You haven't eaten since when? So let's go out to dinner, someplace nice, and relax. Boy, I haven't pulled an all-nighter in a long time."

I nodded. "My hopes are circling the drain. If you had had that kind of money at your fingertips, would you have left it there and hidden out in the middle of no where for years?"

"No. I'm not as smart as they were. There had to be some reason, or motive, why they did."

"They weren't smart enough, they're both dead."

Agent Netz smiled again, "They hadn't planned on running into you."

Agent Wheeling was a local, so he went home. He told us he was going to take a six-hour nap before going to bed and then sleep for eight hours.

I didn't want to sleep; I wanted answers.

In my motel room, I realized what was wrong with my right hand – the battery was going dead. By the time I undressed and removed my legs, it no longer moved. "Great, now what," I said to myself. My left hand was bandaged beyond use. So, I called the front desk and asked for tape and a shower brush. I was back to using my teeth.

After the long, slow ordeal of taking a shower, I felt much better. Now, it took even longer to get dressed, and I literally rubbed my clothes on. The new jeans and shirt were all I had left that were clean. I couldn't get the buttons buttoned, and I felt embarrassed. I would just have to tell Agent Netz I couldn't go out to dinner. I had cut the tape with my teeth on my left hand to remove the wet, dirty bandage. My palm and the inside of my thumb were raw, but without my thumb, I would have remained naked.

Then, the knock on the door, the one I was dreading. I walked to the door with the end of the blue jeans dragging behind me. I opened the door, and all I had to do was push down on the lever. I turned and started walking back toward the bed, holding the front of my shirt closed. My bra wasn't even snapped, all because of a stupid battery.

Agent Netz walked in behind me.

"I won't be able to go to dinner; I'm sorry." I turned and sat on the bed.

I saw the look on his face—astonishment and confusion.

"I had forgotten about your legs. Out in public, you would never know. But why not dinner?"

I was totally embarrassed. "Look at me, I can't even get dressed. The stupid battery in my hand," I held my right hand into the air, "went dead."

"That's all? After what you've been through, you're going to let a battery stop you?" he said.

He had a point. "This is really embarrassing. I can't get my bra hooked, and I can't even get my shirt buttoned." The events of the past two days had me worn down, and I started crying. "I'm sorry, but I'm a cripple without my right hand." I realized how dumb that sounded. "Well, I'm a cripple with it; the left one is too messed up."

Agent Netz looked at it. "Oh, man, we've got to get that bandaged." He regained his composure. "Madie, you are not a cripple, and you have nothing to be embarrassed about. You're the most courageous woman I have ever met."

Tears flowed. I didn't feel courageous sitting on the bed half undressed.

"I can finish getting you dressed and bandage your hand. Then we'll go eat. Deal?"

I wiped the tears on my arm and shook my head 'no.' "I can't hold the silverware."

Agent Netz frowned. "You have to eat sooner or later. Let me take care of it."

He finished dressing me. His fingers were delicate, but I was embarrassed beyond words. There hadn't been a strange man that close to my breasts for many years. I told him how to attach my legs, and after a minor struggle, he had them locked in place.

"Well, at least you don't have to tie my shoes," I laughed. I felt relieved.

No make-up and my shirt wasn't tucked in. I said, "A burger joint will be fine, or pizza."

"Madie, there is nothing wrong with you. On a bad day, you're better than average. I need to go back to my room; I won't be gone long."

He didn't bandage my left hand, and I wondered why. As sore as my hand was, I had to try and do the make-up thing.

I worked away. I managed to hold the brush to apply a little powder, and the mascara took a few minutes. I was doing a real hack job of lipstick when he returned. "Caught me in the act; I didn't want to look too scummy," I smiled.

"I found an Applebee's maybe fifteen or twenty miles from here. We have time now for your hand."

Agent Netz wrapped my hand, and he did a good job for a Fed. "Thank you."

When we pulled into the parking lot at Applebee's, it was full. I noticed he was driving slowly, looking at each car. The few empty slots he drove past. "Looking for bad guys?"

"No, one good guy in a blue car—a Ford," he said.

The first thought that came to mind was Agent Wheeling was meeting us. Then he stopped behind a blue Ford. The driver got out and was carrying a small case. I quickly ran the scenario – another agent, someone with information about the day.

The man walked up to my window, and Agent Netz rolled it down from his side. "Hi, are you Jeff?"

"Yes. Thank you for meeting us."

I quickly looked back at Agent Netz. "Jeff?"

He nodded.

"Madie, would you get in the backseat with me?"

I looked back at Agent Netz, frowning. "He's here to help you."

The man carried a gun and I had trusted him enough to call him to come here. Whatever this was, he had set it up. I got in the backseat, and the stranger got in on the other side.

"Hi, my name is Troy. Can I see your hand?"

Then, I figured it out. Troy went to work instantly, and within seconds, he had my hand removed. He sat his case on his lap and opened it. Within minutes, he had the battery removed as I watched intently. Even after seeing it done, without two good hands, I wouldn't be able to replace it on my own. Five minutes later, the hand was back on my arm. I opened and closed the fingers, and then I picked up a small screwdriver sitting on the seat between us. I rotated the wrist left and right and tilted the hand forward and back. It was the happiest I had been all day.

"You're very good with your movements, holding something so small. You've had that for a while?" Troy asked.

"Two weeks," I replied.

"Wow! I'm impressed," Troy said.

"You have no idea," Jeff said.

I wish people would quit saying that.

Jeff got out of the car, and I watched him pay Troy.

We ordered and were sitting in a booth along the window. "I'll pay you back; just tell me how much. This means more than you know. To tell you the truth, I had all intentions of sitting here and watching you eat. I had planned on getting a new battery when I returned home."

"What – go two more days without eating?"

"I learned a lot through that experience. A few days without food was just a thing."

We both ordered steaks with garlic mashed potatoes and steamed vegetables. "This really tastes good. Do you mind if I call you Jeff?" I asked.

"I prefer it, as long as I can stop calling you Ms. Chanhansen."

"Yes, you can." We were quiet while we ate.

"Tomorrow, they will have the autopsy report and anything on the truck. Then we can return home. After that, it's gathering information and interviews with everyone possible. They don't need us here," Jeff said.

"Is it alright if we fly back together?" I asked.

"Sure, I don't see a problem with that," Jeff answered.

"I don't see a ring. Are you married, Jeff?"

"I was, not anymore."

"I'm not getting into your personal business. I was just wondering if we could fly into Philadelphia. I know tomorrow is Saturday, so do you mind if we drive home from there?"

"If that's what you want to do."

"It is." I decided not to tell him; showing was better.

CHAPTER 47

We walked into the huge empty warehouse at seven a.m. The men were already there working. Al was looking a bit rougher around the edges. The truck and steel box was forty feet from the front door and he didn't see us walk up.

"Good morning, Al," Jeff said.

"Oh, geez!" he said surprised. "Oh, man, look what we found." He held out a small box. "Electronic scrambler for easy definition."

Jeff nodded that he understood. I didn't.

"I think this answers some questions. Nothing could get in or leave. The GPS and radio waves were lost. The theory is that it was activated miles away. They were traveling blind and didn't even know it. They heard nothing from the other end. They assumed no news was good news and kept going on their route."

"More than likely. Where did you find it?" Jeff asked.

"Underneath the engine on the passenger's side," Al answered.

Now we knew something.

As the morning wore on, I learned nothing else. The early morning rush faded away to boredom. Al said they would be finished by noon. I wasn't going to get the answers I so badly wanted. Maybe after digging up several more, something would be found—a mistake they made that was overlooked.

The slight smell Jeff had noticed was cyanide gas. Al had, in with stacks of boxes, a gas detector. The traces had diminished to a non-lethal dose over the years.

Just before noon, the autopsy report came to us, and it was confirmed that the cause of death was cyanide poisoning.

Jeff and I left for the airport. I felt defeated, one more for the death dealers.

At the check-in terminal, Jeff flashed his badge. He was escorted off by airport security. Like all other government officials of his status since 9/11, extra security on planes was always welcomed. Before he left me, he said, "I'll meet you on the plane. Can you make it through, ok?"

"Sure," I said. I had traveled through airports many times in my life. "Piece of cake," I told myself.

As I walked up to the line to go through the metal detector, I saw the people taking off their shoes. I had been thinking deeply about the past days' events that I hadn't thought of my new condition. It would do no good to take off my shoes so I didn't get in line. I slowly walked up to the security people, standing between the two machines. I stood there, waiting, saying nothing. Then, as the closest man noticed me, I smiled.

"You need to get in line, ma'am," he said.

"If I walk through that, it will light up like a Christmas tree. It won't do any good if I take off my shoes," I said.

He looked at me, not sure of what to say.

"I'll show you." I saw a chair sitting just on the other side of the metal detector. "If you would like me to sit in that chair, it would be much easier for me."

He continued to stare at me, and his expression was easy to read. I was different, and he wasn't sure if he trusted me. I sat in the chair he had carried to my side of the machine. I raised my left leg and raised my pant leg. He saw the exposed metal pole of my leg. Then I did the same with the right. I didn't get up. "My right hand also." I twisted it back and forth, then up and down. The mechanical movement of it made it no doubt as to what it was. The glove couldn't hide that.

"Wow! Anything else?"

"No, that's enough for one person."

"Ok, come over here with me. This is going to take some time, I'm sorry, just procedure."

I was led over to the far side. The manual wand was moved all around my body several times. I had to show them physically the starting points of each limb. Then, I had to go through the manual inspection with the bomb sensor. The whole ordeal took time and many people traveled through the line. I saw many of them staring at me. I knew what they were thinking, 'What did they see to alert them?'

Jeff and I sat next to each other on the plane. I didn't feel like talking and he didn't try. All I could think about were questions, and the numbers kept growing. Time passed and the flight attendants were passing out drinks.

"Why do the number of my questions keep growing? It seems that when I learn one thing, I have ten more to ask," I asked.

"You'd make a good detective. Because that's just the way it is. Even after the truth is found, you still have more questions," Jeff answered.

That was definitely my case. No lawyer, judge, or jury would ever ask the death dealers why.

"So where would you get cyanide if you wanted to poison someone?" I asked.

"It's not hard, many places, like industrial settings. It's used to extract gold from ore. It's also used in metal plating; a jeweler uses it. Exterminators can get it, and any chemical lab has it."

That answered that question. "Is it a painful way to die?"

"Yes, the most excruciating pain you could imagine for two or three seconds, then it's over."

I didn't need to ask anymore on that subject. More unnecessary deaths. I felt sad for two men that I never met.

We landed, retrieved our luggage, and headed for the car rental.

While walking there Jeff said, "You do remarkably well."

I wasn't sure what he meant and I looked at him.

"No one would ever know your condition, and you don't limp."

"I was lucky enough to keep my knees. If I had lost them, I believe it would be different."

We signed the papers, thanked the car rental agent, and headed on our way. Before we hit the interstate, I had to know. I wanted to see both spots again, I was pretty sure. Now that I knew what I was looking for, I needed to know.

"Agent Netz, would you do me a favor?"

"Uh oh, why do I think something's wrong? Agent Netz? What happened to Jeff?"

"Would you take the scenic route home? I'd like to go to Boston and see an old acquaintance."

"Yes, I owe you. Call it returning a favor."

For the next thirty minutes, we didn't talk. I was thinking about where we were going. I assumed Jeff was also, or what we had found. I was wrong.

"Did it hurt?" Jeff asked.

That shocked me. I had no idea that's what he was thinking about.

"Being frozen like that, was it painful?"

I sat in the passenger's seat, looking out the windshield. "To tell you the truth, I didn't know what hurt the most: the physical fatigue, the mental pain, lack of sleep, food, and water. And the cold, it was relentless. Walking twelve to sixteen hours a day, everything blended together. At the time, I had a good idea of what was happening, but I had to go on. Getting started in the morning was the worst – unbearable. My feet would sting so bad I would cry. During the day my legs would make me forget about my feet. At times it would take all I had to just make the next step, and then the next. My hands just shut down quietly, and I used them very little. You know what the worst part of it was?"

Jeff shook his head 'no'.

"Sleeping, or trying to sleep. No matter what I did or tried, piling pine limbs on top of me along with snow. I couldn't stay warm. I'd wake shivering and aching so badly I couldn't stand it. I even skinned one of the wolves the bear killed and used that for a blanket."

"A wolf? The bear killed a wolf?"

"Three, one of the many times it saved me." I had told him that part. I went on and told him many other things. It helped the time go faster, and the trip.

During my talking I told Jeff to turn at the right places and continued talking, which happened many times. I didn't need the GPS; I remembered how to get there. Several more turns, and then I saw the spot coming up ahead.

"Ok, you can slow down," I said. "Pull over, please; I need to get out."

Jeff stopped the car, and I got out. "There's nothing here," he said.

Jeff got out anyway. I looked around at the surroundings. It was just as I remembered it. Then I looked at the road – there it was, the crack running from the edge of the road to the center, unnoticeable to the eye that wasn't looking for it.

Jeff was looking around, wondering what we were doing here. I walked to the driver's door, opened it, popped the trunk lid, and then opened it. I removed the cover on the spare tire and removed the tire iron.

I walked in front of the car three feet before the crack. I dropped down onto my knees. By now, the tears were flowing, and I kept sniffling, trying to hold back my runny nose. I struck the ground with the point of the tire iron. I wiped my eyes with my sleeve; I knew there were two more dead men below me.

"Madie, what are you doing?" Jeff asked.

I looked up. I pointed my finger, moving it from where I knelt to the center of the road, then down the center and back to the dirt.

Jeff followed the imaginary line I had just drawn. Then, I saw his shoulders slump.

"Oh, my God! Another one?"

I went back to digging and crying. Jeff walked over and put a hand on my shoulder, but I didn't stop. I had to find the wire. Each pick from the tire iron wasn't resulting in much dirt removal. I was only scratching the ground but I wasn't stopping until the battery in my right hand wore out or I found the wire.

"Here, let me do that."

While Jeff continued to dig, I tried my best not to cry.

"You know, you didn't have to lie to me. If you would have told me I would have still dug here."

"I didn't lie to you. I told you I wanted to go see an old acquaintance. I've been here before, and this is the second location I stopped at before going on to Chicago. At the time, I didn't know what was here."

Jeff stopped digging. "You mean there's another one? Three?"

I started crying harder, thinking of twenty dead men at ten locations. I nodded and then started rattling off the numbers. "Thirty nine, three, ten and one o four, seventeen and twenty. Forty, thirty eight, two and eighty two, nineteen, nineteen. Thirty seven, twenty two, fifty four and ninety three, thirty three, twenty one. And that's just a start, beyond the first three," I said.

Jeff's frame collapsed as if he just melted into a pile of flesh. "How many are there?"

"Ten total," I said.

"Oh, my God," Jeff said slowly.

I nodded. "Twenty dead mean, and I'll never have an answer," I said.

When Jeff faced the bitter reality of what I had just told him, he went back to digging. He dug as I did in Chicago, like he was possessed. I laid my bandaged left hand on his arm. "Slow down, or your hands will end up looking like mine. We already know what's down there."

"I can't believe this. I thought one was an undertaking of unbelievable conception, but nine more? Who were these guys? How did they accomplish something I can't even believe without getting caught? I remember hearing about it years ago. I never worked the case, very few did. No leads were ever found, then it just went away."

"Now, here's your chance to make history; I'm counting on you. I want Craig to know who killed him. If you want, I will stay with you to the end. The only help I can be is to give you each location, but, I'd really like to be there."

"I'd have it no other way. Without you, this would have never happened. What you went through is as unbelievable as this. You're the one who should make history."

I felt the lump in my throat again and swallowed hard. "Thank you, but this is all about Craig."

Jeff continued to dig, and ten minutes later, the wire was found six inches below the surface. It was an exact replica of the first wire.

It was early afternoon, so we decided to cover it back up, drive to the first spot I had stopped at, and confirm that one. Then, Jeff was to make plans to start removing them, one at a time. Then, move to the next until all were removed.

On the drive to the spot closest to where I lived, I asked Jeff if it would be alright if I had the crew, my friends, come down and witness one being dug up. He saw no problem with that. His answer was, "They saved your life. They need to see the reason why they did it."

The first location was confirmed—the cracks in the asphalt and the wire.

As Jeff replaced the dirt, he said, "It's been here for five years. Two more days isn't going to change the outcome. Can your friends make it down tomorrow? If so, I can use the day to get everything lined up. We know what we need, and now, with the proof of what was found in Chicago, everything will be rushed through."

"I don't see why not." I made the call as we drove on to my house.

Jim answered, "Hi, it's Madie," I said.

"So, are you finished? Are you flying up tomorrow?" Jim asked.

"That's why I called. Can you and the rest of the gang fly down here tomorrow? I know it's kind of short notice, but I'd like you guys to be here. I have something to show you."

It was agreed on. They would be here before dinner, and Jim would bring fresh fish. I couldn't wait to see them and I also couldn't wait to eat fresh walleye.

CHAPTER 48

Jeff was at my house waiting for them to arrive. He had the equipment lined up and waiting to start by seven a.m. the next morning. Only this time, the entire road was going to be closed from the beginning and two big track hoes were going to be digging simultaneously to speed the process up. Lee and his crew were assigned to the inspection of it, and the warehouse had been prepared. Things happened fast which had taken a great deal of manpower. But when the FBI was involved and the priority of the project, nothing was questioned.

I heard the car pull into my driveway. I got up and nearly ran out of the house. Jonathon was driving and Mary sat in the passenger's seat. Jerry, George, and Jim sat in the back. I laughed, and I cried; I was so happy to see them.

I introduced them to Jeff. While hands were shook, I hugged Jim several times. Silently, I said to him, "I miss you. I'm glad you came down. I wanted you here."

Bottles of wine were opened, and many caps were removed from beer bottles. While Jim and Mary cooked, the men naturally fell into storytelling. Some I had heard, others were new. I was glad to hear them all. Jeff was fascinated with them. He sat back, listening and smiling, and I could see that he liked them. But how could one not? They were the greatest.

For hors d'oeuvres, there was fish soup made with walleye, potatoes, onions, and light cream, and pickled northern with melted butter. It was just as Jim said it was. The poor man's lobster—both were fantastic.

The main course was baked and broiled walleye cooked in three different ways. Those turned out to be better than fantastic, served with rice pilaf with mushrooms and baked potatoes.

"My Lord, one thing is for certain: that is the best fish I have ever eaten," Jeff said.

The laughter and the story telling continued on into the night. Dishes were done and put away. The men told some of their rescue stories in bitter cold dozens of miles from nowhere and some lasting for days. Not all had good outcomes.

Jeff was in awe. "How do you do it? I mean, how can you stand being out there days at a time in sub-zero temperatures?" he asked.

All went silent. George spoke, "It's nothing compared to what Madie went through."

They'd heard it before, like some of their stories, but I told them again. "I only ran because of what I knew they would do to me. My death wouldn't have been as fast as Craig's. The last half I did for Craig. I made a promise I don't think I'm able to keep."

"So that brings me to a few questions I've wanted to ask all night. What happened to your hand? That's a lot of bandage, must be hurt severely," Jim said.

"No, not really. Jeff just used a good deal of gauze."

Jim grinned, "Nice way to skirt around the answer."

"Oh, alright! I was digging, and that's the truth. I have an FBI agent here to testify to that."

Jim nodded. "So what is it that you called us down here for? What did you find?" Jim asked.

Jeff looked at me. I answered, "You'll see tomorrow; it's unbelievable. The only bad part is that I'm still light-years behind them. I don't think I'll ever have an answer."

"Madie, I've said this before, don't underestimate us. We've found answers with a lot less."

"Not even a hint?" Jerry asked.

The next morning, we were up at four. The gang stayed at my house. Two pots of coffee disappeared, and then we were on our way. I was feeling several different kinds of emotions – excited, nervous, and worried – even though I knew the outcome. I only hoped there would be something new or different, one more clue.

We met up with Jeff at the edge of town.

We arrived twenty minutes before seven. "Good Lord, would you look at all that heavy machinery?" Jonathan said.

"What in the world is going on?" Jerry asked.

"I don't see anything around here," George said. "It's in the ground, isn't it?"

George was the quietest one of the gang and he had earned my respect. He was intelligent.

I said nothing.

We got out. I followed Jeff up to the men in charge of the equipment. Both track hoes were sitting along the road, ready to go to work. The crane and semi, with its extra-long trailer, sat further down the road. Six men who were with the road commission stood waiting, and they had barriers set up at each end.

"So, what's going on? We weren't told what to do," the man said. He was one of the road crew.

"There's a reason for that. You didn't need to know. What you're about to see here remains with you. This doesn't leak out to the papers until I say so. If it does, I guarantee you the FBI will interrogate each and every one of you. Does anyone here need to sign a paper stating that?" Jeff said firmly. He was back in the agent mode.

Some of the men whistled, and others mumbled, but no one said yes.

"Good. What we have here is a steel container." Jeff walked out on the road. He was standing on the crack that ran from the gravel to the center. He started pointing, "It starts here. It's thirty feet long, and the width is wider than this lane. It weighs approximately eighty thousand pounds. So, let's dig it up and get it on that trailer."

Most of the men started talking at once, and I listened to their comments. They ranged from 'no way,' 'you've got to be kidding,' to 'who put it there.' I assumed it was the boss of the road crew who spoke next.

"If something like that was down there, we'd know about it. You're going to dig up the road on a hunch?" he said.

"Believe this, it's no hunch. And no, you didn't know about this."

"Let me check our records," he said.

"There's no need to; you won't find it. To cut through all the legal hassles and to not waste time, I have a signed court order. So, let's start digging." Then Jeff spoke directly to the machine operators. "If you have it sitting on that trailer by noon, you will be paid double."

The drivers practically ran to their machines.

Jim and the rest circled in close to me. "Madie, what's going on?" Jim asked.

"It has to be something important, or you wouldn't have asked us here," Jerry said.

"It's why Craig was killed. I wanted you to see why I have no answers as to who they were."

The machines started in the middle, each working their way to opposite ends. In less than an hour, the top was uncovered.

With the exception of Jeff and myself, no one could believe the massive size. Then they started down the sides. The larger machines were much faster and Jeff didn't need to stop them to inspect – we knew.

Three hours from the start, it was completely unearthed, and the machines were backed away. While the crane moved into position, the rest of the men stood around the edge of the hole, looking down in amazement. 'If only they knew,' I thought.

Jonathon walked up to me, "What did you get into, Madie?"

"I've been asking myself that since the day Craig was killed." Mary and the others stood next to me. "You won't believe what's inside," I said, even though I knew I still had a hard time grasping reality.

We followed it to the warehouse, arriving there just past noon. Lee and his group were there waiting. I saw the look on his face – another one.

While it was being unloaded from the semi, Lee, Jeff, and the rest of us stood back, watching. "I can't believe there's another one. This just blows me away."

I looked at Jeff, "Does he know?" I asked.

"Know what?" Lee said to me.

Jeff nodded no.

"There's eight more, scattered across the country."

"Unbelievable," Lee said.

That seemed to be the phrase for everyone, but that's what it was.

Lee said the same thing I thought, "Twenty dead men, how sad—just for greed."

Mary grabbed my arm, "Madie, is that true?"

"Yes," I answered.

The advantage of having Lee and his group there is they knew what equipment they needed and what to do. Thirty minutes later electricity was hooked into the wire running out of the box.

Before the lid started opening, I said to the crew, "Watch this. It gets better."

The lid started rising. "Oh, my God! What's in there?" Jim asked.

I didn't want to ruin the shock, "You'll see."

It took them an hour to cut the end of the steel box loose, and then it was removed. Everyone walked to the opening and looked in.

To their shocked and surprised look, I said, "An armored truck."

The back of the truck was opened. Now, to Jeff's and my surprise, there were no dead men inside, just bags of money. We looked at each other, wondering why.

"What does this mean?" I asked.

"Another clue – another question," Jeff said.

Before the truck was removed, it was dusted for prints. Only two sets were found, no surprise there.

We watched the truck roll out backward, like the first truck. The little black box was found underneath the engine, but nothing else.

There was nothing more for me to see there. I told Jeff we were going back to my house. He said he would call if anything new was found. I wouldn't get a call.

On the drive back to my house, I was depressed. The guys talked non-stop about what they had just seen. They asked more questions than I had asked myself. The only answer I had which covered them all was, I don't know.

We sat around the kitchen table. The only topic of conversation was the death dealers. I listened. They were as dumbfounded as I was. Why leave that much money buried for five years? And how did something that complicated get pulled off?

I had given up on the idea as soon as my walkout was over. Due to the vast amount of wilderness I had walked, added in, I had no idea where I was on any given day; I didn't know where each of the death dealers had died. My question would simply be answered – if I had their dental imprints. I had learned in the past few months never to underestimate my friends. They were highly skilled at what they did. As I listened to them, I had an idea.

"You guys are the best friends I could ever ask for. Without you, I wouldn't have survived this. So, what I'm about to ask you, if you say no I totally understand. Do you think we could go back and find one of them? If we could bring back one of their skulls, they could get the dental records. I believe that's the only way I will ever know who they were."

The men looked at one another. I thought I was about to get a 'no.'

Jim spoke first. "I'm sure that idea has gone through all our minds."

"More than once," Jerry said. "We have plenty of time before winter sets in."

"What we need from you is anything at all you can remember at each location," Jonathan said.

"It won't be that hard to narrow it down to a few square miles. We can show you topographical maps. With hills, valleys, lakes, and streams, we can find them," George said.

"That's right. What else would help is counting days. If you can remember how many days you walked to where the bear killed the first one or how many you walked to where you found Jim's house after the second died would be really helpful," Jerry said.

My spirits lifted. I had the best crew in all of Canada finding lost souls, and mine was lost. I could feel the tears building on the surface, trying to break through. These were tears of happiness. Then, the fragile wall broke, and tears ran down my face.

"Madie, why are you crying?" Mary asked.

"Because you guys are way too good to me, and there's nothing I could possibly do to ever repay you."

"There is. Come live with us," Jim said.

I nodded, "When this is over, I will. Eight more to go."

The rest of the day was spent talking, and plenty of beer was consumed. My wine rack was getting short in supply, but I was happy. Many ideas were discussed on how to go about finding a set of teeth in the middle of nowhere. Often, the conversation drifted back to the day's event. I just listened; I had nothing to add to the talk.

Late in the evening, my cell phone rang; it was Jeff.

"Hello, Madie. It's as you said it would be; nothing was found out of the ordinary," Jeff said.

I knew the outcome but I still slumped in my chair. That one desperate glimmer of hope vanished. "What happened to the men that were inside?" I asked.

"That is what we will find out. Tomorrow, a team of agents will scrutinize their records. The armored truck company will have records of who worked that night or whose route it was. Like I keep telling you, it's just a matter of time. Oh, and by the way, another four point two million was recovered. These guys definitely did their homework. They knew which trucks carried the most money. The armored truck company is greatly indebted to you. This is something that has baffled them for years. They would like to meet you," Jeff said.

"Did you tell them there are eight more?" I asked.

"No, only because we don't know if they are all their trucks. There are several companies like that throughout the country. We thought it would be best just to notify them as each one is removed."

That made sense to me.

"I'll call you first thing in the morning. I've already started making plans to dig up the next one," Jeff said.

I hung up. The gang was looking at me, waiting to hear the news. "Four point two million was in the truck, but nothing else. The absence of the two men gives me hope. Maybe they haven't murdered as many as I thought," I said.

George broke the silence and said what everyone was thinking, "Wow! That's a lot of money."

"To sit underground for five years," I added.

The next morning, the gang left for the airport. They made me promise, repeatedly, that I would return when this was over. In my mind, it would never be over. I had started it, and I would remain with it until the last eight were dug up.

I sat around waiting for Jeff to call. The morning passed, and nothing. The nervous energy was building, so I cleaned the house. I thought doing that would keep my mind off of it – it didn't.

Two p.m., and the phone finally rang. "Madie, Jeff. Sorry, it took so long to call you. I've been in one long meeting all day. My boss, myself, and some pretty big hitters in the organization.

We came up with a game plan. Pack your bags; there will be a car there in an hour to pick you up. You will be brought here to the office and plan on a long night. They want to sit down with you and discuss several things. One is the location of the eight remaining locations. Also, they would like each and every little detail you can remember – what they said, what they did, and what they didn't do. Then you'll be with a sketch artist. If at all possible, they would like a drawing of both men."

I didn't tell Jeff that when I returned to Canada, we were going back to try to find one of them. That was as about as big of an odds as finding anything useful in the armored trucks.

At two a.m., I was driven to a motel. The car was going to return at six a.m. to pick me up. The game plan was, with the next location being so close, to dig it up in the morning. Then, after that, one every three days – the first day to travel and locate the place, the second day was to be spent locating the equipment to dig it up, and the third day sifting through what was found. Then, on to the next.

What the FBI was working so diligently on was the driver and the guard who was supposed to have been with the truck. That was the only difference, the only positive lead to go with. I was told within two days, they would know. The armored truck company records would be sifted through thoroughly.

After three hours of sleep, I was up. Now, with the findings of the last truck, I was more than ready to see what was in this one. Hopefully, there wouldn't be any dead guys. Greed was one thing; killing to obtain that greed was another.

I walked over to the dirt pile and sat on it. It was where I felt more comfortable like I had some connection with what was under the ground. Maybe it was the death dealer still chasing me. I didn't have one, and they weren't. But I had a bad feeling; there were dead men inside.

Jeff walked over and sat beside me. He no longer wore the suit and tie, blue jeans with a cotton button down shirt was his new attire. I didn't tell him what I felt.

"I know you by now. When you sit on the dirt, something's bothering you," Jeff said.

"They still haunt me. I will never be able to outrun them." My thoughts started drifting back. "You know, the first blizzard that hit, it was snowing so hard I couldn't see the hand in front of my face. At that time, they were close – at most, several hundred yards back. I was so scared I couldn't stop. I ran into several trees trying to put more ground between us. I was blind. The sheer panic I was feeling was unimaginable. I got down on my hands and knees and crawled my way forward. I just knew at any moment, I was going to feel a hand grab me from behind. I kept telling myself that if I could go on, the snow would cover my tracks. I thought if I could get far enough ahead, they would never find me. I went for several hours like that. Then, I became so exhausted I gave up. I sat with my back against a tree. I feared that if I lay down, I would suffocate. The next morning, I was up at daybreak and would be gone, but they always found me. They were good, and now I know how good they were."

"Madie, every time you tell me another part of your story, it amazes me."

By noon, the box was sitting on the trailer. Before it was lifted out of the hole, I told Jeff that I wanted to go inside and see. My feelings were right: two unfortunate dead men. I wanted to scream; I wanted to cry. My question was, why? I remained silent as I walked out of their steel tomb.

CHAPTER 49

We were on the plane heading for the next location. Nothing was found the previous day that would give me a name. Several million dollars was inside the truck with two dead men and traces of cyanide. Depression was slowly setting in. I didn't talk.

"Madie, remember, don't underestimate us. We're only days into one of the biggest puzzles I've ever encountered."

I didn't respond, and he knew what I was thinking.

"Usually, we're following leads and chasing live criminals. This time, we're chasing dead men; you are our only lead. We will find out."

"Is it true what is said about a Texas Ranger – one riot, one ranger?"

Jeff smiled, I think on my behalf. "So they say. They were a rare breed."

I was ninety-nine percent sure how the remaining seven locations were going to turn out. This was going to be finished with me. I had a group of four Texas rangers. There was nothing they couldn't do in their natural surroundings. I started crying.

I sat in my room throughout the afternoon while Jeff made the arrangements for the following day. My spirits hadn't lifted any, so I called Jim. I told him nothing useful was found.

"Madie, we've been searching through stacks of maps. Right now, we're trying to figure out the route you took. It's mostly just speculation right now," Jim said.

I could remember vividly what the location looked like where the second death dealer had died. Where that location was we had to figure out. "Jim, I can remember what the lake looked like when I walked out on it. It was larger than the others. I entered it on the east side and it was much longer than wide. It was sort of pear-shaped. I do recall the terrain on the south side where I ran back into the woods. There was a deep ravine running into it. Beyond that, I believe it was a big swamp; at least, that's what it looked like. Many dead trees, just bare poles sticking up out of the ground. The cliff running alongside it is what saved my life." The silence between us was eerie. "I know that's not much to go on."

"It's a start," Jim said.

"Also, if this helps, the rolling hills were a day or two behind me."

"We'll keep researching. But that's not why you called – what's bothering you?" Jim asked.

Tears pooled. "No, it's not. We're not getting anywhere here. It's rather disheartening."

"All is not lost. No one's perfect, and they had to slip up somewhere."

I only hoped so.

The next day, I sat through the grueling process of digging the next one up. My mind was totally wrapped up in the past. All I could think of was getting back to Jim and the gang. I wanted to be near them. I had to try and find the second death dealer.

As I already knew, nothing more was found inside the fourth truck.

Jeff and I spent the next twenty-four days flying all over the country, and I was becoming exhausted. I always held the hope of finding something at the next location, but we never did. I was becoming immune to seeing two dead bodies inside each truck. I thought how sad that was, but I was glad I wasn't the one who had to tell their families. Nothing surprised me with dealing with the death dealers. They got what they deserved. That was my saving grace. But, on the other hand, I didn't get what I needed.

Finally, at the last location, I was glad this was about to be over. Lee and his group were looking as rough as I felt. They gave each truck attention as if it were the first. Even though they knew what and where to exactly look for everything, they still spent the time to diligently look at every square inch of each truck. The dollar amount was staggering, the total tally I no longer kept track of. At each location there were new faces standing around waiting for the bags of money. My hand shook so many times that I lost count, each time telling me how grateful they were.

Jeff and I were back on another plane, heading east, our last flight together. This ordeal still consumed me, "There's a reason they left that much money hidden in the ground for five years. Another reason as to why they were hiding so far north. I keep asking myself, why? I mean, to this day, no one knows who they were. Why freeze your butt off to remain hidden when you're already unknown around the world," I said.

"As soon as we can answer that, you'll be the first to know. It would have been nice to have interrogated them. Sometimes, it's nice for us good guys to talk to people like that. They were logistical geniuses. What we learn from them, sometimes we can use the next time to catch people like that."

I thought about Mother Nature. As smart as they appeared to be, they didn't beat her. She took them too early from me. I had no doubt she didn't care.

I was glad to be home; I was totally exhausted. I called Jim. The plan was I was going to sleep for a day and then Randy was to fly down and pick me up the following day. Then when I returned to Jim's, the day after was to be spent looking at maps. They had several locations picked out that looked similar to what I had described. Then Randy was to fly us up and drop us off. It was late September, and time was running short. If needed, we were going to spend a month up there looking, searching for my answer.

When I woke I had slept for ten hours. Physically, I still felt worn out, but mentally I was excited. I was returning to the land where I had once said that I would never return, taking half my body and my whole life. But now I have new friends who I love dearly, and I know they would do anything for me. That was far more than anyone could ask for.

I was packed and had called the cab company. Luckily, Tore was working. I told them I needed a ride to the small airport outside of the city. It was the one used by independent pilots.

What lay ahead of us was a monumental task. If it couldn't be achieved, I would be greatly disappointed. But I still had the lazy days, sitting in the boat, fishing with Jim and the gang, listening to the stories and laughing, always enjoying their companionship. That is what I looked forward to the most.

Tore pulled into the driveway. My three large suitcases sat in the garage. I waved to him before the cab stopped moving.

Tore got out. "Hi, Madie! It's been a long time. How are you?" he asked.

"I'm fine, and you? How's the family?"

"Great! To be honest with you, I didn't think I'd ever see you again. With your new parts, I didn't think you'd need my services. I'm glad you called."

"I need a ride to the airport."

Tore looked at my suitcases. I could see the disappointment on his face. "Looks like you're going to be gone awhile."

"Yes. I'm returning to where it all started."

Tore said nothing. During the thirty-minute drive to the airport, I kept the conversation going on Tore's family. He loved to talk about them, and I loved to listen.

When we pulled into the small airport I saw Randy's plane sitting out on the tarmac. He would be inside waiting for me. We got out of the cab and Tore opened the trunk and removed my bags. Slowly, he looked up into my eyes. I saw the sadness.

"The bravest woman I will ever know. You take care of yourself, Madie. I will miss our short trips together," Tore said.

Was this it? Did Tore have a premonition that we would never see each other again? I hadn't thought of that; I was too preoccupied with what was ahead of me. I hugged him. "Tore, you're a wonderful man. I like the way you talk about your family. Always cherish them; life is precious," I said.

Tore looked at me. "You know your way back. You've had to go through more than a dozen people combined. You can't change the past; work on what you believe."

I hugged him tighter and was instantly crying.

"If you let the bad consume you, you have no future."

Now, I was bawling my eyes out. How could someone not like Tore? He was right. "Thank you, Tore, you're the greatest."

I looked toward the movement at the front door, Randy was walking toward us. I quietly said, "Thank you," and kissed Tore on the cheek. I would miss him dearly.

Randy carried the two largest bags as we walked in the front door. "You know, every time I'm near you, I feel so sad and guilty. This sure doesn't help that."

I wiped the remaining tears away.

"When I fail at something, I fail miserably; it's my curse."

New ones returned.

"I will fly you to all ends of the earth. It's all I can do, and it will never be enough. I gave up too easily which haunts me each and every day. Since then, I have thought of at least ten things I should have done differently. I want you to know how sorry I am."

Too weak to go on, I stopped. Crying, I said, "Randy, I've told you before, it was not your fault. It was already over by then."

"Your life wasn't; it's still ahead of you. I've never told anyone this. When I heard you were found and the condition you were in – if you would have died after walking out that far, I would have given up. I was going to sell the business and move far away. I wouldn't have been able to live with the guilt."

I felt like I was going to fall forever and never land. I was so fortunate to be surrounded by people who now were my friends and so good to me. Crying, I said, "I don't deserve all the kindness everyone has given me. There are so many, you included. I'm just me. I'm the one who failed."

"You are one in a hundred billion. I'll never be lucky enough to meet the next one."

Now I hugged Randy, thankful he was on the long list of people that were my friends.

"There was one who was far greater than me; I'm sorry you didn't get to know him."

"Come on, you've got a group of people further north anxiously waiting for your return. They have a small surprise for you, but you didn't hear that." Randy smiled.

I sat in the plane, looking down at the trees far below. The hum of engine noise relaxed me and I was thinking of what Tore said. He was right, some day I would put this behind me enough so I could go on. Right now I couldn't. I was also thinking about how many lives this has touched. Randy's had been the hardest. I didn't realize it then, but now I do. I somehow had to think of something to ease his guilt.

"I was told I had to circle around the lake and then fly across from east to west," Randy said.

Why? I wondered.

Then, I saw it, even before we reached the edge of the water on the east side of the lake. We were high enough to see Jim's yard. Before I had time to register what I was looking at, fireworks went off. And by fireworks, I don't mean the over-the-counter stuff. Huge rockets started shooting up in the air, one after another, sometimes two and three at a time. I couldn't believe my eyes. It was magnificent! When we reached the far side of the lake, they stopped. Randy banked the plane around to the left. Then he brought it down to a landing on the water facing Jim's home.

"Boy, that was something. I haven't seen fireworks like that since I was a kid."

The plane idled across the water before I had a chance to reply. A ground display went off, and I quickly glanced around Jim's yard. There were dozens of people and a large banner that read 'Welcome Home Madie.' Through the tears, I could see many tables set up with food. Randy shut off the engine, and the plane coasted to a stop several feet from shore. I opened my door and could hear the crowd cheering and the fireworks stopped. I looked to the edge of the water; there, I saw my gang standing together. I didn't wait for the plane to be pulled to shore, and I jumped out. I landed in thigh-deep water, but I didn't care. I was crying so hard I would soon be soaked with my own tears. I ran as hard as I could through the water. When I reached the ground, I ran directly into Jim's arms. I was crying so hard I couldn't speak. I went from Jim to Mary, Jonathan, Jerry, and then George. The crowd continued to cheer, and I continued to cry. I whispered in George's ear, "Today, I am the luckiest person alive."

When I regained my composure I hugged them all again, this time thanking them.

As the day passed, I never left their side; I kept the five of them close to me. I met new people and I met a few that I had before. All had come out from town for this.

Then, I noticed Randy. He had remained in the shadows while everyone ate. I walked over to him, "Come on, you're part of this group. If you think I'm letting you stay out of it, you're crazy."

Everyone came up to me throughout the afternoon. In some form, they all had the same thing to say. They had heard so much about me and admired my willingness to survive. Some even said they were sorry for my loss. I thanked each and every one of them.

Beer was consumed by the gallons; dozens of corks were pulled from wine bottles, and the liquor flowed. The Canadians knew how to drink.

CHAPTER 50

I woke the next morning with a bit of a headache and I could hear commotion out in the kitchen. I looked at the clock next to my bed, and it was almost eight. I stumbled out to the kitchen, there everyone sat drinking coffee. I couldn't believe it. I slid on my stumps across the kitchen floor, heading for the coffee pot. "Don't you guys ever sleep?"

"Not when there's work to do," Jerry said.

"Oh, and by the way, with all the commotion going on yesterday, if I haven't thanked you guys for the party, thank you. It was unbelievable."

"Oh, only about a hundred times," Jim said.

"And the fireworks, I mean, geez, what a display," I said.

"That's just a hobby of ours. We make our own," Jerry said.

"Make your own! Is there anything you guys don't do? What haven't you told me?"

They laughed. "No, that just about does it," Jonathan said.

I walked back to the kitchen table. In the center of it sat a tall stack of maps. "Wow!" I said, looking at it.

"Yes, without you to narrow it down, the possibilities are endless," Jim said.

They let me drink one cup of coffee before they started in. After the first question was asked, I was hit with a barrage of them. The maps with the elevations, tree density, and location of lakes meant nothing to me. It was all Greek. My best answer was 'could be'. Mostly, it consisted of 'I don't know' or 'It doesn't look right.'

Then, Jerry pulled out a big map, and I saw two red circles on it. Jerry pointed to the first. "This is where you started." Then, he pointed to the second. "This is where you are now. There are two hundred forty-seven point three miles in between. Giving it a rough guess, you wandered off the straight line at least twenty miles east and west, some days probably more. So with that in mind, there's 4,946 square miles to cover."

I sat back in my chair and let out a long sigh.

"All is not lost. We've had many discussions on how many miles you walked each day," Jonathan said.

George spoke for the first time. "By many, we mean hours and hours. The first week running from them in light snowfall, and the hours per day you walked, we estimated you covered fifteen miles a day. The second week is twelve at best, probably slightly less. The third week is eight, and the fourth week is six. The last week, given the condition you were in when you arrived here, three, maybe four at best, but unlikely. We've seen people in far better condition than you only out there for a few days that only managed to walk two. We've learned a lot tracking people through the years. So, with that said, we can narrow it down to a thirty or forty-mile stretch of your trail. We did the math – number of days and walking time times the amount of miles each day.

I felt my shoulders slump. I had to be walking more than three miles a day at the end. "I know I was tired and malnourished, but I walked more than three miles each day. I started at first light and always walked an hour or two past dark; that's at least eleven hours a day."

"Madie, when I first saw you, you were doubled over. Momentum and sheer determination kept you going. Your body had consumed itself, and there was nothing left."

"Yes, at best, you covered six inches per step. Mentally, you thought you were still traveling at a decent speed. Physically, you couldn't; the mind plays many tricks on you."

"You were bordering on complete hallucination. Do you remember drinking hot chocolate?" Jim asked.

"No. All I remember is you shoving me back into the cold without my clothes on." But what I knew was that I was only covering more than six inches per step and more than three miles per day. They were helping me to arrive at a point that wouldn't prove a thing.

Pots of coffee were made and drank. Hours passed, and stacks of maps were looked at. Everything looked the same to me; not one thing looked familiar. They kept showing me aerial photos of lakes, asking me if it looked right, the lake the death dealer chased me across on his death run.

Finally, I sat back in my chair. "As much as I hate to say this, the only way I can say that it's the correct lake is to see it physically. I'm sorry."

Jim nodded, "We knew that. We've planned on spending up to a month up there if necessary. Provisions have been packed and every situation has been planned for. Randy will be here just after the first light. We're ready. We'll show you what and how to pack before dark."

As the men worked loading their gear in the trailer, waiting for the trip down to the water in the morning to be loaded on the plane, Mary took me to the side.

"Madie, aren't you scared? I would be. I am, and I'm not even going," she said.

"No, look who I have around me. I've been blessed with the best. Even if we don't find what we're looking for, we'll find our way home."

Mary smiled. "Every time they go out, I worry. The unforeseen could happen."

445

That was true; I had learned the hard way. I smiled back. "Nothing will happen. We'll be fine."

We were up at five. By five thirty, Jerry, Jonathon, and George arrived. Each person's backpack contained one sleeping bag and an extra set of clothes. The temperature wouldn't drop below freezing. After that, the men each carried a GPS, and two satellite phones were packed—one for backup. Light, minimal fishing gear, several knives, one axe, and each of us carried freeze-dried packages of food, one flashlight with spare batteries, and plenty of matches and lighters. That seemed more than enough to me, but we were going to live comfortably while there.

Randy landed the plane forty minutes after sunrise. I was nervous about returning to the land that took so much from me. I tried not to show it. Jim walked up to me and put his arm around my shoulder.

"Don't be nervous. Mary's doing enough of that for both of you."

It showed. I smiled. "So, how did you get so good at this?" I asked.

"I learned from them." Jim looked at the three men loading the plane. "Just sit back and watch, you'll be amazed."

I already was.

We were in the air. Jerry sat in the front seat next to Randy. Jim, Jonathon, George, and I sat on the benches that ran down each side of the plane. Our gear was on the floor between us. In the tail of the plane sat several five gallons of extra fuel.

I was sitting right behind Randy, that's where they wanted me so Jerry could look at maps and ask me questions.

Randy turned and looked back at us. Nearly shouting to overcome the noise in the plane, he said, "We're heading into a strong headwind, so we're using more fuel than I had calculated. That means we're only going to have time to fly over three, maybe four lakes before we have to set down and drop you off."

Randy had to return safely. Too many lives had been lost in this—nineteen—excluding the two death dealers; that was their own doing.

Forty miles from Jim's house and then another one hundred miles further north. If I couldn't spot the lake we needed, so be it; we would walk.

The first lake we flew over, approaching it from the east, wasn't right. It wasn't long enough from east to west. Jerry shuffled through the maps.

"Next one is northeast from here, five miles," Jerry said to Randy.

That one wasn't right, either. From the air, two hundred feet above the treetops, nothing looked familiar. I was sure down on the ground, it would be no different. I had spent so much time walking in the dark that land references were lost. Even in the daylight, trees were trees. At the time, I didn't care. Now, I wished I had taken the time to leave a mark, some sort of a sign. I didn't have the energy then but it would have been helpful now. If I had chopped down several trees, maybe even set them on fire.

"Next one is northwest, maybe eight miles," Jerry said.

We were zig-zagging. I continued to look out the window, hoping to see something I recognized. I didn't. The third lake was wrong also. I sat back, thinking, *What did I get everyone into?* I was feeling guilty. I had my friends on a wild goose chase and, in a way, their safety. I looked at Jim, "There isn't anything I wouldn't do for you guys. This is ridiculous; let's go home."

Jim bunched up his lower lip, and he reminded me of Wilford Brimley. "The show hasn't even started yet. We have thirty days. You've never given up before."

He had me there.

Randy flew to a fourth lake. I looked down, 'No,' was all I could say.

Jerry went back to the maps. He chose a small lake that was presumed to be in the middle of the wide path I had walked out on.

The plane landed on the water and floated up to the edge of the trees along the shore.

Everyone stepped out in knee-deep water to unload our gear. "Geez, this water is cold. Doesn't it ever warm up up here?" I smiled.

Jim shook his head in disbelief, and the others laughed.

They helped Randy refuel the plane from the five-gallon cans. I waded through the water next to Randy. "Why did you use the extra fuel to fly to so many lakes? You better make it home, ok," I said.

Randy looked down at the water, "This isn't even close to one end of the earth. I'm sorry I couldn't do more."

I didn't know what to say.

"If you don't return this time, I will stuff this plane nose first, right here in this lake. I will find you, whatever it takes; even if I have to get down on my hands and knees and crawl, I will. Never again," Randy said.

Randy held a guilt, like me, that would remain with him for the rest of his life.

"Look who I have around me—the best. Nothing will happen, and they will see to that."

"They're better than the best; they're the elite. That's the only reason I'm leaving you behind."

"So are you, Randy. What happened before was of no control of yours. Never forget that." I didn't know what else to say to Randy. I only hoped that that would help. I hugged him goodbye.

We stood in the trees along the edge of the lake. We strapped on our backpacks as we watched Randy take off. Then, it hit me; I was back—only this time, it was different. I remembered thinking, in the end, I would never return, and now I had. It felt good. As the noise from the plane faded away, I looked around. My eyes soaked in the beauty, my heart absorbed the feeling, and my lungs inhaled the smell. The land that took my future was peaceful. I looked at each man standing around me, and they were doing this for me. My axe to grind was with the two dead men. I wouldn't, or couldn't, do it without them. Someday, I would repay them. One thing I couldn't avoid out here was when I looked into the midnight sky. I would always feel pain. I hoped Craig was looking down at us, happy to see we were trying to set the wrong right.

Seconds after the last sound from Randy's plane was heard, we were off. Jerry and Jonathon discussed the route we were going to take. I heard them talk as they walked ahead of me. Jim was right behind me, and George was the last in line. What they said to each other was that Randy had flown over two more lakes than the original plan was which saved us two, maybe three days.

The pace they set surprised me. There was no lolly-gagging. Soon, Jonathon faded back to where George was. I heard them talking to each other. I paid no attention to what they were saying. I was too busy trying to keep up with Jerry. After about an hour of walking, something didn't feel right to me. I looked back over my shoulder, and Jim was the only one behind me. I stopped dead in my tracks, and Jim nearly ran into me.

"What?" Jim asked.

"Where did they go?"

"To do what they do best. One went left and the other right to see if they could find anything."

"I never heard them leave."

"You won't. Like I said, sit back and watch; they are amazing."

"When will they catch back up to us?"

"Sometimes by suppertime, once in a while, it's dark."

It was kind of eerie, and they reminded me of the death dealers, moving like ghosts.

By mid-afternoon, we had covered a lot of miles. We walked onto another lake. I saw Jerry flanking us on our right, and then he walked toward us. When he reached us, I saw him shake his head 'no.'

"Where's George?" I asked.

"Does this look familiar to you?" Jerry asked.

I walked to the edge of the water. It definitely wasn't the lake he chased me across. "No, this isn't it." Something about it did trigger a memory as I continued to look out across the lake.

If only I could stand out on the water and look back, I would be sure. I looked up and down the shoreline – I wasn't one hundred percent sure, but it was close. "We're too far north – days – maybe even a week," I told them why. I left out the fact that I had that nagging feeling, something they wouldn't take into being a factor in this. I had learned the hard way not to ignore it. "I believe this is the last lake I fished. I did really well here; that stupid bear ate four or five of the fish. I can't be positive, but the south shoreline looks familiar."

"Why was this the last lake you fished, Madie?" Jim asked.

"Because it was too cold. The ice was really thick here, and it took me hours to chop through the ice to reach the water. I didn't have the strength after that. I thought then the time spent wasn't worth the energy wasted."

No one said anything. No one had answered my question, so I asked again, "Where's George?" This time, they looked at me like they couldn't believe I asked that.

"He's out looking; he'll be back," Jonathon said.

Out looking for what? We aren't even close to where the death dealer died. I chose not to ask any more questions. I would do what Jim said to do—sit back and watch.

We walked to the south side of the lake. I didn't recognize anything, but I still had that feeling. Whatever unforeseen thing was telling me, I wasn't going to let it go. "We have to go south. Why, I don't know; I just know that's what we have to do."

We walked the rest of the day. No one said much. The men I knew, sitting around telling stories, laughing, and drinking beer, weren't the men I saw now. It was all business, pure professionalism. This was their office.

Occasionally Jerry looked at his GPS, although, I was the one that knew what we were looking for. I was just along for the ride. I relaxed as we walked. Early September and the leaves were in full color. This far north, that didn't surprise me. The walking was so much easier than my last journey; no deep snow to plow through. No pain jolting up through my legs with each step, and my hands didn't ache.

The four of us walked on. I listened to the crunching of the leaves under our shoes. The dry leaves covering the ground were calming to me. The wind didn't blow like it had during winter. Mother Nature can be wonderful—at times.

"Another mile, and we'll break for supper," Jerry said.

We walked what I had thought was a mile. I could smell something—smoke. *How could that be,* I thought. Another hundred yards, and then I saw the source of the smoke. George was kneeling beside a small fire as we walked up to him. The questions were reeling through my head. How could this be? How did George get ahead of us? How did we walk up on him in this exact place, in the middle of nowhere? I looked at Jim. I was puzzled, and he noticed.

Jim smiled. "It's just what they do."

I saw George nod his head 'no.' I wondered what that meant. They started talking as we removed our backpacks. Jonathon looked at his compass. "Madie says we need to go south, maybe several days."

George nodded 'yes' this time. "We knew this wasn't going to be easy, but hey, this is only the first day. Couldn't think of anything I'd rather be doing."

I wanted to hug George – all of them, really. We ate. Our meal consisted of freeze-dried stew and water. It was the best, far better than raw fish or nothing.

The next three days were a repeat of the first. George and Jonathon would disappear early in the morning and then would meet up with us by the end of the day. We were covering many miles per day. I was getting tired by the end of each day, but I wasn't going to let it show. What bothered me the most was how out of shape I had become. The months of downtime had taken a toll on my physical endurance. The few years of running 10K marathons with Craig, I learned the only way to get back in shape was to do it. In this case, that was to walk all day. The stumps on my legs were hurting, but I said nothing. I wasn't going to be the anchor of the group.

We lay on our sleeping bags around the fire. I listened as they talked, and I looked up at the stars. For the first time since Craig's death, I felt really good. I felt the tears run down my cheek because of the four men around me. Who had friends like this that would do this for them? I could think of no one.

Each morning, we had fresh brewed coffee. We were allotted one large cup each, homemade biscuits, and beef jerky. The men were carrying a much heavier load than I was. They had brought food for thirty days, plus all the basic cooking hardware and amenities. Everything was cooked over the campfire. It was very primitive, simple, but good.

Some days, the temperature would reach up into the lower fifties, and most of the time high forties was the best Mother Nature could do. That was fine with me. I knew she was warming up for her months of a bad attitude. This time, I would be long gone, sitting at Jim's in front of the fire when she hit us with her full rage.

The trees and landscape had become monotonous, and the lakes were far apart. Walking from one to the next was taking too long. Jerry was in the lead, and Jim was behind me. George and Jonathon were out and about.

"Why didn't we just have Randy fly us from lake to lake? Wouldn't that be faster than this?" I asked. "I feel kind of guilty having you guys go through this."

"Randy wanted to; he all but insisted on it and said that he would return us home each night. I think he feels he's to blame for what happened to you. He said that it would be of no expense," Jim said.

"Yes, you're right. He's mentioned that to me. I've tried many times to convince him it was no fault of his. They smashed our satellite phone and took the GPS. From that point on, I was walking blind. I had no idea how to reach the pick-up point. He doesn't listen. But still, I would have at least paid him for the fuel."

"Why? And miss all the fun? It doesn't get any better than this. It's rare that we get to go out and find somebody when it isn't freezing or a raging blizzard out. This is what the city people say about a stroll in the park – nothing to it," Jerry said.

'Too bad they didn't find me,' I thought. It was as though Jerry was reading my mind. "We would have found you if we had known you were out here," Jerry said.

I had no doubt about that, but it wasn't meant to be.

"We've asked Randy why he didn't contact us. That I do blame him for," Jerry said.

'But, why?' I thought. It wasn't Randy's fault.

"He does feel bad about the whole deal. He said that each day, he expected a call from you giving him new coordinates to come and get you."

"Well, it wasn't Randy's fault. It was theirs. How else would I have found what I did if they hadn't chased me? I believe that's the reason for it. I'm just sorry Craig had to die for it. So tell me, how can this be any better?"

"Well, unlike tracking someone in the snow, which is much easier. The tell-tale signs are always there. Maybe just a dimple in the snow, a footprint left behind that the blowing snow hadn't completely covered up, or just a trench through a snow drift. Something is always there to be found, as it is now. This is just harder. But believe me, you left something behind to be found that couldn't be found from the air. To put you at ease, I don't look for us to be out here more than a week or two at the most. As soon as we find that one thing, we'll know your trail."

"So that's what George and Jonathon have been doing each day? Looking for that one thing?" I asked.

"And us. You've given us a list of things to look for while telling your story. While we listened, we took notes – chopped branches making snowshoes, pine beds you've left behind, and places where you scraped the ground to sleep. They're here, waiting to be found. Nothing is impossible. The nice thing here is we're not racing against time; no life is at stake. This one is a different kind of challenge for us. It will sharpen our skills," Jerry said. We never stopped walking. I looked back at Jim. He smiled. Jerry was right about everything.

"Tonight, we're going to fish. All these good, never fished lakes can't go to waste. How does fresh cooked fish sound for dinner?" Jim asked.

"Wonderful," I said. My legs needed the extra rest. I could feel my stumps becoming raw.

We walked for almost another hour.

Then, I heard a new noise. It was faint, and I listened harder. Beep beep beep—it was coming from Jerry's pocket. He reached inside and removed it. I watched him. It wasn't the bulky satellite phone; it was a small, palm-sized radio.

"Hey, we're here," Jerry said.

Instantly, I wondered who he was talking to, George or Jonathon. I didn't even know they had these with them.

We heard a set of GPS numbers being said in sequence. It was George.

"On our way." Then, Jerry looked at me. "We just found that one thing."

My heart raced. I wanted to jump up and down. What had I left behind? It wasn't much. Jerry looked at his GPS, reading the numbers that would have meant nothing to me. "It's maybe four to five miles southeast from here." He put the GPS back in his pocket.

Was I the only one excited? Jerry just acted matter-of-factly, and Jim said nothing. "Geez, guys, you act like it's nothing."

Jerry shrugged, "Four days, good or bad. Considering the circumstances, it's ok."

Ok! It's phenomenal, I thought. Given the hundreds of square miles to find something so small, the odds were tremendous.

Excitement and adrenaline overcame the pain in my legs. We walked faster than normal. I couldn't wait to see what I had left there. "What about Jonathon? Shouldn't somebody call him and tell him the news?"

"Don't worry, he heard. He's already on his way," Jerry said.

I was breathing heavily, silently grunting as each step landed and then sending my weight forward into the next step. It was my way of dealing with it, as I did then. I remembered the pain I felt in my feet – the thousand needles piercing my skin as my feet slowly froze. Mentally, the drive was different this time. I ignored the pain.

"He's just up ahead," Jerry said.

I looked through the trees, but I didn't see him. Fifty yards passed behind us, and then I saw him. George was standing beside a tree. I waved at him, "Hi, George," I said.

George smiled at me.

We walked up to the spot, and I walked past Jerry. I stopped and looked down at a pile of pine branches lying on the ground. The needles were no longer green. As I continued to look at the brown, dried branches, I couldn't remember being here. I looked around at the surrounding area, and nothing looked familiar. The one thing that I was sure of was I had done this. The telltale sign was where I had chopped the branches from the trees. The axe had made diagonal cuts through the limbs. I slowly looked at each tree. There, I saw where the branches had once been alive.

"I'm sorry, but I don't remember this spot." I thought hard, "I can't tell you which day I did this or how many days it was before he caught up to me on that lake." I felt defeated.

"You don't have to. To be honest, we didn't expect you to. By what you've told us, stopping at night in the dark, you'd have nothing to remember. From this point on, maybe you'll see some sort of landmark you remember seeing during the day," Jerry said.

"Yes, now we can narrow our search down a mile or so on either side. Just up ahead is another spot where you made a new set of snowshoes. The old, battered set lies in two piles," George said.

Instantly, I headed in that direction. George walked behind me, guiding my direction. It wasn't far until I saw them. I remembered doing it, "I remember the morning I got up and did this. I knew he was close behind, and I had to have new ones if I was going to stay ahead of him. But I still can't say how many more days it was to his end."

"You're right. We have to go further south. That's all that matters."

CHAPTER 51

As the next two days passed, I became more and more amazed. What they did, what they found, and how they moved and worked together was amazing—Jerry, Jonathon, and George. Jim, as he had said earlier, was just along for the trip. George and Jonathon would find a sign left behind, showing that I had been there. Some were so small and insignificant that it would scare me. Once, it was a broken, dead branch that I had walked into. When it was snapped loose from the tree it had fallen forward before landing on the ground south, the direction I was walking. I had asked how they knew that. Their answer was if it had fallen naturally, it would have dropped straight down. My next question was, maybe an animal had done it. No, was the next answer. Even at night, animals can see, they would walk around it. Then, we would adjust our course. As I watched them I learned how to trail something or someone. George and Jonathon would come and go like ghosts. They would appear and disappear without a sound. I was thankful they weren't the ones who were chasing me then. There would have been no escape. As good as the death dealers were at finding me, they weren't in the same league. Somehow, these guys always found the spot where I had slept each night.

We were getting close, and I could feel it. I hesitated to tell them that. They worked on facts and hard telltale signs. Intuition was nothing more than speculation. In the middle of nowhere, that meant nothing; I had learned not to ignore what I felt, so I told them. It was mid-afternoon, and we had met up and were taking a break.

"We're close, and I can feel it. I know that means nothing to you guys. Each time they were getting close to me I had a funny feeling between my shoulders. I know that sounds stupid but it always came true. I even learned to read the bear. When it was acting different, I knew. It did so much for me—saving my life and companionship. All I did for it was feed it fish." Tears were building.

"Madie, the small things mean a lot. To the bear, that meant everything," Jim said.

Now I was crying. "But why? Why would a wild bear befriend me?"

"Because this far north, it wasn't tainted by the cruelty of humans. It was a young one, curious as to why you were there," Jerry said.

"Every living creature enjoys company. You were his – or hers. Luckily for you, it was too young to find one of its own yet. I'm sure it has by now," George said.

I hoped so. "I hope it becomes the King Kong of the north woods. It deserves it."

We took time each day to fish. It never took more than an hour to catch enough fish for the evening meal. Some days, either George or Jonathon would show up for our outing, and always at the end of the day, we would mysteriously walk up to one of them, and there would always be a nice campfire burning, its hot bed of coals waiting to cook the fish.

Today was no different. George opted to miss our fishing. We walked into his already-made camp. A stack of firewood sat off to the side, enough to burn throughout the night. The tripod was set up over the fire, and a pot sat on the wire mesh rack with boiling water. The ground had been cleared of fallen branches.

"You guys scare me." I smiled.

"Why?" George asked. "I smuggled in tea bags. Who wants hot tea?"

"Millions of acres, and you always find each other," I said. "I would, thank you, George."

George shrugged his shoulders. "Does this place look familiar to you?"

"No, why should it?" I asked.

George pointed behind his back. I looked in that direction and there I saw a pile of dead pine limbs—another one of my beds. I shook my head in disbelief. "You guys are utterly unbelievable. You need to do this professionally. Contact the Canadian government and tell them you're for hire. You could find anything."

"No, it's just a hobby," George said.

"Besides, if we do that, we would have to have equipment that could transport us quickly. We just stay locally, within snowmobile range," Jerry said.

I walked around studying the area, trying to remember being here and what day. Something told me that this was the last night of sleep with the last death dealer chasing me. I had no way of proving it. Now, without the snow, everything looked different.

I walked back to the men. "We're close. If I'm right, there's a lake about two miles from here."

Jim was already cleaning the fish for dinner, and Jonathan was helping. Jerry removed the maps from his backpack. I waited patiently, watching Jerry study the map. "Yes, there is," Jerry said.

"With a deep ravine flowing into it on the south side," I said. By now, my heart was thumping in my chest. Fresh fish just fell secondary, and dinner didn't seem as important. I wanted to get up and run, not stopping until I arrived at the spot. I remained cool.

"Unfortunately, the aerial view of this map doesn't give a clear enough view of that."

"What do you want to do, Madie? Want to break camp and head that way?" Jim asked.

Yes, I wanted to. It had been another long day, and I was sure the men were hungry. "No, let's eat first. There's enough daylight left to go after we eat, isn't there?"

"Sure," George said. "It's just a hop, skip, and a jump away."

I loved George – I loved all the guys. "Regardless of what we find, what you guys have done for me means the world to me. Very few people have friends that would do this for them. I'm lucky to have you. There's no way I could ever repay you for this; it means that much to me."

"There is," Jonathan said. "Remain our friend. We're the ones who are lucky."

That did it. I cried. I wiped the tears away, "That's a given," I said.

We ate, and the fire was covered with dirt. "I'm sorry, George," I said.

"For what?" he asked.

"You gathered all that wood, and now we're leaving it behind."

"It's just wood; that's not the reason we're here." George stood, "Let's go find a dead man's bones."

As we walked, I was worried. We could be walking the same path as I had before. I recognized nothing, and when we reached the lake, that would be no different. The one true thing I would know was the ravine and the two hundred yards south along the vertical bank. I would remember the dead tree I climbed that saved my life.

As we walked, I was taking short, rapid breaths, and the anticipation was killing me. The odds were fifty-fifty. The wolves, had they destroyed his body? Had they carried the remains off, never to be found?

The two miles passed fast. We walked to the edge of the lake; we were on the north side. I looked to the east, nothing but more trees and I looked to the south. My emotions were racing in high gear; aggravation from everything always looking the same. Hope—that this was the right lake; fear—that it wasn't. Anxiety—that all was lost.

I started walking to the east side of the lake. Nothing would be found there; it was a means to an end. The men followed behind me. The further I walked, the faster I went. "Madie, you're almost running. You can slow down if you want; nothing is going to change," Jerry said.

He was right, but I couldn't help myself.

I didn't stop until we were on the south side of the lake. Standing on the edge of the ravine, I wanted to drop to my knees. I felt too weak to hold myself up. I wanted to cry yet again. The men stopped behind me, breathing heavily.

"This is it, just up in the woods; the bank on this side levels out. A vertical wall is where he leaned up against and died."

I had to go on. We would rest when we got there. I was off and moving at twice the speed.

"Geez! I'm really glad we weren't the ones chasing you," Jonathon said. "I don't believe we would have been able to keep up."

I stopped, surprised. "From what I've learned on this trip, I think just the opposite. I wouldn't have survived many days with you guys on my heels. For the first time since this has happened, I'm glad it was them chasing me and not you. You are way better at tracking someone than they ever thought of being."

"Well, thanks for the compliment. But something tells me you were just cruising now. I'm sure it was different then," Jonathan said.

It was… a matter of my life. "I only did what I was forced to do."

When the vertical wall on our right grew as I said it would, it was as I remembered it. I saw the tree I had pushed over. The difference was the ground—now, it wasn't frozen—there wasn't standing water. It wasn't the type of swamp I thought. Tall grass almost to my knees, now turning brown because summer was over and below that soft, thick mud. I sunk several inches into it. The swamp grass was the barrier; it kept us from sinking into the ooze.

I kept walking. "This isn't good." I was thinking there might not be any remains left. My heart was pounding out of my chest. I held my breath as I walked the final steps up to the dreaded spot. "This is where he died," I said.

The men walked on both sides of me. We were all looking down at the ground, where we saw bits of clothing. Jerry and George started digging through the grass. Instantly, I felt lost, and I was expecting to see something lying right there.

The grass was thick, but within a matter of seconds, they found more shredded clothing. Then, to my surprise, they found more—a piece of a human. It was tangled in what was left of his jeans, part of his leg. The foot was missing so I couldn't tell which leg it was, not that it mattered. What did matter was that it was gross. Whatever had chewed on it didn't do a good job. In places, there were pieces of what was probably once skin, but it no longer resembled it. Each of the men had a slight look of 'yuck' on their face. If you didn't know them, you wouldn't have noticed it. The four of them went to work. Each man dropped their backpacks and so did I, glad to be free of the extra weight. My stumps were hurting.

Jim removed latex gloves and each man put a pair on. Then, Jim removed the black garbage bags. "These aren't body bags, but we'll make do with what we have." Just as it was—dirt, grass, and what was left of the blue jean material was put in the bag, then wrapped up and sealed with duct tape. Again, he had planned ahead.

I was happy and excited – we had found the spot. I hugged Jim but said nothing. It was all I knew what to do.

There was nothing else in the immediate area. George walked further out, away from the cliff. The ground was getting soft as he went. I watched him sink deeper into the ooze as he went.

"When I got to this tree, I looked back. I saw him coming into the clearing. He was carrying his gun. I felt the most scared I had ever been. I remember the ringing inside my head. I knew at any moment I was going to hear a shot fired. I did the only thing I knew what to do, so I cut the snowshoes loose. I climbed up that dead tree, knowing I would never reach the top. I saw him running toward me, bent over forward, but the shot never happened. I reached the top, and then I pushed the tree over so he couldn't follow. Then, I realized I was clear of one problem and into the next. If he had followed somehow, I would have had no snowshoes and no time to make new ones. Then, he told me what little he did and died."

They stopped, looking and listening to me. "To your good fortune, he probably couldn't. The pain in his chest was overwhelming. I'm sure he was having a heart attack. I'm surprised he made it this far," Jim said.

They searched the rest of the area. Pieces were scattered around in a large area, and almost all the body parts were found. It was disgusting, and many times I felt nauseous. What was needed the most was still missing—the skull. It was needed for the dental records.

We searched and searched. An hour had passed, and I was losing hope. Then, Jerry yelled from down in the middle of the ravine, almost to the lake. We all went in that direction.

Jerry was standing there smiling. I looked down. He had removed the leaves covering it, and I felt sick again. The eyes and lips were gone, but small tufts of hair were still attached. To keep from looking at it any longer, I walked up to Jerry and hugged him. "Thank you." I started crying. "I thank all of you. The next to impossible was accomplished, something I couldn't have done without you guys."

"Madie, you did accomplish the impossible. You survived what wasn't survivable. This will never compare to that," Jonathon said.

I went to each man and hugged him. I kissed each one on the cheek, and tears of happiness flowed. "So, what do we do now?" I asked.

"Call Randy. It's too late in the day to be flown out of here. One more night won't hurt," Jerry said.

"Good, fishing it is," Jim said.

I didn't know if I could eat. "After you call Randy, can we call Agent Netz? I'd like to tell Jeff what we found." I looked down at the skull one last time. "The devils water isn't so sweet now, is it?" I walked away. I had given Craig meaning to his death.

All his body parts were wrapped in garbage bags and then packed into one large plastic duffle bag. Then, we made camp by the edge of the water.

"Do you want to make that call now?" Jerry asked.

"Yes, I was thinking he could make arrangements with Randy and fly up here tomorrow with him," I said.

"I don't see why not. It might delay our departure, but hey, a down day would be good. We've got all the fish we can catch and eat and pretty fair company," Jerry said.

I asked Jim, George, and Jonathon. It was unanimous. "As for the company, there is no better. Your friendship is equal to none," I said.

I called Jeff on the satellite phone. After hearing my plan, he agreed, but he had to get the okay from his end. Randy was ready to fly down and pick him up first thing in the morning and then transfer to a seaplane at Randy's base. Randy said they would arrive mid-afternoon tomorrow.

The men fished, and we ate. Business was over. They told stories, and we laughed; they were back to being the crew I knew and had grown to love. Just before dark, we were sitting around the fire when Jim removed two bottles of wine from his backpack. "I was saving these for this special occasion. A very good ending to a very bad story."

"Yes, but at least it was good," I said. "One I'm sure we'll talk about for years to come." We were quiet. I was thinking, "As time passes by, some bits you lose, and some bits you keep. I have no choice in what I retain. I'm sorry Craig had to die to figure this out. Here's to you, Craig, you didn't deserve it. The number one love of my life—you—I will always retain. You made me happy, and you kept me alive long after I should have perished. I'm sorry you're not here to enjoy this, and thank these men who made it possible." I wiped the tears away.

Jim's eyes were wet, and George looked away. Jonathon and Jerry held their coffee cups in the air, full of wine. "And here's to Madie. The bravest, most courageous woman we will ever know. It will always be our honor to help you," Jonathon said.

"Here, here!" they said.

I couldn't speak, and I could barely breathe. I was crying so hard.

CHAPTER 52

I woke to a crackling fire, and the smell of coffee overpowered the smell of pine. I rolled over in my sleeping bag to see who was up. To no surprise, I was the only one still sleeping.

"Good morning, Madie," Jerry said.

"Good morning. The coffee smells good," I said. I saw movement out on the lake. There, Jim and Jonathon stood in knee-deep water, already fishing.

"We get to splurge today and drink all the coffee we want. Last day, and there's plenty left."

Quietly, I said, "If I were here alone, I wouldn't take that for granted. But with you guys, I don't worry."

Jerry nodded, "I can only imagine what you went through."

"Where's George?" I asked.

"He was up and gone before I got up."

"What's he doing?"

Jerry tilted his head, "Just scouting around, that's what he does."

"Why?"

"There's something about George you don't know. He has a photographic memory. He can remember every tree from every rescue we've ever been on. Ninety-nine percent of the time, we're always in new territory. But if we have to backtrack or just get ourselves out, he always knows the way. That helps in the middle of the night when we're racing against time to save a life. We just let George do his thing. It's so much faster than GPS or a compass," Jerry said.

"Is that why he's always so quiet?"

"No, that's just his personality. But maybe that's why he sucks so much at fishing."

I didn't see why that had anything to do with it, but I didn't ask.

"George is different. He thinks differently from the rest of us. I guess that's why he never got married. But rest assured, his difference is still normal. We all bring something with us on one of our trips. Without George, we wouldn't be as successful as we are."

I knew there was something special about George. Now I knew why it was.

I spent the first several hours of the day sitting on my sleeping bag, drinking coffee, and watching the men fish. I didn't put my legs on, which was a huge relief. I never removed the donning sockets. Like before, in the cold, when I wore boots, I knew what I would see, and to take them off might mean a grave mistake. The pain wasn't nearly as severe, and I would tough it out until we got back to Jim's.

Several hours passed.

My jeans were covering my stumps. I was still sitting on my sleeping bag when Jim walked out of the lake and up to the fire. He looked at me.

"I've noticed you've made no attempt to move yet," Jim said.

"No, it feels good to relax." I wasn't lying, I just didn't tell everything.

Jim stared at my legs. "Uh huh, so how bad are they?"

He knew me too well. To answer his question, either way, would draw far too much attention to myself. I was going to make it again on my own. "It's nothing that I can't make it back to your house on my own."

"Uh-huh, that's what scares me. You walked out the first time on practically no feet."

"I'll be fine," I said.

We were within two hours of having Randy and Jeff arrive. As much as the downtime felt good, it was always bad. While moving, my body adjusted to the pain – before, I remembered each morning and what I went through – pure agony. To do that now would be noticeable. I had saved some of the heavy-duty pain medication. I had brought those along with me and took two when no one was looking.

Slowly, I attached my legs. I would be ready when the plane landed.

We heard the plane approaching from the south. While Randy was landing on the lake with the men watching, I stood. The bolt of pain shot through my body, and I grimaced. Like before, I leaned forward as if that was going to lessen the weight bearing down on my legs. It didn't. Before anyone noticed, I stood straight. I couldn't imagine what I would be feeling without the medication.

We watched Randy drive the plane toward the shore. He shut the engine off as the plane coasted in. Then, Randy climbed out and stood on one of the pontoons and threw a rope toward the shore. The men caught it and started pulling the plane toward dry land. Within ten feet of the bank, Randy jumped off into the water and walked quickly to the shore. He walked directly toward me, never taking his eyes off of me. He never said 'Hi' to any of the men; he just walked right up to me. I could see tears in his eyes. He hugged me so tightly I had trouble breathing.

"I worried about you each and every day. I'm glad you're ok," Randy said.

I hugged him back. "Did you forget who I was with? These men are the best," I said.

"I know, but regardless, something can always happen out here." Randy looked into my eyes, then kissed me on the cheek. "You have no idea how happy I am to see you."

The relief was clearly evident in Randy's eyes. My ordeal haunted Randy as much as it did me.

"I let you down once. If I were to do that a second time..." Randy shook his head. "I was serious as a heart attack. I would have stuffed my plane in a lake."

I wouldn't let myself cry. I returned a kiss on Randy's cheek. "You are a good man – as good as the men standing around us," I said.

"No, not hardly," he said quietly.

Jeff jumped from the float on the plane to the shore. He greeted each of the men and then looked at me. I waved. We had become very good friends through the whole deal of digging up the ten armored trucks. Words weren't needed.

Then, I pointed to the bag. "There he is—what's left of him anyway. It's really sick, but I feel no remorse for him," I said.

Jeff stared at the bag. Shaking his head, he said, "I can't believe you found one of them. It's incredible, more like unbelievable. How did you do it? I mean, look where we are, in the middle of nowhere."

"It wasn't me, give credit where it's due. These four men are the ones responsible. I wouldn't have 'ever' returned here without them. What they did is incredible."

"Now I know why you didn't answer my calls. You were here," Jeff said.

"Come on, we'll show you where he died," Jerry said.

I had to walk, so I braced myself for the pain.

Jerry led the way and I let the rest of the guys fall in behind. My plan was to go last, but Jim wouldn't let that happen. I started in that direction—at least in front of Jim; he couldn't see me make any grimaces of pain if I did.

"I'm here for you. Your physical well-being is my concern. Something is wrong, and I believe I know what it is," Jim said softly.

"You know me too well," I said.

"How bad?"

"We're almost home," I responded.

We walked the short distance back to the cliff. "This is it," Jerry said.

Jeff looked at the surrounding area and then at me.

"I was up there when he died," I said.

Everyone looked up at the top of the cliff.

"This one needs to go into the files as the most incredible find – right along with the ten trucks," Jeff said.

"Yes, but they are unequal to the most unimaginable feat ever. She walked out of here. An impossible physical possibility for any human," Jim said.

I looked at Jim. I didn't know what to say.

"Madie, is there anything you do that's normal?" Jeff asked.

"It's all normal. I did what I was forced to do, nothing more," I answered.

"You might have been forced to, but there's nothing normal about it," Jeff said.

Back at the fire, Jeff said, "I've had some news for you. Good or bad, I hold nothing back. Some you'll want to hear, some you won't."

I looked at him. I had no idea. I was thinking thoughts at such a rate I almost couldn't comprehend.

"I'll start as we learned the sequence of information."

Everyone made a small circle around the fire. Some of the men were sitting on the ground, and others were standing.

Jeff looked around, taking inventory. "Are you sure you want to hear this with everyone?"

"They are all family. Please continue," I said.

"Well, we know their names. At least, we're ninety-nine percent sure. What's in that bag will confirm it. Anyone with that kind of security clearance has to have an extensive background check plus a DNA test upon employment. This will make it easy. It's quite a complex series of events of what they did. So, to keep from going on for hours, I'll give you the shortened version. The reason for the only truck that contained no dead men is the direct company they worked for. They drove that truck, which was the first one that went missing. That's what made it easy for us. Those two men disappeared from the face of the earth immediately afterward. How they made connections across the country we're still working on. What they did was find the routes holding the most money. Once inside, it's quite easy. Some trucks only pick up small sums – actually most. There are a few trucks that make the big pickups, and by that I mean big, go to major accounts. Those companies try to make that kind of stop tally small on each route, so one, maybe two major pickups per truck. Occasionally, it can't be helped. Any one truck makes different stops per night, with no given set route to follow, making it harder to do what they did. They hit the big trucks. The total amount in those ten trucks was forty seven million dollars," Jeff said.

Everyone listened intently.

"Good Lord, what a cash haul," Jonathon said.

"Yes. Now for the good and bad news. I'll give it in order as I go on. Madie, some you won't want to hear, but I will tell you as it is. What you do with it is up to you."

I quit breathing. What could I possibly not want to hear?

"The company your husband worked for built those ten boxes. Eight years ago, they were all delivered to a warehouse. Since then, that warehouse has been torn down, removing any further leads – how fortunate for those two men. More than likely, they had something to do with that. Your husband helped design them, so that leaves us with two possibilities. There have been extensive discussions on what I'm about to tell you next. Your husband was part of this, meaning he was a partner with them, or he had figured out what they had done."

I felt sick. My head was spinning, and my skin became hot. It couldn't be.

"Maybe he had no positive proof of what they had done and was threatening to turn them in, or they just removed him. They thought of him as a loose cannon, leaving more for them."

I was shaking my head 'no'. "That can't be. Craig wasn't partners with them. He wasn't evil like they were. He never mentioned a single word of any of this to me, and we kept no secrets." I didn't cry. I was too shocked.

"Think about it, Madie. How else did two men know your exact location, hundreds of miles from civilization, and happened to be there at the same time you were," Jeff said.

Jeff was right, but I didn't want to believe it. I had been so engrossed in Craig's death and then figuring out the whole truck ordeal that I never gave that any thought. I remained speechless.

"Either way, we'll never know; there's no paper trail and no one left to question. I'm sorry, Madie, for having to tell you this. In the beginning, I said I would keep nothing from you. You trusted me from the beginning, and for that, I'm grateful. Look what we accomplished."

I looked around at the men beside me. "Craig was the perfect husband. It's hard for me to think he was part of their evil plan."

No one said anything. Like me, they didn't know what to say.

"Again, I'm sorry, Madie. Now, for the good news, each insurance company representing each armored truck company, actually there were only three, paid a reward as a finder's fee. Without you, that money would have been lost forever. They decided to pay you an eight percent reward totaling three million, seven hundred and sixty thousand dollars," Jeff said.

Then, Jeff did something that made me even more speechless. He reached inside his coat pocket and handed me an envelope. "I told them, my boss, mainly, that I would like to personally deliver it to you for what you had done for us. I just had an idea it would be here. This is your check, Madie."

I stared at the envelope in my hand, thinking of what he had just told me. Craig. I didn't know what to believe.

The men that were sitting stood. They all started clapping and cheering, telling me I had accomplished the impossible and other things. I barely heard them.

On the plane trip back to Jim's, I sat in the back of the plane. I didn't listen to the conversations going on. All I could think about was Craig. I removed the check from the envelope and looked at it again. The large sum of money was more than I would ever need. It wouldn't change the past, and it wouldn't bring Craig back to me, nor would it give me my feet and hands back. As I sat there looking at it, it would change the future. I had decided what I was going to do with some of it.

Back at Jim's house, the goodbyes were said. I hugged them all, and I couldn't tell them or thank them enough. What they had done for me I appreciated way beyond the words that could be said.

The shock had worn off, what Craig had known and the check. Of Craig, I will always think the latter. It just wasn't in him to kill people for money. Maybe he knew what they had done and kept it from me to protect me. Maybe he knew how bad the two death dealers were. If so, he didn't know enough, he died.

Inside the house, I didn't unpack. I sat on the couch. "I really need to get these donning socks off. My legs are killing me."

Jim was instantly by my side, helping. We removed them. "Jesus, Madie!" Jim said.

What we saw wasn't good. Raw, torn flesh and dried, crusted blood filled the inside of the donning sockets. My stumps burned, and it felt good to have them exposed to the air.

"Why didn't you say something? You knew how bad it was. I knew it wasn't good, but I had no idea."

"There was no way I was going to slow the crew down. I didn't help much in finding anything, but I wasn't going to be an anchor. It's just a thing, and it'll pass," I said.

"You didn't have to do this. This time, it wasn't a matter of life or death. Why did you force yourself to endure this much pain?"

"Compared to last time, this is nothing." That seemed to pacify Jim, he said no more.

As Jim bandaged my legs, he said, "Well, this has set you back at least two weeks."

"I wasn't going anywhere unless you get tired of me and send me home."

"That will never happen," Jim responded.

"I've been thinking. What do you think of the idea of me taking some of the money and building a house here beside yours?" "Are you serious? I don't like it. Contrary to what people believe, I'm not a hermit. I want you to live here, in this house, until we grow old."

"It's a deal," I said.

CHAPTER 53

Three weeks passed, but by the beginning of the third week, I was getting around pretty good. The nights were freezing hard, and some days, the temperature didn't get but a degree or two above aero. Mother Nature was coming. Soon, she would be knocking on the door with all her fury.

"Madie, if you're going to return, you had better do it soon. If you want to come back anytime soon, it better be a short trip," Jim said.

"Why?" I asked. We had talked about my returning for a week. I had a few things I needed to do, but I just hadn't told Jim what they were.

"The weather is going to turn fast and when that happens, no planes in or out. Sometimes, it takes up to two weeks," Jim said.

I frowned, but I didn't understand why.

Jim saw the expression on my face. "Once the ice starts, there's no more landing on the water. The ice isn't thick enough to support the weight of the plane."

Then, I remember Randy throwing the rock from the plane. "Yes, you're right. I'll go tomorrow."

I called Randy. He would be here early in the morning to pick me up. It was Tuesday, and I would return on Sunday, weather permitting.

I packed a small bag. The rest of the gang, Mary included, came for dinner. It was a good time. They acted like I was going to be gone for a long time.

Randy landed one hour after daylight. Jerry, Jonathon, and George had returned to see me off. This time, I didn't cry.

"I'll see you on Sunday. Have the wine bottles opened," I said.

"You can count on it," George said.

"We'll have a large spread cooked; we'll celebrate," Jim said.

"I am counting on it."

The first full day home I had a lot to do. The first thing I did was go to the bank. I had called the bank manager since I wanted to deal with him directly. I was excited about what I was doing. It took two hours, but I left there with eight certified bank checks. Before I left the bank,

I called Sharon. I asked her if she and Mia could meet me for lunch. She agreed. It was eleven o'clock, and I called the cab company. I asked if Tore was working this afternoon, and he was. I asked if he could pick me up at my home at three o'clock.

I arrived at the restaurant and got a table in the back. I didn't wait long; Sharon and Mia were also early.

Mia walked up to me and held out her arms, "I missed you," she said.

"Oh, Mia! I've missed you too," I said. "How have you been, Sharon?"

"Wonderful. Life has been great. Kyle and I owe it all to you. Since the night you invited us over to dinner, it opened our eyes. I was as much at fault as he was."

We ate and talked, and time passed quickly. To me, it was a lot. I enjoyed being around them almost as much as the crew.

"I'm really glad you called. I've tried to call you, but I never got an answer."

"I know," I said. "I've been up in Canada, and I plan to return Sunday."

"Well, I have bad news to tell you. Kyle got promoted at his job. That promotion is in Chicago, and we're moving in three weeks. I really wanted to see you before we left."

I felt sad. I didn't want to show it since I was really happy for them. "I have something for you." I reached into my purse, and it took me a few seconds to fumble around and remove the envelope I needed. "It's for Mia." I handed Sharon the envelope. "I want you to send her to the best college in whatever field she chooses."

Sharon looked at me, frowning, and then she opened the envelope. She gasped, and instantly, the tears ran down her face.

"That should cover everything. By the time she's old enough to go, the interest will have grown. Give her the best; she deserves it." I wanted to cry; Mia was something I would never have.

Sharon cried, "I don't know what to say. A thank you is so insignificant to this much money."

It was two hundred fifty thousand dollars. "You don't need to say anything. It will give you and Kyle piece of mind to enjoy your lives."

"Oh, we will," Sharon said.

"Mia won't remember as time passes and that's ok. You don't need to tell her. Just take extra care of her; she's an extra special girl." I looked down at Mia. "Mia, I hope you go on and become the first woman president or do something wonderful. I will always remember you." Now, I was crying.

"She will remember you; I will see to that," Sharon said.

I said goodbye to them. My heart was sad, and I knew I would never see them again.

I got in my car and drove away. I didn't look back. Behind, there was always sadness, and I was going forward. Regardless of what the FBI thought of Craig, I knew he had nothing to do with them.

I sat at the kitchen table. My house felt so empty. It would always be here, mine until death—Craig's shrine, my loss, with unforgettable memories into eternity.

I heard a cab pull into the driveway. Tore was right on time. I walked through the garage and out to the cab. Tore got out smiling.

"Hello, Tore. It's been a long time," I said.

"Yes, it has. It's good to see you. How have you been?" he asked.

"Better now. I've learned a lot and found out things I needed to know – some good, some bad."

"Yes, life is that way, every day," Tore said.

How right he was. "I don't need a cab today."

The look on his face was clear. "I wanted to say thank you." I handed him the envelope. "It's not much but I hope it will help you buy your family a home."

Tore opened the envelope and stood motionless for a long time. Then his eyes watered, and he sat down on the driveway, too shocked and too weak to hold himself up. "But why?" Tore asked.

"Because you are my friend. You didn't look at me like a freak and didn't walk in the other direction. You didn't treat me like an invalid – you treated me as a friend from the very first time we met. I'm very grateful for that and for having you as a friend."

It had been years since I had seen a grown man cry, but that's what Tore did. I waited, as had so many people in my recent past when that's all I ever did. Now, I returned the favor. "I want you to buy a house and take your family there. Always take care of them."

"I will, I promise you that. Will you come and visit us?" Tore asked.

"I'm returning to the land that took everything from me. Somehow, it's found a way to give me a new life. In a way, it has given me more than I ever expected: friends who I don't want to be without."

Tore nodded and then stood. He hugged me, and I returned the friendship.

"Maybe someday our lives will cross paths again," I said.

"I hope so. I will never forget you."

After a goodbye that lasted forever, Tore was gone—like so many people of my past and so many people who I knew and called a friend.

I sat back down at the kitchen table and looked around at the empty house, so many memories in such a short time. Then, my phone rang.

It was Jim. "Madie, it's me. If you're going to return, you have to do it tomorrow. The ice is starting. I talked to Randy, and he said he can still land on a quarter inch of ice. After that, it's waiting. It melted off today. From tomorrow on, there's no break in the weather. The weatherman predicts below freezing from here on out."

"I'll be there. I'll pack now. If at all possible, I'll get a flight out tonight. If not, first thing in the morning. Can you call Randy?"

"Yes."

"See you tomorrow night," I said.

I rushed around the house. I packed several things, things I didn't have there and knew I would need.

I had to settle for the first flight out in the morning. I was up at three, called a cab, and locked the door behind me at three thirty. We pulled in front of the terminal at four a.m. My flight didn't leave until five forty. The window of opportunity was narrow and closing. I wanted to be extra early. This flight I wasn't going to miss.

After the big ordeal of going through security, I walked down to the gate. I was the only one there. Just as I sat down, my phone rang, and I answered.

"Good morning, it's Randy. I'm here at the airport waiting for you."

"Geez, you must have gotten up as early as I did."

"Well, actually, I've been here all night. Plan ahead, in case something goes wrong, you know. They'll have the seaplane warmed up and running before we land at base camp. We should land at Jim's shortly after one o'clock," Randy said.

It was. A shuttle met us before Randy had time to shut down the plane, and we were quickly escorted out to the seaplane. Two men transferred my bags and we were there less than ten minutes, then we were in the air again.

As we flew toward Jim's, I thought now was as good of a time as any. I didn't know what Randy's plan was, if he was staying for a while, or if he was going to make the return trip back.

I removed the envelope from my purse and handed it to him. "I hope this alleviates your guilt; you should have none. This should tell you I hold nothing against you."

Randy opened it and, like Tore, stared at it. Seconds passed; it took time for him to register what he was looking at. "Oh, my God! This isn't right. I can't take this."

The check was made out for five hundred thousand dollars.

"It's way too much. I don't want anything. I don't deserve it, not for what happened."

"It's ok, Randy. I want you to have it. Buy a faster or bigger plane, maybe something you can land on water with," I said.

"But I have that now."

"Expand your business. Use your new plane to help the men rescue people."

Randy had tears. "I will, but I promise one thing that they will never be charged."

"You have to because it takes money to operate. Besides, I have that taken care of. They have more money than they need; they just don't know it yet."

Randy smiled and nodded in agreement.

One million distributed with another one million and a half to go. That left me with just over two million back at the bank collecting interest. More than I will ever need.

We circled the lake. The gang was standing at the shore. As Jim said, the plane broke a thin sheet of ice as we landed. "It isn't thick enough to hurt the pontoons, but any thicker, it starts ripping holes in them. Then, the plane sinks."

"Not good," I said. "Are you going to stay awhile?"

"I wasn't, but I am now. I wouldn't miss this. You are the nicest person God put on this earth."

The plane was tied to Jim's dock, and I hugged everyone. As Jim said, dinner was cooked. Fresh walleye—baked, fried, and broiled, and for an appetizer, homemade fish soup. Bottles of wine were emptied, and empty beer bottles filled the wastebasket.

Everyone sat around the kitchen, enjoying their full stomachs. I got up and went for my purse. I handed the four men their envelopes at the same time. I held on to the fifth one. "This doesn't even come close to what you have done for me. It's just a small thank you. Each and every day, I will always thank you. Though I may never say it, I will always think it. The people here, in this room, have given me a new life. A life I don't want to be without." I was crying.

No one opened them, and they were looking at me. "Well, open them," I said, smiling while wiping away the tears.

They did. I saw the same reaction.

"That's what I did," Randy said.

Jerry, George, and Jonathon talked at once.

"That's what I said," said Randy.

"Madie, why did you do this?"

"I have one more for the entire group. I don't care who is in charge of it. Take it and buy equipment. Faster snowmobiles or one of the snow machines, even a used helicopter. It's up to you guys." I handed it to the closest person which happened to be George. He opened it.

George whistled, "Golly! That's a lot of equipment."

The check made its way around the table. Now Mary was crying. She got up and hugged me. "You never cease to amaze me. What would we do without you?"

"That's what I think of you, the crew. That's what I call you guys—the best ever."

They all got up and hugged me; George and Jim's eyes were wet.

"Let's go save lost souls," I said, crying.

As the weeks passed, I had time to think. I was as happy as I was when Craig was alive. I had a new goal: I was going to be the first handicapped woman ever to win the Boston Marathon. Craig would like that.

Made in the USA
Columbia, SC
27 July 2024

d0deba9a-da9d-4e3a-9283-263da3c0f3cfR02